Building 4.6/5.4L FORD HORSEPOWER ON THE DYNO

RICHARD HOLDENER

CarTech®

Copyright © 2006 by Richard Holdener

All rights reserved. All text and photographs in this publication are the property of the author, unless otherwise noted or credited. It is unlawful to reproduce – or copy in any way – resell, or redistribute this information without the express written permission of the publisher.

All text, photographs, drawings, and other artwork (hereafter referred to as information) contained in this publication is sold without any warranty as to its usability or performance. In all cases, original manufacturer's recommendations, procedures, and instructions supersede and take precedence over descriptions herein. Specific component design and mechanical procedures – and the qualifications of individual readers – are beyond the control of the publisher, therefore the publisher disclaims all liability, either expressed or implied, for use of the information in this publication. All risk for its use is entirely assumed by the purchaser/user. In no event will CarTech®, Inc., or the author, be liable for any indirect, special, or consequential damages, including but not limited to personal injury or any other damages, arising out of the use or misuse of any information in this publication.

This book is an independent publication, and the author(s) and/or publisher thereof are not in any way associated with, and are not authorized to act on behalf of, any of the manufacturers included in this book. All registered trademarks are the property of their owners. The publisher reserves the right to revise this publication or change its content from time to time without obligation to notify any persons of such revisions or changes.

Edited by: Travis Thompson
Designed by: Christopher Fayers

ISBN-13 9781613250082

Printed in the U.S.A.

CarTech®

CarTech®, Inc.,
6118 Main Street
North Branch, MN 55056
Telephone (651) 277-1200 • (800) 551-4754 • Fax: (651) 277-1203
www.cartechbooks.com

Cover Images:
Main: This '97 4-valve Cobra runs in the NMRA Mod Motor Mustang class. It gets its motivation from a Vortech T-Trim making 26 psi. (Photo courtesy Bob McClurg)

Inset Left: A given combination will put down more power on an engine dyno than a chassis dyno. There's no drivetrain loss on the engine dyno, and you can also run an electric water pump, no A/C, and no power steering, which gives you higher power numbers.

Inset Right: There's a lot of buzz around the 3-valve 4.6L GT, and rightfully so – it puts out near-4-valve numbers in stock trim. This '05 GT looks right at home on the chassis dyno. (Photo courtesy Travis Thompson)

Title Page: Just before this book went to print, we witnessed Kenne Bell testing a couple of twin-screw blowers on an '05 3-valve Mustang GT. Of course, it put down impressive numbers with either the 1.7L or 2.2L blower.

Back Cover Images:
Top: Whenever you see an '03 Cobra with a Kenne Bell blower and Mickey Thompsons all the way around, you know it means business. This car made 651 hp and 675 ft-lbs of toque after we installed a set of Crower Stage 2 cams.

Lower Right: The results of the back-to-back testing in this book will help you decide what parts will work best for you. We tested all of the available throttle-body inlet elbows for the 4.6L 2-valve GT. They all improved the power output over the stock combo, but which made the most power?

Lower Left: You might have to take this turbo kit off the engine before you install it in your car, but you get the idea. We tested this twin-turbo kit against centrifugal, roots, and twin-screw superchargers.

Table of Contents

Introduction: On the Dyno 5

Chapter 1 *Throttle Bodies and Inlet Elbows* 8
Test 1: PI 2-Valve GT: Throttle Body & Intake Elbow Shoot-Out
Test 2: Vortech Supercharged PI 2-Valve GT: Throttle Body & Intake Elbow Shoot-Out
Test 3: Ford Racing Supercharged PI 2-Valve GT: Ford Racing 70-mm Throttle Body
Test 4: Kenne Bell Supercharged Early 2-Valve GT: Cold Air, MAF, & Throttle Body
Test 5: Kenne Bell Supercharged 2-Valve 5.4L Lightning: Throttle Body Upgrade
Test 6: 4-Valve Cobra: Accufab Throttle Body
Test 7: Eaton Supercharged 4-Valve '03 Cobra: Accufab Throttle Body & Inlet
Test 8: 5.0L Stroker 2-Valve: Accufab 75-mm Throttle Body & Inlet

Chapter 2 *Intake Manifolds* 30
Test 1: 2-Valve GT: PI Intake vs. Truck Intake
Test 2: 4.6L 2-Valve Truck Divided Intake Plenum Test
Test 3: 2-Valve GT: PI Intake vs. Ford Racing Bullitt Intake
Test 4: 2-Valve GT: PI Intake vs. Reichard Racing Short-Runner Intake
Test 5: 2-Valve GT: PI Intake vs. Fox Lake P51 Intake
Test 6: 4-Valve Cobra: SHM Ported '01 Cobra Intake vs. Ford Racing FR500 Intake
Test 7: Ford Racing FR500 Intake: Long vs. Short Runners
Test 8: Vortech Supercharged 4-Valve '03 Cobra: Effect of Runner Length
Test 9: 5.0L Stroker 2-Valve GT: Variable Runner Intake

Chapter 3 *Cylinder Heads* 50
Test 1: Early 2-Valve GT vs. PI 2-Valve GT
Test 2: Early 2-Valve GT Heads vs. TEA CNC-Ported PI 2-Valve GT Heads
Test 3: Early 2-Valve GT vs. FPS Early 2-Valve GT Heads, Cams, & PI Intake
Test 4: PI 2-Valve GT: Effect of Compression Ratio
Test 5: Kenne Bell Supercharged 2-Valve GT: Effect of Compression Ratio
Test 6: 4-Valve 5.4L: Effect of Compression Ratio
Test 7: ATI Supercharged 4-Valve 5.4L: Effect of Compression Ratio
Test 8: 2-Valve PI GT vs. 3-Valve '05 GT

Chapter 4 *Camshafts* 68
Test 1: Early 2-Valve GT: Comp Cams XE274H Camshafts
Test 2: PI 2-Valve GT: Six Sets of Comp Cams Xtreme Energy Camshafts
Test 3: Ford Racing Supercharged PI 2-Valve GT: Comp Cams XE262H Camshafts
Test 4: Vortech Supercharged Early 2-Valve GT: Comp Cams XE274H Camshafts
Test 5: Naturally Aspirated '03 4-Valve: Cobra Cams vs. Comp Cams XE262AH Camshafts
Test 6: 4-Valve Cobra: Degreeing Comp XE262AH Cams
Test 7: Eaton Supercharged '03 4-Valve Cobra: Comp Cams XE262AH Camshafts
Test 8: Kenne Bell Supercharged '03 4-Valve Cobra: Comp Cams XE262AH Camshafts
Test 9: Kenne Bell Supercharged '03 4-Valve Cobra: Crower Stage 2 Camshafts
Test 10: PI 2-Valve GT: Crane Cams HR-212/550-25-15 Camshafts

Chapter 5 *Nitrous Oxide* 92
Test 1: Early 2-Valve GT: With a 100-hp Zex Kit
Test 2: Early 2-Valve GT: With a 125-hp Zex Kit

Table of Contents

    Test 3: Naturally Aspirated 4-Valve '03 Cobra: With a 125-hp NOS NOSzle Setup
    Test 4: Naturally Aspirated 4-Valve '03 Cobra: Effect of Reduced Timing in Anticipation of Nitrous
    Test 5: Eaton Supercharged 4-Valve '03 Cobra: With a 125-hp Zex Kit
    Test 6: Kenne Bell Boost-A-Spark Cured Misfire with Supercharger & Nitrous
    Test 7: Paxton Supercharged 4-Valve Cobra: With a 75-hp Zex Kit
    Test 8: '05 3-Valve GT: With a 75-hp Zex Kit

Chapter 6: 2-Valve Supercharging 110
    Test 1: PI 2-Valve GT: Ford Racing Supercharger
    Test 2: Ford Racing Supercharged 2-Valve GT: 3.6-inch Pulley vs. 3.4-inch Pulley
    Test 3: Early 2-Valve GT: Kenne Bell Supercharger
    Test 4: PI 2-Valve GT: Kenne Bell Supercharger
    Test 5: PI 2-Valve GT: Vortech T-Trim Supercharger
    Test 6: Vortech T-Trim Supercharged 2-Valve GT: 12 psi vs. 16.9 psi
    Test 7: Kenne Bell Supercharged PI 2-Valve GT: 1.7L vs. 2.2L
    Test 8: 2-Valve 5.4L Lightning: Kenne Bell Supercharger Upgrade
    Test 9: PI 2-Valve GT: Vortech T-Trim vs. JT-Trim

Chapter 7: Supercharging 3- and 4-Valve Modular Engines 130
    Test 1: 4-Valve '03 Cobra: Naturally Apirated vs. Eaton Supercharger
    Test 2: Eaton Supercharged 4-Valve '03 Cobra: Pulley Upgrades
    Test 3: 4-Valve '03 Cobra: Eaton Supercharger vs. Kenne Bell Upgrade
    Test 4: 4-Valve '03 Cobra: Eaton Supercharger vs. Vortech T-Trim Upgrade
    Test 5: 3-Valve '05 GT: Paxton Novi 1200 Supercharger
    Test 6: Kenne Bell Supercharged 4-Valve '03 Cobra: 16.5 psi vs. 19.5 psi
    Test 7: 4-Valve 5.4L: ATI F2M Supercharger
    Test 8: 4-Valve Cobra: Paxton Novi 2000 Supercharger
    Test 9: Paxton Supercharged 4-Valve Cobra: Effect of Intercooling
    Test 10: 3-Valve '05 GT: Kenne Bell Supercharger

Chapter 8: Turbocharging 152
    Test 1: Early 2-Valve GT: HP Performance Twin-Turbo Kit
    Test 2: HP Twin-Turbo Early 2-Valve GT: 10 psi vs. 14 psi
    Test 3: Early 4-Valve Cobra: HP Twin-Turbo Kit
    Test 4: 4-Valve '03 Cobra: Turbo vs. Blower, Blower, & Blower (11 psi)
    Test 5: 4-Valve '03 Cobra: Turbo vs. Blower, Blower, & Blower (14 psi)
    Test 6: 4-Valve '03 Cobra: NA vs. HP Twin-Turbo Kit (20.8 psi)
    Test 7: Mihovitz 4.6L Twin-Turbo Race Motor: 25 psi vs. 29 psi
    Test 8: 3-Valve '05 GT: HP Twin-Turbo Kit

Chapter 9: Exhaust Systems 174
    Test 1: Early 2-Valve GT: Hooker Long-Tube Headers
    Test 2: PI 2-Valve GT: Ford Racing Shorty Headers
    Test 3: PI 2-Valve GT: Kooks 1⅝-inch Long-Tube Headers
    Test 4: Eaton Supercharged 4-Valve '03 Cobra: Flow-Tech Long-Tube Headers
    Test 5: Kenne Bell Supercharged 4-Valve '03 Cobra: Bassani Cat-Back Exhaust
    Test 6: 3-Valve '05 GT: JBA Long-Tube Headers
    Test 7: Kenne Bell Supercharged 4-Valve '03 Cobra: Kooks 1⅝- vs. 1¾-inch Headers
    Test 8: 4-Valve Cobra: Ford Racing Shorty Headers
    Test 9: 4-Valve Cobra: Hooker Long-Tube Headers

Chapter 10: Engine Buildups 194
    Test 1: 407-hp PI 2-Valve GT
    Test 2: 490-hp 5.0L Stroker PI 2-Valve GT
    Test 3: 800-hp Vortech Supercharged PI 2-Valve GT
    Test 4: 990-hp Twin-Turbo 4-Valve '03 Cobra
    Test 5: 1,350-hp ATI F2M Supercharged 5.4L 4-Valve

INTRODUCTION: ON THE DYNO

The aftermarket performance world didn't exactly welcome the new 4.6L modular motor with open arms when it came out in the '96 Mustang, but who can blame them? Imagine trying to fill the shoes of the now-famous 5.0L Mustang. Antiquated to be sure, the venerable fuel-injected 302 was still a force to be reckoned with out on the street, especially since nearly every one you came across was modified in some way. Though considerably less powerful than GM's LT1 and LS1, the 5.0L motor spawned an entire aftermarket industry. It could even be argued that the 5.0L Mustang single-handedly ushered in the performance era we now enjoy. Think about it: not since the big-blocks of yesteryear has there been so much performance machinery offered directly from the factory. Now glance back at the early to mid 1980s and check out the performance stats offered by the heavy hitters of that era. Heck, we have SUVs making more power than a mid-'80s 'Vette or even the mighty turbocharged Buick Grand National.

While the 5.0L Mustang got things started back in the mid-'80s, the fuelie motor, to say nothing of the Fox chassis, was getting a little long in the tooth by 1993, and the SN95 chassis update only prolonged the inevitable. Loyal as we were to the 5.0L, it was time for something radically new. What we hoped for and what we got were actually two different things. On paper, the new 4.6L

Imagine what a 4.6L 4-valve might run like with a pair of twin turbos and a centrifugal supercharger feeding a Kenne Bell twin-screw blower. Actually, the three forms of forced induction were only mocked up on the 4.6L 4-valve Cobra motor, but all three (as well as the stock M112 roots blower) were tested on the '03 4-valve motor at the same boost level. Check out Chapter 8 for details.

modular motor (so named for its crossover potential versatility) looked impressive. Ford finally awarded us with not just an aluminum-headed V-8, but one equipped with overhead cams. All the cool (high-RPM) race motors have overhead cams. Come to think of it, so did all the economy cars – or at least the imports. Regardless, we finally had factory-equipped aluminum heads and an overhead cam configuration to boot. Life was looking good, as the

Introduction

The 4.6L 2-valve was first introduced in the Mustang GT in 1996. Equipped with the right set of CNC-ported heads, cams, and intake, the 2-valve motors can exceed 400-flywheel hp without much trouble.

Camaro continued to rely on the time-honored cam-in-block configuration first seen back in 1955 (never mind that the configuration eventually produced over 400 hp in LS6 guise and an honest 500 hp from the 7.0L LS7).

Yep, we Mustangers were excited about the on-paper potential of the new overhead cam (OHC) modular motor, especially when we heard news of the DOHC Cobra waiting in the wings. Unfortunately, the early 4.6L never delivered on the promised performance. In fact, it could be argued that the early 215-hp 4.6L was actually a step down compared to the 225-hp 5.0L (which was curiously re-rated to 205 hp in the SN95 models—just before the introduction of the new 4.6L). With the 5.0L performance industry in full swing cranking out dozens of different intake configurations, 30 to 40 different sets of performance cylinder heads, and every conceivable displacement stroker assembly imaginable (to say nothing of the huge forced induction market), 5.0L fanatics were somewhat tentative to jump on the 4.6L bandwagon. As of early 2005, no one has produced aftermarket SOHC 4.6L GT heads, and aftermarket intake manifolds can be counted on one hand. With Ford's recent switch to the 3-valve head, the likelihood of AFR, Edelbrock, or Trick Flow (TFS) tooling up to satisfy the hunger for an aftermarket 2-valve GT head grows slimmer by the hour. Too bad, as the ported heads tested in the pages of this book indicate that modular motors (like most) respond well to increased airflow.

Though the 4.6L was met with less fanfare than anticipated by Ford, things changed somewhat when they finally realized the error of their ways and upped the performance in 1999. The now-famous Power Improved (PI) version of the 4.6L came with a full 260 hp. No matter which power numbers you use, the 260-hp 4.6L was a significant step up in performance compared to the original 225-hp (or 205-hp) 5.0L. PI-equipped Mustang GTs were dipping down into the 13s and to the benefit of all the early non-PI headed GTs out there, the late-model heads were a direct bolt on. Seemingly as an apology to the early Mustang owners, installing the late-model PI heads on the early motor raised the compression ratio beyond either the stock PI or non-PI motors to further improve performance. For this reason, owners of the early non-PI 4.6L GTs need not be so quick to trade in their Mustangs. We took an early GT motor right from the wrecking yard and upped the power output to 655 hp without so much as touching the stock (high-mileage) short block. All it took was a set of CNC-ported PI heads and matching intake, an Xtreme Energy cam, and a Vortech supercharger. Naturally this same combination can be applied to the Power Improved motors as well.

The bread-and-butter GT 2-valve engines vastly outnumber the more expensive and powerful 4-valve motors, but it is the 4-valve Cobra that carries the fight to the Vipers and 'Vettes of the world. When originally introduced in the Mustang in 1996, the 4-valve Cobra motor offered nearly 90 horsepower more than the similar-sized (non-PI) 2-valve GT. This power deficit was cut significantly when Ford introduced the 260-hp PI, despite the jump to 320 hp for the 4-valve Cobra. Though the most obvious difference between the 2-valve and 4-valve 4.6L motors is the number of valves and attending valvetrain, the reality is that the power difference between the two motors is not due solely to improved head flow. True enough, the 4-valve heads do outflow the 2-valve versions, but the Cobra motor is also blessed with additional static compression, revised cam timing, and an improved intake design, which included a high-flow, dual-blade throttle body. Though the 4-valve Cobra motor went through a black period where the power output was supposedly somewhat less than advertised, the 4-valve motors have always proven to be powerful performers, especially in modified trim.

Ford teased us with a number of limited-production performers like the FR500 and 4-valve 5.4L Cobra R, but experiments like these eventually gave us some serious power in the form of a supercharger. Some may argue that forced induction is the easy way out of producing a powerful naturally aspirated powerplant, but true enthusiasts saw the introduction of the force-fed 5.4L Lightning truck and the '03 Cobra as proof positive that Ford was finally serious about the modular engine program. The 5.4L Lightning takes (nearly) everything

Introduction

from the PI version of the 4.6L and adds displacement and boost from an Eaton roots-style supercharger. Folks like Johnny Lightning have already managed to run 9s in these supercharged two-ton 5.4L monstrosities, thanks in no small part to the additional power supplied by a twin-screw Kenne Bell supercharger upgrade. Street supercharged Cobra owners have managed to go well into the 9s, while a full-tilt effort by Accufab's John Mihovitz has put turbocharged 4-valve Cobra motors well into the 6s at over 200 mph! These 4-valve motors have serious power potential.

While the aftermarket industry has not embraced the 4.6L in the same way as the 5.0L, there are still a great many performance parts available for nearly all of the available modular motors. In this book, we put these performance products to the ultimate test – direct back-to-back dyno comparisons. Only by comparing the products using regimented testing procedures can the real benefit (or lack thereof) be shown. Forget the advertisers' hype and all the useless Internet rubbish, *Building 4.6/5.4L Ford Horsepower on the Dyno* has real data, generated by real test procedures. While most of the concentration is on the Mustang and Cobra engines, the information and power gains can also be applied to the other modular-motored Ford vehicles. We've also included dyno testing on everything from the supercharged 5.4L Lightning to full-sized 4.6L trucks. Need to know what nitrous does on a supercharged '03 Cobra? No problem. Which cam works best on a 4.6L GT? We tested six different sets of cams on the same motor, so you can choose for yourself. What about throttle bodies and intake elbows on a 4.6L GT? Same deal, we tested all of them – naturally aspirated and supercharged! We covered intakes, head swaps, and forced induction (blowers and turbos). Heck, we even have information on the new 3-valve motors and the supercharged 4-valve 5.4L used in the Ford GT super-car. Whether you're looking for real-world back-to-back dyno results on an air intake, cat-back exhaust, or anything in between, *Building 4.6/5.4L Ford Horsepower on the Dyno* has you covered.

Ford hit a home run when they introduced the supercharged 4-valve motor in the 2003 4-valve Cobra. Later, upgraded with twin turbos and Comp Cams, we managed to produce 990 hp from an otherwise stock supercharged Cobra crate motor from Ford Racing.

Vortech and Paxton quickly introduced blower kits for the 4.6L 3-valve GT motor. With JBA headers and a Vortech blower, this 4.6L 3-valve exceeded 600 hp on the engine dyno.

Chapter 1

Throttle Bodies and Inlet Elbows

While many enthusiasts think of the throttle body as a simple air door, the reality is that there is much more to a good throttle body than the sheer size. Whether single blade, as on the 2-valve motors, or dual blade, like the 4-valve motors, the throttle body acts as a valve to control airflow to the motor. One of the biggest misconceptions about throttle bodies is that installing a high-flow unit (whether larger or of an improved design) will result in a gain in power. Building a better throttle body, or at least one that flows more air than a production piece, is oftentimes a simple matter of increasing the flow area. By this we mean that a 70-mm throttle body (like the 2-valve unit from Ford Racing) will usually outflow a smaller 65-mm version (like the stock 4.6L 2-valve piece). Unfortunately, the simple fact that one throttle body outflows the other does not guarantee power gains. Power gains are only realized by increasing the flow through the motor, not just improving a single component. The exception to this rule is when the single component happens to be the restriction in the system that is limiting the engine's ultimate flow rate.

An example works well here, as the 4.6L 2-valve motors seemed to respond well to throttle body and inlet elbow (also referred to as upper intake)

Blower motors respond very well to throttle-body upgrades, like this Accufab throttle body and inlet system for the '03 Cobra.

upgrades. Having run hundreds of tests on the effect of 2-valve throttle body upgrades on everything from stock to supercharged combinations (both centrifugal and positive displacement), it is safe to say that throttle body upgrades on the 2-valve motors are a worthwhile endeavor. The same cannot be said (universally) about the 4-valve motors, especially the naturally aspirated versions. Testing on stock and mildly modified 4.6L 4-valve motors showed little, if any, power gains offered by throttle body upgrades. This does not mean that the throttle bodies tested didn't outflow their stock counterparts – they did. It simply means that the stock throttle body was not the restriction in the inlet system. Obviously, the wilder the combination, the more likely it is that a throttle body upgrade will be effective, as the stock system was designed with a specific airflow (and power level) in mind. Exceeding that power level with modifications to cylinder-head flow, intake manifold configurations, and cam timing will likely increase the flow requirements of the engine, making a larger (or higher flowing) throttle body a necessity.

It's not surprising that supercharging a motor will dramatically increase its airflow needs, but does that automatically mean that a large throttle body will be necessary or beneficial? In the case of the 4.6L 2-valve GT motors, the stock throttle body and elbow were certainly restrictive, even in stock form. The stock throttle body and inlet elbow become ever more restrictive as the power output of the naturally aspirated combination is increased, meaning that a throttle body upgrade will be worth more power on a 360-hp 4.6L 2-valve motor than a 260-hp version. Adding a centrifugal supercharger to the mix obviously increases the airflow through the throttle body under pressure, but a throttle-body upgrade is still worthwhile. Running the stock throttle body on a draw-through application with a Kenne Bell or a Ford Racing blower eliminates the inlet elbow portion of the equation, but the power gains are still impressive as the air is now being drawn (and not pushed) through the throttle body. Since a positive-displacement supercharger will easily add 100 hp (or more), you'd better think about a larger throttle body to feed all that extra airflow.

When considering a throttle body upgrade, think first about restrictions that may be present upstream in the filter box, mass-air meter, and inlet tubing. If a restriction exists upstream of the throttle body, it is unlikely that changes to the throttle body and/or inlet elbow will yield power gains. Again, the higher the power output of the combination, the more restrictive the stock components can become. A perfect example of this can be seen in Test 4 where we replaced the stock induction system on the Kenne Bell supercharged early 4.6L 2-valve motor. On this supercharged non-PI 4.6L, the stock throttle body represented a restriction, but so too did the filter box and mass-air meter. It was necessary to replace the whole system to achieve the power gains realized in the test. While the power gains on a stock early 4.6L may not have been significant

Testing performed on all of the available throttle-body inlet elbows on the 4.6L 2-valve showed that they all improved the power output over the stock combo.

Running stock boost and power levels, the factory twin-blade throttle body performed very well on the '03 Cobra motor.

Run on a draw-through application like this Ford Racing supercharged 2-valve motor, throttle body upgrades (like the 70-mm unit from Ford Racing) can offer significant power gains.

or even present, adding a supercharger to the mix will certainly tax the flow rate of the stock components. Positive-displacement superchargers are especially sensitive to inlet restrictions, as they cause a drop in boost pressure. The same is true of the inlet system on a centrifugal supercharger, as the induction system should be as free flowing as space will allow. Why limit the power gains offered by that supercharger with a restrictive induction system?

Chapter 1

Test 1: PI 2-Valve GT: Throttle Body & Intake Elbow Shoot-Out

While we all crave stroker motors with blowers, turbos, or nitrous, the reality is that the vast majority of us can't afford to plop down the big bucks for a complete engine buildup right away. The most popular route to improved performance is usually to save up a few bucks and then decide on how best to spend it. Often the decision process goes beyond the monetary considerations, as many enthusiasts have no idea how to build a stroker motor or install a complete turbo system even if they managed to save up the coin. Without the knowledge and experience, the only way to have such systems installed is to pay even more money. For these reasons, simple and inexpensive bolt-on components will always outsell the more expensive items, desirable though they may be. Tops on the list of relatively inexpensive and easy-to-install parts is the throttle body. In the case of the 4.6L GT motor, the throttle body works in conjunction with a 90-degree inlet elbow. Often called an upper intake, the cast aluminum inlet does little more than provide a smooth transition for the airflow from the throttle body to the plenum in the actual intake manifold. This upper and lower designation needs to be left with the 5.0L stuff where it belongs.

Due in part to the ease of manufacturing, the throttle body/inlet elbow combination has become so popular that higher-flow versions are available from a number of aftermarket companies. Throttle bodies have been popular upgrades since the 5.0L fuelie Mustang. Part of the reason for the popularity is the ease of installation. Even the most inexperienced Mustang owner can easily tackle the job of replacing the throttle body and elbow on the 4.6L. There's nothing better than the feeling of your first successful performance modification, especially if you accomplished said installation

The stock elbow and throttle body don't look like a restrictive combination, but these tests proved otherwise. Since the throttle body/elbow combo is right on top of the engine, swapping them out is a relatively painless process.

The engine used in this test features ported PI heads, long-tube Hooker headers, and a set of Comp XE274H cams. It's pretty potent for a naturally aspirated 2-valve combination.

without resorting to a trip to your local tuner shop. As indicated earlier, a number of performance elbows are currently available for the 4.6L 2-valve mod motor, and what better way to demonstrate the effectiveness of each than to gather them together and run them all on the same test motor? When you start talking about a comparison, the only way to achieve the desired results is to run all of the components on the same day on the same motor.

The test motor started out life as an early ('98) 4.6L, originally rated at 225 flywheel hp. The motor was basically your average medium-mileage wrecking-yard special. The early (non-PI) 4.6L short block remained stock, but the stock early heads were replaced with a set of CNC-ported PI heads from Total Engine Airflow (TEA). The ported PI heads offered substantially more airflow than the early models, while upping the static compression thanks to a smaller combustion chamber. Naturally, the PI heads were run in conjunction with the matching PI intake manifold. The 4.6L test motor also received Comp Xtreme Energy XE274H cams, a set of Hooker long-tube headers, and a Meziere electric water pump. All of the testing was performed with a F.A.S.T. electronic (and programmable) fuel-injection system. All of the modifications eventually improved the power output to 393 flywheel hp, making this modified 4.6L the ideal test bed for the larger throttle body/elbow combinations. Check out the results of each system (the stock system vs. Accufab 70 mm, Accufab 75 mm, Dragon, C&L, TFS). They each offered a sizable gain over the stock setup, so it's hard to go wrong with any of the combinations.

Throttle Bodies and Inlet Elbows

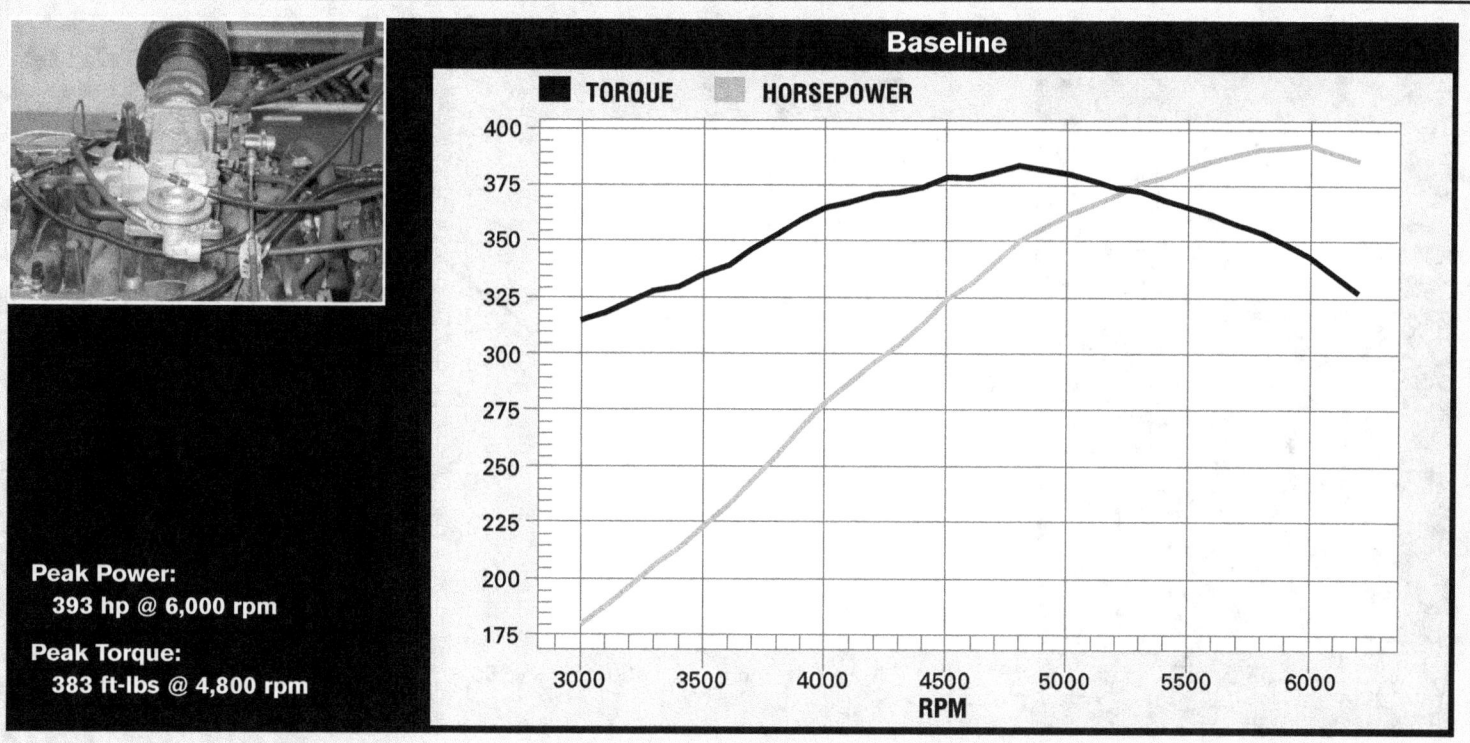

Peak Power:
393 hp @ 6,000 rpm

Peak Torque:
383 ft-lbs @ 4,800 rpm

Stock Throttle Body/Elbow
The baseline test was run with the stock throttle body and elbow. Equipped with the stock components, the 4.6L produced 393 hp and 383 ft-lbs of torque.

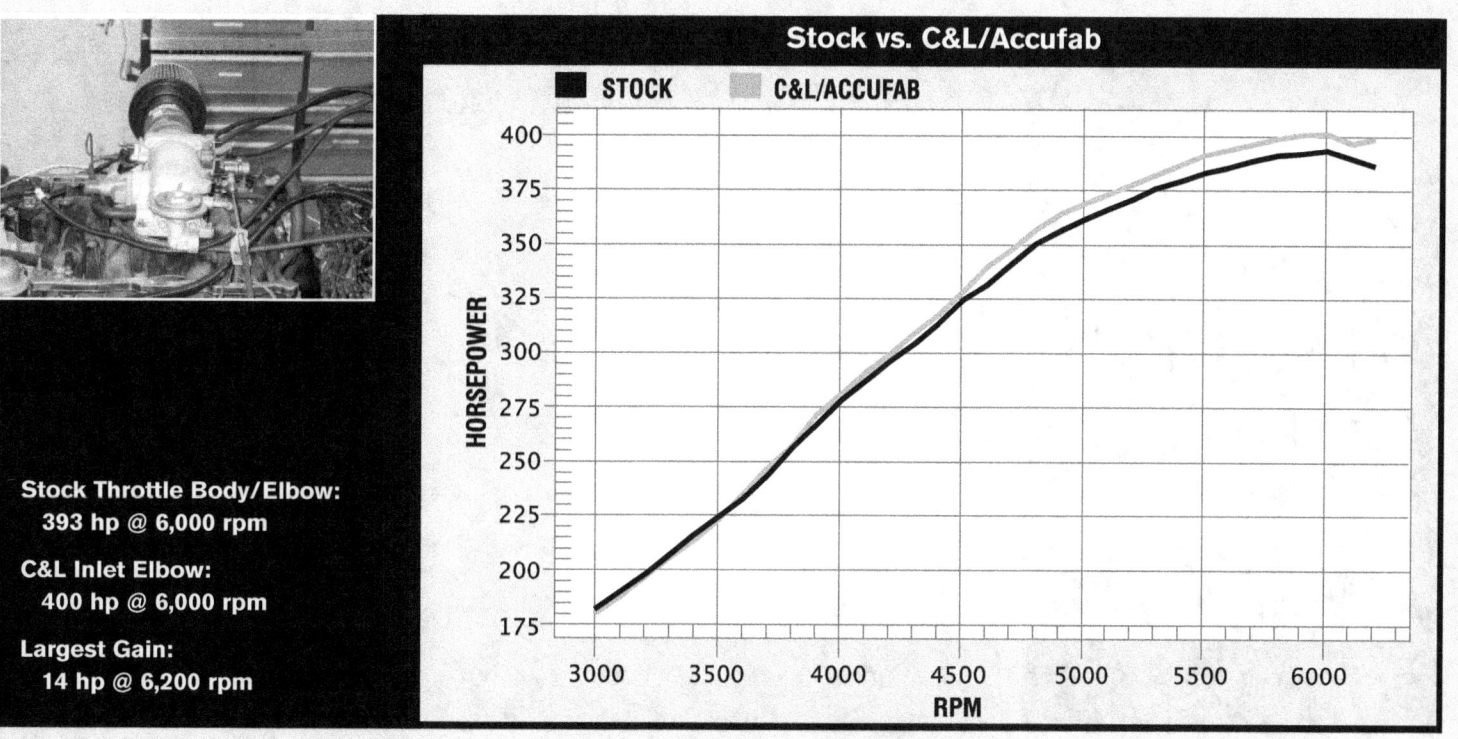

Stock Throttle Body/Elbow:
393 hp @ 6,000 rpm

C&L Inlet Elbow:
400 hp @ 6,000 rpm

Largest Gain:
14 hp @ 6,200 rpm

Stock Throttle Body/Elbow vs. C&L Inlet Elbow & Accufab 75-mm Throttle Body
The C&L inlet was combined with a 75-mm Accufab throttle body for testing. Equipped with the C&L inlet and 75-mm Accufab throttle body, the peak power jumped to 400 hp. The C&L elbow upped the power output by as much as 14 hp.

Building 4.6/5.4L Ford Horsepower on the Dyno

Chapter 1

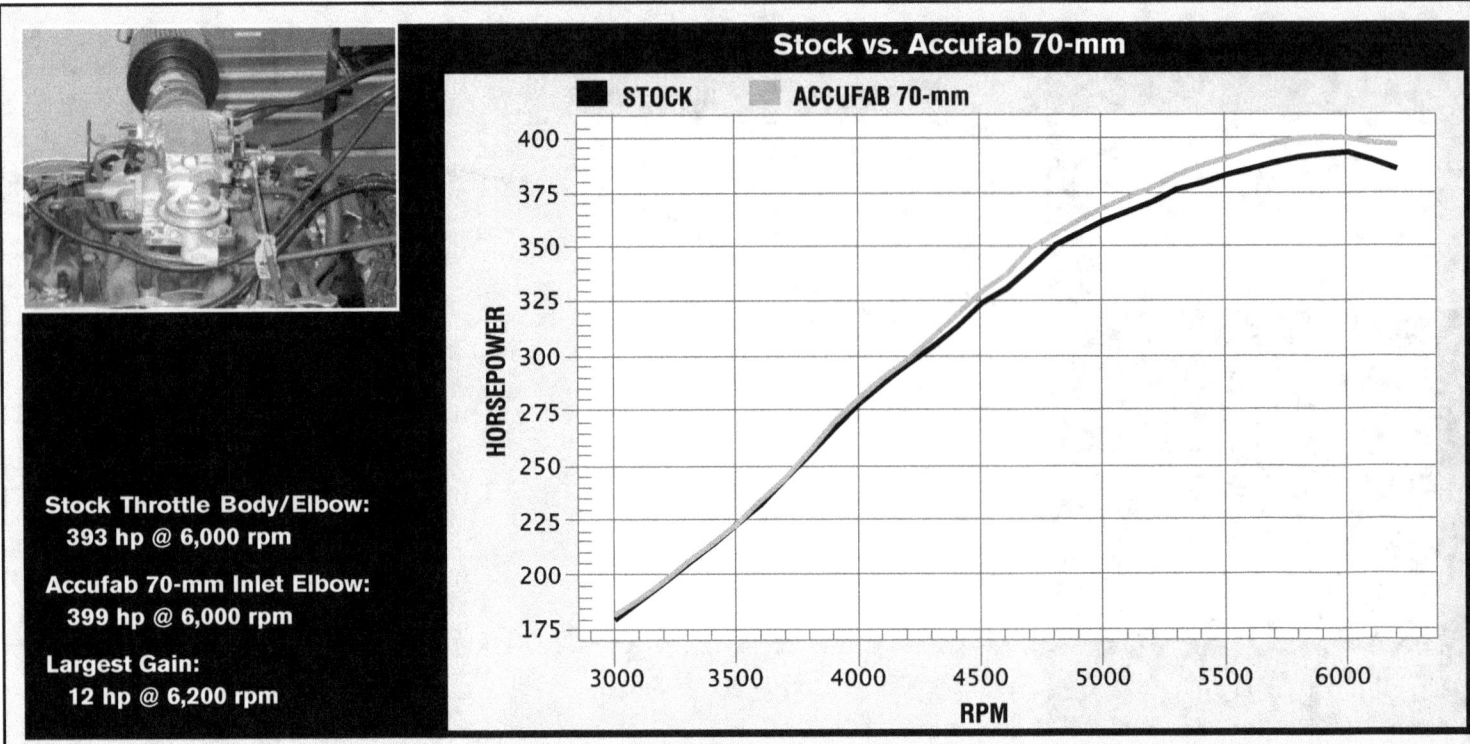

Stock Throttle Body/Elbow:
393 hp @ 6,000 rpm

Accufab 70-mm Inlet Elbow:
399 hp @ 6,000 rpm

Largest Gain:
12 hp @ 6,200 rpm

Stock Throttle Body/Elbow vs. Accufab Elbow & 70-mm Throttle Body
The Accufab 70-mm throttle body and inlet elbow upped the peak power of the modified 4.6L to 399 hp; the largest gain was 12 hp over stock. As with all the other inlet elbows, the gains increased with engine speed. This was the only system to utilize the 70-mm throttle body.

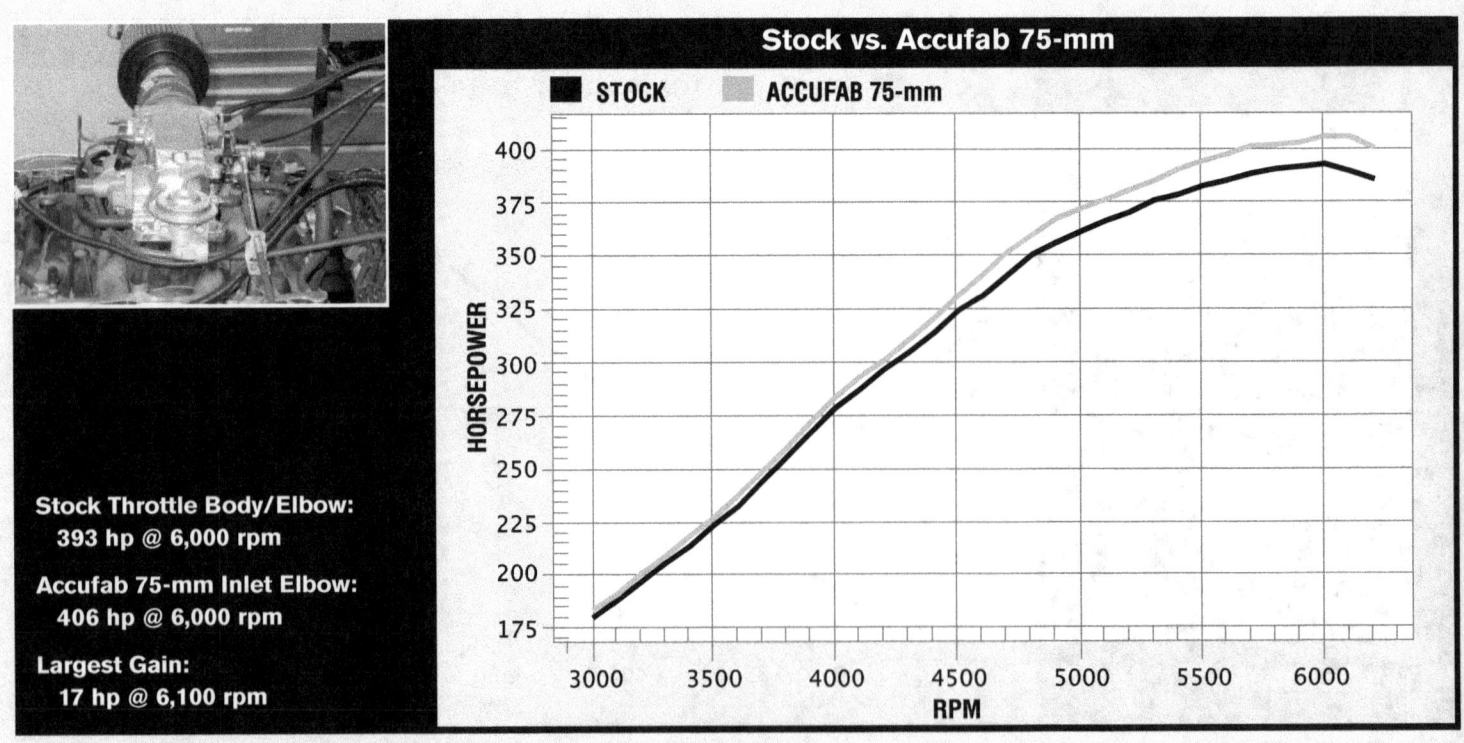

Stock Throttle Body/Elbow:
393 hp @ 6,000 rpm

Accufab 75-mm Inlet Elbow:
406 hp @ 6,000 rpm

Largest Gain:
17 hp @ 6,100 rpm

Stock Throttle Body/Elbow vs. Accufab Elbow & 75-mm Throttle Body
Combining the 75-mm Accufab throttle body with the 75-mm inlet elbow resulted in the largest gains of the test. The Accufab components upped the peak power to 406 hp and offered as much as 17 additional horsepower.

Throttle Bodies and Inlet Elbows

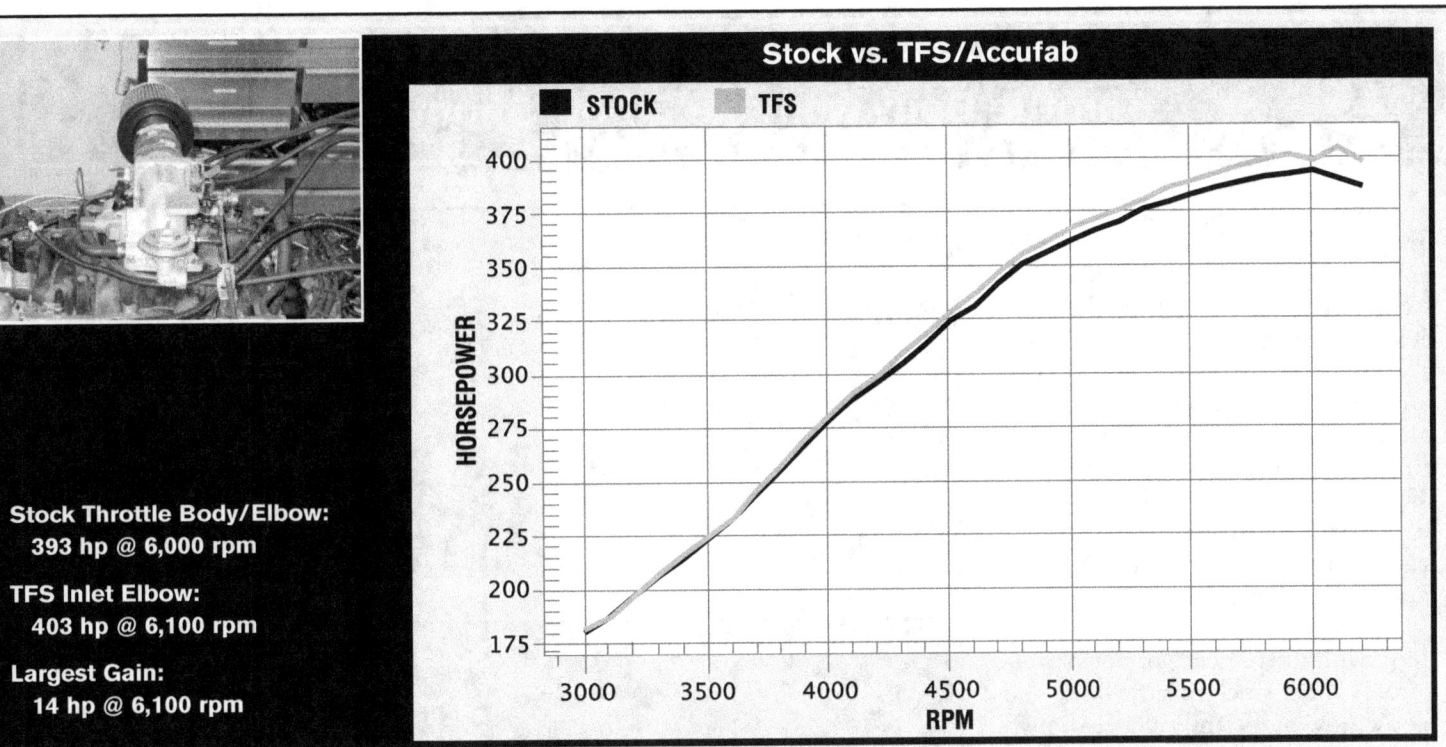

Stock Throttle Body/Elbow:
393 hp @ 6,000 rpm

TFS Inlet Elbow:
403 hp @ 6,100 rpm

Largest Gain:
14 hp @ 6,100 rpm

Stock Throttle Body/Elbow vs. TFS Elbow & Accufab 75-mm Throttle Body
The TFS elbow was the least expensive of the bunch but by no means did that mean it was the least powerful. Equipped with the TFS cast-aluminum elbow, the 4.6L produced 403 hp.

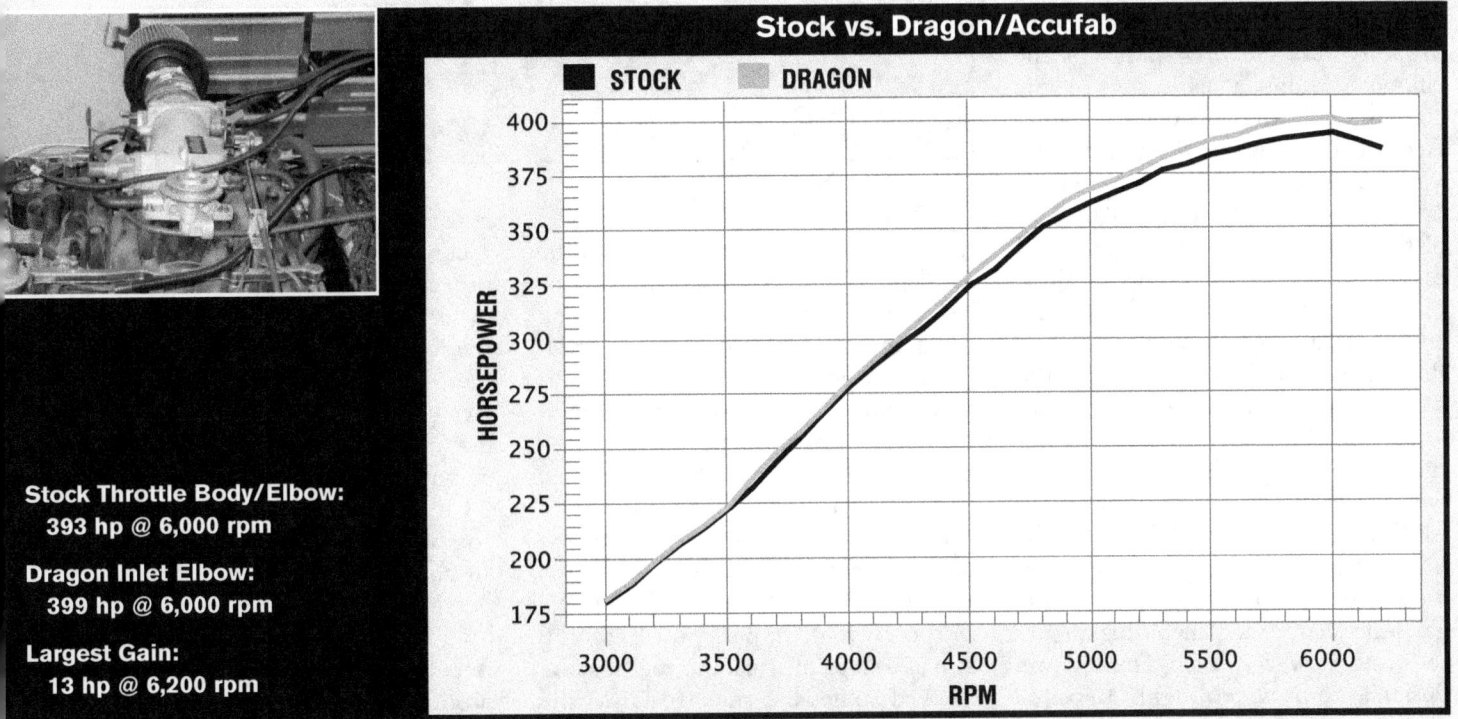

Stock Throttle Body/Elbow:
393 hp @ 6,000 rpm

Dragon Inlet Elbow:
399 hp @ 6,000 rpm

Largest Gain:
13 hp @ 6,200 rpm

Stock Throttle Body/Elbow vs. Dragon Elbow & Accufab 75-mm Throttle Body
The Dragon inlet elbow differed from the others in that the elbow featured a divider to equalize the airflow distribution (prevented stacking against the far wall) through the elbow. The peak power checked in at 399 hp, while the largest gain was 13 hp.

Chapter 1

Test 2: Vortech Supercharged PI 2-Valve GT: Throttle Body & Intake Elbow Shoot-Out

After running the throttle body/elbow combinations on our 390-hp naturally aspirated 4.6L GT motor, we retested the throttle bodies and elbows after installing a Vortech supercharger. Even in naturally aspirated form, the stock throttle body/elbow presented a restriction, as all of the aftermarket combinations increased the power output. Would the test results be repeated once we installed the supercharger? After all, the Vortech supercharger artificially improved the flow rate of even the stock throttle body with the presence of boost pressure. Will the stock throttle body and elbow flow sufficiently under (boost) pressure, or will the extra airflow requirement (more horsepower) offset the improvement in flow rate? In short, will the stock throttle body and elbow still represent a restriction under boost?

Those of you who read Test 1 know that we had an ideal motor to properly test the flow limits of the elbows. Equipped with any of the elbows and the matching 75-mm Accufab throttle body, our naturally aspirated 4.6L GT motor exceeded 400 hp and just missed cresting 400 ft-lbs of torque. The combination consisted of a bone-stock 1998 2-valve short block topped with a set of CNC-ported PI heads from Total Engine Airflow, a set of XE274H cams from Comp Cams, and a set of Hooker long-tube headers. The motor also featured a matching PI intake manifold as well as a Meziere electric water pump, MSD ignition coils, and Denso Iridium spark plugs. To this combination we added a complete Vortech centrifugal supercharger kit, including an air-to-water Power Cooler. The kit was designed to provide roughly 10 psi of boost to a stock 4.6L, but we upgraded our kit with a high-flow T-Trim supercharger. The T-Trim had no problem supplying 10 psi of boost to even our modified 4.6L motor.

The intake charge was now being pushed through the throttle body and elbow by the Vortech T-Trim supercharger. Though each of the throttle bodies will flow more air under boost pressure, the results show that it wasn't enough to keep the throttle bodies/ elbows from becoming a restriction.

The intake elbows used for testing from left-to-right: Accufab 75 mm, Dragon, Trick Flow, C&L, Accufab 70 mm.

The supercharged and intercooled 4.6L GT motor was run first with the stock throttle body and elbow to establish a baseline. Equipped with the stock components, the supercharged 4.6L produced peak numbers of 612 hp at 6,000 rpm and 539 ft-lbs of torque at 5,600 rpm. Eagle-eyed readers will no doubt recognize the fact (on the graphs) that we actually revved the motors to 6,100 rpm and that (nearly) all of the aftermarket throttle body/elbows produced more power at 6,100 rpm. We purposely took the peak power reading at 6,000 since the final number may be skewed somewhat since that was the final reading gathered as the dyno pulled the motor off the test. In other words, the final number might be off by a few horses. Choosing 6,000 rpm as our peak number did not change the outcome in any way, it just ensured we had accurate data. First up was the combination that finished at the bottom of the order on the naturally aspirated motor, the 70-mm Accufab setup. Unlike all of the other aftermarket elbows, this Accufab elbow was set up to accept a 70-mm throttle body. All others were tested with a larger 75-mm throttle body. As it turned out, the smaller 70-mm combo nearly got the last laugh, besting all comers in torque production and missing out on top horsepower honors by 1 hp. Equipped with the 70-mm Accufab system, the supercharged 4.6L produced 631 hp at 6,000 rpm and 556 ft-lbs of torque. The smaller Accufab throttle body/elbow combo bettered the stock system by as much as 22 hp at 5,900 rpm (the largest difference offered by any of the aftermarket systems).

Throttle Bodies and Inlet Elbows

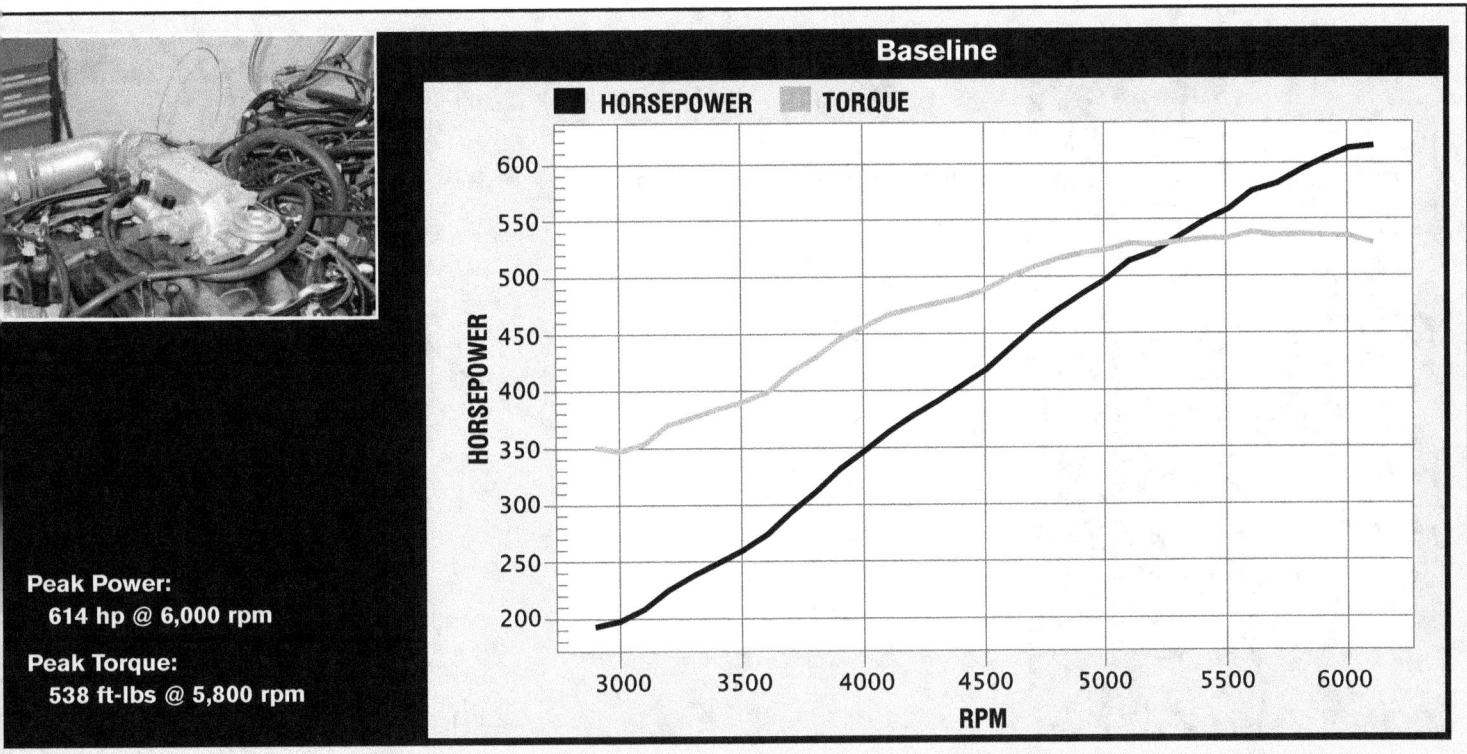

Peak Power:
614 hp @ 6,000 rpm

Peak Torque:
538 ft-lbs @ 5,800 rpm

Stock Throttle Body/Elbow
Naturally we baselined the supercharged 4.6L 2-valve motor with the stock throttle body and inlet elbow. Equipped with the stock components, the supercharged 4.6L produced 614 hp and 538 ft-lbs of torque.

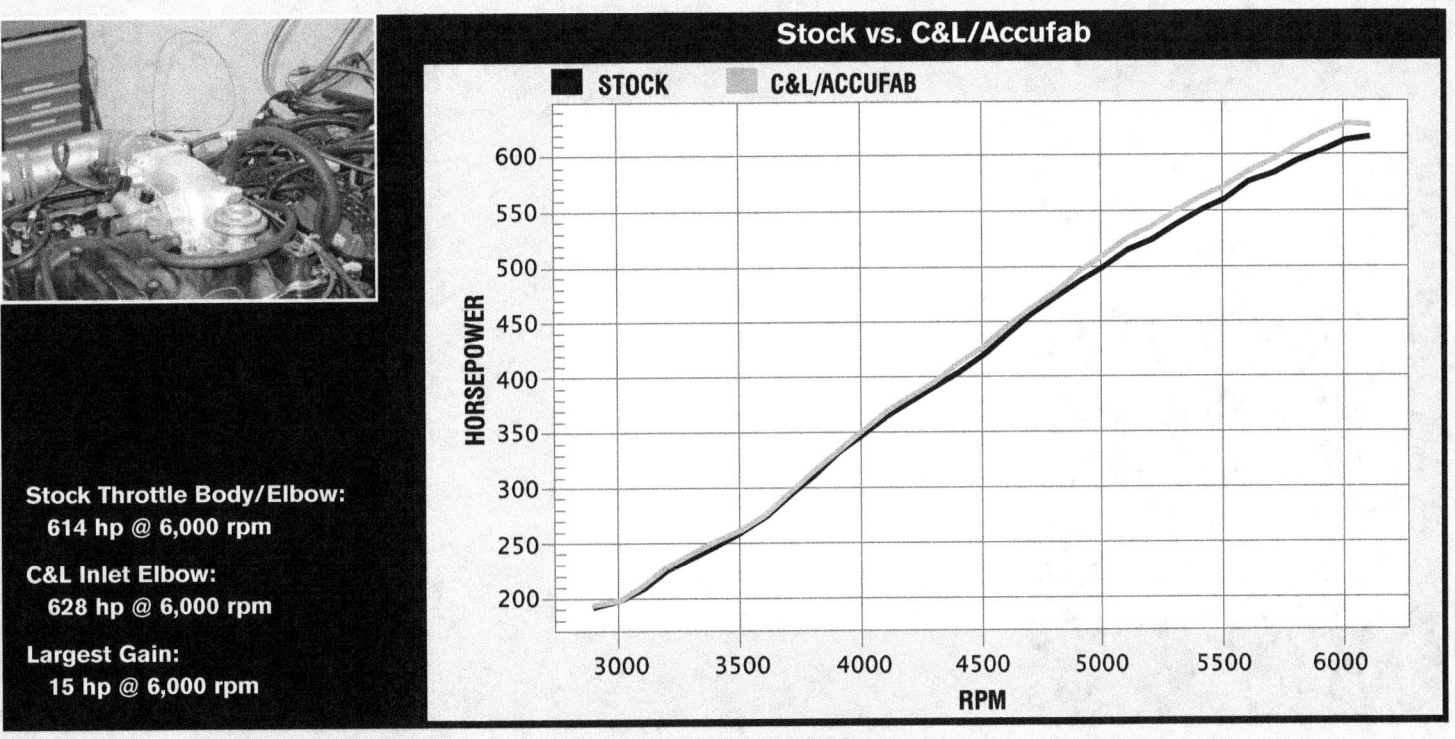

Stock Throttle Body/Elbow:
614 hp @ 6,000 rpm

C&L Inlet Elbow:
628 hp @ 6,000 rpm

Largest Gain:
15 hp @ 6,000 rpm

Stock Throttle Body/Elbow vs. C&L Elbow & Accufab 75-mm Throttle Body
Installing the C&L inlet elbow and 75-mm Accufab throttle body increased the power output of the supercharged 4.6L. The gains increased with engine speed, and the peak was up from 614 hp to 628 hp.

Building 4.6/5.4L Ford Horsepower on the Dyno

Chapter 1

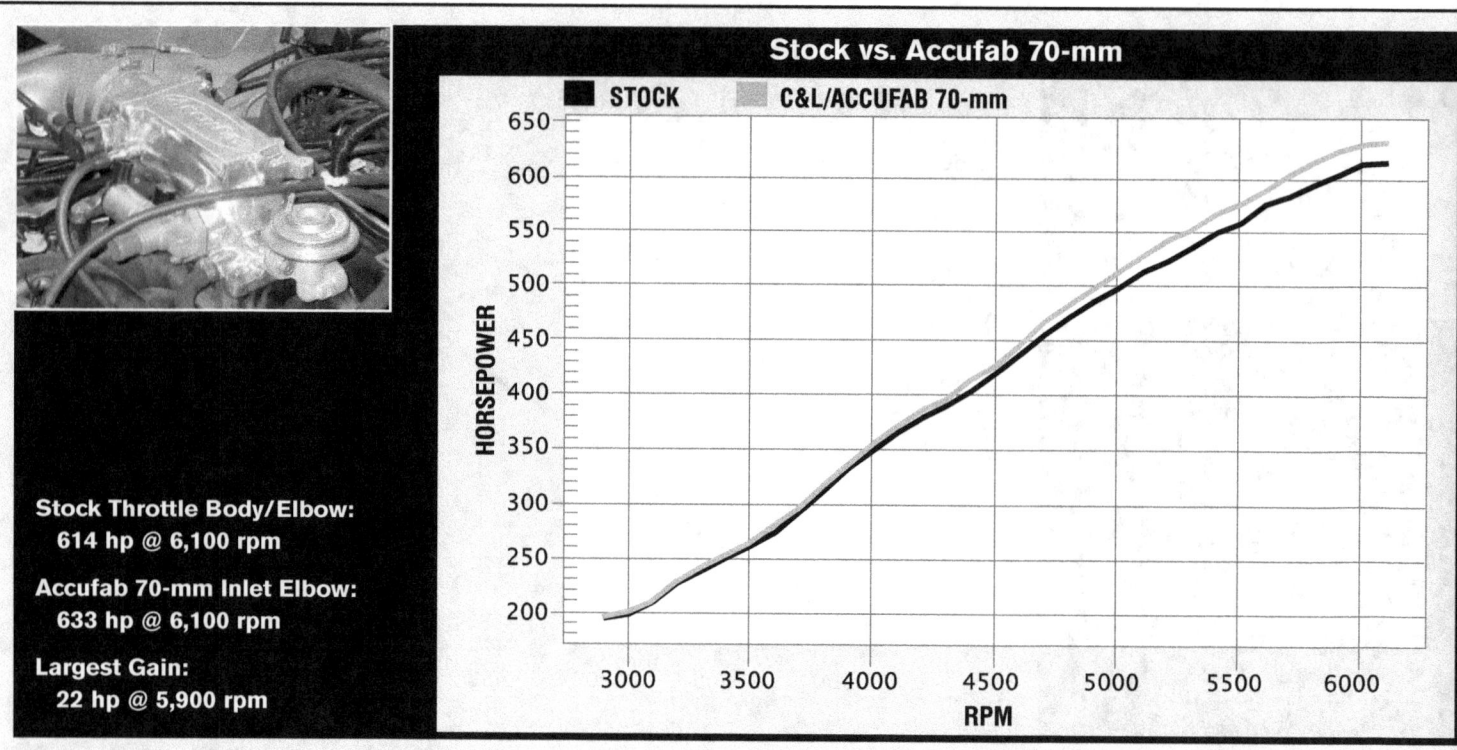

Stock Throttle Body/Elbow:
614 hp @ 6,100 rpm

Accufab 70-mm Inlet Elbow:
633 hp @ 6,100 rpm

Largest Gain:
22 hp @ 5,900 rpm

Stock Throttle Body/Elbow vs. Accufab Elbow and 70-mm Throttle Body
The smaller 70-mm Accufab throttle body and elbow surprised us by posting nearly the greatest gains of the bunch, peaking at 633 hp, with a maximum gain of 22 hp.

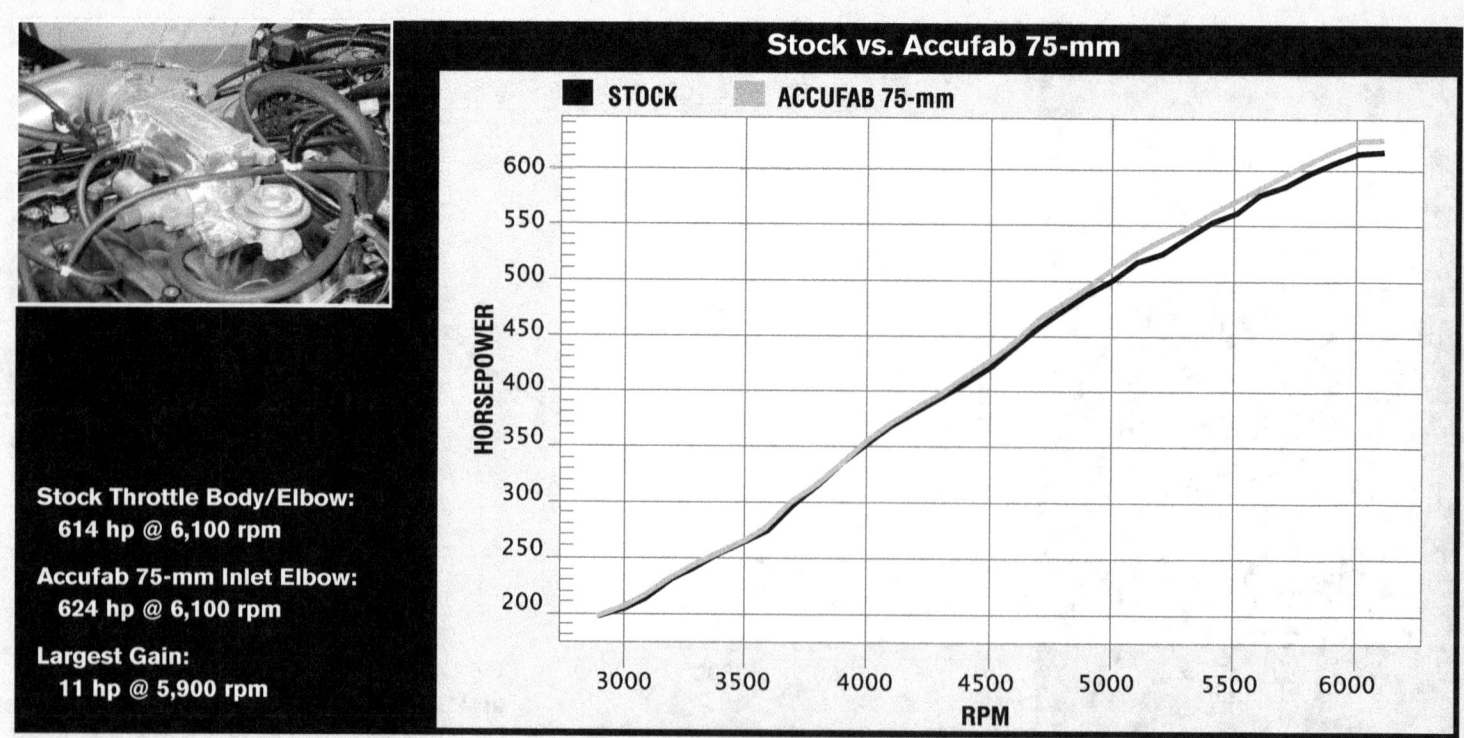

Stock Throttle Body/Elbow:
614 hp @ 6,100 rpm

Accufab 75-mm Inlet Elbow:
624 hp @ 6,100 rpm

Largest Gain:
11 hp @ 5,900 rpm

Stock Throttle Body/Elbow vs. Accufab Elbow & 75-mm Throttle Body
Oddly enough, the larger 75-mm Accufab throttle body didn't seem to perform as well as the smaller 70-mm version. Equipped with the larger 75-mm throttle body and elbow, the supercharged 4.6L produced 624 hp.

Throttle Bodies and Inlet Elbows

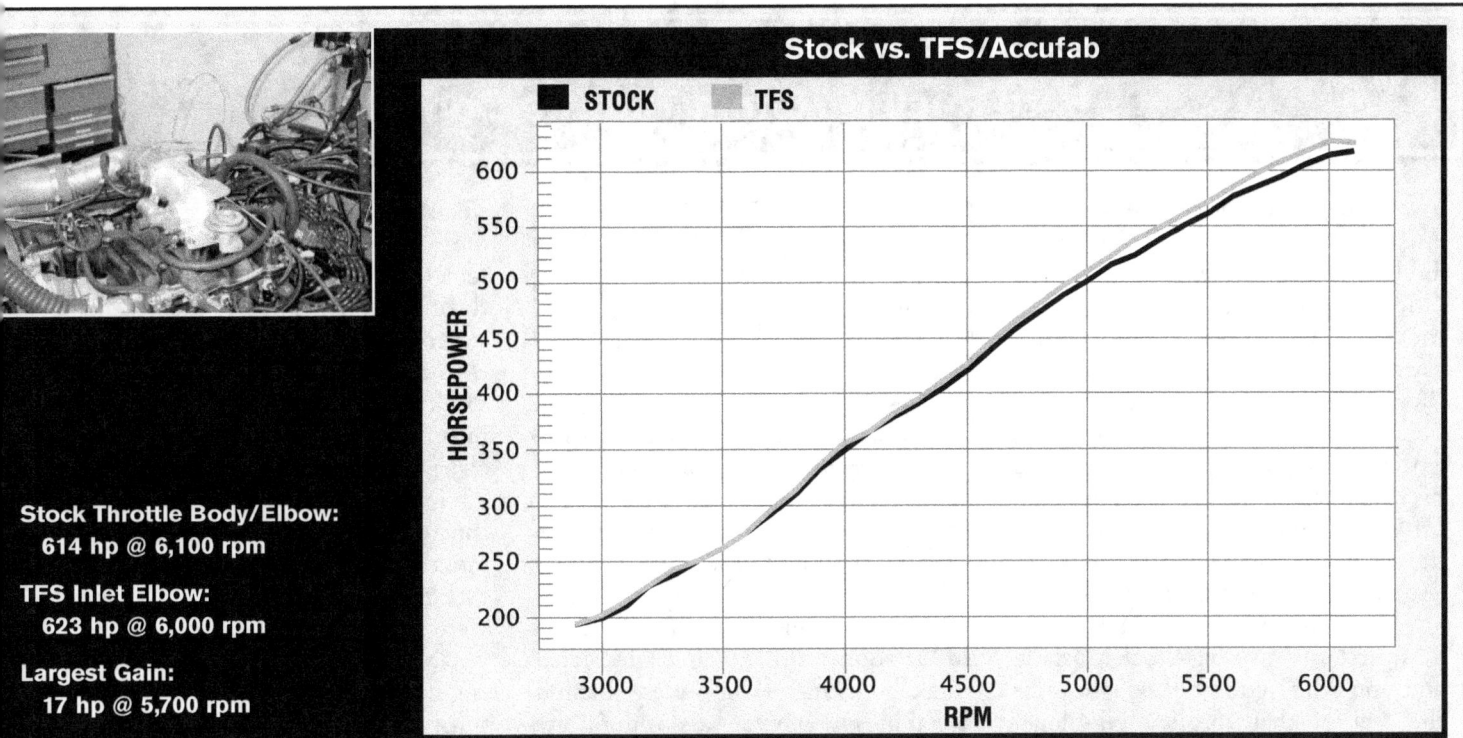

Stock Throttle Body/Elbow:
614 hp @ 6,100 rpm

TFS Inlet Elbow:
623 hp @ 6,000 rpm

Largest Gain:
17 hp @ 5,700 rpm

Stock Throttle Body/Elbow vs. TFS Elbow & Accufab 75-mm Throttle Body
The TFS elbow was the least expensive of the bunch, but it showed its worth by producing 623 hp, with a gain of as much as 17 hp over the stock system.

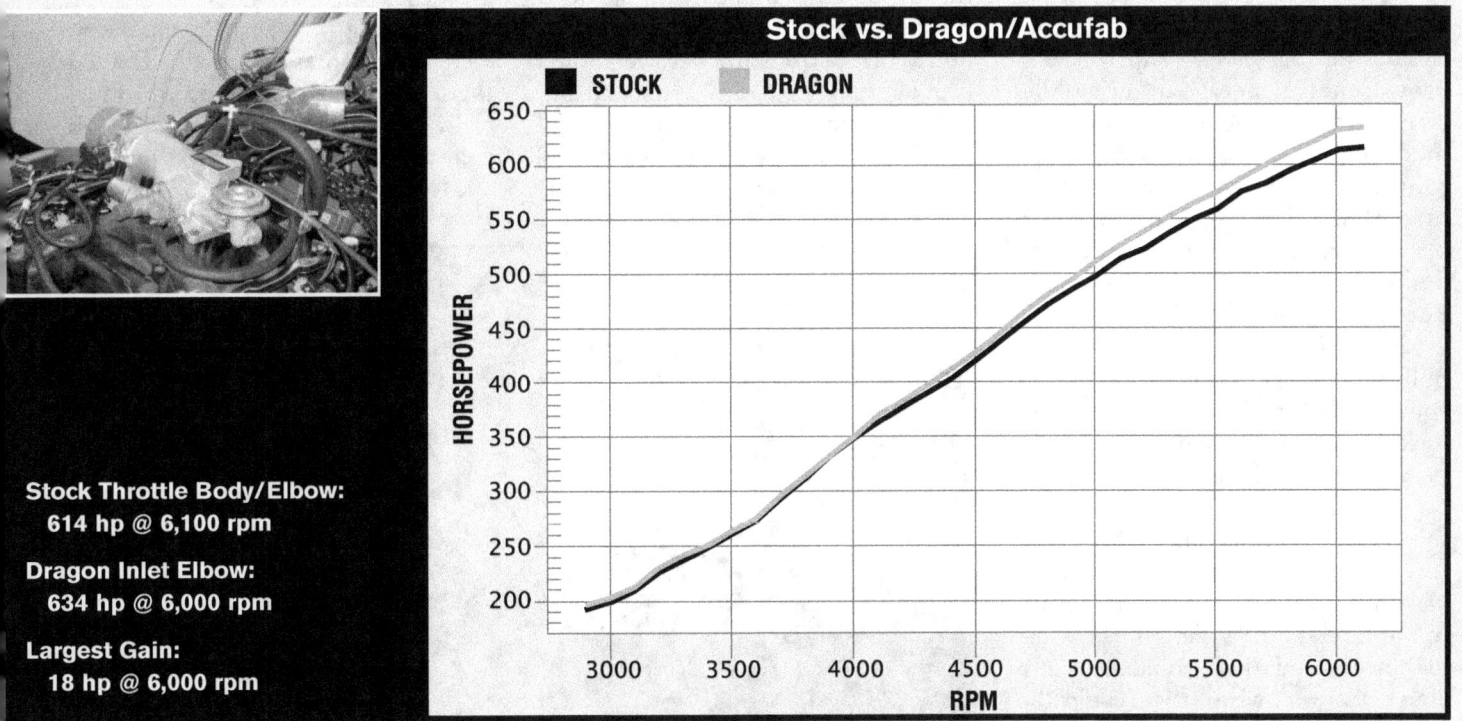

Stock Throttle Body/Elbow:
614 hp @ 6,100 rpm

Dragon Inlet Elbow:
634 hp @ 6,000 rpm

Largest Gain:
18 hp @ 6,000 rpm

Stock Throttle Body/Elbow vs. Dragon Elbow & Accufab 75-mm Throttle Body
The divided path offered by the Dragon elbow seemed to work well on this supercharged application, as the peak power was up to 634 hp, while the largest gain was 18 hp.

Building 4.6/5.4L Ford Horsepower on the Dyno

Test 3: Ford Racing Supercharged PI 2-Valve GT: Ford Racing 70-mm Throttle Body

It's possible that no one since Tim Allen's alter ego Tim "The Tool Man" Taylor uttered those famous words, "More Power," has anyone captured the true spirit of a performance enthusiast. While we all seem to want more, the reality is that not every engine buildup seeks maximum power output as the desired goal. Not everyone wants his or her street 'Stang to be able to rip off 10-second ¼-mile times or out-handle a Ferrari. Some of us just want to add a little more performance to what is already a decent performer. Suppose your first car was a big-block Mustang and you'd like your 4.6L GT to offer the feel of that torquey big-block. Nothing crazy, just the snappy throttle response and instant torque that only large displacement can provide. You could install a 429 or 460 in place of your late-model mod motor, but why ruin a perfectly good Mustang when you could just use what you've got? Besides, no big-block swap will ever provide the fuel mileage and driveability offered by a modern fuel-injected mod motor. Why not try for big-block torque while retaining all that mod motor fuel efficiency and driveability?

Maximum power wasn't the desired goal for this particular test, so I decided to start with a basically stock 2-valve GT motor. The 2-valve GT mill supplied by Sean Hyland Motorsport (SHM) (which we affectionately nicknamed Canadian Bacon) actually featured a forged steel Cobra crank, a set of forged connecting rods, and forged aluminum pistons. The reason for the forged reciprocating assembly was that I planned to crank things up in the future, but for now I had a solid bottom end that would take any abuse (power wise) that could be thrown at it. The forged pistons produced a stock static compression ratio to go along with the stock PI cylinder heads and camshafts. I installed a Ford Racing supercharger kit (see Chapter

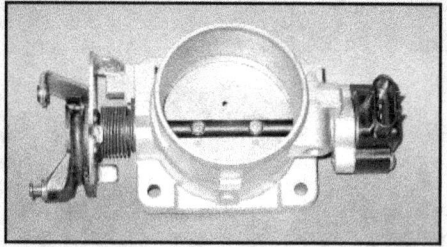

A look down the throat of the stock 65-mm throttle body doesn't reveal any unexpected restrictions, but you can only flow so much air through 65 mm.

6 for dyno results), which includes an M90 roots blower and dedicated intake casting. The idea behind installing the blower was to duplicate the torquey feel of a big block with all the advantages offered by the fuel-injected mod motor. Installing the blower also allowed me to test the effectiveness of a Ford Racing 70-mm throttle body. Equipped with the Ford Racing blower and stock throttle body, the SHM 4.6L 2-valve motor produced 383 hp at 5,600 rpm and 386 ft-lbs of torque at 3,400 rpm.

While the supercharged combination was indeed torquey, like "The Tool Man," we naturally wanted just a bit more. The quest led me to the inlet system, more specifically to the stock throttle body. Positive-displacement superchargers are very sensitive to inlet restrictions and I suspected that the stock throttle body was restricting the inlet flow of the Ford Racing supercharger. As luck would have it, the Ford Racing catalog offers a larger (70-mm) throttle body to replace the stock 65-mm throttle body. Replacing the stock throttle body was easy and the results were impressive. The high-flow Ford Racing throttle body allowed the engine to exceed 400 ft-lbs. The larger throttle body upped the peak power to 394 hp, while the peak torque jumped to 402 ft-lbs. As expected of an airflow improvement, the majority of the power gains offered by the throttle body occurred after 3,300 rpm. The 4.6L was now just a half dozen horsepower away from making an honest 400 hp, but we were most impressed with the fact that the supercharged mod motor had officially exceeded 400 ft-lbs of torque. In fact, the little 4.6L thumped out over 390 ft-lbs from 3,300 rpm to 5,100 rpm.

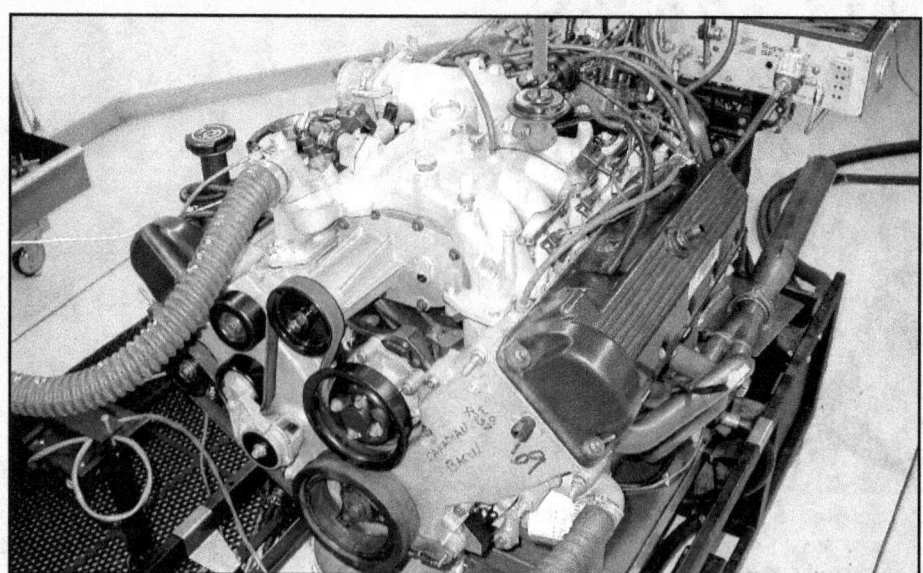

The Ford Racing 70-mm throttle body was tested on this 2-valve GT engine with a forged bottom end and a Ford Racing roots-type supercharger.

Throttle Bodies and Inlet Elbows

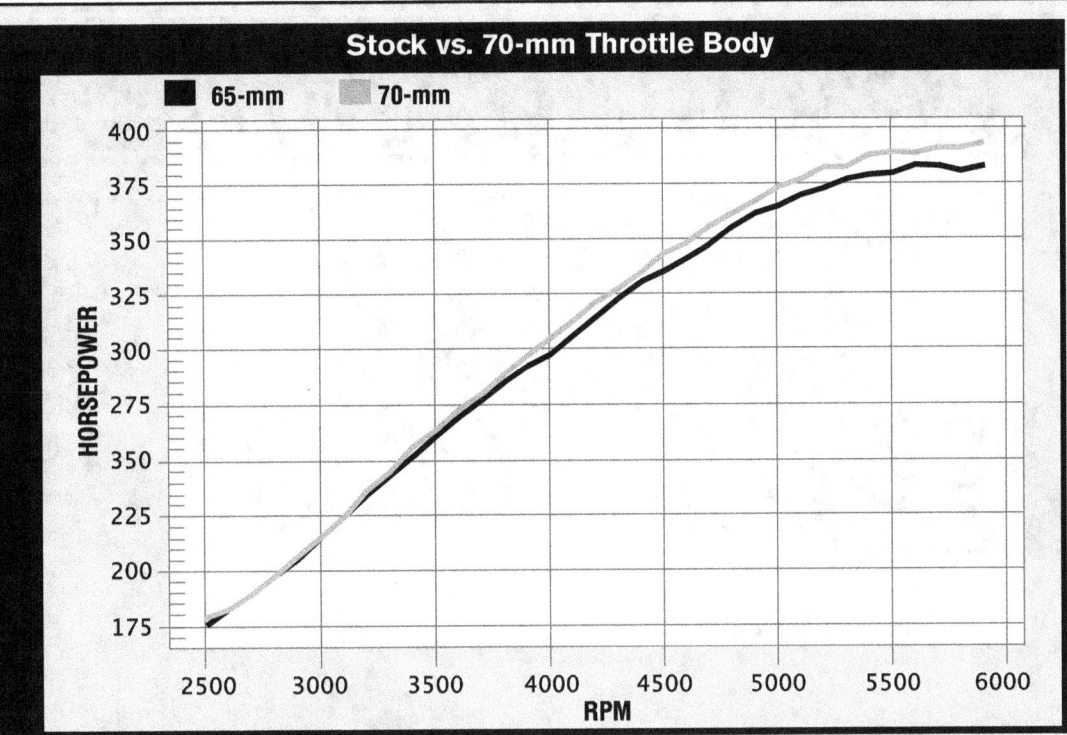

Stock Throttle Body:
383 hp @ 5,900 rpm

Ford Racing 70-mm Throttle Body:
394 hp @ 5,900 rpm

Largest Gain:
11 hp @ 5,900 rpm

Stock Throttle Body vs. Ford Racing 70-mm Throttle Body (Horsepower)
The larger 70-mm throttle body from Ford Racing showed its worth by increasing the power output of the supercharged 4.6L by 11 hp. The diameter of the stock throttle body (shown here) is just 65 mm.

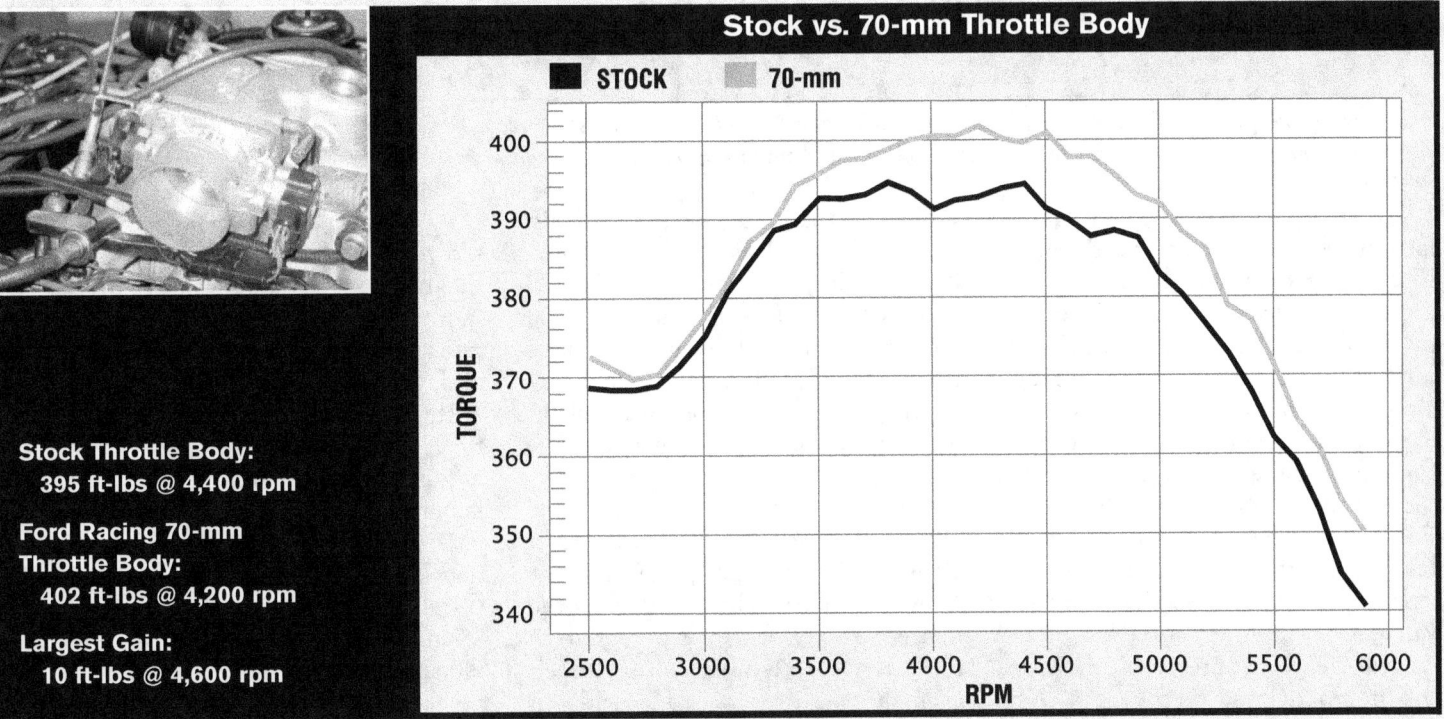

Stock Throttle Body:
395 ft-lbs @ 4,400 rpm

Ford Racing 70-mm Throttle Body:
402 ft-lbs @ 4,200 rpm

Largest Gain:
10 ft-lbs @ 4,600 rpm

Stock Throttle Body vs. Ford Racing 70-mm Throttle Body (Torque)
Though we expected gains at the higher engine speeds, the 70-mm throttle body (shown here) actually offered torque improvements from as low as 3,000 rpm.

Building 4.6/5.4L Ford Horsepower on the Dyno

Test 4: Kenne Bell Early 2-Valve GT: Cold Air, MAF, & Throttle Body

Don't trade your pride-and-joy off just yet. Early (1996-'98 pre-PI) GT owners can stack the deck in their favor with a Kenne Bell twin-screw supercharger. You add even more power to your boosted engine with a free-flowing induction system.

With the new 260-hp PI motor introduced in 1999, many early non-PI 4.6L GT owners were left scratching their collective heads. Like the proverbial redheaded stepchild, the early 4.6L owners were stranded alone, out in the cold. Things look even worse if you compare the performance of the early 2-valve GT to the 4-valve Cobra, especially when Ford introduced the '03 Cobra. Imagine the nightmare of pulling up to a stoplight next to a supercharged 4-valve motor in your naturally aspirated wheezer GT. Sure, you'd have to run him and hope he missed a shift (probably two), knowing in the back of your mind that you just showed up to the gunfight with what amounts to nothing more than a margarine utensil. Nice handle, shinny blade, works well on toast but comparatively speaking, as dull as the day is long. Am I getting down on the early GT owners here? Not on your life – the same events that transpired to make the early 4.6L GT Mustangs uncompetitive in stock trim also make them much more affordable than a new GT, Mach 1, or Cobra.

All you have to do to make the early GTs competitive is to add a Kenne Bell supercharger. While the blower dramatically changes the image and performance potential of the early 4.6L 2-valve motor, there's even more power available with an induction upgrade. Sure, we could have opted for the "more boost" route, as the Kenne Bell 1.7L supercharger is capable of easily exceeding 500 wheel horsepower if your motor is up to task. Rather than change the blower (or crank) pulley to increase the boost, we wanted to see if the motor responded to any of the usual performance bolt-ons, namely a cold-air intake, a mass-air meter, and a larger throttle body. With very little dyno time available, we swapped out the entire induction assembly, from the factory air filter assembly all the way back to the stock throttle body. We installed the Kenne Bell ram-air intake system, a 90-mm mass-air meter, and a 75-mm Accufab throttle body. The induction improvements upped the power output of our 1998 GT motor to 369 hp, a gain of 20 hp. Most of the power gains occurred past 3,500 rpm, or right where they will be put to maximum use while accelerating past a stock '03 Cobra.

Throttle Bodies and Inlet Elbows

Stock Intake Setup:
347 hp @ 5,600 rpm

Kenne Bell Induction:
369 hp @ 5,800 rpm

Largest Gain:
24 hp @ 5,800 rpm

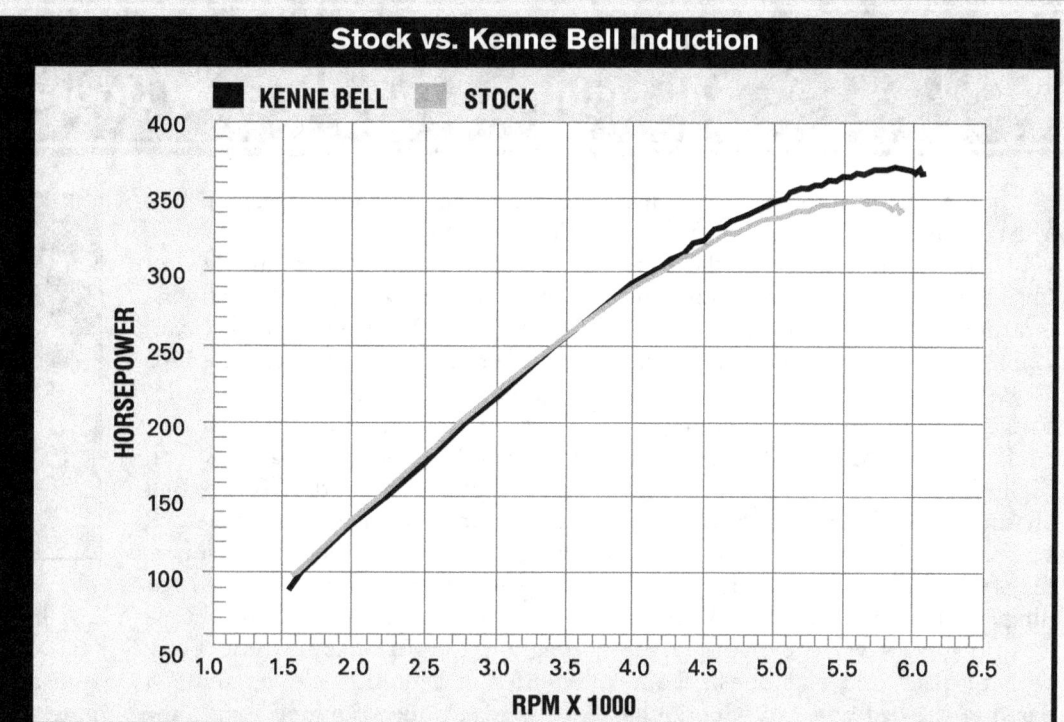

Stock Intake Setup vs. Kenne Bell Induction (Horsepower)
The induction upgrades (CAI, MAF, and 75-mm throttle body) showed their worth by improving the power output by as much as 24 hp on the Kenne Bell-supercharged 1998 2-valve GT motor.

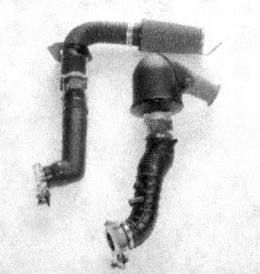

Stock Intake Setup:
385 ft-lbs @ 3,400 rpm

Kenne Bell Induction:
386 ft-lbs @ 3,700 rpm

Largest Gain:
20 ft-lbs @ 5,800 rpm

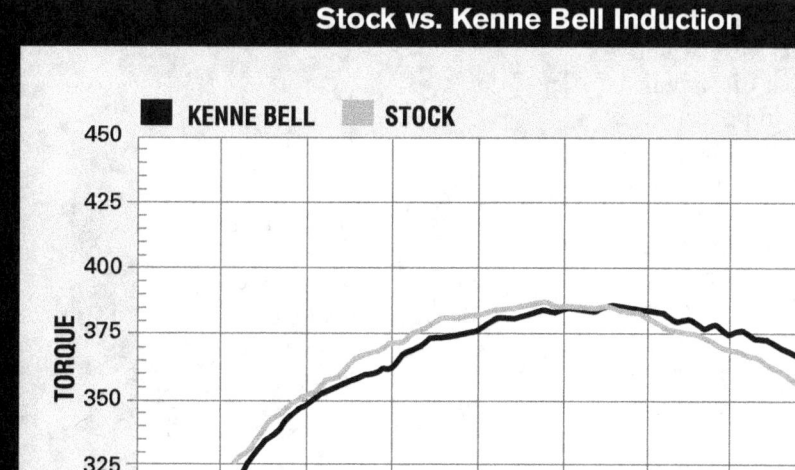

Stock Intake Setup vs. Kenne Bell Induction (Torque)
Though the peak-to-peak torque gains were minimal, the induction upgrades posted big gains out past 3,700 rpm.

Building 4.6/5.4L Ford Horsepower on the Dyno

Chapter 1

Test 5: Kenne Bell Supercharged 2-Valve 5.4L Lightning Throttle Body Upgrade

It sure chapped the hides of some Mustang owners out there when, for a while, the hottest horse in the Blue Oval stable was a truck. Before the introduction of the supercharged '03 Cobra, the naturally aspirated, DOHC 4-valve motors had to take a back seat to the mighty Lightning. In all fairness to Mustang owners, the Lightning was no ordinary truck. Sharing its SVT origin with the 4.6L Cobra, 2.0L Focus, and 351-ci Lightnings of yesteryear, the 5.4-liter Lightning more than made up for those free-flowing, 4-valve cylinder heads with displacement and boost. Compared to the bad boy 4.6L Cobra, the SVT Lightning's 2-valve modular motor seems a trifle unsophisticated. Though valvetrain deficient, the Lightning found the needed motivation via displacement and boost. At 5.4 liters, the Lightning motor sports .8 liters (48 cubic inches for those not metrically inclined) of additional displacement over the 4.6L. With that displacement came something very important, and something decidedly lacking in the SVT Cobra motor, namely torque, for even more torque (necessary to motivate the portly 4,500-lb curb weight) boost provided by an Eaton M112 positive-displacement supercharger. The combination of displacement plus boost makes for one impressive hauler, but just because it's good, doesn't mean it can't be even better!

By now, most Lightning owners should be aware that their heavy haulers are capable of sub-14-second ETs at nearly 100 mph right off the showroom floor. If not, take the damn thing to the drag strip where it belongs! Credit the ultra-flat torque curve offered by the positive-displacement Eaton supercharger for all that performance. The best route to additional horsepower for the Lightning is through a blower swap. Check out Chapter 6 for the story of what happened when we added a Kenne Bell blower to this Lightning motor.

This particular test involved a comparison between the stock twin-blade throttle body and a single (oval) throttle body from Accufab. The 5.4L Lightning was tested on a DynoJet chassis dyno and equipped with a 9-inch crank pulley and a 3.00-inch blower pulley with the Kenne Bell blower upgrade. Running the stock twin-blade throttle body, the supercharged Lightning motor pumped out 484 hp and 543 ft-lbs of torque. Swapping on the Accufab throttle body resulted in a jump to 499 hp and 558 ft-lbs of torque. Equipped with the high-flow Accufab throttle body, the Lightning motor exceeded 500 ft-lbs of torque at the wheels from 3,300 rpm to 5,200 rpm. These 5.4L Lightning motors obviously excel at torque production, especially when you replace the Eaton with a Kenne Bell blower.

The inlet restriction on the 5.4L Lightning was measured using a vacuum gauge.

The Lightning engine for this test was already equipped with a Kenne Bell twin-screw blower. It's making a lot more horsepower and torque than stock, so it follows that it needs more air. Note the extensive data logging wiring and equipment used during testing.

Throttle Bodies and Inlet Elbows

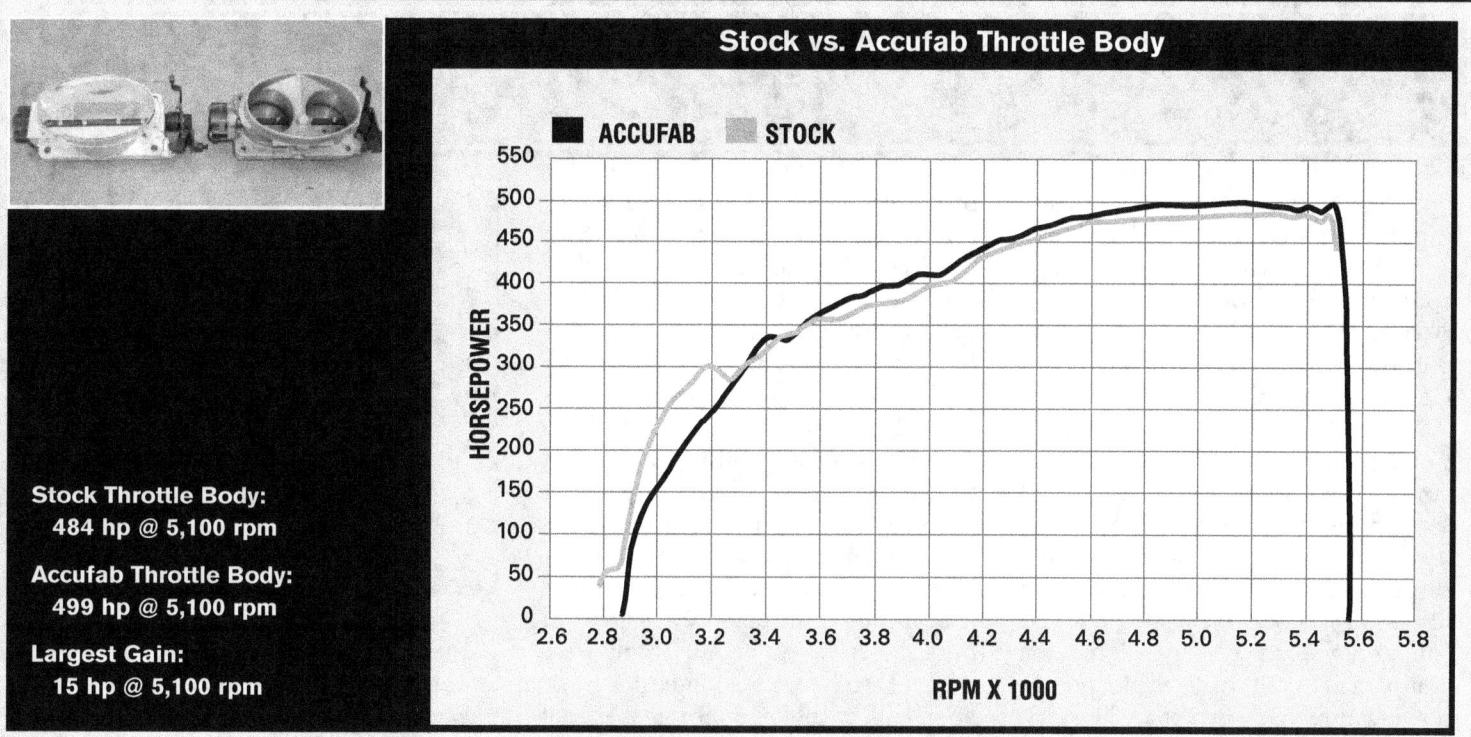

Stock Throttle Body:
484 hp @ 5,100 rpm

Accufab Throttle Body:
499 hp @ 5,100 rpm

Largest Gain:
15 hp @ 5,100 rpm

Stock Throttle Body vs. Accufab Throttle Body (Horsepower)
Obviously, the stock throttle body was restrictive at this elevated power level, as the Accufab throttle body was worth an additional 15 hp.

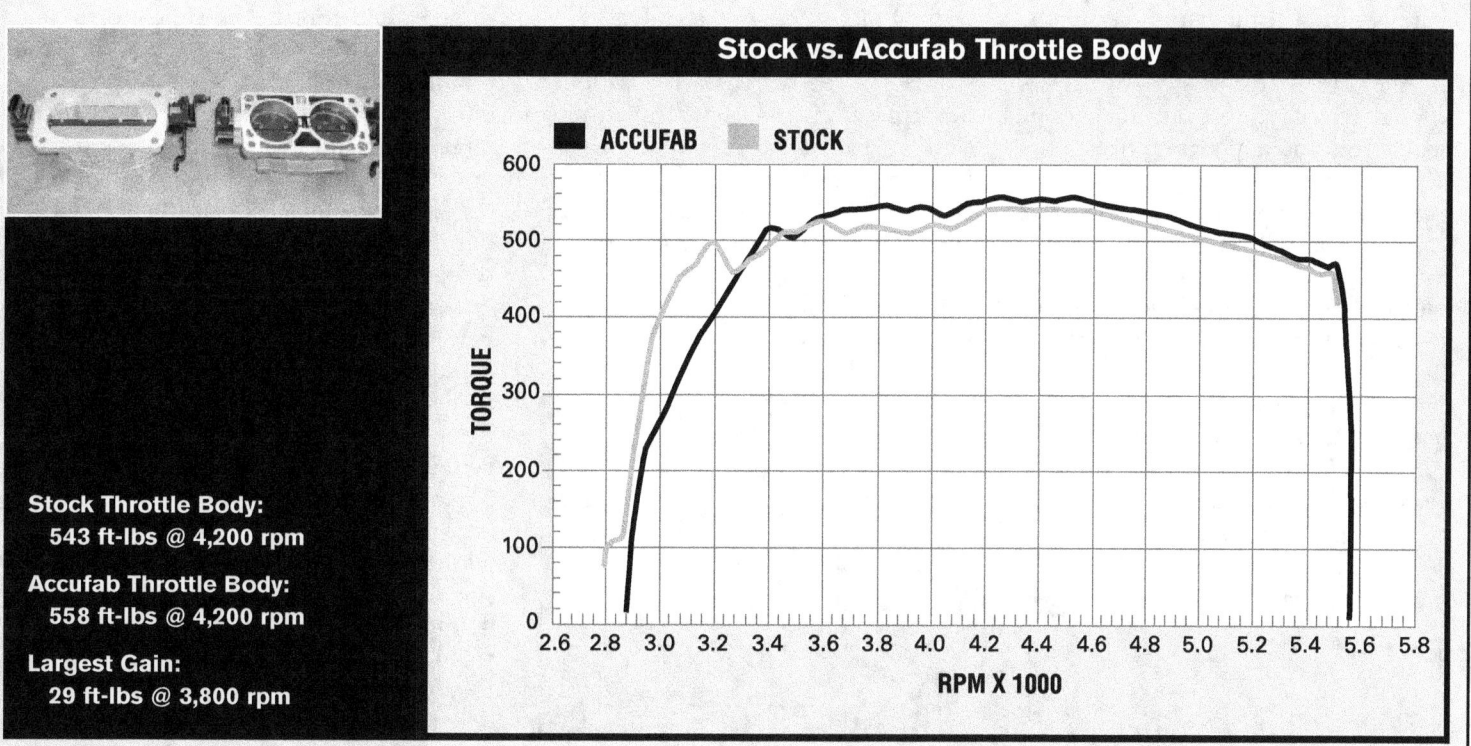

Stock Throttle Body:
543 ft-lbs @ 4,200 rpm

Accufab Throttle Body:
558 ft-lbs @ 4,200 rpm

Largest Gain:
29 ft-lbs @ 3,800 rpm

Stock Throttle Body vs. Accufab Throttle Body (Torque)
The Accufab throttle body showed some impressive torque gains as well, even as low as 3,600 rpm. The maximum gain was 29 ft-lbs.

Test 6: 4-Valve Cobra: Accufab Throttle Body

Though they're little more than a simple air door, throttle bodies can be a confusing performance part. The confusion stems from the ability of the aftermarket throttle body to easily outflow the production counterpart. Compared on the flow bench, the Accufab throttle body outflows the stock twin-blade unit by 150 to 180 cfm, but this doesn't mean that it will offer measurable power gains. Conversely, when you install a high-flow throttle body on your combination (especially a stock one) and you see no gain in power, the reason isn't that the component you installed is poorly manufactured; it's just that the stock throttle body didn't represent an airflow restriction. Whether the motor will respond to the additional airflow offered by a larger (or higher flowing) throttle body depends on the power output of the combination versus the flow rate of the original throttle body. If the stock throttle body flows enough to feed the engine, a larger one won't give you any extra power.

This particular test was a perfect example that not every 4.6L 4-valve combination will respond to a larger throttle body. The 4-valve Cobra motor used for the test was supplied by Sean Hyland, and was a duplicate of the one used in his book *How to Build Max-Performance 4.6L Ford Engines*. The 4.6L Cobra motor featured a forged steel crank, rods, and flat-top pistons, mildly ported 2001 heads and intake, and a set of Stage 1 SHM cams. The flat-top pistons pushed the static compression ratio to near 10.5:1, which is just about perfect for daily street use. The flat-top design also provided optimum flame travel without interference from a dome. The Stage 1 cam specs checked in at .452 inches of lift and 209 degrees of duration at .050. The mild cams were designed to offer good midrange power and allow the mod motor to exceed 400 hp on the engine dyno. The intake manifold was treated to internal porting. The lower portion of the intake was cut off to provide access to the internal passages, and then welded back in place after porting. The SHM motor was set up with a stock 4-valve Cobra throttle body, a set of Hooker headers, and a 3.0-inch open-pipe exhaust system was used on the dyno. No accessories were used (we ran an electric water pump) and the air/fuel and timing curves were dialed in using a F.A.S.T. management system. After playing with various timing curves, we were finally rewarded with peak num-

The factory Cobra throttle body featured dual 57-mm openings. In this test, it proved adequate even for a modified naturally aspirated 4-valve engine.

bers of 426 hp and 393 ft-lbs of torque.

After running the stock twin-blade throttle body, we swapped on the Accufab throttle body. Unfortunately, the swap was not an easy bolt-on affair, as it was necessary to grind out the center divider in the upper intake lid. The stock upper intake lid features a pair of holes that align with the twin-blade stock throttle body, but the Accufab throttle body featured a large, single oval blade. The center divider had to be removed before the Accufab throttle body could fully open without coming into contact with the center divider. Though the Accufab throttle body certainly out-flowed the stock dual-blade throttle body, the 425-hp SHM motor could not take advantage of the additional airflow. The throttle body upgrade resulted in a gain of 3 hp (to 429 hp) and 3 ft-lbs of torque (to 395 ft-lbs). This test indicates that the factory Cobra throttle body is probably adequate for even modified naturally aspirated 4-valve motors. Of course, the Accufab piece was worth a few extra ponies and there is no denying that it looks a ton better than the dull factory piece.

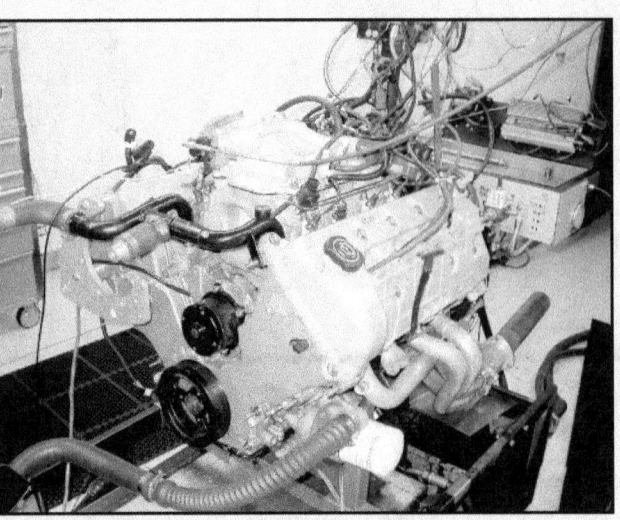

The 4-valve engine for this test was a 2001 Cobra engine with mildly ported heads, a ported intake, SHM Stage 1 cams, Hooker headers, and a compression ratio of about 10.5:1.

Throttle Bodies and Inlet Elbows

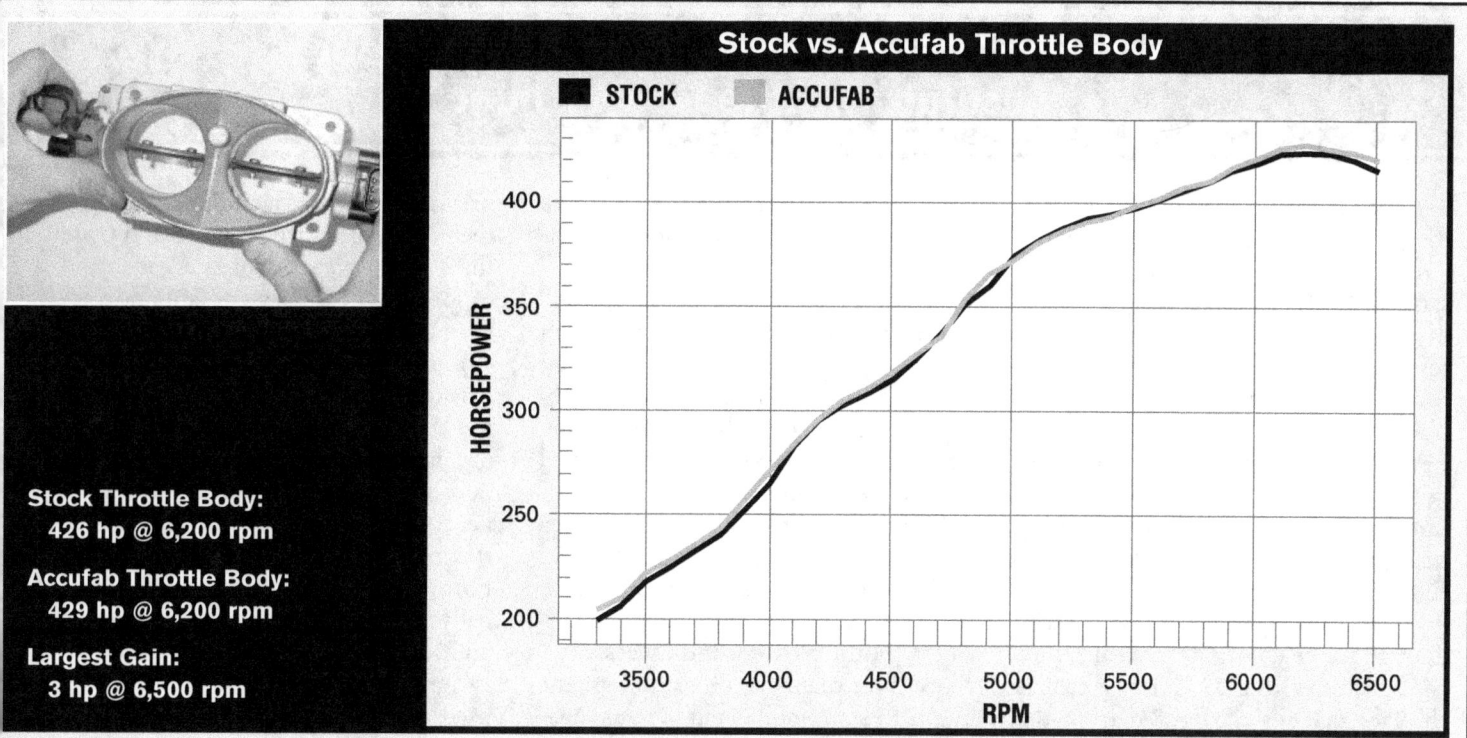

Stock Throttle Body:
426 hp @ 6,200 rpm

Accufab Throttle Body:
429 hp @ 6,200 rpm

Largest Gain:
3 hp @ 6,500 rpm

Stock Throttle Body vs. Accufab Throttle Body (Horsepower)
How much is an extra 180 cfm worth? In this case the gain was only 3 hp. This indicates that the stock throttle body did not represent a restriction.

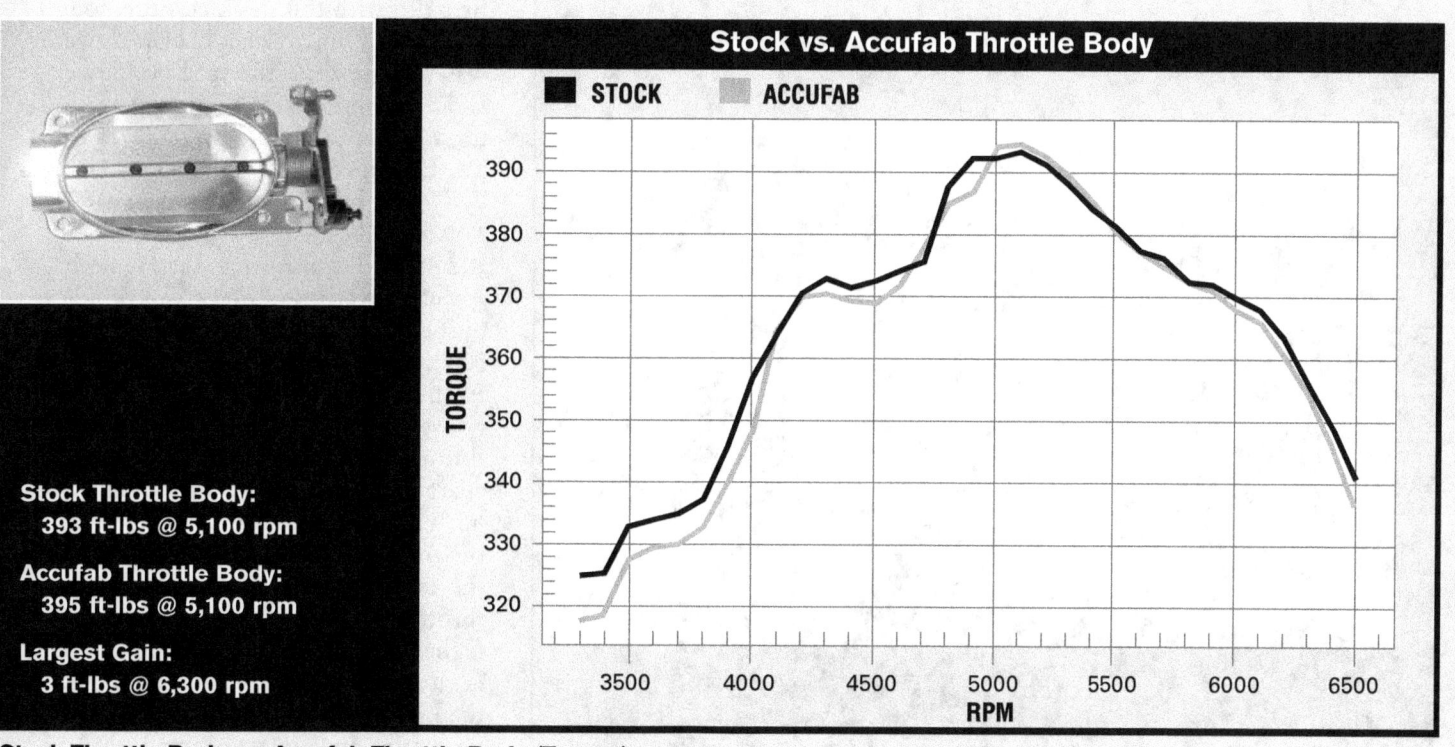

Stock Throttle Body:
393 ft-lbs @ 5,100 rpm

Accufab Throttle Body:
395 ft-lbs @ 5,100 rpm

Largest Gain:
3 ft-lbs @ 6,300 rpm

Stock Throttle Body vs. Accufab Throttle Body (Torque)
On this naturally aspirated 4.6L 4-valve combination, the Accufab throttle body was worth only 2 ft-lbs of torque at the peak, and 3 ft-lbs up higher.

Chapter 1

Test 7: Eaton Supercharged 4-Valve '03 Cobra: Accufab Throttle Body & Inlet

Not long after beginning the testing for this book, the good people over at Ford Racing saw fit to bless me with an '03 Cobra crate motor assembly. Talk about the ultimate 4-valve test mule! The beauty of the '03 Cobra motor was that in addition to every nut and bolt being brand-spanking new, the motor was factory equipped with a number of desirable features, not the least of which is a hefty chunk of forced induction in the form of an Eaton supercharger. While the presence of the supercharger was cause enough for celebration, the real key to the success of the '03 Cobra motor is the fact that it's configured from the factory to accept the rigors of supercharging. This engine features desirable (for forced induction) low compression, free-flowing 4-valve heads, and even an efficient air-to-water intercooler to help lower the inlet charge temperature to suppress detonation. It also comes with forged rods and pistons to stand up to all that power. Having seen '03 Cobra motors already exceed 700 wheel horsepower, naturally I was anxious to get started with some modifications.

My first task was to get the motor installed on the engine dyno. The '03 Cobra motor was shipped complete, including the serpentine drive assemblies (both blower and accessory). Since we planned on running the F.A.S.T. stand-alone engine management system, we removed a number of factory components that were unnecessary. We removed the clutch and pressure plate to facilitate mounting the motor, plumbed water to and from the air-to-water intercooler, and capped the necessary coolant and vacuum lines. Just as with the 2-valve 4.6L GT motors, the F.A.S.T. engine management system allowed us to delete the factory mass-air meter and attending inlet tubing. The stock throttle body and inlet into the blower were necessary, as they are the subjects of this particular dyno test. Though the Ford Racing Cobra motor was originally equipped with a coil-on-plug ignition system, we replaced the factory ignition with the coil-pack system used previously on the 4.6L GT motors. This in no way changed the power potential of the motor; it simply allowed us to use an existing management system on the 4-valve motor.

The 4-valve Cobra motor was first run with the stock throttle body (CTB) and inlet. The M112 blower was still sporting the factory blower and crank pulleys, which caused it to produce a peak boost pressure of 8.8 psi. Equipped with the stock throttle body and inlet, the supercharged '03 4-valve Cobra motor produced 501 hp and 461 ft-lbs of torque. Installing the Accufab throttle body and inlet pushed the peak power up slightly to 508 hp. Then we retested the stock vs. Accufab combination at a higher boost level. Equipped with the stock throttle body and inlet, the supercharged Cobra motor produced 524 hp. This was increased to 532 hp with the Accufab components. Once again, the testing shows that the high-flow throttle body is most effective on higher-horsepower combinations. The greater the airflow needs of the engine, the more restrictive the factory throttle body and inlet become. Many Cobra enthusiasts purchase the Accufab components on looks alone, but the power gains can be impressive on wilder combinations.

Aftermarket throttle bodies and inlet elbows are available for nearly every modular engine tested in this book. For '30-'04 Cobra engines like this one, you can upgrade the throttle body and the supercharger inlet – let that thing breathe.

Throttle Bodies and Inlet Elbows

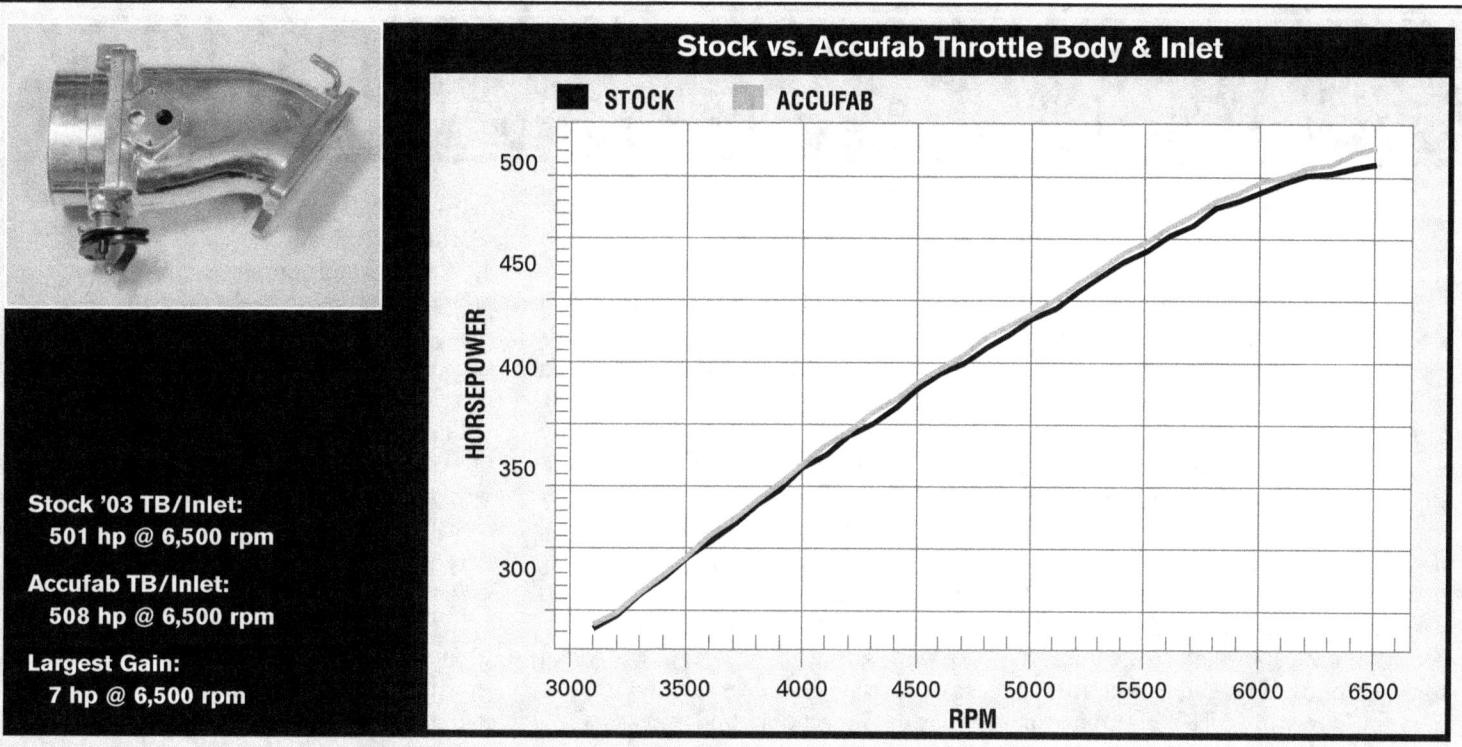

Stock '03 TB/Inlet:
501 hp @ 6,500 rpm

Accufab TB/Inlet:
508 hp @ 6,500 rpm

Largest Gain:
7 hp @ 6,500 rpm

Stock '03 Cobra TB/Inlet vs. Accufab TB/Inlet (Horsepower)
Though the gains from installing the Accufab throttle body and inlet weren't tremendous, they were consistent from 3,500 rpm to 6,500 rpm. The Accufab throttle body and inlet were worth as much as 7 hp.

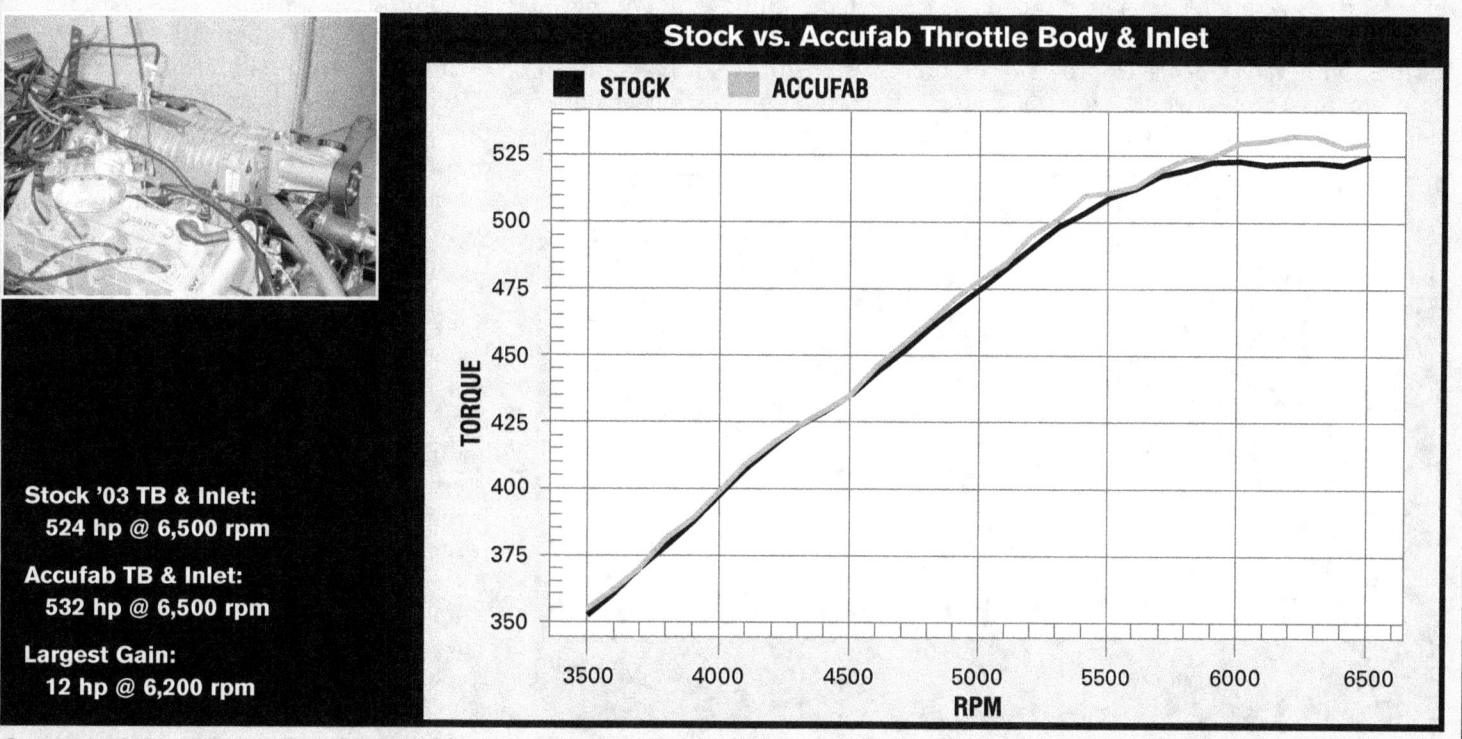

Stock '03 TB & Inlet:
524 hp @ 6,500 rpm

Accufab TB & Inlet:
532 hp @ 6,500 rpm

Largest Gain:
12 hp @ 6,200 rpm

Stock '03 Cobra TB/Inlet vs. Accufab TB/Inlet (Torque)
With an extra 2 psi, the '03 Cobra picked up more power from the Accufab throttle body and inlet. It's intuitive that an engine making more power would need more air.

Building 4.6/5.4L Ford Horsepower on the Dyno

Chapter 1

Test 8: 5.0L Stroker 2-Valve: Accufab 75-mm Throttle Body & Inlet

Given the popularity of stroker motors, it was only natural to include a throttle body test on a 5.0L stroker version of the 4.6L 2-valve motor. The stroker combination was built using a 5.0L kit from Coast High Performance (CHP). Thanks to CHP, installing the longer 3.75-inch stroker crank into the 4.6L block wasn't any more difficult than picking up the phone and ordering. CHP offers 5.0L and 5.1L combinations, the difference being the maximum allowable bore size of .070 over. The CHP stroker kits come complete with the 3.75-inch stroker crank, forged connecting rods, and forged aluminum pistons. The combination will drop right into your professionally machined 4.6L block (iron or aluminum Cobra version) or the kit can be ordered as a dedicated short block. The mod motor kits are available in a variety of different compression ratios, but for this motor, I chose a set of flat-top pistons with valve reliefs to provide sufficient piston-to-valve clearance for our rather larger XE278AH Comp cams. The flat-top pistons combined with the additional stroke and polished combustion chambers in our CNC-ported 4.6L Power Improved (PI) cylinder heads to produce a static compression ratio of 11.25:1. Though a tad on the high side for street use with 87 octane, the motor was run successfully with 91-octane premium unleaded pump gas.

With the short block taken care of, I turned my attention to supplying sufficient airflow to the hungry mod motor. All those additional cubic inches were going to be worthless (or at least considerably less effective) without a decent set of cylinder heads. Given the lack of aftermarket cylinder heads, I chose to have the stock PI heads ported. The heads were shipped off to Total Engine Airflow. The heads were given TEA's Stage 3 treatment, which included full CNC porting of the intake and exhaust ports, new Hi-Chrome valve seats (plus bowl blending), and even combustion chamber polishing to minimize the threat of detonation. The chamber was further worked to unshroud the oversized 47.7-mm Manley intake valves and 36.8-mm stainless-steel exhaust valves. Mod-motor maniac John Mihovitz, who performed the necessary vacuum test and valve job to ensure perfect sealing, finished off the ported heads. Given the dissimilar valve lengths, it was necessary to install a .063 shim under each intake valve lash adjuster. The shims ensured adequate preload on the hydraulic lash adjuster.

The CNC-ported PI heads were topped off with a set of Xtreme Energy cams from the Comp Cams catalog. Given the displacement and compression of this 5.0L stroker and the fact that our newly ported heads flowed so much better than stock (the intake flow increased to 235 cfm at .550 lift), we selected a set of appropriate cam profiles. The XE278AH cams offered .550 lift (both intake and exhaust), a 242/246 duration split (at .050), and a 113-degree lobe separation angle. We knew that the .550 lift offered by the Comp cams would take full advantage of the airflow offered by the CNC-ported heads and that the duration figures would allow the motor to continue to make power right to 6,000 rpm and possibly beyond. Finishing off the 5.0L stroker was a stock composite PI intake manifold. Running the stock throttle body and inlet elbow on the stroker motor produced 417 hp and 418 ft-lbs of torque. Replacing the stock components with a 75-mm system from Accufab increased the power output from 417 hp to 434 hp, a gain of 17 hp. The big-inch mod motor also responded to the larger throttle body with additional torque, with the peak jumping from 418 ft-lbs to 430 ft-lbs. Obviously, the additional cubic inches responded well to the increase in airflow provided by the Accufab throttle body and elbow.

The mouth of the 75-mm Accufab is clearly larger than the stock piece. The Accufab pieces flow more air and look better than stock.

Throttle Bodies and Inlet Elbows

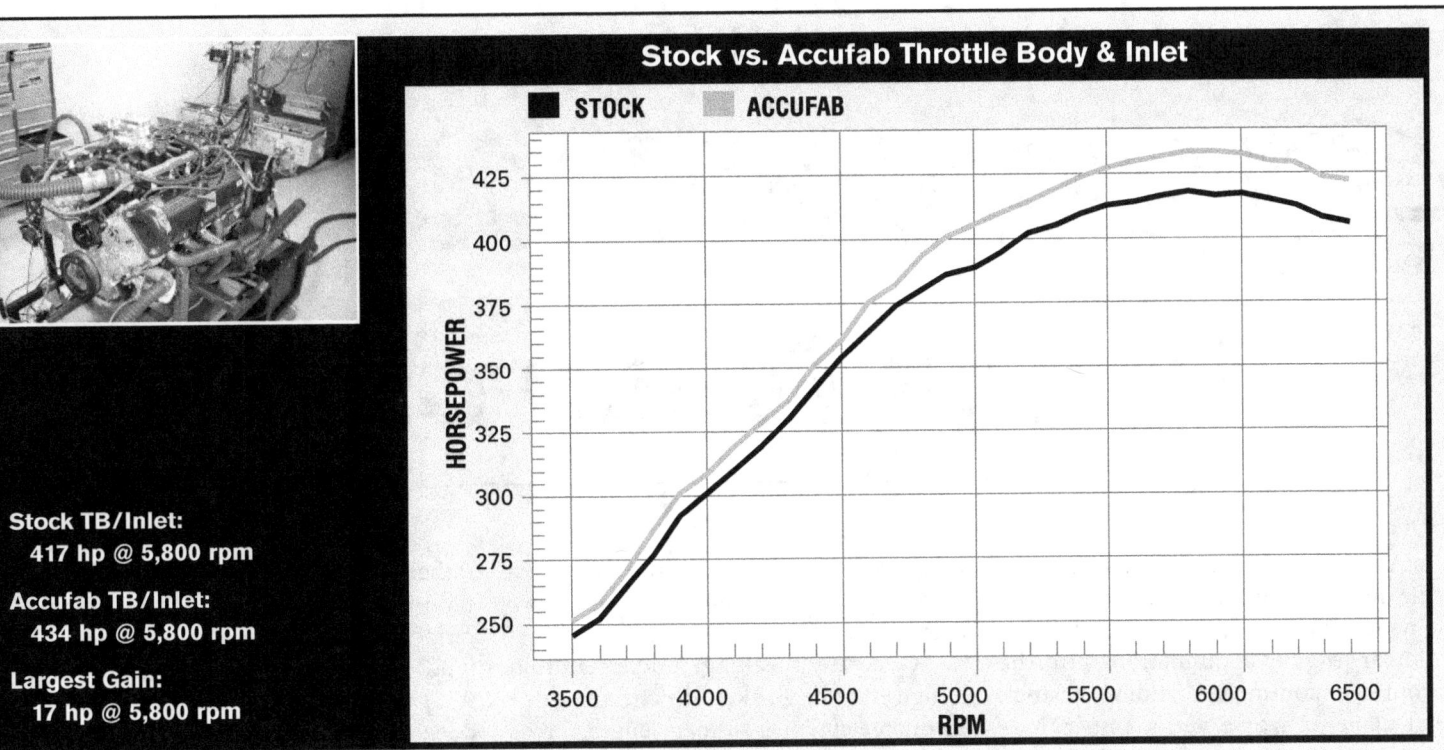

Stock TB/Inlet:
417 hp @ 5,800 rpm

Accufab TB/Inlet:
434 hp @ 5,800 rpm

Largest Gain:
17 hp @ 5,800 rpm

Stock TB/Inlet vs. Accufab TB/Inlet (Horsepower)
Obviously the stock throttle body and inlet elbow were restricting the power output of the 5.0L stroker, as the Accufab components showed power gains from 3,000 rpm all the way to 6,400 rpm. The 75-mm Accufab throttle body and elbow were worth as much as 17 hp on this 2-valve stroker.

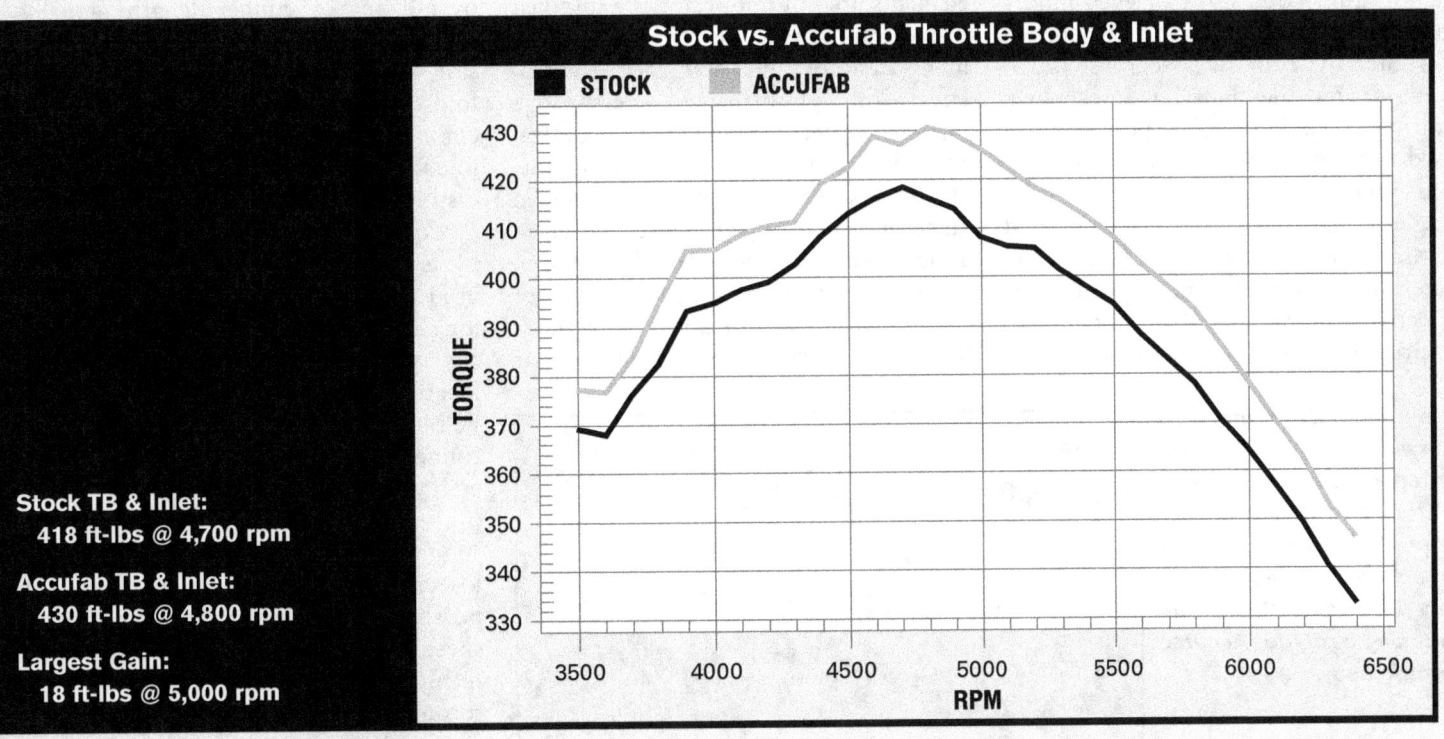

Stock TB & Inlet:
418 ft-lbs @ 4,700 rpm

Accufab TB & Inlet:
430 ft-lbs @ 4,800 rpm

Largest Gain:
18 ft-lbs @ 5,000 rpm

Stock TB/Inlet vs. Accufab TB/Inlet (Torque)
A gain of 17 hp at the peak is always welcomed, but a consistent gain of 10 to 18 ft-lbs is even more so. The larger throttle body and elbow not only improved the peak power (as expected), but the combination added a sizable chunk of torque throughout the rev range.

Chapter 2

INTAKE MANIFOLDS

As with any other type of engine, your intake manifold is one of those key elements that can make or break your modular engine combination. For the carbureted contingent, adding a stock dual-plane or worse yet, a cast-iron 2-barrel intake to your 12.0:1, roller-cammed stroker will be a sure recipe for lackluster power. For the mod-motor fuelie Ford fanatics, the same thing happens when you stick a short-runner manifold on your stock or even mildly modified 4.6L 2-valve. Just as a manifold can literally ruin an otherwise good combination, the right intake can help you produce impressive power when used in conjunction with the right cams and cylinder heads. More than any other single component, the intake manifold (most specifically the runner length) will determine where the motor will make effective power. Match the runner length to produce power in the same operating range as the cam profiles and you are a long way toward making an impressive combination.

Generally speaking, intake manifold design may be broken down into three distinct elements: runner length, cross section (and taper ratio), and plenum volume. These elements are listed in order of importance or in the order they most affect the performance of a given manifold. This is not to say that all of the elements are not important, it's just that proper care should be given to the elements in accordance with their eventual effect on performance. Perspective intake designers should take note of this, as I have seen fabricators spend countless hours altering the plenum volume in an attempt to change the effective operating range when they should have been increasing (or decreasing) the runner length. Manifold design is sometimes limited by production capability, or rather, ease of construction. Building a set of runners with a dedicated taper ratio and a compound curve is difficult, if not impossible, for the average fabricator. Despite the fact that this design produces the best power, it simply isn't going to get produced unless a major intake manufacturer steps up and pays the cost of such a complex combination.

In my opinion, the first element in intake design is the runner length. The overall intake runner length actually includes the head ports, but the discussion will be limited to those in the manifold. Unlike their carbureted counterparts, fuel-injected intake manifolds seem to be broken down into two distinct groups, long and short. This obviously isn't very scientific terminology, as it doesn't describe a complete manifold design. The reason for the simple long and short designations is that generally speaking, the longer the runner length, the lower the effective operating RPM. The opposite is also true; shorter runner length will improve top-end power. If you take a given intake combination (like our 4.6L PI intake) and decrease the runner length, the motor will definitely lose power at lower engine speeds and possibly pick up power at higher engine speeds. It's possible to design an intake manifold that will offer better low-speed torque and top-end power than a stock manifold, but at some point, compromise is the name of the game. It should be pointed out that the "ideal" intake design will vary with engine configuration, as the power gains offered by a given design

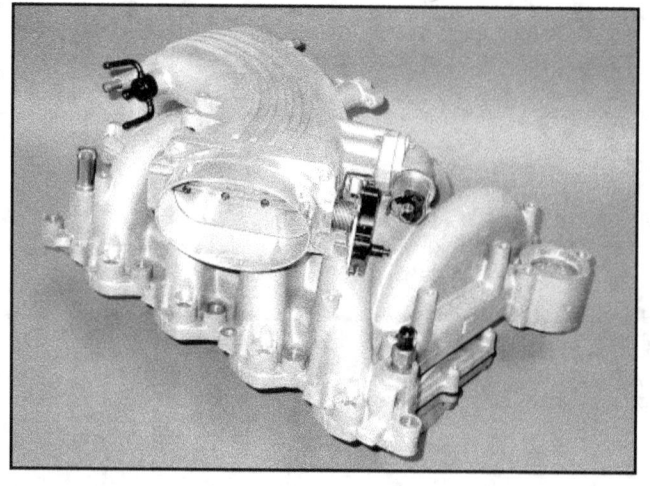

The right intake manifold can make or break the power curve offered by your motor. This Bullitt intake from Ford Racing offers improved flow over the factory PI intake. Check out the single blade Accufab throttle body.

on a stock motor will most likely be different than on a wilder combination.

The next element in intake design is cross section, or port volume. A related issue is taper ratio, but we will cover that shortly. The port volume or cross section of the runner refers to the physical size of the flow orifice. Suppose you have an intake manifold that features 14-inch (long) runners that measure 1.5-inches in (inside) diameter. It's possible to improve the flow rate of the runners by increasing the cross sectional area. Suppose we replace the 1.5-inch runners with equally long 1.75-inch runners. Naturally the larger 1.75-inch runners would flow a great deal more than the smaller 1.5-inch runners, thus improving the power potential of our motor. The increase in cross section will retain the same volumetric efficiency, but it will just occur at a slightly higher engine speed. This differs from a change in runner length in that the longer runner (with a constant diameter) will actually increase the volumetric efficiency at lower engine speeds.

Taper ratio refers to the change in cross section over the length of the runner. Typically, intake manifolds feature decreasing cross sections, where the runner size decreases from the plenum to the cylinder head. The decrease in cross section helps to accelerate the airflow, thus improving cylinder filling.

The final element is plenum volume. Plenum volume refers to the size of the enclosure connecting the throttle body to the runners. Typically, the plenum volume is a function of the displacement of the motor. Most production intake manifolds feature plenum volumes that measure smaller than the displacement of the motor (somewhere near 70 percent), but this depends on the intended application. As a rule of thumb, the plenum volume is increased with the RPM potential of the motor, but as one of our tests demonstrated, increasing the plenum volume offered changes in low-speed power only. A number of manufacturers including Ford and Porsche incorporate devices in the intake manifold to alter the plenum volume to enhance the power curve. We tested Ford's version on the dyno with interesting results. Increasing the plenum volume does increase the air reservoir allotted to the motor, but the real change comes from the resonance wave. When excited, the area in the plenum resonates at a certain frequency. Changing the plenum volume changes the resonance frequency. The Helmholtz resonance wave aids airflow through the runner (sometimes referred to as acoustical supercharging). Where this assistance takes place in the RPM band is determined by (a number of things), but primarily by the plenum volume.

This system from Reichard Racing is one of the very few aftermarket intake manifolds available for the 4.6L 2-valve motor. The shot runners relegated this intake to effective use on high-RPM 4.6L motors only, as the factory PI intake outpowered it all the way to 5,900 rpm.

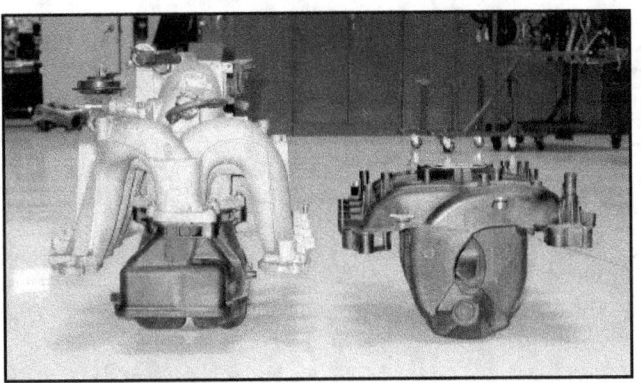

Here is a shot of the 4.6L (aluminum) truck intake versus the 4.6L (composite) Mustang GT intake. The truck manifold featured longer, smaller runners to help promote torque production. The truck manifold also featured a dual-plenum resonating chamber to enhance low-speed power production.

Since long runners enhance low-speed power production and short runners do the same for top-end power, why not combine them in one intake for the best of both worlds? This FR500 Variable Geometry intake from Ford Racing features dual runners to help produce a broad power band.

Test 1: 2-Valve GT: PI Intake vs. Truck Intake

To illustrate the difference in power offered by different intake manifold designs, I gathered two factory Ford intakes and subjected them to the rigors of the dyno. By dyno testing the two on the same engine combination I could properly isolate and illustrate the difference caused by the change in intake manifold design alone. Our test motor for this one features TEA ported heads, a set of Comp cams, and higher compression.

The Power Improved (PI) manifold differs from the 4.6L truck manifold in terms of construction (aluminum/composite to composite) and total height. The additional hood clearance on the truck applications allowed the engineers to increase the height (or length) of the runners. Raising the runners on the truck manifold allowed the engineers to incorporate the trick divided plenum. Both manifolds feature long runners, but the runner length (and cross section) differs between the aluminum truck and composite PI intake. Though shorter, the PI intake made full use of the available space (extending well down into the dry valley between the heads). According to common theory, the manifold with the longer runner length should produce more low-speed torque, while the shorter runner should elevate top-end horsepower. True to form, the long-runner truck manifold out-powered the PI manifold up to 4,000 rpm, but fell off thereafter. Where the modified 4.6L produced 340 hp with the truck intake, the PI manifold upped the peak power to 365 hp. The PI manifold also managed to produce the most peak torque (372 ft-lbs vs. 356 ft-lbs), though the PI intake was only beneficial above 4,000 rpm.

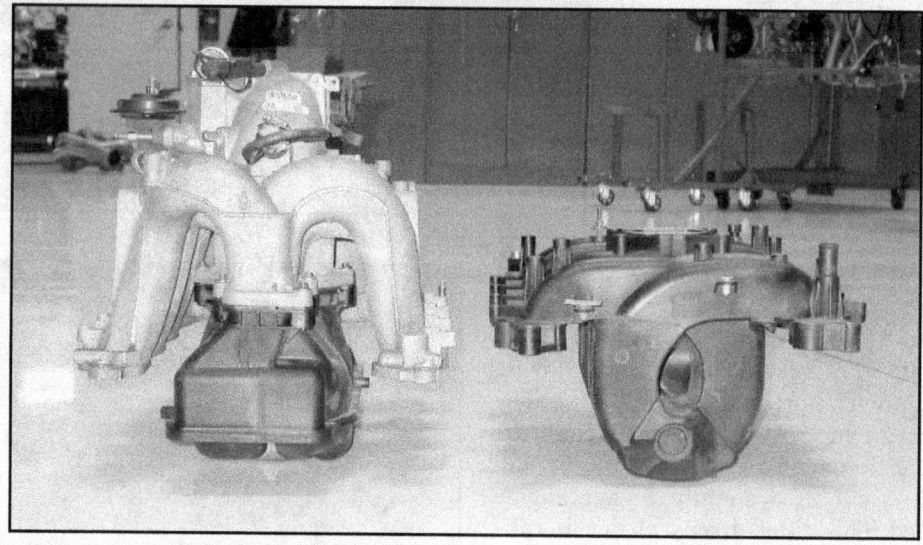

When you look at the truck (left) and PI (right) intakes side-by-side, you can really see the difference in runner length. Besides the difference in power bands, the shorter Mustang intake fits better under the lower Mustang hood.

We completed this test by swapping only the intake manifolds right on the dyno. This allowed us to isolate the gains/losses caused by the different manifolds.

Intake Manifolds

4.6L Truck Intake:
340 hp @ 5,600 rpm

4.6L 2-Valve GT PI Intake:
365 hp @ 5,900 rpm

Largest Gain:
31 hp @ 5,900 rpm

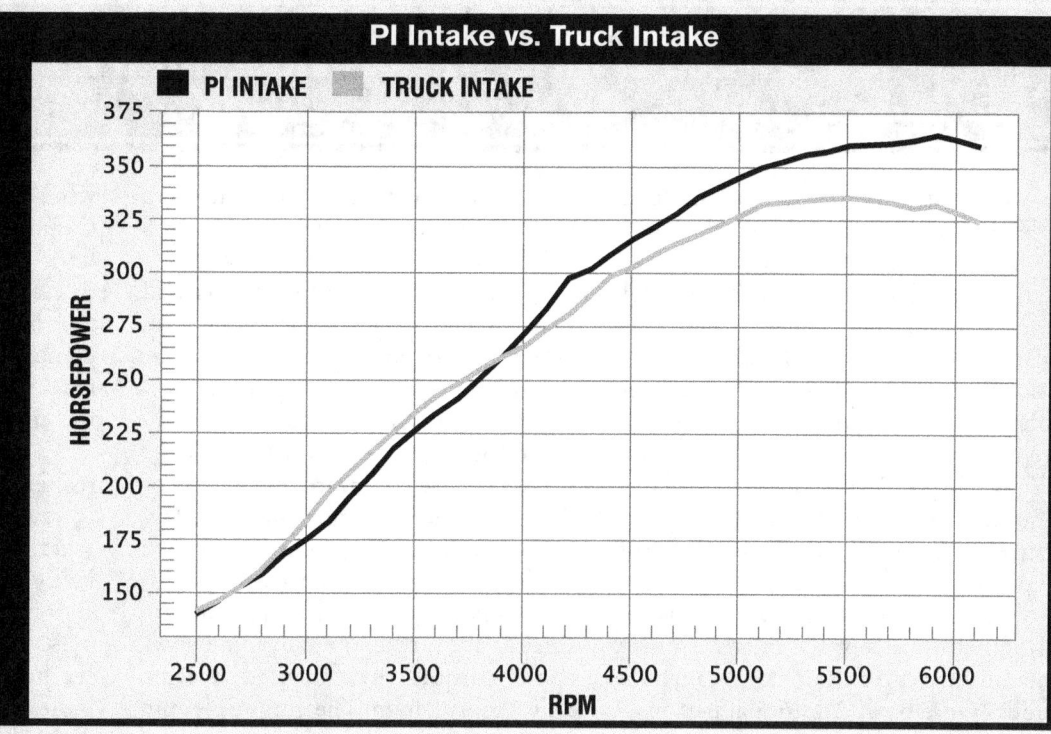

4.6L Truck Intake vs. PI Intake (Horsepower)
Obviously, the PI intake out-powered the 4.6L truck manifold (365 hp to 340 hp), but note that the long runners used in the truck intake made themselves known up to 4,000 rpm. It's a simple matter of the intake working for a specific application. Since most truck owners never see 6,000 rpm, the truck intake is a better choice, especially for heavy hauling. For wide-open-throttle runs in a 4.6L GT, the PI manifold is definitely the choice.

4.6L Truck Intake:
356 ft-lbs @ 4,600 rpm

4.6L 2-Valve GT PI Intake:
372 ft-lbs @ 4,200 rpm

Largest Gain:
28 ft-lbs @ 5,900 rpm

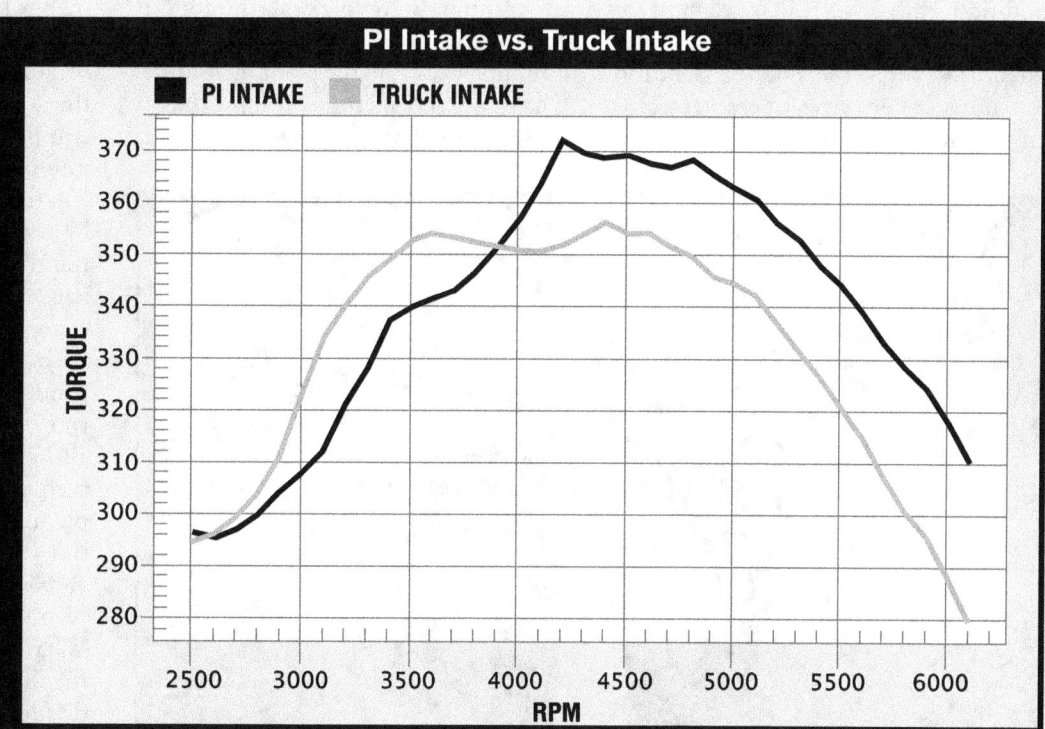

4.6L Truck Intake vs. PI Intake (Torque)
The 4.6L long-runner truck intake offered as much as 22 additional ft-lbs of torque over the PI manifold (below 4,000 rpm). The added grunt would be most welcomed when lugging a small trailer (think jet skis). The PI manifold added a solid 25 to 30 ft-lbs from 4,200 rpm to 6,000 rpm, right where it would be most useful during a ¼-mile run.

Building 4.6/5.4L Ford Horsepower on the Dyno

Test 2: 4.6L 2-Valve Truck Divided Intake Plenum Test

This test run on the divided plenum on the Ford 4.6L truck motor is a perfect example of what happens when you change just one element of the intake design. The test mule consisted of a stock 4.6L 2-valve GT block and crank combined with a set of forged connecting rods and stock replacement forged pistons from Coast High Performance. The augmented 1998 short block was topped off with a set of CNC-ported early 4.6L heads from Ford Performance Solutions. The heads were further modified to accept the later PI intake manifold and Accufab 75-mm throttle body and elbow. Additional performance came in the form of a set of Comp Xtreme Energy XE262AH cams. The cams featured .550 inches of lift (both intake and exhaust) and a 226/230-degrees duration split. The additional lift took full advantage of the airflow offered by the CNC-ported heads, while the hike in duration extended the effective operating range of the motor. The final mods included a set of Hooker long-tube headers, a set of 24-pound injectors, and a F.A.S.T. engine management system.

Though both the Mustang GT and F-series trucks are blessed with a 4.6L 2-valve modular motor, they differ greatly in their power-curve requirements. Given the necessity for low-speed torque, the 4.6L for the F-series was configured to improve power production in the RPM range most used by truck owners. To promote a broad power band, Ford designed a long-runner, small cross section aluminum intake. To further improve the low-speed torque, they devised a trick adjustable plenum. The unique plenum in the 4.6L truck intake features a divider attached to a stepper motor. When you apply voltage to the motor, the divider rotates. Rotating the divider effectively joins each side of the divided plenum, allowing the motor to breathe through both sides, effectively doubling the available plenum volume. Changing the plenum volume has a decided effect on the power curve, but what exactly would that effect be on this modified 4.6L? To find out, I ran a back-to-back test after installing the truck manifold on the test motor. The motor was run with the divided plenum and then again with the divider rotated to allow the motor to breathe through the combined plenum volume.

This plenum volume test is a perfect example of why it is so important to supply complete power graphs when running dyno tests. Had I (like many of the enthusiast's magazines) simply provided peak power numbers, you would not have been able to see how the power curve changed as indicated by the graph. With the divided plenum (each bank breathing through half of the available plenum volume), the motor produced 338 hp at 5,500 rpm and 354 ft-lbs at 4,500 rpm. Down at 2,500 rpm, the truck manifold helped the 4.6L produce 313 ft-lbs of torque. The divider was then rotated to combine the two halves of the plenum and run again. So equipped, the motor produced peak numbers of 336 hp at 5,500 rpm and 356 ft-lbs at 4,400 rpm. The difference in peak numbers could well have been the difference associated from run to run, but the real change in power came below 4,000 rpm. Equipped with the divided plenum, the motor produced more torque up to 2,950 rpm. From 2,950 rpm to 4,000 rpm, allowing the motor to breathe through the common (undivided) plenum improved the power production by as much as 20 ft-lbs. From 4,000 rpm to 6,000 rpm, the change in plenum volume had very little effect. What we learned from this test is that the ideal operation point (to rotate the divider) was at 2,950 rpm. This way, the motor would offer the power advantage of the divided plenum up to 2,950 rpm and the extra power offered by the undivided plenum up to 4,000 rpm.

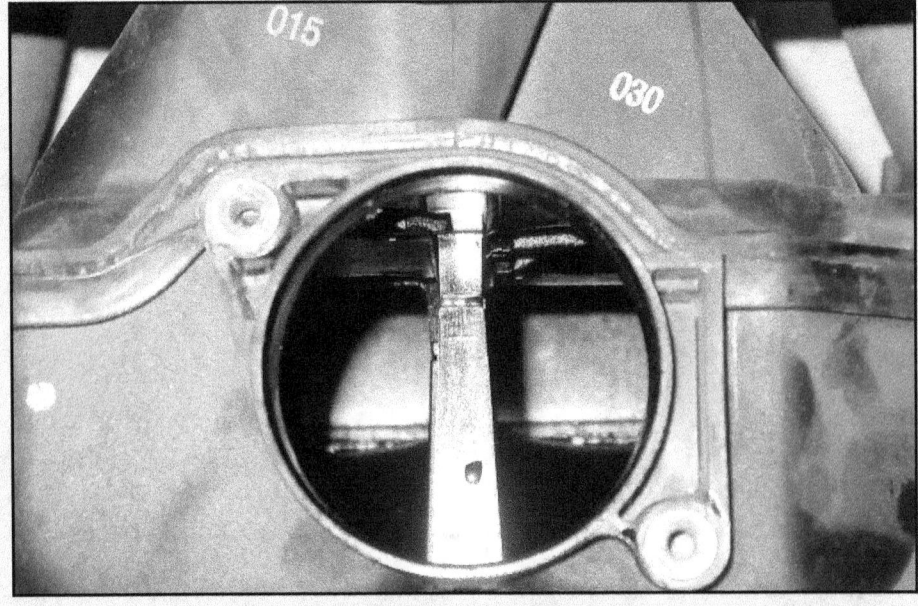

The plenum of the truck intake is divided in half until a stepper motor opens it up. By disabling the stepper motor, we were able to keep the plenum divided at all RPM, and then open at all RPM.

Intake Manifolds

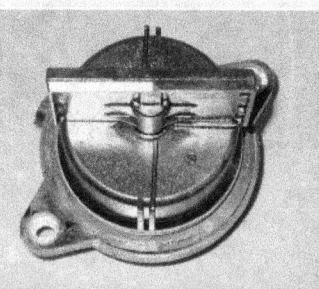

Undivided Plenum:
338 hp @ 5,500 rpm

Divided Plenum:
340 hp @ 5,600 rpm

Largest Gain:
14 hp @ 3,400 rpm

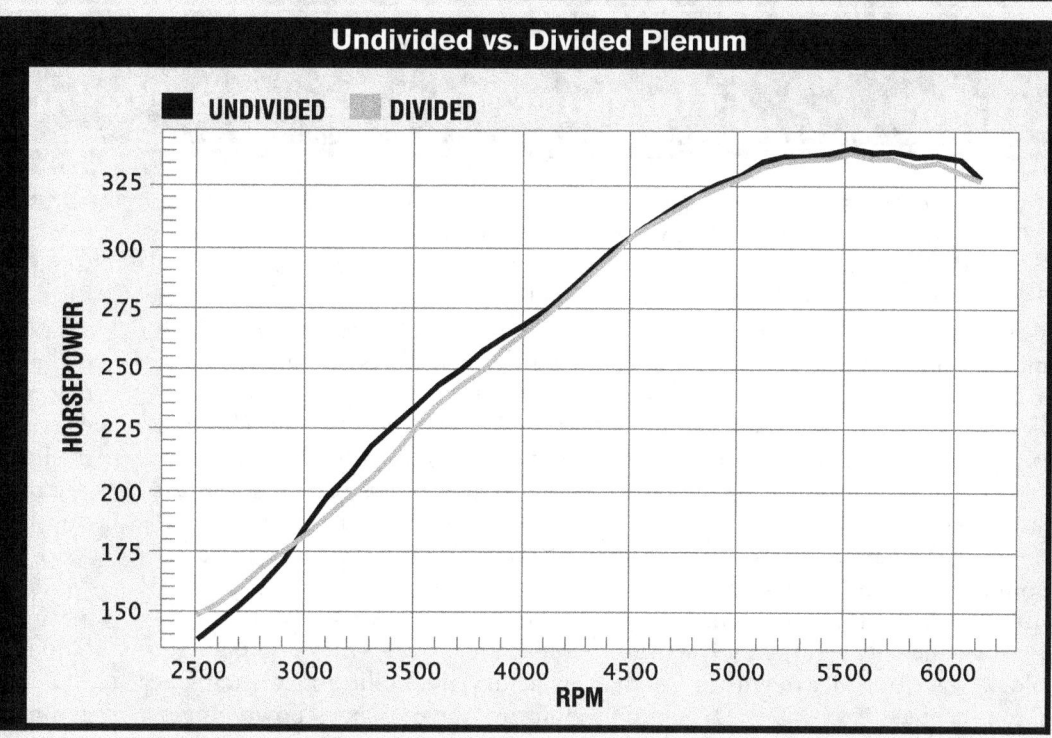

4.6L Truck Intake: Undivided vs. Divided Plenum (Horsepower)
Despite little to no change in peak horsepower or torque values, the divided plenum in the 4.6L truck manifold made a significant change in the power curve. Divided, the low-speed power was better up to 2,950 rpm, and then the undivided plenum configuration took over until 4,000 rpm. After that, the plenum trickery had little to no effect on the horsepower curve. The plenum stepper motor is shown here.

Undivided Plenum:
354 ft-lbs @ 4,500 rpm

Divided Plenum:
356 ft-lbs @ 4,600 rpm

Largest Gain:
19 ft-lbs @ 3,300 rpm

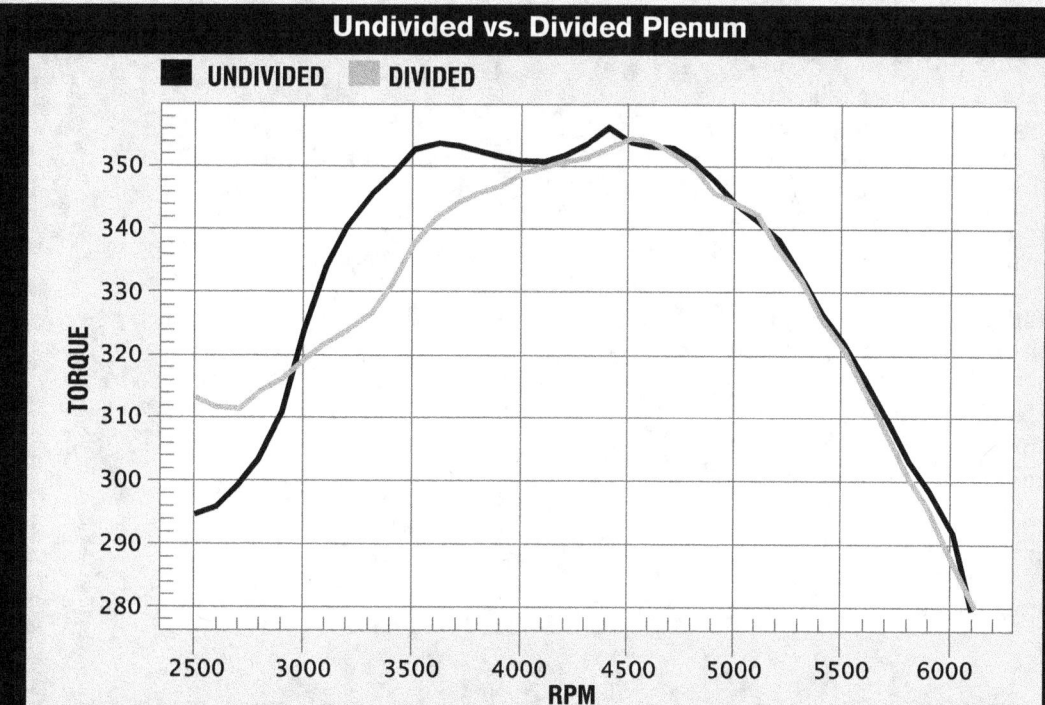

4.6L Truck Intake: Undivided vs. Divided Plenum (Torque)
The torque curves tell the real story, as a 4.6L truck owner is probably most concerned with low-speed torque production. Altering the plenum (divided vs. undivided) swung the torque curve by 20 ft-lbs. Believe me, you can feel an extra 20 ft-lbs (or miss it when it's gone). Tricks like these keep the Ford engineers busy coming up with ways to improve power in the most desirable and usable range for a given application.

Chapter 2

Test 3: 2-Valve GT: PI Intake vs. Ford Racing Bullitt Intake

This test was run to compare a 1999-up 4.6L 2-valve PI intake to the Ford Racing Bullitt manifold. Like Tests 1 and 2, the Bullitt intake test was run on a modified 4.6L 2-valve motor. The thinking behind running a modified motor was that the high-flow Bullitt intake would certainly run best on a wilder-than-stock combination. The test mule consisted of a stock 4.6L (2-valve) GT block and crank combined with a set of forged connecting rods and stock replacement forged pistons from Coast High Performance. The forged 1998 short block was topped off with a set of CNC-ported non-PI 4.6L heads from Ford Performance Solutions. The early heads were further modified to accept the later PI intake manifold and Accufab 75-mm throttle body and elbow. Additional performance came in the form of a set of Comp Xtreme Energy XE262AH cams. The PI-spec Comp cams featured .550 inches of lift (both intake and exhaust) and a 226/230-degrees duration split. The additional lift took full advantage of the airflow offered by the CNC-ported head, while the hike in duration over the stock cams extended the effective operating range of the motor. The final mods included a set of Hooker long-tube headers, a set of 24-pound injectors, and a F.A.S.T. engine management system.

After we tested the stock PI manifold, we installed a Bullitt intake manifold from Ford Racing. The Bullitt manifold features a unique entry designed to accept a larger oval (4-valve Cobra) throttle body. The intake also features slightly shorter runners with a larger cross sectional area than the PI manifold. The changes in the intake design showed what could happen when you continue to push the envelope without regard to the remainder of the components. Installing the Bullitt intake did indeed improve the peak horsepower number from 360 to 369 hp, but the peak torque number actually dropped from 369 ft-lbs to 367 ft-lbs. The changes to the Bullitt intake manifold made themselves known once the tach read 5,500 rpm, but the power output suffered somewhat below that RPM range. The PI manifold bettered the torque production of the Bullitt by as much as 11 ft-lbs at 4,200 rpm. This is not to say that the Ford Racing Bullitt intake doesn't have a lot to offer, it's just that the manifold was applied to the wrong combination, or at least the wrong camshafts. The Bullitt intake would work well with wilder cam timing that would allow the motor to take better advantage of the additional airflow (and design parameters) of the Bullitt. The Bullitt will always trade power compared to the PI manifold, it's just that the mild cam timing and possible head flow didn't allow the motor to run effectively to the engine speed where the Bullitt could really shine.

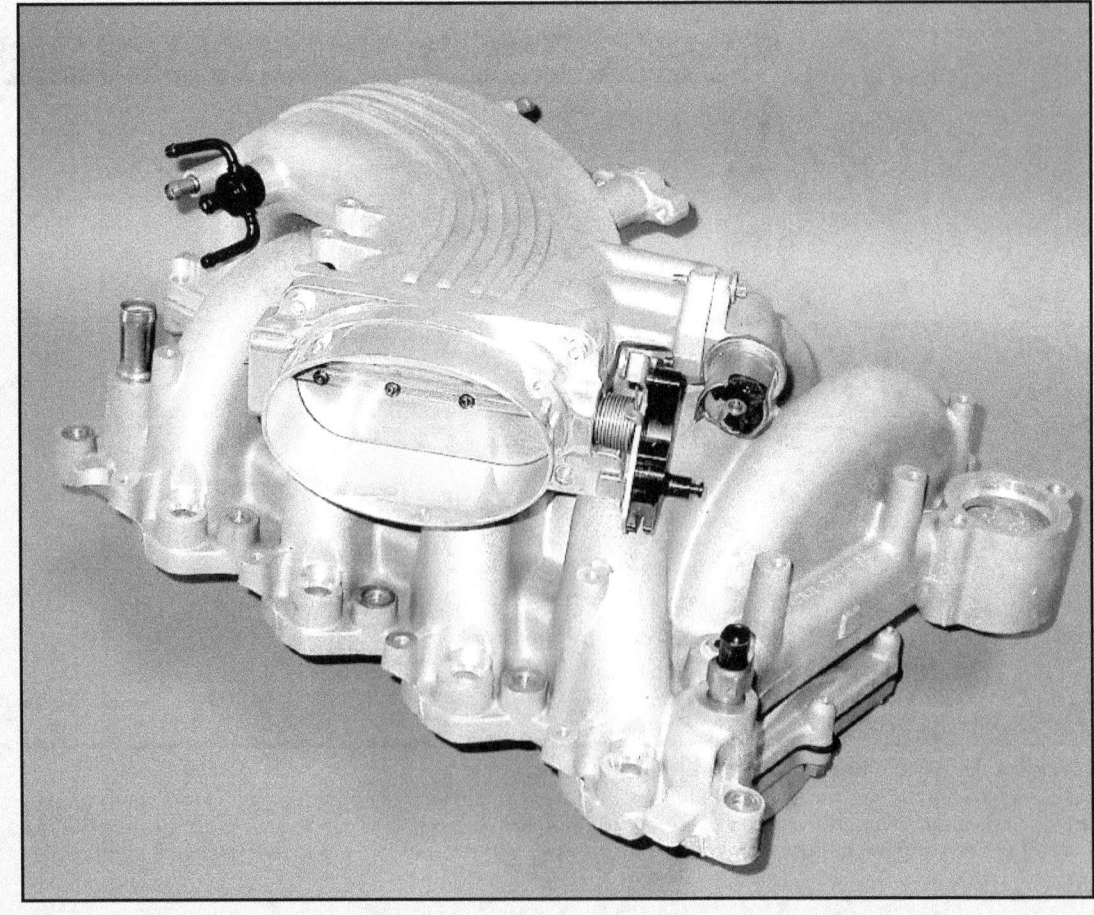

This test compared the aluminum Bullitt intake with the regular PI intake. The Bullitt intake features a top-mounted oval (Cobra style) throttle body.

Intake Manifolds

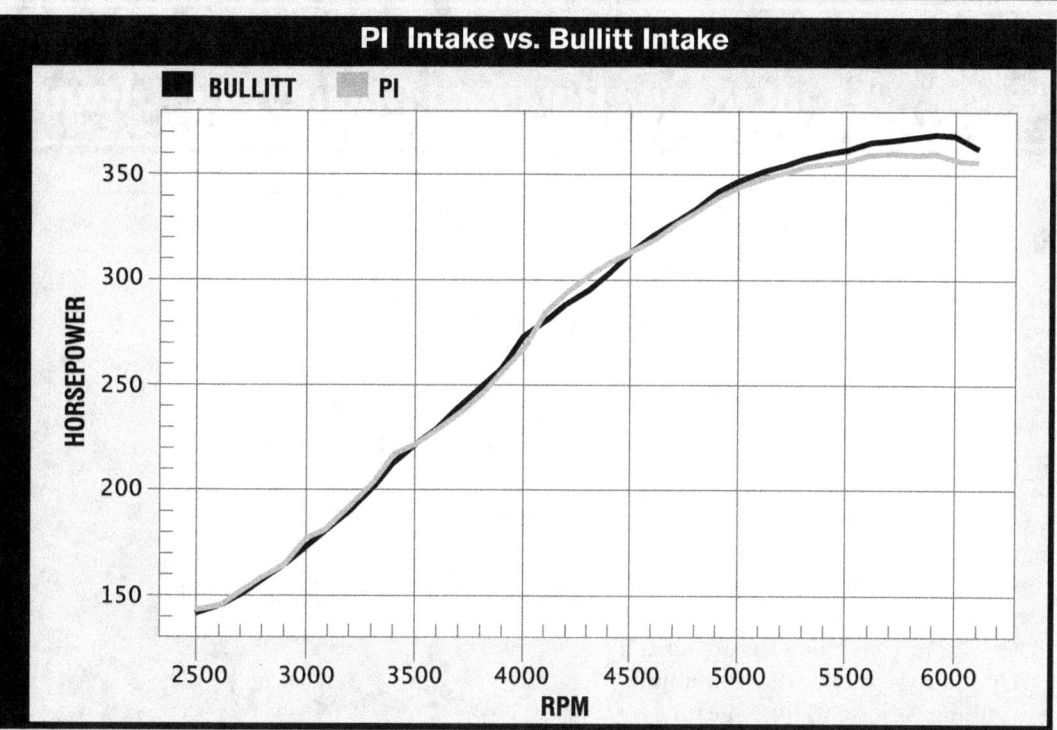

4.6L PI Intake:
360 hp @ 5,700 rpm

FR Bullitt Intake:
369 hp @ 5,900 rpm

Largest Gain:
14 hp @ 6,000 rpm

4.6L PI Intake vs. Bullitt Intake (Horsepower)
The Ford Racing Bullitt intake has always proven powerful, but just how much better is it than the stock PI intake on a mild combination? Tested back-to-back, the Bullitt intake showed power gains above 4,500 rpm, but lost out to the PI intake from 3,100 rpm to 3,600 rpm and then again from 4,100 rpm to 4,500 rpm. My guess would be that the Bullitt intake would need a stronger motor to take full advantage of its airflow. I almost wish I had tested it in supercharged configuration.

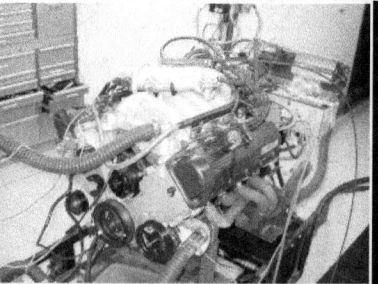
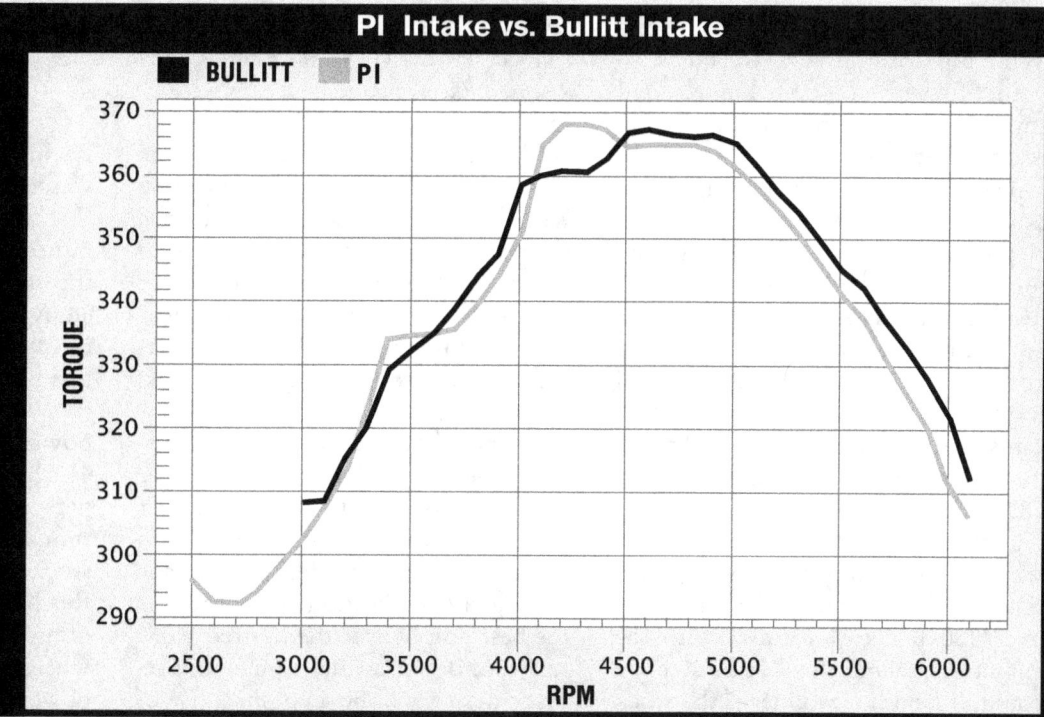

4.6L PI Intake:
368 ft-lbs @ 4,300 rpm

FR Bullitt Intake:
367 ft-lbs @ 4,600 rpm

Largest Gain:
8 ft-lbs @ 5,900 rpm

4.6L PI Intake vs. Bullitt Intake (Torque)
It's not unusual for an intake design that adds power at high RPM to lose power down low. This is especially the case with short-runner manifolds. The Ford Racing Bullitt intake lost out to the PI intake over a very narrow RPM range, but bettered it from 3,600 rpm to 4,000 rpm and then again from 4,500 rpm to 6,100 rpm.

Test 4: 2-Valve GT: PI Intake vs. Reichard Racing Short-Runner Intake

I'm often questioned about the power capabilities of a stock 4.6L and modular owners are surprised to hear that 600+ hp is not out of the question with proper tuning. The stock motor not only survived the abuse of 600 supercharged horsepower, but it will live a long, happy life provided you take one important step: proper tuning. The only reason this high-mileage 4.6L is still alive is that it was never starved for fuel or run with excessive timing for the conditions. Never install something as powerful as a supercharger or nitrous oxide and go out and put your foot in the throttle hoping everything is all right. Miss the tune by just 1 to 2 degrees of timing and say goodbye to those pistons; forged or not. Obviously, testing things on the dyno allowed me to sneak up on the tune and eventual full-throttle runs, but it's important to decide if your motor is worth the added expense of a dyno tune. Enthusiasts are quick to point fingers at Joe-Schmoe's bad supercharger or turbocharger, when in reality they are to blame. The right tune will allow you to make impressive power on a stock motor and exceptional power on a built one. The wrong tune will destroy both; the stock motor just blows a nanosecond quicker.

With a healthy 4.6L test motor equipped with TEA CNC-ported heads, a PI intake, Comp XE274H cams, and an Accufab 75-mm throttle body, the 4.6L produced 393 hp and 383 ft-lbs of torque. While 393 hp is a big number given the displacement, what was most impressive was the fact that this little mod motor produced over 380 ft-lbs of torque. With the engine scratching to exceed 400 hp, I couldn't help but wonder if the stock PI intake was restricting the power output. To find out, I contacted Reichard Racing for one of their trick fabricated intakes. I had high hopes that the additional airflow would

Our 4.6L 2-valve GT motor was tested first with the PI intake (shown) and later with the Reichard Racing intake.

work well in conjunction with the CNC-ported heads and aggressive XE274H Comp cams. Given the shorter runners in the Reichard Racing intake, I knew a tradeoff in power was in order, but for this exercise I was actually searching for a big peak number and not so much for improved torque or driveability.

When it comes to intake manifolds, the rule of thumb is that longer runners promote low-speed power while short runners improve top-end power. The key is to design an intake for a given application that produces the best power over the desired RPM range. Short of a dual-runner intake, every design will be a compromise of sorts. This is especially true of production manifolds, as they must meet a number of design criteria including cost, fuel efficiency, and average power production. Installing the Reichard

Racing intake was pretty straightforward. It's designed to accept an oval (Lightning or Cobra) throttle body rather than the traditional round throttle body used on the stock 4.6L elbow. The large Accufab Lightning throttle body ensured that the intake had plenty of unrestricted airflow. As expected, the intake did improve peak power, bumping our 393 hp 4.6L to 415 hp. True to form, the short runners produced peak power at 6,600 rpm, some 600 rpm higher than the stock PI intake. Unfortunately, the Reichard Racing intake traded plenty of torque – as much as 42 ft-lbs – elsewhere in the curve for the added peak power. What this intake really needed was a 7,000+ rpm 2-valve motor, but unfortunately even our modified 2-valve motor was lacking the RPM potential to take full advantage of the trick design.

Intake Manifolds

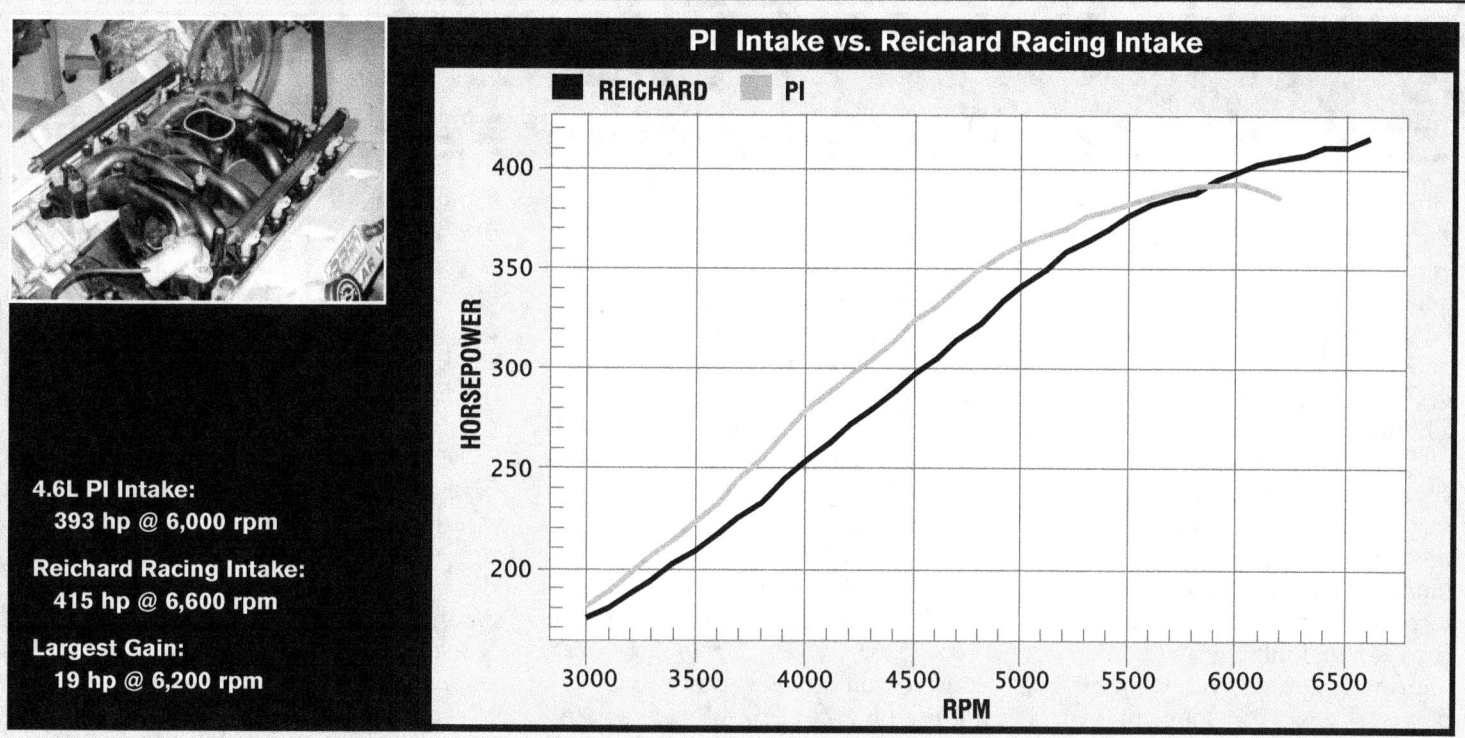

4.6L PI Intake:
393 hp @ 6,000 rpm

Reichard Racing Intake:
415 hp @ 6,600 rpm

Largest Gain:
19 hp @ 6,200 rpm

4.6L PI Intake vs. Reichard Racing Intake (Horsepower)
If only this test motor was designed to run out at 7,000 rpm or even 7,500 rpm, the Reichard Racing intake would have shown its worth even more. Even at 6,600 rpm, it is likely that the short-runner design would have out-powered the stock PI intake by a wide margin, as the stock power curve was falling off rapidly. Unfortunately, it wasn't until past 5,900 rpm that the short-runner design bettered the stock intake.

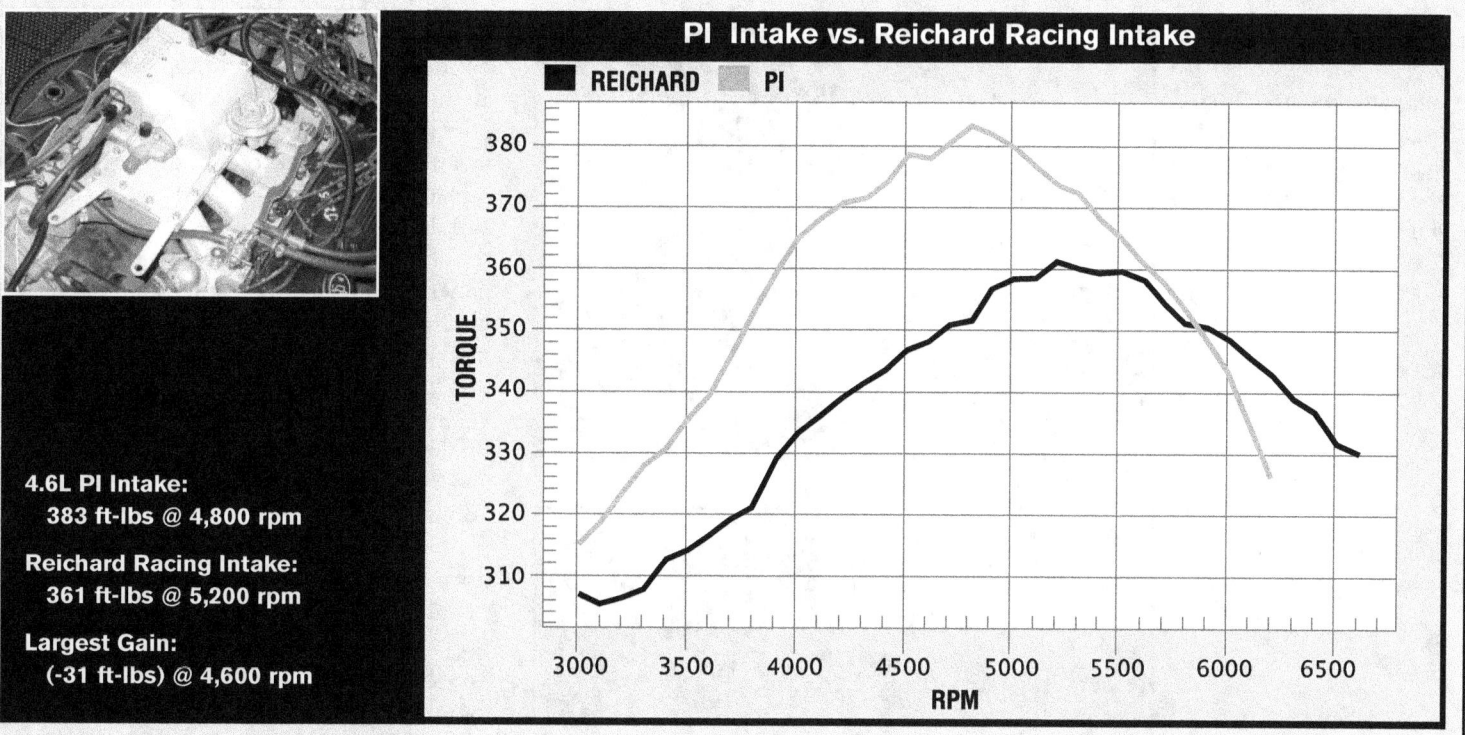

4.6L PI Intake:
383 ft-lbs @ 4,800 rpm

Reichard Racing Intake:
361 ft-lbs @ 5,200 rpm

Largest Gain:
(-31 ft-lbs) @ 4,600 rpm

4.6L PI Intake vs. Reichard Racing Intake (Torque)
The torque curve answers the question about which intake to choose on this motor. The PI manifold was up to the tune of over 30 ft-lbs and a solid 20+ ft-lbs from 3,000 rpm all the way to 5,900 rpm. In a heads-up race, the PI intake would show heals to the fabricated intake.

Test 5: 2-Valve GT: PI Intake vs. Fox Lake P51 Intake

I have to admit I was skeptical about testing the Fox Lake P51 intake, especially after being told it would improve high-end power over the PI intake *and* sacrifice little low-end and midrange power. When it comes to designing an intake manifold, it's actually pretty easy to increase the power output at any given RPM range. Build short runners for high-end power; increase the runner length and watch the low-speed (or midrange) torque improve. The power tradeoff is similar to changing the cam profile. The real trick when building an intake is to improve the power without sacrificing power elsewhere along the curve. Believe me, this is a difficult proposition, as optimizing a runner configuration (length, cross section, and taper ratio) for a particular operating range will almost surely reduce power elsewhere along the curve. You also have to factor in the application. An intake designed for a 260-hp stock motor will likely not work as well on a 450-hp stroker. In a sense, intake manifolds are both application and RPM specific. The fact that the stock PI manifold is so flexible, both in terms of RPM and applications, is a testament to the original designers.

Having tested more than my fair share of intakes on all types of engines, I expected the testing on this P51 to follow suit. I expected that the more power gained up top, the more power would be lost down low. As it turned out, the gang at Fox Lake actually seemed to do their homework, as their promise of additional peak power with a minimal tradeoff in low-speed power was actually pretty accurate. As indicated, the test motor is important in that a wilder combination will likely work best with a different intake than a bone-stock motor. Our Sean Hyland-built test motor consisted of a forged short block with stock PI compression, a set of stock PI heads, and matching PI intake and throttle body. The factory PI cams had since been replaced by a set of Xtreme Energy XE262H (non-PI) cams that offered .500 inches of lift, a 224/232-degrees duration split, and a 114-degree lobe separation angle. Additional changes included a set of Kooks 1⅝-inch headers, MSD ignition, and F.A.S.T. management system to control the 36-pound injectors. Basically, we had a 4.6L 2-valve PI motor equipped with cams and headers, run without any of its accessories.

With the factory PI intake, throttle body, and inlet elbow, the engine produced 331 hp at 5,700 rpm and 342 ft-lbs at 4,200 rpm. It performed best with 30 degrees of total timing and an air/fuel ratio of 13.0:1. The Fox Lake P51 intake was every bit as easy to install as the PI, though we did have to replace the factory fuel rails with the supplied aluminum ones. A peek inside the aluminum P51 via a removable side panel revealed a cross-ram design covered by a common plenum. The P51 intake was also equipped to accept a 75-mm throttle body, so we used a billet version from Accufab. With the P51 intake, the 4.6L produced 341 hp at 5,800 rpm and 346 ft-lbs at 4,400 rpm. While a peak gain of 10 horsepower isn't huge, the P51 offered as much as 16 hp at 6,000 rpm. More importantly, (as promised) the P51 intake traded almost no low-speed power (from as low as 2,500 rpm) for the gains achieved from 4,300 rpm to 6,000 rpm. Though I'm happy with the gains posted by the P51, it should be noted that the gains were almost identical to those achieved with a simple Accufab throttle body and elbow upgrade on the stock PI intake.

The P51 intake manifold goes on just like the PI intake comes off. You will need to use the supplied aluminum fuel rails, and the associated fittings and hoses.

Internally, the P51 intake is a cross-ram design covered by a common plenum.

Intake Manifolds

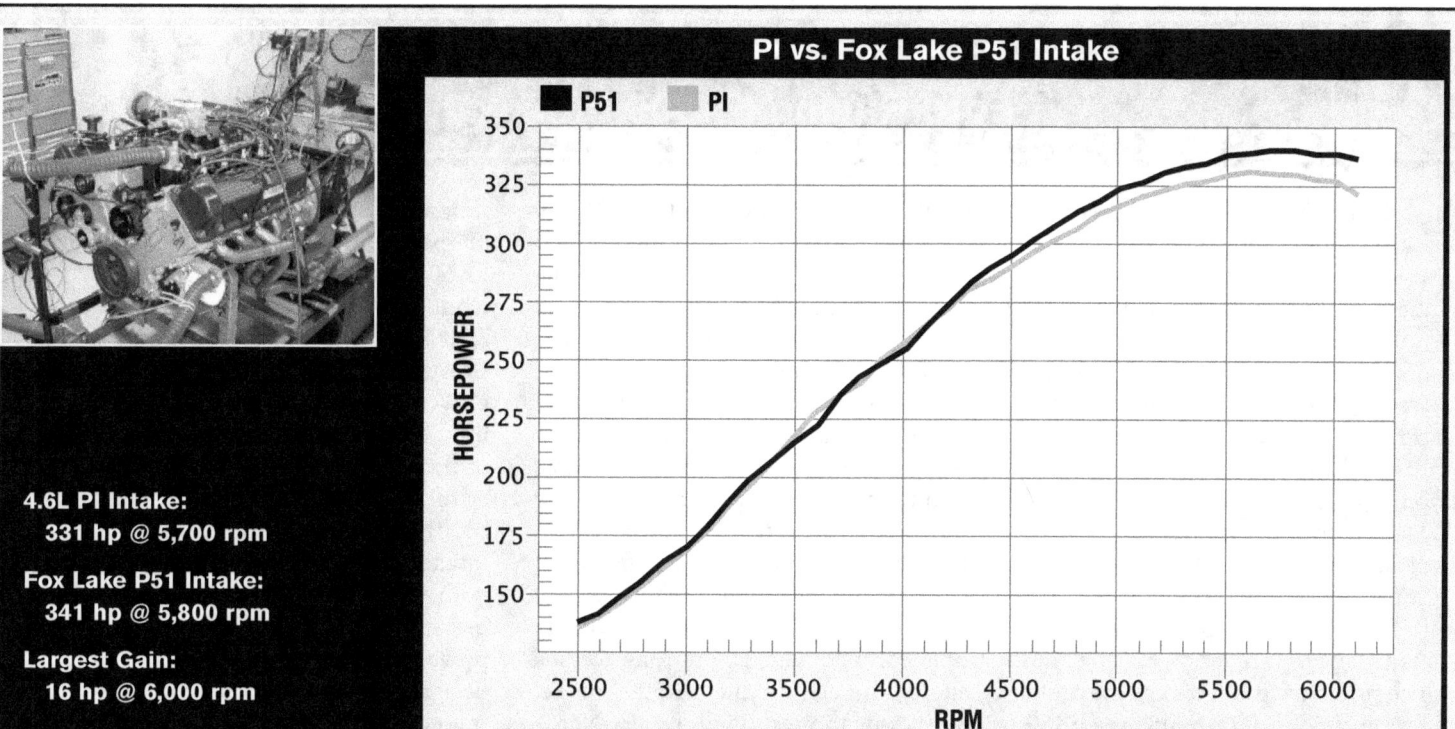

4.6L PI Intake:
331 hp @ 5,700 rpm

Fox Lake P51 Intake:
341 hp @ 5,800 rpm

Largest Gain:
16 hp @ 6,000 rpm

4.6L PI Intake vs. Fox Lake P51 Intake (Horsepower)
As expected, the P51 intake improved the power output of the mild 4.6L. The peak-to-peak gain was 10 hp (331 hp to 341 hp), but at 6,000 rpm the P51 added as much as 16 hp.

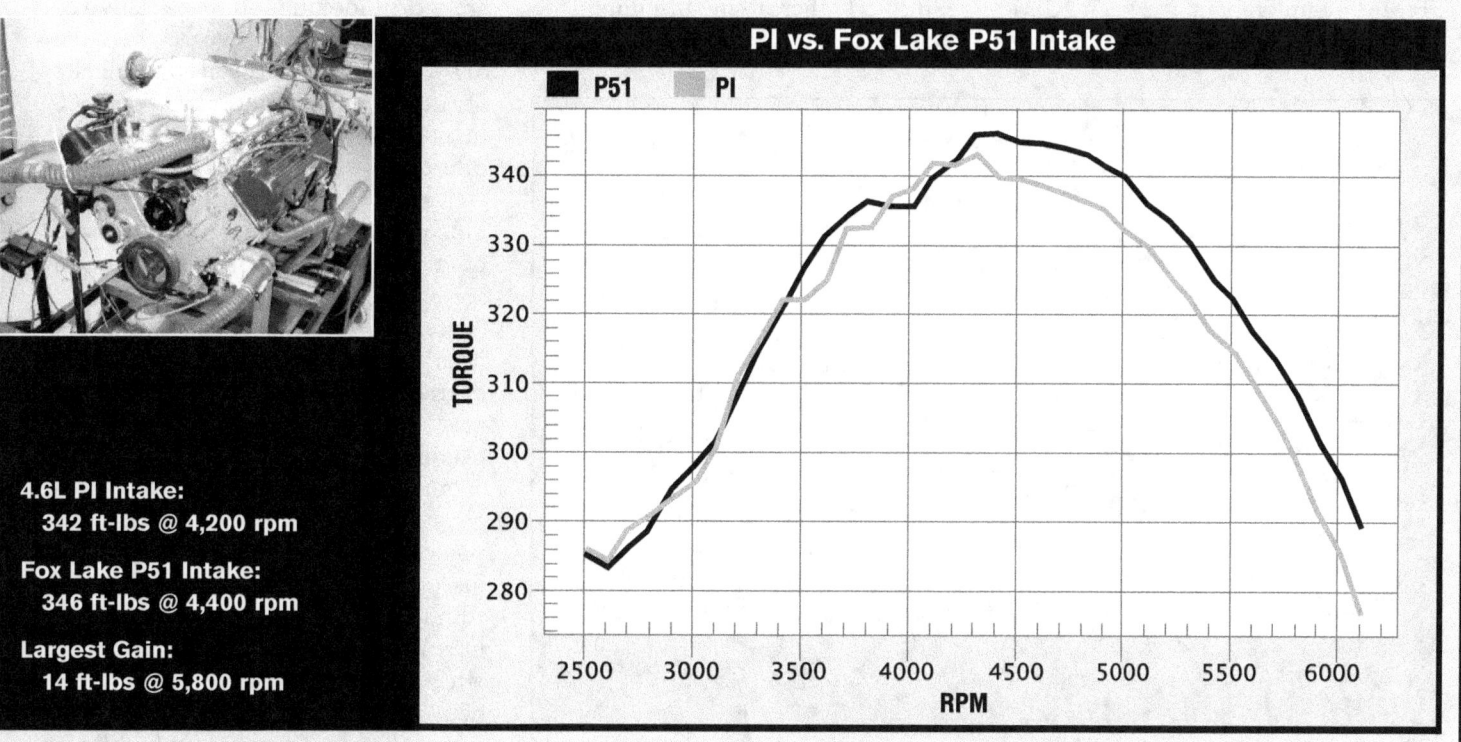

4.6L PI Intake:
342 ft-lbs @ 4,200 rpm

Fox Lake P51 Intake:
346 ft-lbs @ 4,400 rpm

Largest Gain:
14 ft-lbs @ 5,800 rpm

4.6L PI Intake vs. Fox Lake P51 Intake (Torque)
The additional power past 4,300 rpm is evident by the torque curve, but most important is the fact that the P51 lost no power below 4,300 rpm. Even down at 2,500 rpm, the P51 matched the stock PI intake.

Building 4.6/5.4L Ford Horsepower on the Dyno

Test 6: 4-Valve Cobra: SHM Ported '01 Cobra Intake vs. Ford Racing FR500 Intake

While testing a Sean Hyland 4-valve Cobra motor, I decided to compare the SHM-ported 2001 Cobra intake with the Ford Racing FR500 Variable Geometry intake. The unique Ford Racing intake offers dual runners to maximize the power production over a broad power range. Short runners help promote power production at high RPM, while (well-designed) longer runners do the same at lower engine speeds. The ideal situation is to combine the power curves offered by each into a single intake. Intake swaps are easy on the 4.6L since no water passages are disturbed. I was excited about running the FR500 intake on the SHM 4.6L since in addition to the elevated static compression, the motor was equipped with ported 4-valve heads and more-aggressive cams. It's possible that the SHM 4.6L might put the high-RPM power offered by the short runner sections in the FR500 intake to good use. The Variable Geometry intake was installed with the stock 4-valve dual-blade throttle body. Since the upper intake lid was designed to accept the dual blade, mods would have been necessary to install a single-blade piece. The last thing I wanted to do was hack into the magnesium manifold to install a throttle body. I can see the headlines now: "author killed in fiery porting accident" – no thanks.

The FR500 intake was installed and run with the short runners opened. For details on long versus short runners on the FR500 intake, check out the results of Test 7. Naturally, the motor was tuned using F.A.S.T. management with each intake. The SHM-ported long runner 2001 Cobra intake offered exceptional power from 3,500 rpm to 6,200 rpm, falling off thereafter. Installing the FR500 intake in short-runner configuration resulted in a dramatic increase in peak power. The Ford Racing FR500 intake raised the peak power from 435 hp at 6,200 rpm to 483 hp at 7,400 rpm. As is usually the case with short-runner intakes, the low-speed power production suffered. It wasn't until 6,200 rpm that the power output of the FR500 intake matched the power of the SHM-ported factory intake, but from 6,200 rpm on up, the FR500 intake pulled away rapidly. Luckily, with the FR500's long runners working too, much of the lost low-speed power is added back. A single-runner design is pretty much stuck with the tradeoff in power. Your best bet is to choose the intake for the engine combination and intended operating range.

The power curves offered by the SHM-ported stock and FR500 intake are worth looking into, especially the high-RPM stuff. In truth, even the SHM 4.6L was not the ideal candidate for the high-RPM nature of the FR500 intake. The mild SHM Stage-1 cams offered just 209 degrees of duration, well short of what you should be running with an intake that wants to make peak power at 7,400 rpm. I'd like to see a minimum of another 10 to 15 degrees of duration. Heck, I wouldn't hesitate running more than 230 degrees of duration and something near .475 inches of lift in a quest for maximum peak power. The motor should be good for an easy 8,000 rpm given the forged SHM internals. If you combined the additional cam timing with a set of heads like ported FR500s, I think 500 hp was well within reach. On such a combination, the effective operating range would likely be from 6,000 rpm to 8,000 rpm, right where the short runners in the FR500 intake are tuned for. You would sacrifice some power down low, but boy what a wild ride it would be once the motor came up on the cams.

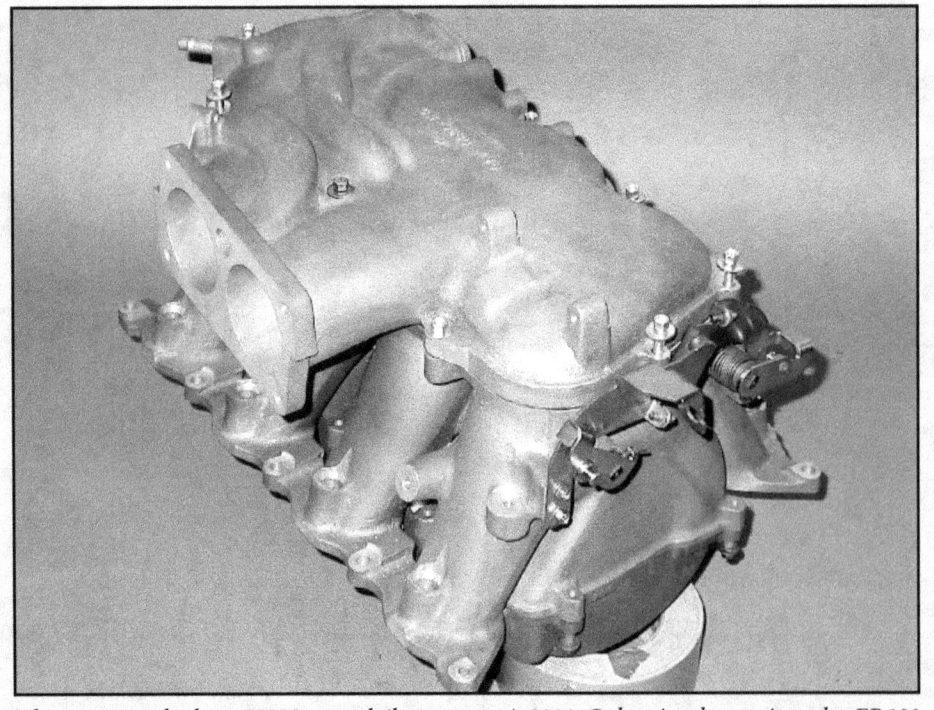

This test matched an SHM ported (long-runner) 2001 Cobra intake against the FR500 Variable Geometry intake. The FR500 would be tested with only its shorter runners operational, so the peak power should be impressive.

Intake Manifolds

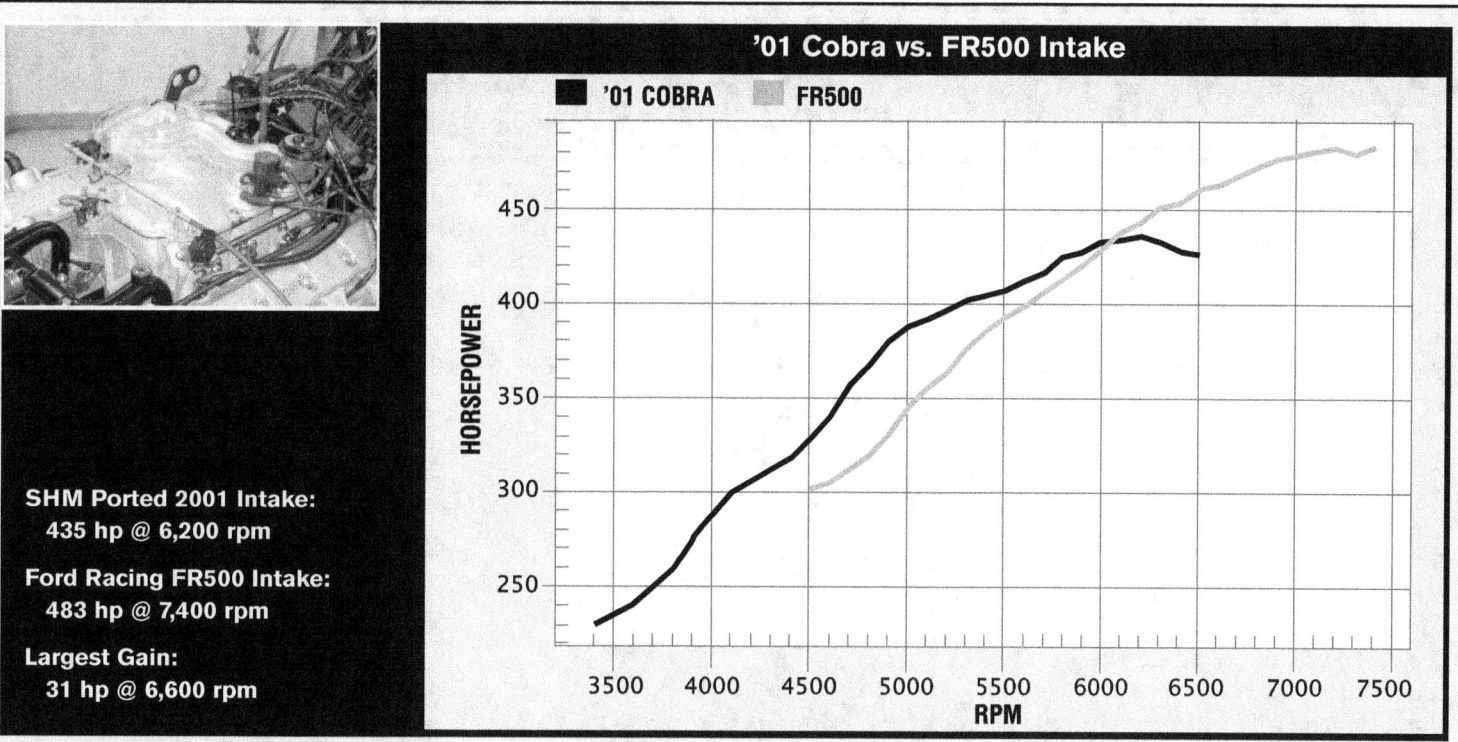

SHM Ported 2001 Intake:
435 hp @ 6,200 rpm

Ford Racing FR500 Intake:
483 hp @ 7,400 rpm

Largest Gain:
31 hp @ 6,600 rpm

SHM Ported 2001 Intake vs. Ford Racing FR500 Intake (Horsepower)
From a peak horsepower standpoint, there is no comparison, as the FR500 intake produced 483 hp versus just 435 hp with the SHM-ported 2001 Cobra manifold. If you look closer, you'll see that the short runners in the FR500 intake offered significantly more power above 6,200 rpm, but lost out below 6,200 rpm.

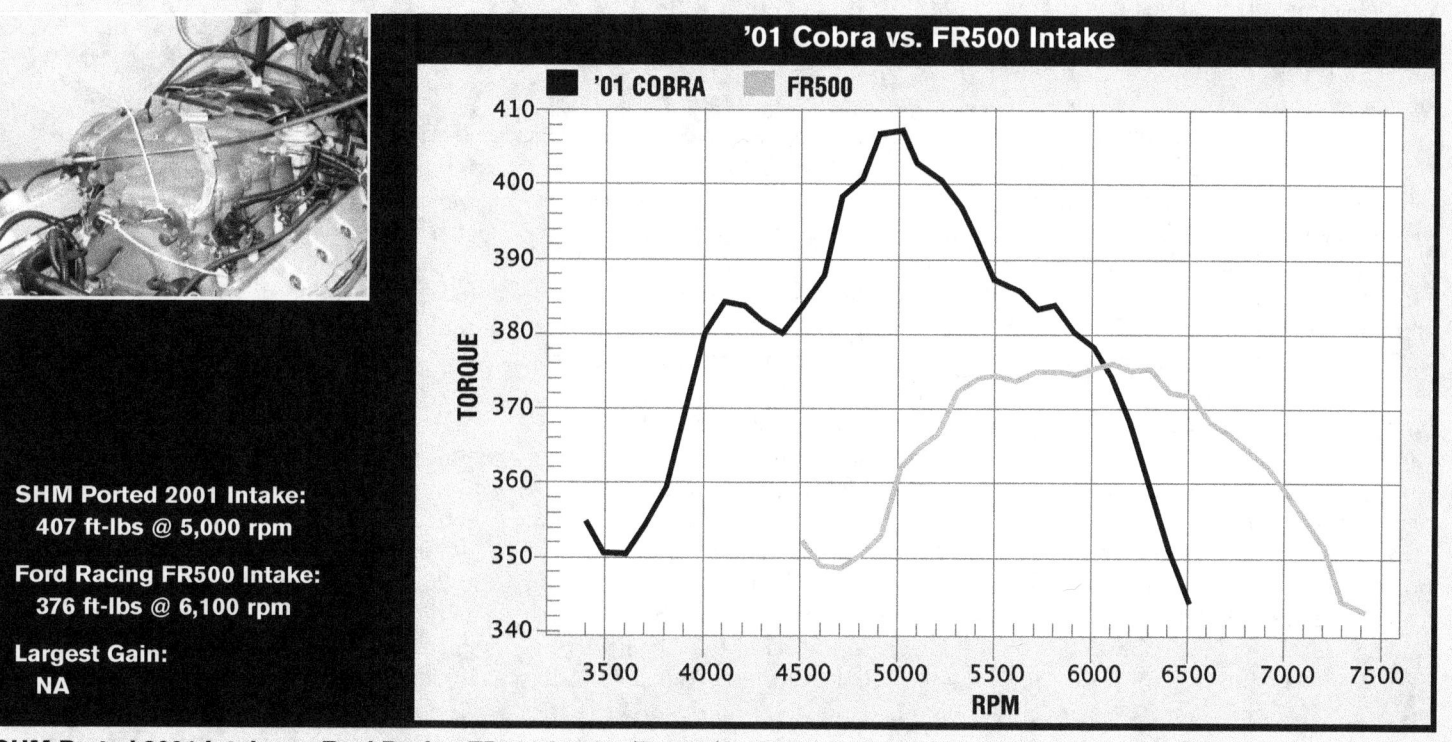

SHM Ported 2001 Intake:
407 ft-lbs @ 5,000 rpm

Ford Racing FR500 Intake:
376 ft-lbs @ 6,100 rpm

Largest Gain:
NA

SHM Ported 2001 Intake vs. Ford Racing FR500 Intake (Torque)
The torque curve illustrates why it is so important to choose the effective operating range of your motor. The FR500 intake was down by over 45 ft-lbs near 5,000 rpm, but kept higher in the rev range the short-runner intake really motored. For street driving, the ported stock intake would be best, but for all-out drag racing, the FR500 would offer superior ETs and trap speed, especially if combined with wilder cam timing and even better head flow. Remember, this is with only the FR500's shorter runners working.

Chapter 2

Test 7: Ford Racing FR500 Intake: Long vs. Short Runners

Though originally equipped with an Eaton supercharger (see Chapter 7), I took the liberty of removing the blower and running this '03 Cobra motor in naturally aspirated trim for this test. The '03 Cobra motor was equipped with a set of Hooker Super Comp headers and a set of Comp Xtreme Energy cams (see Chapter 4). The Xtreme RPM grinds (designed for a naturally aspirated motor) featured low .425-inch lift figures that allowed me to run them with the stock valvesprings. The dual-pattern XE262AH cams offered 226 degrees of intake duration, 222 degrees of exhaust duration, and a 114-degree lobe separation angle to go along with the .425 lift (both intake and exhaust). As it turned out, the XE262AH cams worked great on the '03 Cobra motor, offering significant power gains in naturally aspirated trim. The power gains were slightly less when tested with the blower(s), but the new cam profiles sure worked well with the turbos.

After running all manners of blower tests, I decided it was time to take a look at the 4.6L Cobra Variable Geometry intake available in the Ford Racing catalog. Variable Geometry is Ford-talk for dual runner, as the lightweight magnesium FR500 features both long and short runners designed to enhance power production at both ends of the power curve. The long runners were designed to enhance low-speed power while the short runners improve top-end breathing. The trick is to find the optimum crossover point to switch from one to the other. On a cool scale of 1 to 10, this Ford Racing intake ranks about a 27. Unfortunately for me, the low-compression '03 Cobra motor was not the ideal candidate for this sophisticated dual-runner intake, but it would help demonstrate the difference in the power curves offered by the dual-runner setup. Even better, this intake would allow me to run my favorite long- versus short-runner intake test without even having to swap the intake.

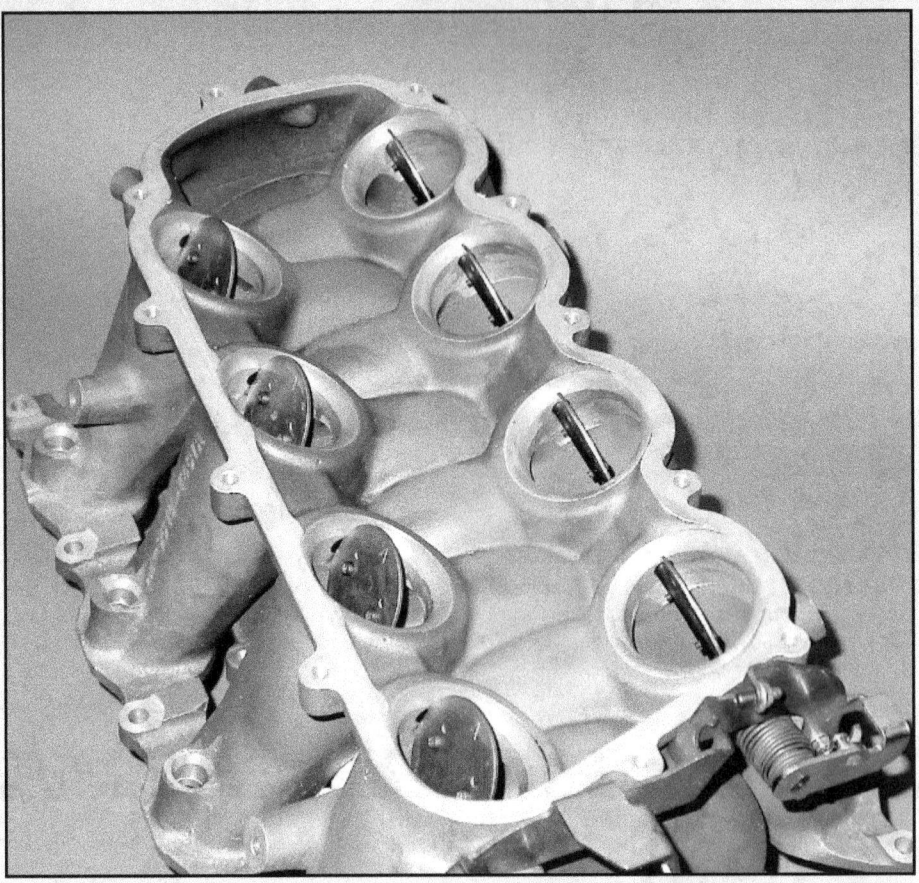

The Ford Racing FR500 Variable Geometry intake offered both short and long runners, but for this test, we're only running one set at a time. As expected, the shorter runners produced more top-end power, while the longer runners ruled down low.

To demonstrate the effectiveness of the dual-runner design, I installed the Ford Racing intake on the naturally aspirated '03 Cobra motor and ran each runner setup from 3,000 rpm to 6,500 rpm. As it turned out, 6,500 rpm was not quite high enough to find the power peak offered by the short runners, but I eventually ran it to 7,000 rpm in a quest to find the power peak. Equipped with the long runners (designed to promote low-speed power), the Ford Racing intake produced just 364 hp and 365 ft-lbs of torque. The peak power was a far cry from the 400+ hp produced with the factory intake, but remember, the long runners were not designed for top-end power. After switching over to the short runners, I found the peak power numbers I was expecting. After some tuning, the short runners eventually netted a peak power output of 446 hp at 7,000 rpm. Note that this was a solid 20 hp stronger than the stock 2001 intake and that the peak power was shifted up by 600 rpm (6,400 rpm vs. 7,000 rpm). I suspect that the Ford Racing intake would show even larger gains on a slightly wilder combination with higher compression and wilder cam profiles to take advantage of the high-RPM potential of the short runner section.

Intake Manifolds

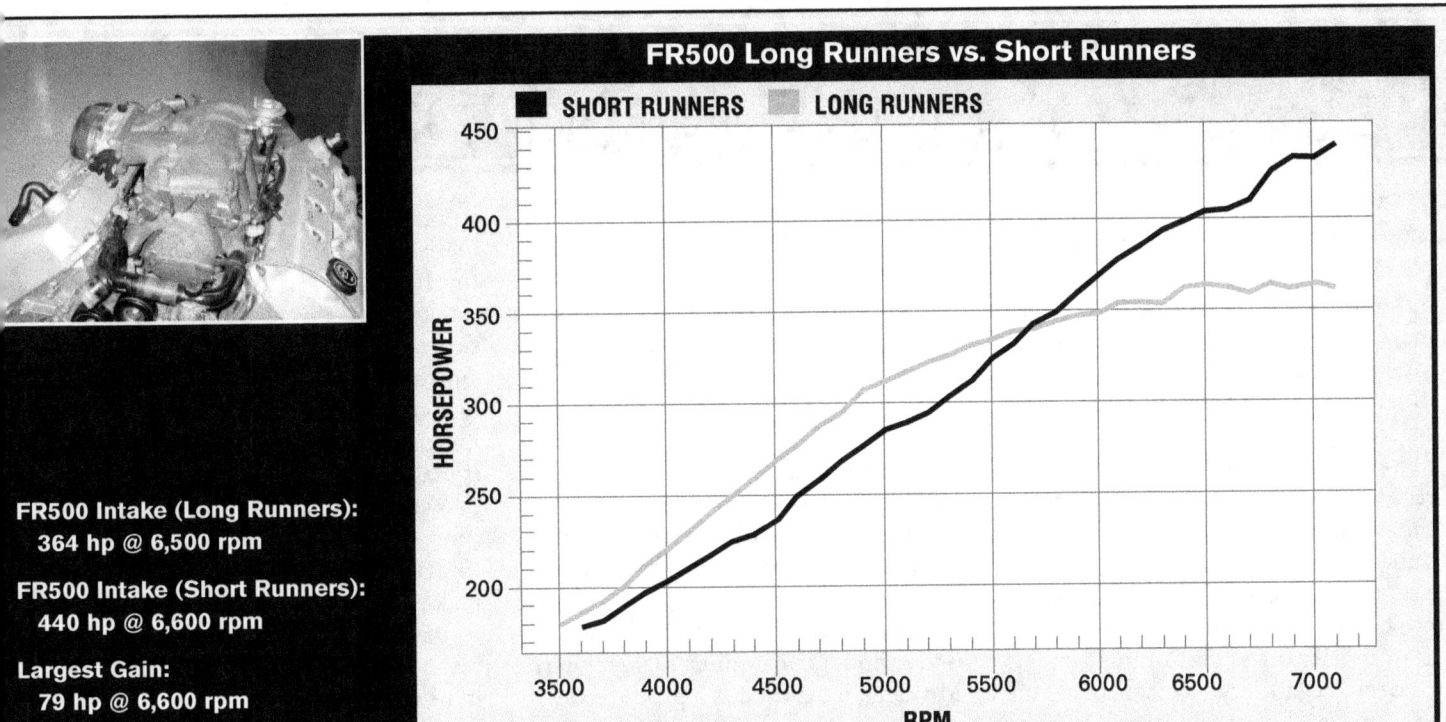

FR500 Intake (Long Runners):
364 hp @ 6,500 rpm

FR500 Intake (Short Runners):
440 hp @ 6,600 rpm

Largest Gain:
79 hp @ 6,600 rpm

FR500 Intake: Long Runners vs. Short Runners (Horsepower)
The graph shows the two power curves generated by running the Ford Racing Variable Geometry intake in each runner configuration. The long-runner produced more power up to 5,200 rpm, at which point the short-runner version took the lead. From this graph we can conclude that the ideal switchover point (from long to short) would be 5,200 rpm.

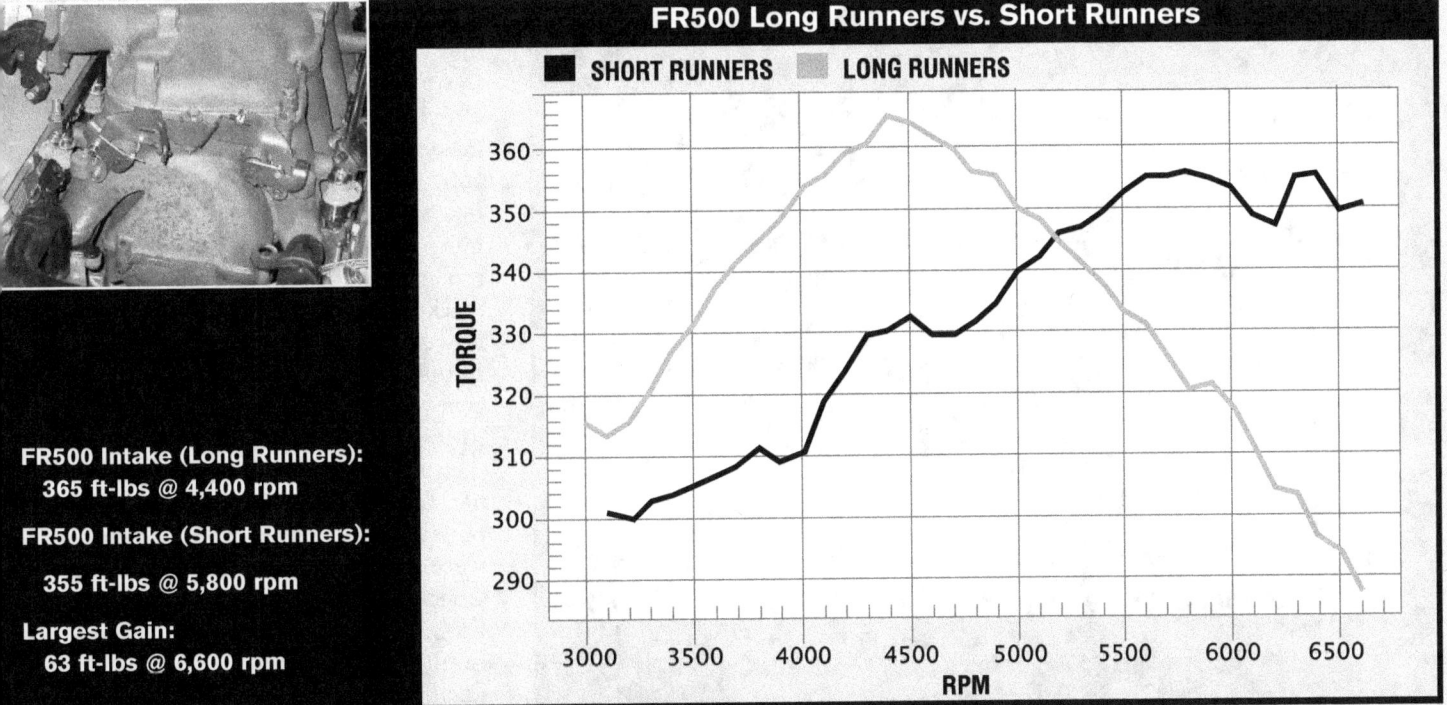

FR500 Intake (Long Runners):
365 ft-lbs @ 4,400 rpm

FR500 Intake (Short Runners):
355 ft-lbs @ 5,800 rpm

Largest Gain:
63 ft-lbs @ 6,600 rpm

FR500 Intake: Long Runners vs. Short Runners (Torque)
This graph once again illustrates the typical long- versus short-runner comparison, where the long runner configuration excels at low-speed (and midrange) torque production. The great thing about this scenario is that the fully functional FR500 intake gives you the best of both worlds.

Chapter 2

Test 8: Vortech Supercharged 4-Valve '03 Cobra: Effect of Runner Length

While running the boost comparison for Chapter 8, I saw an opportunity to once again illustrate the difference in power caused by intake manifold runner length. I blame the intake manufacturers and unknowing tuners for the confusion that exists regarding intake manifold design. Here it is one more time for the record: intake runner length is one of the primary design features that determine the effective operating range of the motor. Longer runners produce peak power at a lower operating range than shorter ones. This tuning effect is present regardless of whether the motor is turbo or supercharged. The presence of boost pressure *does not* dictate a shorter runner length. Shortening the runner length in every case will reduce power at a lower RPM but has the potential to increase power at higher engine speeds. The terms long and short can be misleading, as a 19-inch runner should certainly be considered long, but is 14 inches still long? A runner length of 11 inches is certainly long compared to a runner length of just 4 inches, but just where do you draw the line?

The primary reason for the runner length for fabricated intakes doesn't come from some scientific calculation, or even equally (sometimes more) effective trial-and-error testing. It is dictated by production convenience. Given the under-hood constraints of a modern Mustang, it's difficult to produce sufficient runner length without resorting to some seriously complicated bends. Since difficult, expensive bends are out of the question, the vast majority of fabricated sheet metal or aluminum intakes feature straight runners. The runner length needs to be short (usually 4 to 7 inches) to be both straight and fit under the hood. Voilà, instant performance intake. All you need now is to apply some Internet logic in your advertising and the customers will eat it up, especially if you call it a blower or turbo intake. Unfortunately, all you've done (at best) is make an intake with a runner length that's suited for an 8,000-rpm motor, not (I repeat), not a forced-induction manifold (unless that forced induction motor makes peak power at 8,000 rpm).

Stepping down off my soapbox, I can now get to one of the hundreds of dyno tests that support the runner-length discussion. The Vortech '03-'04 Cobra replacement supercharger kit comes equipped with an intake designed to use the factory '03 air-to-water intercooler and lower intake. Unfortunately, the factory lower intake on the '03 Cobra features almost no runner length, just radiused openings leading into the head (talk about short runners). Vortech did this in an effort to retain the factory pieces and keep the cost down. Adding a factory 2001 intake (like the one tested) and one of Vortech's Power Coolers to the mix would drive the price of the Cobra replacement kit up beyond what the market would bear. To illustrate the power gains offered by the change in runner length, I ran the Vortech supercharged '03 Cobra motor at 15 psi with their adapter/intercooler system, and then again after installing the long-runner factory 2001 Cobra intake. The pulley ratio, air/fuel ratio, and timing were all kept constant for the two tests. Check out the difference in power: From 3,500 rpm to 6,600 rpm, the long-runner intake upped the torque production by a solid 50 ft-lbs, with gains as much as 72 ft-lbs at 4,400 rpm and 5,500 rpm. The factory '01 intake offered as much as 75 hp over the short-runner version at 5,500 rpm and carried a 50-hp gain right through 6,600 rpm.

This test illustrates what a difference a well-designed intake manifold can make. We're comparing a 2001 Cobra intake with the short-runner intake that comes with Vortech's '03-'04 Cobra blower upgrade kit.

Intake Manifolds

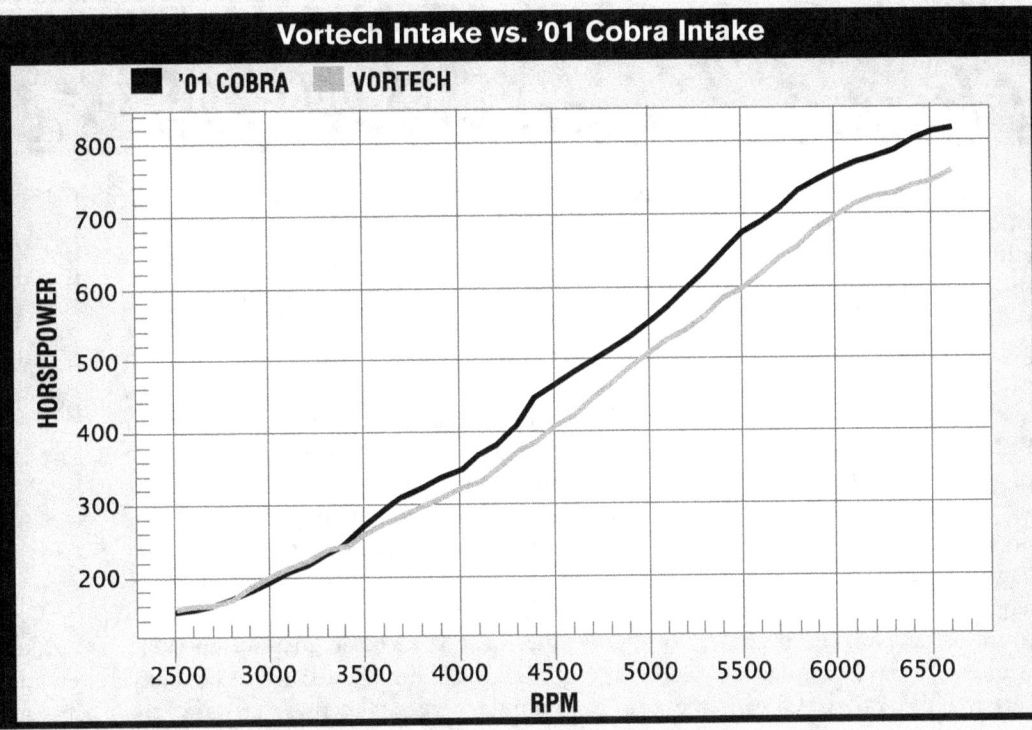

Vortech Intake:
756 hp @ 6,600 rpm

2001 Cobra Intake:
815 hp @ 6,600 rpm

Largest Gain:
74 hp @ 5,700 rpm

Vortech Intake vs. 2001 Cobra Intake (Horsepower)
What can you say about a (long-runner) intake manifold change that adds power (nearly 75 hp) from 3,500 rpm all the way to 6,600 rpm? Installing the 2001 factory Cobra intake in place of the fabricated upper intake (part of Vortech's '03-'04 Cobra blower upgrade) resulted in a significant jump in power, thanks to the increase in runner length. ATI also offers a similar kit for the '03-'04 Cobras and the results would be similar on their kit as well. Ultra-short runners will always cost power.

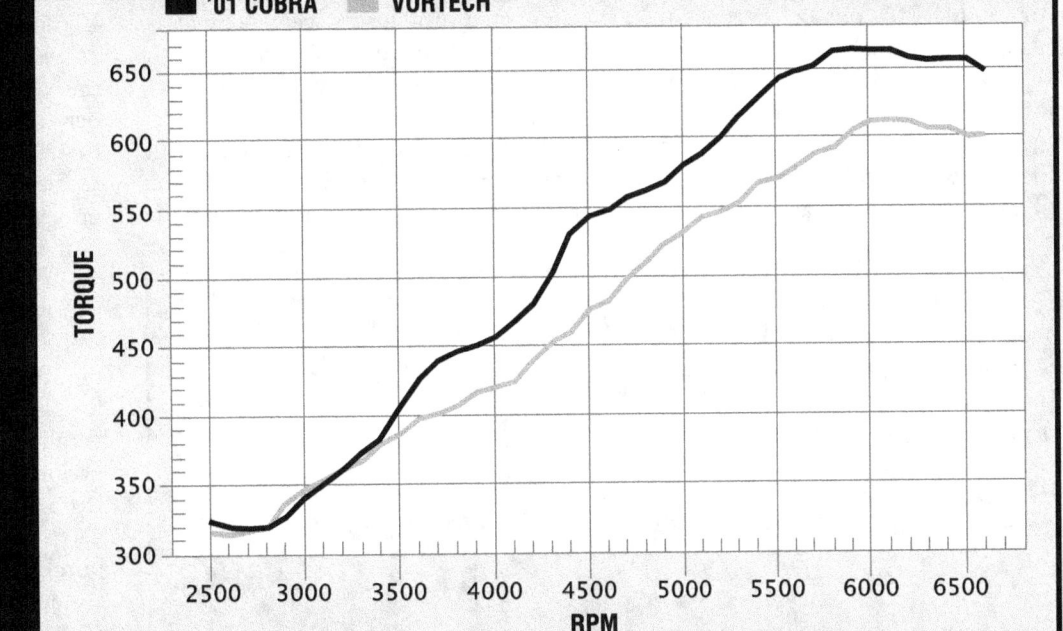

Vortech Intake:
612 ft-lbs @ 6,100 rpm

2001 Cobra Intake:
663 ft-lbs @ 6,600 rpm

Largest Gain:
70 ft-lbs @ 5,700 rpm

Vortech Intake vs. 2001 Cobra Intake (Torque)
Who couldn't use an extra 70 ft-lbs of torque or a solid 50 ft-lbs from 4,500 rpm to 6,500 rpm? Runner length improves cylinder filling, even on forced induction applications. Someone telling you otherwise either has never been on the dyno or is trying very hard to sell you something.

Building 4.6/5.4L Ford Horsepower on the Dyno

Chapter 2

Test 9: 5.0L Stroker 2-Valve GT: Variable Runner Intake

This custom Variable Runner Intake (VRI) was designed by the author to demonstrate the worth of a proper intake manifold design. A great deal of time and effort, not to mention considerable math (something I don't excel at), went into the design. After testing the non-PI, PI, 4.6L Truck, P51, Reichard Racing, and Bullitt intakes for the 4.6L 2-valve, I decided something could be done to improve on what was currently available. The usual trend is to shorten the runner length (a la Reichard Racing), but this route usually results in an intake that is only effective in a narrow (and elevated) RPM range. One of the common misconceptions is that the short-runner intakes work universally well with forced induction, but this isn't the case. The intake runner length determines the effective operating range, regardless of whether boost is present or not. Short-runner intakes sacrifice low-end and midrange power for high-RPM power, even with a blower or turbo.

While most enthusiasts (and intake manufacturers) concentrate on the intake runner length, the reality is that there is a great deal more to intake design. Besides the absolute airflow offered by the intake, three different types of ram tuning (Inertia, Reflected Wave, and Helmholtz Resonator) need to be addressed when designing an intake. Next time you are on the phone with one of the intake manufacturers, mention any one of these three types of ram tuning and see if they can provide a decent definition, let alone the math behind calculating the optimum RPM range (crank angle) for each. You can go one step further and ask them how their design ensures (or minimizes) wave interference between the three forms and just watch them struggle. The reality is that not many manufacturers take these criteria into account when designing an intake. They seem to be content with making it look cool, making it fit, and then marketing it to unsuspecting customers. Until the VRI manifold was designed, every intake ever tested on the 4.6L 2V (and 4V) lost power to the stock intake at some RPM range. In some cases, the losses were as great as 40 ft-lbs of torque! Not one of them ever offered a significant enough power gain to offset the losses.

The VRI intake was tested on every conceivable combination, but the results of these tests are from a 5.0L

Check out the full-radiused, bell-mouthed entries on the custom intake.

stroker (3.75-inch stroker crank) from Coast High Performance. The motor featured flat-top pistons that produced an 11.0:1 compression ratio, and a set of Stage 3 CNC-ported heads from Total Engine Airflow. For a full rundown on the 5.0L, check out Chapter 10. We installed a set of Comp XE278AH cams and ran the motor with Kooks 1⅝-inch headers and a F.A.S.T. management system. Equipped with the stock PI intake, the 5.0L produced 426 hp and 427 ft-lbs of torque. After installing the VRI prototype intake (in long runner form), the peak power jumped up to 460 hp and 440 ft-lbs of torque. The revised intake design increased the power output throughout the rev range, even down at 2,500 rpm. Altering the configuration to include the short runners resulted in a significant shift in the power curve. The peak numbers jumped to 490 hp and 421 ft-lbs of torque. Due to the shift, the peak torque value dropped, but the combination produced huge power gains from 5,000 to 7,000 rpm. Production versions of this intake (the rights were purchased from the author) will include the ability to adjust the runner length. The VRI version will be made available for the early 4.6L 2-valve non-PI, the 4.6L 2-valve PI, 4.6L 4-valve motors, as well as the new 3-valve motors (if testing proves promising).

The author is hard at work installing the new intake on the dyno. The idea was to design an intake that allows enthusiasts to adjust runner length for a particular event or purpose, giving them the best intake for their application.

Intake Manifolds

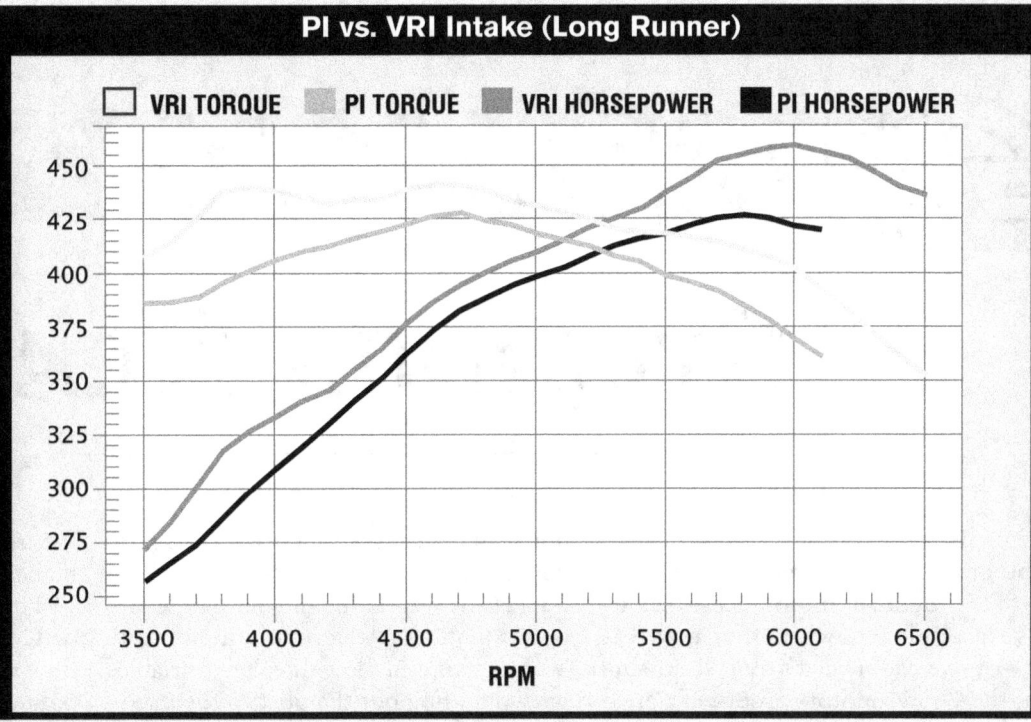

PI vs. VRI Intake (Long Runner)

Stock PI Intake/TB:
424 hp @ 5,800 rpm

VRI Intake (Long Runner):
460 hp @ 6,000 rpm

Largest Gain:
36 hp @ 6,100 rpm

Stock PI Intake/TB vs. VRI Intake (Long Runner)
As you can see, the custom VRI (Variable Runner Intake) manifold offered significant power gains over the factory PI intake on this modified 5.0L stroker 2-valve motor. The important thing to realize about this graph is not so much that the custom VRI intake (in this configuration) produced more peak power, but that it produced more power and torque throughout the rev range.

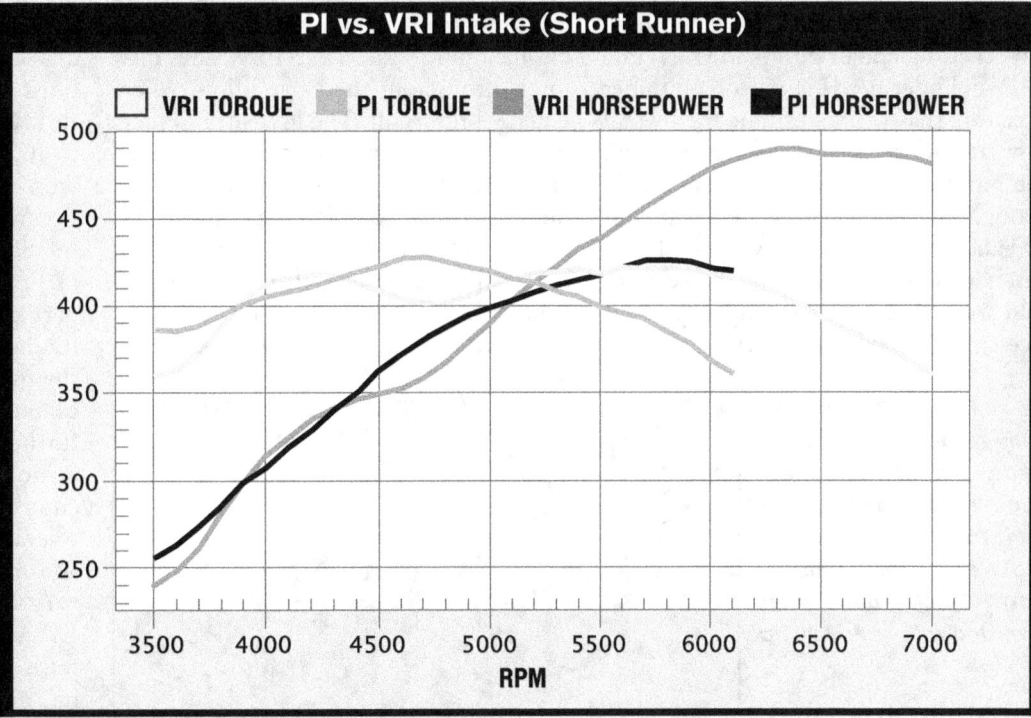

PI vs. VRI Intake (Short Runner)

Stock PI Intake/TB:
424 hp @ 5,800 rpm

VRI Intake (Short Runner):
490 hp @ 6,300 rpm

Largest Gain:
75+ hp @ Above 6,000 rpm

Stock PI Intake/TB vs. VRI Intake (Short Runner)
Running the VRI intake in the short-runner configuration resulted in a significant shift in the power curve. Note that the change in runner length (and taper) resulted in a drop in power from 4,300 rpm to 5,100 rpm, but that was offset by huge horsepower gains up to 7,000 rpm. This configuration would be best for a high-RPM combination, but this intake performed significantly better than the other intakes for the 4.6L 2-valve.

CHAPTER 3

CYLINDER HEADS

Cylinder heads are a major contributing factor to power production on the 4.6L modular motor. Since the 2-valve heads flow nowhere near as well as the 4-valve Cobras, it's not surprising that the 4-valve motors produced a great deal more power. The new 3-valve heads seem to be positioned right between the two in terms of airflow, though the variable cam timing certainly provides a benefit not realized by either the 2-valve or 4-valve motors. Since the modular motor (like every engine) is nothing more than a giant air pump, the flow rate of the cylinder heads is one of a number of factors that will determine the overall flow rate (we see as power) of the motor. The more air the motor can process (in through the induction system and out the exhaust), the more power it will ultimately produce. As with the intake manifold and exhaust system, bigger doesn't necessarily mean better when it comes to ports. In many cases, increasing the port volume can increase absolute airflow, but (as always) there's much more to the power equation than maximum flow. Were maximum flow the key variable, we would hog out the port to the maximum available dimension and watch the power grow. If only life were that easy!

While peak-lift flow (measured at the maximum valve lift offered by the cams) is important, the reality is that the valve spends more time running up to and away from maximum lift than it does at maximum lift. Therefore, the flow rates throughout the valve lift curve are equally important. The low-lift numbers are even more important on overhead cam motors, as the architecture generally does not allow for high-lift values. This is especially true on the 4-valve motors, as the lift values even for performance cams generally do not exceed .500 inch. The 2-valve motors attempt to make up for their lackluster port design with higher lift (.550 to .600 inch), but when you only have .500 lift to work with, you better make every effort to maximize the flow rates at all the lift values below that point. After all, it's the average airflow achieved throughout the lift range that produces the best power curve. Lucky for us, the 4-valve configuration lends itself to impressive low-lift flow numbers. While down on maximum available lift, the 4-valve heads also flow more at .500-inch lift than the 2-valve heads do at .550-inch lift (or even .600). In fact, a ported set of 4-valve heads might outflow a set of ported 2-valve heads by 80 to 100 cfm. All the extra lift in the world won't make up that kind of deficit.

While most of the attention is paid to the flow rate through the ports, the reality is that the port flow rate is only part of the power potential offered by the head. In Chapter 4, I'll explain that the bank-to-bank cam timing can be off dramatically. A related problem that can further skew the power output (even on a stock motor) is the lifter (or lash adjuster) preload. Due to production tolerances in the components, castings, and machining, the lifter preload can vary from .025 to .100 inch (or more). Excessive lifter preload can actually push the valve off the seat, greatly reducing or eliminating valve sealing in that cylinder. The reduced dynamic compression naturally causes a drop in power. In addition to the lifter issue, the actual valve sealing from the production valve job can also hurt cylinder pressure.

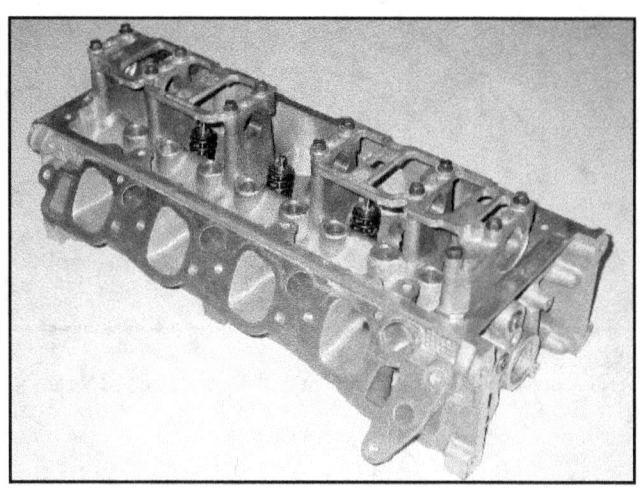

The 4.6L 2-valve motors really respond to ported PI heads. We installed these Stage 2 CNC-ported heads from Total Engine Airflow (TEA) on a 1998 (non-PI) short block and were rewarded with nearly 90 hp.

Since both the valve job and valve length ultimately affect the installed height, which in turn affects lifter preload, all of these variables are interrelated. Miss the valve job, valvestem length, or lifter preload, and the power will suffer. Since a valve job (and possibly new valves) is mandatory when performing head porting, care must be taken when it comes time to reassemble the new components.

In addition to cylinder head testing, this chapter also includes results on the effect of changes in compression. The compression ratio will affect power, with higher compression offering more power, but how much does the drop in compression hurt? Suppose you are in the market for a new short block and want to add a blower down the line, or maybe you already have one on your existing combination and you want to build (or buy) a dedicated forged short block to withstand the rigors of boost. With your current 4.6L, the static compression is around 9.2:1 for a 2-valve or 10.0:1 for a 4-valve. Dropping the compression by a full point will result in a sizable change in power. Many enthusiasts have built or bought a forged low-compression short block thinking that it will make more power than their stock setup, but run at the same boost pressure, the low-compression motor will most certainly make less power than before. Of course, the drop in compression may be necessary to allow you to run safely on pump gas.

The guys at Accufab put the effect of compression to the ultimate test on an assembled 5.4L 4-valve motor. The benefit to the increased compression is actually greater when you add boost into the equation, as the boost pressure becomes a multiplier. On the 5.4L motor, the increase in static compression from 8.2:1 to 11.5:1 resulted in a gain of over 60 hp. Testing on the supercharged versions of the same motors resulted in a gain of over 200 hp. Thus any gains produced by the increase in compression ratio were multiplied by the pressure ratio supplied by the blower. Therefore, every effort should be made to improve the power output of a naturally aspirated motor, including increasing the compression ratio. This is especially true if you are building a motor for a specific drag racing class that limits the size and/or speed of the blower or turbo. If the blower or turbo is limited, you must do everything you can to maximize the power output at the predetermined boost/impeller speed limit. Reducing the boost pressure at any given impeller speed can increase the flow rate of the blower. This is accomplished by improving the power output of the naturally aspirated combination.

It's too bad the aftermarket has not embraced the 4.6L 2-valve motor, as a set of TFS Twisted Wedge heads for the 4.6L 2-valve would sell like hot cakes. The only option for 2-valve owners is to have the stock heads ported like these Stage 3 heads from TEA.

Most enthusiasts opt to lower the static compression when building a motor specifically for supercharging or turbocharging. The drop in compression will allow higher boost levels on pump gas, but it will decrease off-boost efficiency, mileage, and absolute power.

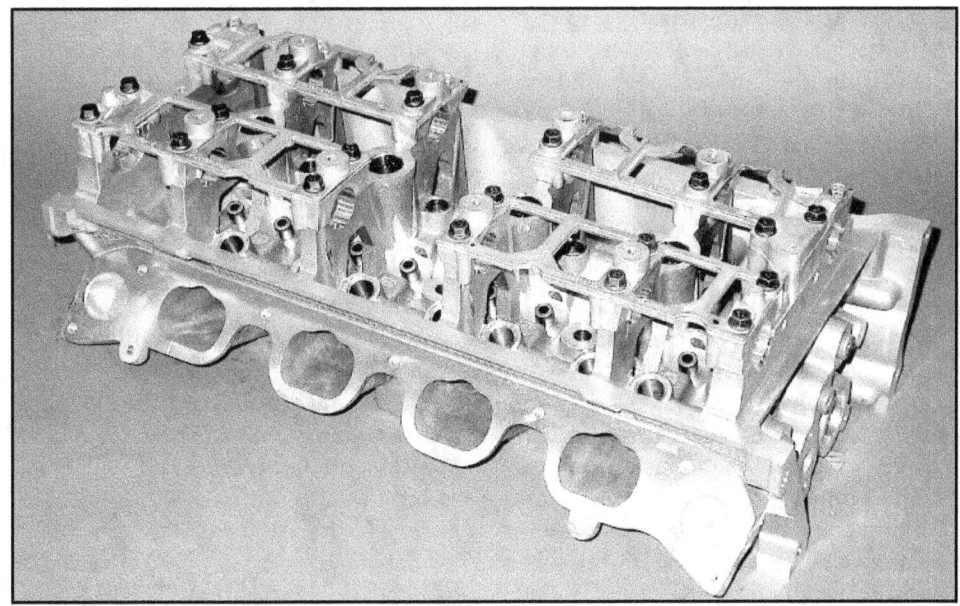

Production 4-valve heads easily outflow even a set of ported 2-valve heads, but these F500 heads from Ford Racing can really wake up a 4-valve Cobra motor.

Chapter 3

Test 1: Early 2-Valve GT vs. PI 2-Valve GT

When first introduced to replace the venerable 5.0L (I'm only just starting to warm up to the impressive 4-valve stuff), the 2-valve 4.6L mod motor was rated at 215 horsepower (upped to 225 hp in 1998). In reality, even the 225 hp version never seemed to match the horsepower output of the similarly rated 5.0L, and it certainly never equaled the torque. In 1999, Ford introduced a revised version of the 2-valve 4.6L GT motor that offered 260 hp. Improvements included additional static compression, a revised cylinder head and intake manifold package, and higher-lift cam profiles. These later Power Improved (PI) heads differed from their early non-PI counterparts primarily in combustion chamber size. The PI heads offered a much smaller combustion chamber. The smaller chamber was offset by a piston design with a larger dish to maintain a reasonable compression ratio, but the combination produced an overall increase in static compression compared to the early 4.6L motors. The PI heads flowed slightly better than the early heads, too.

The PI motors also received a dedicated intake manifold to mate to the revised intake ports. A significant portion of the power gains offered by the PI motors can be attributed to the PI intake manifold. In fact, adapters are available through the aftermarket to install the later PI intake on your early non-PI cylinder heads. This allows early motors to take advantage of the superior breathing potential and power production of the PI intake. This allows early 4.6L owners to port their existing cylinder heads, which can be made to nearly equal the flow of the ported PI heads, and nearly match the power of a PI head swap. Of course, you won't have the jump in compression ratio offered by the PI head swap, but nor will you have the expense either. The early non-PI

How does the non-PI engine stack up against the later PI version? By testing these engines on the dyno, we can find out what the power difference really is.

motors also had cams with less lift. The later PI heads were designed to run cams with .550-inch lift, while the early heads maxed out at just .500. The early non-PI cams can be run in PI heads (see Chapter 4) but the reverse is not true without modifications to the valvetrain to accept the higher lift.

As luck would have it, I was able to run both the early non-PI and PI motors on the engine dyno in the exact same configuration. Both motors were equipped with all factory components but were run with an electric water pump (no accessories), a set of Hooker Super Comp long-tube headers, and an open inlet system (no MAF or intake tubing). The F.A.S.T. management system was used to dial in the air/fuel and timing. Run in this configuration, the early (1998) non-PI motor produced 260 hp at 4,900 rpm and 342 ft-lbs of torque at 3,500 rpm. Note the early power peaks; the 1998 4.6L was designed with torque and throttle response in mind, rather than ultimate power. As expected, the later PI motor exceeded those power numbers significantly. Run in the same configuration, the PI motor produced 293 hp at 5,000 rpm and the same 342 ft-lbs of torque at 4,100 rpm. The peak torque values were identical; the PI motor just produced it later in the rev range, which led to more peak horsepower. Shifting the torque curve did result in a slight loss in low-speed power, as the early non-PI motor actually out-powered the PI up to 3,800 rpm.

The engines were set up with no accessories or intake tract. They also benefited from a set of Hooker Super Comp headers.

Cylinder Heads

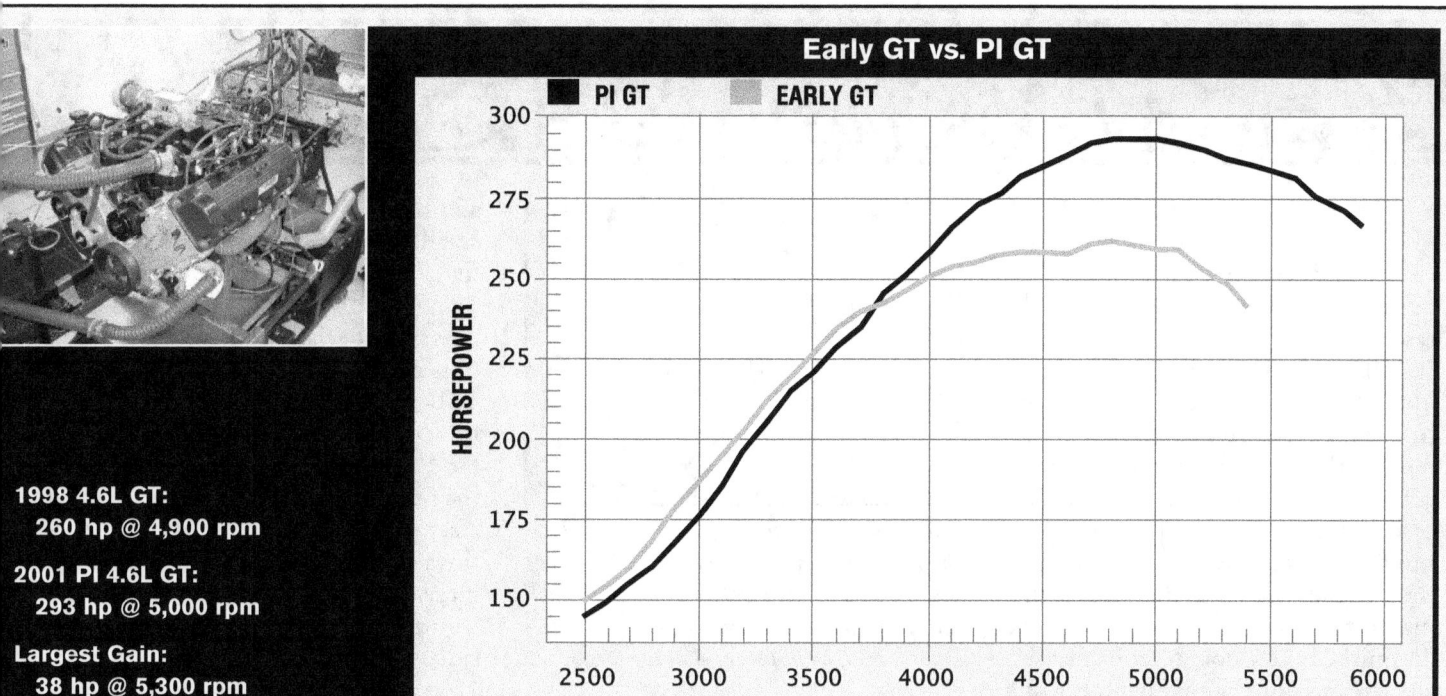

1998 4.6L GT:
260 hp @ 4,900 rpm

2001 PI 4.6L GT:
293 hp @ 5,000 rpm

Largest Gain:
38 hp @ 5,300 rpm

Early 2-Valve GT vs. PI 2-Valve GT (Horsepower)
It should really come as no surprise that the PI motor out-performed the earlier non-PI version, but the early motor was on top until 3,800 rpm. The revised cam timing, improved cylinder heads and intake, and higher compression ultimately won out, allowing the PI version to produce nearly 40 more horsepower.

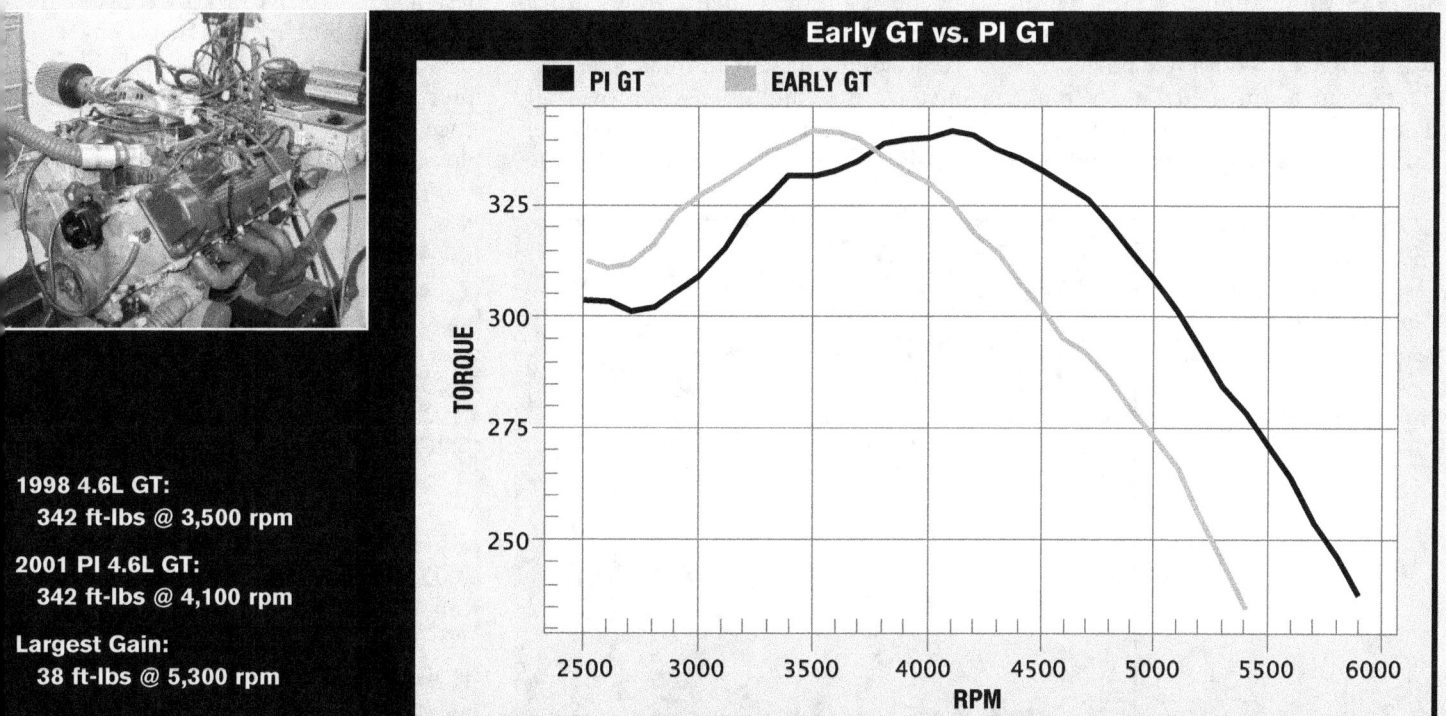

1998 4.6L GT:
342 ft-lbs @ 3,500 rpm

2001 PI 4.6L GT:
342 ft-lbs @ 4,100 rpm

Largest Gain:
38 ft-lbs @ 5,300 rpm

Early 2-Valve GT vs. PI 2-Valve GT (Torque)
This test was very illuminating, as the early 4.6L motors always felt better down low than the PI motors, despite the difference in advertised power. The torque curve illustrates why the early 4.6L Mustang motors felt like they belonged in a truck. Who builds a performance motor for a pony car that produces peak torque at just 3,500 rpm? No wonder they designed the PI motor and later 3-valve 4.6L.

Building 4.6/5.4L Ford Horsepower on the Dyno

Test 2: Early 2-Valve GT Heads vs. TEA CNC-Ported PI 2-Valve GT Heads

After subjecting an early 4.6L GT to a number of basic bolt-ons, I decided it was time to get a little more serious. This meant replacing the restrictive non-PI heads and intake. Installing the PI heads onto an early non-PI short block adds minor power through additional head flow but primarily through the increased compression. The higher-lift PI cams also offer some extra ponies. The only thing to watch out for when running the PI heads on a non-PI motor is that piston-to-valve clearance will be diminished. It's not a problem with stock cams, but with higher-lift and longer-duration aftermarket cams, clearance should always be checked.

Though the stock non-PI heads were certainly restricting the power, the early intake was partially to blame as well. The early and late 4.6L intakes share very long runner lengths, but the cross section on the non-PI version was designed to optimize power production in a much lower rev range. The intake is a major contributing factor in why the early motors make peak

These CNC-ported heads from TEA should give us even more power than a regular PI swap. The CNC program included improved ports and revised, though somewhat larger, combustion chambers.

torque so much lower than the PI. Unfortunately, the early and late intake manifolds are not interchangeable. (I wanted to compare them directly but could not without running an adapter.) The intake port openings on the cylinder heads differ in shape, and naturally, so do the corresponding intake manifolds. The best method is naturally to swap over all the PI components, including the heads, cams, and intake manifold. The additional flow combined with the smaller combustion chamber makes the PI head swap quite desirable to owners of early non-PI-headed motors, especially considering the lack of performance heads available for the 4.6L Ford. While the additional airflow and compression offered by a PI head swap definitely help, I wanted all the performance I could get. I shipped a set of PI heads to Total Engine Airflow (TEA) for CNC porting. TEA increased the flow rate of the PI heads from 177 to 225 cfm on the intake side, while the exhaust increased from 126 to 208 cfm. There were gains registered throughout the lift range, from .050 to .600 inch.

The one downside of the CNC porting from TEA was that the combustion chamber was included in the procedure. The CNC machining was designed to improve flow by reshaping the chamber, but in doing so, the chamber volume was also increased. I didn't mind the slight loss in compression since I was planning on running a blower at some stage on this test motor.

The early motor had previously been upgraded with Comp Xtreme Energy XE274H cams, a set of Hooker headers, and an Accufab throttle body. Equipped with the non-PI components, the 4.6L produced 301 hp at 5,100 rpm and 346 ft-lbs of torque at 4,100 rpm. After installing the TEA CNC-ported PI heads and matching PI intake (we reused the same XE274H non-PI cams), the peak power jumped from 301 hp to 399 hp at 6,000 rpm. The peak torque was up as well, from 346 ft-lbs at 4,100 rpm to 390 ft-lbs at a slightly higher 4,700 rpm. The ported heads and PI intake bettered the early components by over 100 hp and 95 ft-lbs of torque. The gains would be even more impressive had I run the early non-PI motor out to 6,000 rpm, but the power was falling off rapidly.

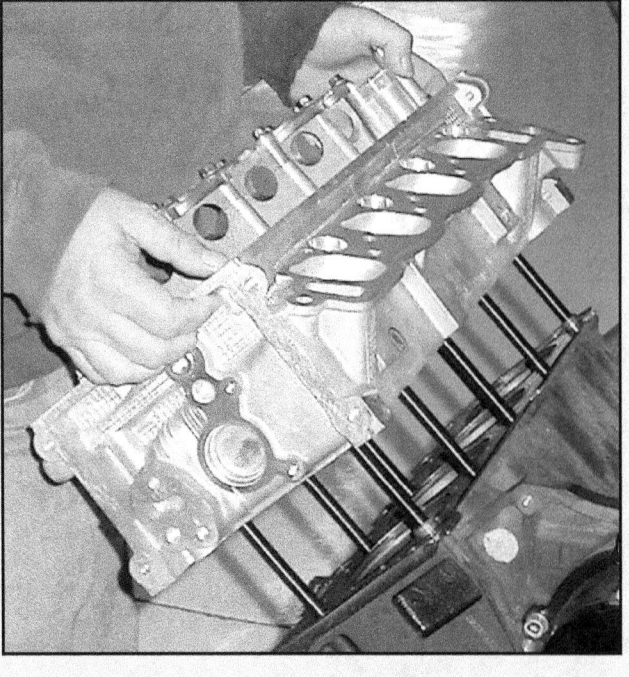

To make sure we got the full benefit of the ported PI heads, we also added a PI intake manifold. The same cams, Comp Xtreme Energy XE274H cams, were used with each setup.

Cylinder Heads

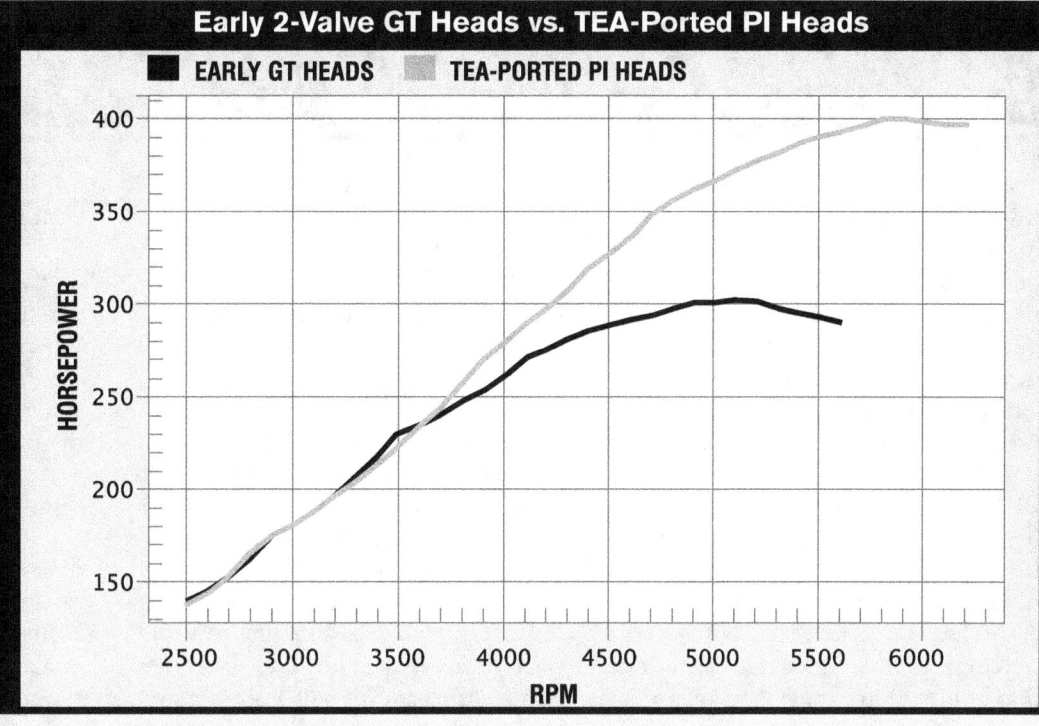

Early 2-Valve Heads:
301 hp @ 5,100 rpm

TEA-Ported PI Heads:
399 hp @ 6,000 rpm

Largest Gain:
100+ hp @ 5,500+ rpm

Early 2-Valve GT Heads vs. TEA-Ported PI Heads (Horsepower)
When you make a major modification to your 4.6L, this is the kind of power gain you want to see. Note that one curve tops out at 300 hp and the other reaches nearly 400 hp. Note also that the later PI motor not only made more peak power but also extended the usable RPM range, something that will further improve acceleration over the non-PI motor. This would make one impressive early GT. I tested 4.6L 4-valve Cobra motors that didn't make this much horsepower, and all it took was a set of TEA-ported heads, Comp cams, and a PI intake on an early stock short block.

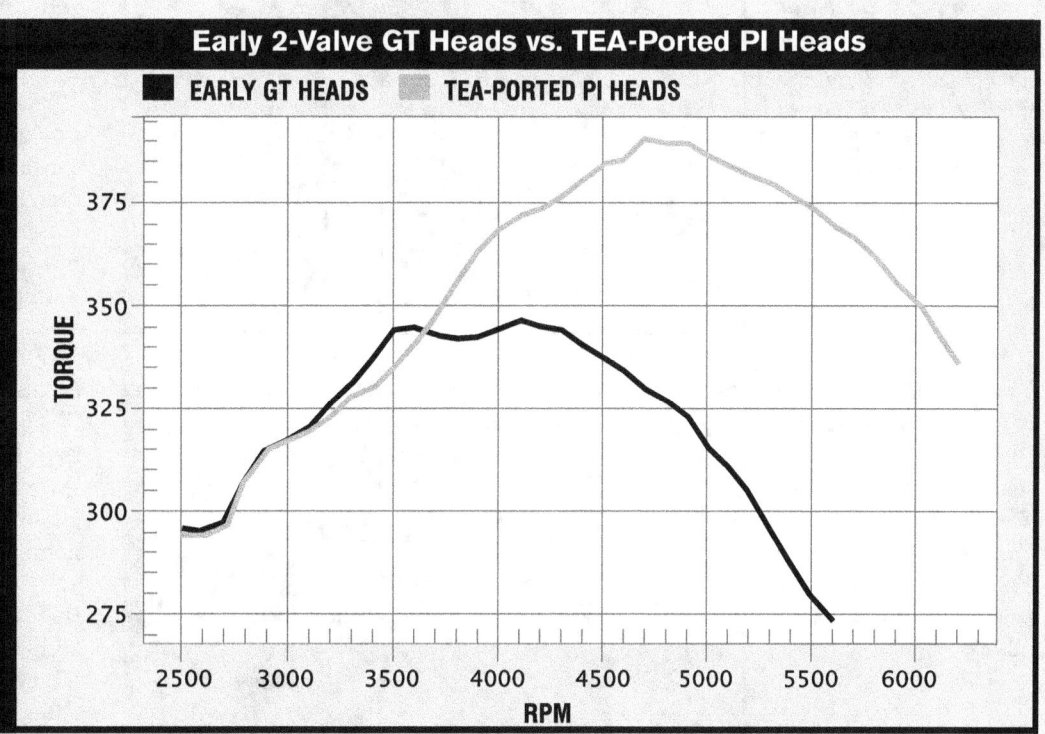

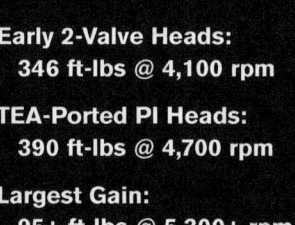

Early 2-Valve Heads:
346 ft-lbs @ 4,100 rpm

TEA-Ported PI Heads:
390 ft-lbs @ 4,700 rpm

Largest Gain:
95+ ft-lbs @ 5,300+ rpm

Early 2-Valve GT Heads vs. TEA-Ported PI Heads (Torque)
The torque gains looks like you just added a centrifugal supercharger to the 4.6L, rather than a set of ported heads and intake. The gang at Total Engine Airflow really did their homework on these 4.6L PI heads. Never known for their torque production, this 4.6L (just 281 cubic inches) produced nearly 400 ft-lbs and bettered the early non-PI torque production by nearly 50 ft-lbs.

Test 3: Early 2-Valve GT vs. FPS Early 2-Valve GT Heads, Cams, & PI Intake

In Test 2 we showed that installing ported PI heads onto your early 4.6L was effective; that extra power doesn't come cheap. The alternative to installing a set of late-model PI heads is to simply have your early heads CNC ported. According to the gang at Ford Performance Solutions (FPS), a set of ported early GT heads will flow just as well as a set of ported PI heads. Plus, porting your existing heads means you don't have to spend the extra green on a set of PI core heads. The downside to porting the early heads (besides the cost of the porting) is that the non-PI intake manifold will limit the ultimate power output. Topping off your CNC-ported early 4.6L heads with a stock early intake would be like asking a marathon runner to compete while breathing through a drinking straw. Unfortunately, the late-model PI intake cannot be used with the early heads due to the revisions in the intake port entry and the water passages. Ford Racing offers a trick aluminum intake for the early heads, but it's pretty pricey. The ideal situation would be to be able to run the cheap PI intake on the non-PI heads – enter FPS.

FPS found a way to adapt the early GT heads to the PI intake manifold, thus providing ported PI-power minus the additional compression. The key to successfully mating the non-PI heads with the PI intake is the custom CNC program performed by FPS. In addition to improving the airflow of the heads considerably, the intake port shapes are modified to resemble the PI heads. Phase two of the transformation includes welding and reshaping the water passages on the early head to mimic those on the PI heads. The welding is performed to reshape the water passages and eliminate any potential water leaks. After the welding and reshaping, the intake mating flange is resurfaced (lightly) to ensure a tight seal using the stock PI intake gaskets. Having already exceeded 400 hp using TEA-ported heads and the stock PI manifold, I was excited to see what these FPS-ported non-PI heads could do.

The stock non-PI motor was first run with Hooker Super Comp long-tube headers, an electric water pump, and F.A.S.T. management (13.0:1 air/fuel ratio and 30 degrees of total timing). In otherwise stock trim, the 1998 4.6L 2-valve motor produced 260 hp at 5,000 rpm and 342 ft-lbs of torque at 3,500 rpm. The motor was then torn down to the short block and reassembled with the FPS-ported non-PI heads, PI intake, and a set of Comp XE262AH (PI-specific) cams. The cams were installed in an effort to take advantage of the added breathing capabilities of the ported heads. The PI-spec Comp cams offered .550 inches of lift and 226/230-degrees duration split with a 113-degree lobe separation angle. Equipped with the FPS components, the power jumped to 347 hp and 350 ft-lbs of torque. Remember that this swap did not include the additional compression offered by the PI heads, but the FPS components added 91 hp and 90 ft-lbs. The slightly wilder cam timing dropped some power below 3,800 rpm, but picked things up big time at the top end.

These FPS CNC-ported heads feature higher-flowing ports that line up with the PI intake manifold, but the non-PI combustion chambers don't get any smaller. As a result, the compression ratio isn't bumped like it would be with a PI head swap.

The FPS heads are CNC ported and otherwise modified to mate up with a stock PI intake manifold. This keeps the cost of the upgrade down by allowing you to use your non-PI heads with the cheap PI intake.

Cylinder Heads

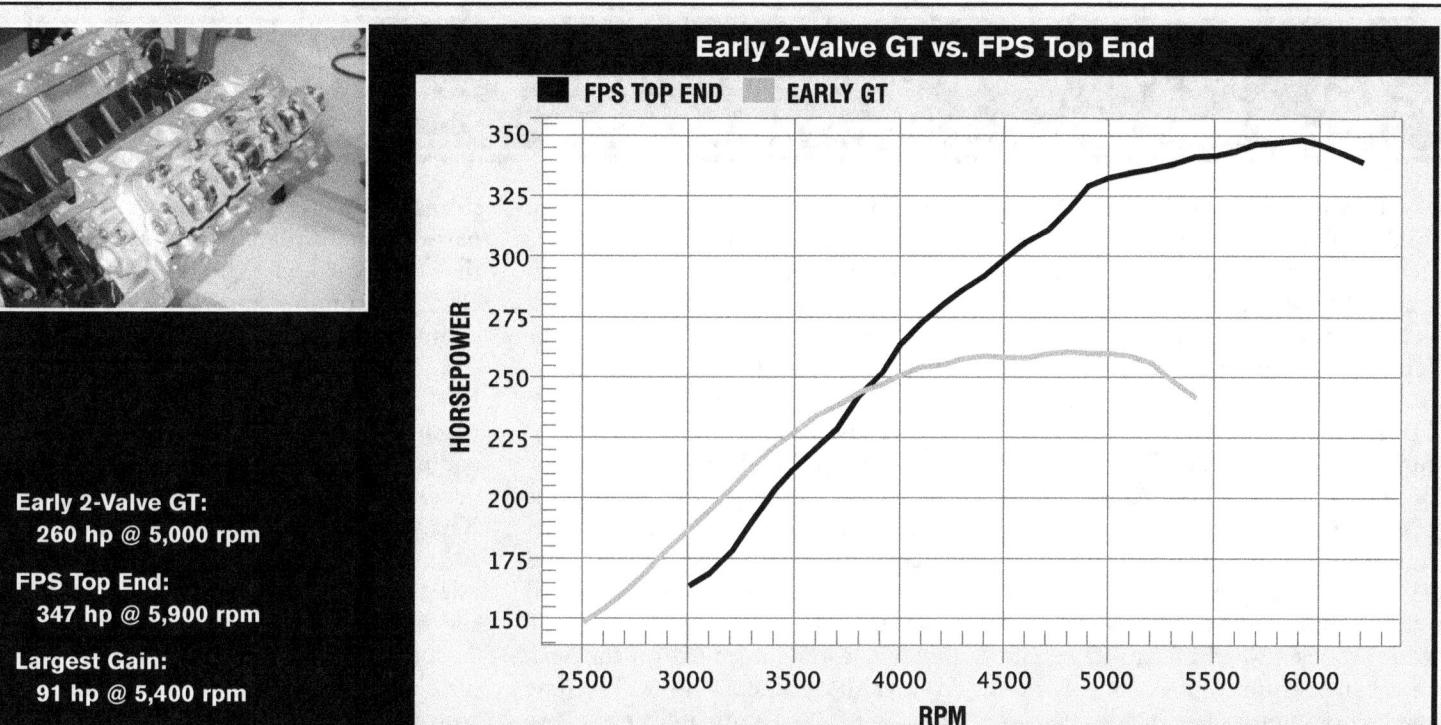

Early 2-Valve GT:
260 hp @ 5,000 rpm

FPS Top End:
347 hp @ 5,900 rpm

Largest Gain:
91 hp @ 5,400 rpm

Early 2-Valve GT vs. FPS Top End (Horsepower)
These early 4.6L motors really respond to ported heads, cams, and a decent intake manifold. Check out the gains offered by the FPS ported non-PI heads, PI intake, and mild Comp cams. Where the stock motor fell on its face after 5,000 rpm, the FPS motor just kept pulling all the way to 6,000 rpm. The porting and cam timing were probably most responsible for the drop in power below 3,800 rpm.

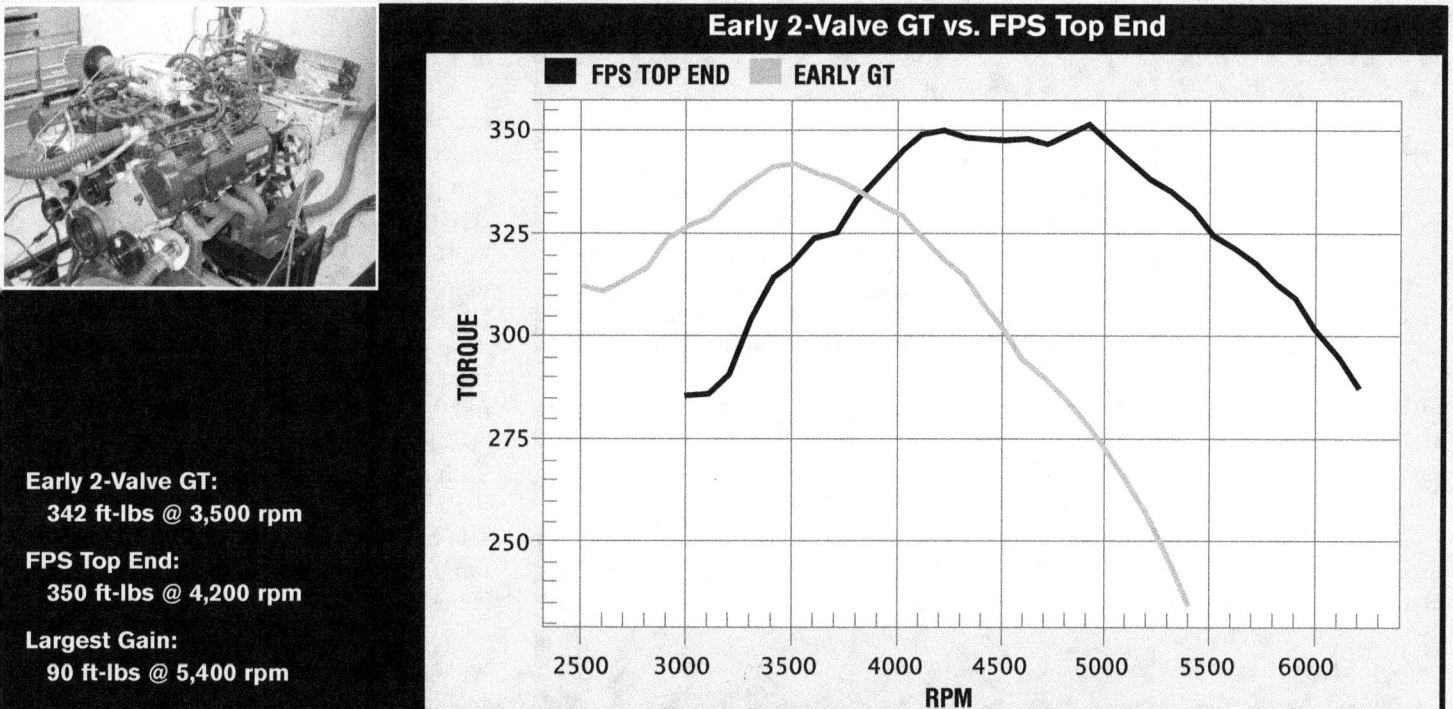

Early 2-Valve GT:
342 ft-lbs @ 3,500 rpm

FPS Top End:
350 ft-lbs @ 4,200 rpm

Largest Gain:
90 ft-lbs @ 5,400 rpm

Early 2-Valve GT vs. FPS Top End (Torque)
Here's a perfect example of what usually happens when you shift the torque curve higher in the rev range. Shifting the torque peak from 3,500 rpm to 4,900 rpm costs some torque down low. It should be noted that the FPS motor actually produced a dual torque peak, producing within 1 ft-lbs at both 4,200 rpm and 4,900 rpm. The drop in torque at 3,000 rpm would be missed but only until you allow the motor to come on the cams and pull strong to 6,000 rpm.

Building 4.6/5.4L Ford Horsepower on the Dyno

Test 4: PI 2-Valve GT: Effect of Compression Ratio

Between all the different heads (and combustion chambers) I was testing for this book, I ended up with quite a few different compression ratios. I was curious to see just how big a difference the compression ratio could make. To make a long story short, Sean Hyland built us a 4.6L short block featuring a steel Cobra crank, forged connecting rods, and a set of dished forged pistons. Common 4.6L piston designs include flat-tops and dish volumes of 11 cc (stock early 4.6L), 17 cc, and 23 cc. Combining the 23-cc dish pistons with a stock 42-cc PI chamber results in a compression ratio of 8.95:1. For reasons of another test, we wanted to further lower the compression ratio, so

Sean Hyland obliged and built a set of custom pistons with a massive 28-cc dish. Combined with a stock PI head, the large dish dropped the compression ratio to 8.44:1. Installing our TEA-ported heads (with 45-cc chambers) dropped the final compression ratio to just 8.1:1.

To properly test the effect of compression, I installed the very same components on each of the two short blocks. The cams, intake, heads, and all other components were removed from the high-compression '98 GT motor and then installed on the Sean Hyland short block. This is very time consuming (and ultimately expensive in terms of dyno time), but I wanted to ensure that every aspect of the comparison was absolutely identical. Only then would I know the results of the change in compression. With all of the compression ratio calculations behind me, I ran the two motors on the dyno. First up was the high-compression combination. The 4.6L GT motor was equipped with the TEA-ported PI heads, a set of Comp Xtreme Energy XE274H cams, and the PI manifold. Additional goodies included 19-lb injectors and Keith Wilson fuel rail, a set of 1⅝-inch Hooker headers, and an Accufab 70-mm throttle body and matching elbow. Run with an MSD coil pack and Meziere electric water pump, the 10.1:1 4.6L produced 401 hp at 6,100 rpm and 393 ft-lbs at 4,800 rpm. The 10.1:1 motor was impressive, never dropping below 320 ft-lbs from 2,900 rpm to 6,200 rpm. Obviously, the Xtreme Energy cams and CNC-ported PI heads were well matched.

Next came the mad thrash to swap everything to the low-compression short block. After swapping on all the components from the high-compression motor, we were ready to run once again. As expected, dropping the compression ratio by two full points (10.1:1 to 8.1:1) resulted in a dramatic drop in power. The peak numbers on the low-compression motor checked in at 365 hp at 5,900 and 368 ft-lbs at 4,700 rpm. Note that not only were both numbers significantly lower than the high-compression motor, but they also occurred 200 rpm lower in the rev range. Looking at the power curves, it's clear that the combination of ported heads and aggressive cam timing worked best with the higher compression. The drop in compression reduced the power curve from 3,000 rpm all the way to redline. It looks like the old adage that each point of compression is worth roughly 4 percent in power is pretty accurate.

Sean Hyland machined these custom pistons with a 28-cc dish. This dropped our compression ratio with our TEA CNC-ported heads (with 45-cc combustion chambers) to just 8.1:1.

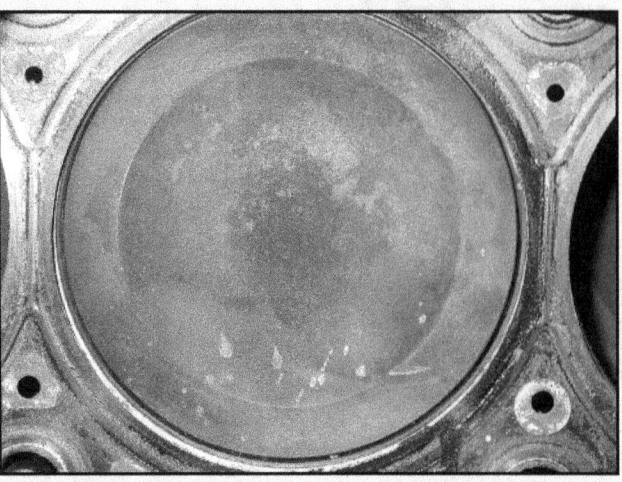

The other short block in the test featured a much higher 10.1:1 compression ratio. We built the 8.1:1 engine for forced induction, but we were curious to see how much power the reduced compression robbed before we installed the blower.

Cylinder Heads

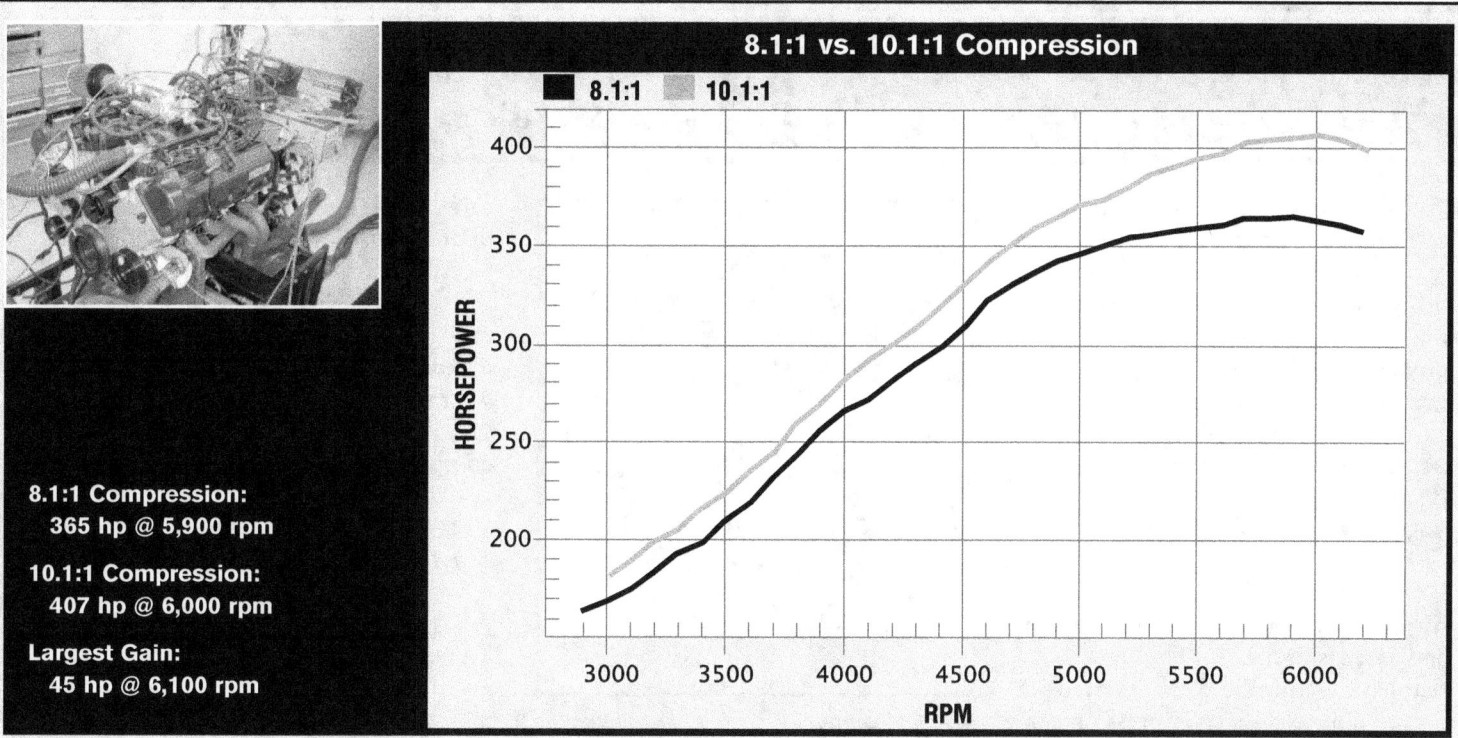

8.1:1 Compression:
365 hp @ 5,900 rpm

10.1:1 Compression:
407 hp @ 6,000 rpm

Largest Gain:
45 hp @ 6,100 rpm

PI 2-Valve GT: 8.1:1 vs. 10.1:1 Compression (Horsepower)
The great thing about adding compression is that the gains will be available throughout the rev range. Of course, the drop in compression was performed in anticipation of forced induction (see Test 5), but the drop in power should make you think twice about dropping the compression down to 8.1:1. Believe me, you will be able to feel 45 hp, especially since the power is down from 3,000 rpm all the way to redline.

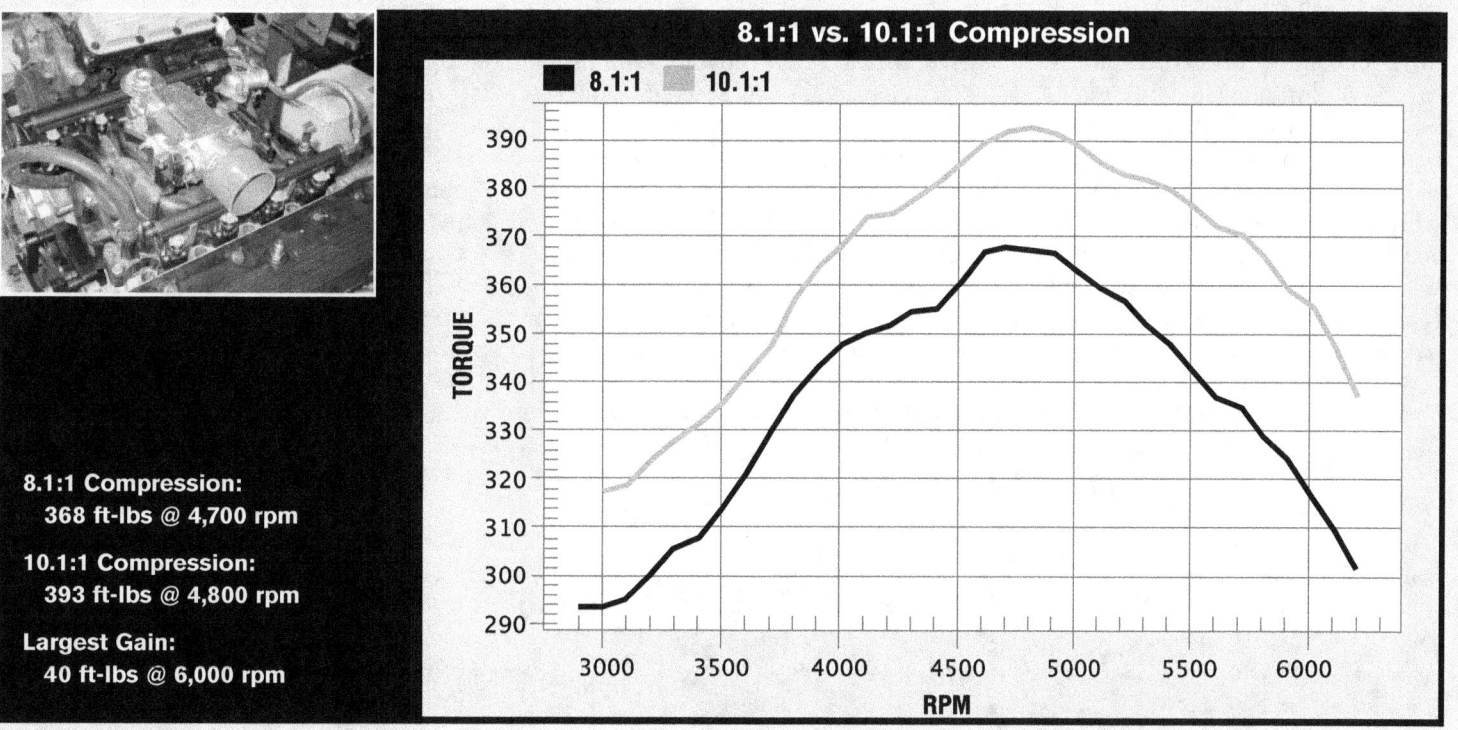

8.1:1 Compression:
368 ft-lbs @ 4,700 rpm

10.1:1 Compression:
393 ft-lbs @ 4,800 rpm

Largest Gain:
40 ft-lbs @ 6,000 rpm

PI 2-Valve GT: 8.1:1 vs. 10.1:1 Compression (Torque)
A drop of two full points of compression feels like someone just pulled a plug wire or two. Where once the motor felt snappy and responsive, it now feels like it wants to stay in bed. Actually, the 8.1:1 motor still produced nearly 370 ft-lbs, thanks to a good set of ported heads, Comp cams, and the PI intake, but 20 extra ft-lbs through most of the curve and an extra 35 to 40 ft-lbs out near redline is hard to pass up.

Building 4.6/5.4L Ford Horsepower on the Dyno

Test 5: Kenne Bell Supercharged 2-Valve GT: Effect of Compression Ratio

Many engine suppliers offer low-compression short blocks designed specifically for boosted street applications. In all instances, a motor with higher compression will make more power, but the combination of high compression and elevated boost pressure will severely limit performance on a street motor due to the resulting detonation. The ideal choice for pump gas on a daily driver is moderate compression (9.0:1) and moderate boost, but it's possible to improve on-boost performance by reducing compression and increasing boost. The tradeoff in detonation threshold is skewed in favor of less static compression and more boost pressure, but off-boost response (and cruise fuel mileage) will definitely suffer with a drop in compression. This is especially true with centrifugal superchargers, as the centrifugal blowers tend to run best near the top of the rev range where they make maximum boost pressure. Due to their climbing boost curve and inherent increased efficiency (defined here as hp per pound of boost), centrifugal superchargers can get away with and will respond better to higher static compression ratios. The instantaneous boost response of a twin-screw and roots blower will not tolerate as much static compression (or

Our low-compression short block made for a compression ratio of just 8.1:1. The lower compression engine made less horsepower for a given boost level, but you can run more boost on a given octane level or detonation level.

timing), but the efficiency of the positive displacement blowers diminishes with elevated boost levels (more so on the roots design than the twin screw).

To see how the high- and low-compression motors respond to boost, we ran one of each with the 1.7L twin-screw Kenne Bell blower. The pulleys (6.5-inch crank and 2.75-inch blower) were not changed between the two motors. We went with 65 lbs/hr injectors (we wanted plenty of injector for higher boost levels later) and a 75-mm Accufab throttle body. The total timing was 24 degrees and the air/fuel ratio was 11.5:1 (for both compression ratios). To keep detonation in check, we ran 100-octane race fuel – necessary because of the relatively high compression.

Run on the high-compression (10:1) short block, the Kenne Bell supercharger pumped out 600 hp at 6,300 rpm and 539 ft-lbs of torque at 4,400 rpm. The pulley ratio produced a peak boost pressure of 10.2 psi at 3,800 rpm and a final boost pressure of 9.3 psi at 6,300 rpm. The boost pressure changed from one motor to the next, despite identical pulley ratios. We attribute this to the fact that more flow was needed to fill the volume in the low-compression motor.

The Kenne Bell 1.7L blower assembly was then applied to the low-compression (8.1:1) 4.6L with equally impressive results. The boosted low-compression setup made 533 hp at 6,300 rpm and 500 ft-lbs at 4,400 rpm. Compared to the high-compression supercharged motor, the peak power was off by 67 hp, while peak torque suffered just 39 ft-lbs. Note that the change in compression reduced the power output across the board, from 3,000 rpm to 6,300 rpm. It's interesting to note that the boost pressure was slightly lower on the low-compression motor than the high-compression version. The peak boost registered on the low-compression motor was 9.3 psi at 3,800 rpm, while the boost finalized at 8.7 psi at 6,300 rpm. Remember, we ran the same pulley ratios on the two motors, so the compression was the only variable responsible for the loss in power and boost pressure. The other side of this test is that the lower-compression motor would allow you to run more boost for a given octane before you experienced detonation.

The other short block made for a 10:1 compression ratio. Though this is a great compression ratio for a naturally aspirated engine, this is less true for high boost. At this reasonable boost level, the 10:1 engine made as much as 64 more horsepower and 54 more ft-lbs of torque.

Cylinder Heads

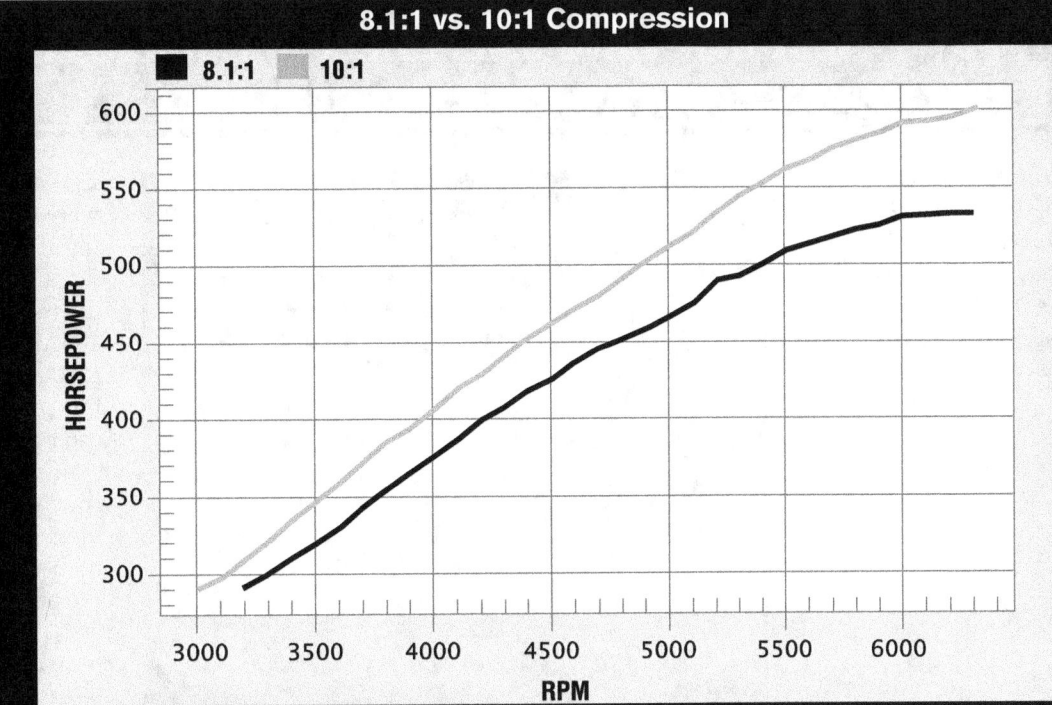

Supercharged (8.1:1 Compression):
533 hp @ 6,300 rpm

Supercharged (10:1 Compression):
600 hp @ 6,300 rpm

Largest Gain:
64 hp @ 6,200 rpm

Supercharged PI 2-Valve GT: 8.1:1 vs. 10:1 Compression (Horsepower)
The additional compression ratio actually had more of an effect on the supercharged combination than the naturally aspirated versions. The reason for this is that the boost pressure multiplies the difference in power. While it's possible to run a higher boost level with lower compression (at a given octane or detonation level), there will always be a loss in power when dropping down from a compression ratio of 10:1 to 8.1:1. For a serious race motor (like the one in Tests 6 and 7), you have to combine the high compression and high boost to maximize power, but for a street application, the best bet is probably a reasonable (9.0:1 or less) compression and a reasonable amount of boost.

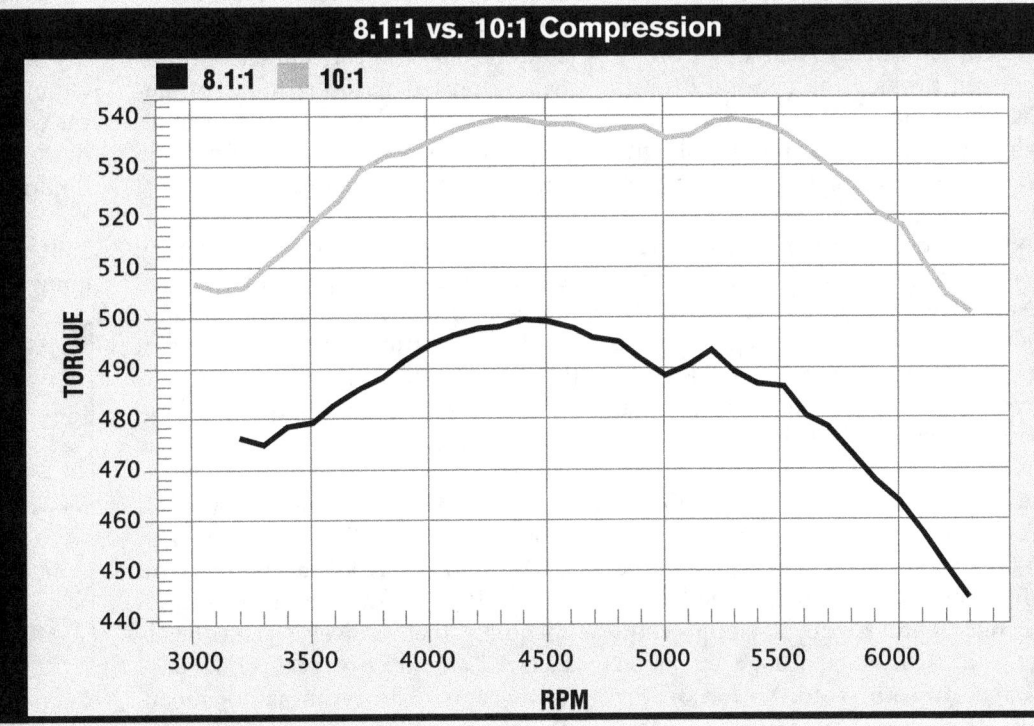

Low Compression:
500 ft-lbs @ 4,400 rpm

High Compression:
539 ft-lbs @ 4,400 rpm

Largest Gain:
54 ft-lbs @ 6,200 rpm

Supercharged PI 2-Valve GT: 8.1:1 vs. 10:1 Compression (Torque)
The drop in compression from 10:1 to 8.1:1 resulted in a consistent drop in torque production. The largest drop was 54 ft-lbs, but the loss was consistently 40 to 45 ft-lbs. This is the equivalent of a good 2 to 3 psi of boost pressure.

Chapter 3

Test 6: 4-Valve 5.4L: Effect of Compression Ratio

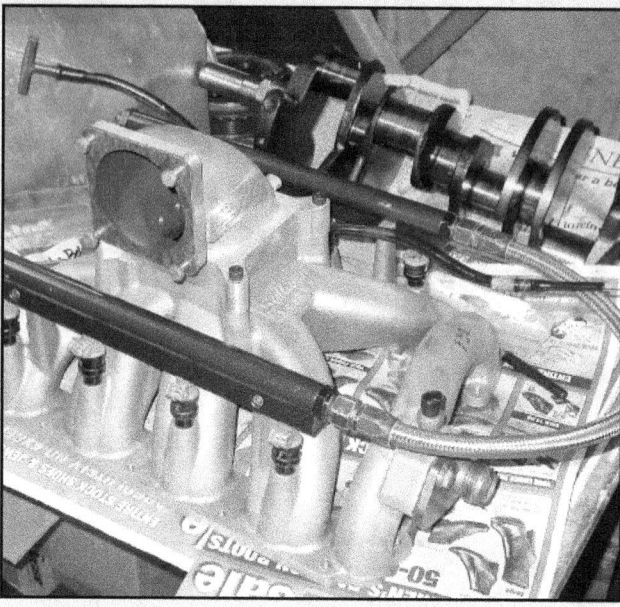

This Sullivan intake for the 5.4L gives you the option of running a carburetor or fuel injection. As you can see, we're running multi-port fuel injection and a throttle-body adaptor.

Sometimes luck is with me while gathering information for a book. More often than not it's me building and testing the motor or components that is in question, but once in a great while I will run across an opportunity that can provide the necessary information. One such opportunity was when Mod motor guru John Mihovitz was running a test on a pair of 5.4L motors. He planned to compare high- and low-compression short blocks using the very same external components. The tests run on this 5.4L 4-valve motor precisely mirrored those run on our own 4.6L GTs. I guess great minds think alike (though it can be added that fools seldom differ). The 5.4L motors were assembled with drag racing in mind, featuring all the right hardware including forged steel cranks, forged rods (aluminum on the low-compression version), and forged pistons. The change in compression ratio came from a change in piston design, as both motors relied on the very same heads, cams (including cam timing), and induction system.

The 5.4L 4-valve motors were built with high horsepower in mind.

The 4-valve heads came from a Navigator, but don't let the humble soccer-mom beginnings fool you. The Navigator heads feature large intake ports that were ported to unleash an additional 50 cfm per runner. Naturally, the ported heads required something other than a long-runner Navigator intake manifold. Knowing the motor would require substantial intake flow, the 5.4L was topped off with a Sullivan intake casting. Designed to accept a conventional carburetor, the short-runner aluminum intake also featured provisions for fuel injectors. A 90-degree inlet elbow was used to mate a 90-mm Accufab throttle body to the carburetor flange. The 90-mm throttle body ensured adequate airflow to the high-RPM 5.4L motor, while 150-lb/hr injectors and an Aeromotive A1000 fuel pump (with Kenne Bell Boost-A-Pump) ensured adequate fuel delivery. The heads received a quartet of Sean Hyland 4-valve cams. The (eventually) supercharged motor was equipped with Stage 2 intake cams (.452 inches of lift and 225 degrees of duration) and Stage 3 exhaust cams (.474 inches of lift and 235 degrees of duration). The cams were installed at 107 degrees.

The 5.4L 4-valve motor was also set up with a set of custom 1¾-to-2-inch step headers, an MSD coil pack, and a F.A.S.T. engine management system. A number of different timing and fuel curves were tested to optimize each combination. The low-compression motor produced 478 hp at 7,300 rpm and 395 ft-lbs at 5,500 rpm. Running the very same components on the high-compression short block upped the power output to 543 hp and 439 ft-lbs. The additional 3.5 points of compression upped the power output by 65 hp. According to the old rule of thumb that every point in compression is worth roughly 4 percent in power, we can calculate that increasing the compression by 3.5 points should yield a gain of roughly 14 percent. If we multiply 1.14 x 478 hp, we get 545 hp, which is very close to our actual peak power of 543 hp. I guess the compression formula is pretty accurate, although it should be mentioned that the gains in power are actually greater in the 8.0:1 to 11.0:1 range and tend to diminish slightly thereafter (upping the compression ratio from 8.0:1 to 9.0:1 will likely yield greater gains than going from 12.0:1 to 13.0:1).

By going with a flat-top forged piston, we're able to raise the compression ratio quite a bit. This piston features valve reliefs to hopefully prevent any piston-to-valve contact.

Cylinder Heads

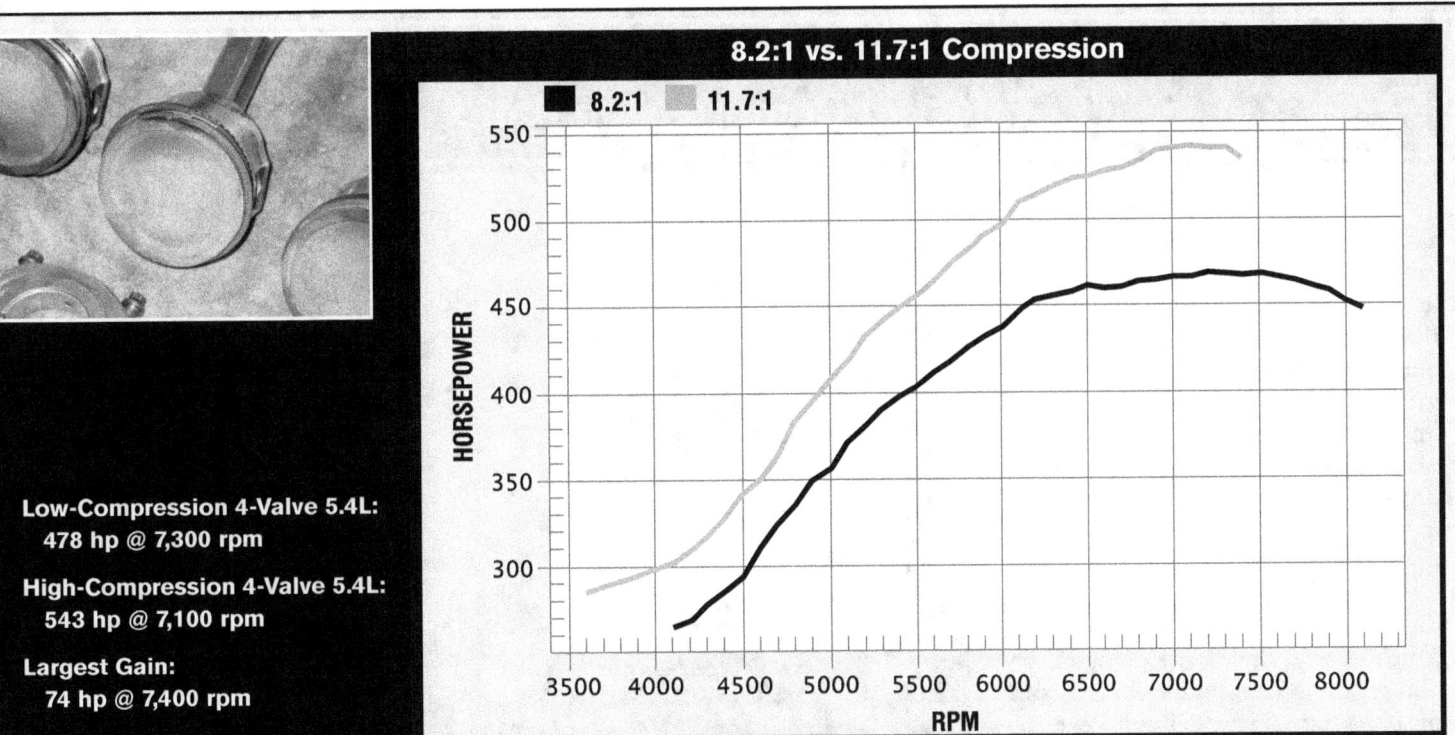

Low-Compression 4-Valve 5.4L:
478 hp @ 7,300 rpm

High-Compression 4-Valve 5.4L:
543 hp @ 7,100 rpm

Largest Gain:
74 hp @ 7,400 rpm

4-Valve 5.4L: Low Compression vs. High Compression (Horsepower)
The nice thing about increasing the compression ratio is that it adds power throughout the curve. Jumping from 8.2:1 to 11.7:1 resulted in a gain of 65 hp (from 478 hp to 543 hp).

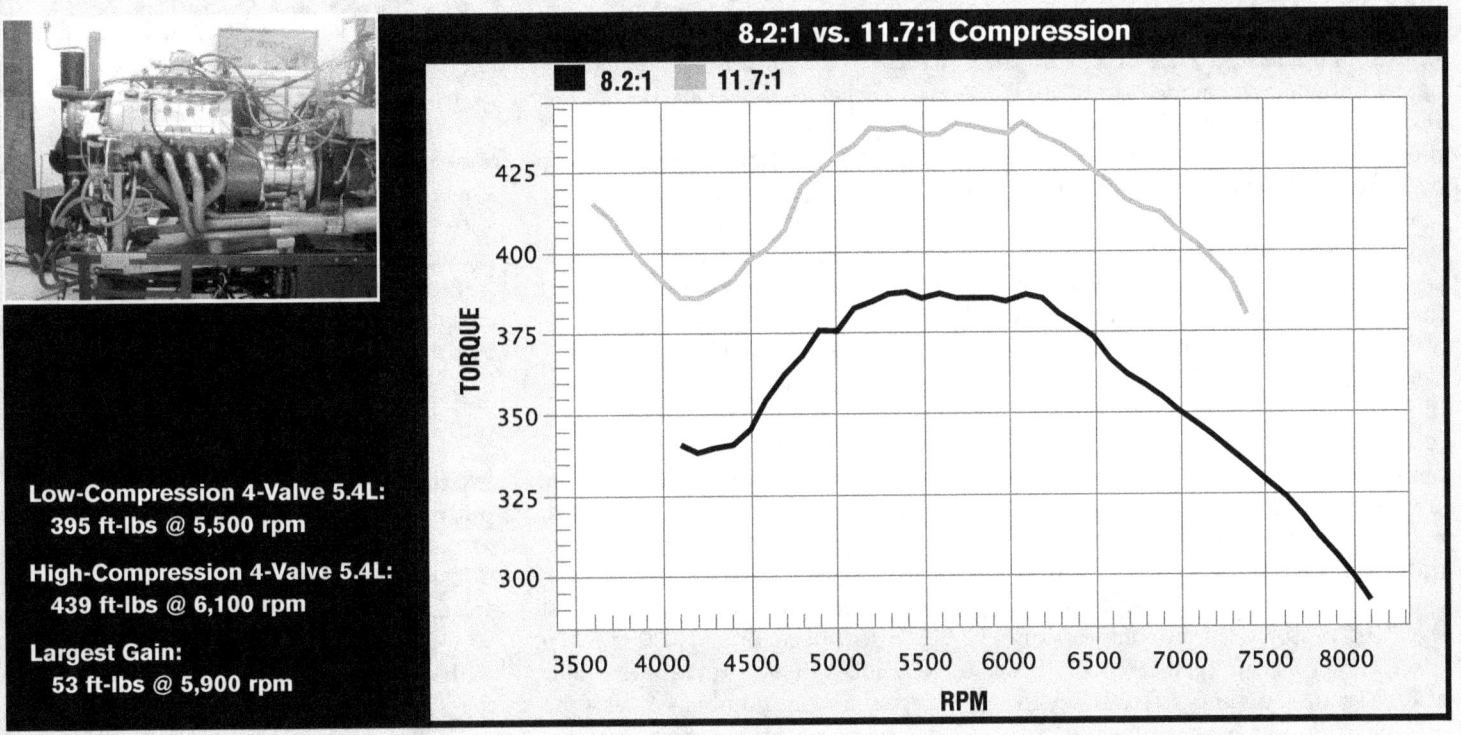

Low-Compression 4-Valve 5.4L:
395 ft-lbs @ 5,500 rpm

High-Compression 4-Valve 5.4L:
439 ft-lbs @ 6,100 rpm

Largest Gain:
53 ft-lbs @ 5,900 rpm

4-Valve 5.4L: Low Compression vs. High Compression (Torque)
Note that the shape of the torque curves remained consistent despite a change in static compression of 3.5 points. The additional squeeze simply elevated the entire curve.

Building 4.6/5.4L Ford Horsepower on the Dyno

Test 7: ATI Supercharged 4-Valve 5.4L: Effect of Compression Ratio

Back in Test 5, I took a hard look at the effect of changes in compression ratio on a 2-valve 4.6L GT motor. The idea behind the test was to illustrate the change in both power and the boost curves caused by a drop in compression ratio. Obviously this was an important (if time consuming) series of tests, as in almost all instances, a drop in static compression is recommended when adding forced induction. This is especially the case when we are talking about street motors, as the limiting factor in terms of power is almost always the octane rating of the pump gas. Sure, you can toss in a tank of 100-octane race fuel and go a bit wilder with boost, compression, or total timing, but running 91 octane will definitely limit power production given the increased risk of detonation.

If you take a look at the results from Test 6, you'll see that we added 65 hp to our naturally aspirated 5.4L motor by upping the static compression from 8.2:1 to 11.7:1. What would happen once we added the ATI Procharger F2M supercharger to the mix? Would the high-compression 5.4L motor still make only 65-hp more than the low-compression version, or would the boost pressure alter the power gains? If you read the results of the previous tests run on the 4.6L, you already know the answer. Adding boost pressure supplied by the ATI blower (and air-to-water intercooler) increased the difference in power between the high- and low-compression motors dramatically. Equipped with a 73-tooth crank pulley and a 46-tooth blower pulley, the ATI supercharger provided as much as 25 psi to the 5.4L motor. In low-compression form, the power jumped from 478 hp at 7,300 rpm to an impressive 1,135 hp at 7,200 rpm. The peak torque jumped from 395 ft-lbs at 5,500 rpm to 882 ft-lbs at 6,400 rpm. According to the power/boost formula, 25 psi should

After testing the differences in compression ratio with a naturally aspirated 5.4L, we performed the same test with an ATI centrifugal supercharger.

have increased the power output to 1,291 hp, but the formula doesn't take into account the parasitic losses associated with driving the blower. Supercharged combinations get much closer to the ideal boost/formula calculation at lower pressures and impeller speeds.

Running the same pulley setup (46/73) with the ATI blower and intercooler on the high-compression motor, the peak power jumped from 543 hp at 7,100 rpm to 1,350 hp at 7,400 rpm. The torque was equally impressive, as the elevated compression pushed the torque curve past 1,000 ft-lbs, peaking at 1,020 ft-lbs at 6,700 rpm. Once again, the formula suggested a peak number of 1,466 hp (2.70 pressure ratio x 543) but the drive losses cost over 100 hp at this RPM and boost level. The difference between the two naturally aspirated motors was 65 hp. Adding the supercharger to the mix upped the power difference to a whopping 215 hp. Like the naturally aspirated versions, the added compression upped the power output not just at the power peaks but also throughout the tested rev range. When you combine the results of this test with those generated by the 2-valve 4.6L GT motor, it's pretty safe to say that the changes in the power output of a naturally aspirated motor are actually multiplied when you add boost. These tests illustrate why I'm so adamant that the best route to a solid forced-induction motor is to start with a stout naturally aspirated motor. Any gains you achieve on your naturally aspirated motor (ported heads, aftermarket cams, or a free-flowing intake) will actually be multiplied after you install the supercharger.

Cylinder Heads

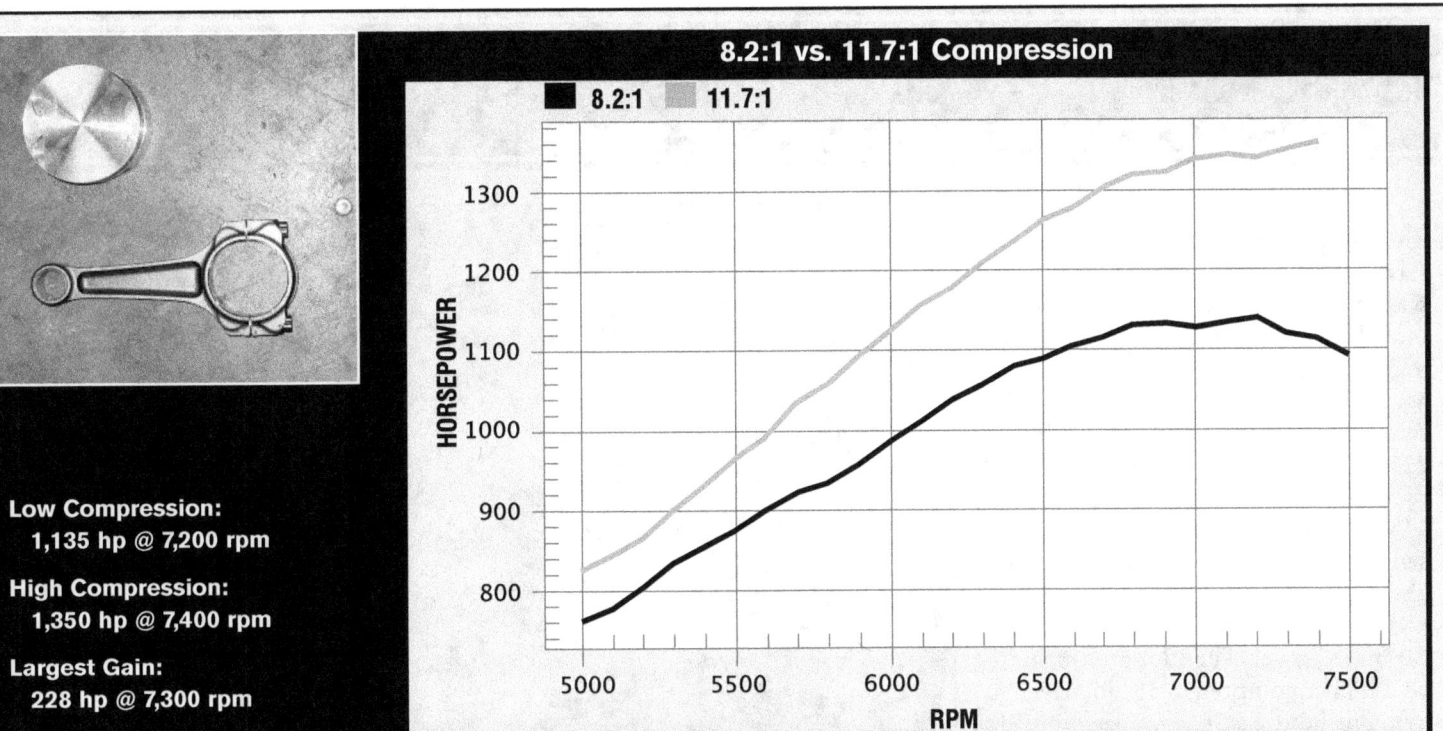

Low Compression:
1,135 hp @ 7,200 rpm

High Compression:
1,350 hp @ 7,400 rpm

Largest Gain:
228 hp @ 7,300 rpm

ATI Supercharged 5.4L 4-Valve: 8.2:1 vs. 11.7:1 Compression (Horsepower)
Adding boost pressure to the equation multiplied the power gains offered by the change in compression. Where the naturally aspirated versions of the 5.4L posted gains of 65 hp, the difference in the boosted motors was 215 hp. I guess it is safe to say that boost has a multiplier effect.

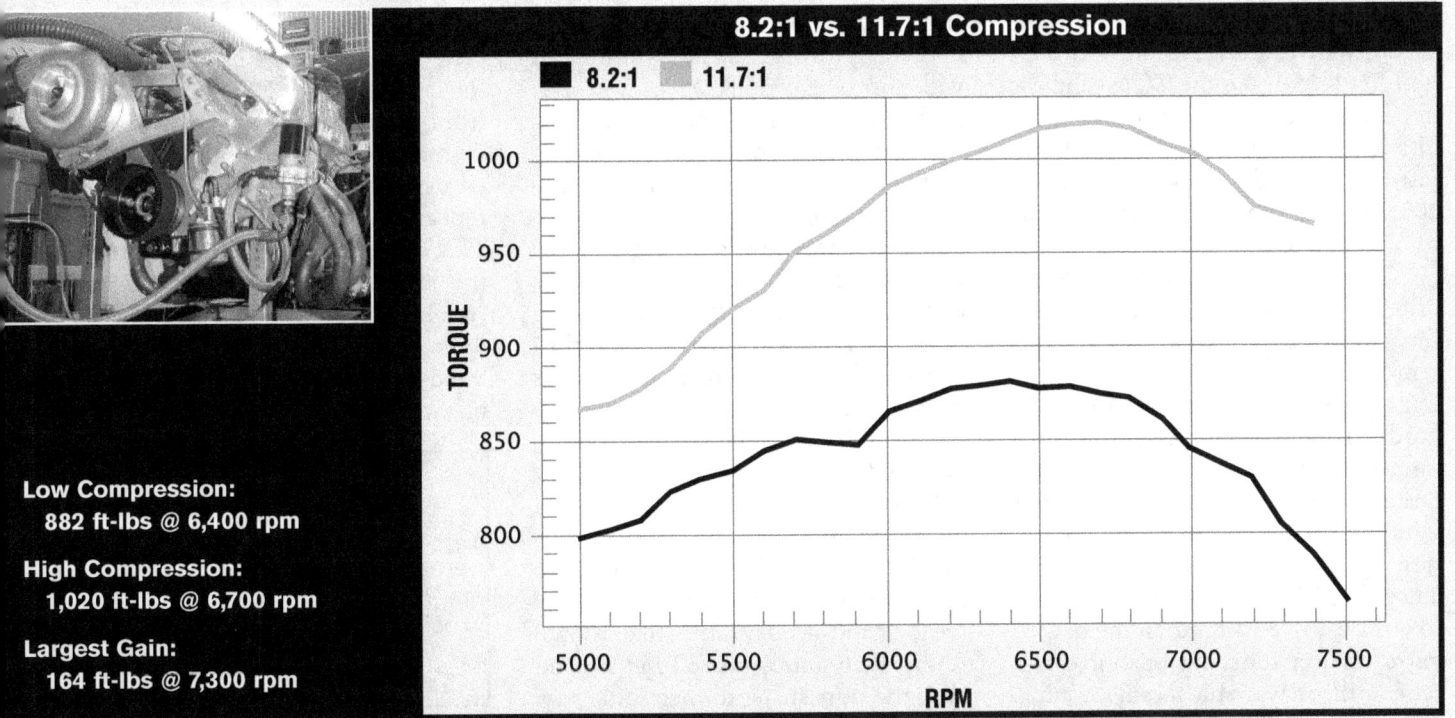

Low Compression:
882 ft-lbs @ 6,400 rpm

High Compression:
1,020 ft-lbs @ 6,700 rpm

Largest Gain:
164 ft-lbs @ 7,300 rpm

ATI Supercharged 5.4L 4-Valve: 8.2:1 vs. 11.7:1 Compression (Torque)
When octane is unlimited (as in many race applications), it makes sense to run as high a static compression ratio as you can. Changing the compression ratio from 8.2:1 to 11.7:1 increased the torque by 46 ft-lbs in NA trim, but by 140+ ft-lbs once we applied the boost. What kind of race motor can afford to give up 140 ft-lbs?

Test 8: 2-Valve PI GT vs. 3-Valve '05 GT

When Ford introduced the 4.6L in the Mustang back in 1996, few enthusiasts stood up and cheered. In fact, it wasn't until the Power-Improved 4.6L introduced in 1999 that people started to take the Mustang GT seriously again. The PI included a number of refinements that upped power from 225 to 260 hp. While still no match for the 285-to-300-hp LT1 or the 305-to-345-hp LS1, the 260-hp 4.6L represented a significant improvement. It also showed Mustang fans that Ford had not turned a deaf ear to their cries for more power. The PI motor included a higher compression ratio, new PI cylinder-head castings, a matching PI intake manifold, and revised cam timing with more lift. Equipped with the new 260-hp PI motor, a well-driven Mustang GT is a solid 13-second car. The PI motor continued basically unchanged until 2004. The Camaro/Firebird twins had since died, but the 'Vettes were running around with 345-hp LS1s (405-hp in the ZO6s) and the import crowd had some pretty heavy hitters as well. Given that Ford was introducing a brand new body style in 2005, this seemed like a perfect time for an upgrade.

The new 3-valve motor included different cylinder heads that featured three valves per cylinder. These heads represented a significant flow improvement over the 2-valve PI heads, even when ported. The flow improvements offered by the 3-valve heads are one of the primary reasons why the 3-valve GT motor pumps out near 4-valve Cobra power numbers. Though the 3-valve motor is SOHC like the 2-valve PI motors, the new 3-valve version adds an impressive system called variable cam timing. Though not quite on par with the legendary dual-cam VTEC systems offered by Honda/Acura, the variable cam timing on the 4.6L 3-valve motor offers improved performance by

The new 3-valve 4.6L features new 3-valve heads, a new intake manifold, and a variable cam timing system. The new front-mounted throttle body also uses a drive-by-wire system instead of a throttle cable.

advancing and retarding the existing cam profile. In most cases, advancing a cam will improve low-end and midrange torque, while retarding it will improve high-RPM power. The problem with advancing or retarding the cam is that the gains achieved at one end of the scale come with a penalty at the opposite end. The key to improving the power throughout the rev range is to advance it at low RPM and retard it at high RPM, something made possible with variable cam timing. Variable cam timing also improves emissions and fuel mileage.

In addition to the 3-valve cylinder head and variable cam timing, the new GT motor also features a redesigned intake manifold. The 3-valve heads featured revised intake ports, which are more like the 4-valve ports in that they are long and slender rather than round. Rather than simply take a PI intake and alter the port shape to match the new heads, Ford engineers designed a whole new manifold. The new intake shares the composite construction with its predecessor but offers slightly shorter runners, a new plenum design, and a

new front-mounted throttle body. The new intake also featured Intake Manifold Runner Controls (IMRCs), complete with throttle linkage, similar to the 1996-'98 4-valve Cobra intakes. The front-mounted throttle body is a new design as well, featuring the sophisticated drive-by-wire throttle actuation to replace the traditional throttle cable. This drive-by-wire system was one of the hurdles I had to overcome when running the 3-valve GT on the engine dyno, but I managed to design and build my own drive-by-wire using a set of Vice Grips and bailing wire.

Ford saw fit to bring back the IMRC plates (sometimes referred to as charge motion control plates) similar to those used in 1996-'98 Cobras. They are actuated using a mechanical linkage system.

Cylinder Heads

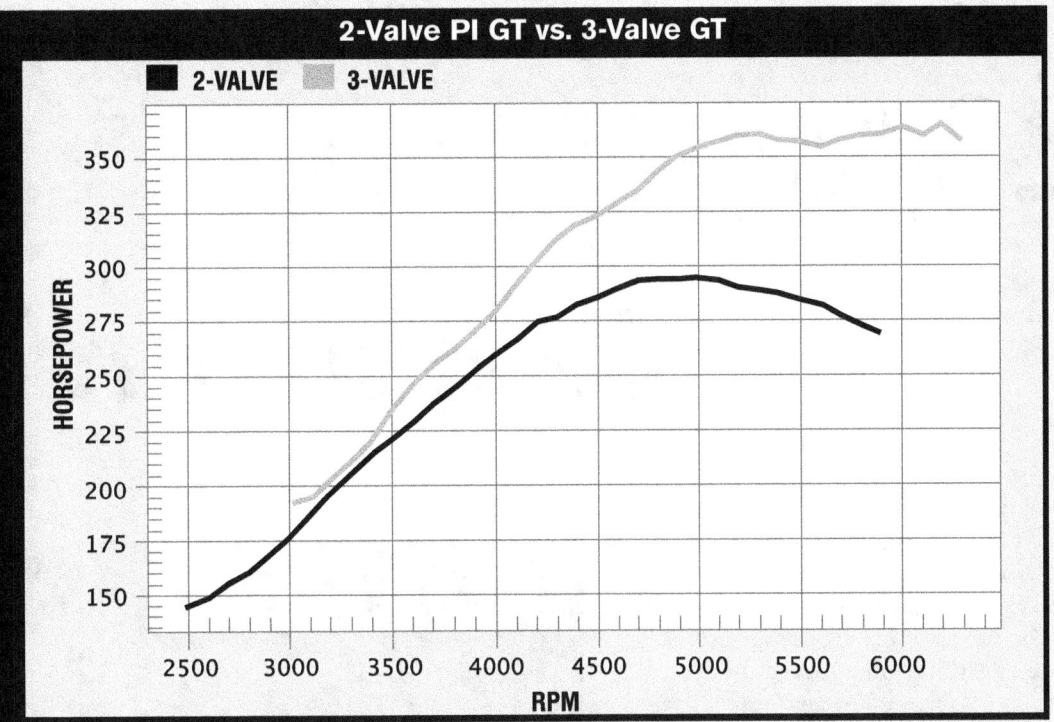

2-Valve PI GT:
293 hp @ 5,000 rpm

3-Valve GT:
362 hp @ 6,200 rpm

Largest Gain:
92 hp @ 5,900 rpm

2-Valve PI GT vs. 3-Valve GT (Horsepower)
While the new 3-valve heads flow significantly better than the 2-valve PI heads, the head flow alone was not responsible for the tremendous gains offered by the new 3-valve motor. The variable cam timing and new intake manifold were also responsible for the significant power gains posted past 3,500 rpm. You can really feel the difference between the old PI 4.6L and the new 3-valve 4.6L.

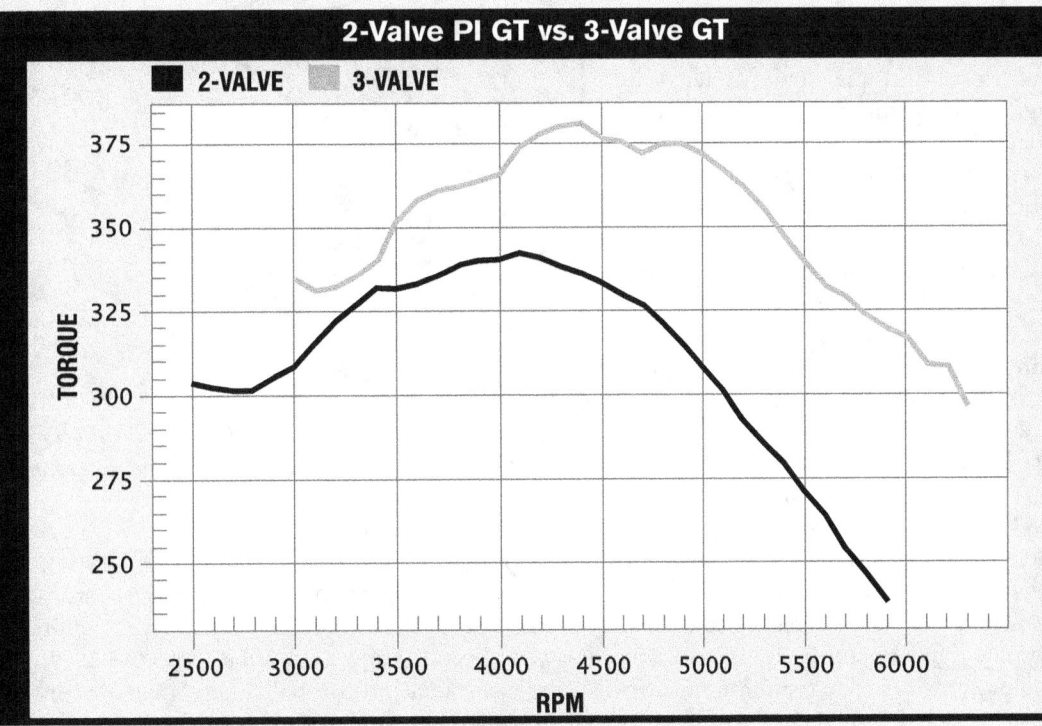

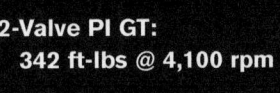

2-Valve PI GT:
342 ft-lbs @ 4,100 rpm

3-Valve GT:
381 ft-lbs @ 4,300 rpm

Largest Gain:
81 ft-lbs @ 5,900 rpm

2-Valve PI GT vs. 3-Valve GT (Torque)
In most instances, significant power gains achieved at one of the rev ranges will be accompanied by losses at the other. The Ford engineers apparently did their homework, as the 2005 3-valve 4.6L offered significantly more peak power (and torque) without sacrificing any low-speed power. Since we weren't using the factory electronics, we had to rig up manual controls for the drive-wire and IMRL systems.

Building 4.6/5.4L Ford Horsepower on the Dyno

Chapter 4

Camshafts

One of the most misunderstood performance components on any motor has to be the camshaft or camshafts. The difficulty is only compounded when you add things like forced induction to the mix. From an anatomical standpoint, camshafts can be likened to the brain, as the cam profile determines how effectively (when and where) breathing takes place. Camshafts are one of the major determining components of the effective operating range of the motor. Of course, the cam timing must be combined with the proper intake manifold, head flow, and primary header tube length for optimum operation over a given RPM range. Stock or ultra-mild aftermarket cams will provide a dead smooth idle, while more radical grinds can transform that mild-mannered motor into one radical ride. The radical route usually includes ill-tempered, cantankerous behavior until the motor comes on the cam, but such is the price for all that high-RPM heaven.

Many mod-motor enthusiasts at least understand the basics of cam timing. They realize that so-called "Saturday-Night Special" grinds are much wilder and potentially more powerful than the production cam profiles. The problem arises when deciding to choose between these two extremes, especially for a daily driver. The temptation is certainly to go big on the cam profile; after all, isn't bigger always better? The problem with going big is twofold. The first problem is that the cam profile must be selected not just for bragging rights at

Degreeing the cams is every bit as important as a cam swap. Advancing and retarding the cams can yield huge power gains. It's time consuming, but ultimately worth it.

the drive-in (or coffee house), but rather to work with your existing components. Adding the right cams to your otherwise stock motor can result in impressive power gains. Adding wild cams to your otherwise stock motor will likely hurt your power throughout the rev range and can even decrease peak power since the cams were designed to run effectively at 8,000 rpm and the rest of your stock components (intake runner length, head, and exhaust flow) sign off at 6,500 rpm. As a general rule, the closer to stock the rest of your engine is, the milder the cam profiles should be. This means leave those weekend warrior cams to the drag racers and stick with mild but effective profiles that will offer power gains not just at high RPM, but also throughout the rev range. After all, what good is it to add 25 hp at the power peak only to loose 35 ft-lbs down at

Camshafts

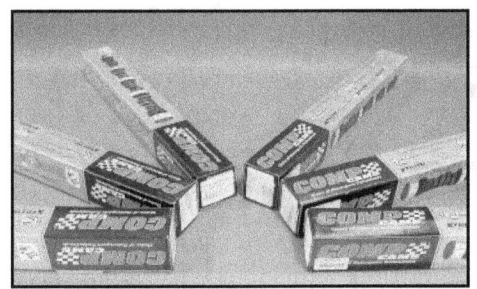

As difficult as cam swaps are on modular motors, what better way to illustrate the differences offered by six different cam profiles than to perform six different cam swaps on the engine dyno?

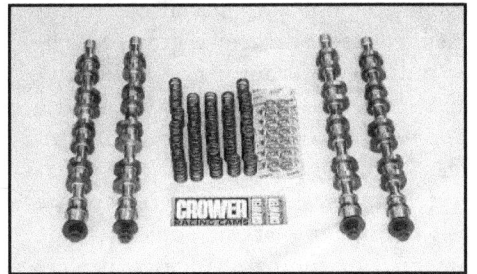

These Crower Stage 2 cams offered a sizable power gain over the stock '03 Cobra cams on a Kenne Bell supercharged 4-valve.

3,000 rpm? Think for a moment about where (what RPM) you spend most of your time driving and choose a cam accordingly!

While naturally aspirated cam choices are difficult enough, just look at any book on the subject of forced induction and skip to the section on camshafts. The recommendation will probably be to run stock cams, or at least to stay away from the dreaded duration or overlap that can cause all that precious boost to escape out past the exhaust valve. While blowers (and turbos) work fine on stock motors equipped with stock cam profiles, like their naturally aspirated counterparts, they respond very well to more aggressive cam timing. In fact, for most street applications, the camshaft chosen for a mild naturally aspirated motor will work equally well with a supercharger. Sure, you can tailor the specific cam timing for supercharged use, but the gains (compared to a naturally aspirated performance cam) will be minimal at most mild boost and power levels run on the street. This is actually good news for enthusiasts, as choosing the right cams for a blower motor is actually as easy as selecting them for a naturally aspirated motor – in many cases you can go with the very same cams. The manufacturers list applications for their cams and many have included profiles for forced induction motors, but the NA cams work well too. How do I know that NA cams work well on forced induction applications? Just check out the results of Tests 5 and 8.

Many mod-motor owners have steered clear of cam swaps, fearing the overhead cam configuration. Know that swapping cams in a 4.6L 2-valve or 4-valve motor is a bit more involved than performing the same task on a 5.0L V-8, but like anything else, once you've done it once or twice, you'll wonder why you avoided all that extra power for so long. As is usually the case, stock cam profiles leave something to be desired in terms of maximizing power. It is possible to add performance cams to your 4.6L (2-valve or 4-valve) and gain power across the rev range, though the wilder (more powerful) profiles will usually cost some low-speed power in trade for the significant gains in midrange and top end. modular motors respond well to aggressive cam timing, though the 2-valve motors are ultimately head flow limited, so ultra-wild cam profiles will be less beneficial than on the free-flowing 4-valve motors. This chapter illustrates the gains offered on naturally aspirated and supercharged 2-valve and 4-valve combinations, but know that similar power gains are available on turbocharged mod motors as well. Don't fear the cam swap on a mod motor, just take things slow and have the factory manual handy as a reference. In a day or so your motor will be up and running with a nasty new attitude.

The one thing missing in the modular world (a deficiency cured by the author after this testing) was the availability of adjustable cam sprockets. While cam swaps certainly offer power gains, they can be maximized only after degreeing the cams. In the case of modular motors, the cams on the right bank of cylinders are not always in alignment with the cams on the left bank. On 4-valve motors, we've measured differences in intake cam timing of 9 degrees (one cam was 9 degrees retarded relative to the other). Naturally, one setting is going to produce more power than the other, but the real concern is that the two banks of cylinders produce different relative power outputs. This unbalanced power production is not desirable, but the only way to cure it is to degree and adjust (synchronize) the cam timing side to side. Power production can be further enhanced by advancing or retarding the cams (in unison), to find optimum power. Additional gains will likely come at the expense of power elsewhere, as advancing the cams (especially the intake) will likely improve low-speed power while retarding them will have the opposite effect. This will change somewhat after adding a blower or turbo, but it will be nice to be able to optimize the power output with adjustable cam sprockets.

The 2-valve cams are a tad easier than the 4-valve swap, but once you've performed the procedure once or twice, it isn't any more technically difficult than a standard 5.0L V-8.

Test 1: Early 2-Valve GT: Comp Cams XE274H Camshafts

After spending some time tuning the base fuel and timing tables, we eventually coaxed this non-PI 4.6L engine to 260 hp and 341 ft-lbs of torque. We managed to match the flywheel rating of the new, more powerful PI GT motors, but before you get all in an uproar about happy dynos and exaggerated power numbers, remember that this reading was taken with long-tube headers, no MAF or air inlet system other than a 3-inch tube and cone filter, and no accessories. The idea was not to exceed the 260 hp offered by the late-model GT motor, but rather to establish a baseline to improve upon.

After I was confident about the repeatability of the baseline power numbers, I decided to start swapping some hard parts. First on the list for the early 4.6L was a set of performance cams. Wanting more than 5 to 10 extra horsepower, I decided to go big in terms of cam profiles and selected the largest Xtreme Energy grinds available for the early 4.6L GT motor.

Comp Cams recommended a spring upgrade to go with their XE274H cams.

The dual-pattern XE274H cams offered a 236/240-degrees duration split, along with .500 inches of lift for both the intake and exhaust. A wide 114-degree lobe separation angle helped tame the cam somewhat, but the duration ensured that these cams lived up to the description of "Hot Street Cams" given in the Comp Cams catalog. Comp Cams also recommended steeper rear-end gears, a higher stall speed (if automatic equipped), and computer upgrades (otherwise known as getting a chip or tune). Our F.A.S.T. programmable ECU obviously fell under the last category, so we felt confident that we could provide any fuel or timing changes that were needed. The new cam profiles required a valvespring upgrade, so Comp Cams supplied a set of 26113-16 springs to provide sufficient seat and open pressure (along with the necessary coil-bind clearance) to ensure proper valve control.

Though designed to operate effectively from 2,000 rpm to 6,000 rpm, we found out in testing that the stock non-PI GT intake manifold kept peak power well below 6,000 rpm. Still, I had high hopes for the cam upgrade. After installing the springs and XE274H cams, the peak power jumped from 260 to 301 hp. The early GT was now making at least as much as (and possibly more than) a later PI GT motor. The peak torque was up as well, by 5 ft-lbs. Not surprisingly, the motor lost a bit of power below 3,400 rpm, but beyond that it was all power. With the effective power band of 3,500 to 5,500 rpm, these cams would do nothing but improve acceleration. With as much as 50 extra horsepower available thanks to the cam swap, the extra acceleration would be significant. In fact, I'd have to say that the wimpy stock intake and heads were now holding back this early GT motor from making serious power.

It's important to degree your new cams and make sure they're right on. The last thing you want to do is take everything back apart.

Camshafts

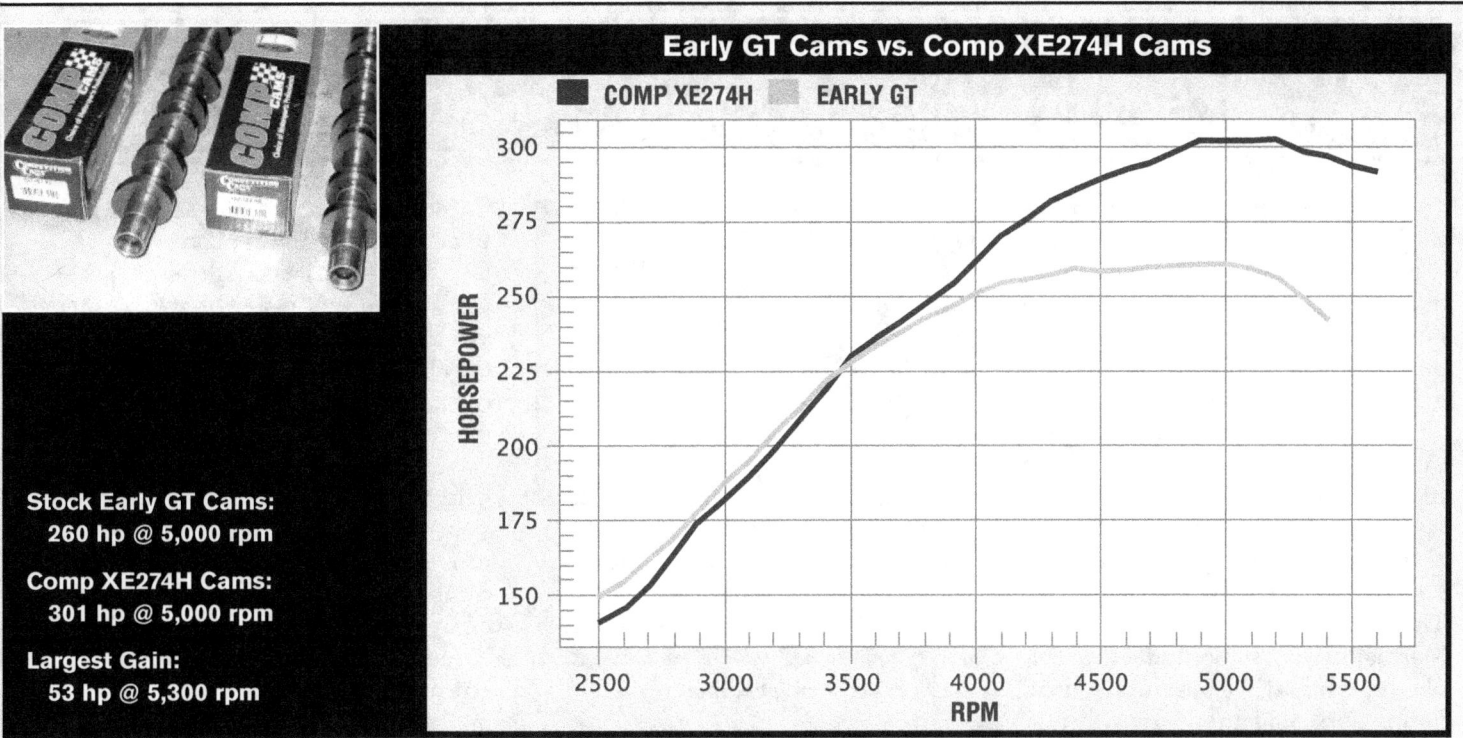

Stock Early GT Cams:
260 hp @ 5,000 rpm

Comp XE274H Cams:
301 hp @ 5,000 rpm

Largest Gain:
53 hp @ 5,300 rpm

Stock Early GT Cams vs. Comp XE274H Cams (Horsepower)
These are the kinds of power gains you dream about when installing performance cams. The Xtreme Energy XE274H cams from Comp Cams added as much as 53 hp to the otherwise stock non-PI 4.6L

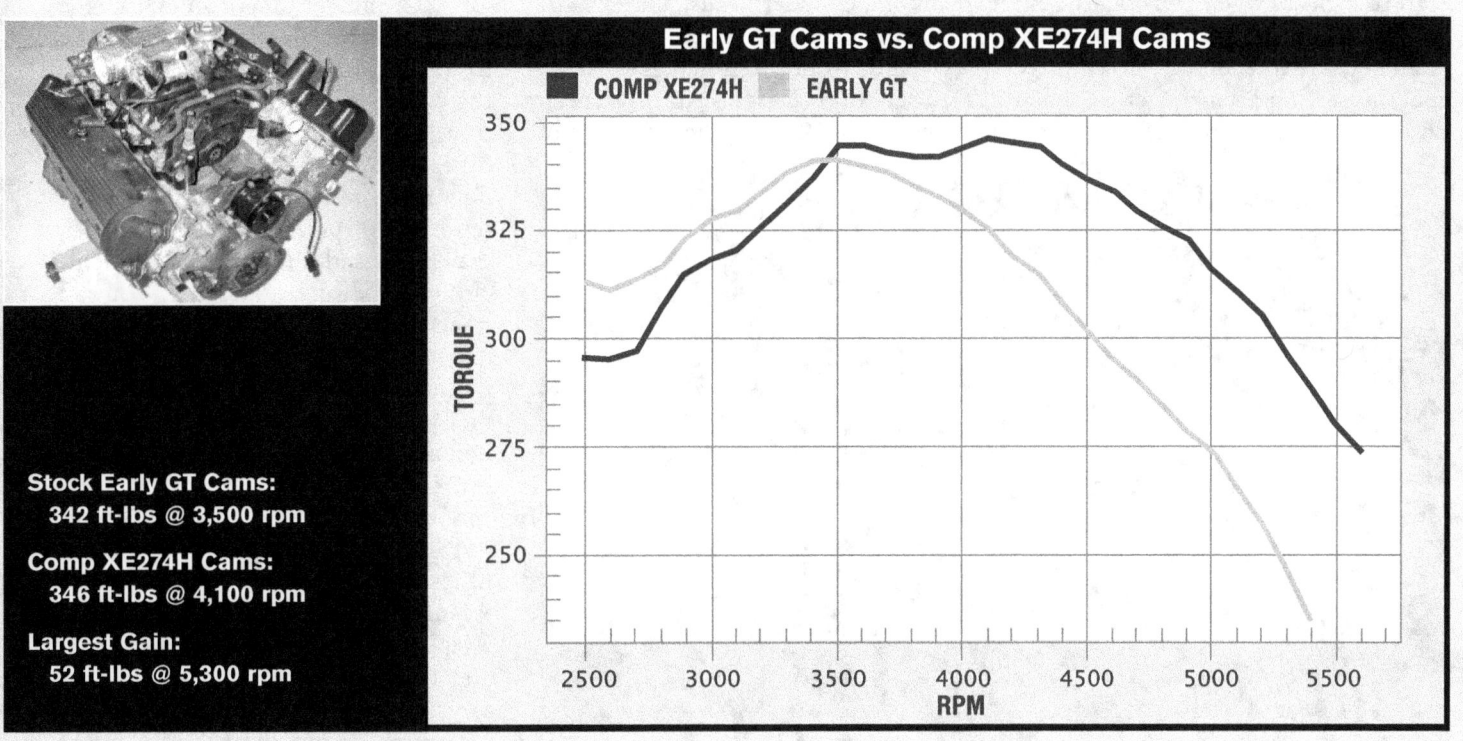

Stock Early GT Cams:
342 ft-lbs @ 3,500 rpm

Comp XE274H Cams:
346 ft-lbs @ 4,100 rpm

Largest Gain:
52 ft-lbs @ 5,300 rpm

Stock Early GT Cams vs. Comp XE274H Cams (Torque)
Note from the torque curve that the wilder cam profiles cost some torque below 3,400 rpm, but significant gains were achieved from 3,500 to 5,500 rpm. The Xtreme Energy cams allowed this early 4.6L to produced PI power and torque numbers.

Building 4.6/5.4L Ford Horsepower on the Dyno

Chapter 4

Test 2: PI 2-Valve GT:
Six Sets of Comp Cams Xtreme Energy Camshafts

If you learn anything from this chapter on performance camshafts it should be that wilder cam timing does indeed improve power. In reality, the question isn't so much whether performance cams will add power, but more of which cam is the right one for your application. The intended application should dictate the cam choice, but the chosen cam may also reflect your personality. Do you have the crust trimmed from your bread while you're watching the cooking channel? Then a stock cam with its (pre-prison) Martha Stewart smooth idle is probably for you. If, on the other hand, your tastes tend more toward Tater Tots and beer while fast forwarding to the Seth Enslo jump on *Crusty Demons of Dirt*, then drop right to the bottom of the cam page where the big ones are. Like you, the idle is a little rough around the edges, but things start to kick ass when you come up on the cam. *Crusty Demons* not withstanding, the intended use is actually the most important factor when choosing a cam. Obviously, the cams

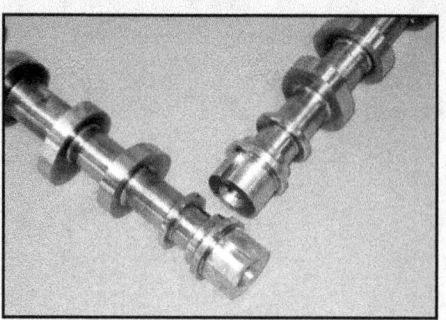

For this test, we ran six different sets of Comp cams against the stock PI cams. Each offered additional horsepower but lost torque down low. Check out the following dyno graphs to help you decide which cams are right for your application.

chosen for a drag-race motor would differ from those optimized for street use or even a road-race application.

Also consider the existing engine combination, as the cam profile must work in conjunction with the intake manifold, cylinder heads, and exhaust system to produce maximum power in a given RPM range. It makes no sense to install cams designed to make peak power at 7,500 rpm when the rest of

the components sign off at 6,000 rpm. In all likelihood, most people won't be building dedicated (single-purpose) motors and will instead have existing stock or mildly modified motors that they deem in need of performance cams. Given that the vast majority of modular motors are of the 4.6L 2-valve variety, this test was designed to help you select the proper cam for your combination. It's impossible to run every cam in every conceivable combination, but I was able to test every one of the six different Comp Xtreme Energy (both PI and non-PI) sets of cams against the stock cams in a modified 4.6L 2-valve motor.

Though all of the Comp Xtreme Energy cams offered power gains over stock, they did so differently, and in every case, the power gains were accompanied by losses in power somewhere in the rev range (usually down low). The milder cam profiles (like the 262H and 262AH) traded very little torque down low (15 to 18 ft-lbs) for the power gains achieved above 4,500 rpm (48 to 58 hp). The larger profiles (like the 278AH) dropped 35 ft-lbs down low, but offered as much as 77 hp at 6,500 rpm. As indicated earlier, the choice is ultimately up to the vehicle owner. Just be sure that you are honest about the intended use, and don't be tricked by the big power numbers out at 6,500 rpm. Your street motor will spend a lot more time driving around from 2,500 rpm to 4,500 rpm than at wide open throttle at 6,500 rpm. Also realize that this DSS-built test motor featured CNC-ported heads from TEA, a PI intake with Accufab 75-mm throttle body and inlet elbow, and a set of Hooker headers. The power probably wouldn't be as great on a milder combination. Be sure to check out all of the following graphs, as this test involved six different sets of Comp cams, as well as the stock PI cams.

You can swap 4.6L 2-valve cams with the engine in the car, but it's easier with the engine on the dyno. It's a little more complicated than a 5.0L cam swap, but it's definitely not impossible.

Camshafts

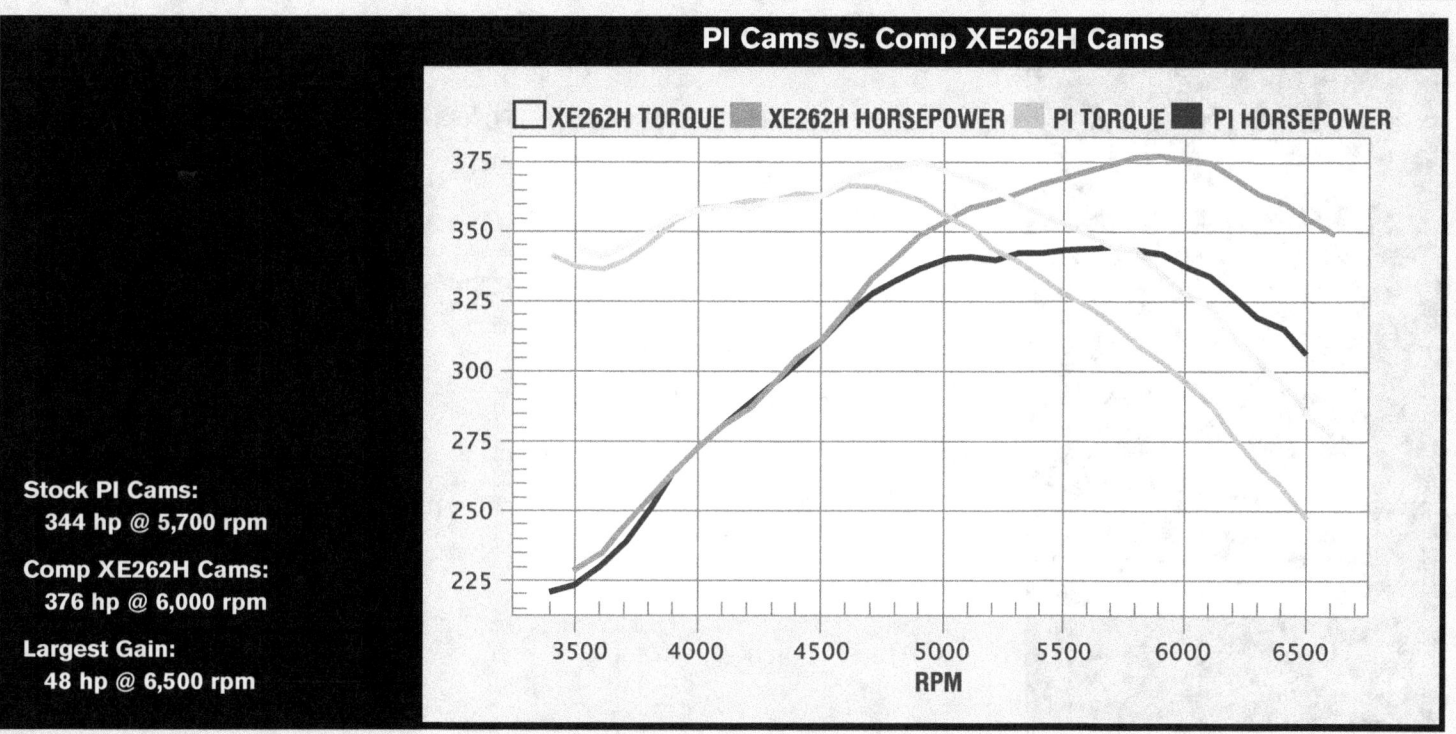

Stock PI Cams:
344 hp @ 5,700 rpm

Comp XE262H Cams:
376 hp @ 6,000 rpm

Largest Gain:
48 hp @ 6,500 rpm

PI 2-Valve GT: Stock PI Cams vs. Comp XE262H Cams
The smallest of the non-PI cams, the XE262H profiles offered significant power gains above 4,500 rpm. The cams were worth an additional 48 hp on this combination and a good 25 to 30 ft-lbs. The tradeoff in low-speed (from 2,500 to 3,500 rpm) torque was minimal, roughly 15 to 18 ft-lbs from 2,500 to 3,000 rpm.

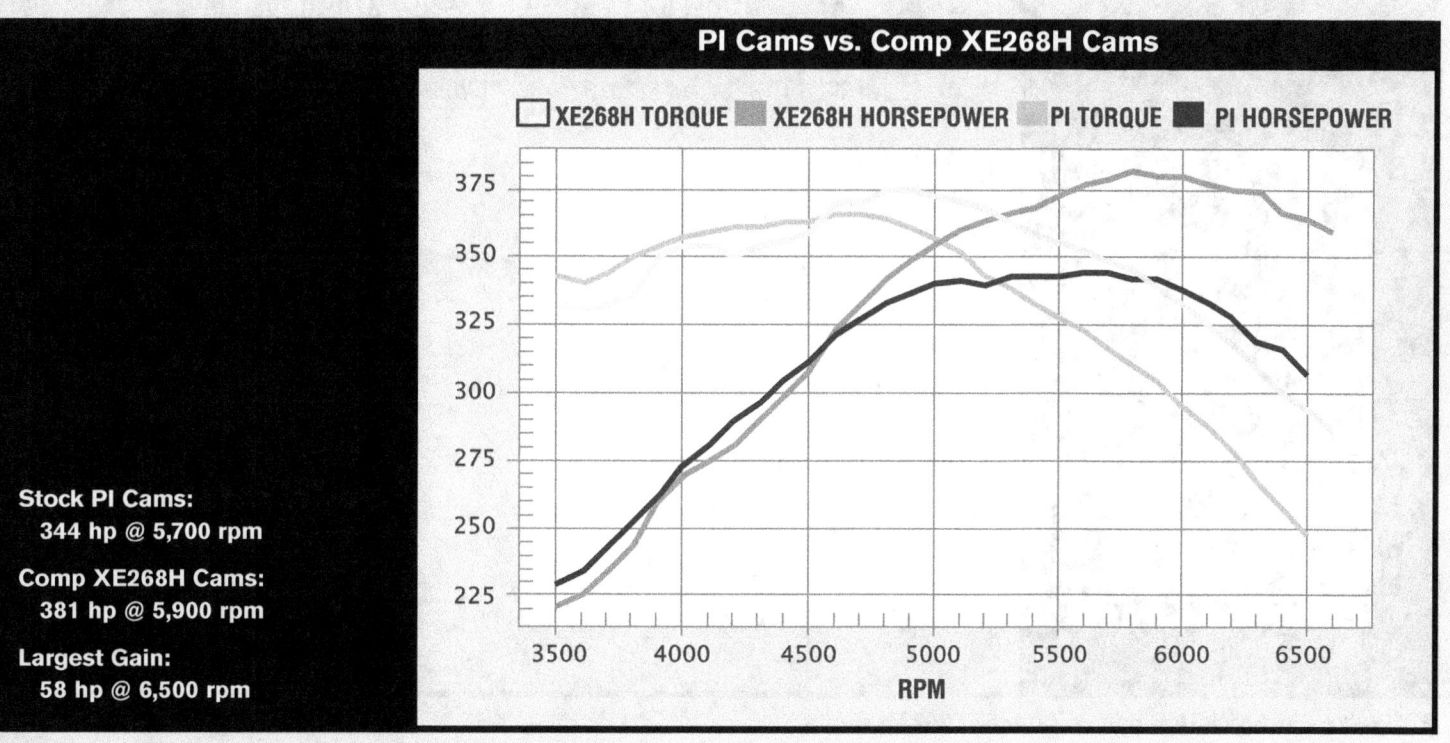

Stock PI Cams:
344 hp @ 5,700 rpm

Comp XE268H Cams:
381 hp @ 5,900 rpm

Largest Gain:
58 hp @ 6,500 rpm

PI 2-Valve GT: Stock PI Cams vs. Comp XE268H Cams
Stepping up to the slightly larger (still non-PI) XE268H cams offered an additional 58 horsepower, but the gains started at 4,550 rpm. Note that the losses were greater down to 3,500 rpm, and this trend continued down to 2,500 rpm as well.

Chapter 4

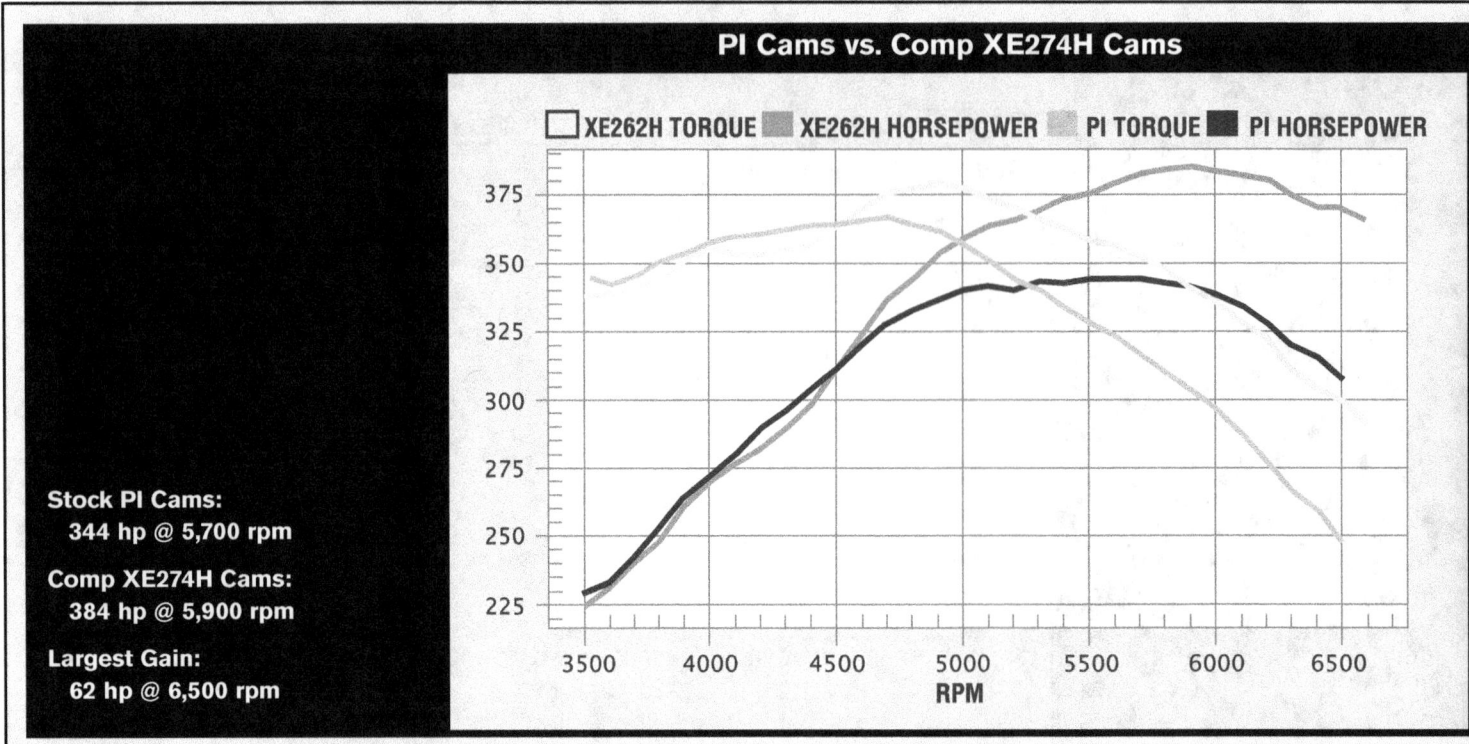

PI 2-Valve GT: Stock PI Cams vs. Comp XE274H Cams
The largest non-PI cams (XE274H) were actually the first Comp modular cams I ever tested. They have proven themselves powerful time and time again, despite offering only .500 lift (the PI cams offer .550 lift). The XE274H profiles improved the power output of the DSS 4.6L by 62 hp, but the trend toward increasing losses below 3,000 rpm continued, as the XE274H cam dropped over 20 ft-lbs of torque below 3,200 rpm.

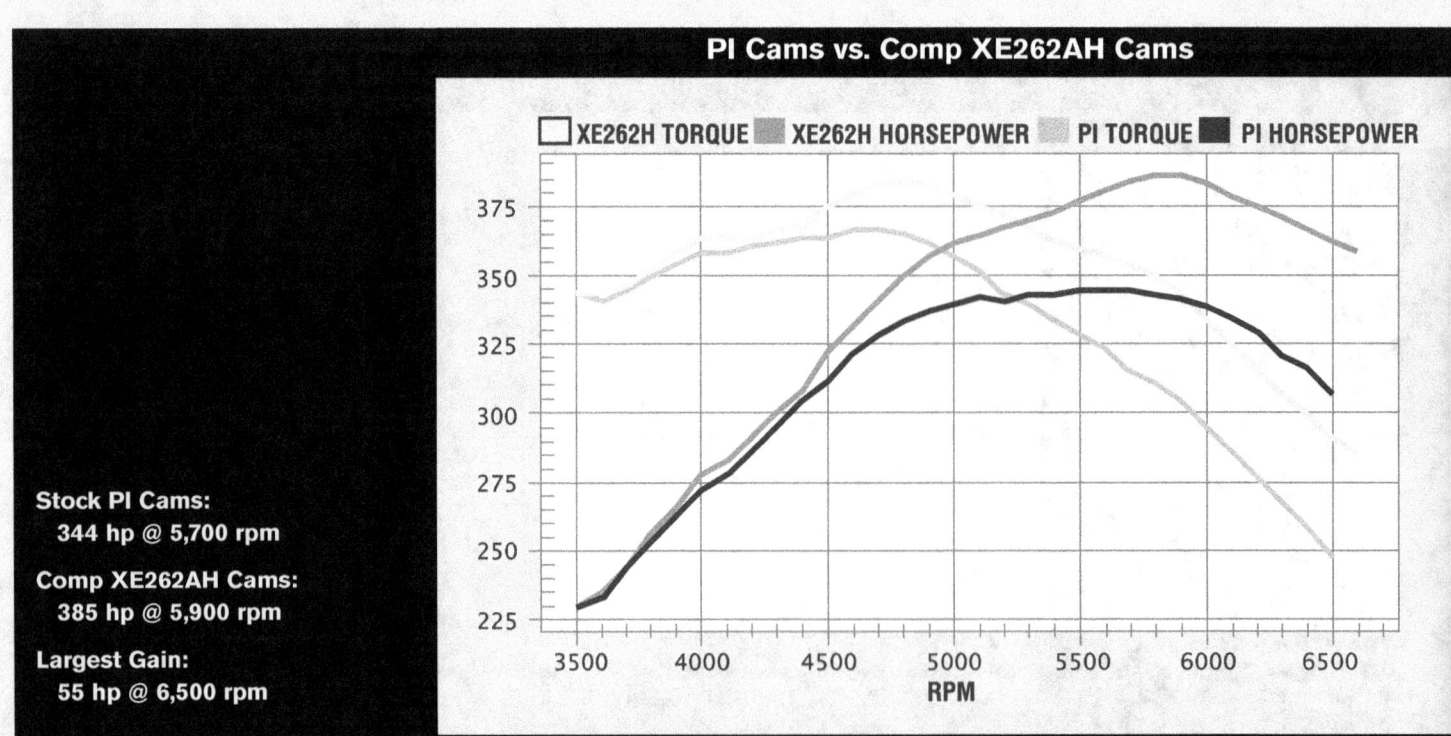

PI 2-Valve GT: Stock PI Cams vs. Comp XE262AH Cams
The XE262AH cams are probably my favorite street cams for the 2-valve 4.6L. These cams offered an additional 55 hp and showed power gains all the way down at 3,700 rpm. The losses were minimal below 3,100 rpm, yet the motor pulled strongly all the way past 6,500 rpm.

Camshafts

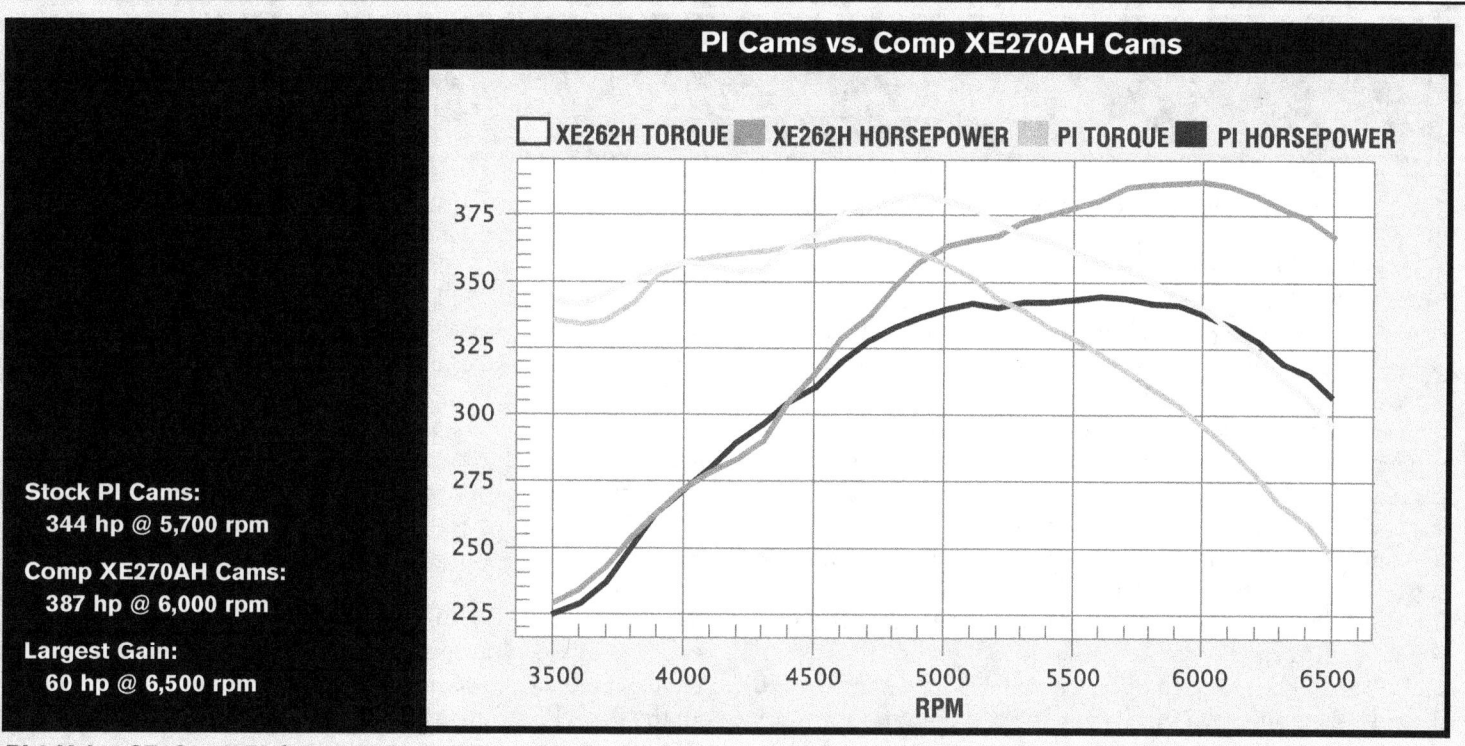

Stock PI Cams:
344 hp @ 5,700 rpm

Comp XE270AH Cams:
387 hp @ 6,000 rpm

Largest Gain:
60 hp @ 6,500 rpm

PI 2-Valve GT: Stock PI Cams vs. Comp XE270AH Cams
The middle PI cams (XE270AH) offered an additional 60 hp at 6,500 rpm over the stock cams, but the losses increased down low compared to the XE262AH. Where the XE262AH cams offered power gains starting at 3,700 rpm, the larger XE270AH cams bettered the stock cams at 4,400 rpm.

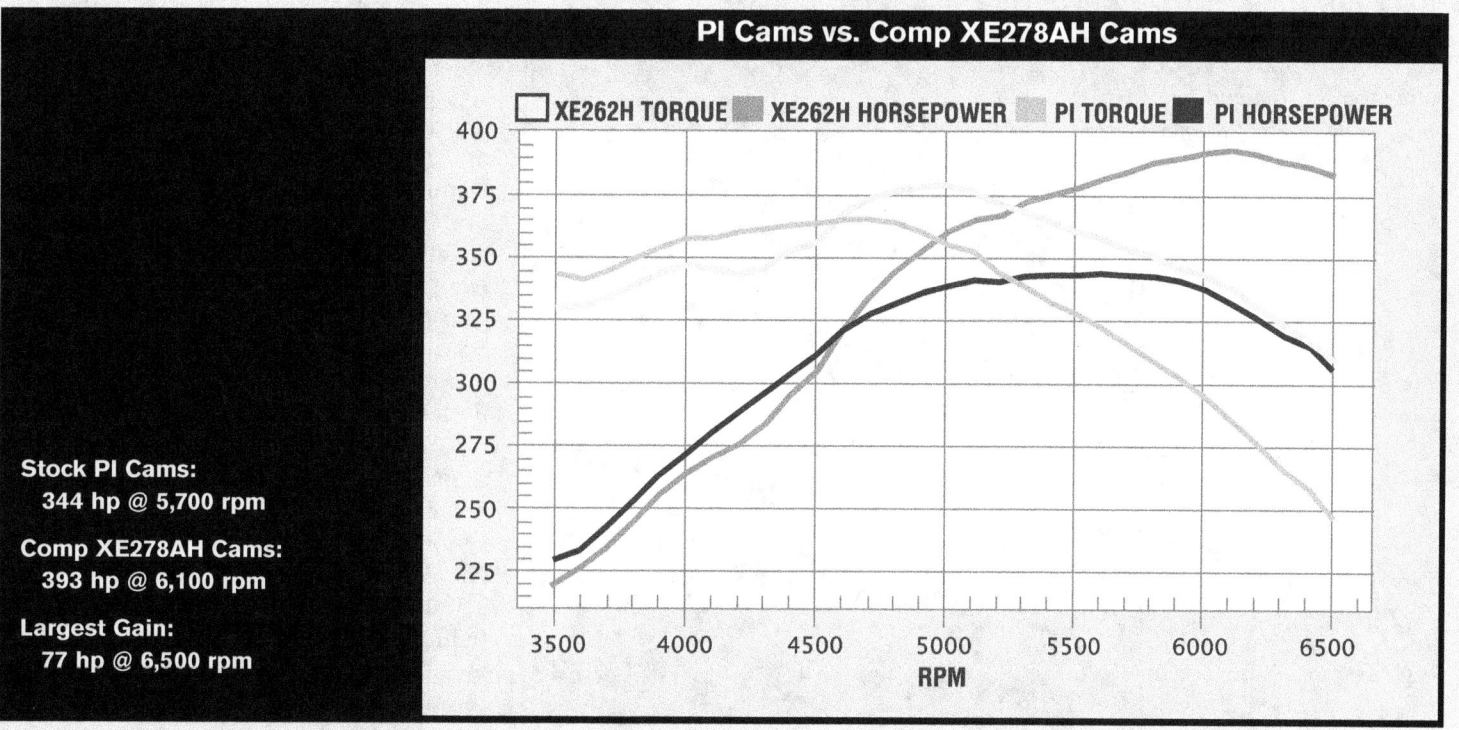

Stock PI Cams:
344 hp @ 5,700 rpm

Comp XE278AH Cams:
393 hp @ 6,100 rpm

Largest Gain:
77 hp @ 6,500 rpm

PI 2-Valve GT: Stock PI Cams vs. Comp XE278AH Cams
The largest of the XE series cams are the XE278AHs. The largest cams dropped power to the stockers up to 4,600 rpm, but added 77 hp at 6,500 rpm. Unlike most of the other cams, the XE278AH cams fell off very little after the power peak at 6,100 rpm.

Test 3: Ford Racing Supercharged PI 2-Valve GT: Comp Cams XE262H Camshafts

The Sean Hyland Motorsport (SHM) 4.6L test motor was one of the more desirable (1999-'04) Power-Improved (PI) engines. It featured a forged reciprocating assembly (stock compression) topped off with bone-stock PI heads, cams, and composite intake manifold. The SHM motor was topped off with a Ford Racing supercharger assembly consisting of an M90 roots-style supercharger and dedicated aluminum intake casting. The supercharger intake features long intake runners designed to optimize power (and torque) production up to 6,000 rpm. The supercharger would provide the additional airflow in the form of boost pressure, but the intake runner length is critical (in both NA and blown applications) for maximizing torque. Combining the immediate boost response of a positive displacement blower with optimized runner length makes for one impressive power curve. In addition to the blower, the motor was also equipped with a 70-mm Ford Racing throttle body, a smaller blower pulley to increase the boost pressure, and 36-pound injectors run by a F.A.S.T. engine management system. The SHM 4.6L was also equipped with a set of Kooks 1⅝-inch stainless steel headers, an electric water pump, and an MSD coil pack.

To illustrate the gains possible with a cam change on a supercharged application, I swapped out the stock PI cams for a set of Xtreme Energy 262H cams (actually designed for the non-PI heads). The main difference in the PI and non-PI cams is the lift value. The PI heads are set up to accept higher (.550 inch) lift cams than the non-PI (.500 inch) versions. The non-PI cams can be run in the PI heads with no trouble, but the reverse is not true without ensuring adequate retainer-to-seal and coil bind (valvespring) clearance. The XE262H cams offered .500 lift (both intake and exhaust) but a dual-pattern duration split. The intake featured 224 degrees of duration and 232 degrees of exhaust duration (@ .050). The wide 114-degree lobe separation angle ensured a broad curve and a relatively smooth idle given the durations specs. The Xtreme Energy cams worked fine with the stock valvesprings, though Comp does offer a valvespring upgrade for both the 2-valve and 4-valve modular motors.

Installing the cams wasn't terribly difficult, but this wasn't my first time. The XE262H cams have been previously tested on a modified naturally aspirated motor and shown to offer impressive power gains on the order of 30 to 35 hp. How well do these "naturally aspirated" cams work on our blown 4.6L? Well, they worked equally well, upping the peak power from 405 to 436 hp (both at 6,000 rpm). In fact, the Comp XE262H cams not only improved the peak power and torque numbers, they didn't lose power anywhere. It's interesting to note that when tested naturally aspirated, the Comp cams showed power improvements starting at 4,500 rpm, while the gains on this supercharged application started as low as 3,300 rpm. Installing the cams actually reduced the peak boost pressure to just 6.9 psi. The drop in peak pressure is not from boost escaping out the exhaust of the wilder cam timing, but rather from the increase in efficiency. The more powerful the naturally aspirated motor, the lower the boost pressure at any given blower speed.

Though originally designed for a naturally aspirated combination, these mild Comp XE262H cams added horsepower and didn't give up any torque on a supercharged application.

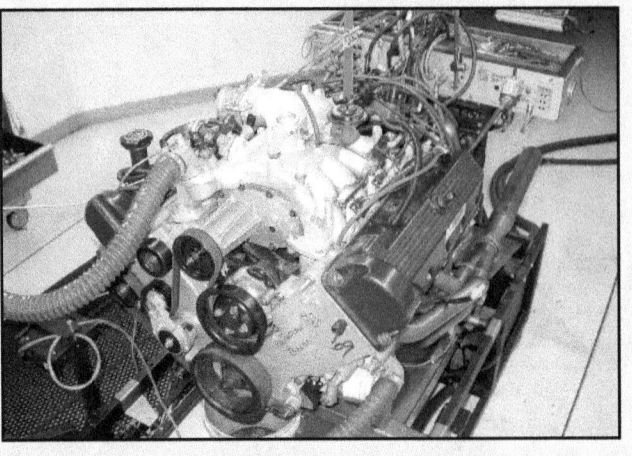

This supercharged 4.6L PI was tested with the stock PI cams and then again with some Comp XE262H cams. The more efficient Comp cams caused the boost pressure to drop to 6.9 psi.

Camshafts

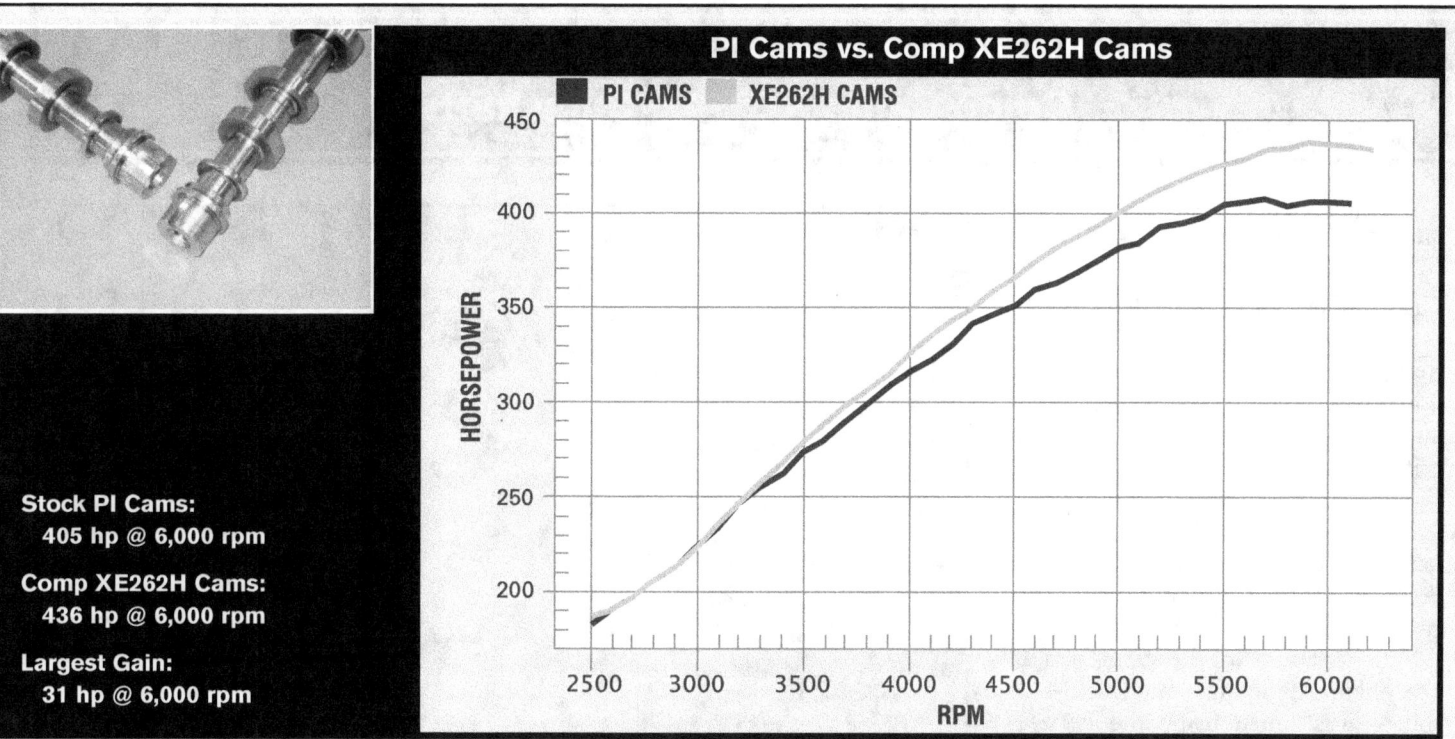

Stock PI Cams:
405 hp @ 6,000 rpm

Comp XE262H Cams:
436 hp @ 6,000 rpm

Largest Gain:
31 hp @ 6,000 rpm

Supercharged PI 2-Valve GT: Stock Cams vs. Comp XE262H Cams (Horsepower)
As expected, the XE262H cams offered impressive power gains. Out near 6,000 rpm, the Comp cams bettered the stock PI cams by over 30 hp.

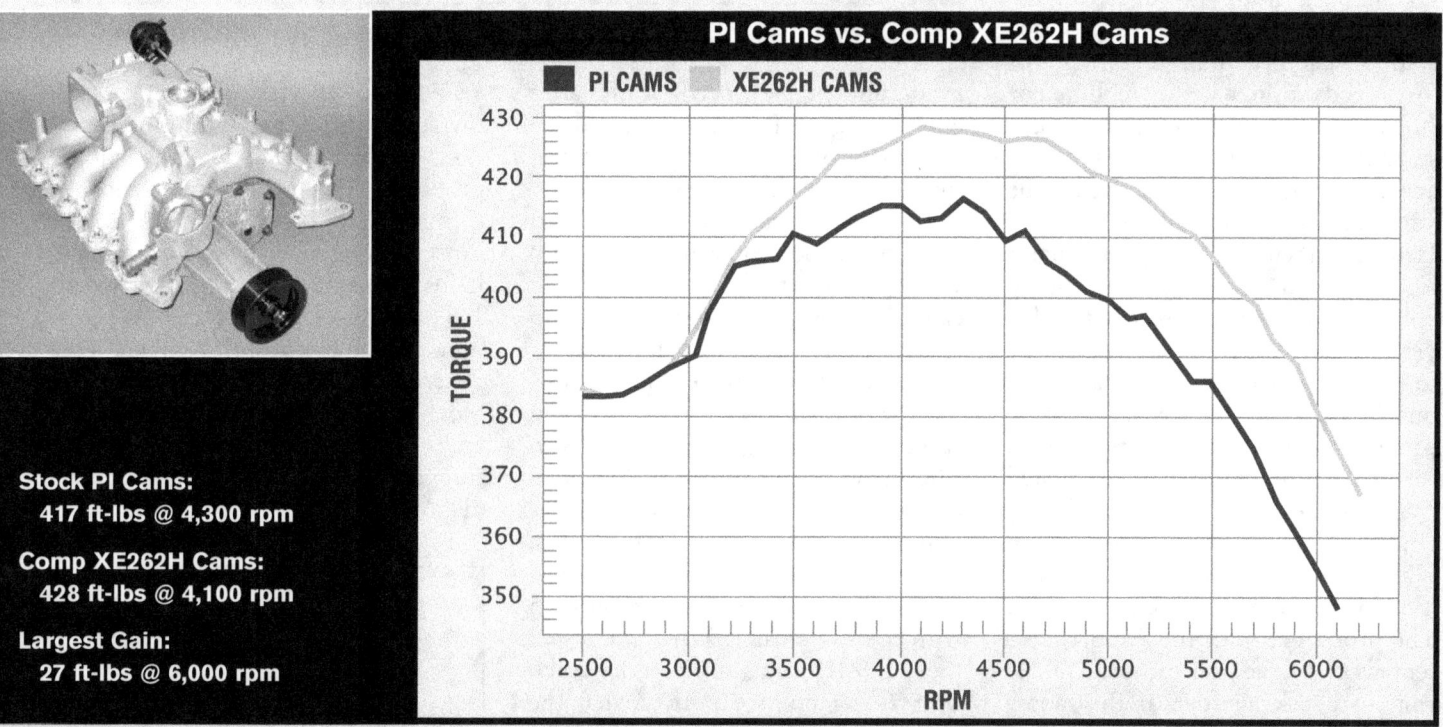

Stock PI Cams:
417 ft-lbs @ 4,300 rpm

Comp XE262H Cams:
428 ft-lbs @ 4,100 rpm

Largest Gain:
27 ft-lbs @ 6,000 rpm

Supercharged PI 2-Valve GT: Stock Cams vs. Comp XE262H Cams (Torque)
Perhaps the most impressive thing about this cam test was that there was no tradeoff in power with the Comp cams on this supercharged combination. The wilder cam timing simply improved the power output from 3,300 rpm all the way to 6,000 rpm.

Building 4.6/5.4L Ford Horsepower on the Dyno

Test 4: Vortech Supercharged Early 2-Valve GT: Comp Cams XE274H Camshafts

This supercharged cam comparison was actually a retest (of sorts) on the Comp 4.6L 2-valve cams used in Test 1. The idea was to demonstrate whether the XE274H cams originally designed for a naturally aspirated combination would work well on a supercharged motor. Due to a snafu with the stock Mustang PI cams (one was lost), I was forced to compare the XE274H cams to a set of 4.6L truck cams that I got at the last minute from Accufab's John Mihovitz (at midnight no less – thanks John).

As with most of the testing run on the engine dyno, this modified 4.6L motor was tuned using the F.A.S.T. engine management system. In no way does that make the results less than applicable for street motors running the factory computer. Custom programming is readily available for the factory ECU and should be considered when installing any type of forced induction, whether modified or stock. I shutter to think of installing a supercharger or turbo on any motor and immediately taking it out on the street and stomping on the throttle. Detonation will kill even the strongest forged pistons, where proper tuning will allow you to run trouble free for years. The F.A.S.T. system allowed us to run any size injector and run without the mass-air meter. Since we were primarily concerned with wide-open throttle tuning (and minor associated transition throttle), the F.A.S.T. system was definitely the way to go. Tom Habryzk from Westech had each combination up and running in no time. The procedure with the F.A.S.T. system was to load the motor at 3,000 rpm to check air/fuel. If the motor was lean at any throttle position, fuel was added via the fuel tables. The total timing was kept at a safe 18 degrees during tuning. This procedure was repeated at 3,500 rpm, 4,000 rpm, and then 4,500 rpm until we reached the maximum engine speed. Only after establishing a safe fuel curve did we load the motor and run a sweep test through the rev range.

Do Comp XE274H cams work on a supercharged application? We're about to find out.

The modified 4.6L (TEA-ported heads, PI intake, and Hooker headers) was run first with the stock 4.6L truck cams and then again with the Comp XE274H cams. Unfortunately, no cam timing adjustments were made to optimize the power; both were installed straight up, using the factory (no adjustable) cam sprockets. Not surprisingly, the two cam profiles required decidedly different fuel cures, as the motor produced a great deal more power with the Comp cams than with the stock cams. When we tested the XE274H cams against the stock 1998 GT cams, we noticed that the motor produced more power with the stock cams up to 3,500 rpm, at which point the Comp cams took over. The very same thing happened on the supercharged motor, as the stock cams made more power from 3,000 rpm to 3,500 rpm, but fell off dramatically thereafter. Equipped with the stock cams, the Vortech supercharged motor produced 550 hp and 505 ft-lbs of torque. With the Comp XE274H cams, the engine made 655 hp and 557 ft-lbs. Imagine, a cam change worth 105 hp and 61 ft-lbs of torque. Keep in mind that these power numbers were generated on the stock 1998 short block with only a set of ARP head studs and Fel-Pro gaskets. Careful tuning is the reason we still have a solid 4.6L eager and ready to test!

These Comp XE274 cams were tested against a set of stock 2-valve truck cams.

Camshafts

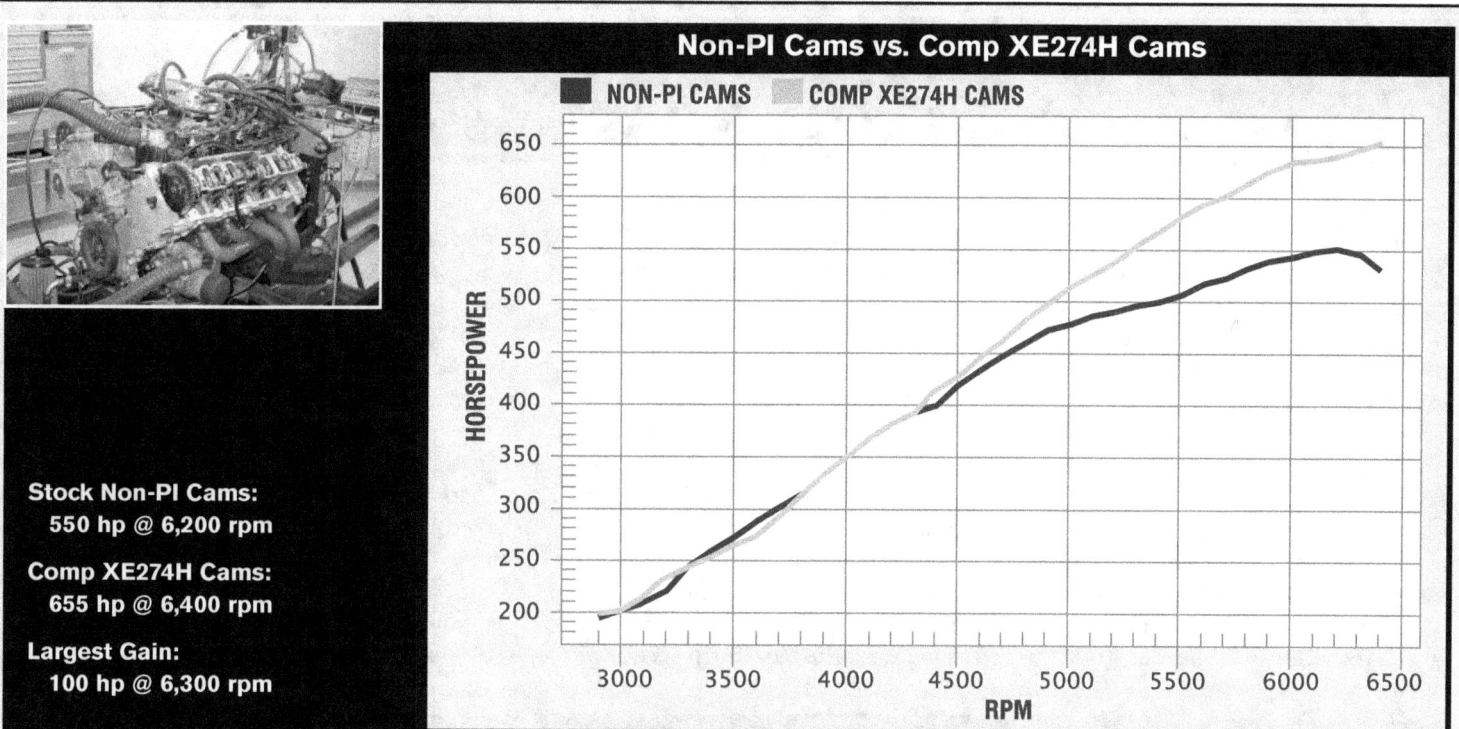

Stock Non-PI Cams:
550 hp @ 6,200 rpm

Comp XE274H Cams:
655 hp @ 6,400 rpm

Largest Gain:
100 hp @ 6,300 rpm

Supercharged Early 2-Valve GT: Non-PI Cams vs. Comp XE274H Cams (Horsepower)
When every other component on the motor has been optimized, the stock cams really restrict the power output of a supercharged 4.6L. Installing the Comp XE274H cams in place of the stock 4.6L truck cams upped the power output by over 100 hp.

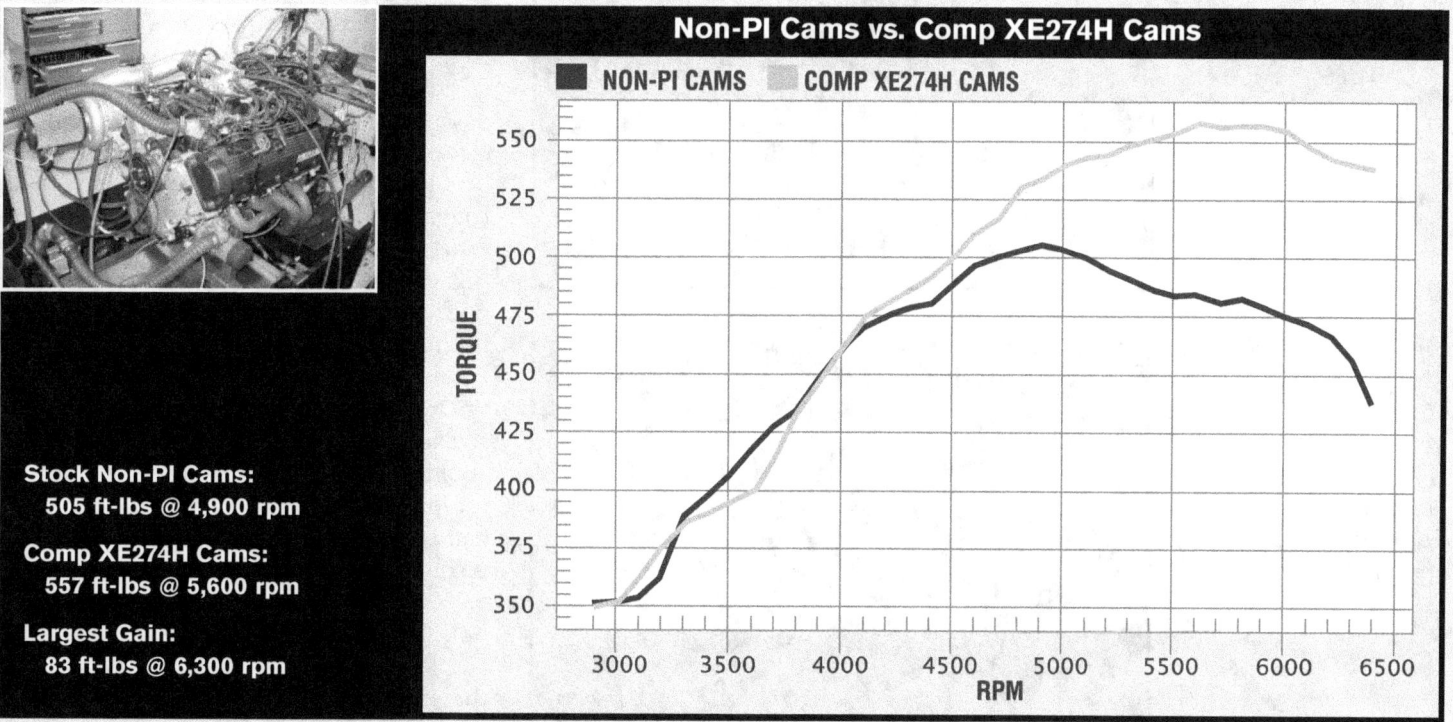

Stock Non-PI Cams:
505 ft-lbs @ 4,900 rpm

Comp XE274H Cams:
557 ft-lbs @ 5,600 rpm

Largest Gain:
83 ft-lbs @ 6,300 rpm

Supercharged Early 2-Valve GT: Non-PI Cams vs. Comp XE274H Cams (Torque)
As was the case with the naturally aspirated test, the stock cams offered slightly more torque up to 3,500 rpm, but beyond 4,000 rpm, it was all Comp cams. The gains down low paled in comparison to the power improvements from 4,000 rpm to 6,000 rpm. Oddly enough, the boost changed very little with this cam change.

Test 5: Naturally Aspirated '03 4-Valve: Cobra Cams vs. Comp Cams XE262AH Camshafts

This test compares the stock '03 Cobra cams and a set of Comp XE262AH cams. Though originally equipped with an Eaton supercharger, the low-compression '03 Cobra crate motor was equipped with a 2001 Cobra intake manifold (and no supercharger). This cam setup was also tested with the Eaton and Kenne Bell superchargers, so be sure to check out Tests 7 and 8. To illustrate the gains offered in naturally aspirated trim, the motor was equipped with the F.A.S.T. management system, a Meziere electric water pump, and Flow-Tech long-tube headers (no mufflers). The motor was tuned for a 13.0:1 air/fuel ratio and 28 degrees of timing. The low-compression 4-valve motor produced 369 hp at 6,000 rpm and 377 ft-lbs of torque at 4,900 rpm. Equipped with the stock cams, the power curve pulled strong up to 5,000 rpm where it flattened out until 6,500 rpm. Despite the low compression, the torque output exceeded 350 ft-lbs from 3,600 to 5,400 rpm. Though this was pretty decent considering the low compression, I knew there was much more power to be had with the right set of performance cams. With the baseline tests out of the way, we tore into the Cobra motor to perform the cam(s) swap.

Before I get to the results of the cam swap, it's important to mention that I checked the position of the stock cams and degreed aftermarket cams before testing. After establishing the baseline power numbers, I installed the degree wheel assembly on loan from Accufab to see how well the factory set up the '03 Cobra crate motor. As it turned out, the stock cams were way off. The right and left intake lobes were as much as 7 degrees different. The exhaust lobes were a little better at just 3 degrees, but we couldn't help wondering how much power was lost due to the stock cams being so far out of whack.

After installing the Comp cams, we went to the effort of degreeing the cams to see how they stacked up against not only the stock cams but also against the supplied cam card. Right to left the Comp cams were perfect, with both intake cams checking in at 117 degrees. The exhaust cams were off by only 1.5 degrees side to side. The odd thing was that the cam card provided the specs at 112 degrees, roughly 5 degrees off from where our cams were currently installed. How this affected power output was anyone's guess, but we'll be looking into it in the very near future. With the new Comp XE262AH cams, we noticed the motor had a slightly more aggressive idle. After the first power pull we could see why. The Comp cams upped the power output from 369 hp to an amazing 426 hp at 6,300 rpm. Since most of the power gains came past 5,000 rpm, the peak torque was up only slightly to 390 ft-lbs. If you check out the graphs, you'll notice that there was a slight loss of low-speed torque from 3,500 to 4,900 rpm, though the torque losses were more than offset by the tremendous power gains past 4,900 rpm.

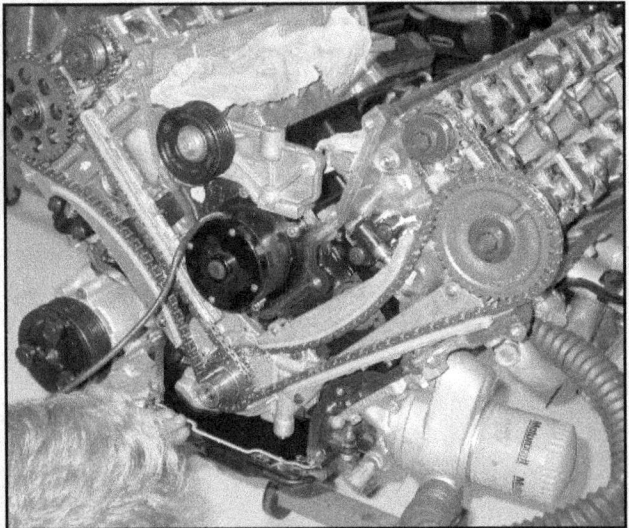

We checked the position of the stock '03 Cobra cams before we removed them from our naturally aspirated test engine. The right and left intake lobes were as much as 7 degrees off, while the exhaust lobes were just 3 degrees off.

After we installed the Comp XE262AH cams, we degreed them and checked them against the cam card. The cams provide a big bump in horsepower, along with a very healthy sound.

Camshafts

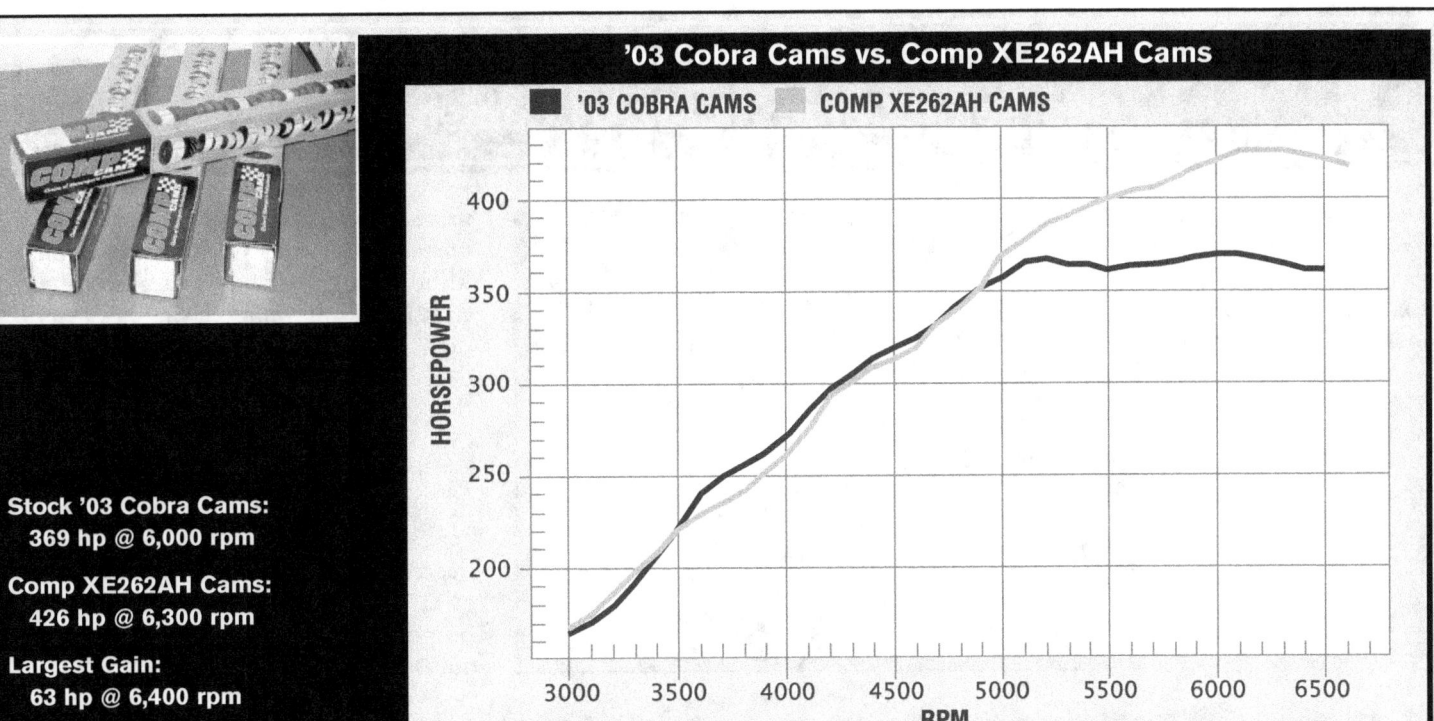

Stock '03 Cobra Cams:
369 hp @ 6,000 rpm

Comp XE262AH Cams:
426 hp @ 6,300 rpm

Largest Gain:
63 hp @ 6,400 rpm

'03 Cobra: Stock Cams vs. Comp XE262AH Cams (Horsepower)
The naturally aspirated '03 Cobra crate motor responded very well to the Comp XE262AH cams. Equipped with the stock cams, the power leveled off at 5,000 rpm but continued to climb past 6,000 rpm with the Comp cams. The Comp cams were worth an extra 63 hp.

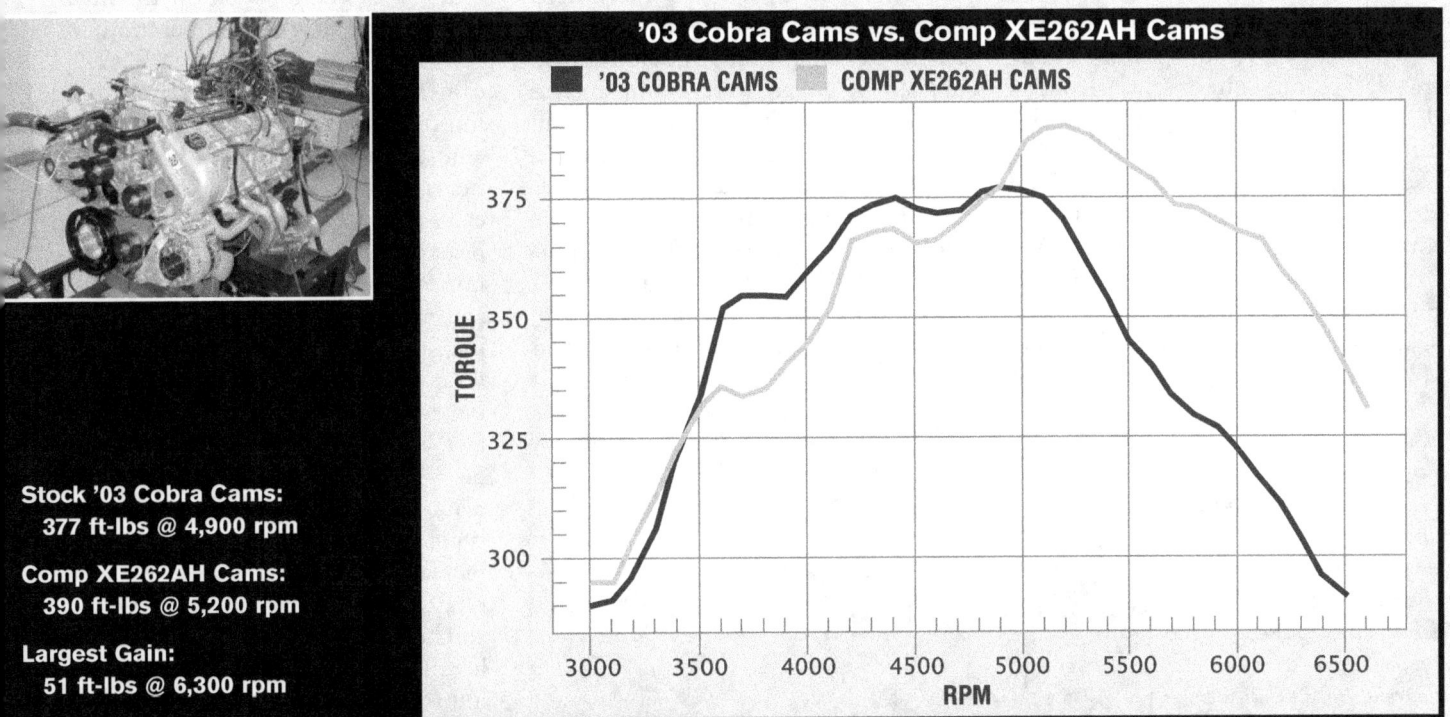

Stock '03 Cobra Cams:
377 ft-lbs @ 4,900 rpm

Comp XE262AH Cams:
390 ft-lbs @ 5,200 rpm

Largest Gain:
51 ft-lbs @ 6,300 rpm

'03 Cobra: Stock Cams vs. Comp XE262AH Cams (Torque)
As is usually the case with cam changes, the huge power gains achieved past 5,000 rpm cost a little bit of torque down low. Despite being off side to side, the stock '03 Cobra cams bettered the Comp cams from 3,000 to 5,000 rpm, but only by 15 to 20 ft-lbs. Additional cam tuning might have decreased the torque loss down low.

Test 6: 4-Valve Cobra: Degreeing Comp XE262AH Camshafts

Degreeing the cams is very important if you want to make as much power as possible. It's imperative that even the factory cams be matched side to side. I've seen the cam timing be off by 8 or 9 degrees.

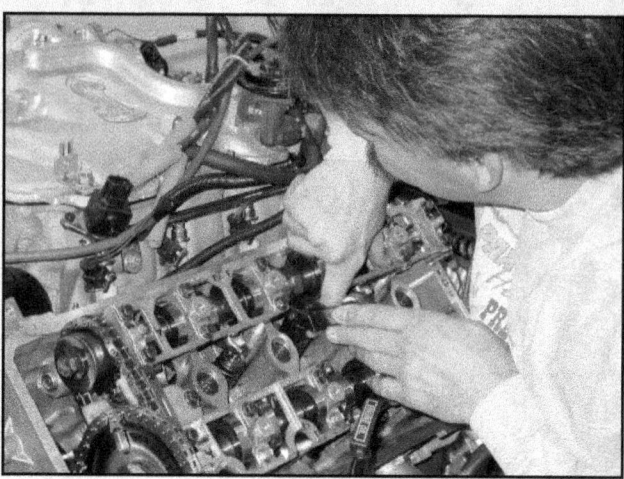

This test features the 4-valve Cobra motor built by Sean Hyland. The 4.6L features a forged steel crank, rods, and flat-top pistons. The flat-top pistons pushed the static compression ratio to near 10.5:1, which is just about perfect for street use. The flat-top design also provided optimum flame travel without interference from a dome. We topped the short block with a set of Ford Racing FR500 heads that had been worked over by Total Engine Airflow, a ported 2001 Cobra intake, and a set of Comp XE262AH cams (the largest that will fit without piston-to-valve interference). The specs on the Comp cams checked in at .425 inches of lift, 226 degrees of intake duration, and 224 degrees of exhaust duration (@ .050). The cams featured a 114-degree lobe separation, though adjusting the cam sprockets can change this. The engine was set up with a stock 4-valve Cobra throttle body and a set of Hooker long-tube headers feeding 3-inch open exhaust. We ran an electric water pump and no other accessories. The air/fuel and timing curves were dialed in using a F.A.S.T. management system. After playing with various timing curves, we were finally rewarded with peak numbers of 426 hp at 6,100 rpm and 394 ft-lbs of torque at 5,000 rpm.

While the power numbers looked good, I was actually expecting a bit more power given the compression, ported heads, and Comp cams. John Mihovitz suggested that we check and adjust the cam timing. Using his years of mod-motor experience, John degreed the cams in their current position and discovered that the intake cams were unbalanced side to side by 6.5 degrees. The driver's side checked in at 114.5 degrees, while the passenger side intake cams were at 108 degrees. Both exhaust cams were even at 113 degrees. To improve the power output of the 4-valve test motor, John advanced both intake cams to 107 degrees. It's imperative that even the factory cams be matched side to side. I've seen the cam timing be off by 8 or 9 degrees. With the two sides so different, one bank of cylinders will certainly be out-powering the other. This is not a desirable situation for maximum power or smooth operation.

After adjusting the XE262AH cams, I ran the SHM 4-valve Cobra motor on the dyno once again. After adjusting the cams, the power jumped up significantly. Dialing both intake cams to 107 degrees resulted in a gain in peak power of 9 hp, though the largest horsepower gain registered from 3,500 rpm to 6,500 rpm was 14 hp. Even more important in the jump in peak power was the fact that the power curve improved throughout the rev range. In fact, advancing the cam(s) resulted in more of a gain at 3,500 rpm than at 6,500 rpm. This is to be expected, as typically advancing the cam timing will increase low-speed power while retarding the cams will improve top-end horsepower. True to form, advancing the cams (even just one intake cam) improved the torque production by as much as 22 ft-lbs. It is this attention to detail that makes the difference between a good-running Cobra and an average one. It also helps explain why some stock Cobras are faster than others right off the showroom floor.

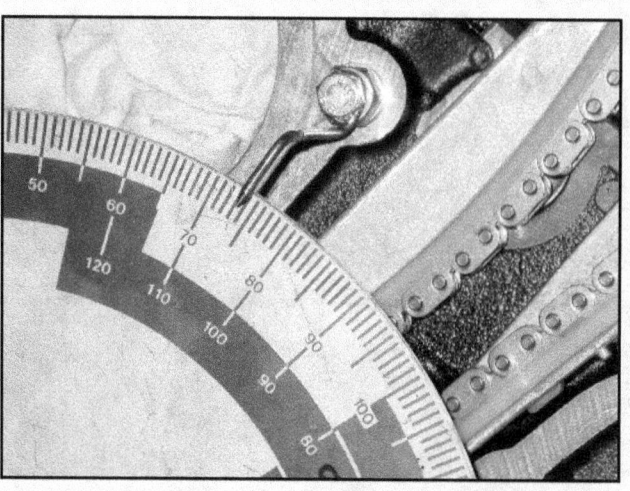

We checked our Comp cams and found that the intake cams were unbalanced side to side by 6.5 degrees. The driver's side checked in at 114.5 degrees, while the passenger-side intake cams were at 108 degrees. Both exhaust cams were even at 113 degrees.

Camshafts

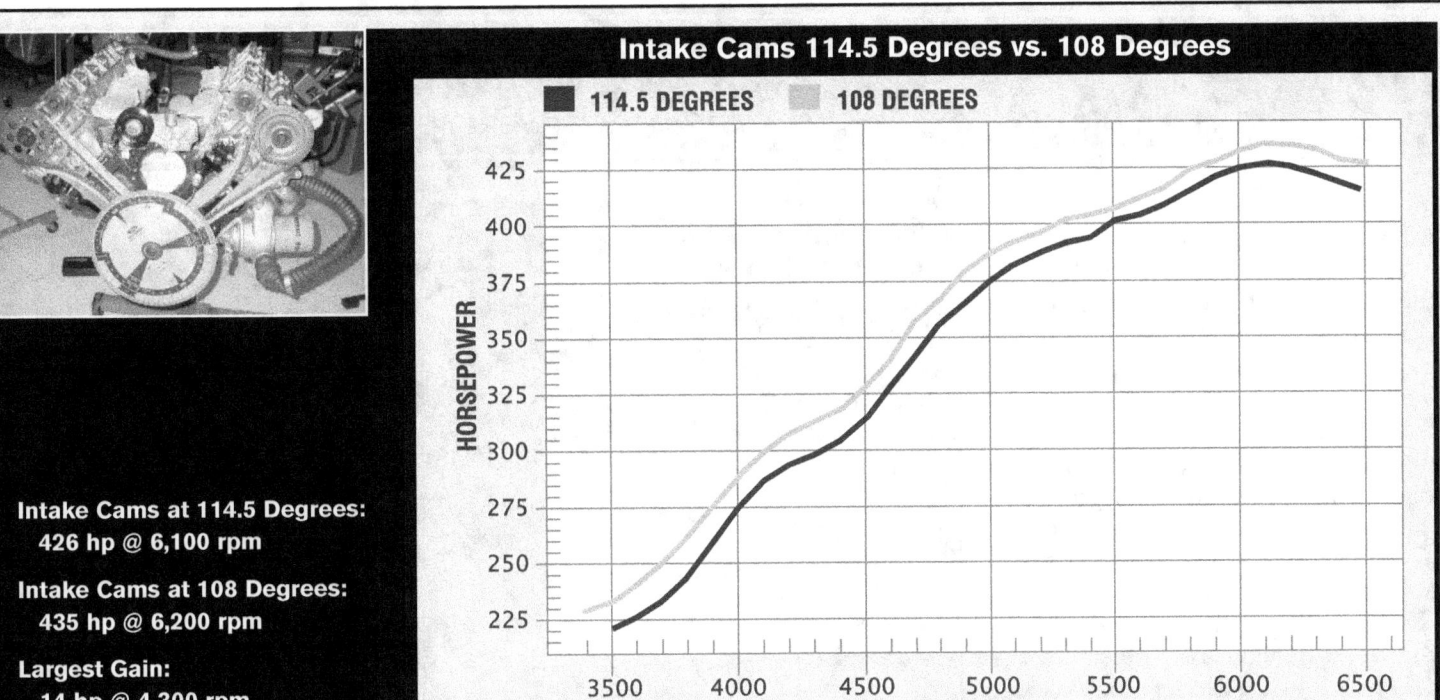

Intake Cams at 114.5 Degrees:
426 hp @ 6,100 rpm

Intake Cams at 108 Degrees:
435 hp @ 6,200 rpm

Largest Gain:
14 hp @ 4,300 rpm

Degreeing Comp XE262AH Cams: 4-Valve Cobra (Horsepower)
When you add power from 3,500 rpm (and below if we bothered to run the motor there) to 6,500 rpm, chances are that you've done something right. With the help of John Mihovitz, advancing the cams from 113 to 114 degrees to 108 degrees was worth a solid 14 hp and a consistent 10 to 12 hp through most of the power curve.

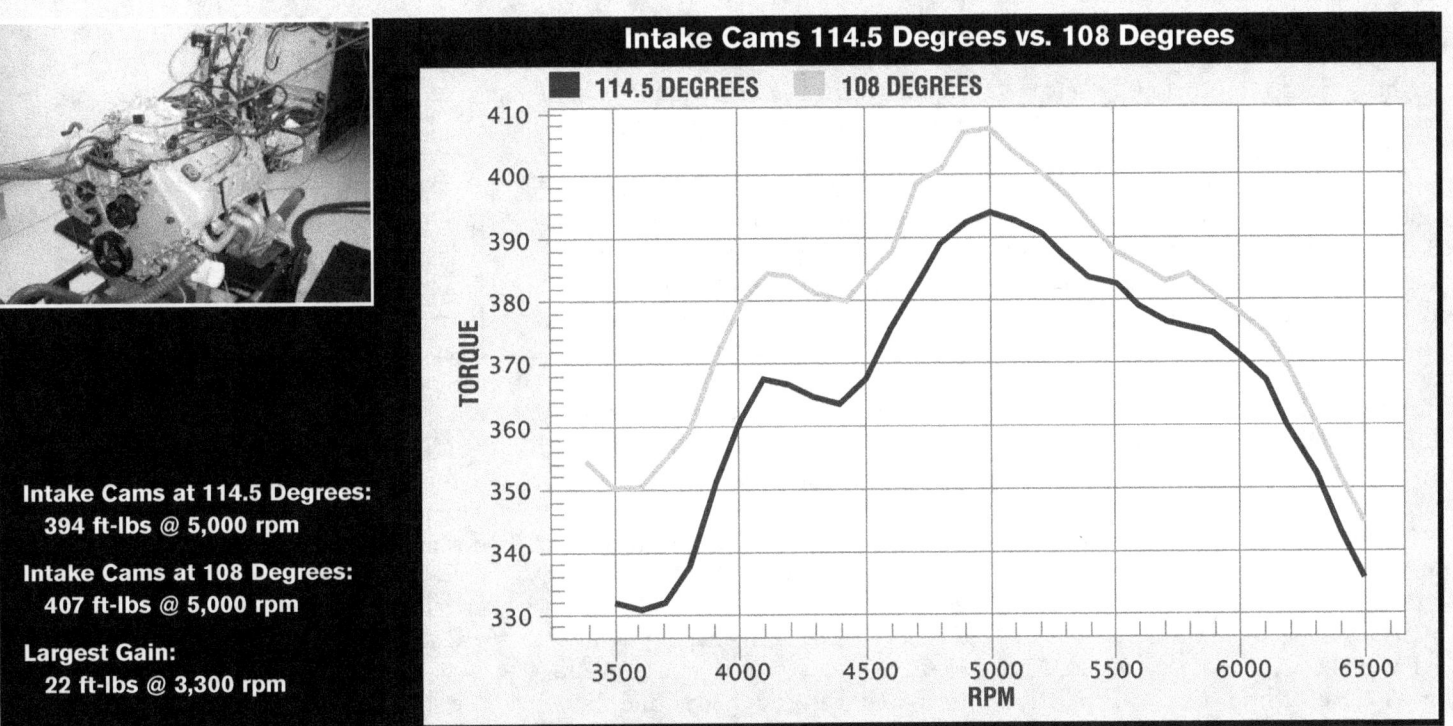

Intake Cams at 114.5 Degrees:
394 ft-lbs @ 5,000 rpm

Intake Cams at 108 Degrees:
407 ft-lbs @ 5,000 rpm

Largest Gain:
22 ft-lbs @ 3,300 rpm

Degreeing Comp XE262AH Cams: 4-Valve Cobra (Torque)
As expected, advancing the cams paid larger dividends at lower engine speeds. Altering the cam timing by nearly 6 degrees increased the torque production by as much as 22 ft-lbs. I guess Mr. Mihovitz knows a thing or two about mod motors.

Test 7: Eaton Supercharged '03 4-Valve Cobra: Comp Cams XE262AH Camshafts

Like their selections for the 2-valve mod motors, Comp Cams offers a wide variety of different cam profiles. Not all 4-valve 4.6L motors (or their owners) will respond to the same cam profile, so Comp whipped up no less than 10 combinations ranging from mild replacement cams to maximum-effort race cams; they even offer cam combos for supercharged and nitrous applications. The new Comp 4-valve modular cam choices are broken down into three series: the Xtreme RPM, the Xtreme XE-R, and the XE-R Supercharged and Nitrous grinds. All of the Xtreme RPM cams feature .425 inches of lift with duration figures ranging from 218 degrees to 234 degrees (@ .050). The remainder of the Comp offerings features a split lift of .475 inches (intake) and .450 inches (exhaust). The Xtreme XE-R series share 114-degree lobe separation angle, while the supercharged and nitrous cams feature slightly wider 116-degree lobe separation angles.

Our first choice of cams for our supercharged '03–'04 Cobra motor is one of the XE-R Supercharged and Nitrous grinds. Unfortunately, these cams required a valvespring upgrade that was not available to meet our dyno schedule. Rather than give up and reschedule the test, I decided to do the next best thing and proceed forward with cams that don't require a spring upgrade. Basically, this meant some Xtreme RPM cams with only .425 inches of lift. The low lift figures allowed me to retain the stock Ford valvesprings without fear of coil bind. After looking over the four Xtreme RPM offerings, I chose the XE262AH cams. According to Comp, the XE262AH cams were designed to provide great street performance with significant horsepower and torque gains without computer modifications. For our F.A.S.T. engine manage-

For this test, we're swapping out the stock '03 Cobra cams for a set of Comp Cams XE262AHs. It will be interesting to see if the supercharged engine picks up more or less power than the naturally aspirated version.

ment, the plug-n-play feature wasn't as important, but it sure would be for the vast majority of Cobra owners running the factory ECU. The dual-pattern XE262AH cams offered 226 degrees of intake duration, 222 degrees of exhaust duration, and a 114-degree lobe separation angle to go along with the .425 inches of lift (both intake and exhaust).

The first step was to run the '03 Cobra crate motor with the stock cams and the Eaton M112 supercharger. The motor was equipped with the F.A.S.T. management system, a Meziere electric water pump, Accufab inlet and throttle body, and Flow-Tech long-tube headers (no mufflers). The motor was tuned to an 11.8:1 air/fuel ratio with 23 degrees of timing using a 7.5-inch crank pulley and a stock blower pulley (for 9.3 psi).

With the stock cams, the engine produced 532 hp at 6,600 rpm and 480 ft-lbs of torque. Equipped with the Comp cams, the peak power jumped from to 557 hp, a gain of 25 hp. Oddly enough, the Comp cams improved the peak power by as much as 63 hp on the naturally aspirated combination. The peak torque was up only 10 ft-lbs, from 481 ft-lbs to 491 ft-lbs. Though the peak-to-peak gains were not as high as the NA combination, there was much less of a tradeoff in low-speed power. In fact, the power gains started much earlier in the rev range on the supercharged combination (3,800 rpm) than the NA motor (4,900 rpm). While the peak-to-peak gains were not quite half as much as with the NA motor, the supercharged motor offered the gains for another 1,000 rpm.

Camshafts

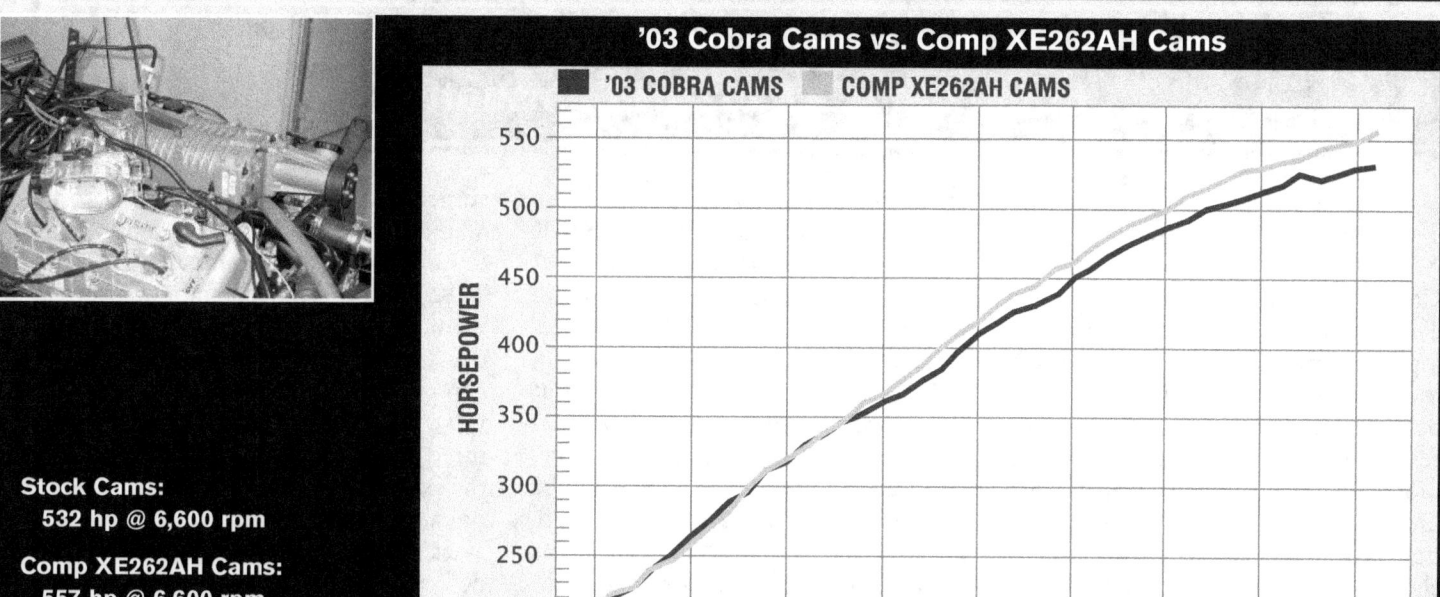

Stock Cams:
532 hp @ 6,600 rpm

Comp XE262AH Cams:
557 hp @ 6,600 rpm

Largest Gain:
21 hp @ 6,400 rpm

Eaton Supercharged '03 Cobra (10 psi): Stock Cams vs. Comp XE262AH Cams: (Horsepower)
The supercharged combination obviously responded favorably to the XE262AH profiles, but the gains were not quite as impressive as on the naturally aspirated combination. It should be noted that the Comp cams out-powered the stock profiles much earlier in the rev range than with the NA combination. Still, 25 extra horsepower and a solid 10 to 15 hp from 3,500 rpm to 6,500 rpm make the cam swap a worthwhile proposition.

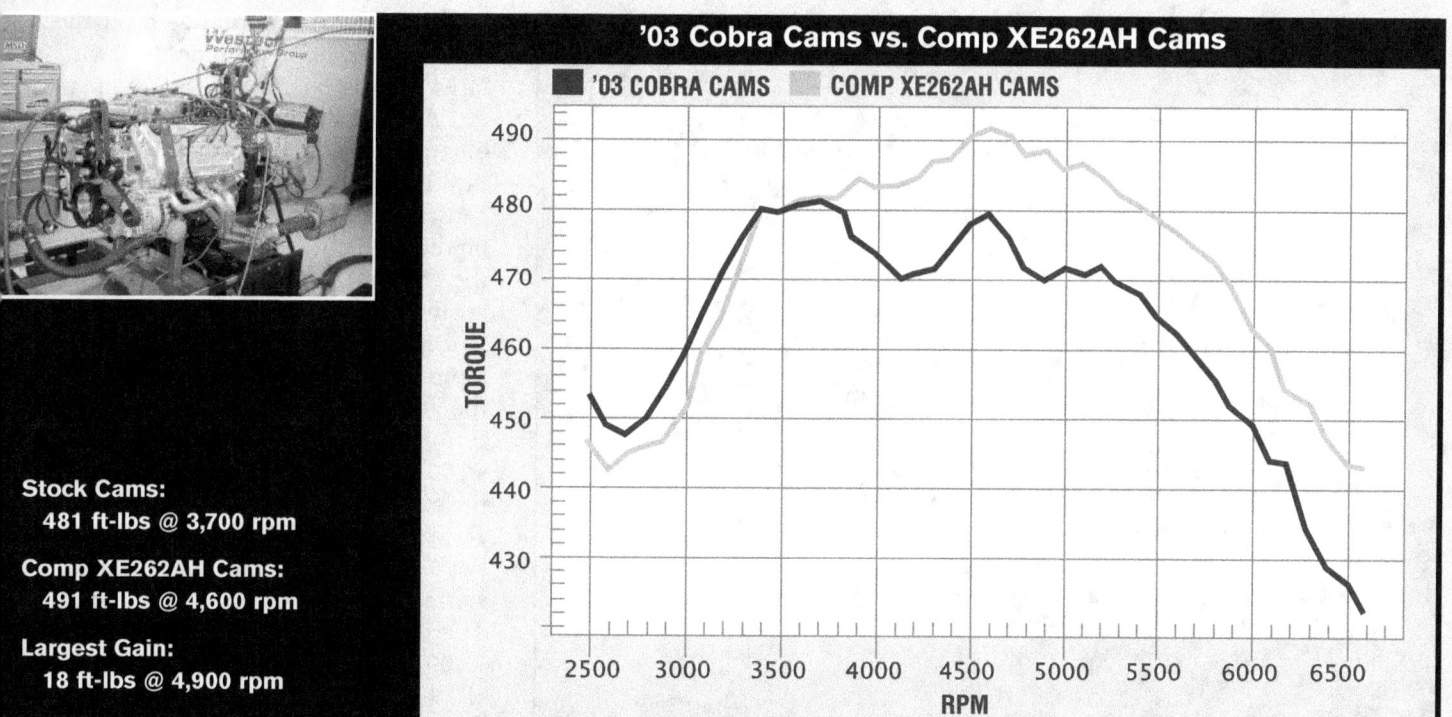

Stock Cams:
481 ft-lbs @ 3,700 rpm

Comp XE262AH Cams:
491 ft-lbs @ 4,600 rpm

Largest Gain:
18 ft-lbs @ 4,900 rpm

Eaton Supercharged '03 Cobra (10 psi): Stock Cams vs. Comp XE262AH Cams: (Torque)
There was a slight loss in low-speed power with the Comp cams, but not nearly as much as on the naturally aspirated combination. The extra 18 ft-lbs would certainly be welcomed. It's possible that additional power was available with adjustments to the cam timing (moving the cam sprockets).

Test 8: Kenne Bell Supercharged '03 4-Valve Cobra: Comp Cams XE262AH Camshafts

Test 8 is actually a continuation of Tests 5 and 7, as I compared the Comp XE262AH cams against the factory '03 Cobra cams on an '03 Cobra motor. The comparison was made in naturally aspirated trim (Test 5) as well as with the Eaton supercharger (Test 7). I also decided to test using a Kenne Bell twin-screw supercharger as I felt the Eaton blower may have been nearing its flow limit and that the more efficient (and powerful) twin-screw blower might show better improvements. Those eagle-eyed readers who have access to a Comp Cams catalog may have checked out the spec box and noticed that the supercharged cam offerings (like the XE262AH) for the 4.6L 4-valve motors are dual-pattern as well. The difference between the Xtreme RPM and XE-R Supercharged cams was that the supercharged versions featured more exhaust duration. Our XE262AH cams offered 4 degrees more intake duration (226 degrees versus 222 degrees), but the comparable supercharged cams featured a 2-degree split (224 degrees versus 222 degrees) skewed in favor of the exhaust. The XE262AH cams were selected out of necessity, as all of the larger (blower specific) cams required a valvespring upgrade that was unavailable at the time of the dyno test.

A huge thanks goes out to Accufab's John Mihovitz for providing the necessary tools for performing the cam surgery on our 4-valve Cobra motor. Without the valvespring compressor, custom piston stop (to precisely locate TDC), and associated components, we would never have been able to perform this 4-valve cam swap. While the main components are very similar to the 2-valve GT motor, the 4-valve also featured a secondary drive assembly from the exhaust cam to the intake. This secondary chain drive naturally required a second pair of cam sprockets and a dedicated chain tensioner. The cam swap required compressing and removing all 32 hydraulic lifters. The 4-valve cam swap was not terribly difficult, just time consuming. Equipped with the stock cams, the Kenne Bell-supercharged '03 Cobra motor produced 670 hp at 6,600 rpm and 578 ft-lbs of torque at 4,300 rpm. Stock cams or not, this was pretty impressive. Check out the chapter on 4-valve supercharging for a rundown on the gains offered by the Kenne Bell twin-screw blower over the stock Eaton.

As with all the supercharged combinations, the air/fuel ratio was set at 11.8:1 and the total timing was kept constant at 23 degrees. The cam swap on the '03 Cobra motor equipped with the Kenne Bell blower offered a greater power gain than with the Eaton, but still less than in naturally aspirated trim. The Comp cams upped the power peak to 704 hp, while the torque peak jumped to 597 ft-lbs at 4,800 rpm. Equipped with the Eaton, the cams showed power gains starting at 3,700 rpm. With the Kenne Bell twin-screw blower, the improvements started slightly lower at 3,400 rpm. The gains really improved starting at 3,900 rpm and were pretty consistent all the way out to 6,500 rpm. The Comp cams improved the peak power output by 34 hp and the peak torque by 30 ft-lbs. There may be even more power available by advancing or retarding the profiles.

The Comp cams XE262AH are tested again in our '03 Cobra engine, this time with a Kenne Bell supercharger running 14 psi. The gains from the cams were higher than with the stock Eaton supercharger, but lower than when the engine was naturally aspirated.

Camshafts

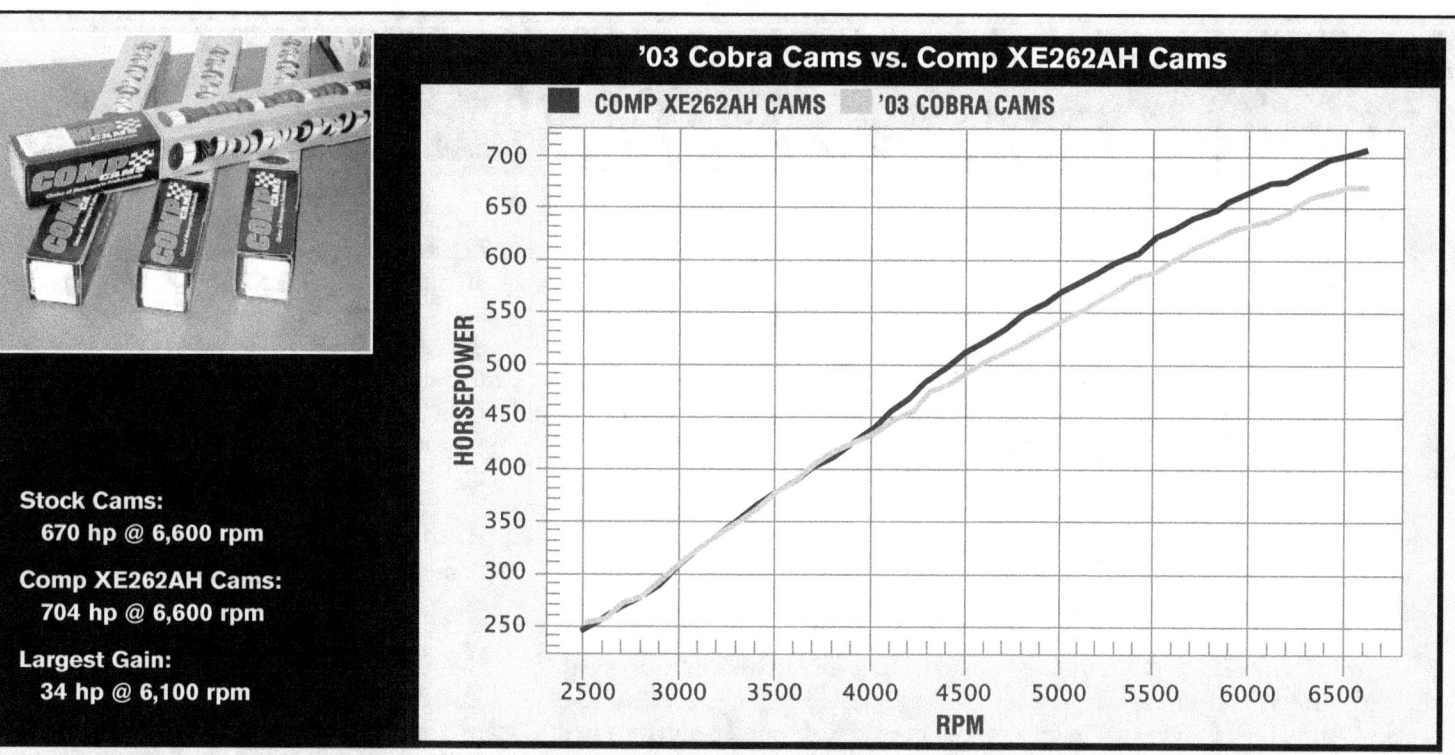

Stock Cams:
670 hp @ 6,600 rpm

Comp XE262AH Cams:
704 hp @ 6,600 rpm

Largest Gain:
34 hp @ 6,100 rpm

Kenne Bell Supercharged '03 Cobra (14 psi): Stock Cams vs. Comp XE262AH Cams: (Horsepower)
As with the Eaton supercharger, the cam swap on the '03 Cobra motor with the Kenne Bell showed earlier improvement compared to the naturally aspirated tests. The Comp cams offered additional power starting at just 3,400 rpm. The additional power (as much as 34 hp) was available all the way out to 6,600 rpm.

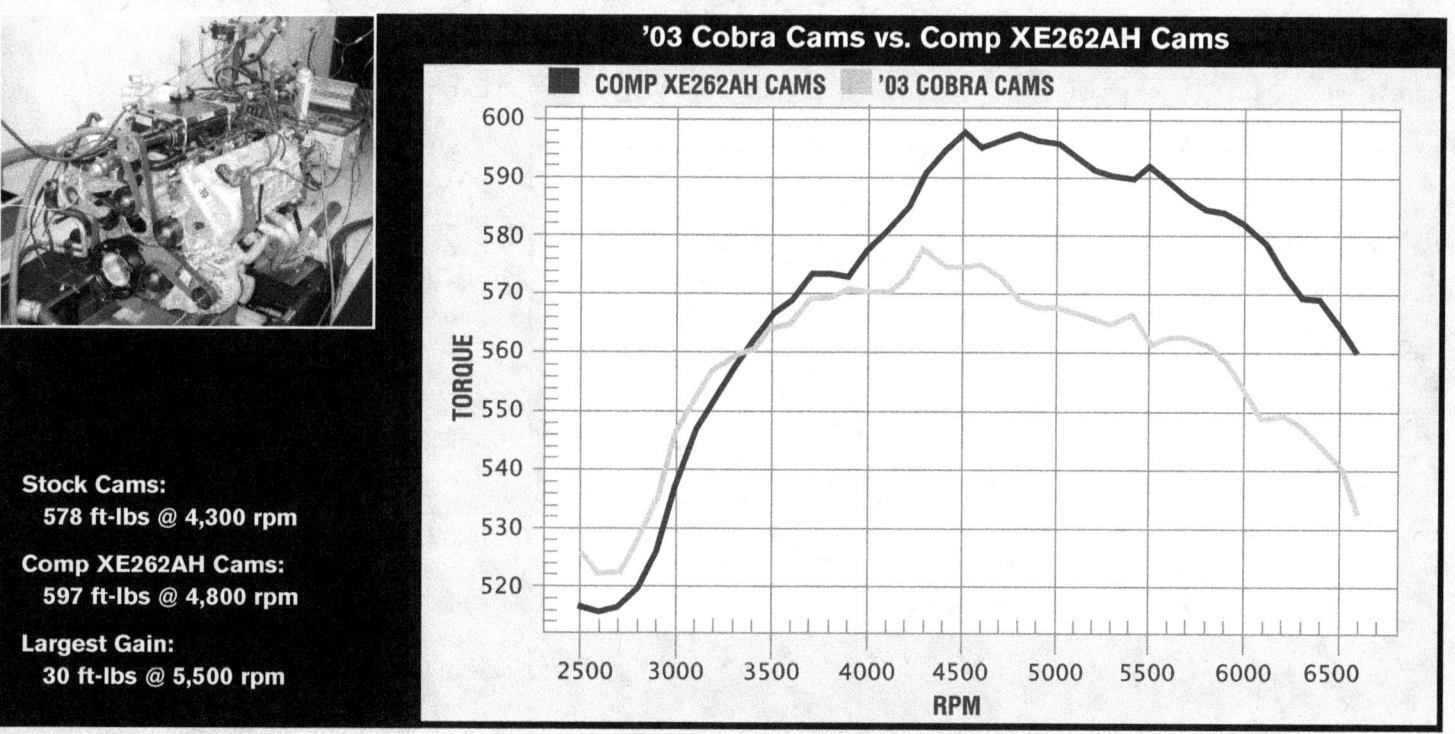

Stock Cams:
578 ft-lbs @ 4,300 rpm

Comp XE262AH Cams:
597 ft-lbs @ 4,800 rpm

Largest Gain:
30 ft-lbs @ 5,500 rpm

Kenne Bell Supercharged '03 Cobra (14 psi): Stock Cams vs. Comp XE262AH Cams: (Torque)
Equipped with the Comp cams, the supercharged 4.6L produced almost 600 ft-lbs of torque. In fact, the supercharged combination produced more than 520 ft-lbs down as low as 2,500 rpm. Such is the benefit of the positive-displacement supercharger.

Test 9: Kenne Bell Supercharged '03 4-Valve Cobra: Crower Stage 2 Camshafts

Rather than testing the Crower Stage 2 cams on a stock '03 Cobra motor, I decided to try them on something a bit more powerful – an '03 Cobra equipped with a Kenne Bell blower upgrade. Though no internal mods were performed to the 4-valve motor, the Cobra did feature a Kenne Bell cold-air intake system, the stock 90-mm mass-air meter, and an Accufab single-blade throttle body and elbow. Given the additional power potential of the modified mod motor, the stock injectors were ditched in favor of a set of 60 pounders fed through ½-inch fuel line by a pair of stock Cobra fuel pumps augmented with a Kenne Bell Boost-A-Pump. During high-boost testing, the motor was run with C16 race fuel, but runs daily on 91-octane pump gas. This Kenne Bell supercharged street car has run in the 9s!

With all that supercharged power forcing its way into the motor, it was imperative to get it all out as well. The

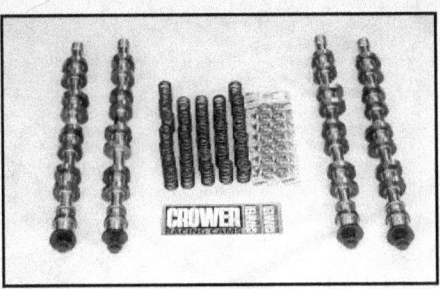

The Crower Stage 2 supercharger cam kit consisted of cams, springs, and retainers.

exhaust system consisted of a set of Kooks headers, high-flow cat pipe, and a Bassani cat-back exhaust system. In a quest for improved ETs, the Cobra-exclusive independent rear suspension was replaced with a standard-issue solid rear axle featuring 3.55:1 gears. The stock tranny has held up to the abuse but the stock clutch was upgraded with a Center Force Dual-Friction setup with matching steel flywheel. Using the new Superchips Custom Tuning Advantage software, a Kenne Bell custom chip was used to dial in the combination with 23 degrees of total timing and a steady air/fuel mixture of 11.7:1. With the stock Cobra cams, the engine produced peak numbers of 618 hp and 642 ft-lbs of torque at a maximum boost pressure of 25.6 psi (to the rear wheels). This peak reading was recorded at 5,500 rpm, as ignition misfire caused some problems with high-RPM power readings. As we have come to expect of twin-screw supercharged Cobra motors, the torque curve was every bit as impressive as the power curve. The KB-augmented '03 thumped out more than 600 ft-lbs of torque from below 2,900 rpm to 5,500 rpm. Imagine what 600+ ft-lbs of torque feels like at 3,000 rpm.

Given that our test motor was a modified supercharged Cobra street motor, we selected Crower's Stage 2 cams designed specifically for supercharged applications. They offer 222 degrees of both intake and exhaust duration (@ .050) along with .475 inches of lift. This compares to a 186/194 duration split and .392/.390 lift split for the factory 4-valve cams (according to literature supplied by Crower). The supercharged motor was run again on the DynoJet, with the only change being installing the Crower cams. The data logging indicated a slight drop in boost with the cams, which is always a sign that the efficiency of the motor has improved. The cams made enough of a difference that minor tuning was necessary to duplicate the 11.7:1 air/fuel ratio curve achieved with the stock cams. Once tuned, the Crowerized Cobra put down 651 hp at 5,500 rpm, while the torque peak jumped to 674 ft-lbs. Measured peak-to-peak, the Crower cams improved the power output by 33 hp and 30 ft-lbs of torque. In a later test with the ignition misfire cured, the motor produced 681 hp.

One unique aspect of this test is that the engine is in the car, so the power gains tested on a chassis dyno instead of on an engine dyno. This means that you have to consider the losses through the drivetrain and running the other accessories when comparing/analyzing the final numbers.

Camshafts

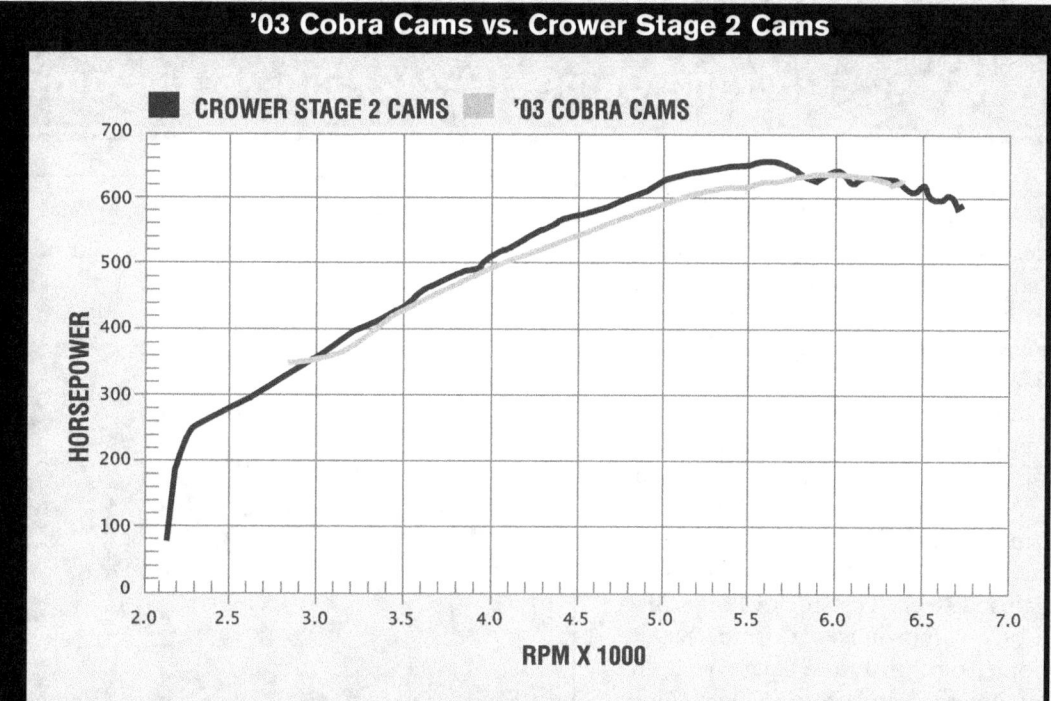

Stock Cams:
618 hp @ 5,500 rpm

Crower Stage 2 Cams:
651 hp @ 5,500 rpm

Largest Gain:
33+ hp @ 5,500 rpm

Kenne Bell Supercharged '03 4-Valve Cobra: Stock vs. Crower Stage 2 Cams (Horsepower)
The Crower cams offered plenty of power from 3,000 rpm all the way to 6,500 rpm. The problem with this test was that the ignition system was not cooperating and would misfire while running 25 psi of boost. It's obvious from the power curves that the Crower cams offered significant horsepower gains that only increased with engine speed. This motor eventually went on to produce 681 hp at the wheels.

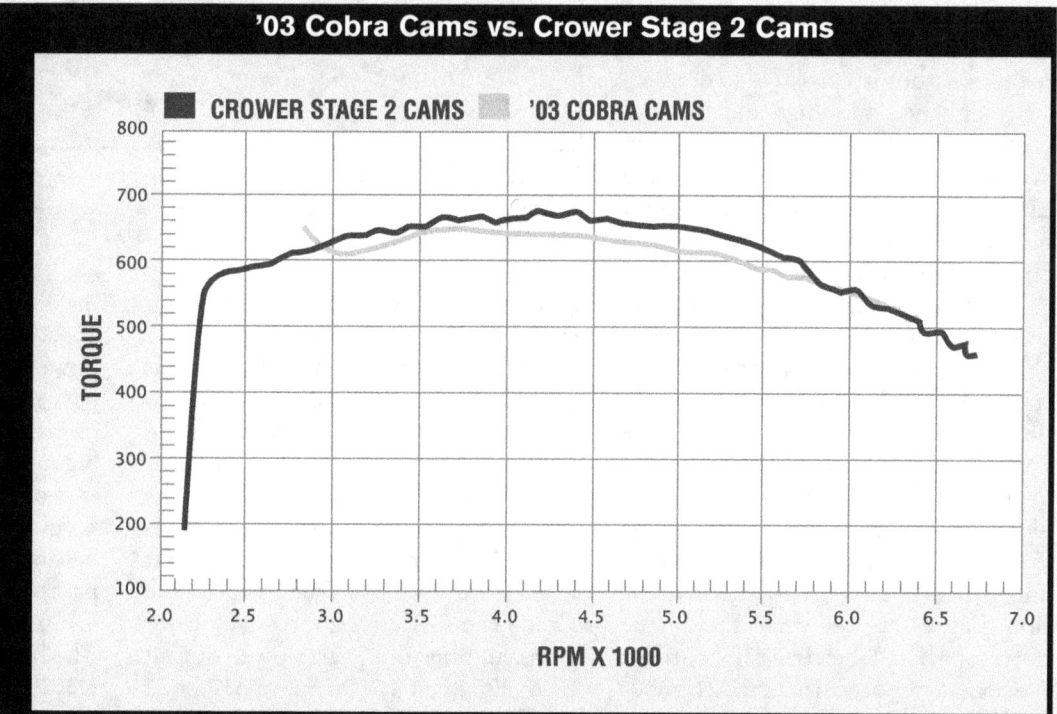

Stock Cams:
642 ft-lbs @ 4,400 rpm

Crower Stage 2 Cams:
675 ft-lbs @ 4,400 rpm

Largest Gain:
33 ft-lbs @ 4,400 rpm

Kenne Bell Supercharged '03 4-Valve Cobra: Stock vs. Crower Stage 2 Cams (Torque)
A street car that makes over 600 ft-lbs not just at some peak but also from 2,500 rpm to 5,500 rpm is bordering on insane. This billiard-table-smooth torque curve is why these '03-'04 Cobras are such fun on the street. Add a set of Crower Stage 2 cams and the fun factor only increases.

Building 4.6/5.4L Ford Horsepower on the Dyno

Chapter 4

Test 10: PI 2-Valve GT: Crane Cams HR-212/550-25-15 Camshafts

The key to successfully choosing a cam profile is to choose one that's designed for a specific operating range. Given that most street 4.6L 2-valve Mustangs operate over a wide RPM range (from say 1,500 rpm to 6,000 rpm), it would be nice to have cams that optimize power production in this 4,500-rpm power band. Unfortunately, no cam profile can offer this type of power band. The very best we can hope to achieve is to minimize the tradeoffs associated with the power gains we seek. The stock PI cams offer a nice compromise. It's important to point out that the factory didn't choose the cam profile solely for its power band, but rather for its combination of peak and average power production, emissions output, and cycle life (or longevity). With so many design variables, it's only natural to assume that the stock cam profiles can be improved upon. The stock profiles are pretty tough to beat in the lower rev ranges, but it's possible to dramatically enhance midrange and top-end power without sacrificing too much down low. In the case of the Crane cams tested on our Sean Hyland mod motor, the tradeoff was skewed way in favor of the additional power.

With daily street use in mind, we selected the mildest cam profiles available from Crane. To properly illustrate the merits of a set of street performance cams, we'll be testing the Crane Cams HR-212/550-25-15 grinds for the 4.6L PI 2-valve motor. The HR-212/550-25-15 cams offer .550 inches of lift for both the intake and exhaust with dual-pattern duration figures. Given that the intake ports of the PI heads easily outflow the exhaust ports, the HR-212/550-25-15 cams offered 212 degrees of intake duration and 218 degrees of exhaust duration. With the cams installed (as recommended by Crane) at 110 degrees (intake) and 120 degrees

This test will show you what some mild cams can do for a PI engine with only headers and a throttle body and matching elbow. You don't have do go to the bottom of the page to find some great cams for your street car.

(exhaust), this left the lobe separation at an idle-friendly 115 degrees.

Previous testing has shown that performance cam profiles for the 4.6L 2-valve motor usually offer significant power gains past 4,000 rpm, but that the additional power can come at the expense of low-speed torque. Such is the tradeoff inherent in a dramatic shift in the torque curve. True to form, the Crane cams offered impressive power gains, upping the peak power output from 297 hp at 4,900 rpm to 332 hp at 5,500 rpm. Interestingly enough, though the engine speed where peak power occurred shifted by 600 rpm, the torque peak shifted by only 100 rpm. Equipped with the Crane cams, the 4.6L PI motor produced 347 ft-lbs at 4,200 rpm. As expected, most of the power gains came after 4,000 rpm. Out past 5,500 rpm, the power output improved by as much as 50 hp. With big power gains on the top end, we expected big losses down low, but the Crane cams sacrificed very little power below 3,700 rpm for the huge gains past 4,100 rpm. From 3,700 rpm to 4,100 the power output was identical. The largest torque loss was 13 ft-lbs at 3,300 rpm – a small price to pay for an extra 50 hp. With maximum acceleration occurring between 4,000 rpm and 6,000 rpm, expect a dramatic drop in ETs with a commensurate increase in trap speed.

Camshafts

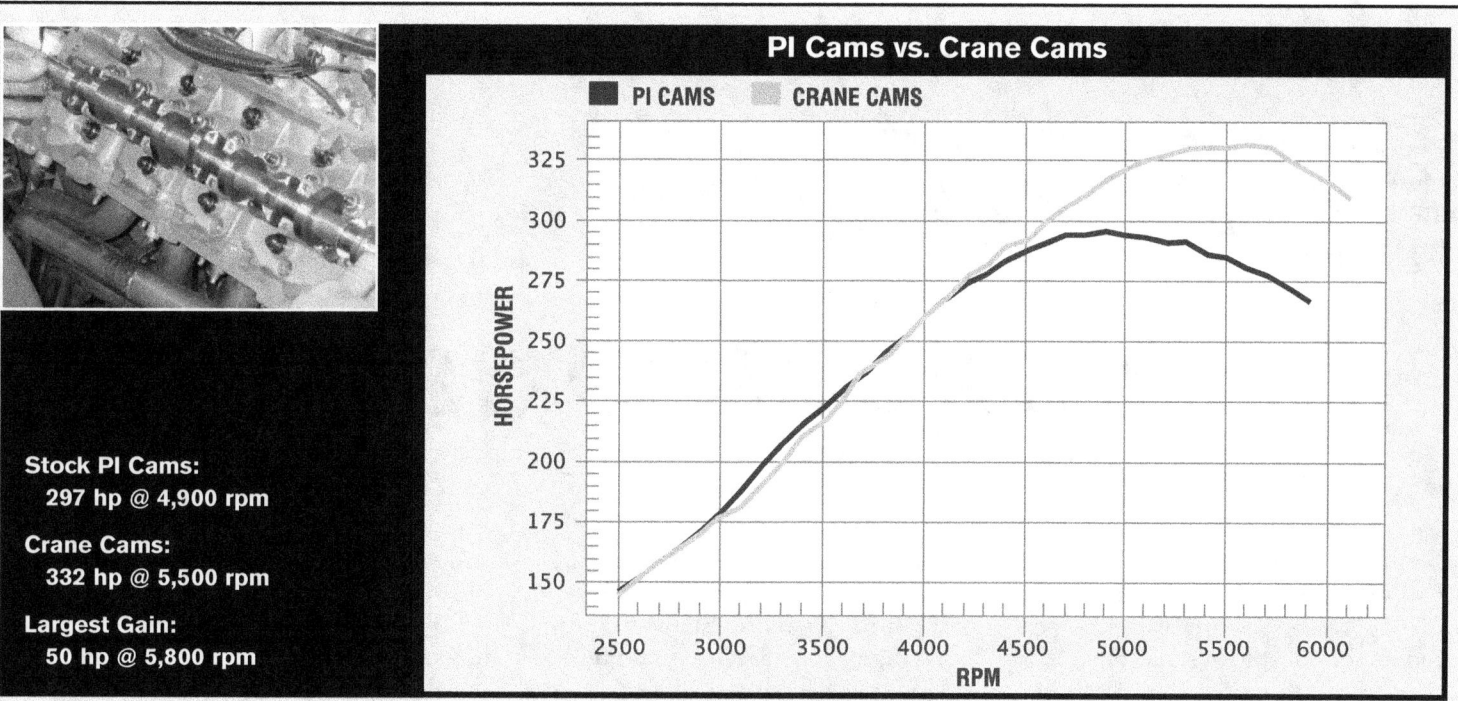

Stock PI Cams:
297 hp @ 4,900 rpm

Crane Cams:
332 hp @ 5,500 rpm

Largest Gain:
50 hp @ 5,800 rpm

PI 2-Valve GT: Stock Cams vs. Crane Cams HR-212/550-25-15 Cams (Horsepower)
The Crane HR-212/550-25-15 cams offered .550 inches of lift, 212 degrees of duration (@ .050) on the intake and 218 degrees on the exhaust. The mild Crane cams produced a solid idle and impressive power gains with only minimal tradeoff in power below 4,000 rpm. Our mild 4.6L PI motor was basically stock; with the exception of Kooks 1⅝-inch headers and Accufab throttle body and elbow. The motor produced 297 hp at 4,900 rpm and 344 ft-lbs of torque at 4,100 rpm. After swapping on the Crane cams, the peak power jumped to 332 hp at 5,500 rpm and 347 ft-lbs of torque at 4,200 rpm. Shifting the torque curve resulted in a dramatic increase in power. The Crane cams offered as much as 50 hp at 5,800 rpm.

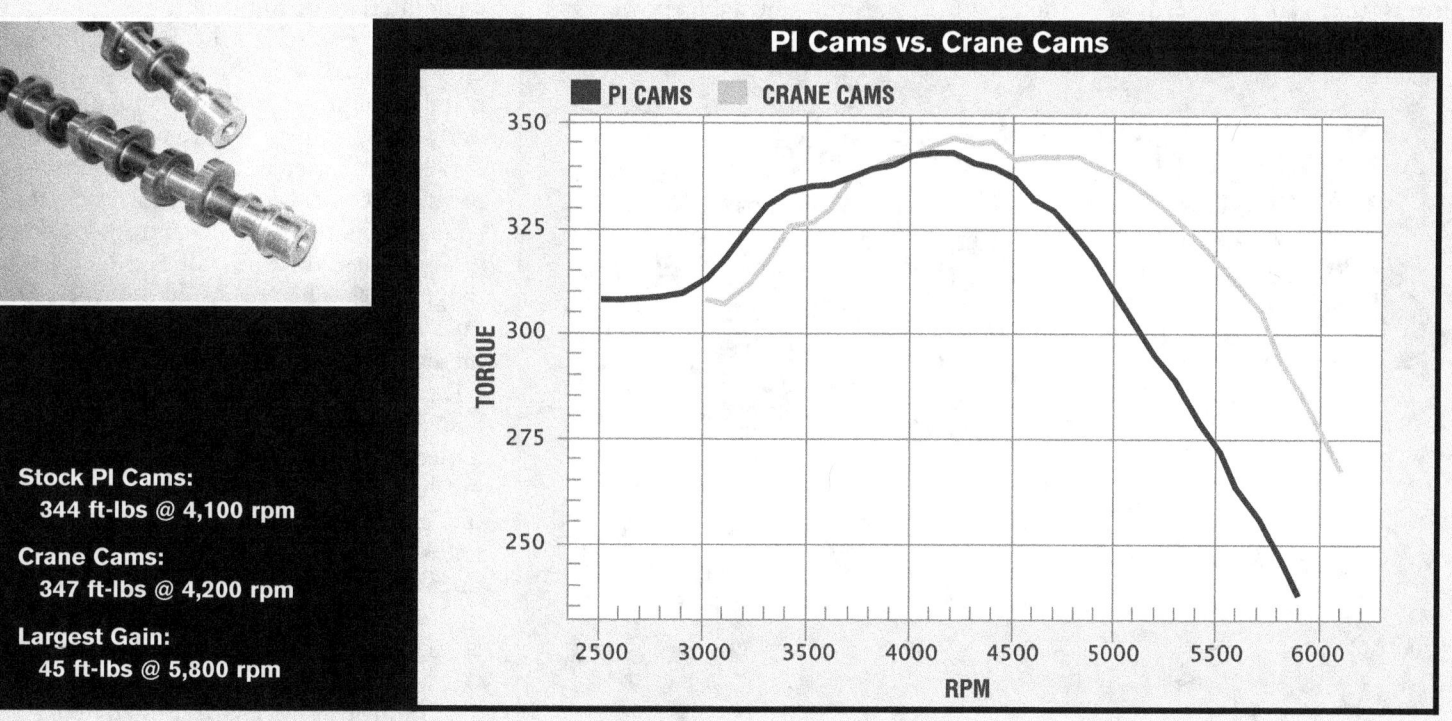

Stock PI Cams:
344 ft-lbs @ 4,100 rpm

Crane Cams:
347 ft-lbs @ 4,200 rpm

Largest Gain:
45 ft-lbs @ 5,800 rpm

PI 2-Valve GT: Stock Cams vs. Crane Cams HR-212/550-25-15 Cams (Torque)
As is evident by the torque curves, the Crane cams lost a tad bit of torque below 3,700 rpm (pretty typical for 4.6L 2-valve cams), but showed big-time torque gains past 4,000 rpm. The stock cam profiles did not offer enough duration to allow the motor to run effectively at higher RPM. Equipped with the stock cams, the torque curve fell off rapidly after peaking at 4,100 rpm. The Crane cams allowed the motor to extend the torque curve another 500 to 600 rpm before falling off significantly. The right cams will really wake up your mod motor.

CHAPTER 5

NITROUS OXIDE

Nitrous oxide is all the rage among mod motor Mustang street racers, and for good reason. Short of a well-prepared turbo or blower, nothing runs harder than a motor on the juice. Nitrous oxide offers a number of benefits, including the ability to adjust the available power level. Much like cranking up the boost pressure on a turbo, jet changes on a nitrous system allow you to literally dial in the extra power. Naturally there is a limit to the amount of nitrous that can be added, something usually dictated by the strength of the internal components of the motor. In addition to the adjustable power, street racers dig nitrous because it can be easily hidden. Of course it doesn't take a genius to figure out that if a '96 Mustang GT dusts off an LS1 Camaro, it's probably sporting something more than a stock 4.6L 2-valve. Nitrous is also cheap. Compared on the basis of available power gains, nitrous offers far and away the best bang for the performance buck. Stealth, adjustable power gains, and easy on the wallet—is it any wonder nitrous has become so popular?

For the uninitiated, nitrous oxide is not a fuel, but rather an oxidizer. Despite the automotive infernos depicted in movies like *The Fast & The Furious*, nitrous oxide does not burn, nor is it likely to incinerate a car. The special effects people in Hollywood – not the compound contained in your shiny blue bottle – cause explosions of the magnitude depicted on the big screen. You could literally open the bottle of nitrous and touch a match to the spray and the only thing that would happen is that the match would go out. No thunderous explosions, no massive fire balls, just an anticlimactic wisp of smoke as the high-pressure, ice-cold stream of nitrous oxide extinguishes the flame. If nitrous oxide doesn't burn, then how does it increase the power? This seems like a logical question, and it's one that has a very simple answer. Nitrous oxide adds power by releasing free oxygen molecules contained in the compound. Since oxygen molecules are a key ingredient in power production (the more oxygen present, the greater the power potential), the release of these oxygen molecules adds to the power potential of the motor. More nitrous equals more free oxygen molecules, which in turn equals more power.

Naturally there's a limit to just how much nitrous can be added to any combination. While most stock motors, even those equipped with cast or hypereutectic pistons, will happily withstand an increase of 40 to 50 percent (depending

Looking for some show with your nitrous-power go? This NOSzle system from NOS is as trick looking as it is powerful.

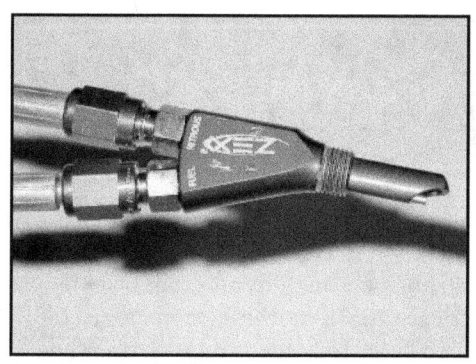

Wet nitrous systems (like this unit from Zex) combine the nitrous and fuel in a single fogger nozzle.

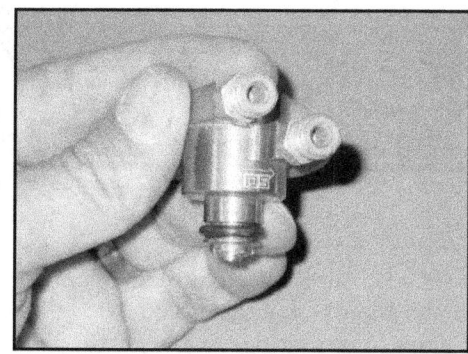

The NOS NOSzle system features these individual nozzles for each cylinder that combines the fuel and nitrous under the injectors.

on the original power output and displacement), adding more power brings the strength of the internal components into play. Building a high-horsepower nitrous motor is not much different than building a high-horsepower turbo or supercharged motor. Short blocks typically include forged rods, cranks, and pistons, with high-strength head gaskets, head studs, and possibly even an O-ringed block. Nitrous and forced-induction motors do, however, differ in their cam timing and cylinder head porting. Nitrous motors tend to like a lot of exhaust flow, since the nitrous adds all the necessary intake oxygen molecules. All that improved intake efficiency must now be allowed to escape, thus the need for greater exhaust port flow and wilder exhaust cam timing (relative to a turbo).

Adding power through nitrous is different than adding the same amount of power through forced induction. Sure, both will add an easy 50, 100, or even 200 hp (or more) to your average modular motor, but how they go about adding the power differs. Both the turbo (or supercharger) and nitrous increase the amount of oxygen molecules available to produce power. Forced induction does so by increasing the mass flow of air. The increase in mass flow is accomplished by pressurizing the air, thus force-feeding the motor more air than it could ingest of its own accord (in naturally aspirated form). The unfortunate side effect of the pressurization (we see as boost) is that the pressure causes heat. Turbos and superchargers heat the inlet air, something not desirable from either a power (less oxygen molecules per volume) or a detonation threshold standpoint. The hotter the air, the easier it is to ignite. In some cases, the heated inlet air can self ignite before the spark plug initiates the burn. The result is an expansion of the air/fuel mixture while the piston is still on its way up to TDC. Naturally the expanding gases resist the upward moving piston. The result of this struggle is sometimes not very pretty. The same thing can happen with excessive ignition advance.

Nitrous, on the other hand, doesn't resort to pressurizing the inlet air, but rather the extra oxygen molecules are carried in the pressurized compound. Once delivered to the inlet tract from a pressurized bottle, the liquid nitrous quickly turns into a gas. The transformation of a compound from a liquid to a gas is a process called vaporization. Vaporization requires an input of energy; in this case the energy is heat. The vaporization of the liquid nitrous absorbs heat from the surrounding inlet air, desirable in any performance application (especially a turbo or supercharged motor). While we associate heat with boiling (for example water turning from a liquid to a gas), the vaporized nitrous does not produce heat (at least not to the inlet air). Though vaporized, the temperature of the nitrous oxide is still at or near -129 degrees (the boiling point of nitrous oxide). Naturally, mixing your inlet air with a gas that is still a chilly -129 degrees provides a dramatic cooling effect. It is this double cooling that not only reduces the chance of detonation, but also increases the density of the inlet air. Denser air equals more oxygen molecules, which in turn (potentially) create more power.

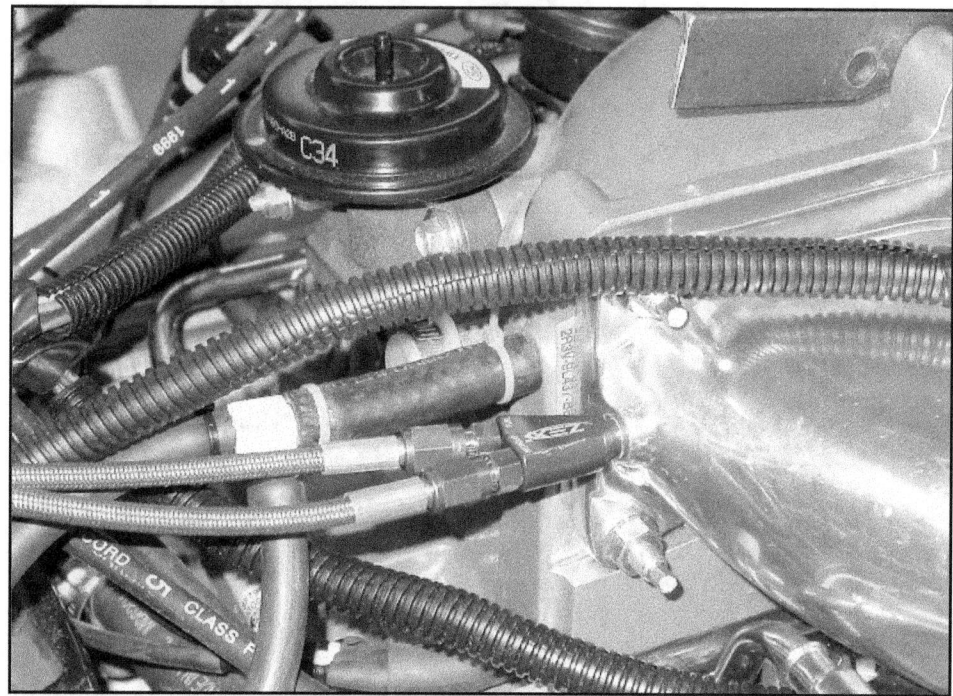

Ever think about combining nitrous oxide and forced induction? This Zex nitrous system was installed on a Supercharged '03 4-valve motor with excellent results. The nitrous actually acts as an intercooler to lower the inlet charge temperature.

Chapter 5

Test 1: Early 2-Valve GT: With a 100-hp Zex Kit

This particular test of a Zex wet fogger system on our 1998 (non-PI) 4.6L GT motor was one of the very first test sessions for this book. Though it took some time, we finally got the 4.6L motor up and running on the engine dyno, thanks to guys at F.A.S.T. and Westech Performance, specifically Tom Habryzk. The F.A.S.T. fuel injection provided us the ability to fine tune each and every combination tested on the dyno. Without the help of Westech Performance, the F.A.S.T. management system, and especially Tom Habryzk, I would never have been able to complete the extensive testing illustrated in these pages.

Before running the nitrous, the test motor was actually modified from its stock form. The '98 4.6L GT (originally rated at 225 hp) was treated to a set of Hooker long-tube headers (see Chapter 9), an Accufab throttle body and elbow (see Chapter 1), and a set of Comp XE274H cams (see Chapter 4) and valvesprings. The naturally aspirated baseline runs also included a Meziere electric water pump, which eliminated all of the remaining accessories. The Hooker headers were run through a 3-inch dyno exhaust system consisting of nothing more than 18-inch collectors and no mufflers. While I usually employ mufflers in my testing, I was curious about the sound potential of the much-maligned (early) mod motor. The F.A.S.T. stand-alone fuel-injection system also allowed me to eliminate the mass-air meter and associated inlet tubing from the power equation. Sure, that dismissed some important (and popular) performance components from the test regiment (such as cold-air intakes, aftermarket MAFs, and inlet tubes), but I knew the power output would not be limited in any way by the air induction system (ditto for the catalytic converters and cat-back exhaust).

Actually, the Zex nitrous turned out to be the final test of the afternoon. The simple wet system combines the nitrous and fuel together in a single fogger nozzle and sends the mixture through the throttle body and into the (rather torturous) intake manifold. We made sure to raise the bottle pressure to the recommended 900 psi before testing. This was accomplished by placing the bottle next to a small space heater, but the preferred method is a dedicated bottle blanket. As expected of almost any nitrous installation, the gains were significant. We managed to increase the power output of the mild non-PI 4.6L from 301 to 400 hp and (more impressively) increase the torque from 346 ft-lbs to a whopping 500 ft-lbs of torque. In reviewing the results, I feel that the extremely long intake runners limited the ultimate power potential as the gains dropped off past 4,800 rpm. Remember that the naturally aspirated motor produced peak power at 5,200 rpm. The 100-hp shot added as much as 118 hp and 151 ft-lbs of torque.

The Zex nitrous setup is unique in that it has the fuel and nitrous solenoids together in this box. This makes it a little easier to mount under the hood.

The Zex kit includes a single nozzle for the fuel and nitrous. Be sure to point the nozzle in the right direction.

Nitrous Oxide

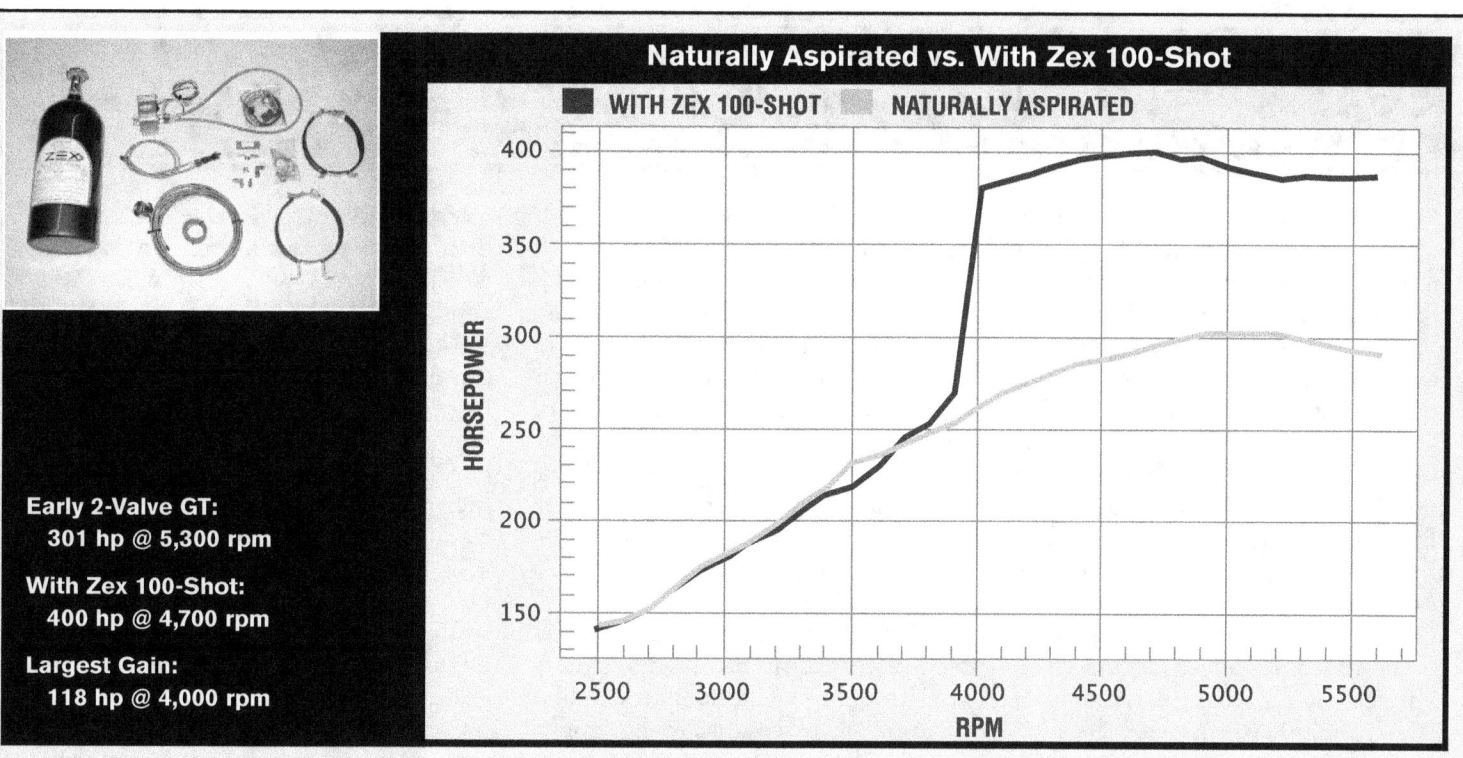

Early 2-Valve GT:
301 hp @ 5,300 rpm

With Zex 100-Shot:
400 hp @ 4,700 rpm

Largest Gain:
118 hp @ 4,000 rpm

Early 2-Valve GT: Stock vs. with 100-hp Zex Kit (Horsepower)
Installing jets to produce 100 additional horsepower actually upped the power output by as much as 118 hp. Our peak numbers jumped from 301 hp to an even 400 hp.

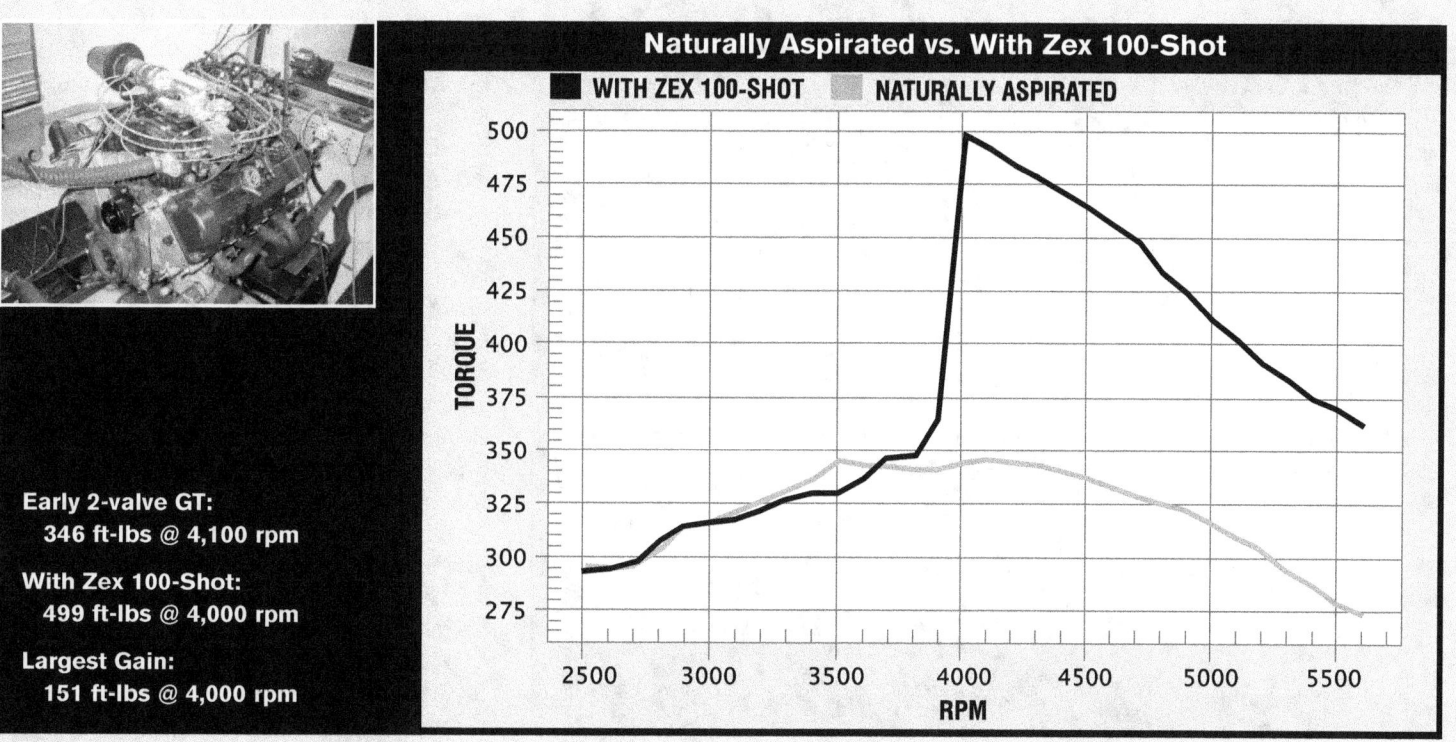

Early 2-valve GT:
346 ft-lbs @ 4,100 rpm

With Zex 100-Shot:
499 ft-lbs @ 4,000 rpm

Largest Gain:
151 ft-lbs @ 4,000 rpm

Early 2-Valve GT: Stock vs. with 100-hp Zex Kit (Torque)
Since we (manually) engaged the nitrous below 4,000 rpm, the torque gains were impressive. The 100-hp shot of nitrous added as much as 151 ft-lbs of torque.

Building 4.6/5.4L Ford Horsepower on the Dyno

Chapter 5

Test 2: Early 2-Valve GT: With a 125-hp Zex Kit

While nitrous oxide is perfectly safe even for a stock motor, this particular test was run on a modified motor. The great thing about nitrous oxide is that the power gains can be applied to just about any combination, from mild to wild, with predictable results. That obviously assumes the timing and fuel parameters are met. While a stock motor might have sufficed for testing this 125-hp shot, I decided to use one that had been beefed up a little. The test mule consisted of a stock GT block and crank combined with a set of forged connecting rods and stock replacement forged pistons from Coast High Performance. The augmented '98 short block was topped off with a set of CNC-ported non-PI 4.6L heads from Ford Performance Solutions. Knowing the early 4.6L intake was very restrictive, the early heads were further modified to accept the later PI intake manifold, though we used the Bullitt intake. Additional performance came in the form of a set of Comp Xtreme Energy XE262AH cams. The final mods included a set of Hooker long-tube headers and a set of 24-pound injectors run by a F.A.S.T. engine management system.

The great thing about nitrous oxide is that it can be added at almost any power level. Check out the results of Test 7 where we add a 75-hp shot to an 841-hp supercharged 4-valve motor. Since nitrous oxide carries its own power-producing oxygen molecules, it doesn't really care what the combination is. The recipe is simple. Inject a given amount of nitrous oxide (dictated by the bottle pressure and flow orifice or jet size) and add the required amount of fuel to support the burning of the oxygen. The additional fuel is critical, as adding the nitrous alone will cause immediate meltdown. This is akin to pumping up the boost on a supercharger without concern for additional fuel delivery. The air/fuel mixture must be kept in check to ensure safe power production. The horror stories you've heard about motor meltdowns can always be traced to either tuning errors (most common) or component failure (extremely rare). Applied properly with the right amount of fuel, a nitrous motor will live a long, happy life.

This test involved installing a 125-hp Zex wet system on our modified 4.6L 2-valve motor. The forged reciprocating assembly was more than stout enough to withstand the extra cylinder pressure of the nitrous. The air/fuel was kept safe and we dialed the timing back by 2 degrees to minimize the chance of detonation. The modified 4.6L 2-valve motor produced 369 hp at 5,900 rpm and 367 ft-lbs of torque at 4,600 rpm. Once we added the 125-hp shot from the Zex system, the peak power jumped to 472 hp, while the torque peak was up to 491 ft-lbs. There is just nothing like seeing the power curve take a 100-hp jump straight up. Even the wildest turbo system won't gain 100 hp (and 125 ft-lbs) in less than 200 rpm. For our testing, the Zex fogger was installed into a silicone hose connector, though it is preferable to drill and tap a more secure location. Like most systems, the Zex fogger is adjustable for more or less power by altering the fuel and nitrous jets in the fogger nozzle.

One of the luxuries of testing on an engine dyno is that you don't have to permanently mount everything. You'd probably want to find a better place to put your Zex kit on your street car.

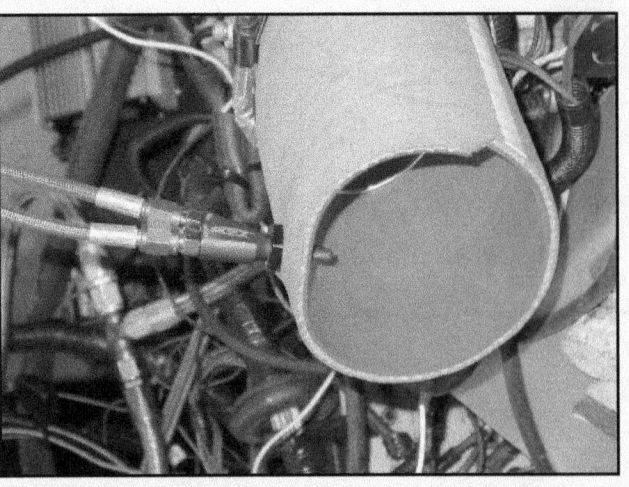

For the sake of our test, we mounted the nozzle in this silicone hose connector. For a permanent installation, the intake tube would be a better place.

Nitrous Oxide

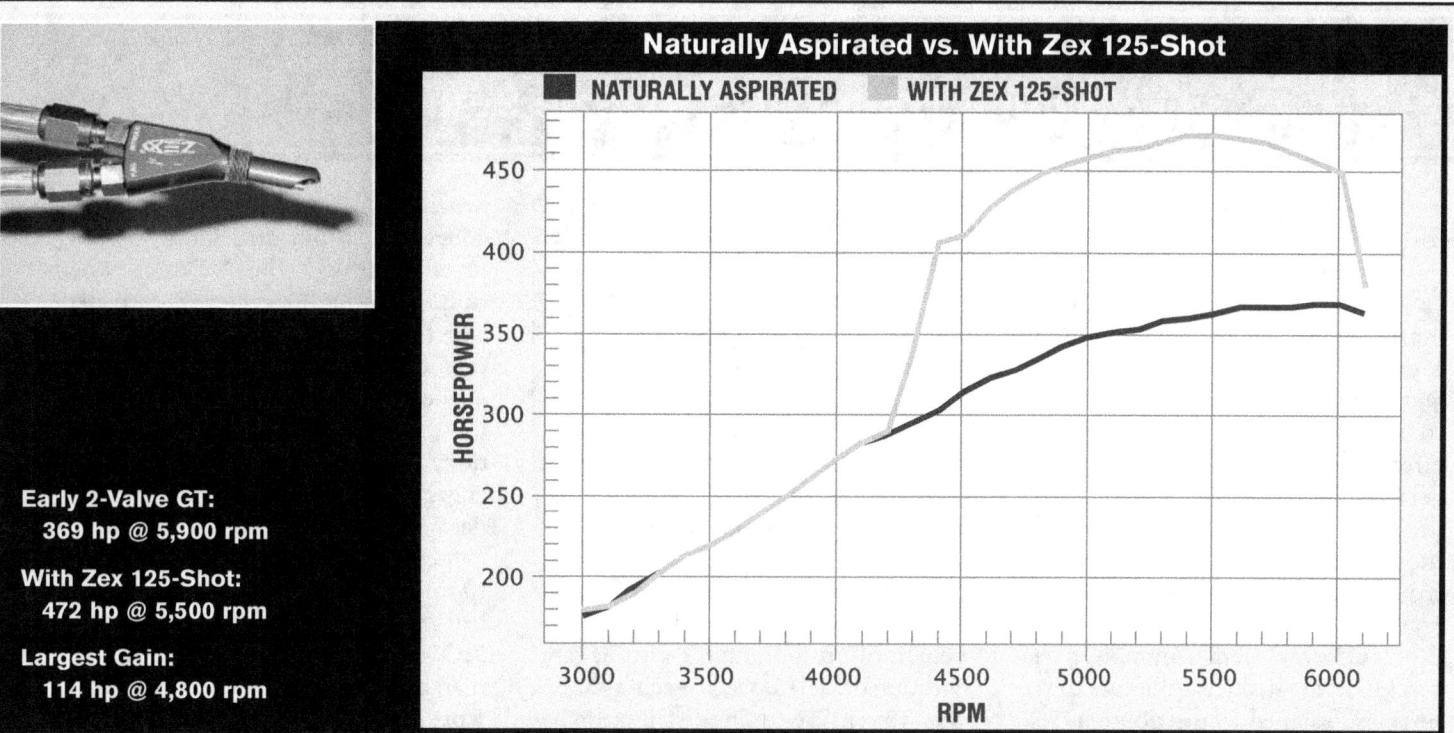

Early 2-Valve GT:
369 hp @ 5,900 rpm

With Zex 125-Shot:
472 hp @ 5,500 rpm

Largest Gain:
114 hp @ 4,800 rpm

Early 2-Valve GT: Stock vs. 125-hp Zex Kit (Horsepower)
Everything was going along nicely and then all of a sudden the mild-mannered Clark Kent immediately became Superman. No wonder nitrous is so popular with street racers. This system increased the power output of the 4.6L from 369 hp to 472 hp.

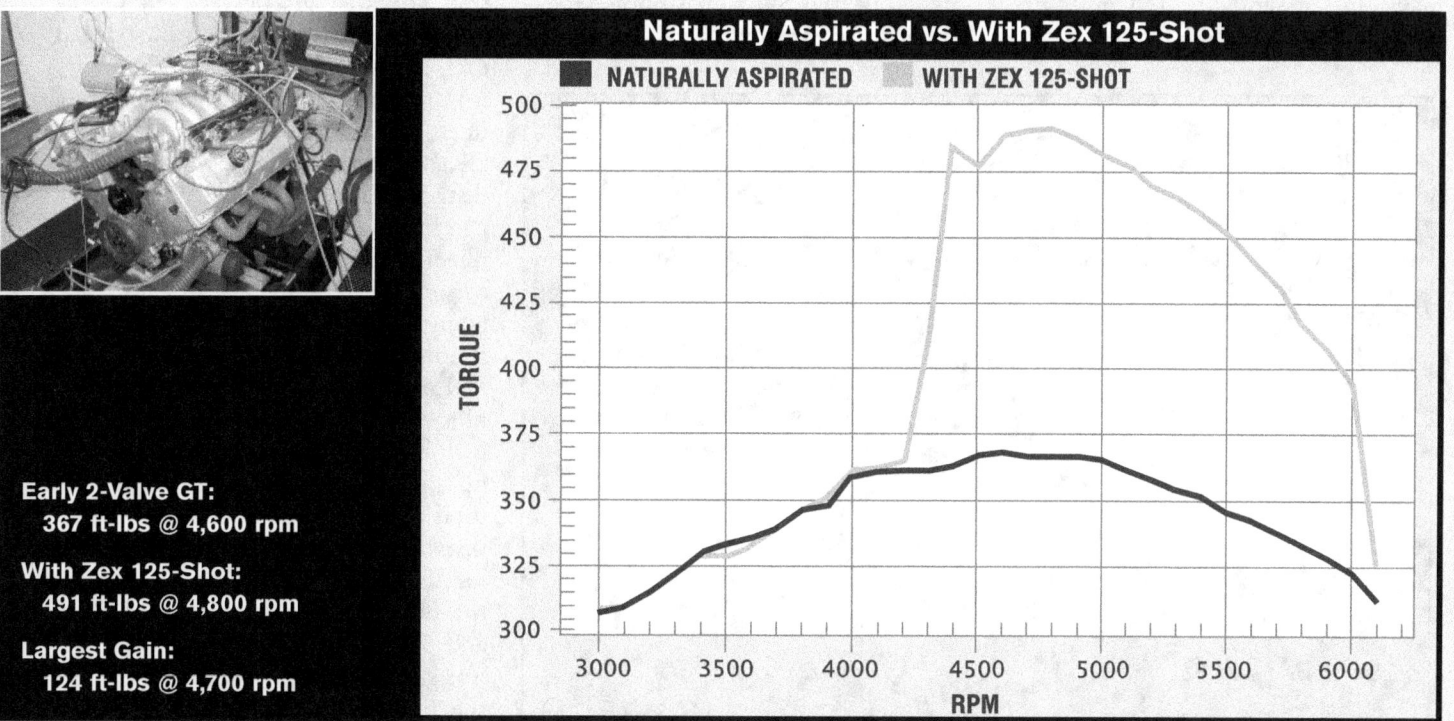

Early 2-Valve GT:
367 ft-lbs @ 4,600 rpm

With Zex 125-Shot:
491 ft-lbs @ 4,800 rpm

Largest Gain:
124 ft-lbs @ 4,700 rpm

Early 2-Valve GT: Stock vs. 125-hp Zex Kit (Torque)
The earlier the engagement point (RPM), the greater the torque gains. This Zex system added as much as 124 ft-lbs of torque. At the flip of a switch, your motor becomes a serious contender.

Test 3: Naturally Aspirated 4-Valve '03 Cobra: With a 125-hp NOS NOSzle Setup

Can you think of a better recipient for nitrous than a low-compression motor factory equipped with a steel crank, forged rods, and (most importantly) forged pistons? Neither could I, but rather than just add your typical wet fogger system, I decided to step up to something trick and impressively effective – enter the NOS NOSzle fogger system. The kit was originally designed for the 2-valve 4.6L GT motor, but I didn't let that deter me from using it on our 4-valve Cobra crate motor. As implied by the name, the NOSzle system from NOS features individual billet aluminum fogger nozzles designed to distribute nitrous and additional fuel to each cylinder. The trick part about this distribution system is that the NOSzles are sandwiched between the injectors and the factory injector openings in the intake manifold. Essentially, the injectors were plugged into the NOSzles, which were in turn plugged into the injector openings in the manifold. The major benefit of positioning the nitrous (and additional fuel) flow at each cylinder was to ensure even distribution of nitrous, which is difficult when injecting the nitrous and fuel through an intake originally designed to flow just air (as was the case with both the 4.6L 2-valve and 4-valve motors).

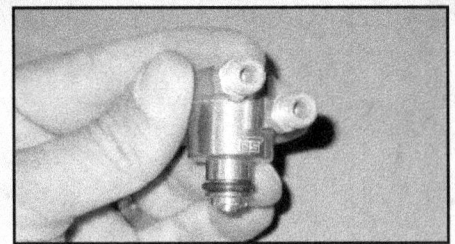

The NOS NOSzles fit between the fuel injector and the intake manifold. They inject nitrous and fuel into the engine.

While the individual-port NOSzles ensured even cylinder-to-cylinder distribution, I couldn't help but be concerned about the injector spray pattern through the NOSzles when running without the nitrous activated. The fuel has to flow out of the injectors and through the opening located in the bottom of the NOSzles. Would this hurt the spray pattern, atomization, and power without the nitrous engaged? Given that NOS was a pioneer in the nitrous field and was *the* name in nitrous for many years, I should have realized that my injector fears were unfounded. Apparently the NOS crew had stayed up late on more than one occasion and did their homework, as this test revealed that not only did the NOSzle system allow the injectors to operate effectively, if anything the power actually improved slightly after their installation.

The NOSzle system is indeed trick looking. Plastic feed lines running from the distribution block feed each of the eight NOSzles. The block is home to eight nitrous and eight fuel lines, one of each running to a NOSzle. Nitrous and fuel flow through the distribution block is controlled by a pair of solenoids. The fuel was supplied via the Schrader valve in the factory fuel rail, while the nitrous came from the ubiquitous 10-lb blue bottle. Before running the nitrous, I ran the 4.6L in naturally aspirated trim. Running through a set of Flow-Tech 1⅝-inch headers, the engine produced 427 hp and 397 ft-lbs of torque with the total timing set at 28 degrees. After installing the 125-hp jets and activating the NOS NOSzle nitrous system, the peak numbers jumped to 547 hp and 526 ft-lbs of torque. The power was still climbing strong when I let off the power button at 6,000 rpm. As advertised, the NOS nitrous system supplied a solid 125-hp gain (actually a tad more in some spots) and a ton of extra torque.

You could probably make it look a little tidier under your hood, but our NOSzle install worked great on the engine dyno. Installing the NOSzles between the fuel injectors and the intake manifold had no effect on power off the juice.

Nitrous Oxide

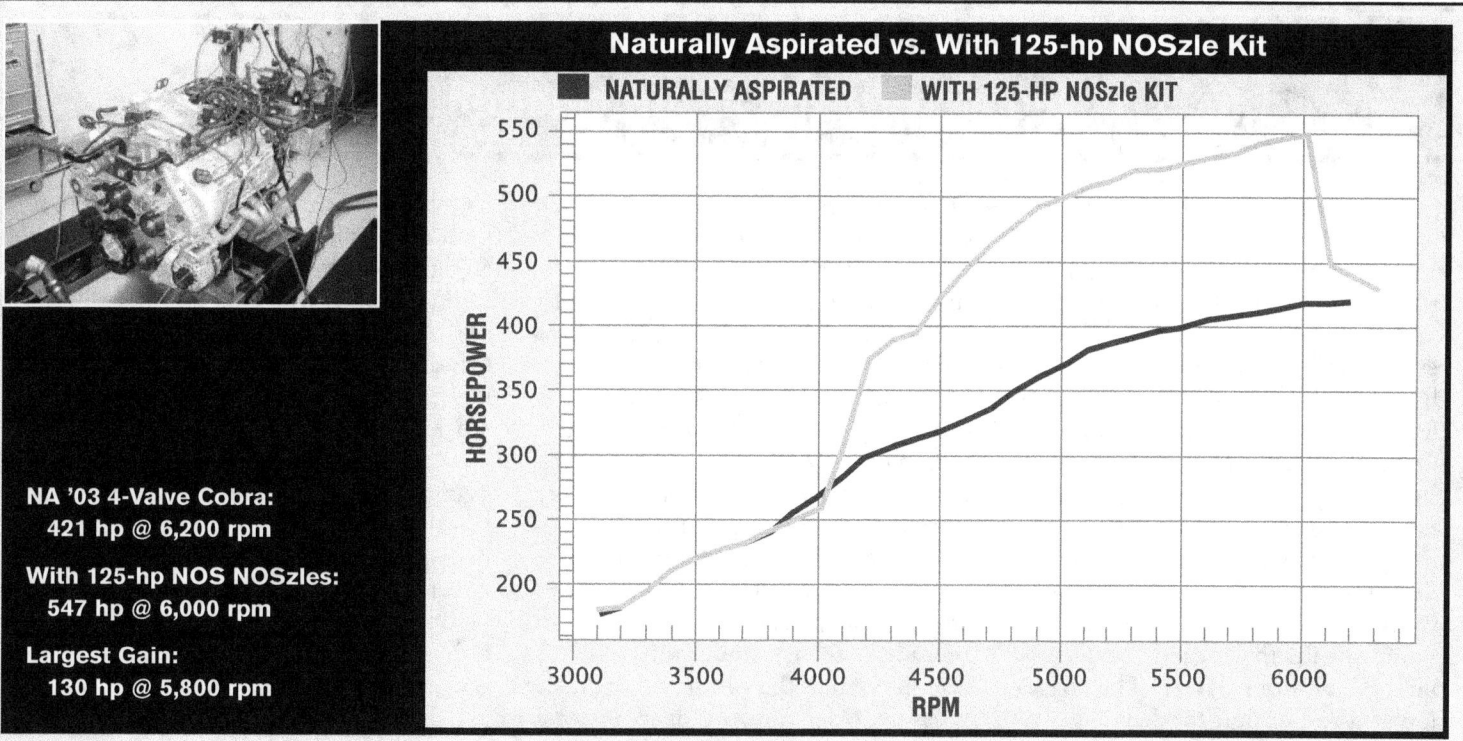

NA '03 4-Valve Cobra:
421 hp @ 6,200 rpm

With 125-hp NOS NOSzles:
547 hp @ 6,000 rpm

Largest Gain:
130 hp @ 5,800 rpm

NA '03 4-Valve Cobra: Stock vs. NOS 125-hp NOSzle Kit (Horsepower)
This was one of those tests where I wish I kept my finger on the trigger for a tad longer. The power output was still climbing rapidly when I let off, but 550 hp is hard to argue with. As it turned out, the NOSzle nitrous system more than made up for the lack of the blower.

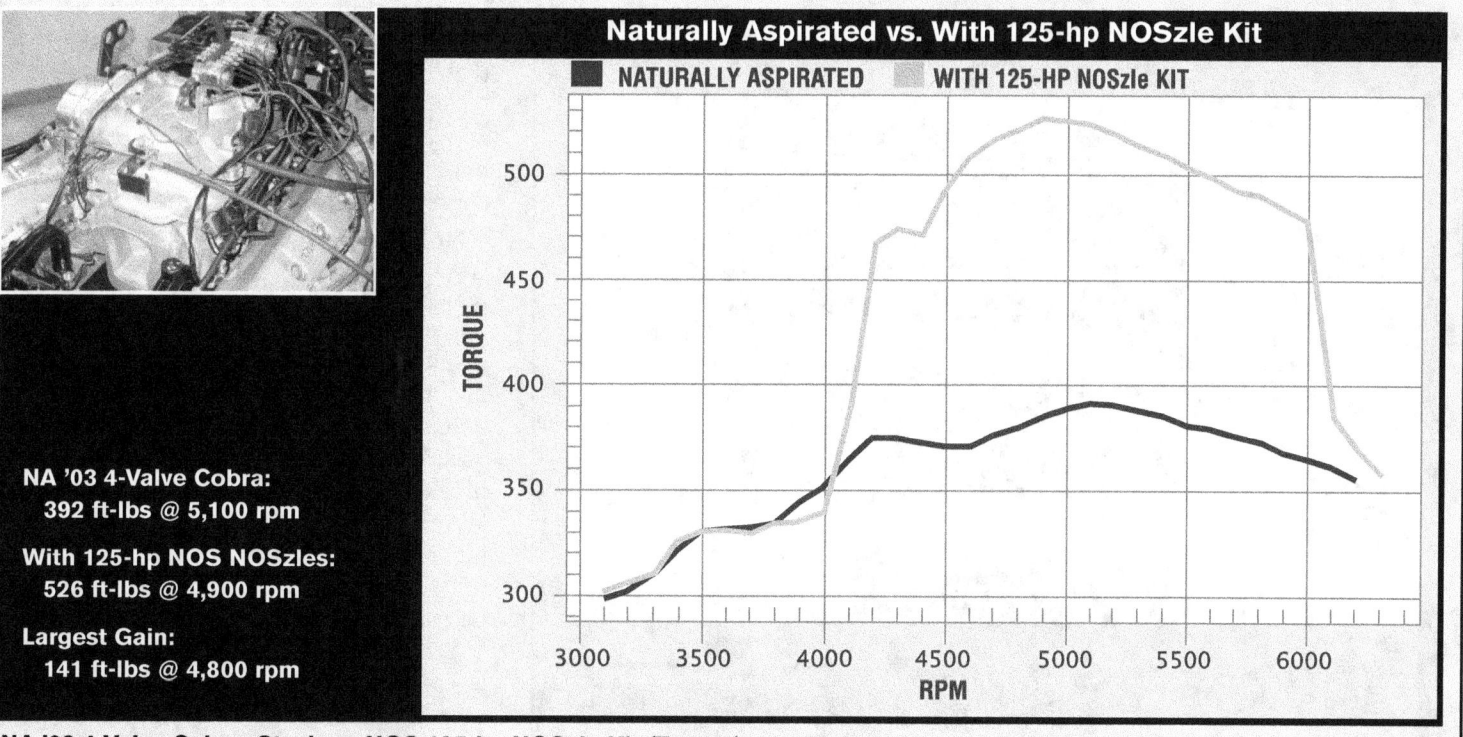

NA '03 4-Valve Cobra:
392 ft-lbs @ 5,100 rpm

With 125-hp NOS NOSzles:
526 ft-lbs @ 4,900 rpm

Largest Gain:
141 ft-lbs @ 4,800 rpm

NA '03 4-Valve Cobra: Stock vs. NOS 125-hp NOSzle Kit (Torque)
Note that the shapes of the two curves were very similar. The additional nitrous simply elevated the torque numbers, in this case from 392 ft-lbs to 526 ft-lbs. The '03 Cobra motor would take this kind of abuse day in and day out.

Building 4.6/5.4L Ford Horsepower on the Dyno

Test 4: Naturally Aspirated 4-Valve '03 Cobra: Effect of Reduced Timing in Anticipation of Nitrous

There is no denying that a good nitrous system can add an impressive amount of power. This chapter illustrates that without fail, nitrous oxide improved the power output of each test motor by the amount specified by the jetting. Just like with forced induction, the tuning must be spot on with nitrous. Since nitrous oxide carries extra oxygen molecules (technically nitrous oxide is not a fuel – it's an oxidizer), the oxygen must be accompanied by additional fuel. In the case of a wet nitrous system, a separate fuel line plumbed into the fogger nozzle supplies the additional fuel. The fogger nozzle is responsible for delivering the metered amount of fuel and nitrous based on the fuel and nitrous jetting and the nitrous bottle and fuel pressure supplied to the fogger. In the case of a dry system, the fogger nozzle delivers only the nitrous and the additional fuel is supplied by an increase in fuel pressure to the injectors. In both cases, the air/fuel ratio is kept safe with the addition of extra fuel.

While the proper air/fuel ratio is critical for safe nitrous use, the ignition timing is even more important. Adding nitrous oxide to your motor is a lot like adding a blower or turbo kit. In both cases, the additional cylinder pressure may require additional octane (you should always run at least premium unleaded when running nitrous). It's also likely that the additional cylinder pressure will require a drop in total ignition timing. Excessive timing has killed more nitrous motors than too little fuel. Unfortunately for mod-motor owners, retarding the ignition timing is best accomplished via a revised computer chip, but it can also be done with an ignition amplifier that features a timing retard. Retarding ignition timing is necessary to reduce detonation (caused by early ignition that leads to the expansion of the gases actually working against the upward moving piston). On the positive side, elevated cylinder pressures increase the speed of the flame travel, so the drop in total timing may not have such a negative effect on the power output. Nitrous (and forced induction) motors will not only tolerate less ignition timing, but the reality is that they require less.

To illustrate the effect of a reduction in timing, I ran my naturally aspirated '03 4-valve Cobra motor with 28 degrees of total timing and then again with just 25 degrees. I purposely reduced the total timing to 25 degrees in anticipation of adding the nitrous on 91-octane pump gas. According to the instructions supplied with the NOS NOSzle nitrous kit, jetting above 75-hp should be accompanied by a reduction in timing of 2 to 4 degrees. Splitting the difference, I retarded the timing by 3 degrees using the F.A.S.T. engine management system. The drop in timing brought the power output of the motor down from 430 to 421 hp, and peak torque dropped just 6 ft-lbs. A drop of 9 hp is a small price to pay for the extra insurance against detonation. On the safety of the engine dyno, where we control all the temperatures, air/fuel, and timing, running nitrous with full timing is not a problem. I wouldn't think about performing the same task on the street. Get a bad tank of gas and bye-bye motor. In reality, it was certainly possible to run a 75-hp shot on his low-compression Cobra motor with 28 degrees, but I wanted to demonstrate the proper way to add nitrous with a high-compression (NA) Cobra motor, so I took the retard route.

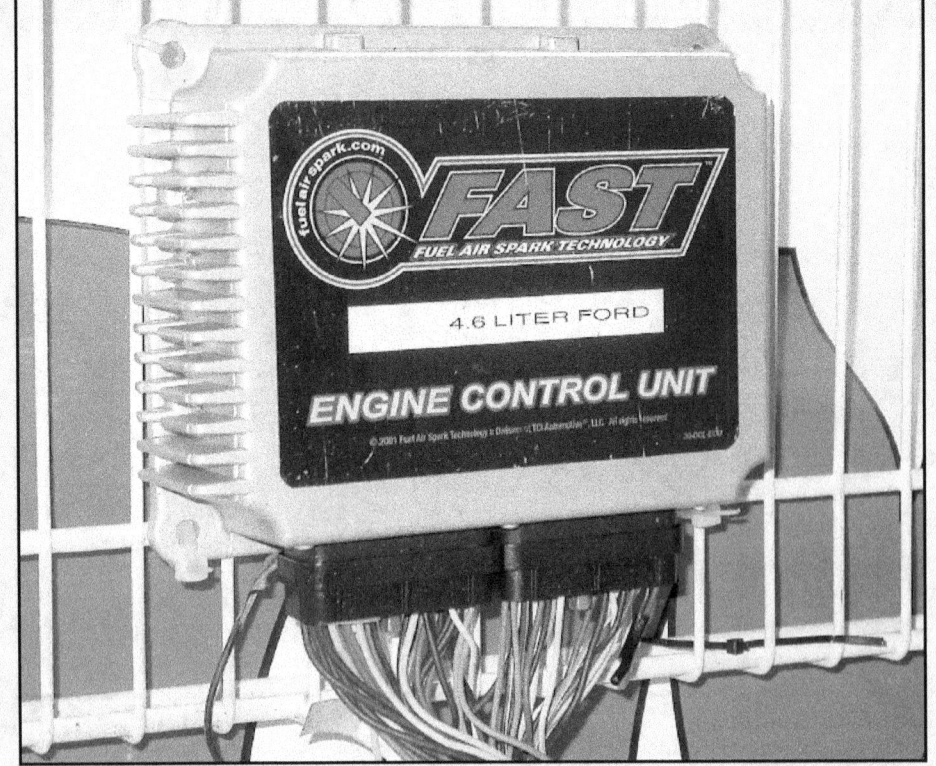

We'll be retarding our timing with the F.A.S.T. engine management system, but you can do it by having a special computer chip tuned for your application, or with some types of ignition amplifiers.

Nitrous Oxide

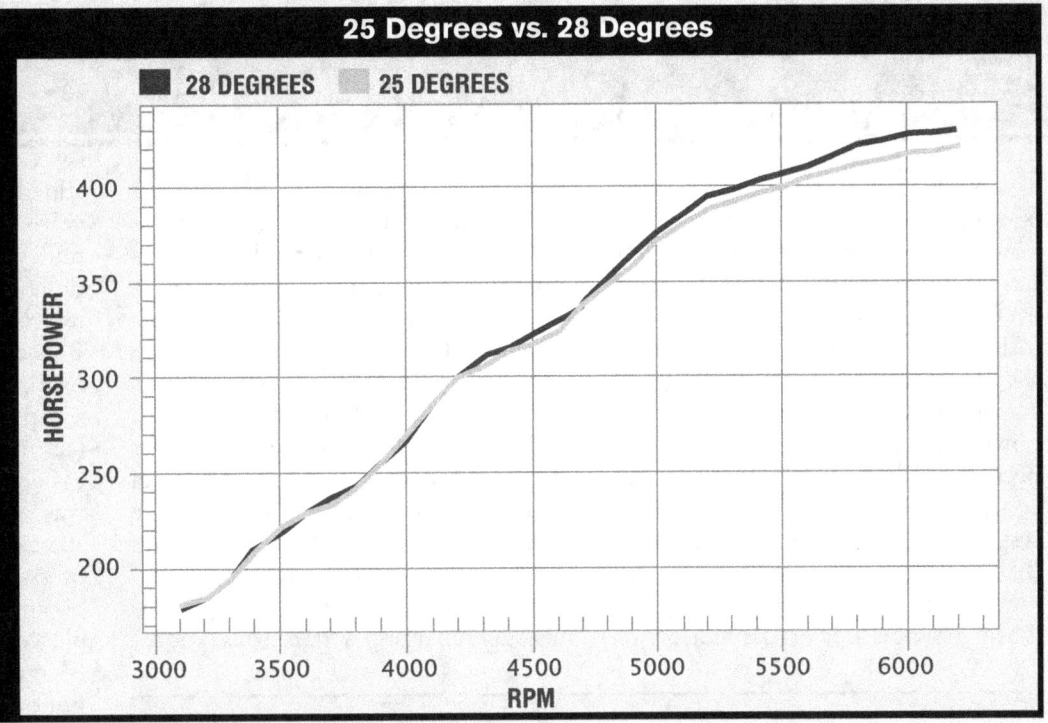

NA '03 4-Valve (25 degrees):
421 hp @ 6,200 rpm

NA '03 4-Valve (28 degrees):
430 hp @ 6,200 rpm

Largest Gain:
9 hp @ 5,800 rpm

NA '03 4-Valve: 25 Degrees vs. 28 Degrees of Total Timing (Horsepower)
This minimal drop in power is a small price to pay for the security of having your motor stay alive. Dropping from 28 degrees of total timing to just 25 degrees will minimize the chance of detonation. You'll probably never miss the power loss when running the juice, but you'll sure miss not having a running motor if you detonate it.

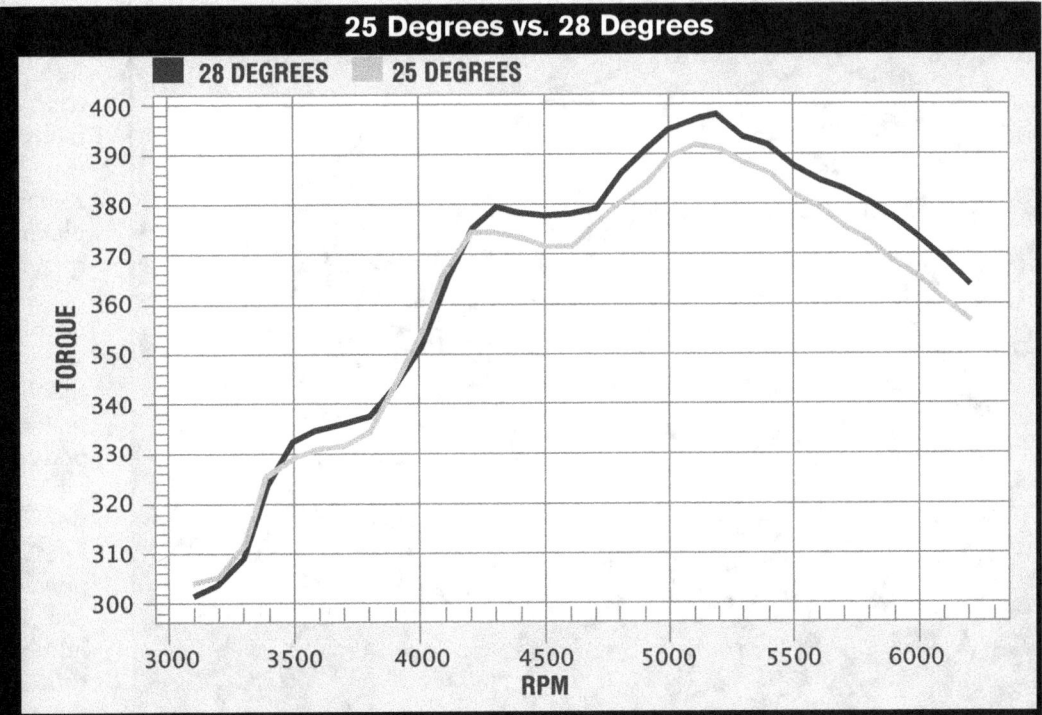

NA '03 4-Valve (25 degrees):
392 ft-lbs @ 5,100 rpm

NA '03 4-Valve (28 degrees):
398 ft-lbs @ 5,200 rpm

Largest Gain:
8 ft-lbs @ 5,800 rpm

NA '03 4-Valve: 25 Degrees vs. 28 Degrees of Total Timing (Torque)
The drop of 3 degrees of total timing had little effect on power up to 4,200 rpm. In this case, it's better to drop 6 or 7 ft-lbs of torque to safely employ the extra 125 hp offered by the nitrous.

Chapter 5

Test 5: Eaton Supercharged 4-Valve '03 Cobra: With a 125-hp Zex Kit

While all-motor cars are fun, there is something special about having a power adder. If you're lucky enough to have a supercharger, turbocharger, or even nitrous oxide, you know what it feels like every time you let loose with the boost or the juice. There's just something about the feeling of extra power exploding in a surge that becomes addicting. Whether the surge comes immediately from the boost response of a good roots supercharger (like the Eaton on our '03 Cobra test motor), the swell of a turbo system when it spools up, or the violent jolt when you hit the nitrous, there's nothing like it. If you check out the various drag racing classes where blowers, turbos, and nitrous all compete head to head, or ask the guys at the local track, you'll probably find competitors who swear by their favorite. After all, it's hard to argue with an additional 100, 200, or even 300 hp (or more) from a well-executed power adder. Rather than choose just one, why not combine the benefits offered by nitrous oxide with the boost from a good supercharger?

To illustrate the effects of combining supercharging with nitrous oxide, I added a little juice to the boost in my 4-valve Cobra motor. The stock blower pulley was replaced with a 3.2-inch pulley as part of the South Florida Pulley Headquarters (SFPH) Dial-Ur-Boost (DUB) system. The DUB features an adapter hub designed to accept bolt-on pulleys to replace the factory press-fit version, which means easier pulley swaps. The DUB system was also incorporated on the crankshaft, as we were able to replace the press-fit crank pulley as well. The combination of interchangeable crank and blower pulleys gave us nearly unlimited range of potential boost pressure. For our test, we chose a 3.2-inch blower pulley and a 7.5-inch crank pulley, resulting in a peak boost pressure of 12.1 psi. At 12.1 psi, the engine produced 533 hp at 6,400 rpm and 518 ft-lbs of torque at 3,700 rpm. The boost pressure started at 11.6 psi at 3,000 rpm, climbed to 12.1 psi from 4,300 rpm to 5,300 rpm then dropped off to just 10.9 psi at 6,500 rpm. The supercharged 4.6L produced more than 500 ft-lbs from 3,000 rpm to 4,800 rpm. We usually ran this supercharged motor at 23 degrees of total timing, but since we planned to add nitrous, we backed the total timing down to just 20 degrees.

Now it was time to add a little nitrous oxide. We used a Zex wet kit equipped with 125-hp jets. To install the fogger nozzle, we removed a vacuum fitting in the Accufab throttle body and tapped the opening with the tap supplied in the Zex kit. This position provided excellent cooling of the inlet air. The 125-hp shot increased the power output by as much as 126 hp and 140 ft-lbs of torque. The peak numbers checked in at 638 hp at 6,300 rpm and an amazing 636 ft-lbs of torque at 4,800 rpm. We let off on the nitrous a few hundred RPM early; otherwise the peak number would have been slightly higher.

Most people are content to run nitrous or a supercharger, but why can't you run both? We took out a little timing and added a 125-hp shot to our supercharged '03 Cobra motor just to see what would happen.

Nitrous Oxide

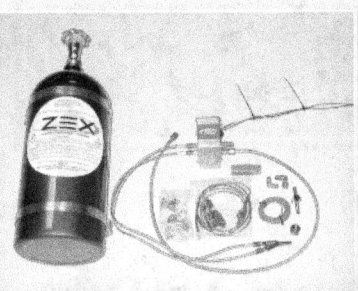

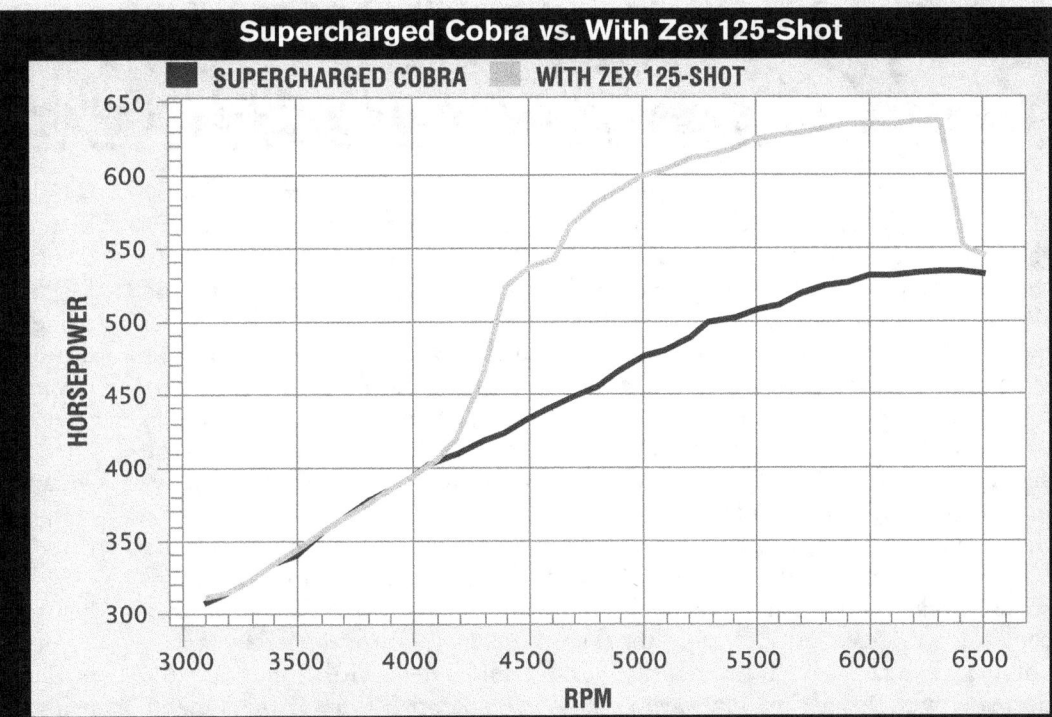

Supercharged '03 Cobra:
533 hp @ 6,400 rpm

With Zex 125-Shot:
634 hp @ 6,000 rpm

Largest Gain:
126 hp @ 4,900 rpm

Eaton Supercharged 4-Valve '03 Cobra: Stock vs. 125-hp Zex Kit (Horsepower)
Most '03 4-valve Cobra owners would be thrilled to have their supercharged 4.6L produce 533 flywheel hp, but check out what happened when we pushed the Zex power button. The power soared from 533 hp to 638 hp. Running jetting to supply 125 hp, the Zex added as much as 126 hp (right on target).

Supercharged '03 Cobra:
518 ft-lbs @ 3,300 rpm

With Zex 125-Shot:
636 ft-lbs @ 4,800 rpm

Largest Gain:
138 hp @ 4,800 rpm

Eaton Supercharged 4-Valve '03 Cobra: Stock vs. 125-hp Zex Kit (Torque)
These supercharged '03-'04 4-valve Cobra motors are all about torque. Note that the torque curve on this modified '03 Cobra crate motor was pretty impressive even before we added the nitrous. The motor exceeded 500 ft-lbs way down at 3,000 rpm. Adding the Zex kit upped the torque peak from 518 ft-lbs to 636 ft-lbs – what a kick ass little street package.

Building 4.6/5.4L Ford Horsepower on the Dyno

Test 6: Kenne Bell Boost-A-Spark Cured Misfire with Supercharger and Nitrous

The results from Test 5 came only after we cured an ignition problem on the dyno. The problem stemmed from the impressive cylinder pressure that resulted from combining supercharging with nitrous oxide. Supercharging is nothing more than force-feeding the motor more air than it can ingest of its own accord. Nitrous oxide can be considered a chemical form of supercharging. Power production is a function of the number of oxygen molecules supplied to the motor. In the case of supercharging, additional oxygen molecules are supplied by increasing the volume of air. Though the density decreases with the increase in temperature (compression or boost causes the air to be heated), the increase in volume more than offsets the decrease in density, providing a net gain in the number of oxygen molecules (or mass flow) present. Nitrous oxide does not increase the airflow per se, but rather increases the number of oxygen molecules present (acts as an oxidizing agent) by releasing free oxygen when it breaks down in the combustion chamber. Nitrous oxide breakes down into its component parts (oxygen and nitrogen) at approximately 572 degrees F. This allows the free oxygen to mix with fuel and burn. Just as with supercharging, the more oxygen molecules that can be fed to the combustion chamber, the greater the eventual power potential.

While both supercharging and nitrous oxide can and do offer exceptional power gains on their own, they can, under the proper circumstances, be combined to further increase the power potential. One of the benefits of adding nitrous to a supercharged motor is that nitrous oxide is stored as a liquid and injected as a gas. This transformation from a liquid to a gas (boiling) requires an energy input. Think about it this way: What happens when you pour water on a fire or hot stove? The water draws heat from the fire or stove causing the liquid to boil. The nitrous works the same way by pulling heat out of the air stream as it turns from a liquid to a gas. Lucky for us, the boiling point of nitrous oxide is an extremely low -129 degrees. Even after having drawn a tremendous amount of heat from the inlet tract (cooling it off), the gaseous nitrous continues to cool things off by equalizing itself with the surrounding temperature. Thus in addition to all those wonderful power-producing oxygen molecules, the nitrous oxide helps further improve power output by dramatically increasing the density of the air through rapid cooling. This helps prevent detonation.

The problem is that the tremendous cylinder pressure, combined with retarded timing, plays havoc on the ignition system. Installing a Kenne Bell Boost-A-Spark (BAS), which increases the supply voltage to the coils, cured a misfire that would have otherwise limited the success of our nitrous/blower test.

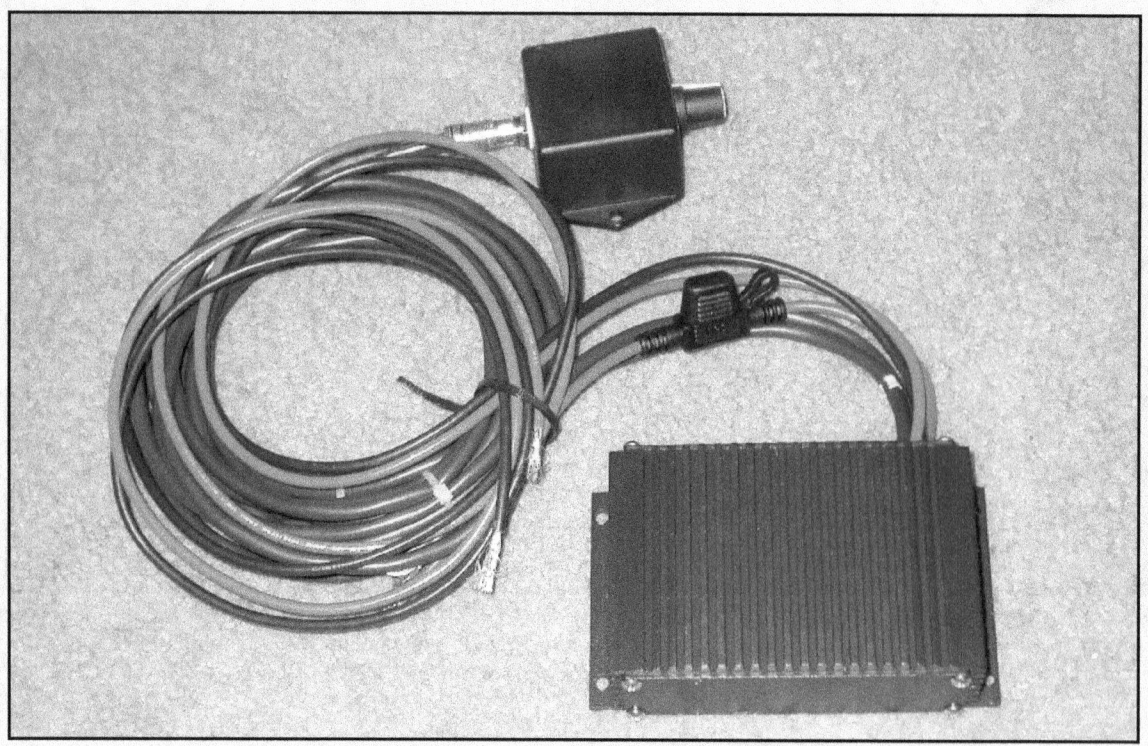

The Kenne Bell Boost-A-Spark increases the amount of energy going into, and thus coming out of, the ignition coils. The extra power helps keep the spark from blowing out at high boost and/or nitrous levels.

Nitrous Oxide

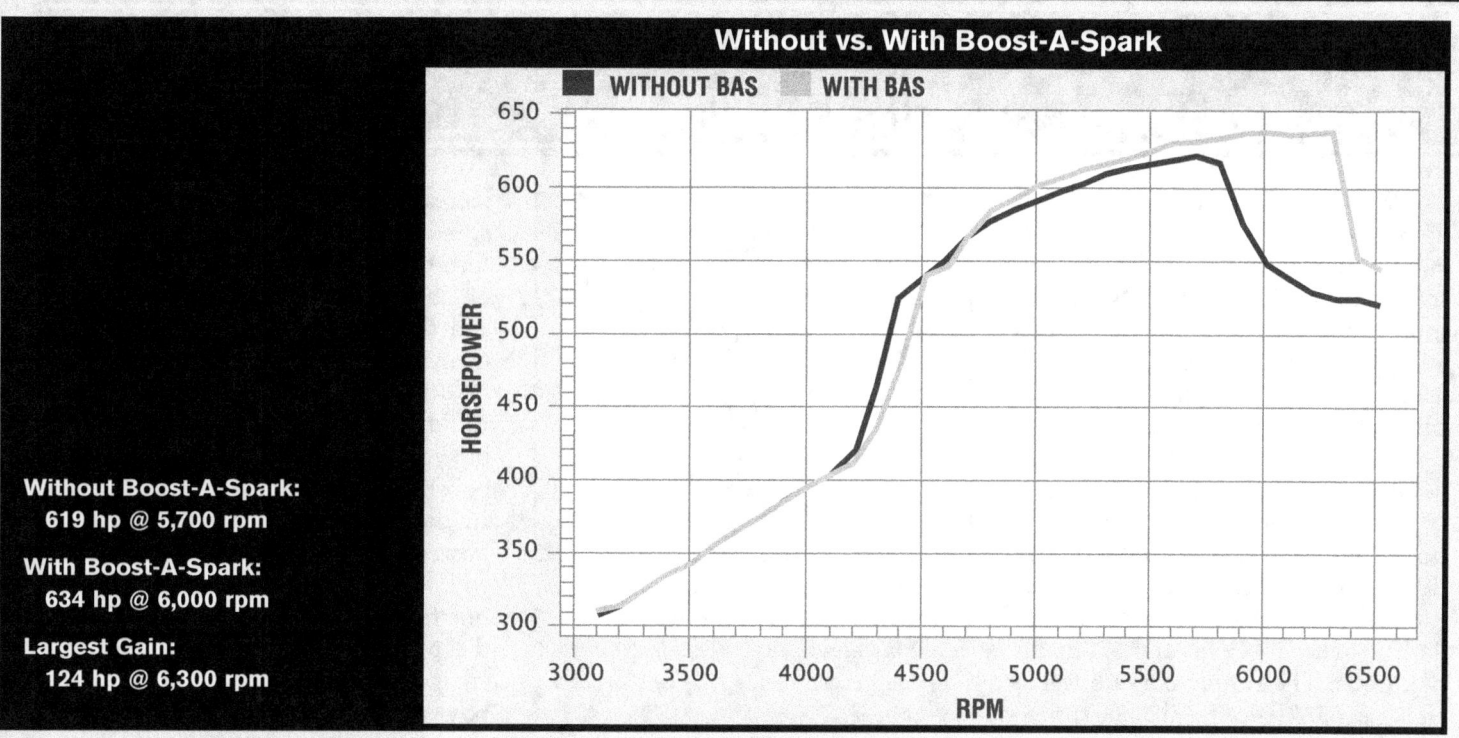

Without Boost-A-Spark:
619 hp @ 5,700 rpm

With Boost-A-Spark:
634 hp @ 6,000 rpm

Largest Gain:
124 hp @ 6,300 rpm

Nitrous/Supercharged '03 4-Valve Cobra: Without vs. With BAS (Horsepower)
The first time we tried combining nitrous oxide with the boost from the Eaton M112 roots supercharger, we were rewarded with an ignition-related misfire. The excessive cylinder pressure (aggravated by retarding the timing) caused the engine to misfire badly at 5,800 rpm. Installing a Kenne Bell Boost-A-Spark, which allowed the supercharged motor to rev cleanly to 6,400 rpm on the nitrous, cured the misfire. The ignition upgrade was worth an extra 124 hp at 6,300 rpm.

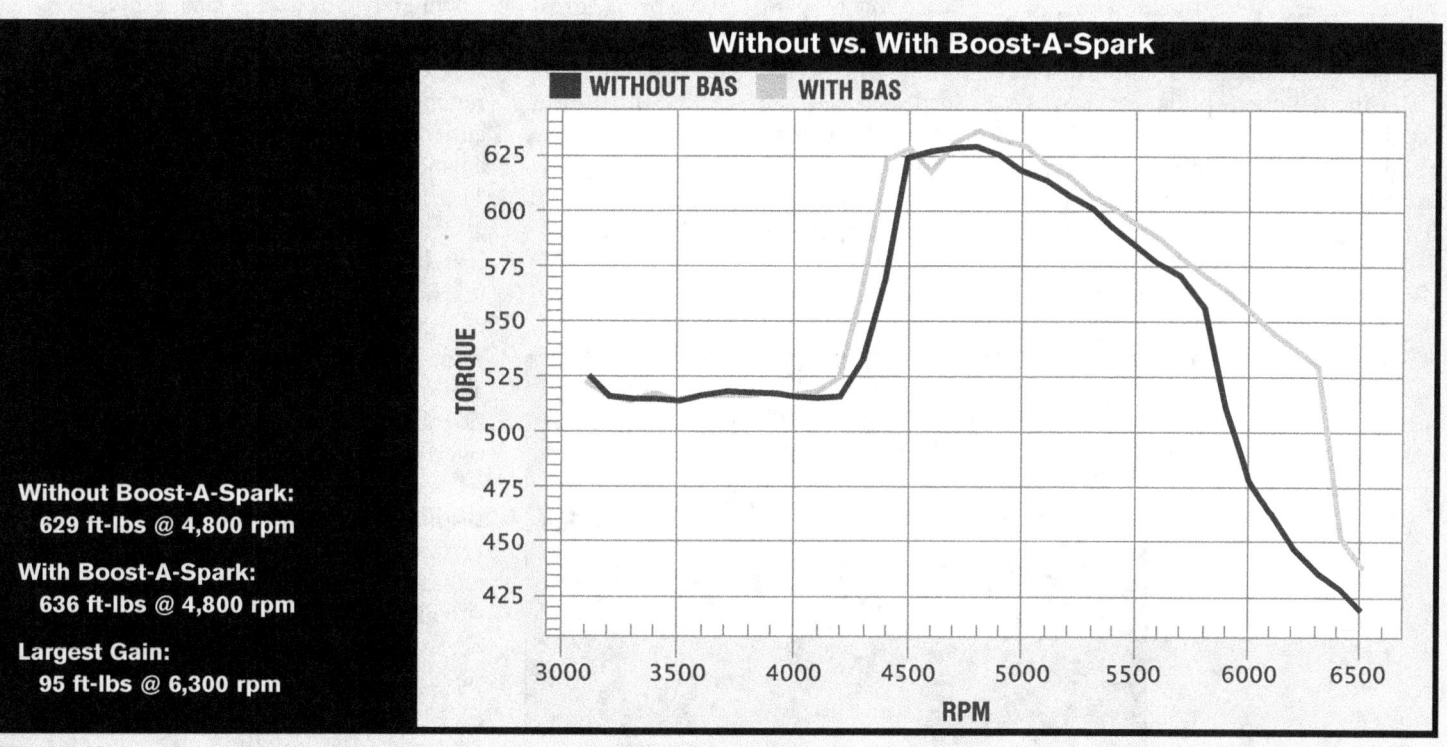

Without Boost-A-Spark:
629 ft-lbs @ 4,800 rpm

With Boost-A-Spark:
636 ft-lbs @ 4,800 rpm

Largest Gain:
95 ft-lbs @ 6,300 rpm

Nitrous/Supercharged '03 4-Valve Cobra: Without vs. With BAS (Torque)
The torque peaks were very similar; it's just that the supercharged motor wouldn't run cleanly beyond 5,800 rpm until we installed the Boost-A-Spark. Sometimes it's the little things that make a big difference. A quality high-powered ignition system is paramount on a high-horsepower motor.

Building 4.6/5.4L Ford Horsepower on the Dyno

Test 7: Paxton Supercharged 4-Valve Cobra: With a 75-hp Zex Kit

While nitrous oxide is always welcomed as a power adder, under the right circumstances, it can be so much more. In this case, the "so much more" was the fact that the nitrous added some much-needed power with a dramatic drop in charge temperature, allowing me to reach a self-imposed 900-hp goal. The 4.6L 4-valve test motor was run in naturally aspirated form with a set of 36-pound injectors. Tuned to provide 28 degrees of total timing and an air/fuel ratio of 13.0:1, the naturally aspirated 4.6L produced 483 hp and 376 ft-lbs of torque. The torque curve hovered right near 375 ft-lbs from 5,300 rpm to 6,500 rpm.

Unfortunately, the valvesprings (though upgraded) limited the maximum engine speed before valve float occurred. This would come back to haunt us even more after installing the supercharger. After the baseline, we installed the Paxton Novi 2000 supercharger kit. The kit was supplied with a 3.5-inch blower pulley that when combined with the stock 6.5-inch crank pulley produced a maximum impeller speed of over 46,000 rpm. Running no intercooler and a custom 6-rib belt (no accessories), the impressive Novi 2000 supercharger provided

This 4-valve Cobra motor featured a set of Ford Racing FR500 heads and the FR500 intake manifold – plus a Paxton Novi 2000 supercharger. This setup fell just short of my 900-hp goal.

a maximum of 16 psi, which pushed the peak power up to 841 hp and peak torque to 630 ft-lbs. Unfortunately, the boost exaggerated the valve float issue (boost pressure on the valve surface works against the spring pressure), limiting our maximum engine speed to just 7,100 rpm. Even there we suspected a loss of valve control, but we had no springs or shims to improve the situation.

The nice thing about centrifugal superchargers (especially ultra-efficient units like the Paxton Novi 2000) is that the boost pressure (and airflow) increases with engine (and impeller) speed. Unfortunately, we couldn't turn our motor to 7,500 rpm because of insufficient valvespring pressure and the resulting valve float. Believe me, you don't want to hear valve float on a 900-hp motor at 7,000 rpm. We could get boost by using a smaller blower pulley, but again, the added boost aggravated the valve float issue. In the end, we decided to cure our power/RPM dilemma *and* an associated inlet charge temperature issue all in one fell swoop: nitrous oxide. Within the purple 10-lb bottle was a magic elixir that offered not only increased power potential (much more than even our built motor could ever handle) but also a dramatic decrease in inlet temperature.

Initially, we wanted to run a small 25-hp shot of nitrous to use primarily as a cooling agent. Unfortunately (or fortunately) for us, the smallest jets we had supplied a 75-hp shot. At first I was a tad skeptical about adding this much nitrous to an already stout supercharged combination, but we had a handle on the tune (18 degrees and an 11.5:1 air/fuel ratio) and the motor had already proven itself plenty stout. We installed the Zex wet nozzle into the discharge tube running from the supercharger to the throttle body. Westech's Tom Habryzk drilled and tapped the aluminum casting to accept the fogger nozzle. The first attempt resulted in an overly rich mixture, but a drop in fuel jet size eventually produced a peak reading of 908 hp and 683 ft-lbs of torque. The nitrous was (manually) engaged at 5,000 rpm and allowed to run all the way to 7,000 rpm. As we've come to expect, the Zex system supplied a steady power jump of 75 to 80 hp through most of the curve, but the gains decreased slightly near the top due to a (still) rich mixture. Properly applied, nitrous will even benefit an 841-hp supercharged motor.

A built engine – with a supercharger – with nitrous? This combo held together to the tune of 908 hp and 683 ft-lbs of torque.

Nitrous Oxide

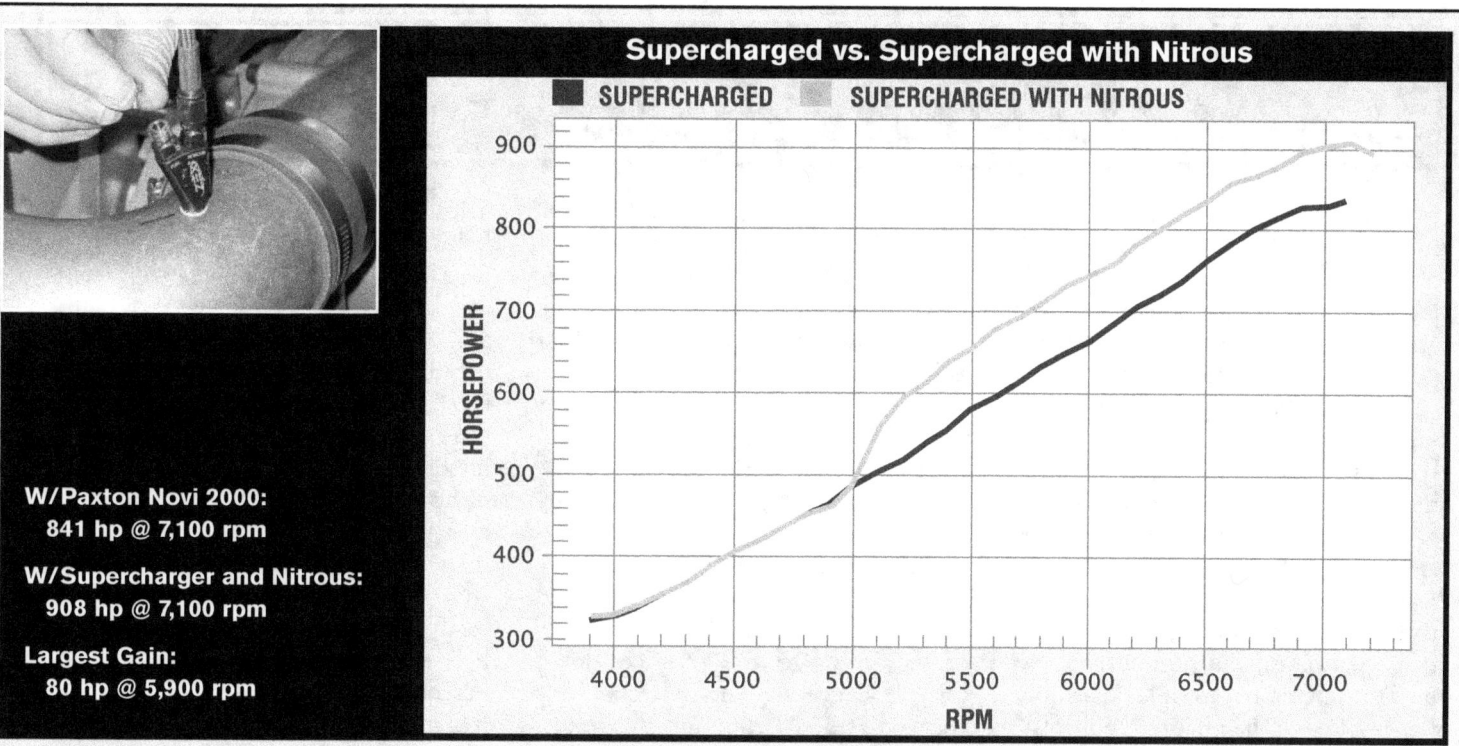

W/Paxton Novi 2000:
841 hp @ 7,100 rpm

W/Supercharger and Nitrous:
908 hp @ 7,100 rpm

Largest Gain:
80 hp @ 5,900 rpm

Paxton Supercharged 4-Valve Cobra: Without vs. With 75-hp Zex Kit (Horsepower)
The last place you would expect nitrous use is on a supercharged mod motor that already makes 841 hp, but the nitrous acted as an intercooler for the blower motor and allowed me to reach my goal of 900 hp.

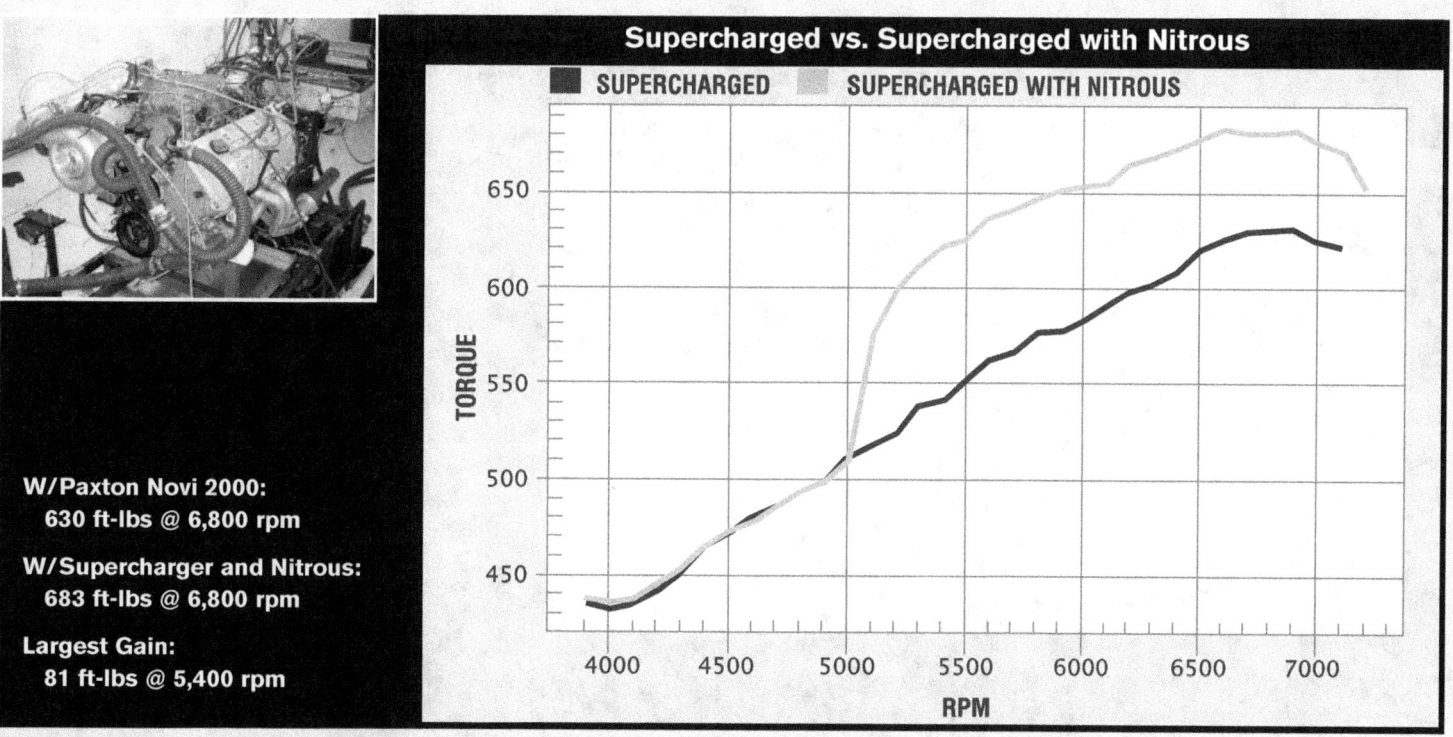

W/Paxton Novi 2000:
630 ft-lbs @ 6,800 rpm

W/Supercharger and Nitrous:
683 ft-lbs @ 6,800 rpm

Largest Gain:
81 ft-lbs @ 5,400 rpm

Paxton Supercharged 4-Valve Cobra: Without vs. With 75-hp Zex Kit (Torque)
Engaging the nitrous at 5,000 rpm produced an impressive torque gain. The gains decreased with engine speed (due mostly to a rich mixture), but the juice still managed to increase the torque output by 81 ft-lbs.

Chapter 5

Test 8: '05 3-Valve GT: With a 75-hp Zex Kit

I was excited about the introduction of the 2005 4.6L 3-valve GT motor. The 3-valve motor was originally equipped with a coil-on-plug ignition, but we replaced this system with a coil-pack system (from a 1998 4.6L 2-valve Mustang). As with all of our modular motors run on the engine dyno, we used the F.A.S.T. management system and a Meziere electric water pump. The 3-valve motor was equipped with a set of JBA shorty headers to replace the factory cast-iron exhaust manifolds, a set of 2.5-inch open pipes, and no mufflers. No mass-air meter or air inlet assembly was employed; the inlet to the throttle body was simply left open until we installed the nitrous. The F.A.S.T. system was used to dial in the air/fuel ratio to 13.0:1 and adjust the total timing to 30 degrees. Run in this configuration, the stock 4.6L 3-valve produced 357 hp at 5,900 rpm and 384 ft-lbs at 4,700 rpm. The horsepower curve leveled off around 5,100 rpm, but the power curve never dropped off as it had on the previous 4.6L 2-valve motors. The torque output was impressive, exceeding 325 ft-lbs from 3,000 rpm to 5,650 rpm. With the baseline complete, it was time to bring on the Zex nitrous.

Out of respect for the new 3-valve motor (with only 200 miles on it and owned by Vortech no less), we retarded the timing from 30 degrees down to 28 degrees. The nitrous was engaged at 3,700 rpm and the results were dramatic. The small (and perfectly safe for street use) 75-hp shot upped the peak power output of the 3-valve 4.6L to 427 hp. The torque gains were very impressive, as the peak torque jumped from 384 to 468 ft-lbs. The 75-hp shot supplied right near 75 additional horsepower from the engagement point all the way to 5,700 rpm where we let off. No modification known to man can supply the type of performance per dollar (or time spent) offered by a well-designed nitrous oxide system. In just a couple of hours, you can add 75 to 125 hp to just about any motor. Improving the power output by 21 percent (a 75-hp shot on our 357-hp 3-valve 4.6L) is easily accomplished, but that same 75-hp shout would represent a gain of 60 percent on a 125-hp 4-cylinder. Regardless, the new 3-valve 4.6L has proven itself powerful in stock trim and willing to accept at least an additional 75 hp without fear of damage. It looks like performance is still alive and well at Ford.

This Zex kit is starting to look pretty familiar, isn't it? The extra 75 hp is just as at home here on this 3-valve 4.6L as it is on the 2- and 4-valve mod motors.

Nitrous Oxide

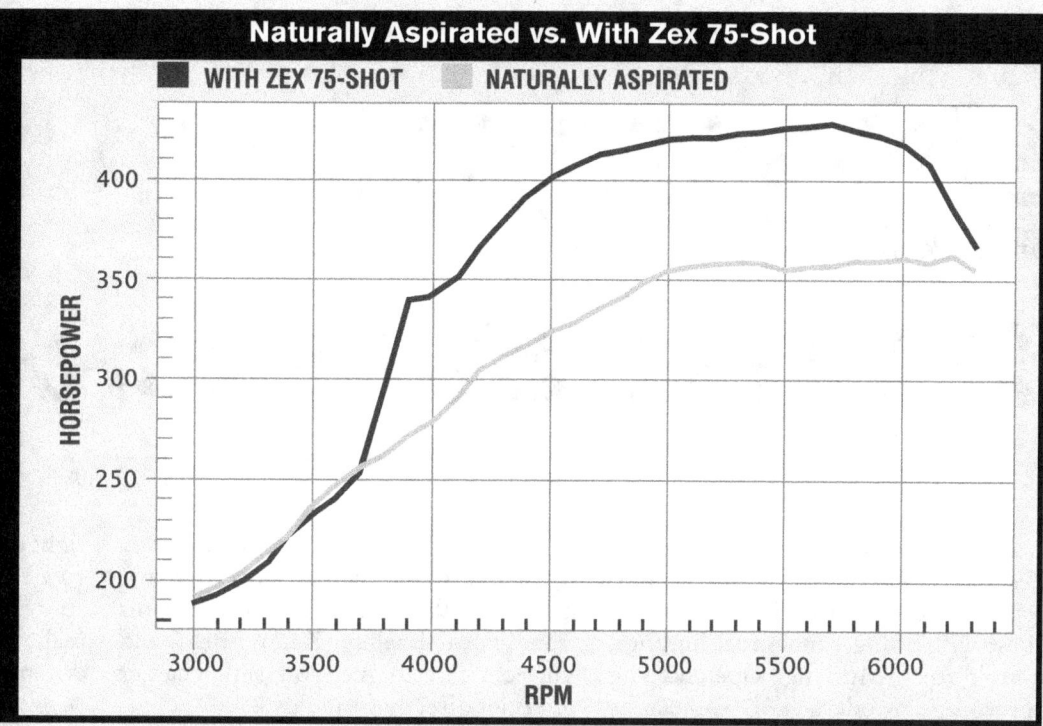

3-Valve GT:
362 hp @ 6,200 rpm

75-hp Nitrous 2005 3-Valve GT:
427 hp @ 5,700 rpm

Largest Gain:
77 hp @ 4,500 rpm

3-Valve GT: Stock vs. With 75-hp Zex Kit (Horsepower)
Adding the Zex wet fogger system to the new 3-valve GT motor upped the peak power output from 362 hp to 427 hp. It looks like these new 3-valve 4.6L motors will take to power adders every bit as well as the 2- and 4-valve versions.

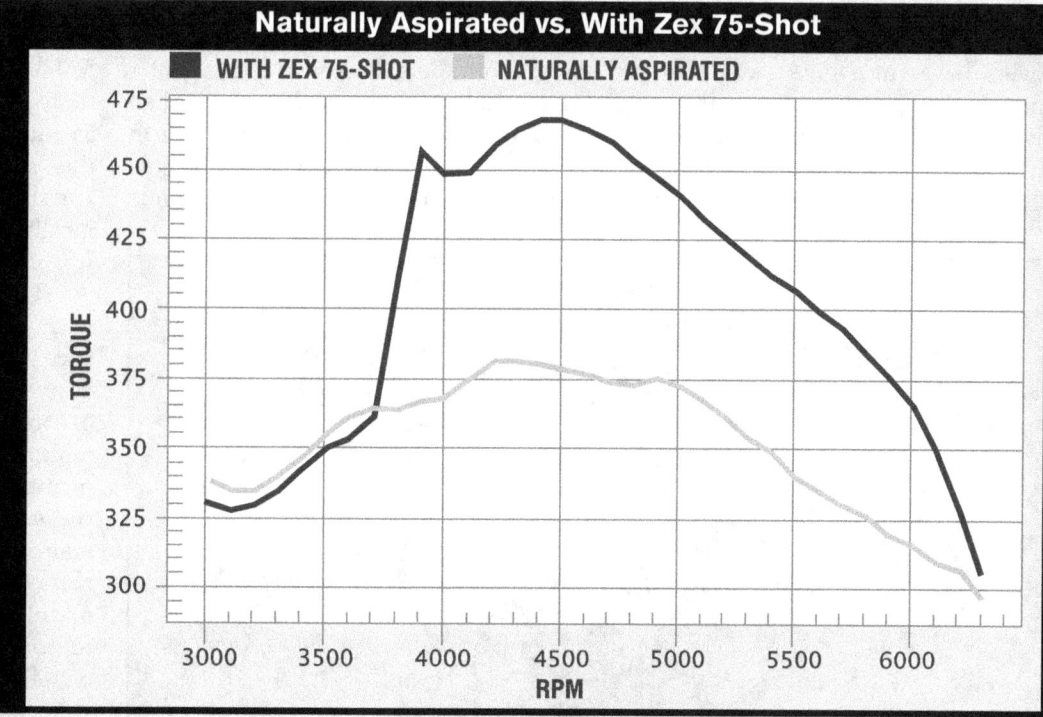

3-Valve GT:
381 ft-lbs @ 4,300 rpm

75-hp Nitrous 2005 3-Valve GT:
468 ft-lbs @ 4,400 rpm

Largest Gain:
88 ft-lbs @ 4,400 rpm

3-Valve GT: Stock vs. With 75-hp Zex Kit (Torque)
Engaging the nitrous down at 3,500 rpm produced a sizable torque gain. The 75-hp shot added as much as 88 ft-lbs of torque to the 3-valve GT motor.

CHAPTER 6

2-VALVE SUPERCHARGING

Though superchargers certainly pre-dated the fuel-injected 5.0L Mustang, it wasn't until Ford replaced the carburetor in 1986 with a long-runner fuel-injection manifold that Mustang supercharging came of age. Modern 4.6L enthusiasts have the 5.0L to thank for the current crop of superchargers available for the modular motors. Those of us with a few years under our belts remember when the Paxton planetary drive blowers were the only game in town and actually running across one on the street was a real surprise. Those early planetary drive Paxton blowers have since given way to such impressive offerings as the gear-driven Novi 1000, 1200, and (my favorite) the ever-impressive Novi 2000. Where the early Paxton blowers were hard pressed to support 500 hp, the modern Novi 2000 is capable of more than doubling that number. In this chapter, we'll test systems from Ford Racing, Kenne Bell, and Vortech, not to mention supercharger offerings directly from Ford.

While Ford offered Paxton supercharged motors back when Carroll Shelby was putting the hurt on Ferrari, the modern era probably started with the Eaton M62 supercharger in the Ford Thunderbird Super Coupe. The 3.8L V-6 was equipped not only with modern fuel injection, but also a positive displacement roots supercharger and intercooler gave it 5.0L performance. Ford supplied truck owners with an impressive gift in the form of the supercharged 5.4L Lightning truck. An easy 14-second machine right off the showroom floor (13s if driven well), the 5.4L Lightning mill demonstrated that the 2-valve mod motors really responded to boost (what motor doesn't?). Ford would later add an Eaton M112 roots supercharger to the 4.6L 4-valve Cobra in 2003, and then apply an even more impressive 2.3L twin-screw blower to the all-aluminum 5.4L 4-valve mod motor used in the Ford GT. To date, this is the ultimate Ford modular motor, and quite possibly the most impressive (if not most powerful) motor Ford has ever offered in a production car. Rated at 550 hp, the supercharged 5.4L 4-valve motor has been tested to produce that 550-hp power rating at the wheels. I'd pit this supercharged mod motor against any stock 427 Cammer (though not technically a production motor), 428 Cobra Jet, or Boss 429 any day.

Though the 5.0L can be credited with introducing the modern performance world to supercharging, the 4.6L has continued to expand the popularity of forced induction. Currently there are a minimum of 10 different supercharger manufacturers that offer kits directly for the 4.6L Ford family. The number of manufacturers involved (and their success) should give you an idea about the popularity of the supercharged mod motors. In the end, it's the enthusiast that benefits from the proliferation of available kits, as competition improves the product line and decreases the cost to the consumer. Having 10 different manufacturers also provides variety. This is an important fact and contrary to some of

This 4.6L 2-valve mod motor cranked out 800 flywheel hp running a Vortech YS-Trim supercharger and a custom dual-core air-to-water aftercooler.

2-Valve Supercharging

the propaganda you read on some of the Web sites there is not one ideal form of supercharging for the 4.6L 2-valve motor. Were there one form that excelled above all others and provided the very best of every comparison variable, no other form would continue to exist. Fortunately for us, this is simply not the case. Variety allows you to pick and choose the best combination to meet your particular needs. Centrifugal superchargers perform a certain way, as do roots and twin-screw blowers. Which one is right for you depends on what you want.

If you are looking for maximum (peak) power production from your (hopefully suitably built) 4.6L 2-valve motor, then you will probably be best served by a centrifugal blower. If instantaneous boost response is more important, then you should be leaning toward either of the positive displacement designs (roots or twin-screw). There are obviously positive and negative attributes offered by each type of supercharger, but in the end, the choice will likely come down to more variables than just peak power; things like cost, kit completeness, ease of installation, availability, customer service, and (*very important*) tuning. Does the supercharger kit come with an ECU program designed to provide maximum safe performance on pump gas? Does the kit include the necessary injector upgrade, fuel pump upgrade, or ignition amplifier? Once installed, how difficult is it to further increase the power output? Is it more involved than a simple pulley change (it almost always is)? I have just scratched the surface in terms of considerations when choosing a supercharger for your 4.6L Mustang, but know that all superchargers offer a significant power gain, just be sure that the tune (air/fuel and especially timing) are spot on before putting your foot in it.

While not quite on par with the 4-valve 4.6L, the 4.6L and 5.4L 2-valve motors respond very well to supercharging. Whether the blower kit is a simple M90 from Ford Racing or an intercooled YS trim from Vortech, adding a blower kit to your mod motor will yield impressive dividends. One convenient way to calculate the power potential offered by any supercharger is to take the power output of the naturally aspirated motor and multiply it by the boost pressure as a function of atmospheric pressure. Since a naturally aspirated motor runs at an atmospheric pressure of 14.7 psi (or 1 BAR), all we have to do to double the power output of the motor (in theory) is to double the pressure to the motor. By this I mean that if the naturally aspirated 4.6L 2-valve motor produced 300 hp, all we have to do to reach 600 hp is to double the pressure or supply 14.7 psi using a supercharger. If we supply only 7.35 psi, we should see a corresponding power gain of roughly 50 percent, since 7.35 psi is 50 percent of 14.7 psi. Using 10 psi, we see that the power gain will be 68 percent, since 10 psi is 68 percent of 14.7 psi, while 20 psi should provide a gain of 136 percent. The simple math formula is as follows: Supercharged HP = NA hp x (Boost pressure/14.7 +1).

Now that I have extolled the virtues of the boost/power formula, I can tell you why motors usually do not reach the stated power outputs. The first problem is that the formula does not take into account the parasitic losses associated with driving the supercharger. In the case of a high-horsepower application, the supercharger may consume 50 to 100 hp (or more) and this power is subtracted directly from the output. If the boost pressure of 10 psi were to supply a mass flow gain able to support a 68-percent increase, then you would still have to subtract the parasitic losses associated with driving the blower. Due to the increase in heat associated with the increase in compression (to 10 psi), the number of oxygen molecules per volume is less than it would be at atmospheric pressure. Therefore, the increase in pressure of 68 percent (to 10 psi) will not likely yield a commensurate gain in power, though intercooling can improve the air density (number of molecules per volume). Despite these seemingly insurmountable odds, we often reach the power suggested by the power/boost formula on 4.6L 2-valve motors by combining a healthy (and powerful) naturally aspirated combination with an efficient supercharger.

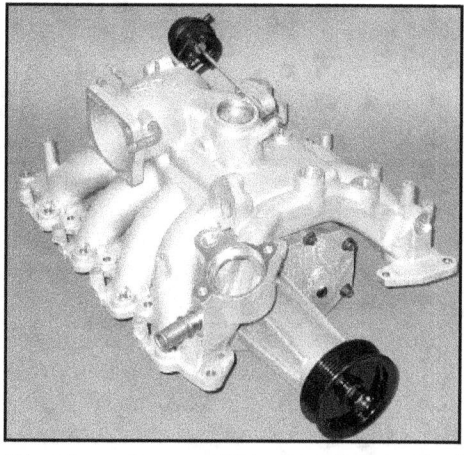

Want to make your 281-ci mod motor feel like it just gained another 100 cubic inches? This roots blower kit from the Ford Racing catalog will provide big-block-like torque from your 4.6L.

Even on a mild 4.6L, a centrifugal supercharger like this T-Trim unit from Vortech will add an easy 100 hp. The air-to-water aftercooler provides the necessary cooling to allow you to run elevated boost levels on pump gas.

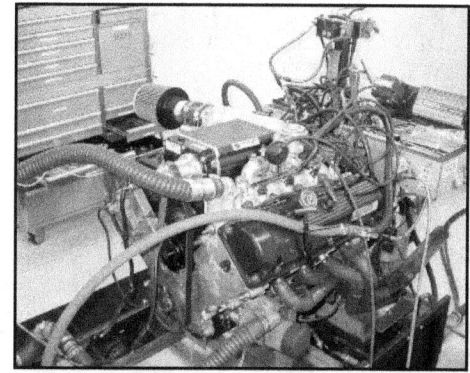

The twin-screw supercharger from Kenne Bell combines the immediate response of the positive-displacement blower with improved efficiency (and power potential) over a typical roots blower.

Building 4.6/5.4L Ford Horsepower on the Dyno

Chapter 6

Test 1: PI 2-Valve GT: Ford Racing Supercharger

One common mistake when reading a book like this is to compare absolute power outputs. If you're concerned only with huge power numbers, check out Test 7 in Chapter 7 with the ATI blower on the 5.4L 4-valve motor, or the 1,600-hp twin-turbo 4.6L in Chapter 8. The reality is that while impressive, the huge power numbers generated by these drag-race-only motors is certainly not what you want for your daily driver. It would be nice to brag to your friends, but the reality is that these massive power outputs are only useable by a dedicated race chassis on a certified drag strip. Believe it or not, the vast majority of modular-powered vehicles rely on stock motors. Owners who opt to modify their motors are actually in the minority, and racers who exceed 1,000 hp are probably less than one percent of that small minority. Most mod-motor guys are just looking for that little extra bit of power to make the daily commute or the occasional stoplight encounter a bit more exciting.

For those 4.6L 2-valve Mustang GT owners not looking to go to the extreme, the Ford Racing supercharger has a lot to offer. If you grew up driving big-block machines (say a 390 GT or (if you were lucky) a 428 Cobra Jet), you no doubt long for the mountains of torque. Despite the similarities in actual ¼-mile performance between the 260-hp 4.6L GT and the big-block muscle cars of old, the 281-ci mod motor will never offer the feel of a big-block. When it comes to low-speed torque production, big motors rule the roost. About the only replacement for displacement is forced induction, and nothing pumps out the torque like a positive-displacement supercharger. The Ford Racing supercharger kit for the '99-'04 PI motor was designed as a direct bolt-on and is available with a complete installation hardware kit that includes a high-flow fuel pump, 30-pound injectors, and a reprogrammed computer designed specifically for the supercharger. Basically, the Ford Racing supercharger is as close as you can get to having a 2-valve GT supercharger available from the factory.

The Sean Hyland 4.6L for this test featured a forged crank, rods, and pistons. The top end was stock PI stuff, including heads, cams, and intake.

The Ford Racing supercharger kit was tested on a 4.6L 2-valve motor built by Sean Hyland. The SHM motor featured forged internals (crank, rods, and pistons) but the upgraded reciprocating assembly was not necessary for use with the blower. The supercharger was designed to be installed and perform on a bone-stock 4.6L motor. The SHM test motor also featured stock PI heads, intake, and cams. The motor was equipped with an electric water pump, a F.A.S.T. engine management system (with 36-pound injectors), and a set of Kooks 1⅜-inch long-tube headers. In naturally aspirated form (running 26 degrees of total timing and an air/fuel ratio of 13.0:1 on 91-octane pump gas), the 4.6L produced 298 hp at 4,900 rpm and 345 ft-lbs of torque at 4,100 rpm. Installing the Ford Racing supercharger upped the power output to 383 hp at 5,700 rpm and the torque to 395 ft-lbs at 3,800 rpm. No longer did the power fall off at 5,000 rpm; it instead kept climbing all the way to 6,000 rpm. The torque curve exceeded 375 ft-lbs from 3,000 rpm to 5,200 rpm while offering a big-block-like reading of 370 ft-lbs.

2-Valve Supercharging

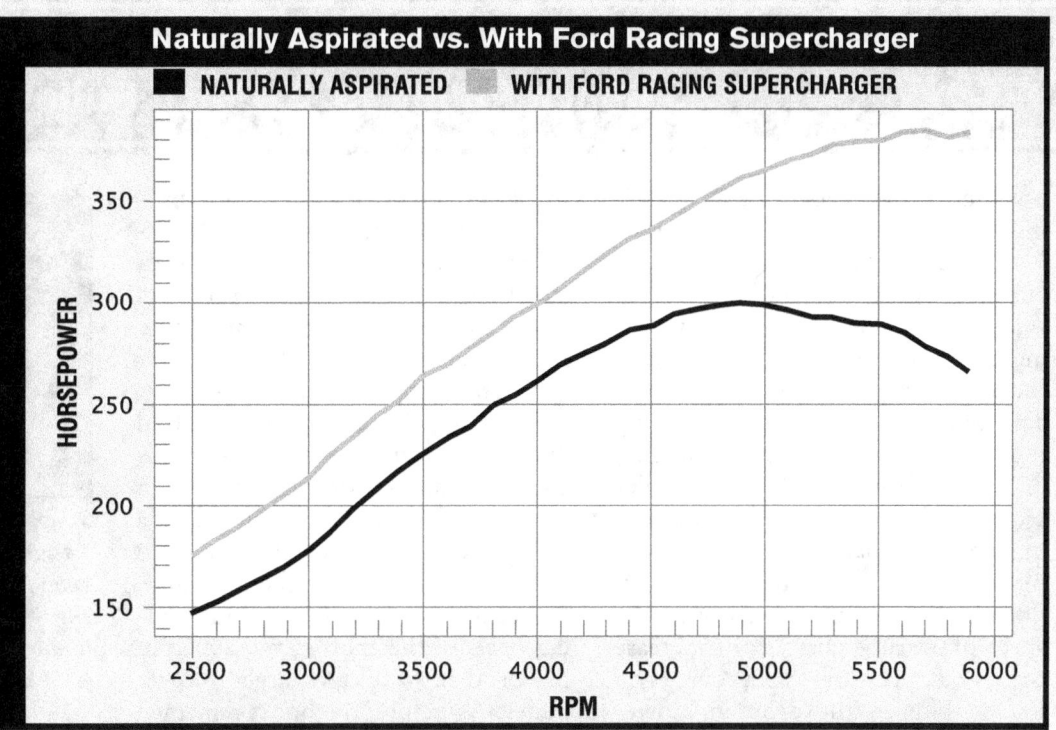

PI 2-Valve GT:
298 hp @ 4,900 rpm

With Ford Racing Supercharger:
383 hp @ 5,700 rpm

Largest Gain:
117 hp @ 5,900 rpm

PI 2-Valve GT: NA vs. Ford Racing Supercharger (Horsepower)
When you're trying to add power to your 2-valve modular motor there's nothing quite like forced induction. In this case, the boost in power came from a Ford Racing supercharger kit. The Ford Racing supercharger system utilizes an M90 Eaton blower and dedicated intake casting that features long intake runners to maximize the power production below 6,000 rpm. Unlike most other supercharger systems, the Ford Racing blower doesn't include an intercooler, but you don't need one at the reduced boost. Adding the blower to the SHM 2-valve 4.6L upped the peak power to 383 hp and the torque to 395 ft-lbs. The peak-to-peak power gain was 85 hp, but the largest gain was 117 hp at 5,900 rpm.

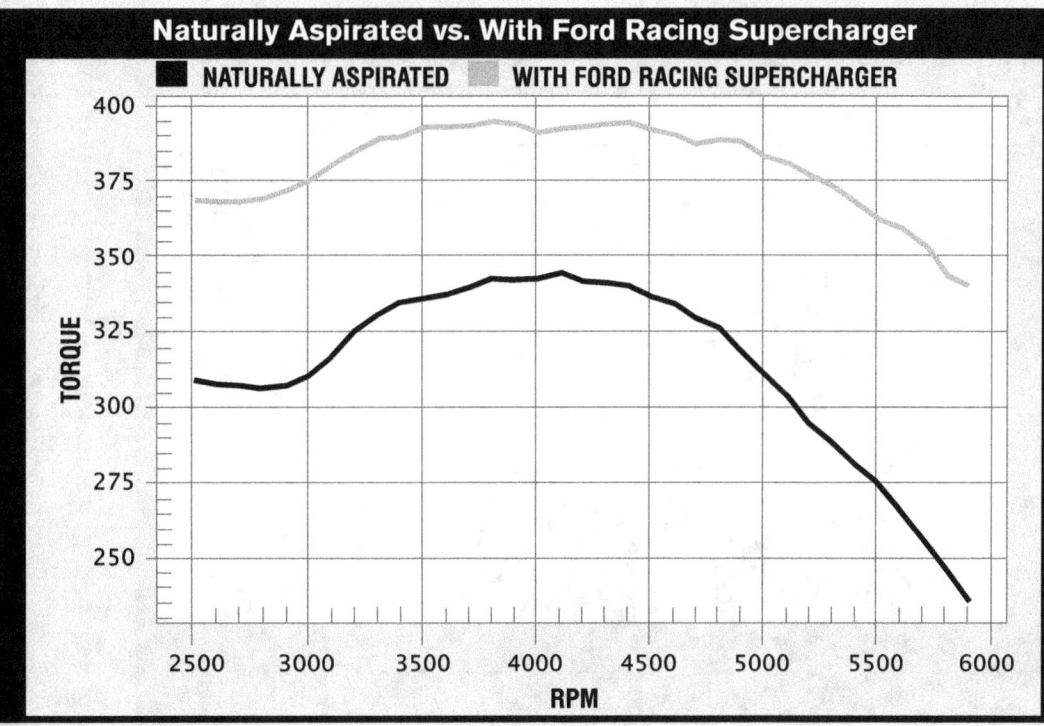

PI 2-Valve GT:
345 ft-lbs @ 4,100 rpm

With Ford Racing Supercharger:
395 ft-lbs @ 3,800 rpm

Largest Gain:
95 ft-lbs @ 5,900 rpm

PI 2-Valve GT: NA vs. Ford Racing Supercharger (Torque)
As expected, the roots supercharger provided instantaneous boost and torque, adding 60 ft-lbs at just 2,500 rpm. In fact, the Ford Racing blower added a solid 50 ft-lbs throughout the rev range. An extra 50 ft-lbs is always a welcomed addition to any 2-valve 4.6L Mustang. The boost pressure reached a peak of 6.8 psi, but was just 4.5 to 5 psi for most of the RPM range.

Building 4.6/5.4L Ford Horsepower on the Dyno

Test 2: Ford Racing Supercharged 2-Valve GT: 3.6-inch Pulley vs. 3.4-inch Pulley

One of the major benefits of having a motor equipped with forced induction is the ability to further enhance the power output. With a supercharger, you can boost power by increasing the blower speed relative to the motor by changing the drive ratio. This can be accomplished by altering the size of either the blower (smaller) or crank (larger) pulley. A smaller blower pulley will increase the speed of the supercharger relative to the motor, which will provide more airflow. In most instances, increasing the speed of the supercharger will increase the boost pressure. With our Ford Racing blower, the drop in blower pulley size from 3.6 inches to 3.4 inches resulted in a jump in peak boost pressure from 6.9 to 8.9 psi.

It should be noted that the SHM 4.6L test motor was treated to a 70-mm Ford Racing throttle body upgrade between installing the blower and this test on swapping pulley sizes, so it was included in the before and the after of this test. Equipped with the stock pulley, the mild 4.6L produced 394 hp at 5,900 rpm and 402 ft-lbs of torque at 4,200 rpm. The boost curve remained below 5.5 psi from 2,500 rpm to 5,100 rpm and only ramped up to the peak of 6.9 psi after 5,100 rpm. This is an indication that boost was stacking in the manifold due to the restrictive cylinder heads and cam timing. Installing the 3.4-inch blower pulley from South Florida Pulley Headquarters resulted in a gain of roughly 1 psi across the rev range. The peak reading of 8.9 psi is misleading because the motor was 200 rpm higher than with the larger blower pulley. As before, the boost remained below 6.5 psi until 5,100 rpm and only ramped up rapidly thereafter. The extra 1 psi resulted in a gain of 11 hp (peak to peak) for a total of 405 hp. The torque gain was even more dramatic, with the additional boost pressure adding 15 ft-lbs of torque for a total of 417 ft-lbs.

One interesting point should be made here regarding the effect of

Swapping the 3.6-inch blower pulley for a 3.4-inch pulley resulted in a jump in peak boost pressure from 6.9 to 8.9 psi. The engine picked up both horsepower and torque, but not as much upper end power as we'd hoped for.

increasing the boost pressure. Some readers may be wondering why we stopped at adding just 1 psi of boost pressure. The reason is quite simple: We were not looking for maximum power output from this combination, but more importantly, the M90 supercharger was nearing its flow limit. One of the ways to judge the merits (or success) of any forced induction application is by the power-per-pound-of-boost scale. In some cases, adding 1 psi can be worth 35 to 40 hp (or more), but on our roots blower the gain was just 11 hp. The reason for this relatively mild gain is due to the fact that the M90 supercharger is actually on the small side for a high-horsepower 4.6L application. The Ford blower is excellent as a bolt on for a stock or near-stock motor where the power output will be less than 450 hp, but running beyond that will put the blower out of its efficiency range. The fact that the increase in boost pressure offered more power (torque) down low than horsepower at the peak is a sure sign that we were nearing the flow limit of the blower. An even smaller blower pulley would likely yield more power (especially low-speed torque) but the gains near the top of the rev range would certainly diminish.

By swapping out the blower pulley on our Ford Racing supercharger, we'll add boost and hopefully some horsepower and torque. You can also change your crank pulley and get the same effect; what matters is the ratio between the two pulleys.

2-Valve Supercharging

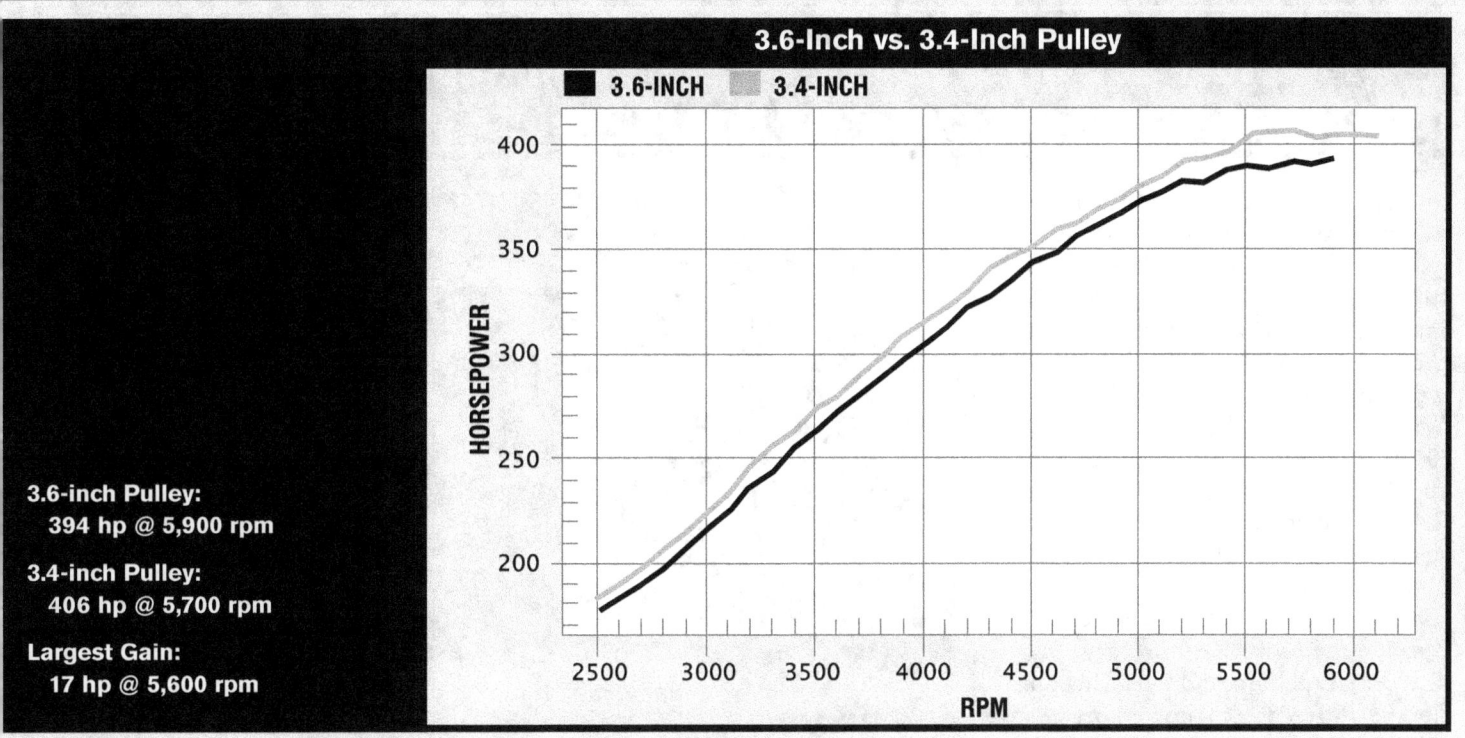

3.6-inch Pulley: 394 hp @ 5,900 rpm
3.4-inch Pulley: 406 hp @ 5,700 rpm
Largest Gain: 17 hp @ 5,600 rpm

Ford Racing Supercharged 2-Valve GT: 3.6-inch vs. 3.4-inch Pulley (Horsepower)
With our supercharged 4.6L now breathing well, thanks to the Ford Racing supercharger, it was time to crank up the boost. The blower pulley that came in the kit measured 3.6 inches. We picked up a 3.4-inch pulley from South Florida Pulley Headquarters. The pulley swap upped the peak boost pressure from 6.9 psi to 8.9 psi, raising power from 394 hp to 405 hp, with a consistent increase throughout the rev range.

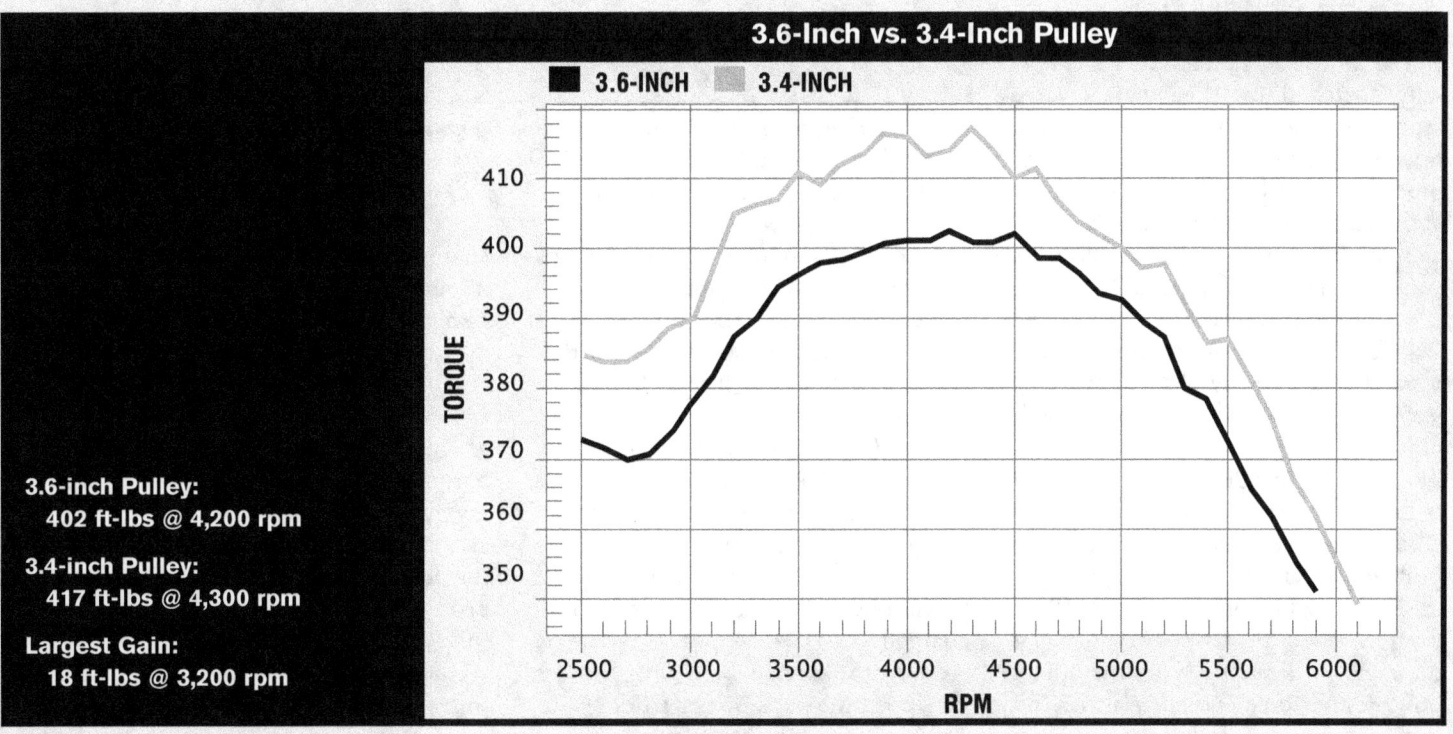

3.6-inch Pulley: 402 ft-lbs @ 4,200 rpm
3.4-inch Pulley: 417 ft-lbs @ 4,300 rpm
Largest Gain: 18 ft-lbs @ 3,200 rpm

Ford Racing Supercharged 2-Valve GT: 3.6-inch vs. 3.4-inch Pulley (Torque)
As expected, the increase in blower speed improved the torque curve. The peak torque was up from 402 ft-lbs to 417 ft-lbs, but gains were available throughout the rev range. The Ford Racing roots blower makes for an impressive package, as the extra torque will provide that big-block feel from your 281-cubic-inch 4.6L.

Building 4.6/5.4L Ford Horsepower on the Dyno

Chapter 6

Test 3: Early 2-Valve GT: Kenne Bell Supercharger

The early 1996–'98 (non-PI) 4.6L motors hardly set the performance world on fire, but it's possible to transform these mild-mannered early GTs into super 'Stangs. Not surprisingly, the route to super 'Stangdom starts with the addition of a supercharger. When you go out hunting for an '03–'04 Cobra, you'd better be sporting some serious hardware. True, the '03–'04 Cobras come factory equipped with a force feeder, but it's possible to choose a superior form of forced induction for your GT. Believe it or not, the twin-screw Autorotor supercharger is capable of more than making up the difference in power between your non-PI 2-valve motor and the much-heralded '03–'04 4-valve Cobra motor. Simply bolting on the new Kenne Bell intercooled supercharger kit will usher forth nearly 350 flywheel hp, up from just south of 200 flywheel hp (in stock trim). This power gain comes at just 9 psi, a number incidentally matched by the stock 4-valve Cobra. It's odd that a 4-valve Cobra boosted to nearly 9 psi makes only as much as the milder '96–'98 GT motor at the same boost. Like we said, the efficiency of the twin-screw blower is far superior to the roots (Eaton) blower.

While I trust that the guys at Kenne Bell did their homework on the kit, I wanted to see for myself. Our test subject was a '98 5-speed GT equipped with only a cat-back exhaust. On the chassis dyno, the GT produced 198 hp and 266 ft-lbs of torque at the wheels. As expected, peak torque came at 3,100 rpm and peak power came less than 1,500 rpm later. The early GT only exceeded 250 ft-lbs from 2,700 rpm to 4,000 rpm, falling off rapidly thereafter. Even the horsepower curve took a nosedive after 5,000 rpm. If you've ever been behind the wheel of an early 4.6L GT, you know that the motors feel pretty torquey at part throttle and at low engine speeds, but mashing your foot to the floor doesn't seem to summon up the demons foreshadowed by the impressive throttle response. Instead, the power surge quickly subsides and you're left with a windshield full of taillights. For kicks, check out the curves offered by the early and late (PI) GT motors in Chapter 3.

If you want to skip a few little steps and jump right in with the big boys, check out a twin-screw supercharger kit from Kenne Bell. This kit takes your stock early GT and brings it up to about 350 hp at the wheels.

While PI 4.6L motors are impressive, installing the Kenne Bell supercharger takes the power output of the early 4.6L well beyond the late-model (even modified) GTs right into supercharged '03–'04 Cobra territory. Adding the Kenne Bell 9-psi blower kit upped the peak power from 198 to 349 hp. The peak torque was up from 266 to 388 ft-lbs. The Kenne Bell kit included everything for the installation, including injectors, a custom (proprietary) computer chip, and an air-to-water intercooler, which allows it run to on 91-octane pump gas. Extensive tuning was employed to optimize the air/fuel ratio and timing curves under boost. Care was taken to ensure the power offered by the blower was available safely without fear of harmful detonation. Rather than waiting for a surge of power that never arrives on the stock motor, stomping the loud pedal with the Kenne Bell produces lots and lots of tire smoke followed by a frantic explosion of forward thrust. The most impressive thing about these efficient positive-displacement superchargers is that the explosive thrust is available at nearly any engine speed, even down at 1,500 rpm! Such is the benefit of a twin-screw supercharger.

2-Valve Supercharging

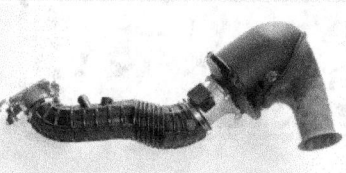

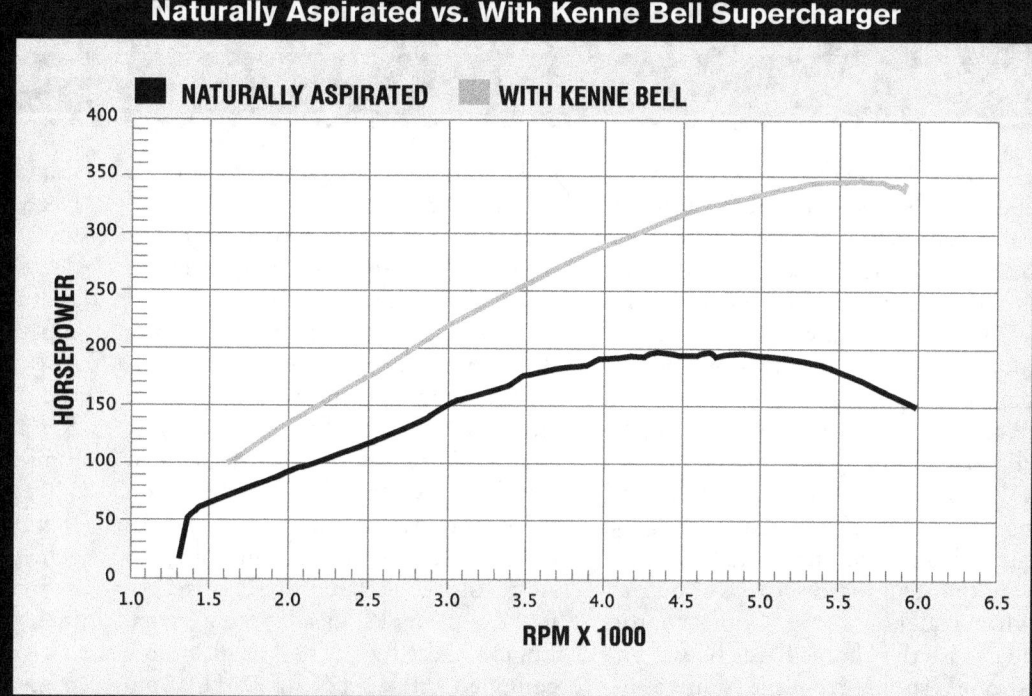

Early 2-Valve GT:
198 hp @ 4,600 rpm

W/Kenne Bell (9 psi):
349 hp @ 5,700 rpm

Largest Gain:
182 hp @ 5,700 rpm

Early 2-Valve GT: NA vs. Kenne Bell Supercharger (9 psi) (Horsepower)
Not surprisingly, installing the Kenne Bell supercharger kit upped the power output of the non-PI 4.6L GT motor significantly. With 349 hp at the wheels, this early GT was now pumping out supercharged 4-valve '03 Cobra power. Besides adding the blower, we've substituted new intake plumbing to replace the restrictive stock pieces shown here.

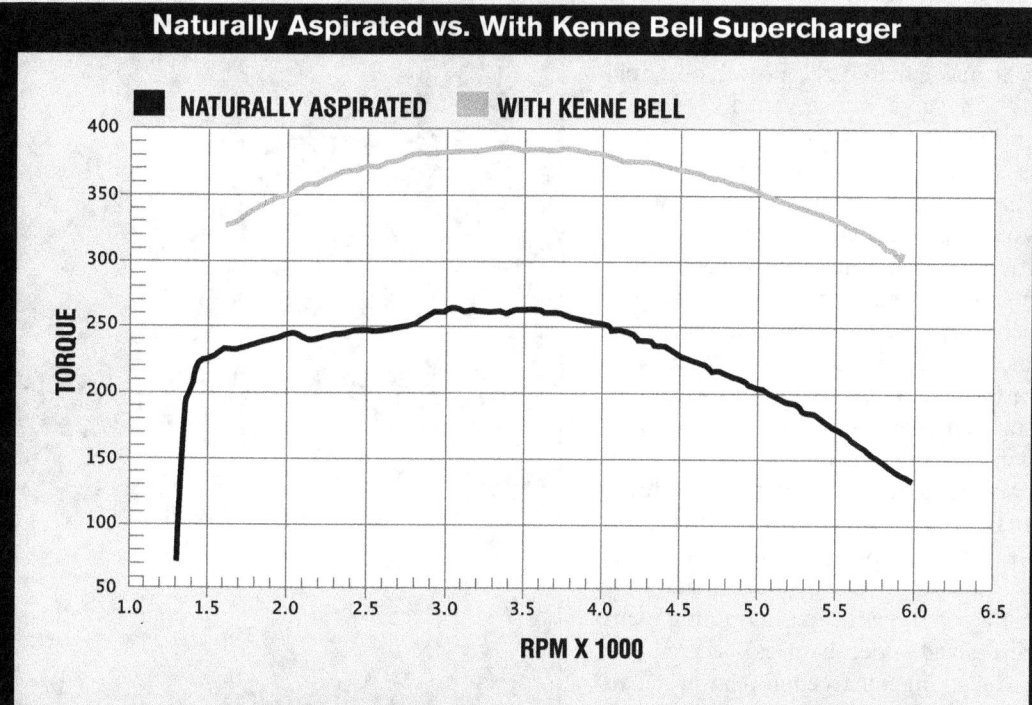

Early 2-Valve GT:
266 ft-lbs @ 3,100 rpm

W/Kenne Bell (9 psi):
388 ft-lbs @ 3,400 rpm

Largest Gain:
175 ft-lbs @ 5,600 rpm

Early 2-Valve GT: NA vs. Kenne Bell Supercharger (9 psi) (Torque)
While big-time horsepower gains are what everyone will be talking about, it's actually the huge torque gains offered from as low as 1,500 rpm that will be enjoyed most often on the street. Equipped with the efficient Kenne Bell twin-screw supercharger, the early 4.6L GT motor produced a peak of 388 ft-lbs at 3,400 rpm. More importantly, the supercharger motor pumped out over 350 ft-lbs from 2,000 rpm to 5,000 rpm. In fact, the torque production of the supercharged motor never dropped to within 40 ft-lbs of the peak produced by the naturally aspirated motor. Cost of the blower kit – a few grand. The look on the face of a destroyed '03-'04 Cobra owner – priceless.

Test 4: PI 2-Valve GT: Kenne Bell Supercharger

While Ford fanatics have been celebrating the '03-'04 Cobra motor, it has definitely widened the gap between 2-valve GTs and Cobras. Even stock, the power potential of a supercharged 4-valve Cobra motor is more than any naturally aspirated GT motor is capable of producing. If you have any hope of producing supercharged Cobra power from your 2-valve GT, you better be ready to add boost. While just about any good supercharger (or turbo) kit will provide the required peak power output, what really sets the Cobra motors apart is the immediate boost and torque response from the positive-displacement Eaton supercharger. Thinking one step ahead, once you meet stock '03 Cobra power levels, what are you going to do when you run up against one of the thousands that are already modified?

Stock to stock, your 2-valve GT will never match the power potential of a 4-valve motor. Lucky for GT enthusiasts, the '03-'04 Cobra motor is somewhat detuned for a long life (and minimal warranty claims). When you combine this with the fact that the roots-style Eaton supercharger is low man on the efficiency totem pole, you can start to see some light at the end of the tunnel. All you need is to install a more efficient positive-displacement supercharger and you cannot only handle a stock Cobra, but you should have enough in reserve for a modified snake. The twin-screw supercharger is decidedly more efficient than the roots style, offering more mass flow for a given revolution (assuming identical sized superchargers), as well as a reduced inlet charge temperature. This extra efficiency adds up to more power per pound of boost. Toss in the fact that the Kenne Bell supercharger kit designed for the 4.6L GT comes with an air-to-water intercooler just like the factory Cobra, and you have the makings for a serious serpent slayer, to say nothing of those pesky LS1s.

The Kenne Bell supercharger kit comes with everything needed to install the kit on a stock or modified 4.6L GT. The kits include injectors, a Boost-A-Pump, and a custom calibrated computer chip to produce safe and effective air/fuel and timing curves. To test it out, we decided to run the blower on a modified 4.6L on the engine dyno. Our modified 4.6L test motor was a high-mileage '98 short block updated with a set of CNC-ported PI heads from Total Engine Airflow. The heads were equipped with a set of XE274H Comp cams, 1⅝-inch long-tube Hooker headers, and 42-pound injectors. A F.A.S.T. engine management system was used to dial in the total timing (30 degrees NA and 22 degrees SC) and air/fuel curves (13.0:1 NA and 11.8:1 supercharged). The naturally aspirated 4.6L produced 393 hp at 6,000 rpm and 383 ft-lbs at 4,800 rpm. With the Kenne Bell, the peak power numbers jumped to 587 hp at 6,300 rpm and 520 ft-lbs at 4,300 rpm and 5,000 rpm (flat torque curve). This power was achieved running dyno water (95 degrees) through the air-to-water intercooler at 9 psi of boost. Incidentally, this is more power than we ever made with the Eaton supercharger on the 4-valve Cobra motor.

This Kenne Bell supercharger more than evens the score between the PI GT and the supercharged '03-'04 Cobra. It comes with everything you need, including an air-to-water intercooler.

2-Valve Supercharging

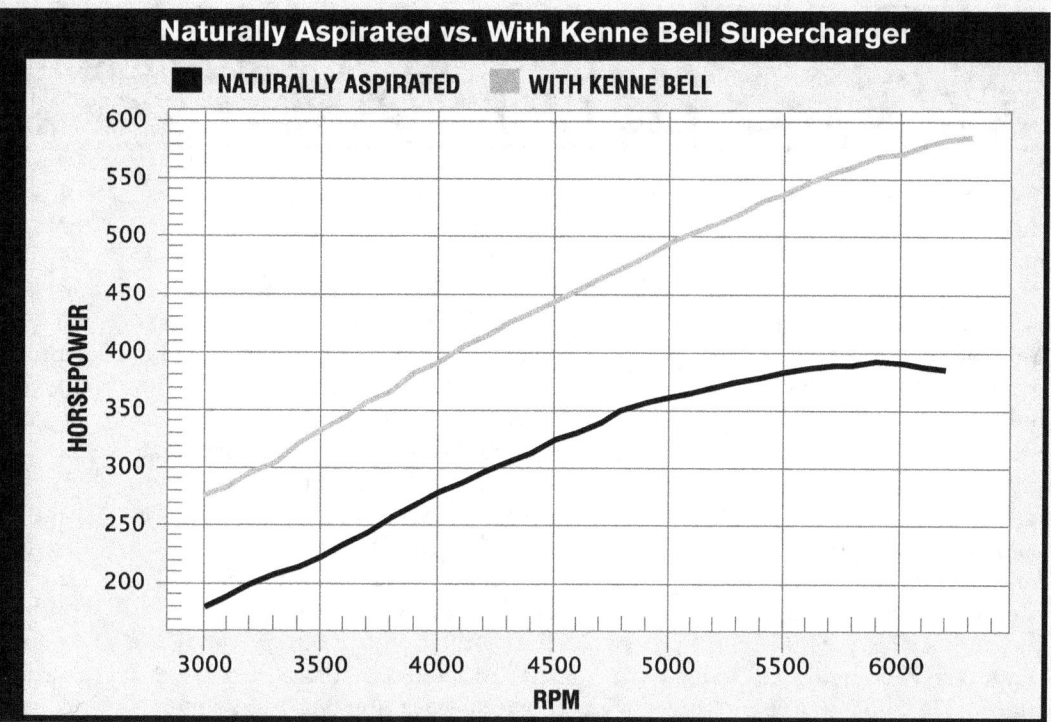

PI 2-Valve GT:
393 hp @ 6,000 rpm

W/Kenne Bell (9 psi):
587 hp @ 6,300 rpm

Largest Gain:
197 hp @ 6,200 rpm

PI 2-Valve GT: NA vs. Kenne Bell Supercharger (9 psi) (Horsepower)
At 393 hp, our modified 4.6L GT test motor was no slouch to begin with, but adding 9 psi from the Kenne Bell supercharger upped the peak power to 587 hp. Even down at 3,000 rpm, the blower added 90 horsepower.

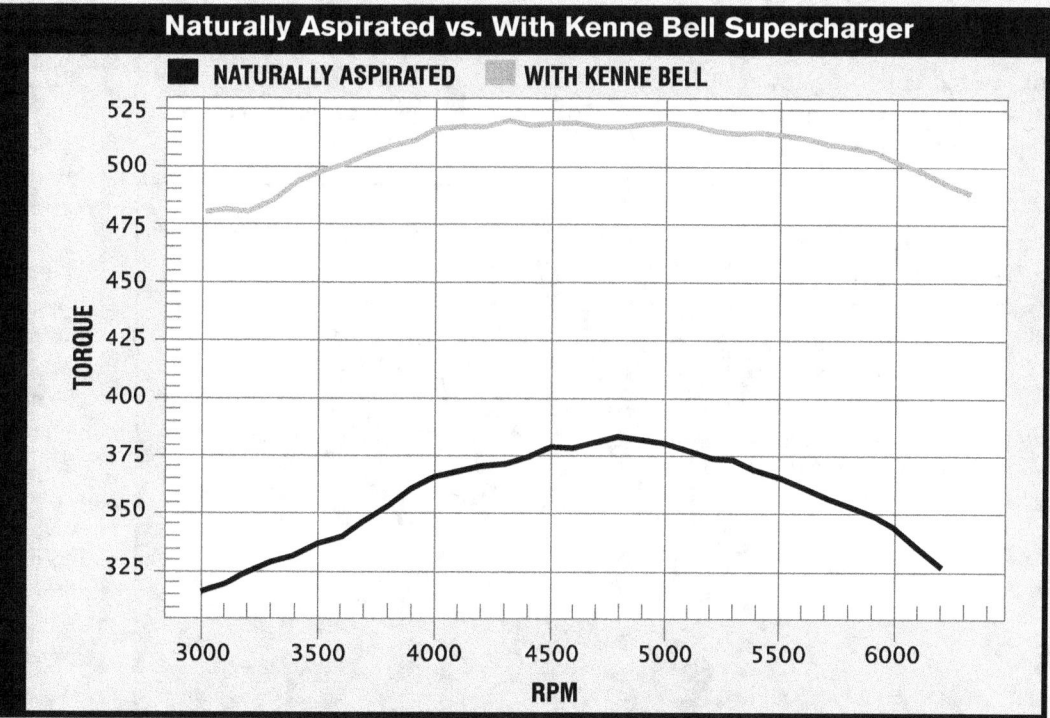

PI 2-Valve GT:
383 ft-lbs @ 4,800 rpm

W/Kenne Bell (9 psi):
520 ft-lbs @ 5,000 rpm

Largest Gain:
165 ft-lbs @ 6,100 rpm

PI 2-Valve GT: NA vs. Kenne Bell Supercharger (9 psi) (Torque)
Check out how flat the torque curves were after installing the Kenne Bell supercharger on our modified 4.6L GT motor. From 4,000 to 5,100 rpm, the torque production never varied by more than 2 ft-lbs (from 518 to 520)! Down at 3,000 rpm, the supercharger increased torque production by 165 ft-lbs. Imagine what an extra 165 ft-lbs of torque would feel like. Now imagine what it would feel like as you showed taillights to the 4-valve Cobra owner.

Building 4.6/5.4L Ford Horsepower on the Dyno

Chapter 6

Test 5: PI 2-Valve GT: Vortech T-Trim Supercharger

Anyone who ever tells you that there is no replacement for displacement has never experienced a well sorted forced induction system. What better way to add 100, 150, or 200 hp? You won't get these kinds of power gains from simple bolt ons, but you can bolt on more than 200 hp to your modified 4.6L GT motor with nothing more elaborate than a Vortech supercharger kit. Okay, so it is a little more complicated than that (the tuning must be spot on), but it is possible to easily add 100 to 150 hp and, with sufficient fuel and octane, you can up the power output of your modified 4.6L to the tune of 265 hp! Where else are you likely to get power gains like that? While the centrifugal supercharger like our Vortech will never provide the immediate boost response of a positive-displacement supercharger, no positive-displacement supercharger (not even the twin-screw) will offer the power-per-pound of boost gains of an efficient centrifugal supercharger at the top of the rev range.

Your typical (street) positive-displacement supercharger is run with a drive ratio ranging from a low of around 1.75:1 (meaning the blower is spun 1.75 times the engine speed) to as high as 3:1 on a high-power twin-screw. This puts the blower speed between 11,500 and 19,500 rpm (though this blower speed is rare) at an engine speed of 6,500 rpm. A centrifugal supercharger can be spun as high as 65,000 rpm thanks to a combination of an internal step ratio near 3.5:1 and a drive pulley ratio between 1.8:1 and 2.75:1. When you multiply the drive ratio by the internal step ratio by the engine speed, things start to get going in a hurry. Similar to a turbo impeller, the impeller on a centrifugal supercharger is small (compared to the rotors on a roots or twin-screw supercharger) and must be spun very rapidly to achieve significant airflow. Once spun into its efficiency range, the centrifugal supercharger will provide impressive power gains at the top of the rev range (arguably where are most needed for in-gear acceleration).

The debate between air-to-air and air-to-water intercooling still rages on, but from a maximum efficiency (defined here as the ability to reduce the inlet charge temp) standpoint, there is no beating the air-to-water system, simply because it's possible to reduce the inlet charge temperature below ambient temp using ice water or some other ultra-cold transfer (cooling) medium. Obviously, ice water would be of limited value for continual street use, but even Ford (as well as other OEMs) combines supercharging with air-to-water intercooling on the Lightning and Cobra motors. For occasional acceleration spurts that make up 99 percent of street use, the choice between air-to-air or air-to-water is less important than choosing to have some form of charge cooling in the first place. Rather than supply the Vortech air-to-water Power Cooler with ice water, we chose ambient (actually slightly warmer) dyno water. With less than 13 psi of boost, the actual gain in charge temperature was relatively small given the length of total run time for the dyno pull.

The test motor consisted of a stock, high-mileage '98 2-valve GT short block topped off with a set of Total Engine Airflow CNC-ported PI heads, matching PI intake, and a set of Comp XE274H cams. The near 10:1 compression was relatively high for forced-induction use, but we ran the test on a mixture of 91-octane pump gas and 100-octane race fuel just to be safe. The naturally aspirated 4.6L produced 393 hp at 6,000 rpm and 383 ft-lbs of torque at 4,800 rpm. Once we installed the Vortech T-Trim supercharger and Power Cooler, the power jumped to 655 hp at 12.6 psi. The peak torque was up to 556 ft-lbs, a number registered from 5,600 to 5,900 rpm. As expected, the boost curve offered by the centrifugal supercharger started out at just 2.4 psi at 3,000 rpm and motored up to 12.6 psi at the power peak of 6,400 rpm.

This Vortech T-Trim centrifugal supercharger and Power Cooler added an insane amount of high-end power to our 4.6L PI GT. If you like racing from a roll, or worry about too much torque when you launch, a centrifugal blower is perfect for you.

2-Valve Supercharging

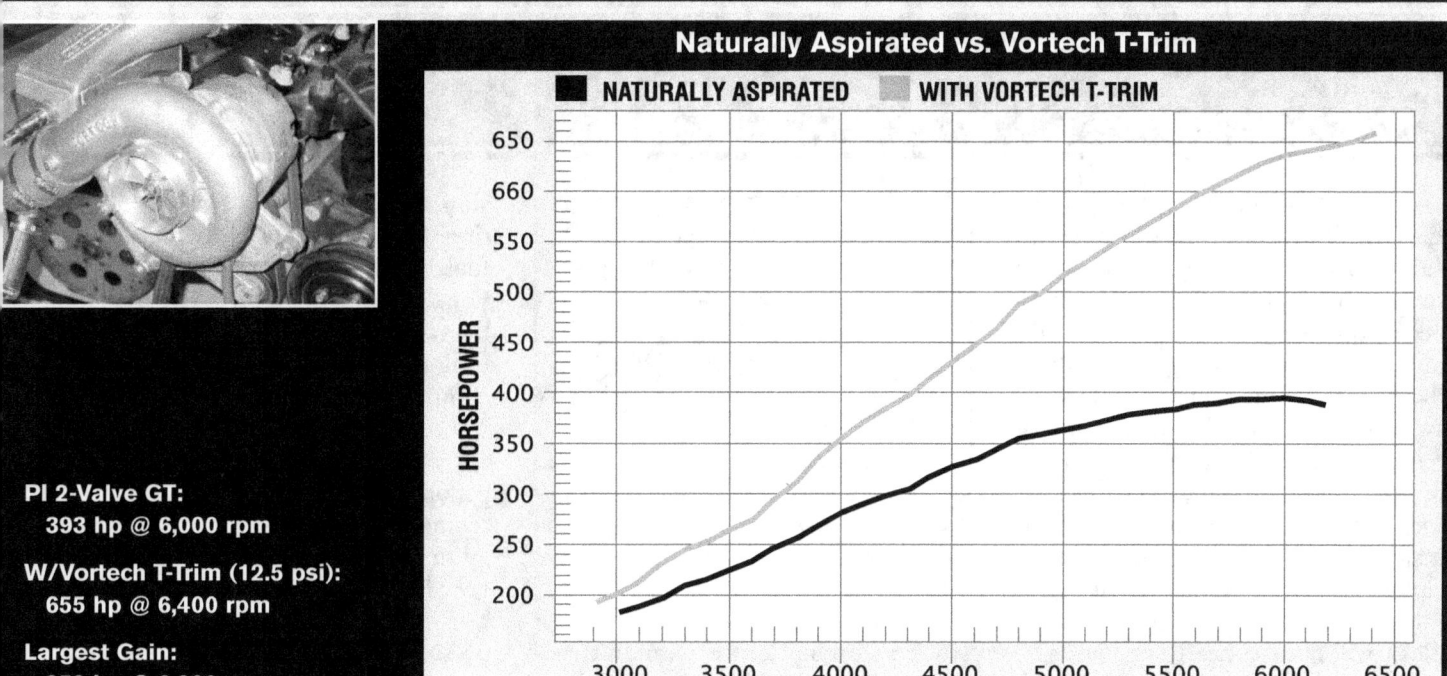

PI 2-Valve GT:
393 hp @ 6,000 rpm

W/Vortech T-Trim (12.5 psi):
655 hp @ 6,400 rpm

Largest Gain:
252 hp @ 6,200 rpm

PI 4.6L GT: NA vs. Vortech T-Trim (12.5 psi) (Horsepower)
Though the low-speed gains don't compare to the positive-displacement superchargers, centrifugal superchargers offer unsurpassed (except by turbos) top-end power gains. Adding the aftercooled Vortech T-Trim to the 4.6L GT motor upped the power output from 393 hp to 655 hp with 12.5 psi of boost.

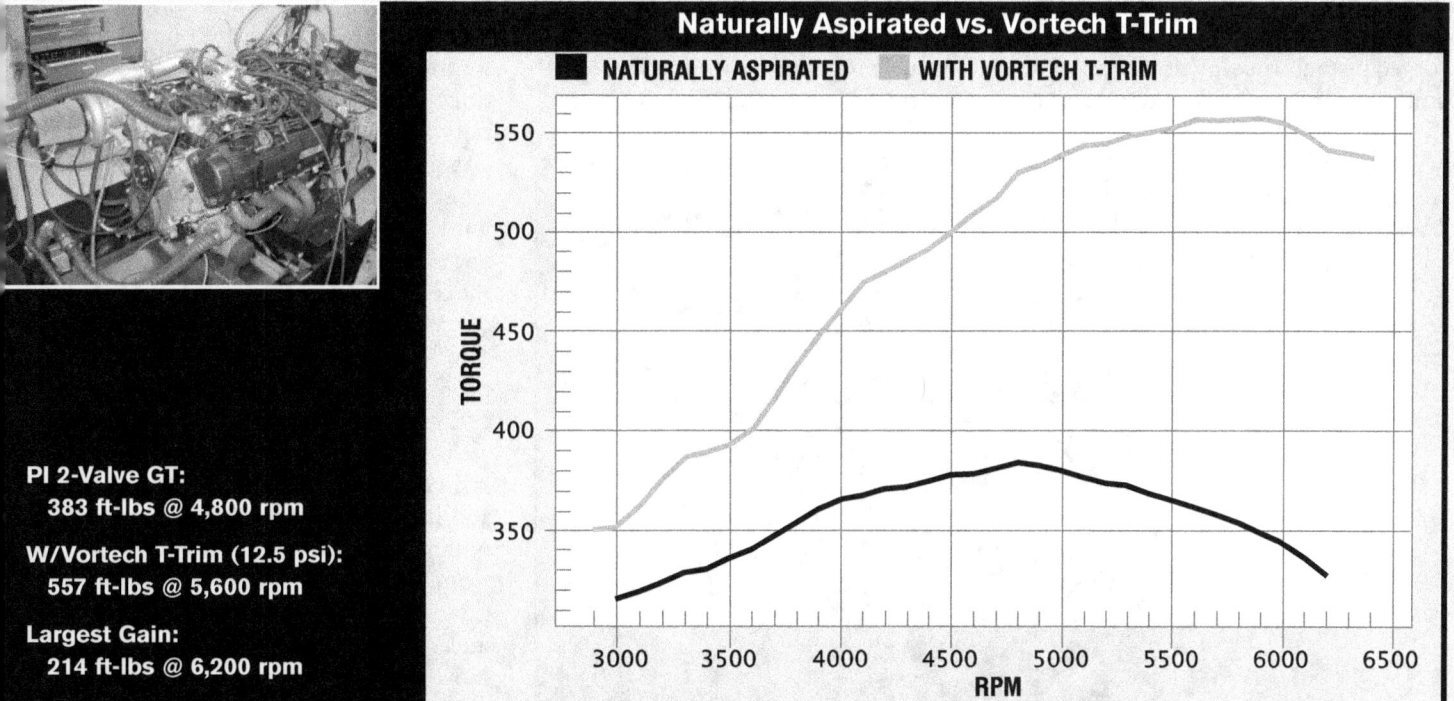

PI 2-Valve GT:
383 ft-lbs @ 4,800 rpm

W/Vortech T-Trim (12.5 psi):
557 ft-lbs @ 5,600 rpm

Largest Gain:
214 ft-lbs @ 6,200 rpm

PI 4.6L GT: NA vs. Vortech T-Trim (12.5 psi) (Torque)
A gain of 40 ft-lbs at 3,000 rpm is nice but it doesn't compare to the gain of over 200 ft-lbs at 6,000 rpm. Equipped with the Vortech, the 4.6L GT motor produced 557 ft-lbs of torque, up from 383 ft-lbs before installing the blower.

Test 6: Vortech T-Trim Supercharged 2-Valve GT: 12 psi vs. 16.9 psi

How do you make a 700-hp 4.6L? Easy: Start with a 600-hp supercharged 4.6L and add more boost. Actually, to successfully build a 700-hp 4.6L, you'll need more than just boost, you'll need a motor that can hold together with all that power. While many enthusiasts swear that any forced induction motor must be equipped with a forged crank, forged connecting rods, and (of course) forged pistons, the reality is that the major contributor to engine failure is almost always the tuning. That's right folks: A poorly tuned forged short block will not last nearly as long as an over-stressed but properly tuned stock short block. Case in point: My stock '98 2-valve short block has been subjected to all manner of heads, cams, and nitrous before getting hit with numerous blowers and even more nitrous. Did I mention we occasionally revved it to 7,000 rpm or more? The little engine that could never once gave up, not even after repeated runs exceeding 650 hp. No forged pistons, rods, or crank, just stock stuff with proper timing and fuel curves.

Check out our custom 7.5-inch crank pulley. It slips over the damper and upped boost from 12 to 16.9 psi.

While we exceeded 650 hp using a stock short block, we wouldn't recommend running this power level for extended periods. Proper tuning will keep things alive, but the right reciprocating assembly can allow even higher performance. Case in point: A change in static compression ratio. You have to choose the proper combination of compression and boost, especially for a daily driver. The choices are: low compression and high boost, moderate compression and moderate boost, and high compression and low boost. Other combinations are available with higher-octane fuel, but (despite what some may have you believe), there's a fixed limit on the amount of boost pressure (and timing) that can be run on a given compression ratio with pump gas. Those who say that it's possible to run a streetable timing curve with 15 to 20 psi on pump gas are obviously not listening for detonation (or they get their "pump" gas from the local airport). A very boost-friendly 8.0:1 compression ratio will allow much more boost pressure (for a given octane fuel) than 9.0:1, but the extra power and off-boost driveability might allow similar power at a reduced boost level. The high-compression boosted motors should be best left to racetracks where the octane is essentially unlimited.

For our 700-hp 4.6L GT motor, we used a static compression ratio of 8.1:1. The ultra-low compression allowed us to run elevated boost (and timing) levels without fear of detonation. The downside was that the naturally aspirated (and therefore boosted) power output was down somewhat from the same combination equipped with 9.0:1 compression. Equipped with the 6⅝-inch (truck) crank pulley, the T-Trim Vortech produced a boost curve ranging from 5.5 psi to 12.0 psi. The low-compression 4.6L GT easily produced 612 hp at 12 psi on 91-octane pump gas using the efficient air-to-water Power Cooler. We then switched over to 100-octane race fuel and installed the larger 7.5-inch crank pulley, which upped the boost curve from 8.4 psi to a max of 16.9 psi. With this setup, the modified 4.6L produced 710 hp and 590 ft-lbs of torque. Note that in both cases, the boost pressure more than doubled in just 1,500 rpm. It was so easy to get 700 hp, maybe we should go for 800 hp (see Chapter 10).

We changed our pulley ratio, and thus our boost level, by swapping the crank pulley. It's also common to just swap the supercharger pulley and keep the crank pulley.

2-Valve Supercharging

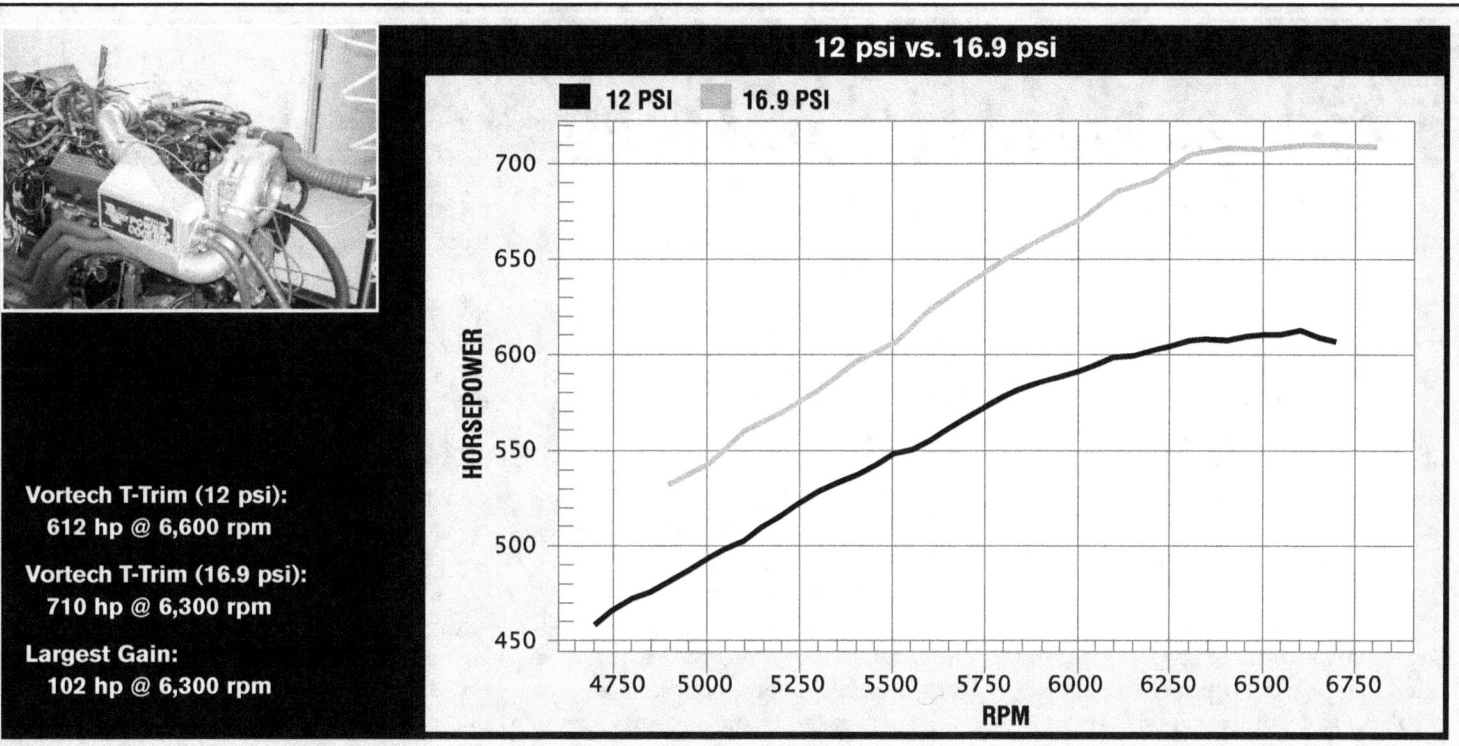

Vortech T-Trim (12 psi):
612 hp @ 6,600 rpm

Vortech T-Trim (16.9 psi):
710 hp @ 6,300 rpm

Largest Gain:
102 hp @ 6,300 rpm

Vortech T-Trim Supercharged 2-Valve GT: 12 psi vs. 16.9 psi (Horsepower)
To demonstrate the type of power potential available from the Vortech T-Trim, we replaced the stock 6-rib crank pulley with a custom 7.5-inch version. The new 7.5-inch crank pulley was actually machined to slip over the existing damper. The 7.5-inch crank pulley was used in conjunction with the 3.33-inch blower pulley. The combination produced a peak boost pressure of 16.9 psi and 710 hp (up from 610 hp).

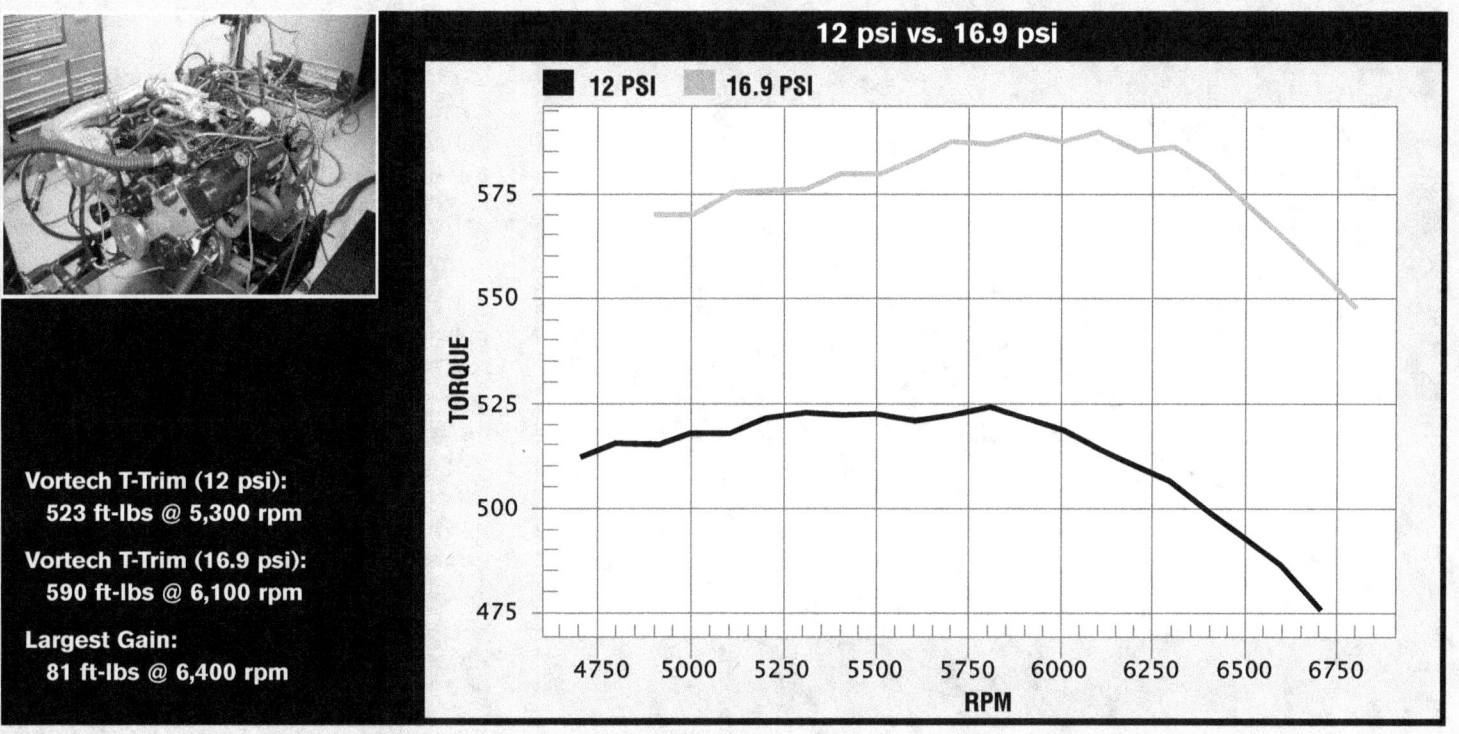

Vortech T-Trim (12 psi):
523 ft-lbs @ 5,300 rpm

Vortech T-Trim (16.9 psi):
590 ft-lbs @ 6,100 rpm

Largest Gain:
81 ft-lbs @ 6,400 rpm

Vortech T-Trim Supercharged 2-Valve GT: 12 psi vs. 16.9 psi (Torque)
As expected, the increase in blower speed upped the torque production everywhere. We suspect belt slippage at the top of the rev range was responsible for the dramatic fall off in torque starting at 6,300 rpm. Imagine what a 700-hp supercharged 2-valve 4.6L motor might feel like in your street GT.

Chapter 6

Test 7: Kenne Bell Supercharged PI 2-Valve GT: 1.7L vs. 2.2L

Kenne Bell's original 4.6L GT kit was supplied with a 1.7L twin-screw Autorotor supercharger. Having already exceeded 500 wheel horsepower with the smaller 1.7L, it was natural to assume GT owners might want to turn the wick up and push their motors to the 600-wheel-hp mark. While the 1.7L was certainly capable of exceeding 500 hp at the wheels, the answer was not more blower speed from the 1.7L but to install a larger supercharger. Enter the 2.2L twin-screw.

The reason for stepping up to a larger blower is that the flow rate (and attending power output) of a positive-displacement supercharger is determined by the size and speed of the blower. A bigger blower can supply more air than a smaller blower; therefore, it can also be spun slower to deliver the same volume. The 2.2L twin-screw blower had already proven itself capable of exceeding 600 wheel hp on both the 4-valve Cobra and 5.4L Lightning, so Kenne Bell decided to apply that power potential to the 2-valve GT motor. The 2.2L kit also comes with the Cobra inlet and throttle body to make sure the big blower doesn't get chocked off.

The Kenne Bell blower upgrade was run on our Sean Hyland 4.6L GT motor. The test motor consisted of a forged steel Cobra crank, a set of forged connecting rods, and low-compression forged pistons with 28-cc dishes. The deep-dish pistons combined with a set of CNC-ported heads from Total Engine Airflow produced a very boost-friendly static compression ratio of 8.1:1. The motor was equipped with a set of Comp XE274H cams, a set of Hooker 1⅝-inch long-tube headers, and F.A.S.T. programmable engine management. First up was the 1.7L blower and standard inlet consisting of a 75-mm Accufab throttle body. Both the 1.7L and 2.2L blowers were run with the same 2.75-inch blower pulley and 6.5-inch crank pulley and dialed in with 22 degrees of total timing at an air/fuel ratio of 11.8:1. Equipped with the 1.7L, the supercharged 4.6L produced 537 hp and 549 ft-lbs of torque at a maximum boost level of 12.4 psi (which dipped down to 10.7 at 6,300 rpm). (Further testing revealed that the inlet system on the smaller blower was restricting the power and boost curves.)

Next we installed the 2.2L Kenne Bell blower upgrade, including the revised inlet system. Equipped with the same pulley ratio, timing, and fuel curve (65-lb/hr injectors), the larger blower upped the peak boost pressure to 14.5 psi and the power output to 664 hp. The peak torque now stood at 577 ft-lbs, though the curve exceeded 550 ft-lbs from 3,500 rpm to 6,400 rpm.

We used the same drive ratio (as opposed to boost pressure) on this test because driving the two blowers at the same speed better illustrates the difference in power potential. It would be difficult to attempt to compare the two blowers at the "same" boost pressure since boost curves offered by the two sizes differ greatly. The 1.7L produced a dropping boost curve (from 12.4 psi to 10.7 psi), while the 2.2L blower produced a rising boost curve (from 13.1 psi to 14.5 psi). Regardless of how you decide to compare them, the Kenne Bell 2.2L blower upgrade for the 4.6L GT has a lot of power potential.

This is the upgraded 2.2L blower from Kenne Bell. It's actually the blower from the 4-valve Cobra kit, so it uses the inlet and throttle body from the Cobra setup as well.

2-Valve Supercharging

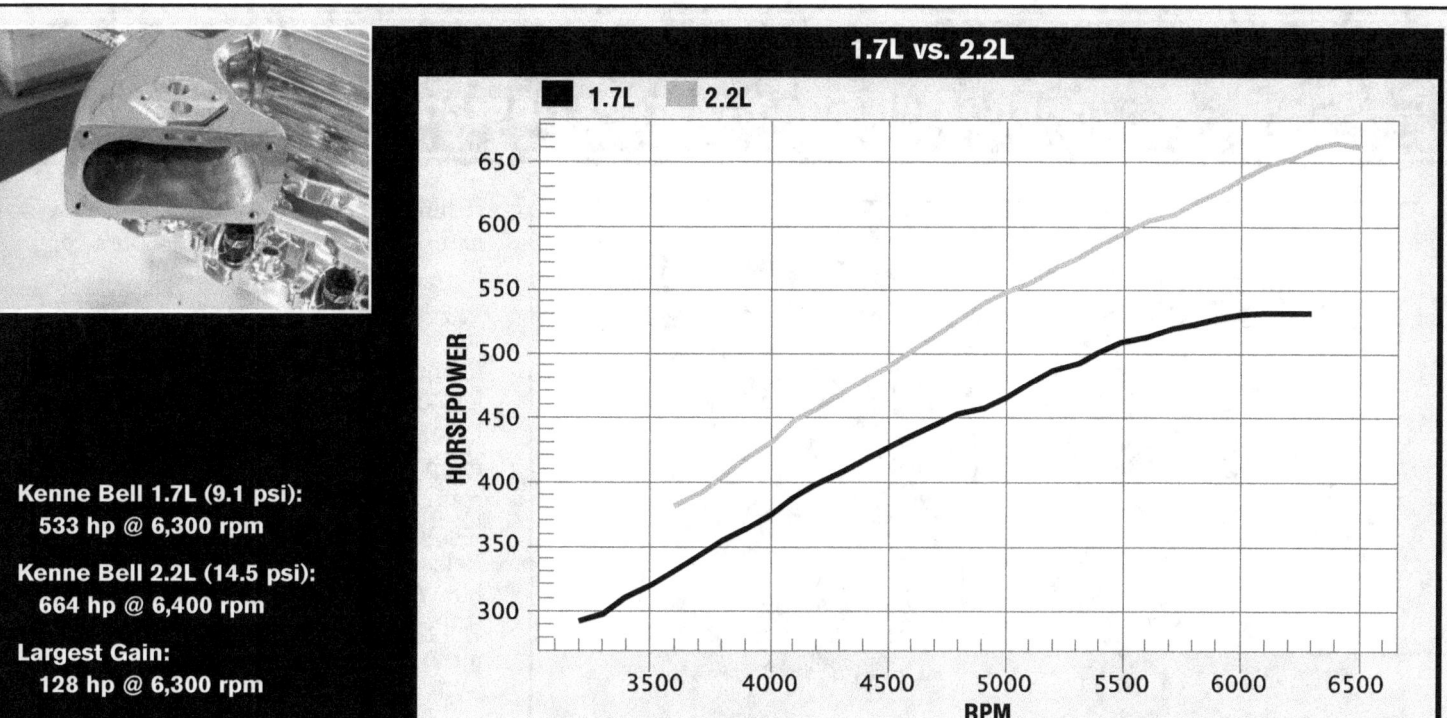

Kenne Bell 1.7L (9.1 psi):
533 hp @ 6,300 rpm

Kenne Bell 2.2L (14.5 psi):
664 hp @ 6,400 rpm

Largest Gain:
128 hp @ 6,300 rpm

Kenne Bell Supercharged PI 2-Valve GT: 1.7L vs. 2.2L (Horsepower)
Installing the Kenne Bell 2.2L blower upgrade in place of the smaller 1.7L resulted in an impressive power gain throughout the rev range. How does a jump from 537 to 664 hp sound?

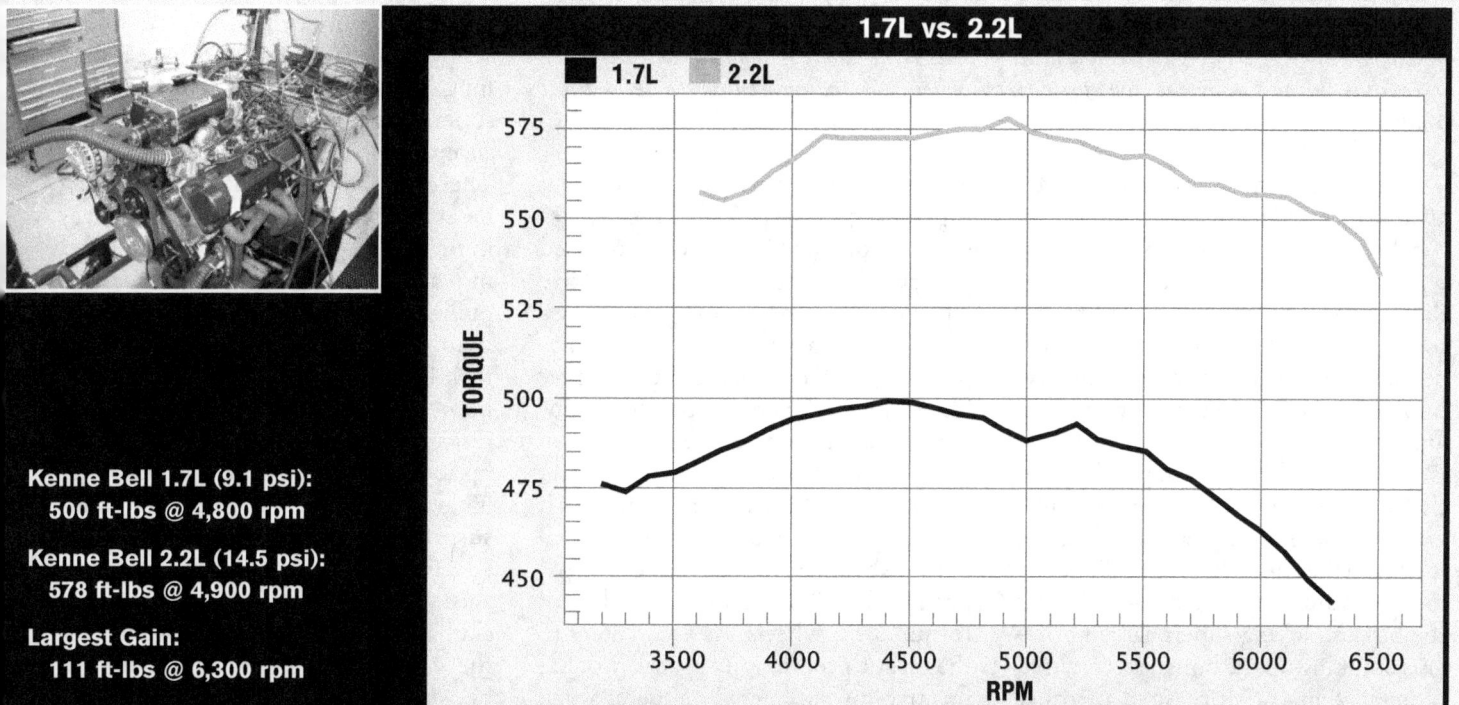

Kenne Bell 1.7L (9.1 psi):
500 ft-lbs @ 4,800 rpm

Kenne Bell 2.2L (14.5 psi):
578 ft-lbs @ 4,900 rpm

Largest Gain:
111 ft-lbs @ 6,300 rpm

Kenne Bell Supercharged PI 2-Valve GT: 1.7L vs. 2.2L (Torque)
Do you think you might be able to feel an extra 75 ft-lbs of torque? The blower upgrade increased the torque peak from 500 ft-lbs at 4,400 rpm to 577 ft-lbs at 4,900 rpm.

Chapter 6

Test 8: 2-Valve 5.4L Lightning: Kenne Bell Supercharger Upgrade

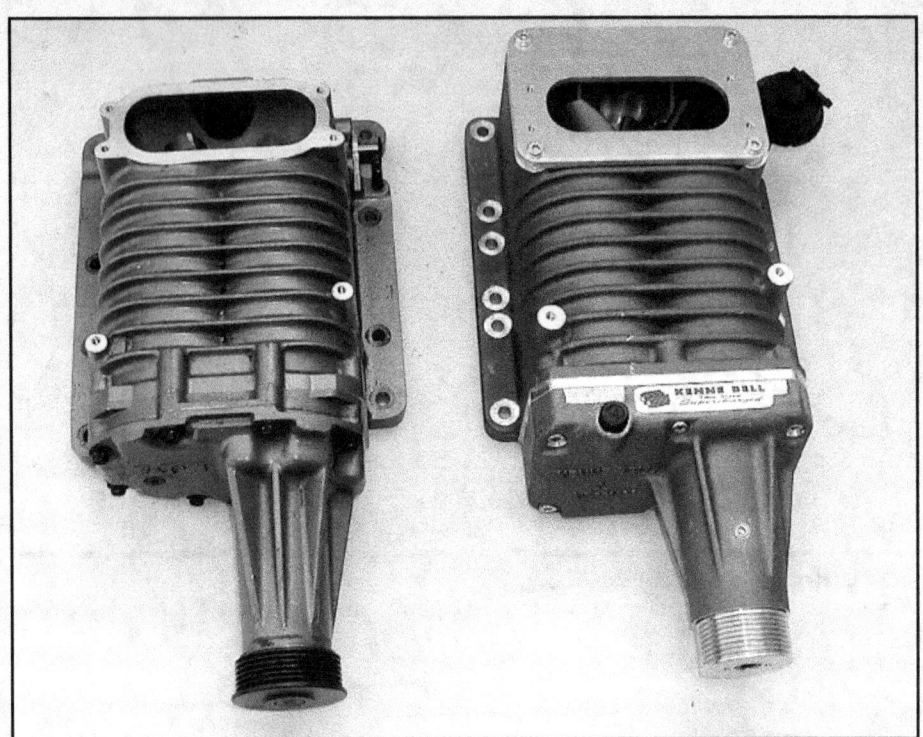

When you look at how close the Eaton M112 and Kenne Bell twin-screw superchargers are in size, it will be interesting to see how much of a difference there is in power. We were able to conduct this test using the same lower intake manifold and intact tract to get a direct comparison between the blowers.

Most Lightning owners are well aware that their heavy haulers are capable of sub-14-second ETs at nearly 100 mph right off the showroom floor. Credit the impressive, ultra-flat torque curve offered by the positive-displacement Eaton supercharger. As impressive as the stock performance is, and as easy as the supercharged motor is to modify, there is always a limit to the power gained with external modifications. One limiting factor is (believe it or not) the supercharger itself. While many enthusiasts inaccurately think the key to making supercharged power is cranking up the boost, rest assured there is a limit. More so than other forms, positive-displacement superchargers were not designed to sustain elevated pressure ratios (high boost levels). Turbos and even centrifugal superchargers run well at higher boost levels, but positive-displacement superchargers, especially the roots-style Eaton M112 supercharger used on the Lightning, are most effective when used on low-boost applications.

To illustrate the benefit of swapping out the Eaton M112 supercharger for a more efficient Autorotor twin-screw design from Kenne Bell, we ran them back-to-back on the DynoJet chassis dyno. Our supercharged 5.4L 2001 Lightning with a modified cat-back exhaust (but factory cat pipe) produced 348 hp and 439 ft-lbs of torque at the wheels. As a testament to the torque production capability of the positive-displacement supercharger, the torque curve exceeded 400 ft-lbs from 3,000 rpm (our lowest load speed) to 4,600 rpm. The Eaton-supercharged 5.4L also exceeded 300 horsepower from 3,700 rpm all the way to redline. These are torque numbers a naturally aspirated 4-valve Cobra (or now 3-valve GT) can only dream of. The 5.4L was equipped with all of the stock components, including a 7.5-inch crank pulley, 3-inch blower pulley, and the factory inlet system. The Eaton supercharger produced a maximum boost reading (taken at 5,000 rpm) of 9.3 psi. According to the data logging equipment set up by Kenne Bell, the charge temperature exiting the blower measured 207 degrees F before being cooled to just 85 degrees F by the ultra-efficient air-to-water intercooler. SVT obviously programmed the processors to produce a safe air/fuel mixture, as the Horiba real-time air/fuel monitor indicated the ratio hovered at a safely rich 10.32:1.

To keep the comparison between the two positive displacement blowers even, Kenne Bell made a custom adapter to mount the Autorotor twin-screw supercharger to the stock Lightning lower manifold. The twin-screw supercharger was further modified to accept the stock factory inlet setup. Therefore, any difference in power can be attributed solely to the differences in the two superchargers. Once bolted in place, the 5.4L was run first with a pulley ratio identical to the stock Eaton (7.5-inch crank pulley and a 3.0-inch blower pulley). The results were impressive. Using an identical pulley ratio, the Autorotor pumped out 403 hp, besting the Eaton by a whopping 55 horsepower. The gains were not surprising, as the boost gauge indicated a full 13.2 psi (the Eaton only managed to put out 9.3 psi). Given the similarities in displacement between the two blowers, the difference in boost production and power output was significant. We eventually took the Kenne Bell supercharged Lightning motor to 522 wheel hp and 600 ft-lbs of torque. The very most the Eaton M112 could muster was 415 hp.

2-Valve Supercharging

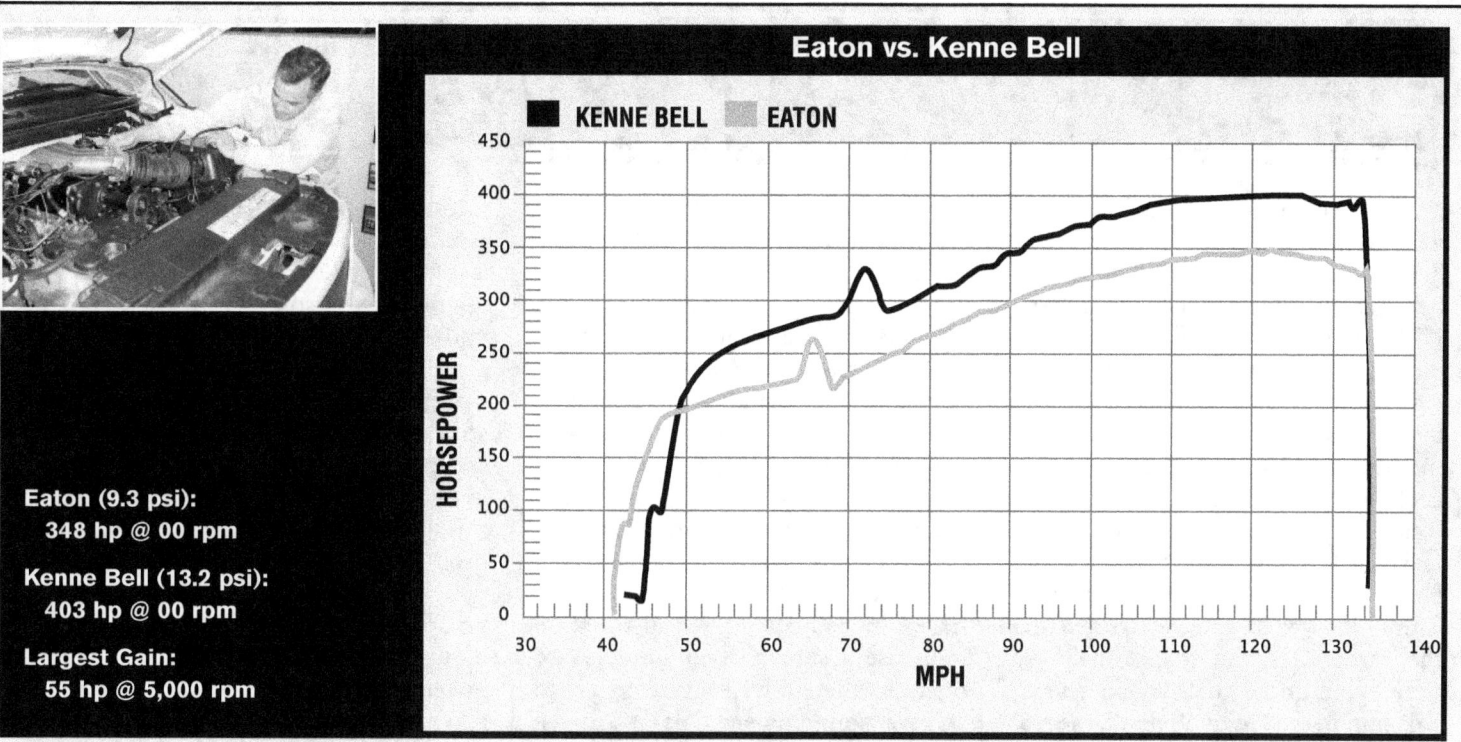

Eaton (9.3 psi): 348 hp @ 00 rpm
Kenne Bell (13.2 psi): 403 hp @ 00 rpm
Largest Gain: 55 hp @ 5,000 rpm

2-Valve 5.4L Lightning: Eaton (9.3 psi) vs. Kenne Bell (13.2 psi) (Horsepower)
The Kenne Bell blower upgrade increased the boost pressure to the 5.4L 2-valve motor and the power right along with it. The increase in boost pressure and improved efficiency improved the horsepower curve everywhere. Just adding the twin-screw blower improved the power output by 55 hp.

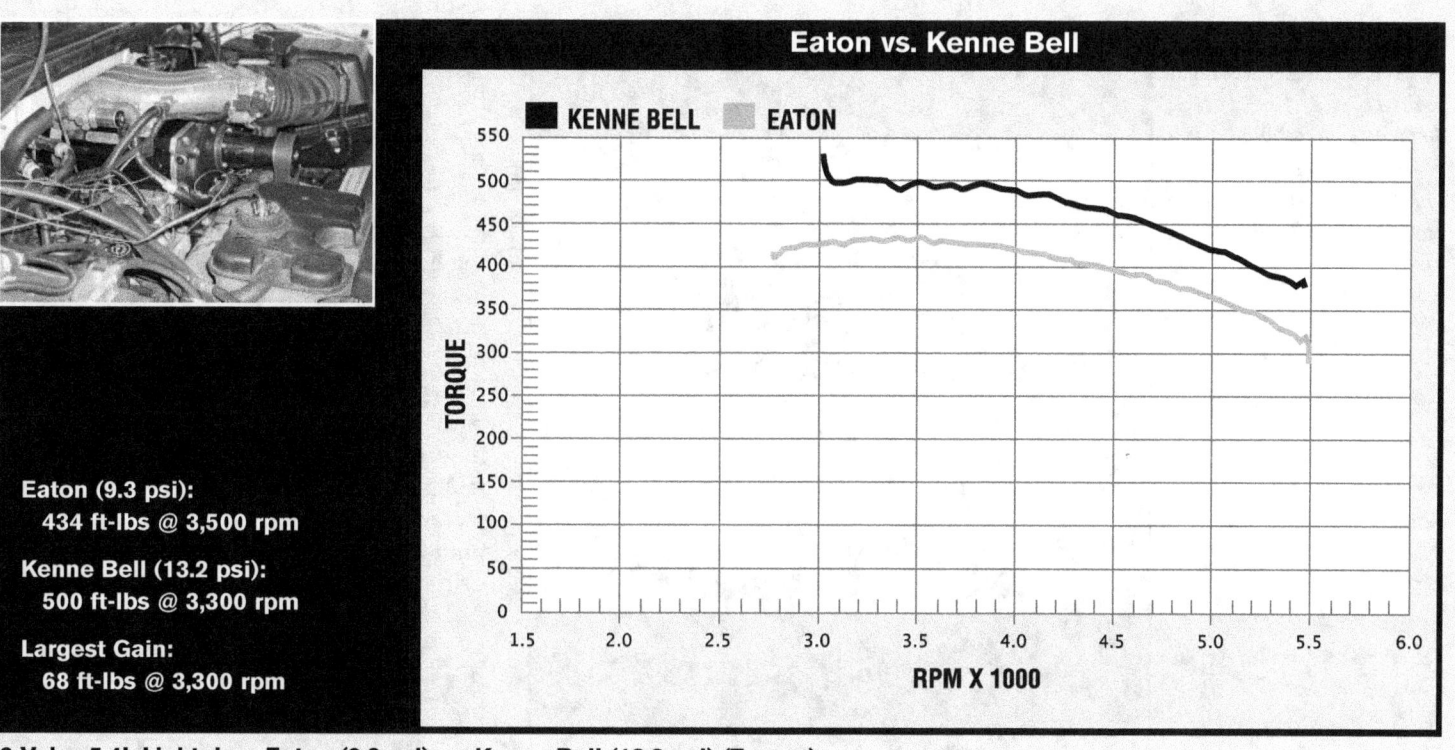

Eaton (9.3 psi): 434 ft-lbs @ 3,500 rpm
Kenne Bell (13.2 psi): 500 ft-lbs @ 3,300 rpm
Largest Gain: 68 ft-lbs @ 3,300 rpm

2-Valve 5.4L Lightning: Eaton (9.3 psi) vs. Kenne Bell (13.2 psi) (Torque)
The torque gains offered by the blower upgrade were equally impressive, jumping from 434 ft-lbs to an even 500 ft-lbs. If there's anything a heavy Lightning truck needs, its extra torque.

Chapter 6

Test 9: PI 2-Valve GT: Vortech T-Trim vs. JT-Trim

Some comparison tests happen by design; others happen almost by accident. Case in point: This comparison between the Vortech T-Trim and the JT-Trim on a modified 4.6L GT motor. The idea was to achieve a solid 800 hp from a supercharged 2-valve motor and not specifically to compare the different Vortech superchargers back to back. During initial testing, John Mihovitz of Accufab volunteered a JT-Trim he had at the shop. Since the comparison only required a simple blower swap, we figured that the larger JT-Trim might help us achieve our goal. While 800 hp is a sizable number in anyone's book, the real handicap turned out to be the 6-rib drive system we stubbornly employed. At this power level, a cog drive, or at the very least, an 8-rib system like on the 4-valve Cobra motors, is preferred. The only thing that kept our hopes alive was the fact that the 6-rib system relied on a very short belt, which minimized stretch. This, along with a few drops of track bite, helped minimize belt slippage.

A common misconception among blower owners (and some manufacturers) is that more power is a simple matter of more blower speed. More mass flow equals more power, but every supercharger has an island of efficiency. Run the blower outside that island and things start to get inefficient in a hurry. The ideal situation is to use a supercharger designed to provide the flow requirements to achieve your power goals at a given pressure ratio. If you start out with a 400-hp naturally aspirated motor, it'll naturally be much easier to reach 800 hp with a supercharger than had you started with a 300-hp motor. Unfortunately, many enthusiasts (and drag racers) miss this very important aspect. This scenario is especially critical when you run the supercharger up near its absolute flow limit (are you listening drag racers?). For any given impeller speed, the flow rate of a supercharger actually diminishes with pressure. Suppose you run a supercharger at 65,000 rpm on your low-compression drag-race motor. At this impeller speed, the race blower produces a maximum of 28 psi and your motor makes 1,000 hp. Were you to increase the efficiency of your motor (by changing cam timing, increasing static compression, or actually increasing displacement), the power would go up and the boost pressure would likely drop. The supercharger will flow more air at 65,000 rpm having to only work against 25 psi, instead of 28 psi.

Enough theory – let's get to the results of the test. The DSS 4.6L motor featured a forged rotating assembly, a set of Total Engine Airflow CNC-ported PI heads, and a set of Comp Xtreme Energy XE278AH PI cams. We topped off the combination with an Extrude-Honed Ford Racing Bullitt intake and channeled all the hot gases through a set of Hooker long-tube Super Comp headers. Both superchargers were run with a 7.5-inch crank pulley and a 3.33-inch blower pulley and fed a custom dual-path Vortech aftercooler. A F.A.S.T. management system was used to control a set of 65-pound injectors, which were fed by an Aeromotive A1000 fuel pump. Equipped with the Vortech T-Trim, the supercharged 4.6L produced 720 hp at a peak boost pressure of 13.4 psi. Adding the larger JT-Trim upped the peak boost pressure to 13.9 psi and brought the peak power output to 745 hp. An increase in the drive ratio upped the boost pressure to allow us to eventually reach the 800-hp mark with the JT-Trim.

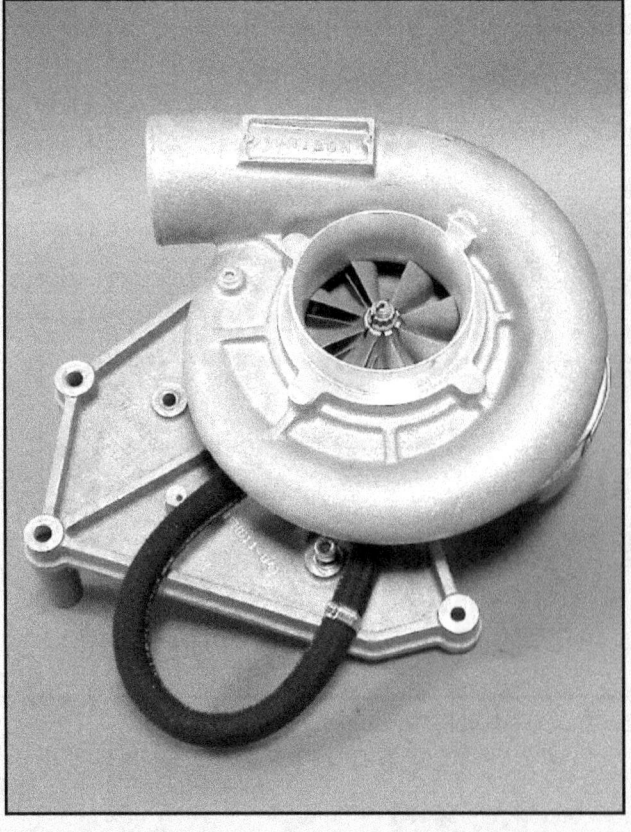

If a centrifugal supercharger is good, then a bigger centrifugal supercharger is better, right? We'll test Vortech's T-Trim against the larger JT-Trim and see how much of a difference there is.

2-Valve Supercharging

Vortech T-Trim (13.4 psi):
720 hp @ 6,300 rpm

Vortech JT-Trim (13.9 psi):
745 hp @ 6,300 rpm

Largest Gain:
25 hp @ 6,300 rpm

PI 2-Valve GT: Vortech T-Trim (13.4 psi) vs. JT-Trim (13.9 psi) (Horsepower)
While building the 800-hp 4.6L GT motor (see Chapter 10 on buildups), we tried a pair of different Vortech superchargers on the modified 4.6L GT motor. The superchargers were run with the same crank (7.5-inch) and blower (3.33-inch) pulleys. Equipped with the T-Trim blower, the modified 4.6L produced 720 hp at a peak boost pressure of 13.4 psi. Installing the larger JT-Trim blower upped the peak boost pressure to 13.9 psi where the motor produced 745 hp.

Vortech T-Trim (13.4 psi):
612 ft-lbs @ 5,900 rpm

Vortech JT-Trim (13.9 psi):
631 ft-lbs @ 6,000 rpm

Largest Gain:
21 ft-lbs @ 6,200 rpm

PI 2-Valve GT: Vortech T-Trim (13.4 psi) vs. JT-Trim (13.9 psi) (Torque)
The torque curves show that the larger blower upped the torque production from 4,800 rpm to 6,500 rpm. The increase in boost pressure supplied by the larger JT-Trim helped push the torque peak to 631 ft-lbs, up from 612 ft-lbs.

Building 4.6/5.4L Ford Horsepower on the Dyno

CHAPTER 7

SUPERCHARGING 3- AND 4-VALVE MODULAR ENGINES

Supercharged modular motors are so popular that I was forced to separate them into two chapters. Given the current concern for emissions compliance (especially here in California), supercharger kits have become extremely popular. Blower kits allow users to dramatically increase the power output of their motor without resorting to the usual array of cams, cubes (cubic inches), and compression, none of which would likely be emissions legal. Adding 100 hp (or more) to your 4.6L or 5.4L modular motor with traditional bolt-ons is a difficult (but not impossible) proposition. Adding the same amount of power with a supercharger is quite easy. Given that the rated power output of a typical Cobra motor is about 300 hp, improving the power output by 100 hp equates to a gain of only 33 percent. Truth be told, most enthusiasts would be disappointed if they received a gain of "only" 100 hp from their blower kit. The gains from a 7 to 8 psi kit would probably be closer to 150 hp (roughly 50 percent), upping the power output of your 300-hp Cobra motor to an altogether more impressive 450 hp. The best thing about the gains offered by supercharging is that additional power is just a pulley change (and proper tuning) away. Suppose you build a dedicated blower motor down the line the right supercharger can easily supply your new power needs.

Though enthusiasts had been installing superchargers on their modular motors for years, things really took off when Ford introduced the supercharged Cobra in 2003. The 4.6L 4-valve motor came from the factory with a forged short block, including a forged steel crank, forged steel (Manley) connecting rods, and even forged aluminum pistons. Naturally, Ford lowered the static compression on the supercharged combination for safe street use on unleaded pump gas. The highlight of the supercharged 4.6L 4-valve was of course the Eaton M112 supercharger. Like any supercharged (or turbocharged) motor offered by the factory, improving the power output was a simple matter of upping the boost pressure. Actually, there's a great deal of power to be had with software tuning, as the factory naturally left the timing and fuel curves pretty conservative. A tad more timing (especially down low) and a slightly leaner mixture up top can give you an easy 30 to 40 hp from a chip change. Add to that the extra boost available from blower and/or crank pulley swaps and '03 Cobra owners were ruling the streets. The supercharged '03 and '04 Cobra motors not only produced impressive peak power numbers (easily more than their rated power), they also produced something decidedly missing in previous modular motors: torque. The positive-displacement roots supercharger belted

Things got serious during testing when Accufab installed an ATI (Procharger) F2M blower on a 5.4L 4-valve motor. Running 25 psi, the high-compression modular motor produced 1,400 hp.

Supercharging 3- and 4-Valve Modular Engines

out impressive low-end and midrange torque like nobody's business.

While the Mustang performance world welcomed the supercharged Cobra, enthusiasts soon found that the limiting factor in terms of power output was actually the Eaton supercharger. Kenne Bell came to the rescue with a more efficient and powerful supercharger. Having already rescued the 5.4L 2-valve Lightning owners, Kenne Bell decided that 4-valve Cobra owners deserved the same respect. Replacing the roots blower with a more powerful twin-screw takes the blown Cobra motor to the next performance level. While Cobra owners struggle to exceed 500 flywheel hp with the stock Eaton (most resorting to nitrous to dip into the 10s with the stock blower), upgrading to the Kenne Bell twin-screw blower (especially the larger 422 model) pushes wheel power numbers over 700 hp. This power potential allows supercharged Cobra owners to dip into the 9s without nitrous. What Cobra owners like most about the Kenne Bell upgrade is that the majority of the components, including the factory air-to-water intercooler, are kept intact. The Kenne Bell twin-screw doesn't suffer the low-speed power losses associated with a centrifugal supercharger, offering all of the immediate boost and torque response of the Eaton roots blower without falling off at elevated engine speeds and power levels. Where the boost pressure (and resulting power) supplied by the Eaton roots blower falls off rapidly, the power just continues to climb with the Kenne Bell.

The centrifugal camp (ATI, Paxton, and Vortech) all jumped on the supercharged Cobra bandwagon, offering to replace the restrictive Eaton supercharger with a much more efficient centrifugal design. While the centrifugal superchargers are capable of easily exceeding the power levels offered by the Eaton roots blower, there is a tradeoff associated with this upgrade, a tradeoff many of the Cobra owners are not willing to accept. Unlike the Kenne Bell twin-screw blower, the boost pressure supplied by the centrifugal blowers increases with engine speed. Pullied to produce 11 psi, the Eaton (or Kenne Bell) blower may offer 10 psi at 2,500 rpm where the centrifugal will only supply 2 psi. Obviously, this significant difference in boost pressure will result in a sizable difference in torque production in favor of the positive-displacement blower. Out on the other end of the rev range, the result is quite different, as the efficiency of the roots blower diminishes where the centrifugal is coming into its element. For maximum peak power, the centrifugal design will offer much more power potential than the stock Eaton M112 roots blower. Given the efficiency of the centrifugal design, it's also possible to run much higher boost levels than with the roots blower while maintaining the same charge temperature. The choice between a positive displacement and a centrifugal comes down to where you want your motor to produce power, down low or up high.

Naturally, in this chapter you'll find testing on the supercharged '03 Cobra crate motor. I replaced the stock Eaton supercharger with a naturally aspirated manifold from the 2001 NA 4-valve Cobra in an effort to demonstrate just how much power the Eaton supercharger supplied to the stock motor. Boost upgrades for the Ford Racing Cobra crate motor are also covered, as is a Kenne Bell twin-screw blower upgrade. I ran a Vortech supercharger on the '03 4-valve motor, and then installed a Paxton Novi 2000 on a Sean Hyland (high-compression) 4-valve test motor to demonstrate the effect of intercooling. In addition to the 4-valve motors, this chapter also includes coverage of a Paxton supercharger kit for the new 2005 4.6L 3-valve motor. Though we hoped to include test results on the new Vortech VF24 race blower, problems arose with the test motor and pushed testing beyond the completion date of the book. We did manage to run a wild 5.4L 4-valve motor with an ATI F2M supercharger and air-to-water intercooler that produced huge power. The 4-valve (and 3-valve) combinations work very well with forced induction, much better than the 2-valve counterparts. Credit the improved head flow offered by the 4-valve motors for the improved power potential. Read on and see for yourself.

The Novi 2000 (shown here in intercooled form) has proven itself an excellent street blower for a modular motor. Though capable of supporting better than 1,000 hp, the Novi even excels at lower (street-oriented) boost levels.

Just before this book was completed, Vortech introduced a supercharger kit for the new 2005 4.6L 3-valve motor. As time goes on, the market for the 3-valve will catch up.

I was excited about testing the new Vortech VF24 supercharger, but damage to the test motor (with another supercharger) meant that I couldn't include results on the impressive new race blower.

Test 1: 4-Valve '03 Cobra: Naturally Aspirated vs. Eaton Supercharger

Though the '03 Cobra motor came factory equipped with an Eaton supercharger, we decided to run it naturally aspirated to demonstrate the effect the factory supercharger has on the power curve. While installing an intake manifold from a naturally aspirated 2001 4-valve Cobra might seem like taking a giant step backward, this is a great way to gauge the gains offered by the Eaton.

The first order of business was to run the 4-valve Cobra motor with the supercharger. The motor was configured on the engine dyno with the F.A.S.T. management system. The dyno setup included long-tube headers (run on both the supercharged and NA configurations), a stock throttle body and inlet manifold (to the Eaton), as well as an electric water pump. No other accessories were run on the motor except the alternator, which was required, as it shared the blower drive belt. No electronics were hooked up to the alternator, so no field was generated. We set it up at 23 degrees of total timing across the rev range, while the air/fuel curve was set at a steady 11.8:1. Equipped as described, the '03 Cobra motor produced a peak boost pressure of 8.7 psi and delivered 501 hp at 6,500 rpm and 461 ft-lbs of torque at 4,000 rpm. The difference between this power output and the rated 390 hp can be attributed to the lack of a complete exhaust system, lack of a complete inlet system (air silencer, filter housing, MAF), not driving any of the accessories, and a better tune. The factory '03 Cobra motors are run significantly richer than this (as low as 10.0:1) and with less total timing at most engine speeds.

After a backup run, we removed the Eaton supercharger to make room for the 2001 Cobra intake. Our job was made much easier by the fact that we didn't have to hook up every last vacuum line, throttle linkage (other than for the dyno), or water lines. Installing the 2001 intake took only a few minutes, as we reused the '03 fuel rail assembly and 65-pound F.A.S.T. injectors. We did have to relocate the throttle linkage, but that was a simple job. Equipped with the 2001 Cobra intake, the naturally aspirated '03 motor produced 369 hp at 6,000 rpm and 377 ft-lbs of torque at 4,900 rpm. The peak power engine speed of 6,000 rpm on the naturally aspirated motor is somewhat misleading, as the power actually leveled off at 5,100 rpm (365 hp). Check out the horsepower curves to see what we are talking about.

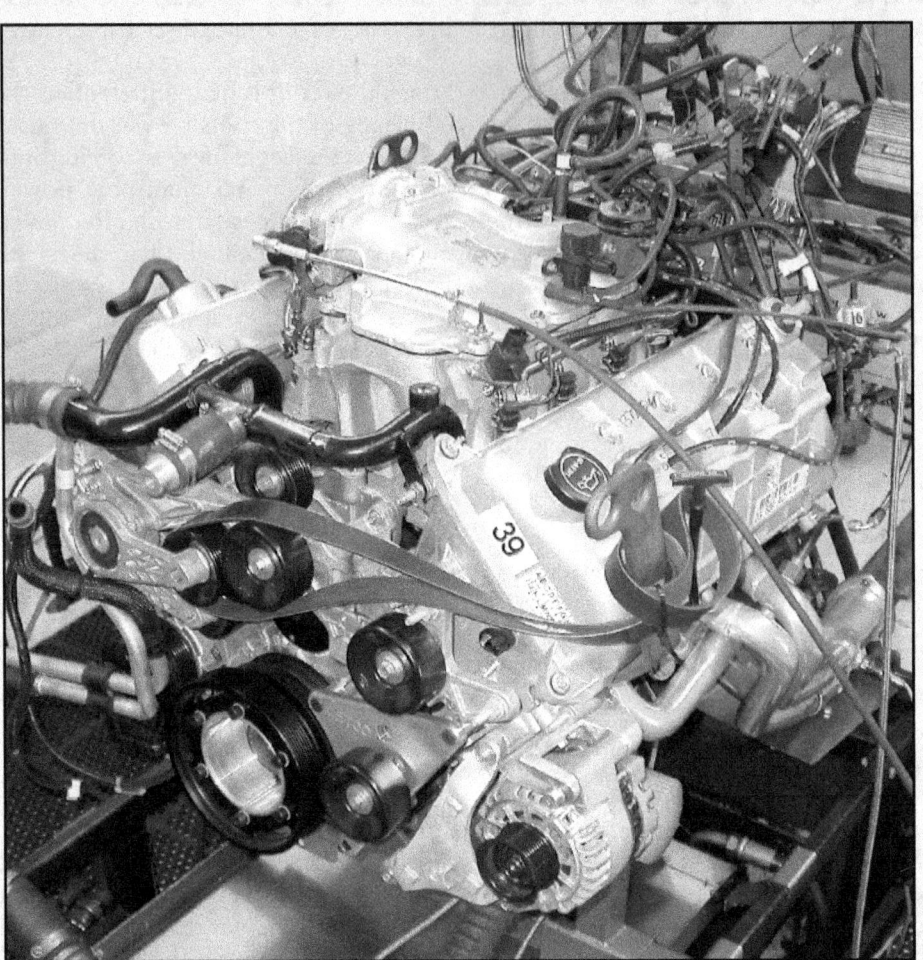

In order to see what an '03 Cobra motor would put out without its supercharger, we replaced the blower with an '01 Cobra intake manifold. The swap was easy enough, especially considering that no water goes through the intake manifolds.

Credit the low static compression ratio, mild cam timing, and the runner length of the 2001 intake for the shape of the naturally aspirated power curve. One thing the long-runner intake did do was to enhance the midrange torque production. It would be nice to have a supercharged Cobra motor that offered the benefit of boost combined with the enhanced torque production of the long intake runners. Unfortunately, combining the Eaton supercharger with an air-to-water intercooler and attempting to keep it all under the hood left very little room for additional runner length.

Supercharging 3- and 4-Valve Modular Engines

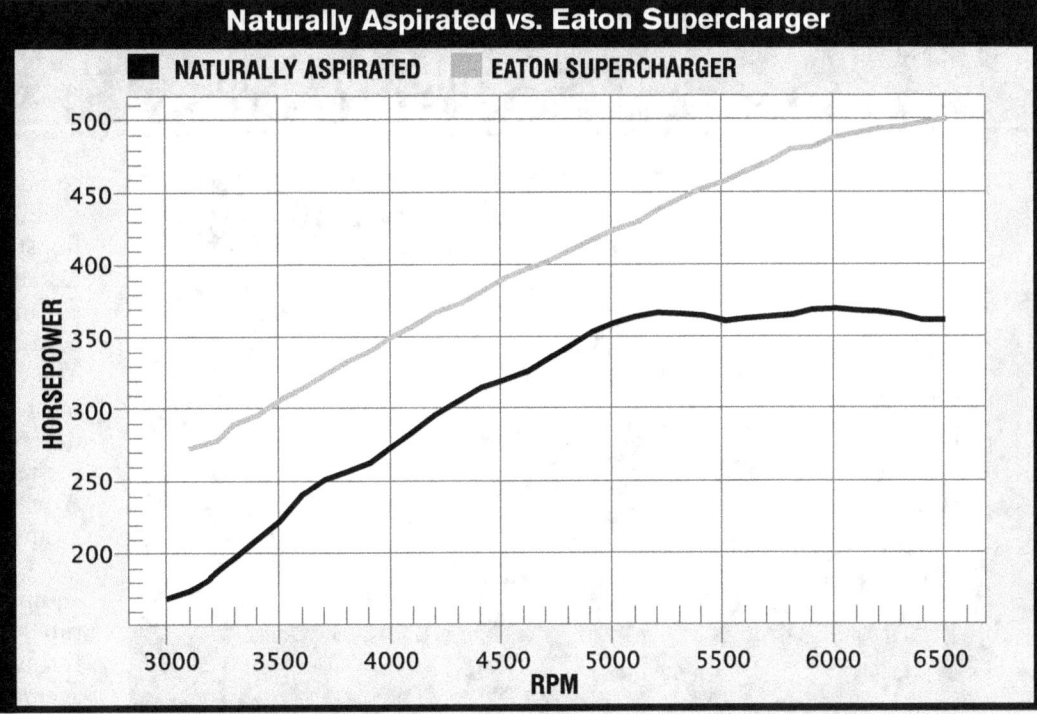

NA '03 4-Valve Cobra:
369 hp @ 6,000 rpm

Supercharged (8.7 psi):
501 hp @ 6,500 rpm

Largest Gain:
138 hp @ 6,400 rpm

4-Valve '03 Cobra: NA vs. Eaton Supercharger (8.7 psi) (Horsepower)
In an effort to demonstrate the effectiveness of the Eaton supercharger on the factory '03 Cobra motor, we removed the blower and installed a 2001 4-valve (NA) Cobra intake manifold in its place. Equipped with the 2001 intake, the '03 Cobra motor produced 370 hp in naturally aspirated trim. This compares to 501 hp with the supercharger in the same trim. Note how the power curve continued to climb with the Eaton but leveled off with the naturally aspirated intake. Equipped with the stock blower (and crank) pulleys, the Eaton supercharger pumped out a peak of 8.7 psi.

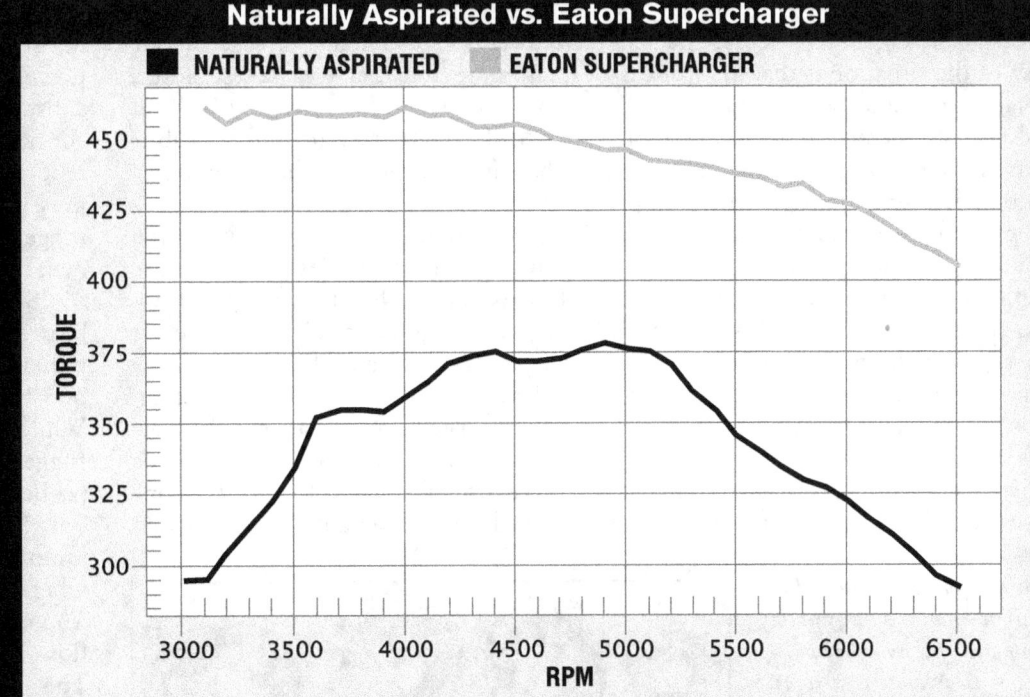

NA '03 4-Valve Cobra:
377 ft-lbs @ 4,000 rpm

Supercharged (8.7 psi):
461 ft-lbs @ 4,000 rpm

Largest Gain:
166 ft-lbs @ 3,000 rpm

4-Valve '03 Cobra: NA vs. Eaton Supercharger (8.7 psi) (Torque)
Check out the difference in the torque curve between the naturally aspirated motor and the supercharged '03 Cobra motor. Note that the long runners in the 2001 NA intake improved the torque production in the middle of the rev range. The Eaton supercharger produced a falling torque curve, though the peak value was up from 377 ft-lbs to 461 ft-lbs.

Test 2: Eaton Supercharged 4-Valve '03 Cobra: Pulley Upgrades

To make pulley swaps easier, we installed the Dial-Ur-Boost (DUB) blower and crank pulley system from South Florida Pulley Headquarters. It allowed us to change pulley sizes in a couple of minutes.

If you're looking for more power from your supercharged Cobra motor, all you have to do is crank up the boost – or so goes the theory. The reality of the situation is that in most cases more boost pressure supplied by the blower does equal more power. Confused? Boost pressure supplied to the motor is a function of the efficiency of the naturally aspirated motor (power output), the size of the supercharger, and the supercharger's speed relative to the motor. "Relative" is important here, as the blower spins faster as you spin the motor faster, but this doesn't always equal more boost. In most cases, the size of the blower and the efficiency of the motor are fixed elements. You can increase the efficiency with ported heads, cams, or a free-flowing exhaust system. It's also possible to increase the size of the blower with a blower swap, but in the case of our Eaton supercharger 4-valve test motor, the motor and blower size were both fixed. That left one remaining variable: changing the speed of the supercharger relative to the motor.

Changing the size of either the blower or crank pulleys can increase blower speed. Not surprisingly, blower pulley upgrades are tops on the list of performance modifications for the '03 Cobra motor. The factory Eaton supercharger features a press-fit pulley to purposely make pulley swaps more difficult. Naturally, Ford is concerned about warranty issues related to raising the boost pressure. Wanting to illustrate the power gains at various boost (and blower speed) levels, we installed Dial-Ur-Boost (DUB) blower and crank pulley systems from South Florida Pulley Headquarters. The DUB system featured a press-fit machined hub to allow you to bolt-on different pulley sizes – just the ticket for testing changes in boost pressure. After installing the DUB hubs, pulley swaps take only a minute or two.

Our '03 Cobra crate motor was equipped with a set of Hooker long-tube headers, an Accufab inlet and throttle body, and the F.A.S.T. management system (tuned for 11.8:1 air/fuel and 23 degrees of timing). Equipped with the stock blower and crank pulleys, the Eaton pumped out 8.7 psi and allowed the supercharged 4-valve motor to produce 508 hp and 463 ft-lbs of torque. Swapping out the stock blower pulley for a smaller 3.2-inch DUB version increased the peak boost pressure to 10.9 psi and the peak power to 530 hp. The torque was up substantially to 506 ft-lbs. As expected, the power gain was pretty consistent with the increase in boost pressure until the very top of the rev range. We would find out why on the next pulley swap.

Stepping down from the 3.2-inch blower pulley to the smaller 2.93-inch pulley resulted in an increase in peak boost pressure from 10.9 to 13.3 psi. While the gain in peak boost pressure suggested a sizable gain in peak power (as before), the peak power was up to only 538 hp. Peak torque took a sizable jump from 506 ft-lbs to 550 ft-lbs, but where was all the extra horsepower? The reality is that we had reached the flow limit of the Eaton supercharger. The additional boost produced power gains lower in the rev range (where the supercharger still had plenty of flow potential), but 538 hp seemed to be closing in on the flow limit.

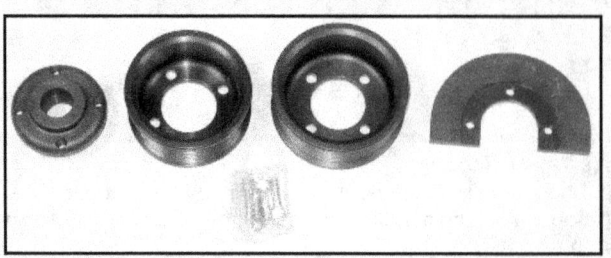

By swapping a couple of different smaller blower pulleys in place of the factory pulley, we raised boost first to 10.9 psi, and then to 13.3 psi.

Supercharging 3- and 4-Valve Modular Engines

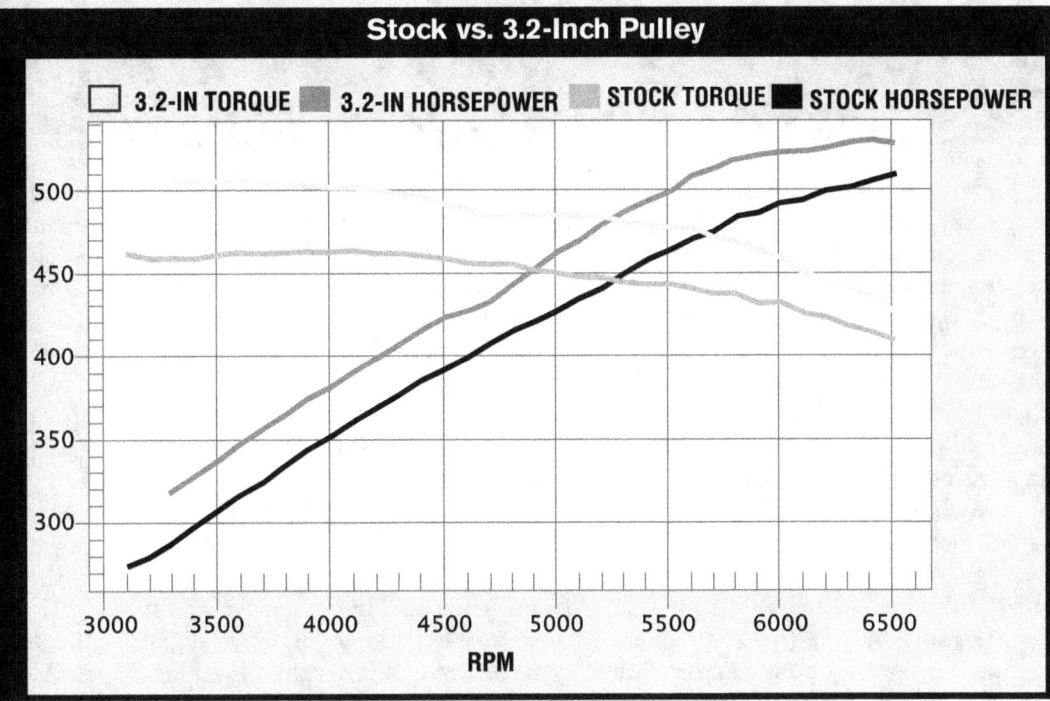

Stock Pulley:
508 hp @ 6,500 rpm

3.2-inch Pulley:
530 hp @ 6,400 rpm

Largest Gain:
38 hp @ 5,600 rpm

Eaton Supercharged 4-Valve '03 Cobra: Stock vs. 3.2-inch Pulley
Since this test involved three different pulley sizes, we decided to include both the horsepower and torque curves on one graph. Replacing the stock '03 Cobra blower pulley on the Eaton supercharger resulted in a jump in peak boost pressure from 8.7 to 10.9 psi. It's important to note that the boost curve is not linear or flat with the Eaton supercharger. The boost pressure climbed from 3,000 rpm to 4,500 rpm, and then fell off thereafter. Adding the 3.2-inch blower pulley from South Florida Pulley Headquarters upped the peak power from 508 to 530 hp and peak torque from 463 to 506 ft-lbs. As expected, the change in blower speed increased the power output throughout the rev range, though the power gains diminished somewhat from 6,000 rpm to 6,500 rpm.

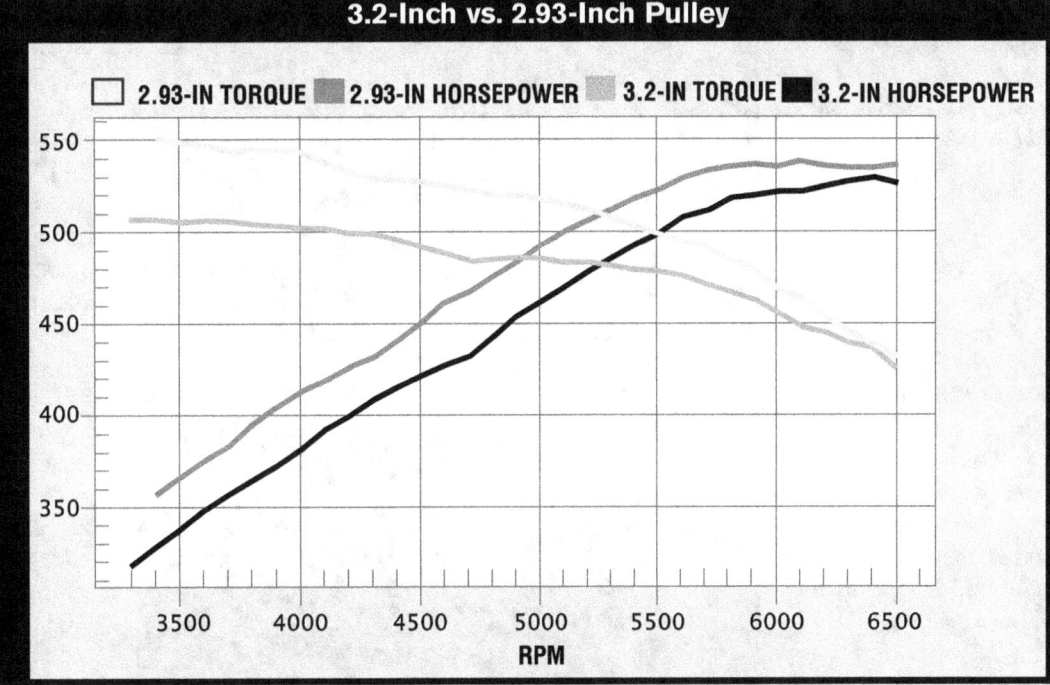

3.2-inch Pulley:
530 hp @ 6,400 rpm

2.93-inch Pulley:
538 hp @ 6,100 rpm

Largest Gain:
35 hp @ 4,700 rpm

Eaton Supercharged 4-Valve '03 Cobra: 3.2-inch vs. 2.93-inch Pulley
The next step down in blower pulley size upped the peak boost pressure from 10.9 to 13.3 psi. The additional boost pressure helped the peak torque number significantly, from 506 ft-lbs to 550 ft-lbs. The gain in peak horsepower was less impressive, jumping from 530 hp with the 3.20-inch blower pulley to 538 hp with the smaller 2.93-inch pulley. The Eaton M112 supercharger was simply running out of flow. Big horsepower and torque gains were available down low (where the blower could support the necessary airflow), but became choked off near the top.

Building 4.6/5.4L Ford Horsepower on the Dyno

Test 3: 4-Valve '03 Cobra: Eaton Supercharger vs. Kenne Bell Upgrade

Previous testing run on the effect of pulley (boost) changes with the Eaton clearly illustrated that the supercharger was limiting the power output once we reached 539 hp. We were able to increase the power output at lower engine speed (below the horsepower peak), but increasing the speed of the supercharger had a minimal effect on the peak power. Once you reach this point, your best option is to increase the flow rate of the supercharger. This can be accomplished by porting, increasing the size of the roots blower (not a practical option for the Cobra motor), or replacing the Eaton supercharger with something that offers more power potential. There are a number of supercharger upgrades (centrifugal and twin-screw) available for the '03 and '04 Cobra, but enthusiasts that appreciate the right-now feel of the torque offered by a positive-displacement supercharger are sure to welcome the Kenne Bell twin-screw blower. Unlike the centrifugal superchargers, which change the personality of the original motor, the Kenne Bell twin-screw retains all that impressive low-speed torque and adds a ton of extra top-end power potential.

We replaced the factory Eaton supercharger with a twin-screw blower from Kenne Bell. In this particular test, the Kenne Bell blower used was slightly larger (at 2.2 liters) than the M112 (roughly 2.0 liters), though extensive testing has been performed with both M90s versus 1.5L twin-screws as well as M112 and the smaller 1.8L twin-screws. The 2.2L blower was chosen by Kenne Bell to not only eclipse the smaller Eaton but to also allow for extensive power gains should the Cobra owner decide to crank up the boost. In this back-to-back test, the factory Eaton M112 supercharger was removed from the '03 Cobra motor after producing 537 hp and 530 ft-lbs of torque at a maximum boost pressure of 12.1 psi. Remember that additional boost pressure had no effect on the power. The Eaton blower was equipped with a 3.20-inch blower pulley and a 7.5-inch crank pulley. The boost curve rose to 12.1 psi at 4,400 rpm then fell off to 10.8 psi at 6,500 rpm. The falling boost curve is a clear example that the flow rate of the blower has been reached.

After running the Eaton supercharger on the motor, we installed the Kenne Bell twin-screw supercharger. The twin-screw blower utilized the factory Cobra air-to-water intercooler and lower intake manifold. Oil, water, intercooler water temps, and even blower pulley size were kept constant. The Kenne Bell stepped up the power output to a whopping 682 hp, while the torque peak was up to 595 ft-lbs. Unlike the Eaton supercharger, the twin-screw blower produced a rising boost curve, peaking at 16.5 psi at 6,500 rpm. With more boost, power, and torque everywhere, it's hard to argue against installing the Kenne Bell blower in place of the factory M112 Eaton. As further testament to the power potential of the twin-screw design, we played the pulley game once again to increase the blower speed. Though ineffective on the Eaton at improving the peak power, swapping out the 7.5-inch crank pulley for a larger 8.5-inch version upped the peak boost pressure to 19.5 psi and the peak power to 704 hp. The torque peak now stood at 631 ft-lbs, with the Kenne Bell supercharged Cobra motor exceeding 600 ft-lbs from 3,500 rpm to 6,100 rpm.

The '03 and '04 Cobras come from Ford with Eaton M112 roots-style superchargers. In the last test, we upped blower speed but maxed out at about 540 hp.

Kenne Bell offers this 2.2L twin-screw blower upgrade for '03 and '04 Cobras. Even with the same pulley ratio, the Kenne Bell produced more boost, horsepower, and torque than the factory Eaton supercharger.

Supercharging 3- and 4-Valve Modular Engines

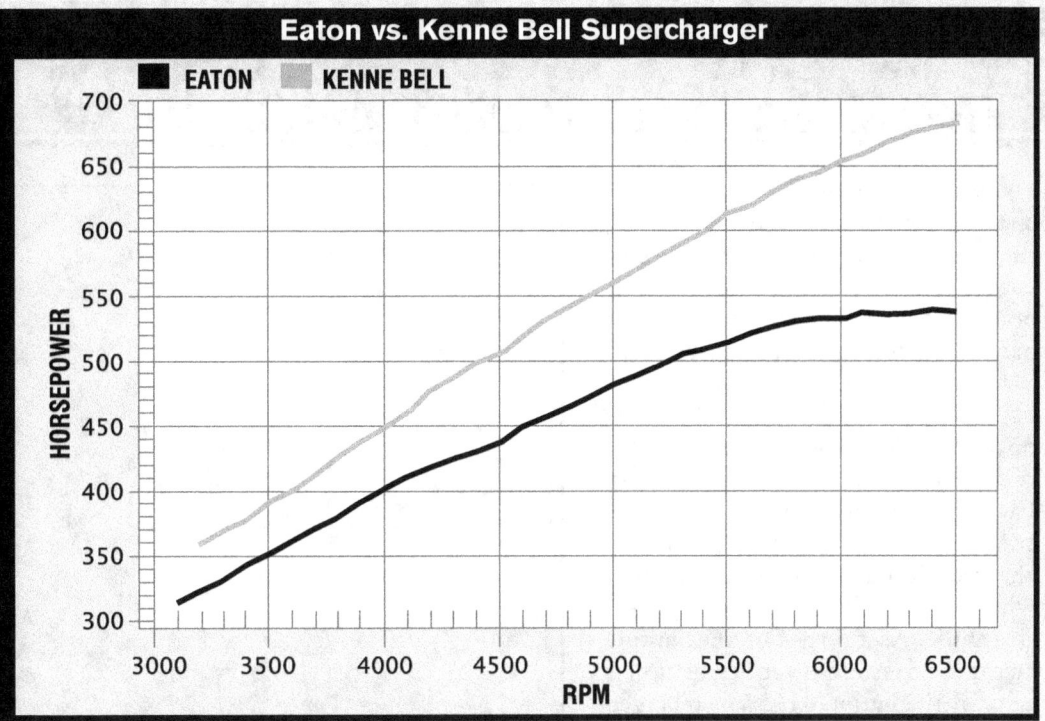

Eaton (12.1 psi):
537 hp @ 6,500 rpm

Kenne Bell (16.5 psi):
682 hp @ 6,500 rpm

Largest Gain:
145 hp @ 6,500 rpm

4-Valve '03 Cobra: Eaton (12.1 psi) vs. Kenne Bell (16.5 psi) (Horsepower)
If you check out the last test with pulley upgrades on the stock Eaton supercharger, you'll see that the Eaton was limited in ultimate power production regardless of the blower speed. What the '03 Cobra motor really needed was a better, more powerful supercharger. Replacing the Eaton with the Kenne Bell twin-screw 2.2L supercharger resulted in a dramatic increase in power. Both blowers were equipped with the same blower pulleys, but the Kenne Bell blower upped the horsepower peak from 537 hp to an amazing 682 hp. Where the boost curve fell off with the Eaton, the boost pressure climbed to 16.5 psi (compared to a peak of just 12.1 psi) for the Eaton.

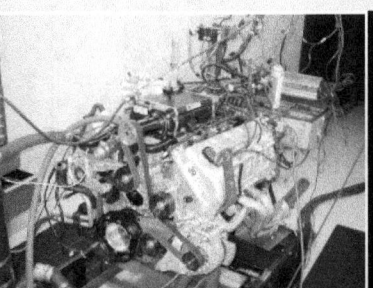
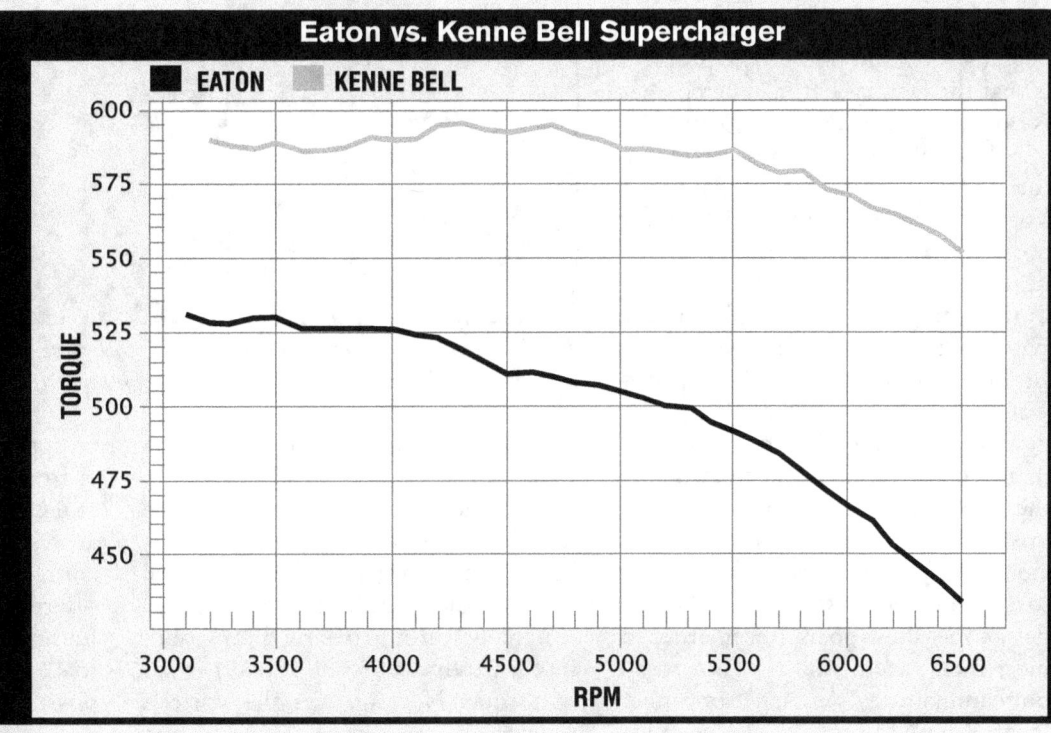
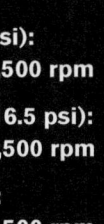

Eaton (12.1 psi):
537 hp @ 6,500 rpm

Kenne Bell (16.5 psi):
682 hp @ 6,500 rpm

Largest Gain:
145 hp @ 6,500 rpm

4-Valve '03 Cobra: Eaton (12.1 psi) vs. Kenne Bell (16.5 psi) (Torque)
The torque curves tell the same story. Installing the Kenne Bell supercharger in place of the less efficient Eaton M112 will result in a dramatic increase in torque. Where the Eaton produced a peak of 530 ft-lbs, the Kenne Bell answered with 595 ft-lbs. With more power potential, a lower charge temperature, and a simple bolt-on replacement, the Kenne Bell supercharger upgrade for the '03 Cobra has a lot going for it.

Test 4: 4-Valve '03 Cobra: Eaton Supercharger vs. Vortech T-Trim Upgrade

When Ford introduced the supercharged 4-valve 4.6L in the '03 Cobra, they gave enthusiasts possibly the best engine to ever come in a Mustang. A bold statement to be sure, but think back to yesteryear and name a motor that had the potential to pump out 990 hp in stock trim! Try running 20 psi on a stock 5.0L, or any Windsor for that matter, and see what happens. Factory equipped with forged steel crank, rods, and pistons, the supercharged Cobra motors can withstand what can only be described as excessive abuse. As it turns out, the limiting factor in terms of power production is actually the Eaton M112 supercharger. That's right – the same component that delivers all that extra power is ultimately the choke point when it comes to making *serious* power. With a stout reciprocating assembly, a set of free-flowing 4-valve heads, and an impressively efficient air-to-water intercooler, the '03-'04 motors are just begging for more boost. The problem is that the factory Eaton supercharger is flow limited to around 600 hp.

After all the hoopla surrounding the factory supercharged Mustang, Vortech decided to do something for those looking to take things to the next level. Vortech came up with a blower upgrade that replaced the Eaton M112 roots-style supercharger. In order to use the factory air-to-water intercooler, Vortech designed a new upper intake manifold. The new intake design had to allow installing the production intercooler core and positioning the throttle body in the stock location for using the factory MAF and inlet system. The Vortech design met these goals, but in order to meet them, the intake also had to all but eliminate any semblance of runner length (the ATI centrifugal system for the Cobra suffers from this same problem). The lack of runner length greatly reduces power production in

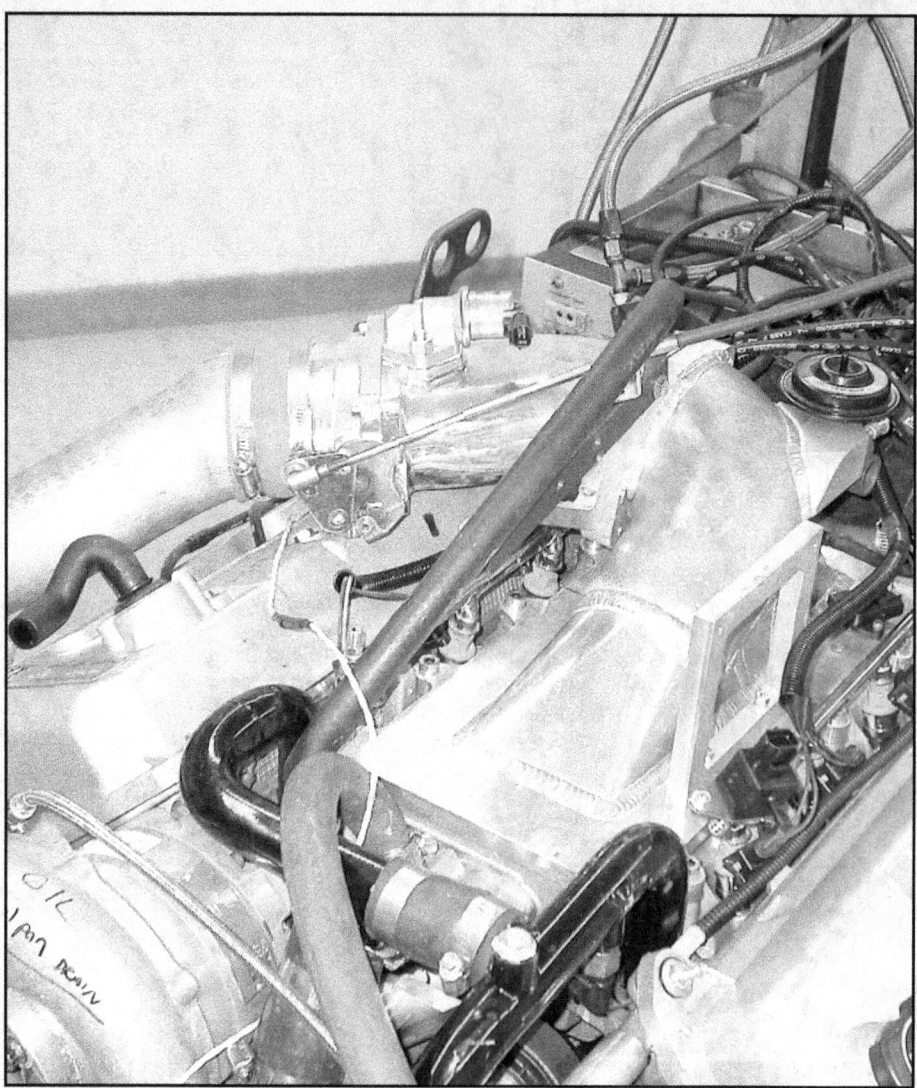

The Vortech supercharger upgrade comes with a centrifugal supercharger and this new intake manifold that meets up with the factory intercooler and lower intake manifold.

the all-important 3,500 to 6,500 rpm range.

Replacing the Eaton M112 on the '03 Cobra motor with a Vortech T-Trim supercharger had a dramatic effect on the power curve. Running 10 psi, the Eaton supercharged '03 Cobra motor produced 557 hp and 491 ft-lbs of torque. Next up was the Vortech blower upgrade. The Vortech was equipped with a 3.12-inch blower pulley, which produced a peak boost pressure of 14 psi. The Vortech blower upgrade upped the peak horsepower from 557 hp to an impressive 725 hp at 6,600 rpm. The peak torque was up as well, from 491 to 576 ft-lbs. Of course, the immediate boost response offered by the positive-displacement Eaton out-powered the centrifugal up to 4,900 rpm. In a drag race where the power band runs from 4,500 rpm to 6,500 rpm, the Vortech would be the clear winner, and with a centrifugal blower, there's always more boost and power waiting in the wings.

Supercharging 3- and 4-Valve Modular Engines

Eaton (10 psi):
557 hp @ 6,600 rpm

Vortech T-Trim (14 psi):
725 hp @ 6,600 rpm

Largest Gain:
168 hp @ 6,600 rpm

4-Valve '03 Cobra: Eaton (10 psi) vs. Vortech T-Trim (14 psi) (Horsepower)
The horsepower curves illustrate the differences inherent in the different blower designs. The roots-style Eaton supercharger offers tremendous low-speed power, thanks to immediate boost response. The problem is that the efficiency signs off with extended rpm and boost pressure. The exact opposite is true of the centrifugal supercharger, as the boost response at lower engine speeds is down compared to the roots but is clearly superior at elevated boost levels. The Vortech T-Trim offered a huge peak power increase (from 557 hp to 725 hp), but this came at a higher peak boost level (14 psi versus 10 psi). The top-end charge of the Vortech has to be experienced to be believed.

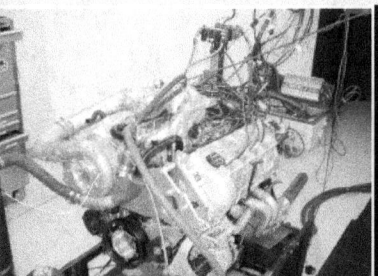

Eaton (10 psi):
491 ft-lbs @ 4,600 rpm

Vortech T-Trim (14 psi):
576 ft-lbs @ 6,300 rpm

Largest Gain:
134 ft-lbs @ 6,600 rpm

4-Valve '03 Cobra: Eaton (10 psi) vs. Vortech T-Trim (14 psi) (Torque)
The torque curve is where you really see the difference between the roots blower and the centrifugal. While the Vortech added 168 hp and 134 ft-lbs of torque at 6,600 rpm, the immediate boost response of the roots blower provided an additional 125 ft-lbs of torque at 2,500 rpm. Whether you could harness all that extra low-speed torque is another question, but extra power is always nice. Given the differences between the two blowers, you simply need to choose where you want your power.

Test 5: 3-Valve '05 GT: Paxton Novi 1200 Supercharger

The new 3-valve motor included different cylinder heads that featured 3 valves per cylinder. These heads represented a significant flow improvement over the 2-valve PI heads, even when ported. The flow improvements offered by the 3-valve heads are one of the primary reasons why the 3-valve GT motor pumps out near 4-valve Cobra power numbers. Though the 3-valve motor is SOHC like the 2-valve PI motors, the new 3-valve version adds an impressive system called variable cam timing. Though not quite on par with the legendary dual-cam VTEC systems offered by Honda/Acura, the variable cam timing on the 4.6L 3-valve motor offers improved performance by advancing and retarding the existing cam profile. In most cases, advancing a cam will improve low-end and midrange torque, while retarding it will improve high-RPM power. The problem with advancing or retarding the cam is that the gains achieved at one end of the scale come with a penalty at the opposite end. The key to improving the power throughout the rev range is to advance it at low RPM and retard it at high RPM, something made possible with variable cam timing. Variable cam timing also improves emissions and fuel mileage.

In addition to the 3-valve cylinder head and variable cam timing, the new GT motor also features a redesigned intake manifold. The 3-valve heads featured revised intake ports, which are more like the 4-valve ports in that they are long and slender rather than round. Rather than simply take a PI intake and alter the port shape to match the new heads, Ford engineers designed a whole new manifold. The new intake shares the composite construction with its predecessor but offers slightly shorter runners, a new plenum design, and a new front-mounted throttle body. The new intake also featured Intake Manifold Runner Controls (IMRCs), complete with throttle linkage, similar to the 1996-'98 4-valve Cobra intakes. The front-mounted throttle body is a new design as well, featuring the sophisticated drive-by-wire throttle actuation to replace the traditional throttle cable. This drive-by-wire system was one of the hurdles I had to overcome when running the 3-valve GT on the engine dyno, but I managed to design and build my own drive-by-wire using a set of Vice Grips and bailing wire.

Setting the 3-valve motor up on the dyno was made easier by the fact that we had previously run both 2-valve and 4-valve combinations. The 3-valve motor was originally equipped with a coil-on-plug ignition, but we relied on a coil-pack system used on the early 2-valve motors. The 3-valve motor was equipped with JBA long-tube headers feeding 2.5-inch open pipes. The F.A.S.T. system was used to dial in the air/fuel ratio at 13.0:1, and the timing curves at 30 degrees total advance. Run in this configuration, the stock 4.6L 3-valve produced 356 hp at 5,800 rpm and 392 ft-lbs at 4,300 rpm. The power curve leveled off around 5,100 rpm, but the power never dropped off like on the previous 4.6L 2-valve motors. The torque output was impressive, exceeding 325 ft-lbs from 3,000 rpm to 5,650 rpm. Adding the Paxton supercharger with a 3.6-inch blower pulley produced a peak boost pressure of 11.3 psi at 6,200 rpm. The Paxton Novi 1200 blower upped the power output of the new 4.6L 3-valve motor to an impressive 559 hp. This number was later increased to 613 hp with a 3.33-inch blower pulley.

For this test, we're adding a Paxton Novi 1200 centrifugal supercharger to the already impressive '05 3-valve Mustang GT engine. The 3-valve motor responded to boost like a 4-valve motor because of its great flowing heads.

Supercharging 3- and 4-Valve Modular Engines

NA 3-Valve GT:
356 hp @ 5,800 rpm

W/Paxton Novi 1200 (11.3 psi):
559 hp @ 6,200 rpm

Largest Gain:
200 hp @ 6,100 rpm

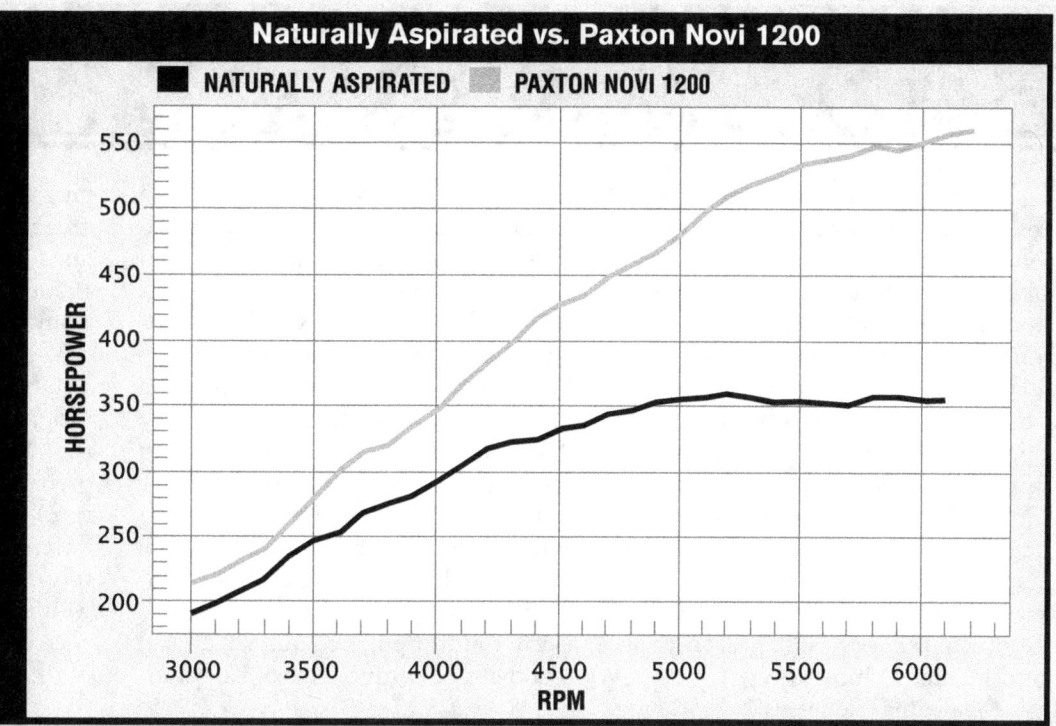

3-Valve '05 GT: NA vs. Paxton Novi 1200 Supercharger (11.3 psi) (Horsepower)
As we have come to expect, the gains offered by the Paxton Novi 1200 supercharger increased with engine speed. Out past 6,000 rpm (11.3 psi), the blower added 200 hp to the already impressive 2005 3-valve motor.

NA 3-Valve GT:
392 ft-lbs @ 4,300 rpm

W/Paxton Novi 1200 (11.3 psi):
513 ft-lbs @ 5,300 rpm

Largest Gain:
175 ft-lbs @ 5,600 rpm

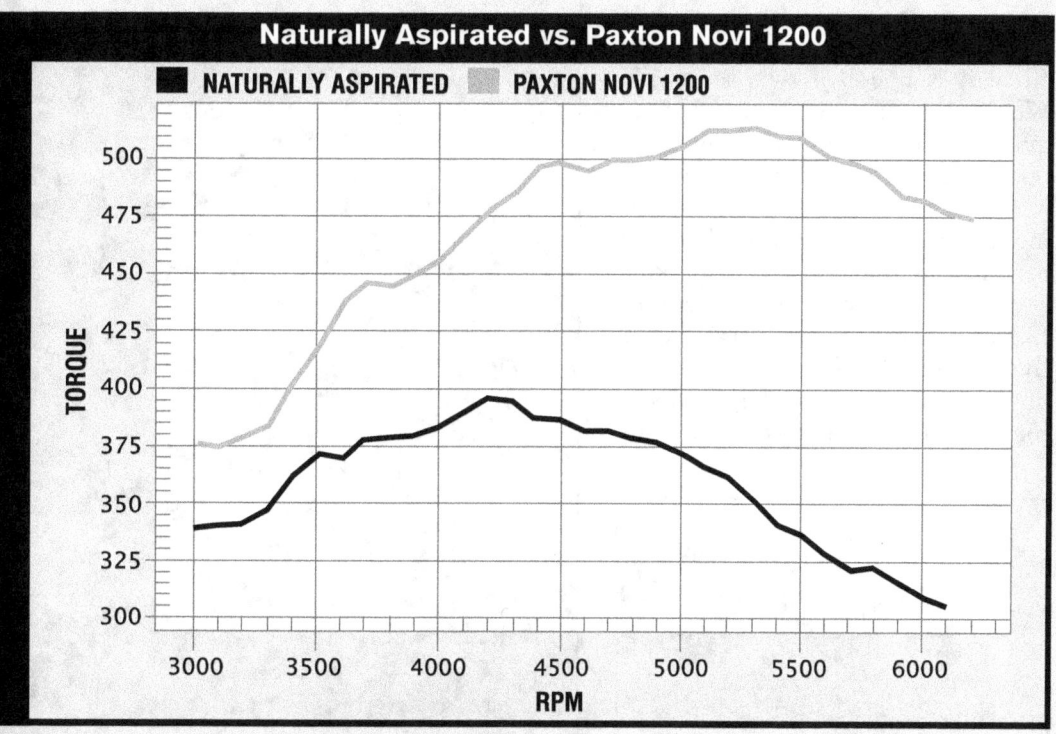

3-Valve '05 GT: NA vs. Paxton Novi 1200 Supercharger (11.3 psi) (Torque)
Even down at 3,000 rpm, the Paxton blower upped the torque output by a solid 35 ft-lbs. The Novi 1200 went on to improve the torque production by as much as 175 ft-lbs, with huge gains from 4,000 rpm to 6,200 rpm, right where it will come in handy during hard acceleration.

Chapter 7

Test 6: Kenne Bell Supercharged 4-Valve '03 Cobra: 16.5 psi vs. 19.5 psi

This test is a perfect example of the kinds of things that can go wrong when you get greedy. Boost has a way of bringing out the worst in people. It hooks people like any good drug. Check under the hood of any supercharged '03 or '04 Cobra and tell me if you don't at least see a blower pulley upgrade. While the stock power is impressive, it's just too easy to add more. Who can resist seeing the boost gauge swing just a little farther? 10 psi starts to get old after a while. But 11 or maybe 12 psi, that would be all you need, right? Pretty soon 12 psi turns into 14, and 14 into 16.

While this tale seems to be leading to some untimely demise, the reality is that upping the boost pressure is a time-honored tradition, especially among '03 and '04 Cobra owners. This is even true of those owners who were lucky enough to swap out their Eaton M112 roots supercharger for the more efficient Kenne Bell twin-screw kit. Where the factory Eaton blower quickly reaches its maximum flow, boost, and power limit, finding the limit of the Kenne Bell supercharger is a bit more difficult. Just know that if you're maxing this one out, you're talking about some serious power. Where the Eaton M112 blower signs off about 600 flywheel hp, the Kenne Bell 2.2L has no trouble exceeding 800 hp (or more for the 2.4L). If you max out a Kenne Bell blower on your 4-valve Cobra motor, chances are you are looking to find a way into the 9s, a level seldom achieved by most daily drivers.

We did experience some belt slippage on this test, but we weren't surprised since we were still running a factory 8-rib serpentine drive belt. The '03 4-valve Cobra motor was all stock with the exception of the Hooker headers and the Kenne Bell 2.2L twin-screw supercharger. Equipped with a 7.5-inch DUB crank pulley and a 3.25-inch blower pulley, the supercharged 4-valve motor pumped out 682 hp and 595 ft-lbs of torque at 16.5 psi. Swapping out the 7.5-inch crank pulley for a larger 8.5-inch version resulted in a jump in boost pressure from 16.5 to 19.5 psi. The power increased as well, from 682 to 704 hp, but the peak-to-peak gains would have been even more significant had we not experienced belt slippage near the top of the high-boost run. The effect on the power curve is pretty evident (it levels off at 6,000 rpm). Given that the maximum power difference was 42 hp and 48 ft-lbs of torque, eliminating the belt slippage would have given us a similar difference in the power peaks. This was one of those frustrating dyno sessions.

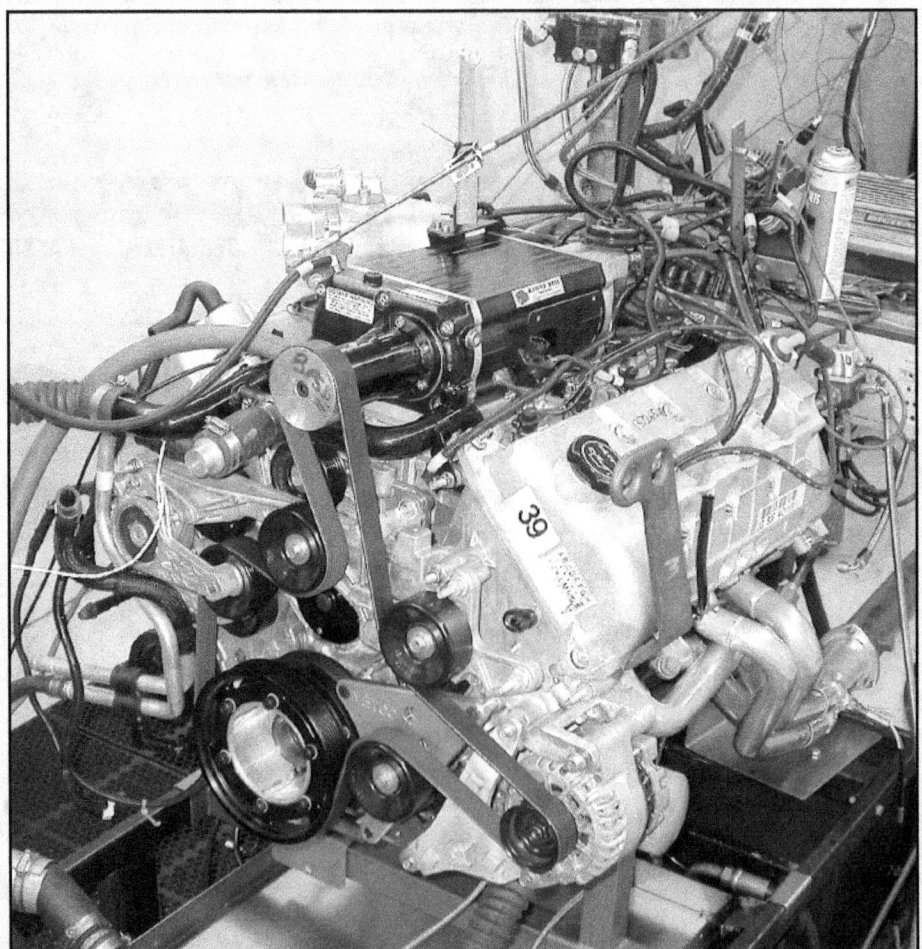

With the Dial-Ur-Boost (DUB) system, we were able to change the crank pulley to bump maximum boost from 16.5 to 19.5 psi.

The '03 Cobra engine for this test was stock except for the Hooker headers and Kenne Bell blower upgrade. I don't know if "stock except for the Kenne Bell blower" is really a reasonable statement.

Supercharging 3- and 4-Valve Modular Engines

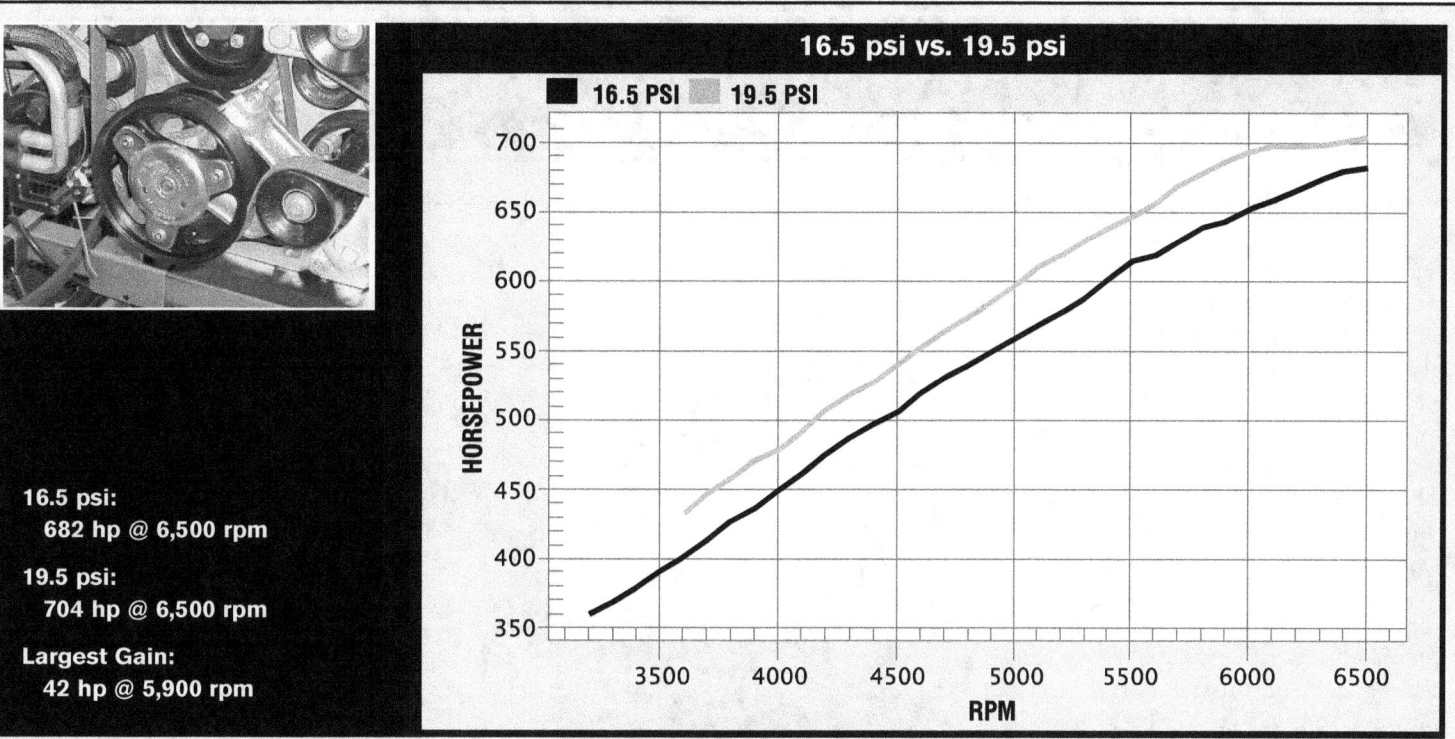

16.5 psi:
682 hp @ 6,500 rpm

19.5 psi:
704 hp @ 6,500 rpm

Largest Gain:
42 hp @ 5,900 rpm

Kenne Bell Supercharged 4-Valve '03 Cobra: 16.5 psi vs. 19.5 psi (Horsepower)
While the Kenne Bell supercharger upgrade offered a significant power increase over the Eaton M112, we wanted to see if the 2.2L twin-screw blower had more power in reserve. To find out, we replaced the 7.5-inch DUB crank pulley with a larger 8.5-inch version. The DUB system made pulley changes a snap. The increase in crank pulley size increased the boost pressure from 16.5 to 19.5 psi, pushing the peak power to 704 hp.

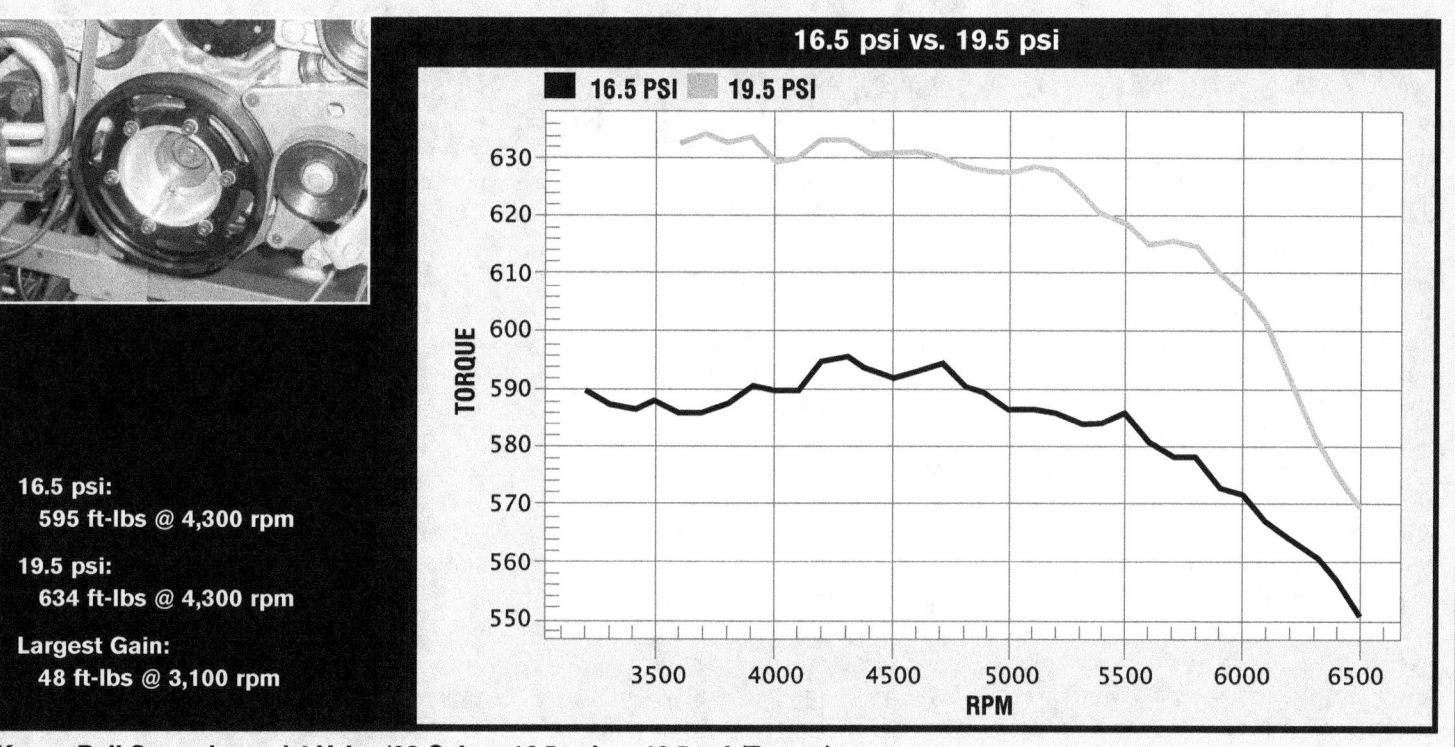

16.5 psi:
595 ft-lbs @ 4,300 rpm

19.5 psi:
634 ft-lbs @ 4,300 rpm

Largest Gain:
48 ft-lbs @ 3,100 rpm

Kenne Bell Supercharged 4-Valve '03 Cobra: 16.5 psi vs. 19.5 psi (Torque)
The torque peak was naturally up as well; from 595 to 631 ft-lbs. The gang at Kenne Bell has produced over 700 flywheel hp using this same 2.2L blower, so additional power production is not a problem.

Test 7: 4-Valve 5.4L: ATI F2M Supercharger

Ford modular motors are available in two different displacements from the factory. The smaller 4.6L has proven itself powerful, but when it comes to maximum performance, it's always easier to make big power with a big motor. Technically, the larger the motor, the lower the specific output required to reach a given power level. The specific output of any motor is in direct proportion to difficulty and expense. If you were looking to produce 460 hp from a 4.6L, it would require a specific output of 100-hp per liter. Achieving the same output using a larger 5.4L motor requires a specific output of only 85-hp per liter, which is much easier. The added benefit of the additional displacement is low and midrange torque, as a hike in displacement improves power not just at the power (or torque) peak, but also throughout the rev range. Since races are won not by peak power numbers, but with average power production over the usable range, extra power is always welcomed.

When you go looking for huge power with your supercharged motor, the best place to start is with a solid naturally aspirated motor. Our 4-valve 5.4L features a steel crank, forged steel connecting rods, and forged aluminum pistons. Despite the fact that this motor was destined for high boost, the short block was assembled with a set of high-compression (flat-top) pistons. Given the fact that this motor was to see nothing less than C16 race fuel, the combination of high compression and high boost was not a problem given the correct tune. The forged short block was topped off with a set of ported 4-valve cylinder heads that also featured a few proprietary touches from mod-motor legend John Mihovitz. Though sworn to secrecy, we can say the valve seats, installed heights, and cam timing was optimized to the fullest extent possible. All time-consuming prospects to be sure, but ultimately worth the effort—especially for a dedicated drag race motor. The 5.4L 4-valve motor was equipped with a rather unique Sullivan intake manifold and 90-mm Accufab throttle body. The high-compression naturally aspirated 5.4L combination netted 542 hp at 7,200 rpm and 439 ft-lbs at 6,100 rpm.

If this blower looks a little bigger than some you've seen on the street, that's because it probably is. This ATI F2M centrifugal blower made 25 psi on our 5.4L engine.

Before installing the ATI F2M supercharger, the 5.4L received 150-pound injectors, replacing the 36 pounders on the NA combination. The 5.4L was equipped with a set of 1¾-inch to 2.0-inch step headers (run on the NA combination as well) and 3.5-inch collector extensions. A F.A.S.T. management system was employed to control the MSD coil packs and large injectors. The ATI F2M supercharger was installed with a custom cog drive system designed by Accufab to eliminate belt slippage. The cog system featured a 73-tooth crank pulley and 46-tooth blower pulley. Given the expected high boost level (north of 20 psi), an ATI intercooler filled with ice water was employed to reduce the all-important intake charge temperature. Run with 19 degrees of total timing, an air/fuel ratio of 11.2:1, and C16 fuel, the ATI blower produced a maximum of 25 psi of boost on its way to 1,350 hp at 7,200 rpm and 1,028 ft-lbs of torque at 6,500 rpm. Though far from a streetable combination, just imagine this kind of power in your street Mustang!

Supercharging 3- and 4-Valve Modular Engines

NA 5.4L 4-Valve:
542 hp @ 7,200 rpm

W/ATI Supercharger (25 psi):
1,350 hp @ 7,200 rpm

Largest Gain:
808 hp @ 6,900 rpm

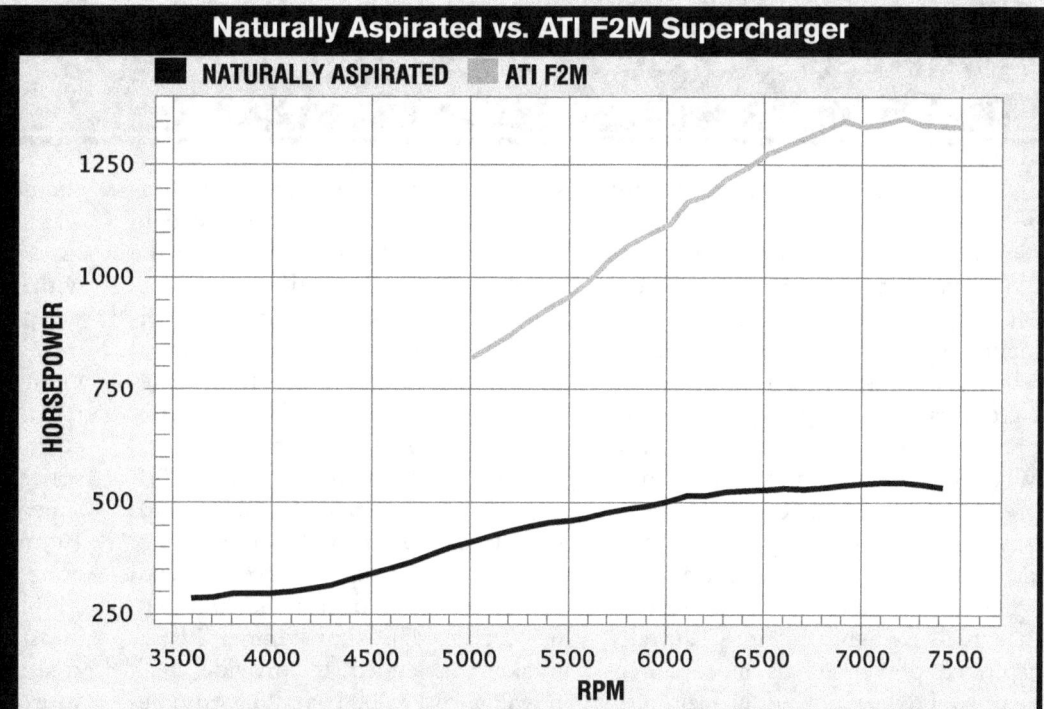

4-Valve 5.4L: NA vs. ATI F2M Supercharger (25 psi) (Horsepower)
As expected, the ATI F2M supercharger had a huge effect on the horsepower output of the modified 5.4L. Where the naturally aspirated 5.4L produced 542 hp at 7,200 rpm, the supercharged motor motored all the way to 1,350 hp at a peak boost pressure of 25 psi. The supercharger increased the power output of the motor by an amazing 808 hp. Having a motor that produces 808 hp would be impressive enough, just imagine adding 808 hp to an already stout naturally aspirated 5.4L.

NA 5.4L 4-Valve:
439 ft-lbs @ 6,100 rpm

W/ATI Supercharger (25 psi):
1,028 ft-lbs @ 6,500 rpm

Largest Gain:
625 ft-lbs @ 6,700 rpm

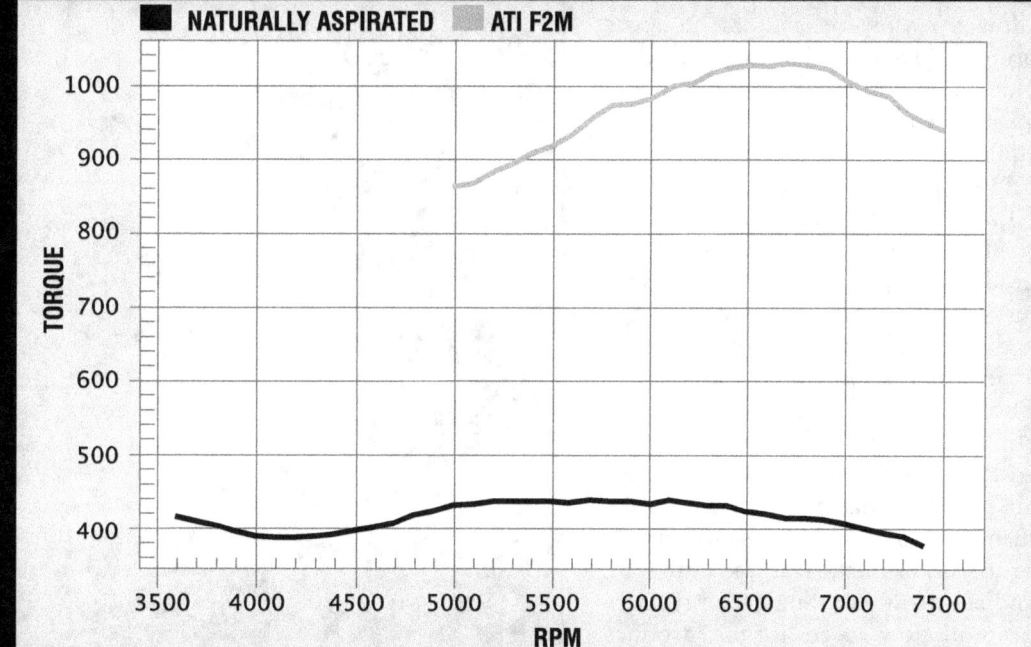

4-Valve 5.4L: NA vs. ATI F2M Supercharger (25 psi) (Torque)
Like the horsepower, the torque output more than doubled as well, up from 439 ft-lbs at 6,100 rpm to 1,028 ft-lbs at a slightly higher 6,500 rpm. The supercharged 5.4L exceeded 900 ft-lbs from 5,400 rpm to 7,400 rpm. The big ATI F2M blower featured a custom Accufab cog-drive system to eliminate the one Achilles heel of supercharging – namely belt slippage. The Accufab cog-drive system completely eliminated any belt slippage to produce consistent (and repeatable) boost curves run after run.

Chapter 7

Test 8: 4-Valve Cobra: Paxton Novi 2000 Supercharger

Our quest for 900 hp started out with a stock 2001 4-valve Cobra motor rated at 320 hp. Our short block was fitted with a Sean Hyland Motorsport forged rotating assembly, including the crank, rods, and pistons, which were basically duplicates of the factory castings, offering a static compression ratio of just over 10.25:1. While you might think the static compression ratio is a tad on the high side for forced induction, this motor was slated for drag-race use and as such will be fed a steady diet of high-octane race fuel. Remember, more naturally aspirated power equals more supercharged power, and additional static compression equates to more naturally aspirated and supercharged power. Were the motor run on the street where octane is the limiting factor, we would certainly think about dropping the compression to around 8.5:1 to 9.0:1. This would take some of the snap out of the motor, but it would allow a reasonable amount of boost pressure given the detonation threshold of 91-octane pump gas.

The 4.6L Cobra short block was equipped with a set of Ford Racing FR500 cylinder heads and Comp XE262AH cams. Though impressive right out of the box, these FR500 heads were upgraded with a Ford Racing valve and spring upgrade package and a full-blown port job from the experts at Total Engine Airflow. These FR500 heads should flow over 300 cfm on the intake side. The TEA-ported FR500 heads were topped off with an FR500 Variable Geometry intake manifold, so named for its dual runner profiles. The intake featured both long and short runners. Since long runners promote low-speed torque production and short runners do likewise for high-speed horsepower, the FR500 intake was able to offer the best of both worlds. A unique throttle linkage operated by a solenoid controlled the switchover point, but for our application we were primarily interested in the power production offered by the short runner configuration.

We ran the 4.6L in naturally aspirated form with a set of 36-pound injectors using the F.A.S.T. management system and MSD coil packs. Tuned to provide 28 degrees of total timing and an air/fuel ratio of 13.0:1, the naturally aspirated SHM/FR 4.6L produced 483 hp and 376 ft-lbs of torque. The torque curve hovered right near 375 ft-lbs from 5,300 rpm to 6,500 rpm. The short-runner FR500 intake was tuned to provide peak power above 7,000 rpm. Unfortunately, the valvesprings (though upgraded) limited the maximum engine speed before we experienced valve float. This came back to haunt us even more after we installed the Novi supercharger. After establishing a baseline, we installed the Paxton Novi 2000 supercharger kit. The kit was supplied with a 3.5-inch blower pulley and when combined with the stock 6.5-inch crank pulley produced a maximum impeller speed of over 46,000 rpm. Running no intercooler and a custom (short) 6-rib belt (no accessories), the impressive Novi 2000 supercharger provided a maximum of 16 psi of boost to push the peak power up to 841 hp. The peak torque now stood at 630 ft-lbs. Unfortunately, the boost supplied by the Paxton exaggerated the valve float issue (boost pressure on the valve surface works against the spring pressure), limiting our maximum engine speed to just 7,100 rpm. Even there we suspected a loss of valve control, but we had no springs or shims to improve the situation.

With a forged short block and FR500 heads and intake, this 4-valve was ready for some boost. With the Novi 2000 centrifugal blower running at about 16 psi, the combo produced 841 hp and 630 ft-lbs of torque.

Supercharging 3- and 4-Valve Modular Engines

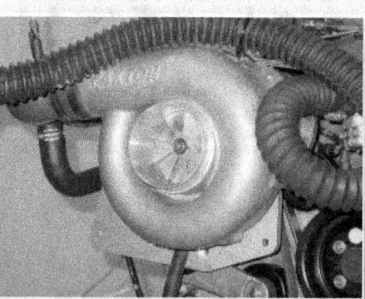

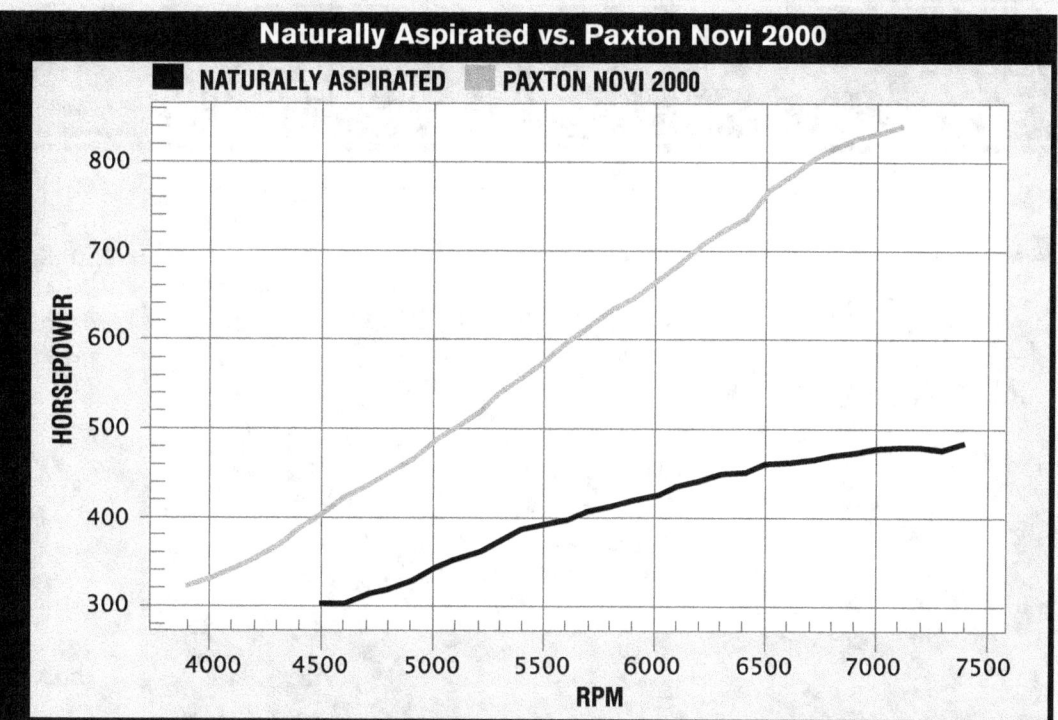

NA 4-Valve Cobra:
483 hp @ 7,400 rpm

W/Novi 2000 (15.9 psi):
841 hp @ 7,100 rpm

Largest Gain:
361 hp @ 7,100 rpm

4-Valve Cobra: NA vs. Paxton Novi 2000 Supercharger (15.9 psi) (Horsepower)
After running the SHM 4.6L with the TEA-ported FR500 heads and intake, we were naturally anxious to install the Paxton Novi 2000 supercharger. In the past, 4-valve mod motors have always responded very well to forced induction, and this combo was no exception. Adding the Paxton Novi 2000 supercharger to the naturally aspirated Cobra motor resulted in a jump in peak power from 483 hp to 841 hp. Check out the shape of the power curve – it was really on its way up. Unfortunately, the valvesprings installed on the FR500 heads limited the maximum engine speed to 7,100 rpm before valve float.

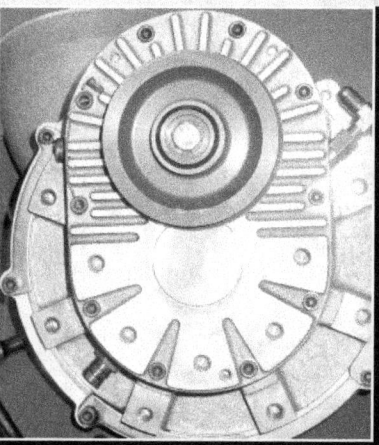

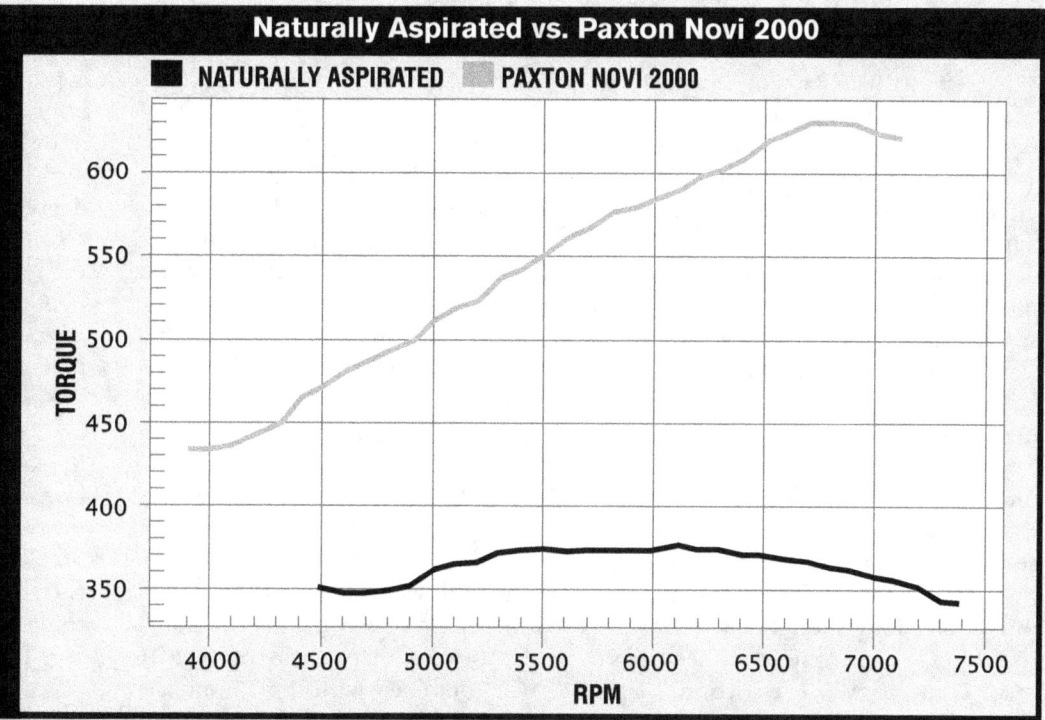

NA 4-Valve Cobra:
376 ft-lbs @ 6,100 rpm

W/Novi 2000 (15.9 psi):
630 ft-lbs @ 6,800 rpm

Largest Gain:
267 ft-lbs @ 7,100 rpm

4-Valve Cobra: NA vs. Paxton Novi 2000 Supercharger (15.9 psi) (Torque)
The Paxton Novi 2000 supercharger was equipped with a 3.5-inch blower pulley and a 6.5-inch crank pulley for a maximum impeller speed of 46,149 rpm and a maximum boost pressure of 15.9 psi. It is evident from the shape of the torque curve that the Novi 2000 had plenty left to offer if our weak valvesprings were not artificially limiting engine speed. Still, a jump in peak torque from 376 to 630 ft-lbs is pretty impressive. The Paxton Novi 2000 blower is an excellent choice for a 4.6L mod motor.

Building 4.6/5.4L Ford Horsepower on the Dyno

Chapter 7

Test 9: Paxton Supercharged 4-Valve Cobra: Effect of Intercooling

Though the Paxton intercooler was designed for about 500 hp, it held up quite well on our 766-hp engine. With a cooler, denser intake charge you can usually run more boost or add timing to make more power.

While there's no argument that intercoolers reduce the inlet charge temperature and therefore the risk of detonation, whether or not they add power is a bit more confusing. On the surface, adding an intercooler to your existing blower seems like a no-brainer, but there is a tradeoff. Not surprisingly, a supercharged motor performs best with an unrestricted flow of air into and out of the supercharger. On the inlet side, you need an unrestricted source of cold air. The same holds true on the discharge side. Installing an intercooler (any intercooler) between the blower and the throttle body results in a flow restriction. The amount of restriction caused by the intercooler is determined by a variety of different design parameters, including the diameter and length of the tubing, the number of bends, and the flow capacity of the core (heat exchanger) itself. The ideal intercooler system is short, free of bends, free flowing, and offers exceptional heat rejection. Unfortunately, a number of these design criteria are at odds, making the intercooler a compromise at best.

To illustrate the intercooler restriction, I talked Paxton into letting me perform this test. The Paxton kit for the 2001 Cobra included the Novi 2000 blower, a 3.5-inch blower pulley, and everything you need to install it. The 3.5-inch blower pulley was combined with the factory 6.5-inch crank pulley to produce a drive ratio of 1.857:1. When combined with the 3.5 internal step ratio and the engine's 6,500-rpm rev limit, the impeller speed maxed out at 42,250 rpm, which produced a maximum boost pressure of 13 psi. Using the F.A.S.T. system, the combination was tuned with 18 degrees of total timing and an air/fuel ratio of 11.7:1. Adding the Novi 2000 supercharger to the 4-valve motor upped the peak power to an amazing 766 hp. The torque peak stood at 618 ft-lbs. The Paxton Novi 2000 made exceeding 750 hp as easy as falling off the proverbial log. Tests like these make me wish for a 4-valve Cobra of my own.

Next up came the intercooler test. We installed the Paxton air-to-air intercooler setup on the dyno. A dual electric fan was used on the intercooler to ensure adequate cooling for the short runs. Keeping the pulleys, air/fuel, and timing the same, adding the intercooler dropped the boost pressure supplied to the intake manifold by as much as 3 psi at 6,500 rpm. Not surprisingly, the drop in boost pressure resulted in a drop in power, but the real key to this scenario is the restriction of the intercooler. No intercooler made could make up for a 3-psi drop in boost pressure, especially given the low initial charge temperature offered by the Paxton to begin with. Were the charge temperature 350 degrees F going in, it's possible to add a sizable chunk of power by dropping the temps to 100 degrees, but since the inlet temp was only around 220 degrees, less power was left on the table for the intercooler to make up. We could install a smaller blower pulley to increase the boost pressure back up to the 13-psi level and make additional power (compared to the non-intercooled 13-psi run), but the idea was simply to illustrate the effect of the restriction. What is the important thing to remember from all this testing? First of all, intercoolers work, just don't be misled into thinking that the drop in charge temperature is primarily responsible for the power gains – it's the tuning and additional boost pressure you can run. Second of all, the Novi 2000 is an impressive blower.

Supercharging 3- and 4-Valve Modular Engines

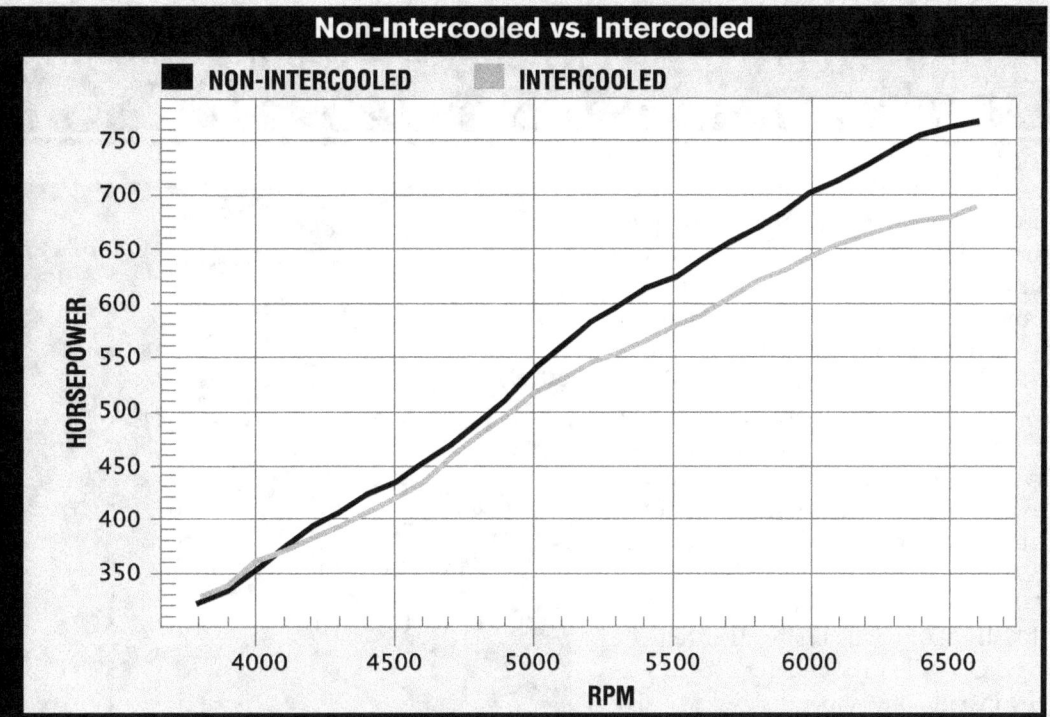

Novi 2000 Non Intercooled:
766 hp @ 6,600 rpm

Intercooled Novi 2000:
687 hp @ 6,600 rpm

Largest Drop:
81 hp @ 6,500 rpm

Paxton Supercharged 4-Valve Cobra: Effect of Intercooling (Horsepower)
The first thing you should notice is that the airflow restriction presented by the air-to-air intercooler increased with engine speed (and engine flow). This is not surprising, but note that the restriction was minimal up to 5,000 rpm but increased dramatically thereafter. Given the fact that this intercooler was designed for a 500-hp application and our motor exceeded that level by 50 percent, the intercooler actually performed admirably.

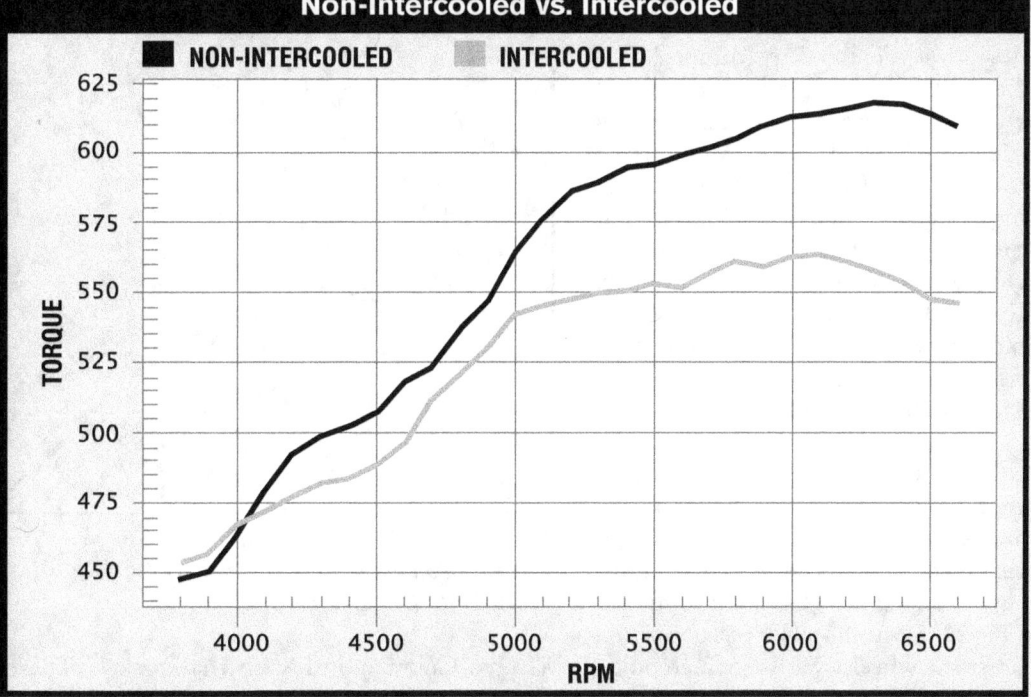

Novi 2000 Non Intercooled:
618 ft-lbs @ 6,300 rpm

Intercooled Novi 2000:
563 ft-lbs @ 6,100 rpm

Largest Drop:
66 ft-lbs @ 6,500 rpm

Paxton Supercharged 4-Valve Cobra: Effect of Intercooling (Torque)
I can remember having an argument with an industry individual about the projected results of this test. He could not be convinced that installing an intercooler between the supercharger and the throttle body represented a restriction. The longer the inlet tract length, the greater the restriction. He assured me that adding an intercooler would add power, thanks to the reduced charge temperature and increased density. He obviously never spent any time on the dyno checking his facts!

Test 10: 3-Valve '05 GT: Kenne Bell Supercharger

Fans of the Mustang GT welcomed the '05 3-valve 4.6L with open arms. In addition to the impressive new body style, Ford increased the power. The new 3-valve 4.6L is nearing 4-valve territory with a factory rating of 300 hp. The extra 40 hp over the 2-valve PI had been a long time coming, but the real question is can the normally aspirated 3-valve Mustang motor be expected to take the fight to the LS1s of the world? Despite the increased 300-hp rating of the '05 GT, the larger 5.7L LS1, to say nothing of the new 400-hp 6.0L, will easily dispatch the new GT. What Ford really needed was to install the supercharged 4-valve Cobra motor in the new body style. Dropping the supercharged Cobra from the lineup in 2004 left the Mustang GT to do battle sans supercharging, at least as far as the factory goes.

While the factory left us without a supercharged Mustang, the aftermarket quickly came to the rescue with upgrades for the '05 Mustang GT. Kenne Bell is a name long associated with supercharged Mustangs, way back to the 5.0L days. Mod motor owners are well aware of their offerings for late-model Mustangs, and their upgrade kits for factory supercharged Cobras and Lightnings. Kenne Bell kits feature a twin-screw blower, which unlike a typical centrifugal supercharger, gives you power throughout the RPM range.

Given the near (normally aspirated) 4-valve Cobra performance from the 3-valve motor, Kenne Bell expected and was rewarded with power outputs that exceeded those of the Eaton-supercharged '03-'04 4-valve motor. Our 2005 Mustang GT put down 268 hp at the wheels. With the intercooled Kenne Bell blower kit, the peak power numbers jumped to 459 hp at just 9 psi in pump-gas trim. This power level compares very nicely to the numbers pumped out by a modified '03-'04 4.6L

Just before this book went to print, we witnessed Kenne Bell testing a couple of twin-screw blowers on an '05 3-valve Mustang GT. Of course, it put down impressive numbers with either the 1.7L or 2.2L blower.

4-valve Cobra motor with the stock Eaton roots blower. Imagine, a gain of 191 hp with just 9 psi of boost! To further demonstrate the power potential, Kenne Bell upped the boost pressure to 14 psi and made an amazing 535 hp.

There was more power available from the blower, but it was at this level that the fuel pump (with Kenne Bell Boost-A-Pump) was getting close to maxing out, to say nothing of the strength of the stock short block.

Supercharging 3- and 4-Valve Modular Engines

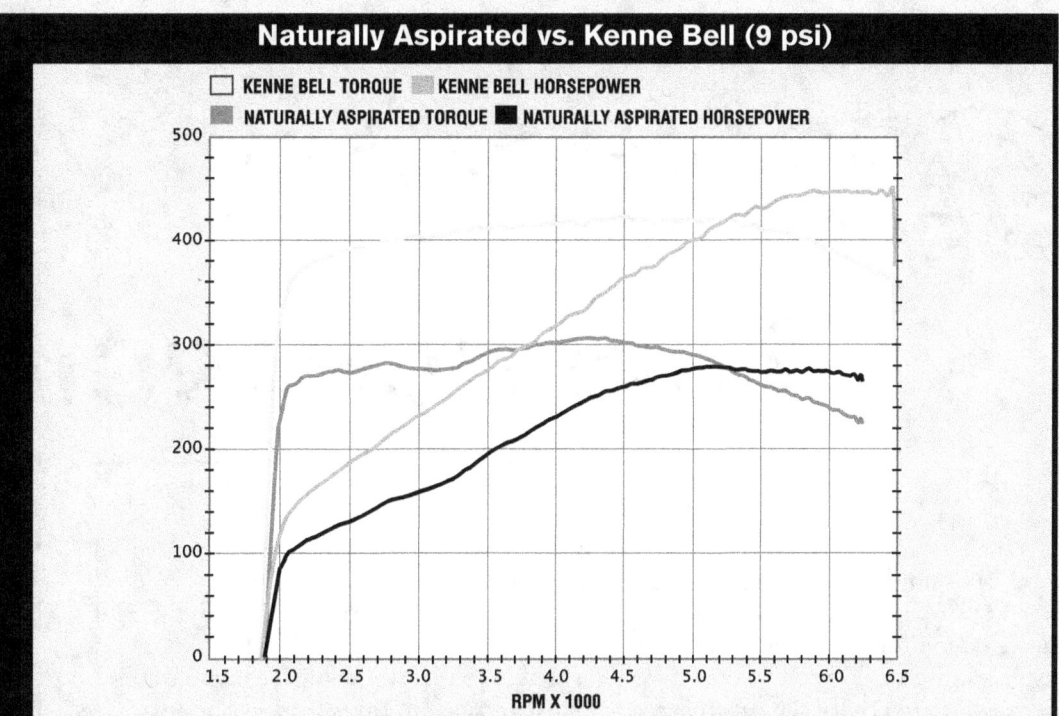

Stock 3-Valve GT:
286 hp @ 5,300 rpm

Kenne Bell Supercharged 4.6L
3-Valve GT (9 psi):
459 hp @ 6,200 rpm

Largest Gain:
179 hp @ 6,300 rpm

3-Valve '05 GT: Stock vs. Kenne Bell Supercharger

The 4.6L 3-valve motor has already proven itself effective, pumping out power numbers right between the 2-valve PI motor and the naturally aspirated 4.6L 4-valve Cobra. Rated at 300 flywheel hp, the '05 Mustang GT 4.6L 3-valve produced 286 hp and 315 ft-lbs of torque on the chassis dyno. After installing the new Kenne Bell supercharger kit, the peak numbers jumped up to 459 hp, a gain of 173 hp. What makes this kit so much fun to drive is the torque curve, which exceeded 400 ft-lbs from 2,500 rpm to 5,700 rpm.

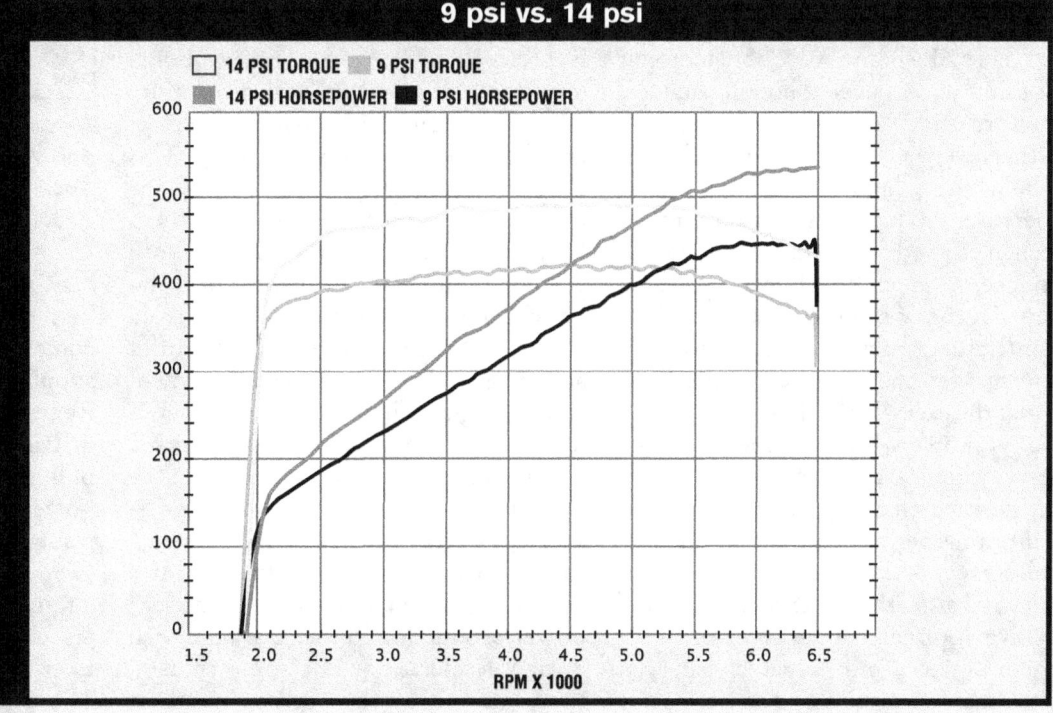

Kenne Bell Supercharged
4.6L 3-valve GT (9 psi):
459 hp @ 6,200 rpm

Kenne Bell Supercharged
4.6L 3-Valve GT (14 psi):
535 hp @ 6,600 rpm

Largest Gain:
251 hp @ 6,500 rpm

3-Valve '05 GT: 9 psi vs. 14 psi

If a little boost pressure is good, then more must be better, right? Yes – provided that the extra boost comes with the appropriate amount of fuel and timing. Upping the boost pressure from 9 psi with the smaller 1.7L blower to 14 psi with the larger 2.2L blower resulted in a dramatic change in power. Running 14 psi, the otherwise stock 4.6L 3-valve produced 535 hp at the wheels. The peak torque checked in at over 500 ft-lbs. At this power level, it might be a good idea to think about a more serious short block, but it's nice to know that the Kenne Bell kit is up to the task of feeding a serious modular motor.

CHAPTER 8

TURBOCHARGING

When it comes to making serious power, nothing beats a turbocharger. Sure, 4.6L superchargers rule the streets, but the reason for their popularity probably has more to do with the manufacturer's ability to certify the supercharger kits than the power potential. Anyone who doubts the power potential of a well-designed turbo system need only check out the results of the comparison between the four forms of forced induction (roots blower, twin-screw blower, centrifugal blower, and turbos) run on the same 4.6L 4-valve '03 Cobra motor at the same boost level. Though catalogs, literature, and Web sites offered by some of the less well-informed supercharger manufacturers may have you believe otherwise, the reality is that no form of mechanically driven supercharger will produce as much absolute power as a proper turbo system. I remember reading literature supplied by one centrifugal supercharger manufacturer that indicated that the excessive backpressure associated with turbos would somehow offset the parasitic losses associated with driving the supercharger. Real-world, unbiased testing performed for this book (as well as every SAE paper ever written) has proven that with the exception of the positive displacement blowers run at low engine speeds, no supercharger can match the absolute or average power production offered by a turbo system. To think or suggest otherwise amounts to nothing more than marketing hype.

While a huge fan (and student) of all things forced induction, my testing on turbo systems was somewhat limited until I hooked up with Jimmy and Nathan at HP Performance. Using their 2-valve, 3-valve, and 4-valve 4.6L kits, I was able to directly compare turbo systems versus all three of the popular supercharger systems. I had never seen a direct comparison of this magnitude using the four forms of forced induction, so I decided it was high time someone showed the modular world the benefits (and deficiencies) associated with each system. From the results it is pretty obvious that at every boost level the turbo system will offer more power per pound of boost than any of the three forms of supercharging. This takes nothing away from any of the blower kit manufacturers, as blower sales should continue to skyrocket until someone finds a way to certify a turbo system for a late-model 4.6L. Even then, superchargers will still offer advantages. The positive-displacement supercharger will always offer more low-speed power than the turbo, though a turbo system (as shown in the results in this chapter) will allow the 4-valve-powered Mustang to accelerate through the 1/4-mile quicker and at a higher trap speed, thanks to the average power production in the rev range used during acceleration. For some though, the peak and average power numbers are not as important as the low-speed response.

How does one form of forced induction produce more power than another at the same boost level? In the

Topping the list of mod motor maniacs is Accufab's John Mihovitz. This twin-turbo 4.6L 4-valve motor thumped out over 1,700 hp.

case of a turbo versus a supercharger, the vast majority of the power difference comes from the fact that the crankshaft supplies the drive for the blower. Remember the power gain received by installing your first set of underdrive pulleys? The underdrive pulleys increase power by reducing the parasitic losses associated with driving the accessories (water pump, A/C, power steering, and alternator). Any of the three superchargers will cause more parasitic drive loss than all of your accessories combined. The worst offender is the Eaton M112 roots blower on the '03-'04 supercharged Cobra motor. The drive losses associated with spinning the roots blower amounts to well over 150 hp at an elevated RPM and flow rate. The twin screw requires less power to drive, ditto for the Vortech, but all three require a significant amount of power to drive the blower. This parasitic loss is power consumed and not produced by the motor, something the turbo system avoids by using the heat energy normally expelled through the exhaust. Properly sized, minimal backpressure is used to generate the equivalent boost pressure (a 1:1 ratio between boost and exhaust pressure is considered very good).

In addition to eliminating parasitic losses, turbochargers usually offer superior efficiency (they are better able to manage air movement). Compared to a typical roots blower, a properly sized turbo system will always offer more power per pound of boost. In terms of efficiency, roots blowers rank at the bottom, while turbos rank at the top. Centrifugal superchargers rank high as well, not surprising given the fact that they are very similar to the compressor section of a turbo (just mechanically driven). The twin-screw blower ranks above the roots blower but a tad below a centrifugal. If you check out the results of the boost comparison, this is basically the finishing order (at least in terms of maximum power). Of course, the efficiency tells us nothing about the overall power curve offered by each, as the least-efficient roots blower bettered all three of the other forms of forced induction in the lower rev range. This low-speed torque production offered by the positive-displacement supercharger makes for an impressive argument, but the rapid response rate soon gives way to the efficiency of the turbo. The most telling aspect of the superior efficiency offered by the turbo system is the fact that the turbocharged motor produced more power than the roots supercharged motor well before the turbo motor reached the same boost pressure (with as much as 3 to 4 psi less boost).

Here are a couple more examples of the power potential offered by combining Ford modular motors with turbocharging. The 4.6L 2-valve motors are usually looked down on by their 4-valve brethren, but we ran a twin-turbo system (from HP Performance) on a mild 4.6L 2-valve motor that produced over

This twin-turbo kit from HP Performance offered an easy 700 hp and over 700 ft-lbs of torque at just 13 psi of boost.

700 flywheel hp with just 13 psi of boost. We struggled like hell to exceed 700 hp with any of the blowers, though I did eventually manage to reach 800 hp with a 2-valve motor using a Vortech YS-Trim. The 700-hp mark came easy with the turbo kit and had I arranged additional dyno time, 800 hp would have come just as easy with more boost pressure. Things got serious while running the '03 Cobra crate motor. Equipped with a small set of Comp cams and an intercooled HP Performance twin-turbo kit, the low-compression 4.6L 4-valve Cobra motor thumped out an amazing 990 hp and over 900 ft-lbs of torque at 20 psi. We may have reached the flow limit of the 57-mm turbos, but the power output was impressive nonetheless. The ultimate expression of turbocharged madness came when I was fortunate enough to be on hand when Accufab's own John Mihovitz was on the dyno with his twin-turbo 4.6L race motor. How does over 1,700 hp from just 281 cubic inches sound?

Replacing the factory Eaton supercharger on this '03 Cobra crate motor with a more efficient twin-turbo system from HP Performance eventually resulted in 990 hp. Note the 2001 intake used on the '03 Cobra motor in place of the supercharger.

On an all-out race motor, the exhaust system is critical. Check out the trick stainless steel tubular headers, centrally mounted wastegate flange, and massive 5-inch exhaust tubing.

Test 1: Early 2-Valve GT: HP Performance Twin-Turbo Kit

The motor used for testing the twin-turbo 4.6L 2-valve kit from HP Performance featured low-compression (9.0:1) forged pistons and forged steel connecting rods from Coast High Performance and a pair of Xtreme Energy cams from Comp Cams. After running all six of the available Xtreme Energy cams on a naturally aspirated 4.6L (see Chapter 4, Test 2), I was better able to choose a suitable street turbo cam. The XE262AH cams provided a broad torque curve, something that would definitely improve turbo response, with impressive peak horsepower and torque numbers. Other grinds offered more peak power (though not much), but I figured that the XE262AH cams were the best choice for a street application. These cams offered .550 inch of lift on the intake and exhaust, but a dual-pattern duration split of 226/230 degrees at .050. The wide 113-degree lobe separation angle minimized overlap. Though our motor featured early non-PI heads, the CNC porting performed by FPS greatly improved the flow rates. We knew that the ported heads could take full advantage of the additional cam lift. We also installed the valvespring upgrade recommended by Comp Cams.

With additional cylinder pressure and power output supplied by the turbo system, it was necessary to upgrade both the ignition and fuel systems. The fuel system was taken care of with an Aeromotive EFI fuel pump capable of supporting 1,000 hp. A Kenne Bell Boost-A-Pump increased the supply voltage to the pump to further improve the flow capacity. The stock injectors were not up to the task of feeding a turbo motor, so I replaced the 19 pounders with a set from F.A.S.T. that flowed 65 lbs/hr. The injectors were installed in a Wilson billet fuel rail. With the fuel system taken care of, I turned our attention to the ignition system. The ignition mods included replacing the stock coil packs with high-energy units from MSD. MSD also supplied a set of plug wires, but the most important part of the ignition equation was the DIS-4 ignition amplifier. Elevated cylinder pressure will require a hotter spark or misfiring will occur. We also ran a set of Denso Iridium IT24 spark plugs, which also helped eliminate the misfires associated with boosted applications.

As always, I ran the modified 4.6L in naturally aspirated form to establish a baseline. The turbo-ready 4.6L produced 347 hp and 350 ft-lbs of torque with an air/fuel ratio of 13.0:1 and 30 degrees of total timing. Installing the twin-turbo kit on the dyno required a number of modifications. It was necessary to relocate the water tower to facilitate proper positioning of the front-mounted air-to-air intercooler. It was also necessary to modify the 2.5-inch exhaust system (after the turbos) to minimize the heat directed to vital dyno components. After the installation, Tom Habryzk had the twin-turbo motor up and running in no time with the F.A.S.T. engine management system. Running vacuum/boost reference lines directly to the dual TiAl wastegates resulted in a maximum boost pressure of 9.8 psi. The motor was run with race fuel for safety, though this boost level was certainly achievable on pump gas. We dropped the total timing from 30 to just 21 degrees and the air/fuel mixture from 13.0:1 to 11.7:1. Once we had the air/fuel and timing dialed in, the twin-turbo motor produced an impressive 612 hp and 606 ft-lbs of torque. Remember that all this horsepower and torque were coming from a motor displacing just 281 cubic inches!

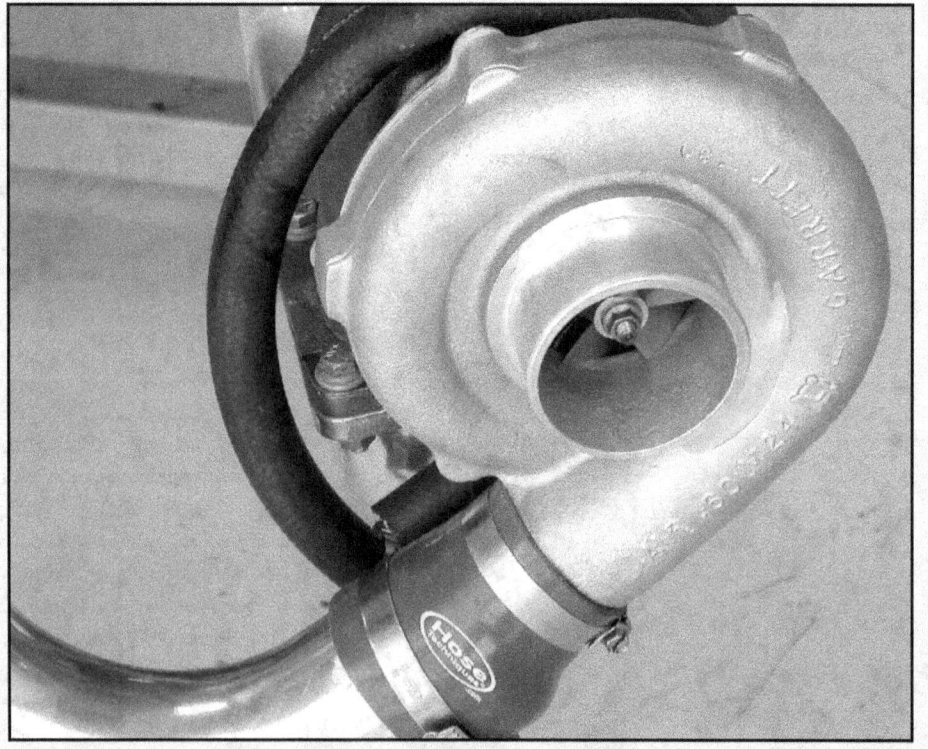

Turbo systems require more additional plumbing than supercharger systems, but the extra horsepower and torque is worth it. Once we got it hooked up and running, the twin-turbo kit made 9.8 psi.

Turbocharging

NA 2-Valve GT:
347 hp @ 5,900 rpm

W/HP Twin-Turbo (9.8 psi):
613 hp @ 6,000 rpm

Largest Gain:
267 hp @ 5,800 rpm

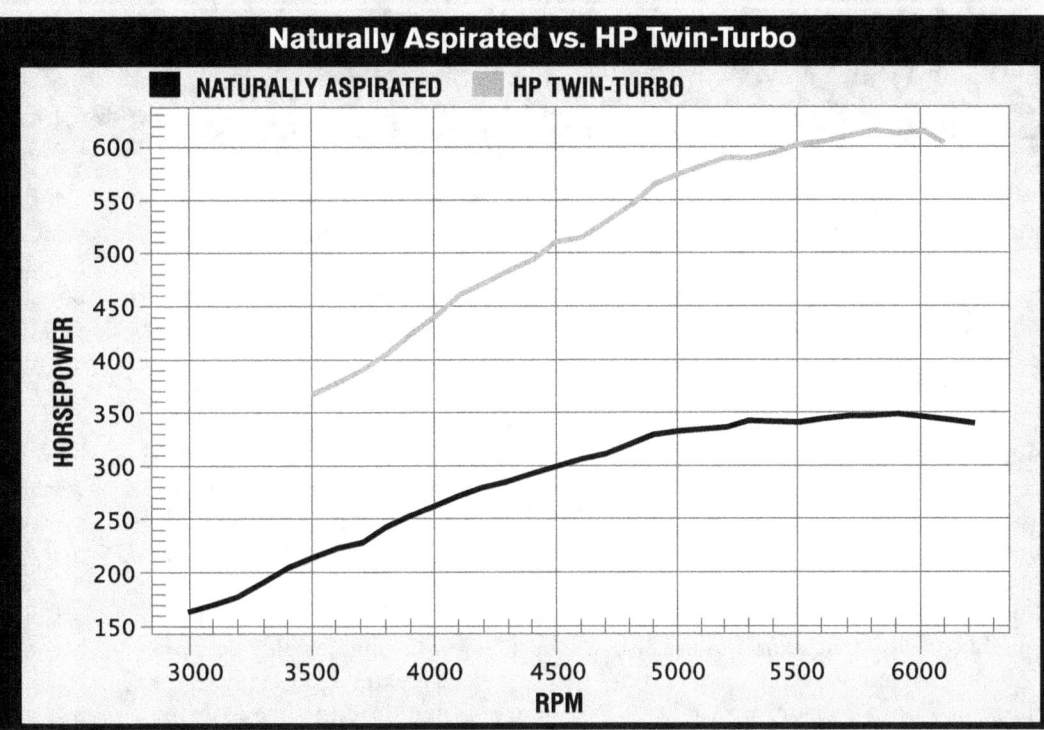

Early 2-Valve GT: NA vs. HP Performance Twin-Turbo Kit (9.8 psi) (Horsepower)
Turbo motors kick some serious ass. A 600-hp 2-valve 4.6L motor will eat modified 4-valve Cobras for lunch. This is even Viper-killing power, all from a mild 4.6L equipped with a twin-turbo kit running less than 10 psi.

NA 2-Valve GT:
350 ft-lbs @ 4,200 rpm

W/HP Twin-Turbo (9.8 psi):
604 ft-lbs @ 4,900 rpm

Largest Gain:
250 ft-lbs @ 4,900 rpm

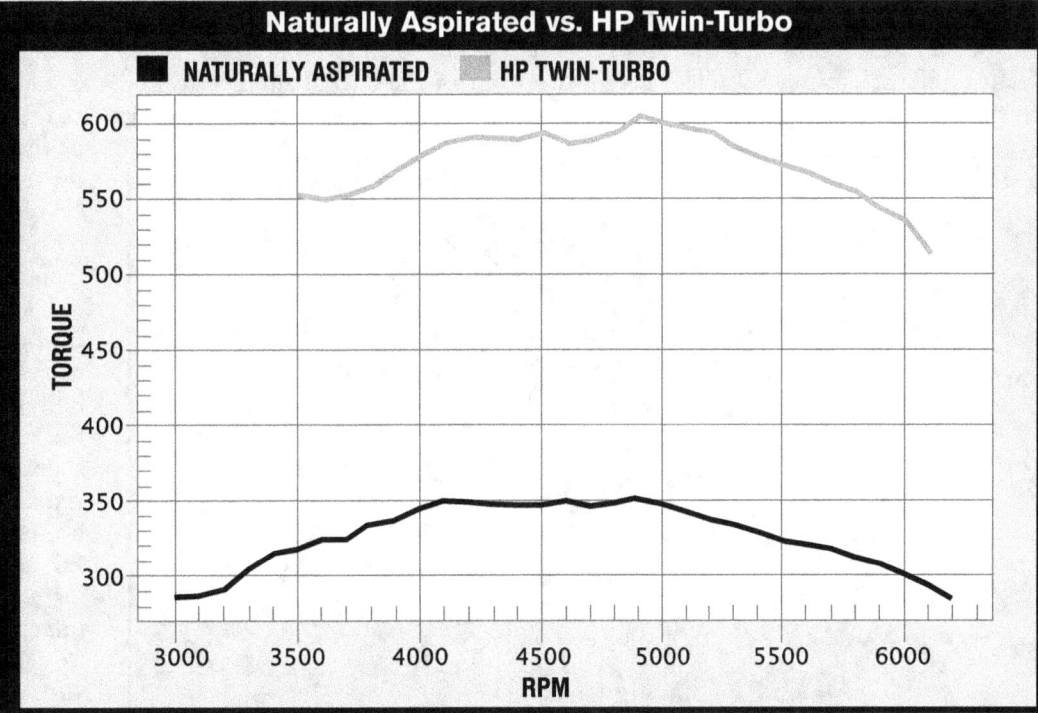

Early 2-Valve GT: NA vs. HP Performance Twin-Turbo Kit (9.8 psi) (Torque)
The motor produced 600 ft-lbs of torque to match the 600-hp reading. Can you really use 550 ft-lbs of torque from 3,500 rpm to 5,800 rpm? You bet!

Test 2: HP Twin-Turbo
Early 2-valve GT: 10 psi vs. 14 psi

The 2-valve 4.6L GT kit from HP included everything needed to install the twin-turbo system on a modern modular motor. There were a couple of changes made to the kit for our dyno needs, one of which was the deletion of the C&L mass-air meter. Our 4.6L test mule was set up to run using a F.A.S.T. stand-alone management system, so the mass-air meter and associated custom chip were unnecessary for our purposes. As supplied by HP, the standard twin-turbo kit includes a pair of T04E-46 turbos capable of supporting somewhere near 750 hp. Originally we planned on running the boost pressure up to 20 psi, so we opted for a set of upgraded T04E-57 turbos. As it turned out, available dyno time and an ignition snafu limited our high-horsepower testing, making the upgraded turbos probably unnecessary. The turbo upgrade also required the use of external wastegates (the standard turbos feature internal wastegates). HP Performance supplied a pair of precision TiAl wastegates to properly control the boost pressure. Since turbochargers are capable of astronomical boost levels, the wastegates are employed to keep the boost pressure at a predetermined level.

Also included in the kit was an ultra-efficient front-mounted air-to-air intercooler. Intercoolers help dissipate some of the heat gained when the turbos compress the inlet air. Turbos heat up the air less than other (less efficient) forms of forced induction, but all forms will increase the heat of the inlet air. The higher the boost pressure, the greater the temperature increase. In addition to the loss in air density (fewer power-producing oxygen molecules per volume), the elevated temperature can also increase the likelihood of harmful detonation. The intercooler greatly lowers the temperature of the inlet charge air by forcing it through the heat exchanger, which uses ambient airflow to help draw the heat out of the charge air. The front-mounted position provides plenty of airflow once the Mustang is at speed, which it will be quite quickly after the installation of this kit. At reasonable boost levels, the intercooler is of marginal value since the efficient turbos do not increase the inlet air dramatically. The large intercooler core will become more and more effective with increase in boost. The intercooler core featured a pair of provisions for compressor bypass valves to eliminate pressure buildup during shifts.

While turbo selection is the critical element in the success of a good turbo system, the gang at HP Performance decided it was also necessary to sweat the small stuff on their twin-turbo kit for the 4.6L Mustang. This was evident in the design of the tubular exhaust manifolds. Looking like a quality pair of shorty headers, the exhaust manifolds offered a significant improvement in exhaust flow compared to the stock (cast iron) exhaust manifolds. Like the remainder of the exhaust and inlet system tubing, the headers featured Jet Hot coating to help maximize the exhaust energy to the turbos. The Jet Hot coating should also help extend the life of the tubing by protecting it from rust and the elements. The barrier coating also helps to keep under-hood temperatures down by retaining the heat inside the exhaust tubing. To eliminate the possibility of exhaust leaks, HP designed the exhaust system with V-band clamps to provide a leak-free seal. Exhaust leaks will definitely limit turbo performance. Along those lines, HP also saw fit to use heavy-wall tubing and extra thick exhaust flanges to improve both sealing and tubing life.

Running the HP kit on the mild 4.6L 2-valve resulted in peak numbers of 613 hp and 604 ft-lbs at 10 psi. Upping the boost pressure to 14 psi (with the appropriate fuel and timing changes) resulted in a jump in power to 707 hp and 718 ft-lbs of torque.

Since our HP twin-turbo kit already had the upgraded turbos and an air-to-air intercooler, upping the boost was no problem. Just as with a supercharger, you need to retune the air/fuel ratio and timing curve for the additional boost.

Turbocharging

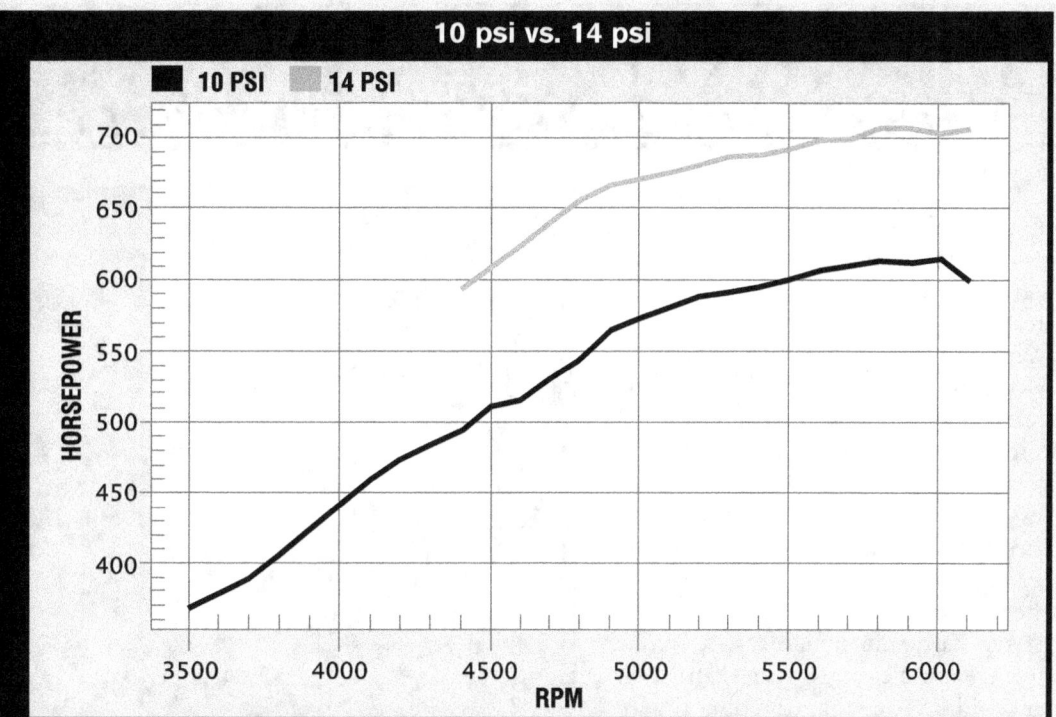

HP Twin-Turbo (10 psi):
613 hp @ 6,000 rpm

HP Twin-Turbo (14 psi):
707 hp @ 5,900 rpm

Largest Gain:
112 hp @ 4,700 rpm

HP Twin-Turbo Early 2-Valve GT: 10 psi vs. 14 psi (Horsepower)
When everything is working right, increasing the boost pressure should offer a consistent increase in power across the rev range (assuming the boost pressure is stable). Upping the boost pressure from 10 psi to 14 psi resulted in a gain of nearly 100 hp, from 613 hp to 707 hp.

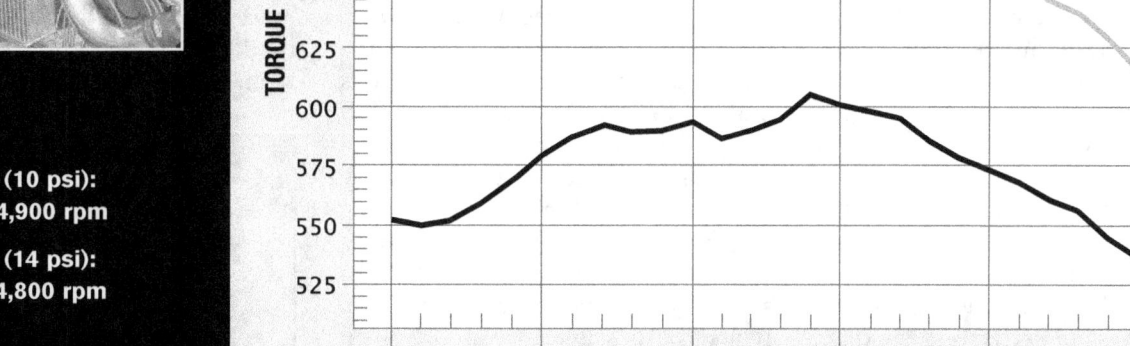

HP Twin-Turbo (10 psi):
604 ft-lbs @ 4,900 rpm

HP Twin-Turbo (14 psi):
718 ft-lbs @ 4,800 rpm

Largest Gain:
127 ft-lbs @ 4,600 rpm

HP Twin-Turbo Early 2-Valve GT: 10 psi vs. 14 psi (Torque)
Due to the mathematical relationship between horsepower and torque, if you have a consistent horsepower gain across the rev range, the torque gains will be greater at lower engine speeds. Upping the boost pressure increased the torque output by as much as 127 ft-lbs (from 604 ft-lbs to 718 ft-lbs).

Building 4.6/5.4L Ford Horsepower on the Dyno

Chapter 8

Test 3: Early 4-Valve Cobra: HP Twin-Turbo Kit

I have to admit; at first the acceleration didn't seem that impressive. Little did I know, Jimmy from HP Performance was doing all he could to keep the rear tires from spinning. While you'd expect any self-respecting V-8 to be able to roast the hides in first gear, things were still pretty hairy well into second. Feathering the throttle was the order of the day and even at less than ½ throttle, traction was still the limiting factor. Don't get me wrong, even fighting the wheel spin, the twin-turbo Cobra was accelerating pretty hard, much harder than your average muscle car. It wasn't until well into third gear that traction finally caught up to the tremendous turbocharged torque. With a clear road and full boost, the 4-valve Cobra finally got a chance to get down to business; the business of going fast, real fast. Doing my best Quint from *Jaws* impression, I said, "I think we're going to need bigger tires." Nothing short of a genuine super car could outrun this twin-turbo 4-valve 540 turbocharged flywheel hp that fast. Heck, I'd even put money down on a match race against one of those fancy Saleen S7s.

Looking at the engine compartment, it's difficult to tell that the motor has been turbocharged. With the turbos tucked in the fender wells, it looked all the world like any other 4-valve Cobra motor sporting a cold-air intake. We liked that stealth approach, as an LS1 Camaro or Corvette owner may not give the Cobra a second look other than thinking here goes another notch on the old Bowtie win belt. Let's face it, early 4-valve Cobras are pretty easy pickings for an LS1-powered machine, but not when they're turbocharged.

Equipped to produce 7 psi, the HP Performance twin-turbo Cobra kit produced an impressive 460 horsepower and 440 ft-lbs of torque. The turbo motor bettered 400 ft-lbs of

From the top, this looks like any other '96-'98 Cobra on the street. It doesn't sound like just another Cobra when you're running through the gears.

torque from 3,900 rpm to 6,000 rpm, right where you'll be doing most of your accelerating as you whip past that LS1 owner. Best of all, the motor can be driven around without ever knowing its turbocharged. Sure, there are hints from the bypass valves and the surge of torque that accompanies each press of the load pedal, but the turbo motors are so quiet compared to a like-powered supercharged combination.

While we're impressed to see the power at 7 psi, we knew there was more to be had. After all, why install forced induction if you aren't eventually going to crank up the boost? By lowering the total timing and tailoring the air/fuel curve to produce a steady (and safe) 11.5:1 air/fuel ratio, HP was able to up the boost pressure to 10 psi. It may be possible to run 10 psi on pump gas, but the 91-octane stuff offered here in California is real junk. Knowing that our 91 acts like the 87 served elsewhere, we took the liberty of mixing in some race fuel just for safety. Upping the boost pressure to 10 psi increased the power output from 460 hp to 511 hp. The peak torque was up as well, from 440 ft-lbs to 475 ft-lbs. Such is the beauty of forced induction. If you need another 50 horsepower, simply turn the knob. Before leaving, we gave the knob one final turn to 11 psi. The result was an increase in power to 539 hp, while torque was over 500 ft-lbs. We hit the streets in the newly twin-turbocharged 4-valve Cobra. We must have smoked that Z06 Corvette by 20 car lengths. As Quint again, I replied "25!"

The underside of this Cobra is definitely the business end. Because of the already cramped engine compartment, the turbos are mounted down in the fender wells.

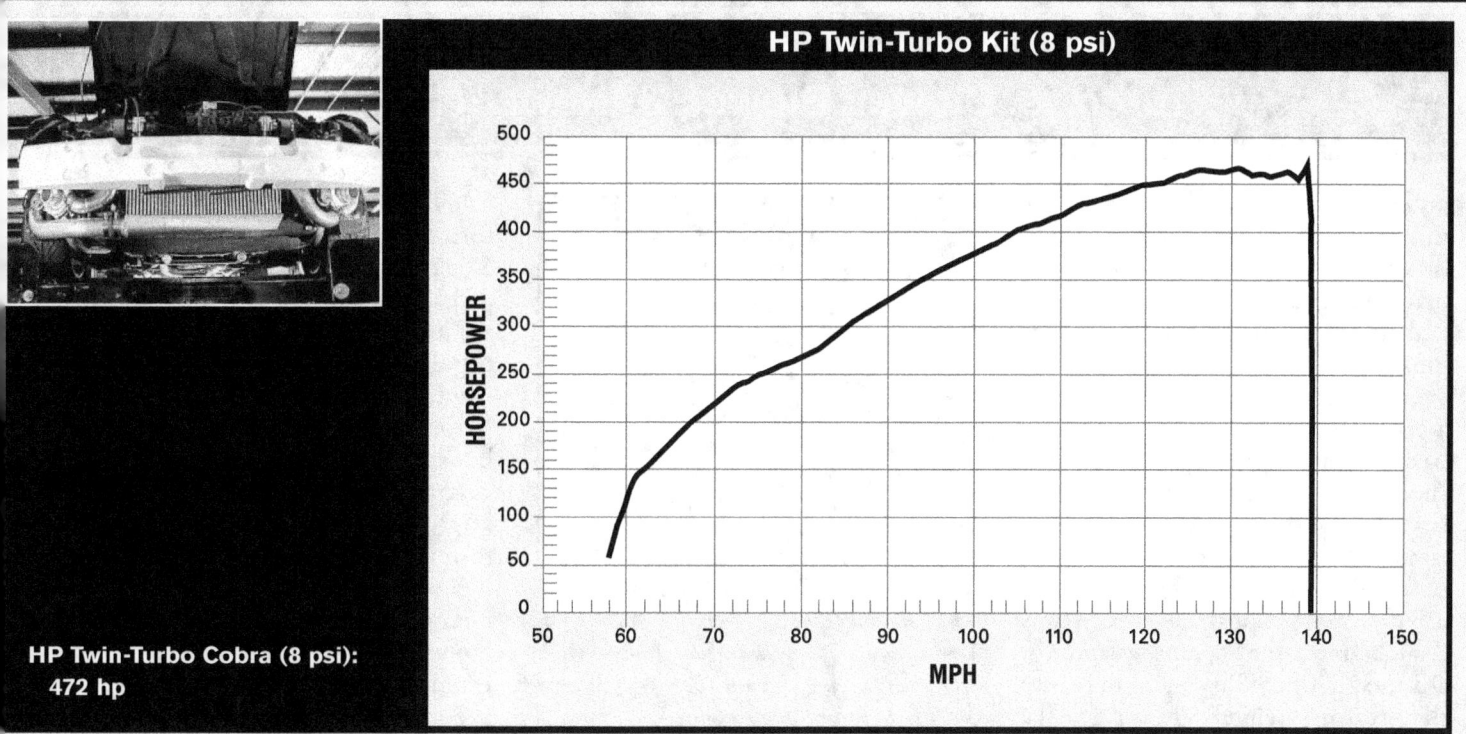

Early 4-Valve Cobra: HP Twin-Turbo Kit (8 psi)
A problem with the tach lead for the dyno prevented me from including the torque values for this twin-turbo early ('96-'98) 4-valve Cobra, but know that they were impressive. Running just 7 psi, the turbo Cobra produced 472 hp to the wheels, a solid 200 hp over the stock power output.

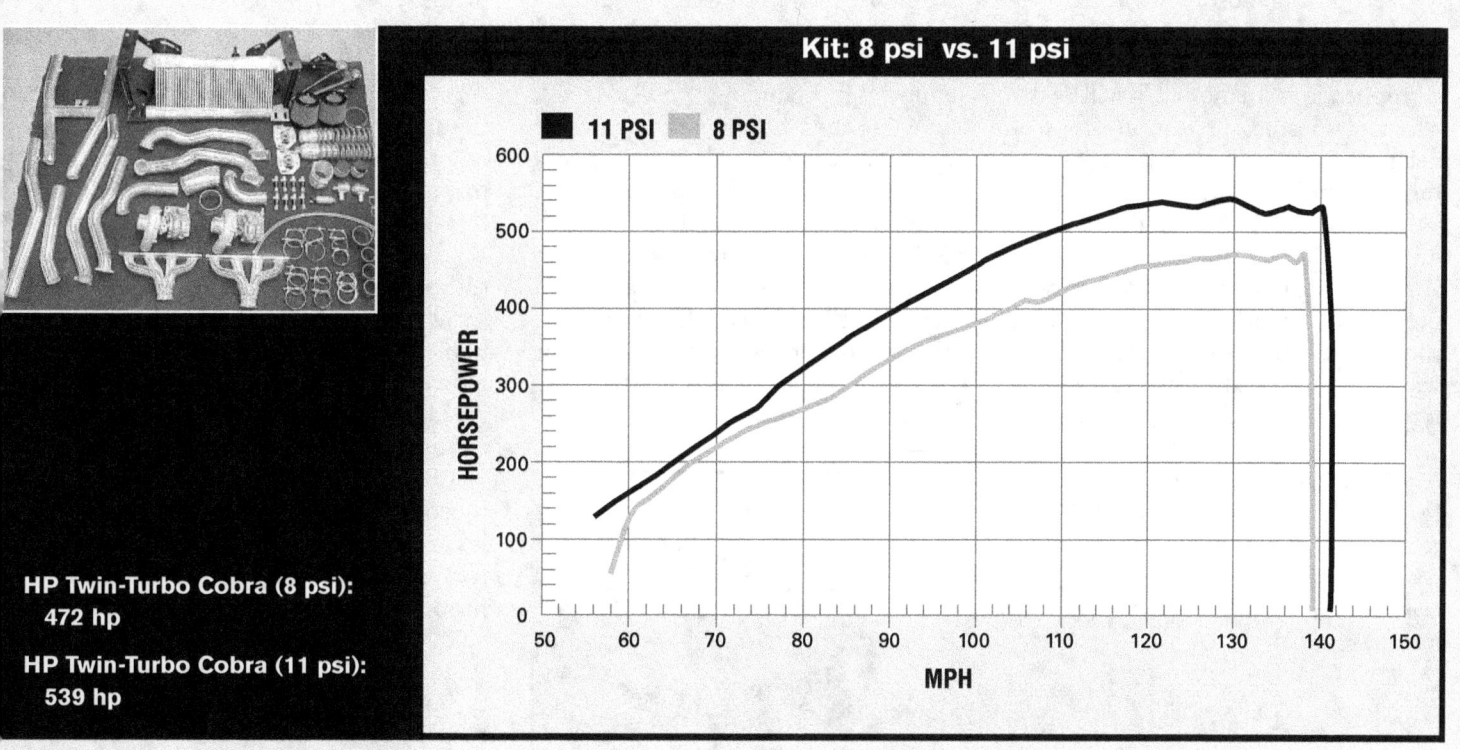

HP Twin-Turbo Early 4-Valve Cobra: 8 psi vs. 11 psi
Like any good boosted application, we decided to run the boost up on this twin-turbo Cobra. On the otherwise stock motor, the HP Performance twin-turbo kit increased the power output from 472 hp to 539 hp. An ignition upgrade later cured the minor misfiring that occurred at the top of the rev range on the 11-psi run.

Building 4.6/5.4L Ford Horsepower on the Dyno

Test 4: 4-Valve '03 Cobra: Turbo vs. Blower, Blower, & Blower (11 psi)

Some of the testing performed for this book was definitely more fun than others. Though this particular test involved a great deal of work, it was far and away the most rewarding (and informative). Imagine, installing nearly every popular form of forced induction available for the 4-valve 4.6L in a boost-bashing, charge-cooling, head-to-head shootout. Okay, so maybe a shootout isn't exactly the right description, but running all four of the different forms of forced induction on the same motor at the same boost level certainly demonstrated the advantages and disadvantages offered by each. In reality, the reason behind this particular adventure was exactly that, to illustrate inherent differences in the boost and power curves, not to crown an absolute winner. It would be nearly impossible to determine an absolute winner, as if one form of forced induction was vastly superior to all others on all levels, for all applications. In the end, it will be the user and specific application that will determine the appropriate form of forced induction that best applies, but before you can choose, you need to see how they all stack up.

The '03 Cobra crate motor was not only factory equipped with a roots-style Eaton supercharger, but it was also configured to easily accept the rigors of forced induction. The forged

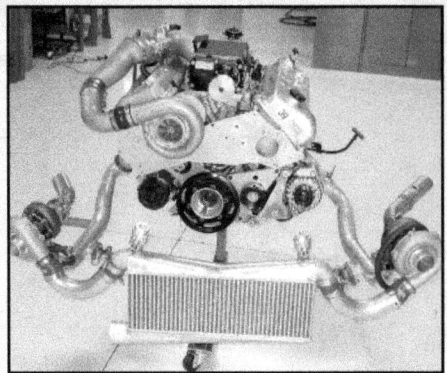

We didn't actually run it like this, but you can imagine what a twin turbocharged, centrifugally supercharged, Kenne Bell blown Mustang would be like. Where should we mount the Eaton?

crank, rods, and pistons provided an ultra-sturdy reciprocating assembly, while the low compression made such an exercise a safe and welcome proposition. The '03 Cobra crate motor had already proven itself plenty capable of supporting prodigious power levels, exceeding the 700-hp mark at elevated boost levels (with a blower upgrade) without ever so much as lifting a valve cover. Who knows exactly how much power these motors are capable of, but I managed to make 990 hp at 20 psi using an HP turbo kit. In addition to the reinforced reciprocating assembly, the '03 Cobra motor also sported free-flowing 4-valve heads.

The motor was run with all four forms of forced induction (Eaton M112, Kenne Bell 422, Vortech T-Trim, and 57-mm twin turbos from HP Performance). Check out the next three pages to see how each system performed. As expected, the roots-style Eaton blower provided immediate boost response and, despite the short-runner factory intake, produced impressive low-speed and midrange torque numbers before falling off at higher engine speeds. The torque output of the Eaton-supercharged 4-valve motor exceeded 500 ft-lbs from 3,100 rpm to 5,200 rpm. Spinning slower to keep the maximum boost pressure in check, the twin-screw lost out slightly at the lower engine speeds, but made up for the difference in blower speed with improved efficiency. Where the boost pressure fell off with the Eaton supercharger, the boost (and power) kept climbing with the Kenne Bell blower. As expected, the Vortech out-powered the other superchargers at the top of the rev range, but lost out in terms of torque production big time compared to the positive displacement blowers. Like the centrifugal supercharger, the turbos lost out at the lower engine speeds until the turbos came up on boost. Below 3,600 rpm, the roots blower was the clear winner, but once the tach needle swung past 3,600, it was all turbo. How do an extra 178 hp and 154 ft-lbs of torque sound? While the turbos were down by as much at 100 ft-lbs at 2,500 rpm, they quickly made up for lost time by eclipsing the Eaton and producing the most impressive (post-4,000 rpm) power curves of the bunch. At this power level, the smaller 46-mm turbos and an electronic wastegate controller (we had 57-mm turbos) would have helped improve the response rate (and low-speed torque production) of the HP turbo kit. Still, boost for boost, the HP turbo kit offered far and away the most power and torque.

For the twin-turbo kit and centrifugal supercharger, we ran our '03 Cobra motor with an intake manifold from a 2001 (naturally aspirated) Cobra.

Turbocharging

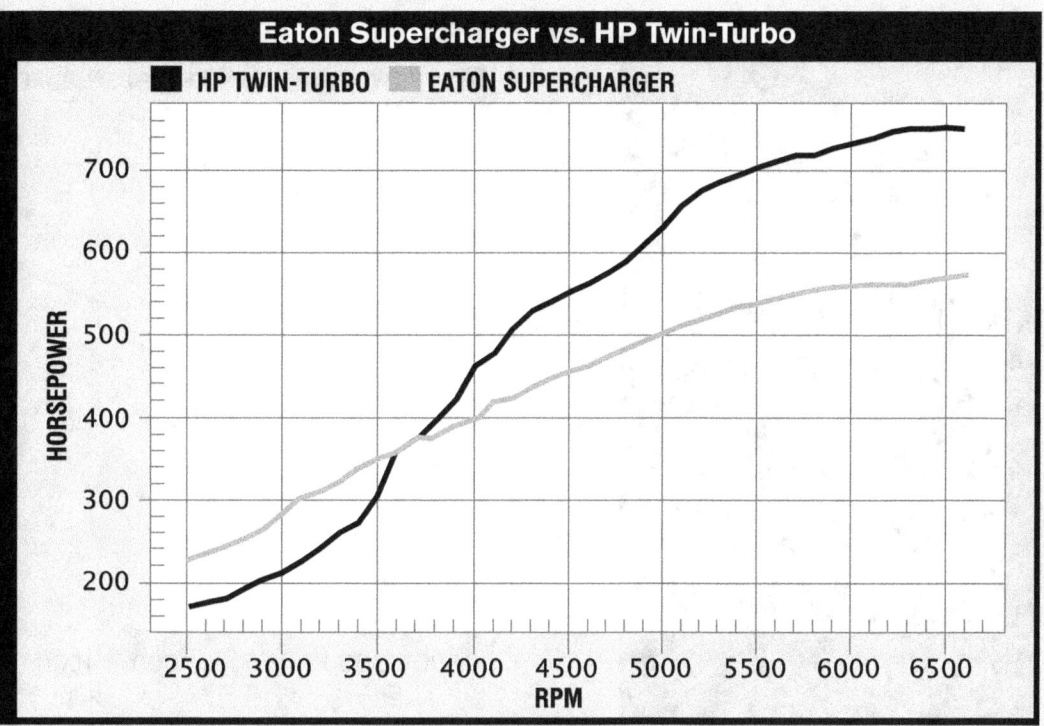

Eaton Supercharger (11 psi):
572 hp @ 6,600 rpm

HP Twin-Turbo (11 psi):
750 hp @ 6,500 rpm

Largest Gain:
183 hp @ 6,300 rpm

Turbos vs. Eaton Supercharger (11 psi) (Horsepower)
It should be obvious from the dramatic difference in the power output that turbos are much more efficient than the factory M112 roots blower. Running an identical peak boost pressure (11 psi), the roots blower produced 572 hp while the HP twin-turbo kit reached 750 hp. Think you might notice a difference of 183 hp?

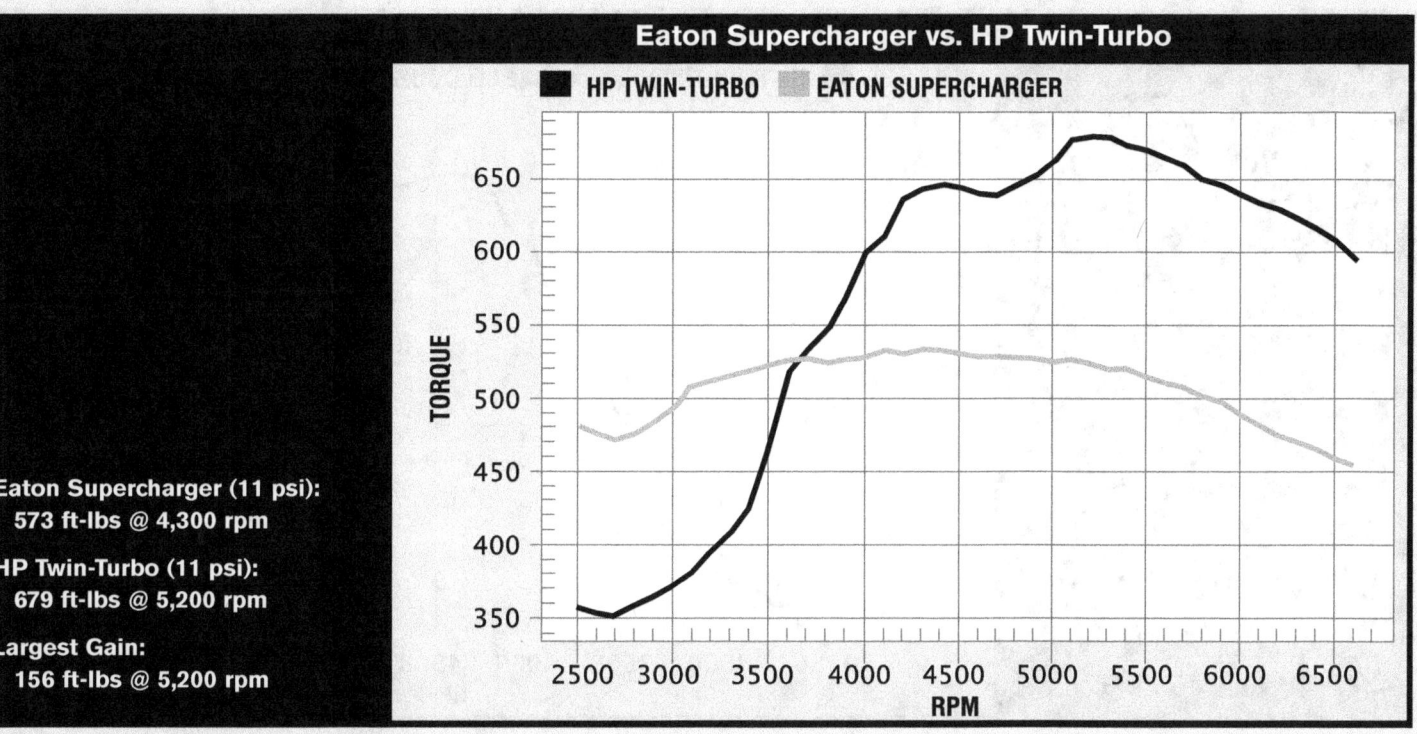

Eaton Supercharger (11 psi):
573 ft-lbs @ 4,300 rpm

HP Twin-Turbo (11 psi):
679 ft-lbs @ 5,200 rpm

Largest Gain:
156 ft-lbs @ 5,200 rpm

Turbos vs. Eaton Supercharger (11 psi) (Torque)
Thanks to the immediate boost response of the roots blower, the 4.6L produced more torque up to 3,600 rpm. This low-speed torque will certainly come in handy around town, but is actually of little value at the strip. With well over an extra 100 ft-lbs from 4,000 rpm to 6,500 rpm (where full-throttle acceleration takes place), the turbo motor would kill the blower motor in any kind of speed contest.

Chapter 8

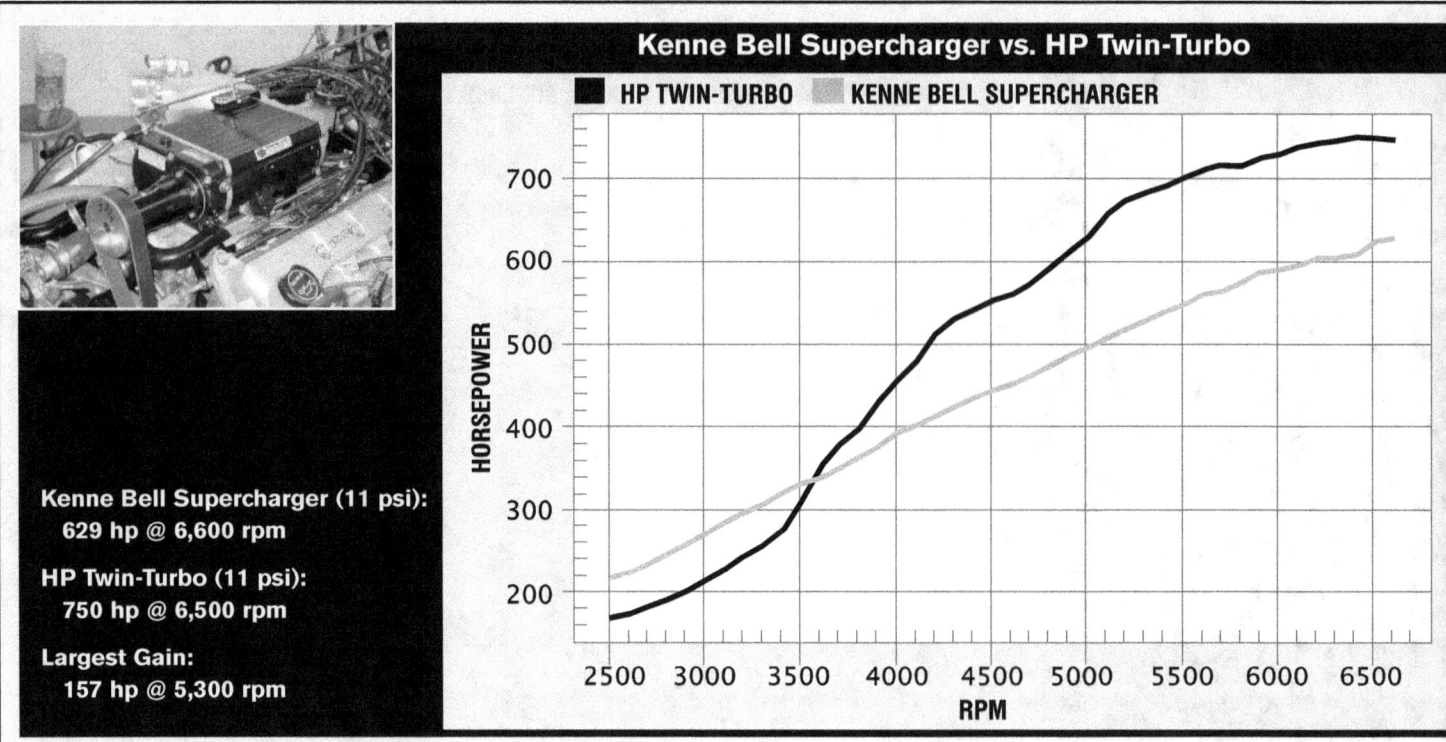

Kenne Bell Supercharger (11 psi):
629 hp @ 6,600 rpm

HP Twin-Turbo (11 psi):
750 hp @ 6,500 rpm

Largest Gain:
157 hp @ 5,300 rpm

Turbos vs. Kenne Bell Supercharger (11 psi) (Horsepower)
Compared to the Kenne Bell supercharger, the HP Performance twin-turbo system added 157 hp at the same 11-psi boost level. The major power difference comes from the fact that the superchargers all require power to drive. This drive loss is subtracted from the power gains offered by the additional boost pressure. The turbos suffer no such parasitic losses. Note that the power gains offered by the turbos were less than on the Eaton – the twin-screw blower is much more efficient (and powerful) than the Eaton M112 roots blower.

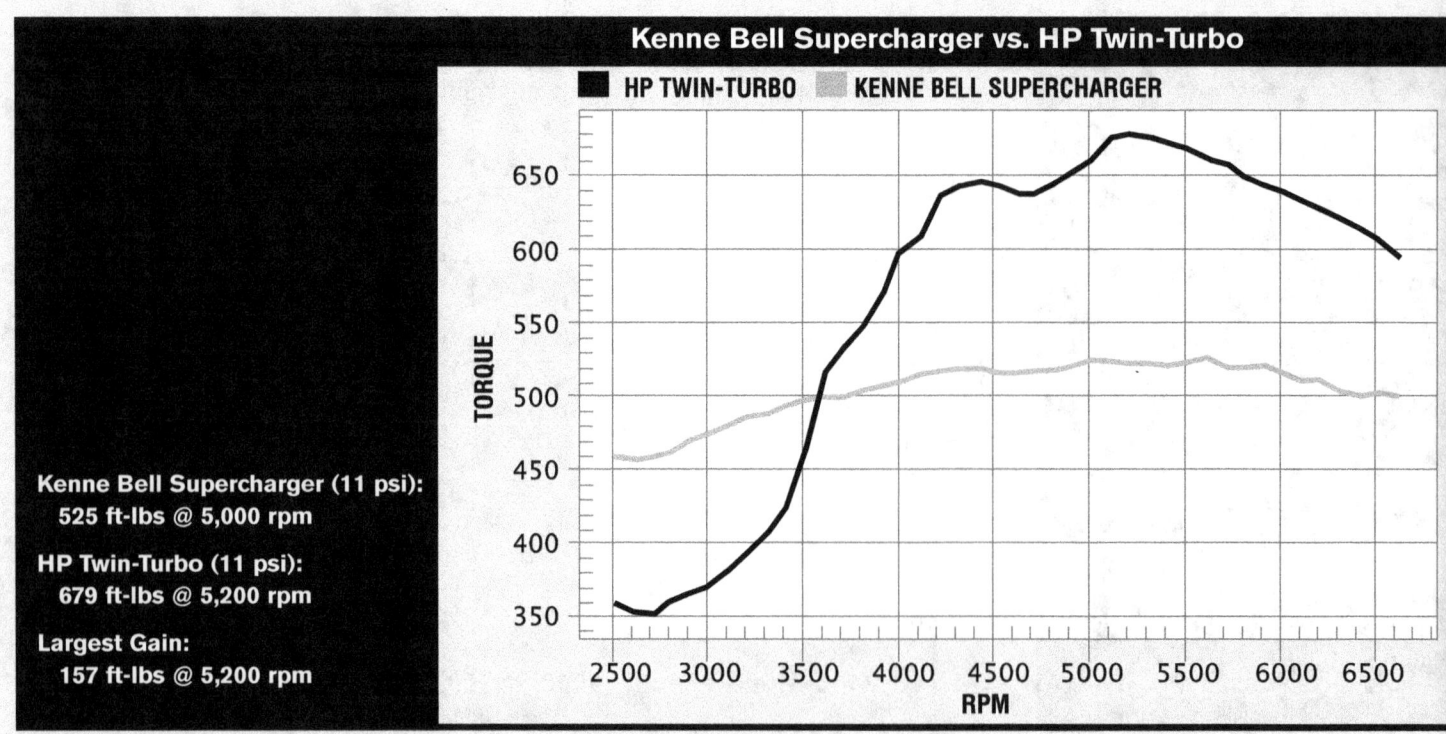

Kenne Bell Supercharger (11 psi):
525 ft-lbs @ 5,000 rpm

HP Twin-Turbo (11 psi):
679 ft-lbs @ 5,200 rpm

Largest Gain:
157 ft-lbs @ 5,200 rpm

Turbos vs. Kenne Bell Supercharger (11 psi) (Torque)
As expected, the positive-displacement (twin-screw) supercharger offered better low-speed power than the turbos. It wasn't until the turbos spooled up and the revs exceeded 3,500 rpm that the torque curves crossed. Just as with the roots blower (though slightly less with this more efficient twin screw), the turbos out-powered the blower by a significant margin. The largest difference was 157 ft-lbs at 5,200 rpm.

Turbocharging

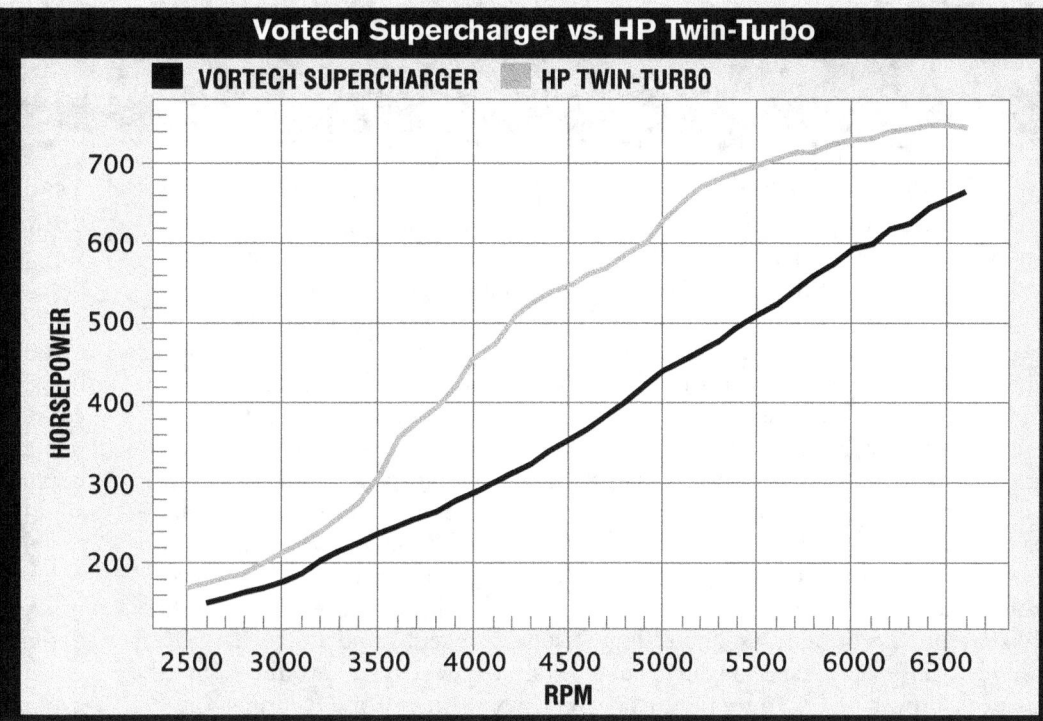

Vortech Supercharger (11 psi):
667 hp @ 6,600 rpm

HP Twin-Turbo (11 psi):
750 hp @ 6,500 rpm

Largest Gain:
204 hp @ 5,200 rpm

Turbos vs. Vortech Supercharger (11 psi) (Horsepower)
Unlike the positive-displacement blowers (both roots and twin screw), the Vortech centrifugal supercharger design did not offer immediate boost response. Actually, the blower did provide immediate response, it was just that in typical centrifugal fashion, the boost (and power) curve provided by the Vortech increased with engine speed. The power output was similar down low, but where the turbos produced 10 to 11 psi starting at 3,500 rpm, the Vortech didn't produce 11 psi until 6,500 rpm. The result was that the centrifugal produced 667 hp (significantly more than the roots blower), which wasn't quite on par with the 750 hp offered by the turbo kit.

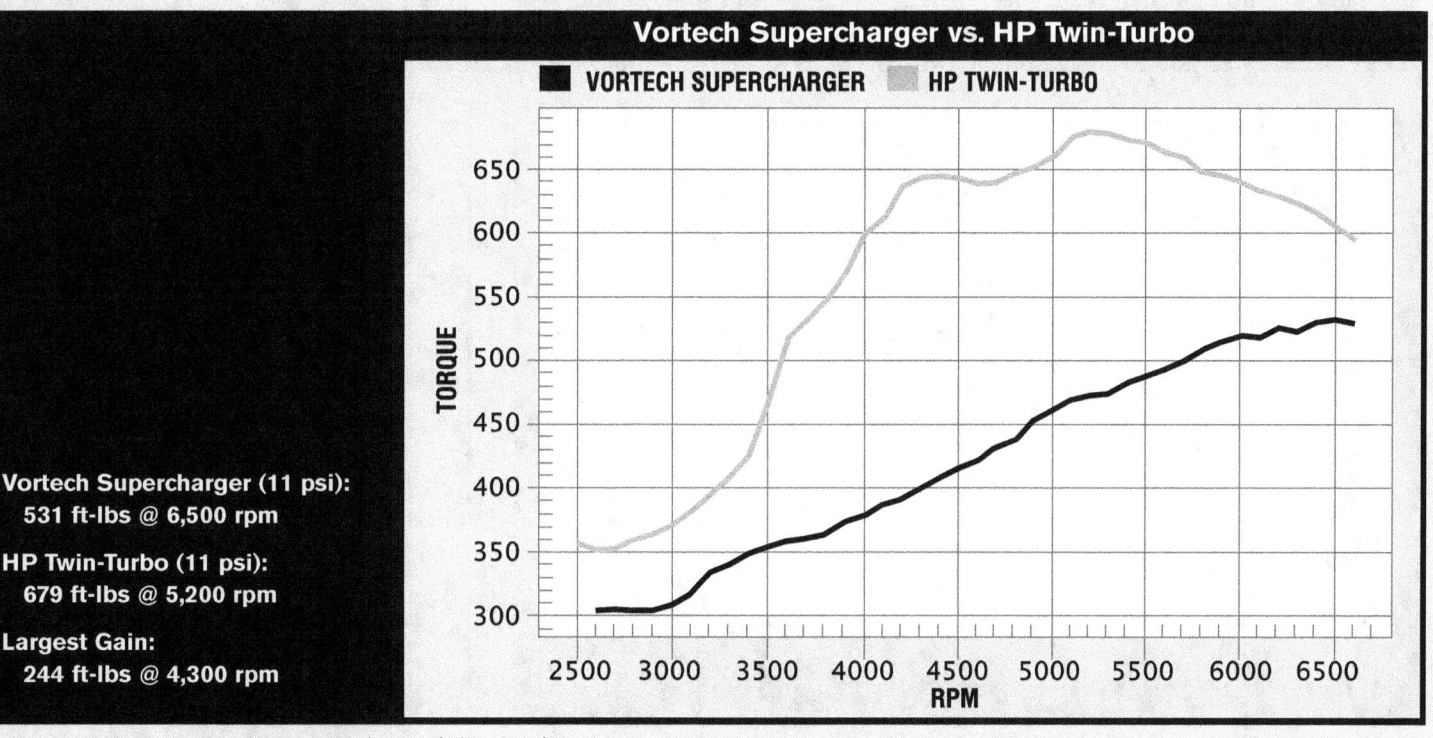

Vortech Supercharger (11 psi):
531 ft-lbs @ 6,500 rpm

HP Twin-Turbo (11 psi):
679 ft-lbs @ 5,200 rpm

Largest Gain:
244 ft-lbs @ 4,300 rpm

Turbos vs. Vortech Supercharger (11 psi) (Torque)
Given the disparity in boost production, it was not surprising that the turbos bested the centrifugal supercharger by as much as 244 ft-lbs. While the centrifugal is ultimately more efficient than the roots blower, the linear boost curve means you won't have tremendous torque production in the midrange.

Chapter 8

Test 5: 4-Valve '03 Cobra: Turbo vs. Blower, Blower, & Blower (14 psi)

If you're interested in the theory behind the various forms of forced induction, here it is in a nutshell. Basically, the positive-displacement superchargers offer immediate boost response, with the twin screw bettering the roots blower in terms of efficiency and power potential. The centrifugal supercharger offers even more power per pound of boost than the positive-displacement superchargers, but lacks the response rate of either the roots or twin screw. In life, there is always a tradeoff, and the turbos are no exception. Despite besting all the forms of supercharging in terms of peak power and torque, the turbo lagged behind the roots and twin-screw blowers at the lower engine speeds. As with the 11-psi comparison (Test 4), I was never trying to declare an absolute winner, but simply to illustrate the differences so the reader can make an informed decision. In most cases, the decision to choose one type of forced induction over another won't be based solely on the maximum (or peak) power potential. These variables might include cost, complexity, ease of installation, and reliability to name just a few. That's the great thing about having a choice; you can pick which one works best for you.

The motor was run with all four forms of forced induction (Eaton M112, Kenne Bell 422, Vortech T-Trim, and 57-mm twin turbos from HP Performance). The supplied graphs indicate how each of the three superchargers stand up to the power and torque curves produced by the HP twin-turbo kit. Running the '03 Cobra motor with the twin 57-mm turbos at a maximum boost of 13.6 psi, the 4.6L 4-valve motor produced 830 hp and 756 ft-lbs of torque.

Swapping over to the M112 supercharger was pretty simple considering the motor came originally equipped with the roots blower. Equipped with a 2.93-inch DUB blower pulley and an 8.5-inch DUB crank pulley, the Eaton supercharger pumped out a maximum boost pressure of 14.2 psi. The peak power checked in at 583 hp, while the torque stood at 574 ft-lbs. This jump in boost versus the 11 psi in Test 4 resulted in only a small gain in peak horsepower but sizable gains in low-speed torque. The Eaton roots blower was simply taxed out at this power level. Installing the Kenne Bell blower resulted in 704 hp and 598 ft-lbs of torque. Like the roots blower, the twin-screw design offered immediate boost and impressive torque production. Equipped with the Vortech T-Trim, the 4.6L produced 725 hp and 576 ft-lbs of torque. (Note: I suspect some belt slippage on the Vortech run, though the boost curve was pretty smooth.) All of the forms of forced induction produced impressive results, but once again the turbos came out on top with 830 hp and 756 ft-lbs of torque.

By raising the boost level to 14 psi, we're introducing another variable into the test. Some forms of supercharging are better at building high pressure than others.

We used this Turbo XS manual boost controller with our HP Performance twin-turbo kit. We jacked the boost up to 13.6 psi (and rounded up to 14).

Turbocharging

Eaton Supercharger (14 psi):
578 hp @ 6,500 rpm

HP Twin-Turbo (14 psi):
830 hp @ 6,500 rpm

Largest Gain:
253 hp @ 6,400 rpm

Turbos vs. Eaton Supercharger (14 psi) (Horsepower)
The power offered by the roots blower diminished rapidly as we increased the boost pressure. Running 14 psi, the roots supercharged 4.6L produced just 578 hp to the amazing 830 hp offered by the turbos. Obviously, the roots blower was nearing its limit in terms of flow while the turbos just seemed to be getting started.

Eaton Supercharger (14 psi):
574 ft-lbs @ 4,500 rpm

HP Twin-Turbo (14 psi):
756 ft-lbs @ 5,100 rpm

Largest Gain:
203 ft-lbs @ 5,300 rpm

Turbos vs. Eaton Supercharger (14 psi) (Torque)
As before, the roots blower out-powered the turbos to 3,900 rpm. Advocates of the roots blower will always point out the immediate boost response offered by the blower, but that won't change the results of a drag race between these two. The turbos offered 756 ft-lbs of torque to the blower's 574 ft-lbs. It's hard to argue with an extra 200 ft-lbs of torque!

Building 4.6/5.4L Ford Horsepower on the Dyno

Chapter 8

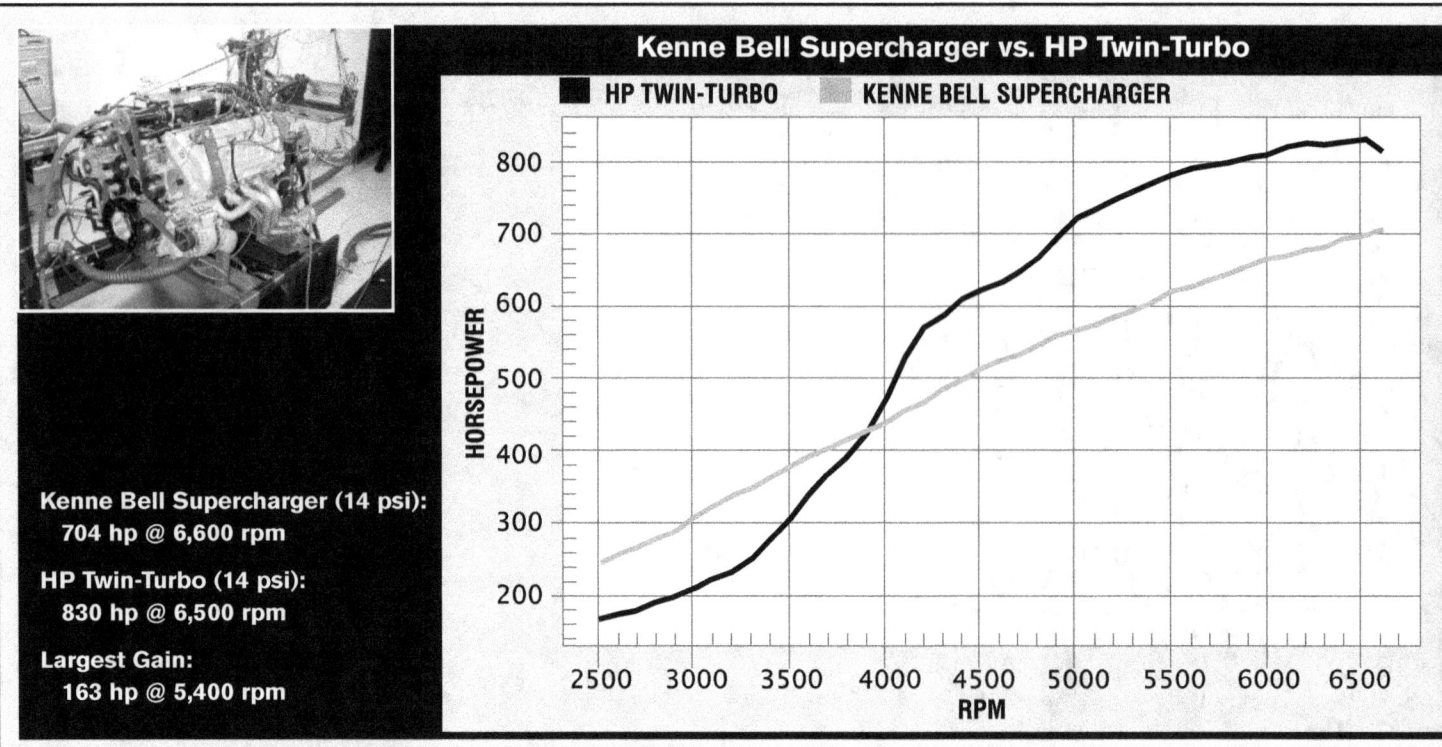

Kenne Bell Supercharger (14 psi): 704 hp @ 6,600 rpm

HP Twin-Turbo (14 psi): 830 hp @ 6,500 rpm

Largest Gain: 163 hp @ 5,400 rpm

Turbos vs. Kenne Bell Supercharger (14 psi) (Horsepower)
Though significantly better than the roots blower (704 hp versus 578 hp), the Kenne Bell twin-screw still lagged behind the turbos (830 hp) in terms of peak power. It's just impossible to get past the parasitic losses associated with driving the blower. The Kenne Bell blower upgrade for the Cobra is nonetheless very poplar due to the ease of installation and impressive power gains compared to the factory Eaton M112 blower.

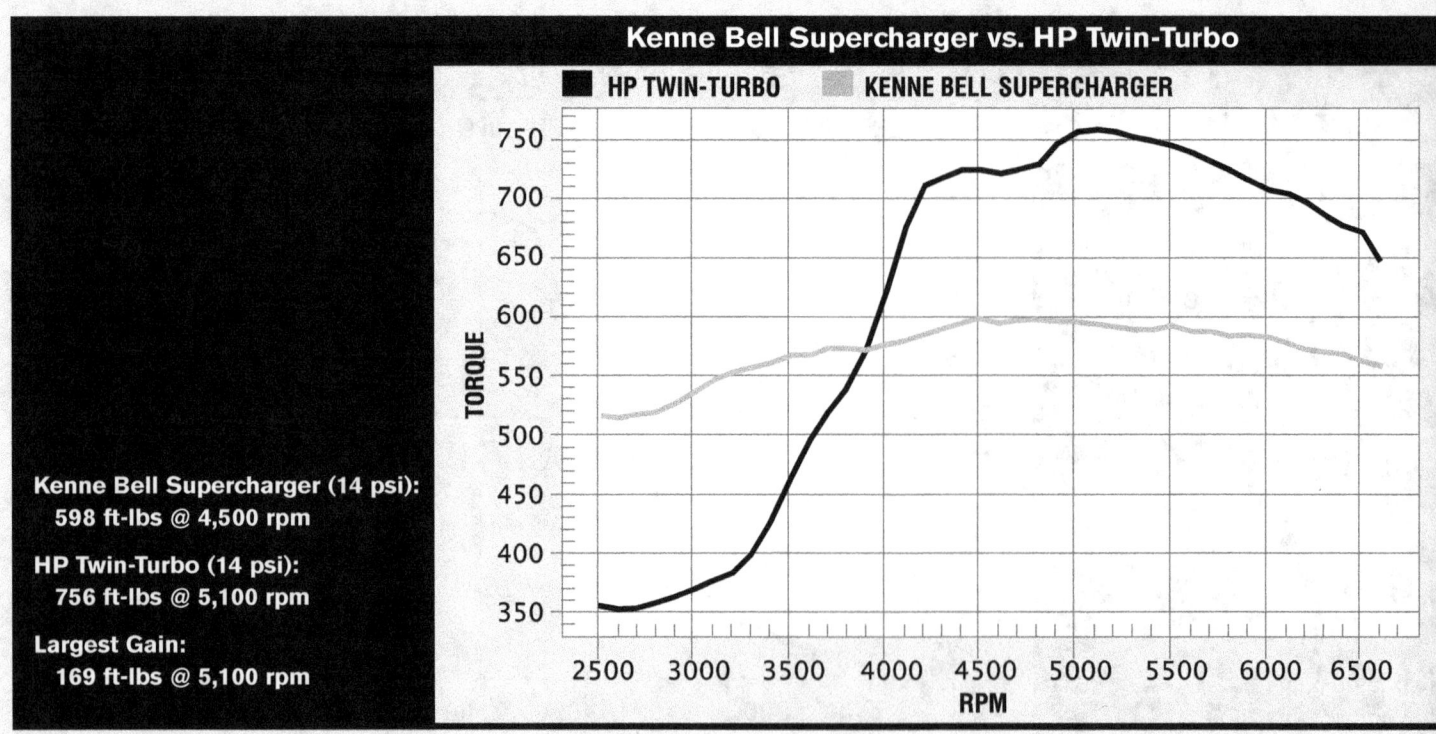

Kenne Bell Supercharger (14 psi): 598 ft-lbs @ 4,500 rpm

HP Twin-Turbo (14 psi): 756 ft-lbs @ 5,100 rpm

Largest Gain: 169 ft-lbs @ 5,100 rpm

Turbos vs. Kenne Bell Supercharger (14 psi) (Torque)
Like the roots blower, the Kenne Bell twin-screw offered significantly more low-speed torque than the twin turbos. Down at 2,500 rpm, the difference was over 150 ft-lbs, but by 4,000 rpm, the turbos were well on their way to offset the low-end advantage held by the blower. The turbos wound up at 756 ft-lbs, with 598 ft-lbs for the twin screw.

Turbocharging

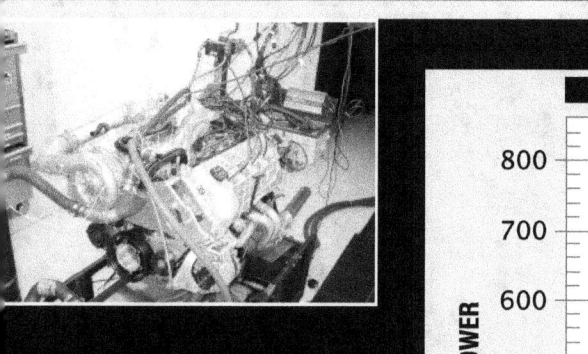

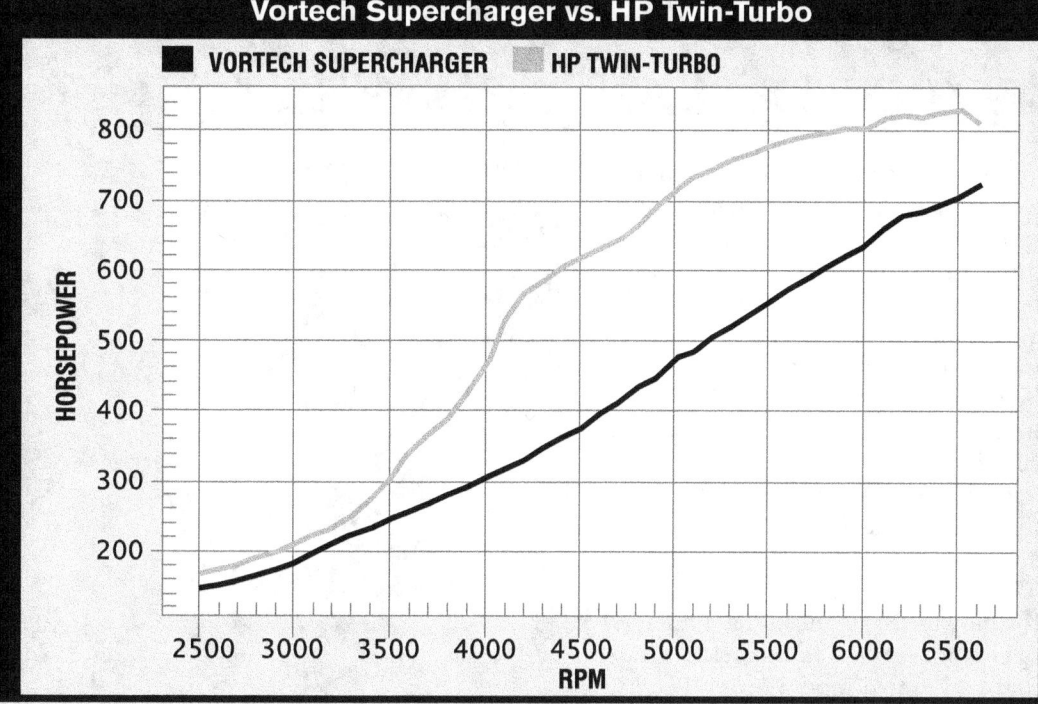

Vortech Supercharger (14 psi):
725 hp @ 6,600 rpm

HP Twin-Turbo (14 psi):
830 hp @ 6,500 rpm

Largest Gain:
247 hp @ 5,100 rpm

Turbos vs. Vortech Supercharger (14 psi) (Horsepower)
As at 11 psi, the centrifugal supercharger lagged behind the power output of the turbos. The Vortech produced the highest peak power of any of the blowers, but the 725 hp was no match for the 830 hp produced by the HP turbos.

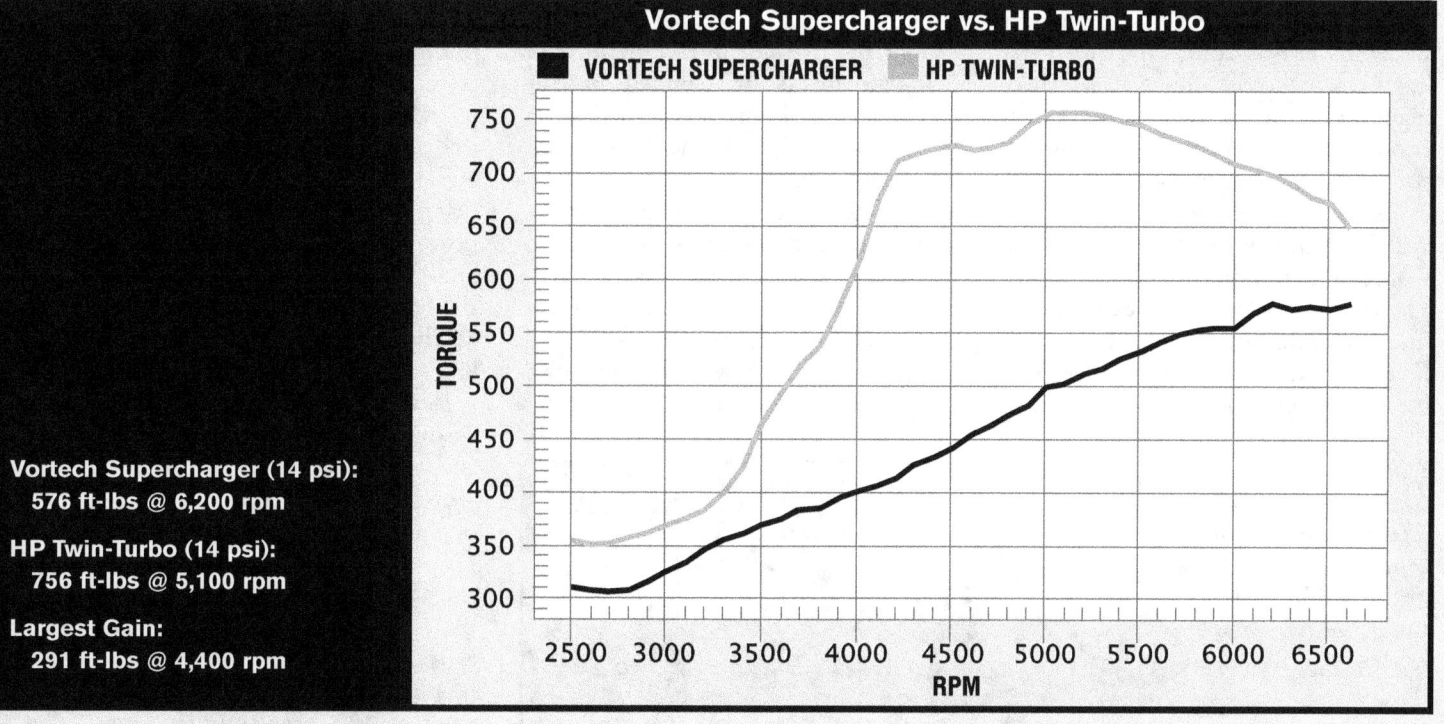

Vortech Supercharger (14 psi):
576 ft-lbs @ 6,200 rpm

HP Twin-Turbo (14 psi):
756 ft-lbs @ 5,100 rpm

Largest Gain:
291 ft-lbs @ 4,400 rpm

Turbos vs. Vortech Supercharger (14 psi) (Horsepower)
Obviously, when one form of forced induction is making over twice as much boost as another, there really isn't much of a comparison. Such was the case with the Vortech and HP turbos, as the turbos ramped up and were making 11 psi at 4,000 rpm, but the Vortech was pumping out just 4.5 psi. The difference was a predictable 291 ft-lbs of torque.

Building 4.6/5.4L Ford Horsepower on the Dyno

Test 6: 4-Valve '03 Cobra: NA vs. HP Twin-Turbo Kit (20.8 psi)

The supercharged 4-valve motor in the '03 and '04 Mustang Cobra sports a number of impressive features. In fact, it might well be the most powerful combination ever offered in a Mustang, or any Ford product for that matter, eclipsing the real-world power output of even the big-block motors of yesteryear. While the Eaton M112 roots supercharger usually garners all the attention, the reality is that the motor is much more than a 4-valve 4.6L with a blower stuffed up top. The '03-'04 Cobra motors were fortified for blower usage, including a number of components not found in lesser naturally aspirated mod motors. The list of blower-specific equipment includes a forged steel crank, a set of Manley forged connecting rods, and forged, low-compression pistons. According to our sources, the cam timing is somewhat milder than the NA motors, something we have come to expect with blower use. Toss in the free-flowing 4-valve heads and a trick intake manifold with an air-to-water intercooler and you have the makings of some serious performance potential.

Before installing the twin-turbo system from HP Performance, the '03 Cobra crate motor was upgraded with a set of Comp XE262AH cams and an intake manifold from a 2001 (naturally aspirated) 4-valve Cobra. The 2001 intake replaced the Eaton supercharger and air-to-water intercooler, as the HP twin-turbo kit included an efficient air-to-air intercooler. Run in naturally aspirated form, the 4.6L produced 426 hp and 390 ft-lbs of torque. We relied on a manual wastegate controller from Turbo XS to adjust the boost pressure to the twin-turbo system. Raising the boost pressure was a simple matter of twisting the small Allen screw in the Turbo XS unit. What could be easier? After

With the same HP Performance twin-turbo kit that has been building boost in the last few tests, we cranked up the boost to over 20 psi and made 990 hp. The air/fuel ratio and timing was regulated by the F.A.S.T. engine management system, and this thing burned only 114-octane race gas.

installation, we started with the boost pressure at the minimum setting of 5 psi. Using the F.A.S.T. system we kept the timing curve steady at 20 degrees and the air/fuel ratio at 11.7:1. With just 4.8 psi of boost pressure, the peak power jumped from 426 to 530 hp, and then to 670 hp at 7.8 psi. Upping the boost pressure to 11.0 psi brought 750 hp, while 13.6 psi pushed things to 830 hp. This thing just seemed to be getting happier and happier with each turn of the screw. With our air/fuel and timing still well in the safe level (combined with the safety of 114-octane fuel), we pushed on to 16.2 psi. Now things were getting serious, as the 4.6L produced 891 hp and 815 ft-lbs of torque. With our fingers crossed, we took the boost up in 1-psi increments until finally getting to a peak of 20.8 psi. Running a peak of 20.8 psi (down to 20.4 psi at the power peak), the twin-turbo 4.6L Cobra motor produced an amazing 990 hp and 912 ft-lbs of torque!

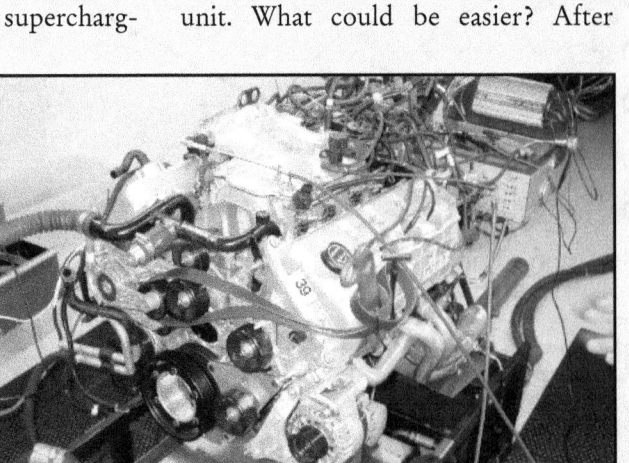

With a set of Comp XE262AH cams and an intake manifold from a 2001 (naturally aspirated) 4-valve Cobra, our '03 Cobra crate motor was ready for a turbo or two.

Turbocharging

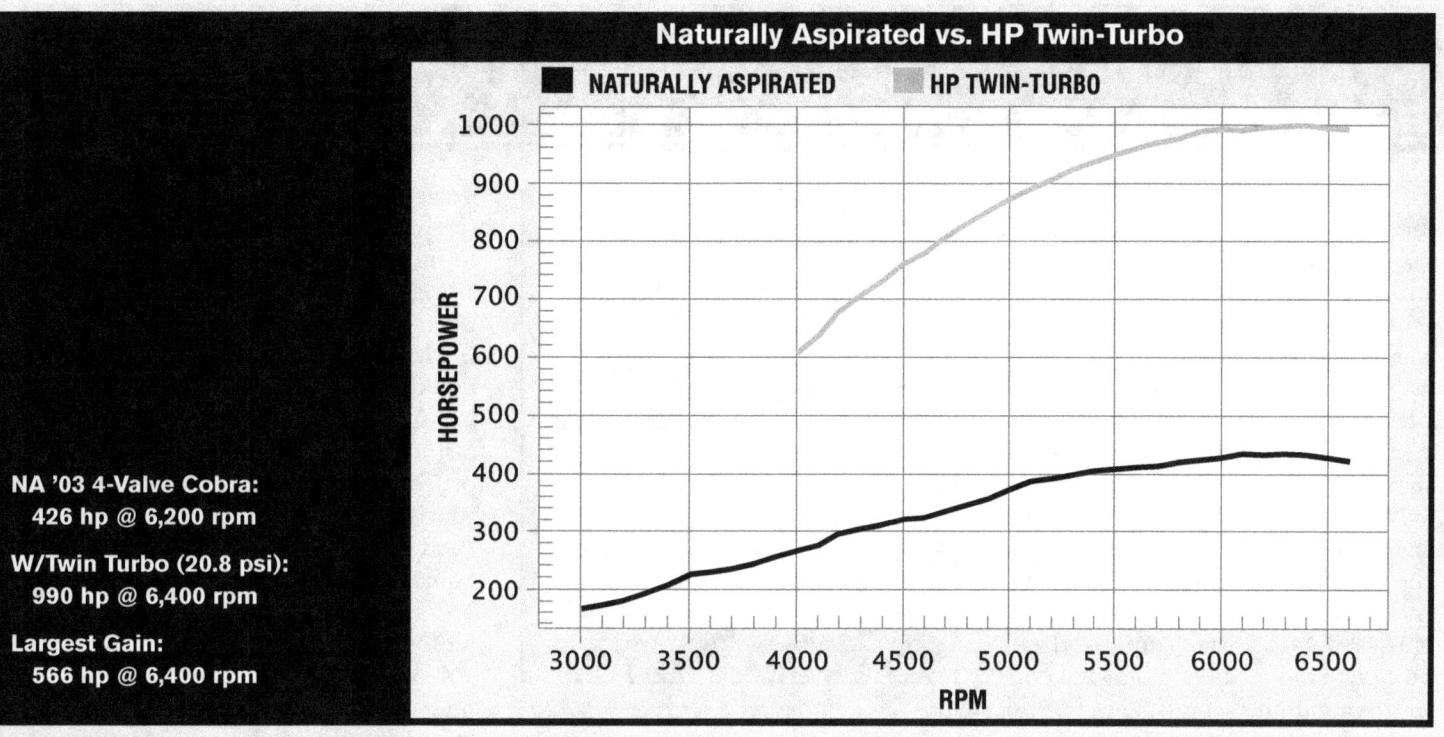

NA '03 4-Valve Cobra:
426 hp @ 6,200 rpm

W/Twin Turbo (20.8 psi):
990 hp @ 6,400 rpm

Largest Gain:
566 hp @ 6,400 rpm

4-Valve '03 Cobra: NA vs. HP Twin-Turbo Kit (20.8 psi)
Naturally aspirated, the '03 Cobra motor made 426 hp. At 20.8 psi it made 990 hp. The huge gains show the potential in both the '03 4-valve Cobra motor and the twin 57-mm turbo system from HP Performance.

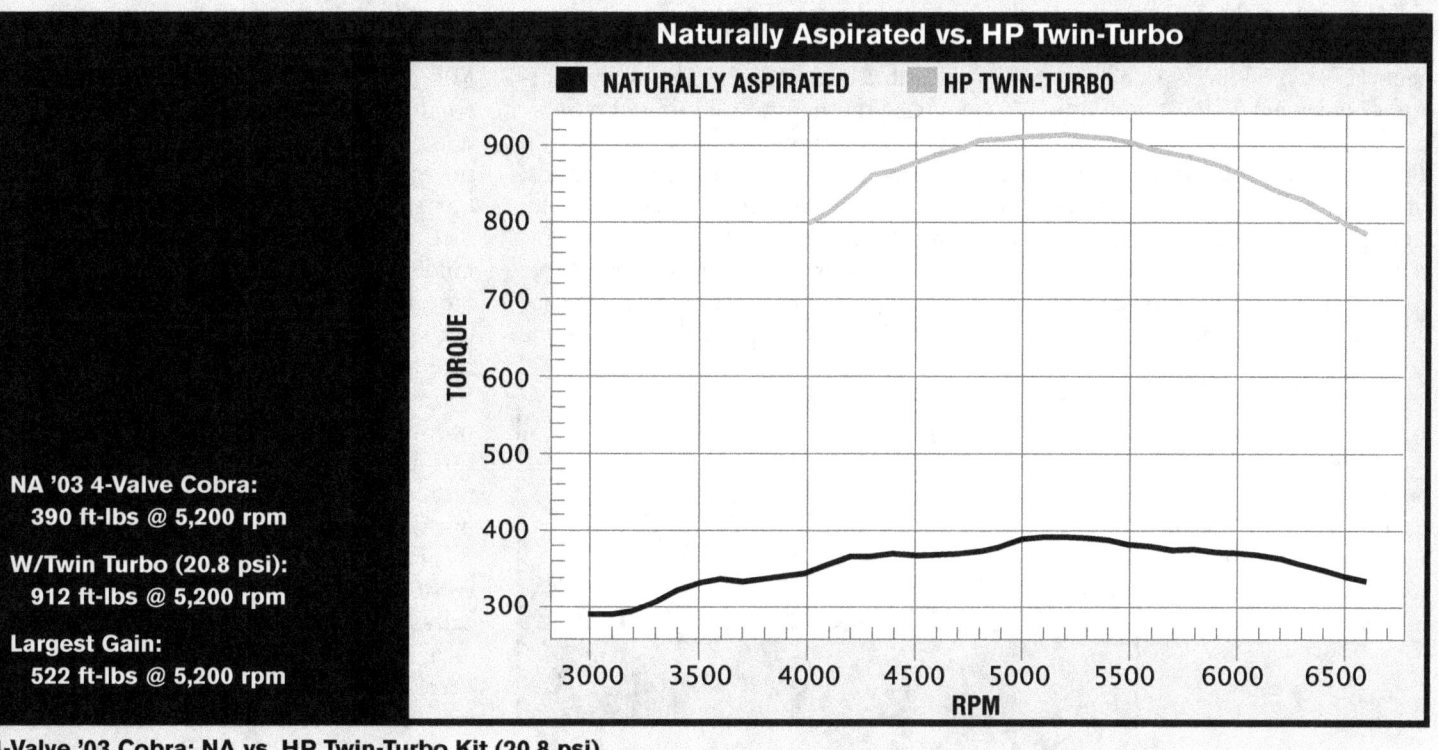

NA '03 4-Valve Cobra:
390 ft-lbs @ 5,200 rpm

W/Twin Turbo (20.8 psi):
912 ft-lbs @ 5,200 rpm

Largest Gain:
522 ft-lbs @ 5,200 rpm

4-Valve '03 Cobra: NA vs. HP Twin-Turbo Kit (20.8 psi)
I guess it's arguable whether a street car can really use over 900 ft-lbs of torque, but there is no denying the power potential of the '03 Cobra crate motor from Ford Racing. Imagine what your Cobra might feel like with 912 ft-lbs of peak torque and over 800 ft-lbs from 4,000 rpm to 6,500 rpm.

Test 7: Mihovitz 4.6L Twin-Turbo Race Motor: 25 psi vs. 29 psi

Let's take a look at some rudimentary turbo math. Suppose you have a 300-hp Cobra motor and are looking to make 600 hp, how should you go about it? When you're talking about turbos, the answer is pretty simple. A naturally aspirated motor relies on atmospheric pressure of 14.7 psi to force air into the vacuum created by the downward moving piston (through the open intake valve). If the motor produces 300 hp at the atmospheric pressure of 14.7 psi, theoretically all we have to do to double the power output is to double the pressure (add 14.7 psi with turbos). If we take our 300-hp Cobra motor and double the atmospheric pressure of 14.7 psi, we should be rewarded with a 600-hp motor. Doubling the atmospheric pressure means we will have to supply 14.7 psi from our turbo or turbos. The math works at any boost level, as adding 10 psi of boost to the 300-hp motor will increase the power output by 68 percent (10/14.7), adding 7 psi of boost will add 47.6 percent (7/14.7), and adding 20 psi will increase the power output by 142.8 percent. This assumes a number of things, such as proper air/fuel and timing curves, the motor will withstand the additional boost pressure, and the turbos are capable of producing the additional airflow and boost pressure.

This big air-to-water intercooler is a little different than the one that comes with the HP Performance kit.

From the formula, we can deduce that boost pressure has a positive effect on power. Not quite so evident is the fact that significant gains are possible by improving the power output of the naturally aspirated combination. Suppose we take our 300-hp motor and add cams, ported heads, and an aftermarket intake manifold, thereby increasing the naturally aspirated power output to 400 hp. If we then apply the boost formula, we see that the same 7 psi will increase the power output from 400 hp to 590 hp (up from just 442 hp with 7 psi applied to the 300-hp combination). Basically, any gains achieved in naturally aspirated form are multiplied by the boost level. Thus, improving the power output of the naturally aspirated motor by 100 hp (from 300 hp to 400 hp) will result in a gain of 148 hp at 7 psi, a gain of 168 hp at 10 psi, and 200 hp at 14.7 psi. If we up the boost pressure to 2 BAR (29.4 psi), our 100-hp naturally aspirated gain will be increased to 300 hp. That means our original 300 hp motor would produce 900 hp, but the 400-hp version would produce 1,200 hp. You can see the importance of improving the power of the naturally aspirated motor when you go looking to make big power.

This was one of the very few times I was not responsible for building and testing the motor and/or components. As luck would have it, John Mihovitz was testing a few different combinations just shortly before this book was due. One such test involved the effect of boost on an ultra-high-horsepower combination. As we have seen in the previous tests run on the milder combinations, 4-valve mod motors readily respond to increased boost pressure. In the case of this 4.6L race motor, the gains were significant. Running 24 psi, the twin-turbo 4.6L produced 1,492 hp and 1,038 ft-lbs of torque. These would be impressive numbers from a 500-inch big-block, but when you consider that this motor displaced only 281 cubic inches, it's truly staggering! For the mathematically inclined, that represents an amazing 5.31 hp per cubic inch. Not surprisingly, this 4.6L motor was far from stock, but when you start talking about nearly 1,500 hp, you need to examine every detail and modify it accordingly. With the boost pressure set at 29 psi, the numbers jumped to 1,577 hp, or 5.61 hp per cubic inch.

If your Mustang didn't have inner fenders (or outer fenders for that matter), a hood, or a firewall, it might fit. Actually, the system is run on John Mihovitz's racecar.

Turbocharging

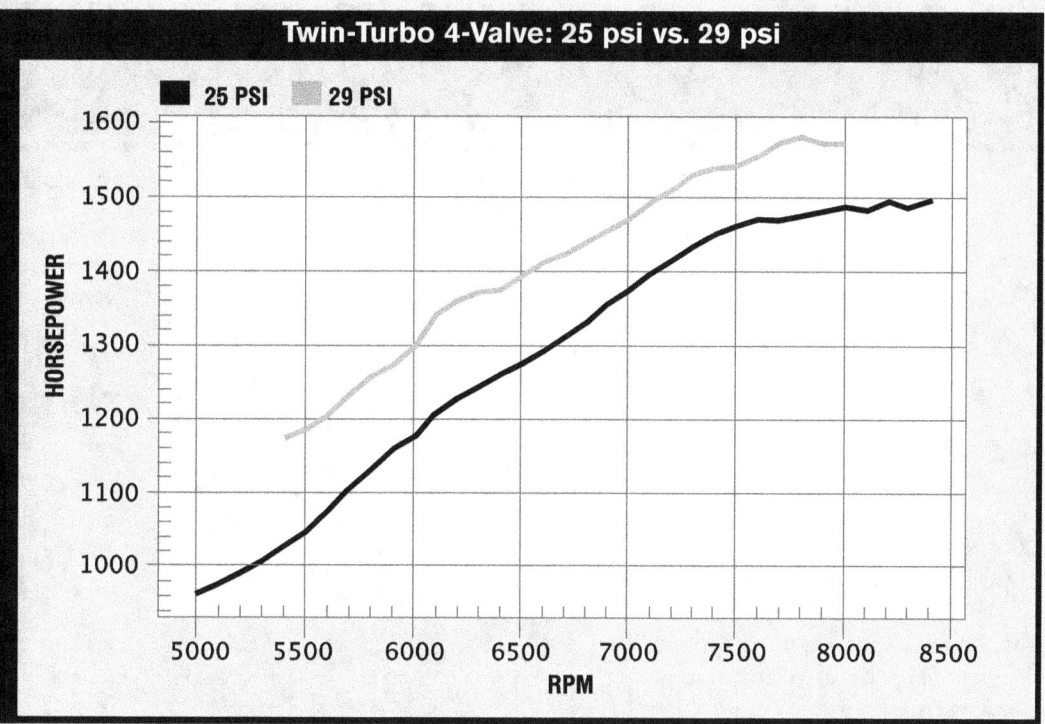

Twin-Turbo 4-Valve (25 psi):
1,492 hp @ 8,400 rpm

Twin-Turbo 4-Valve (29 psi):
1,577 hp @ 7,800 rpm

Largest Gain:
135 hp @ 6,200 rpm

Mihovitz 4.6L Twin-Turbo Race Motor: 25 psi vs. 29 psi (Horsepower)
Hard as it might be to believe, those numbers listed on the side of the horsepower graph are accurate. The power curve really goes to 1,600 hp. In fact, I saw this motor exceed 1,700 hp but was sworn to secrecy about a number of the components that went into making the motor so powerful. As is usually the case, upping the boost pressure supplied by a pair of custom Turbonetics 76-mm turbos from 25 psi to 29 psi resulted in a dramatic gain in power. The peak power jumped from 1,492 hp to 1,577 hp – from a mod motor displacing just 281 cubic inches.

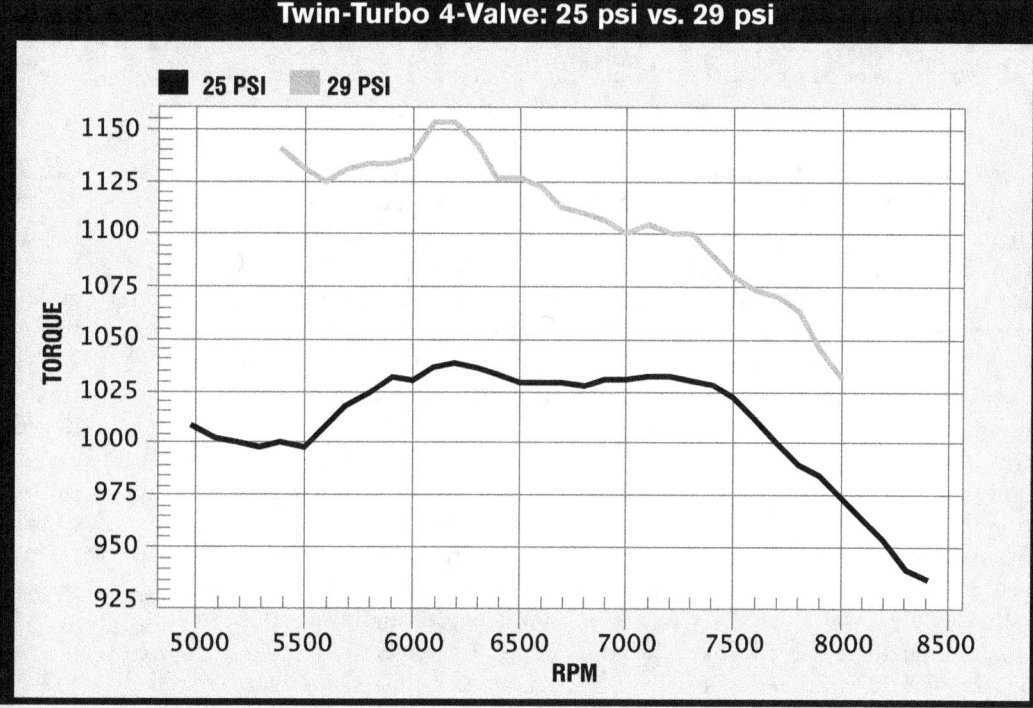

Twin-Turbo 4-Valve (25 psi):
1,038 ft-lbs @ 6,200 rpm

Twin-Turbo 4-Valve (29 psi):
1,153 ft-lbs @ 6,200 rpm

Largest Gain:
133 ft-lbs @ 5,500 rpm

Mihovitz 4.6L Twin-Turbo Race Motor: 25 psi vs. 29 psi (Torque)
As always, the torque gains were greater at lower engine speeds. The additional 4 psi of boost resulted in a gain of 133 ft-lbs of torque. Obviously, these Turbonetics 76-mm turbos had plenty of power left to offer.

Building 4.6/5.4L Ford Horsepower on the Dyno

Test 8: 3-Valve '05 GT: HP Twin-Turbo Kit

The new 2005 Mustang GT has it all over the earlier GTs. The exterior package, with the retro fastback styling, looks like a modern interpretation of an early muscle car ancestor. The previous GT now looks somehow dated, after all the basic bodywork had been around since the introduction of the SN95 chassis in 1994. While good looks will definitely help you get ahead in the world, the new 300-hp 3-valve 4.6L only adds to its appeal. Where the PI Mustang GT made due with 260 hp, the new 3-valve motor sports a more Cobra-like 300 hp. Sales have demonstrated that the Mustang continues to be the pony car choice (the GM competition has disappeared for now), but it's nice to know that Ford has listened to GT enthusiasts begging for more power.

While the new GT promised and delivered additional power, the 300-hp motor is still no match for the 345-hp LS1s or 400-hp LS2s out roaming the streets. Lucky for new GT owners, HP Performance has a twin-turbo kit for the 3-valve 4.6L. To demonstrate the worth of the HP kit, we took a stock 3-valve test motor and ran it both in normally aspirated form and then with the new HP twin-turbo system. The engine was configured for engine dyno use with a Meziere electric water pump (no accessories), a set of JBA long-tube headers, and the F.A.S.T. management system controlling the 36-pound injectors. The 4.6L was run through the stock throttle body after we converted the electronic drive-by-wire throttle body to a manual version. Tuned to produce an air/fuel mixture of 13.0:1 (slightly richer down low) and 28 degrees of total timing, the 3-valve 4.6L produced 351 hp at 5,300 rpm and 374 ft-lbs of torque at 4,400 rpm. As we've come to expect of the 3-valve motor, the torque curve exceeded 350 ft-lbs from 3,500 rpm to 5,250 rpm. Though the power

The 3-valve 4.6L Mustang GT engine looks even more impressive with a pair of turbos and an air-to-air intercooler. The 3-valve motor puts out some impressive 4-valve-like numbers under boost.

peak was reached at just 5,300 rpm, the power curve didn't fall off dramatically thereafter, hovering very near 350 hp all the way to 6,000 rpm. It should be mentioned that we did not have control over the variable cam timing, something that would surely have helped the overall power curve.

After establishing our baseline, we installed the HP twin-turbo kit. To properly cope with the power output of the new turbocharged 4.6L 3-valve combination, we replaced the 36-pound injectors with a set of larger 65-pounders (though the HP kit includes 42-pound injectors and a reprogrammed ECU). Once again we relied on the F.A.S.T. management system to control the timing and fuel and took our time tuning the combination. The initial 6-psi runs were made on pump

gas, but we eventually replaced the pump gas with race fuel before cranking up the boost. The last thing I wanted to do was ruin a perfectly good 3-valve motor. With the twin-turbo kit, we ran the motor at an 11.7:1 air/fuel ratio and 20 degrees of total timing. The combination produced an impressive 500 hp and 529 ft-lbs of torque at a maximum boost pressure of 6.2 psi. As we have come to expect, the power curve offered by the turbo motor was a duplicate of the normally aspirated curve, just elevated. Upping the boost pressure to 9.1 psi resulted in a jump to 578 hp and 617 ft-lbs of torque, while our final runs at 11 psi produced 624 hp and 666 ft-lbs of torque. It's obvious that the new 3-valve 4.6L motor will carry the modular banner with honors.

Turbocharging

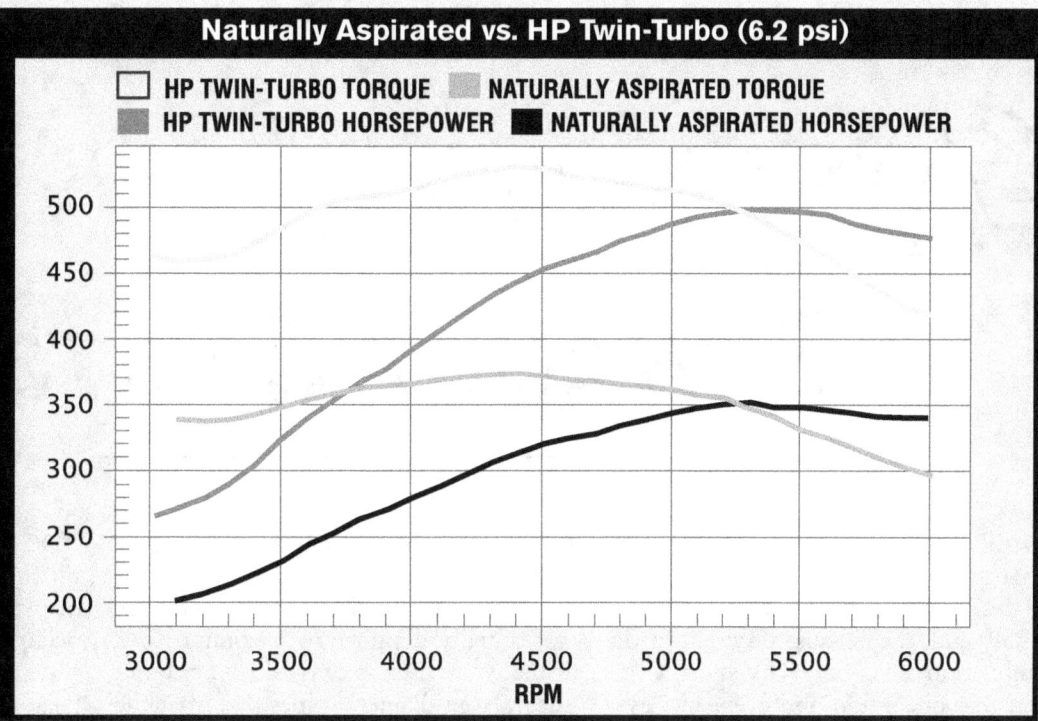

3-Valve GT:
351 hp @ 5,300 rpm

HP Twin-Turbo (6.2 psi):
500 hp @ 5,300 rpm

Largest Gain:
150 hp @ 5,300 rpm

3-Valve '05 GT: NA vs. HP Twin-Turbo Kit (6.2 psi)

The 3-valve 4.6L motor was run on the engine dyno with a set of JBA headers, no accessories, and a F.A.S.T. management system. The otherwise stock motor produced 351 hp and 374 ft-lbs of torque. In stock trim, the horsepower curve peaked at 5,300 rpm but remained close to 350 hp all the way out to 6,000 rpm. Adding the HP twin-turbo kit essentially elevated the curves (both power and torque), upping the peak power numbers to 500 hp and 529 ft-lbs at just 6.2 psi.

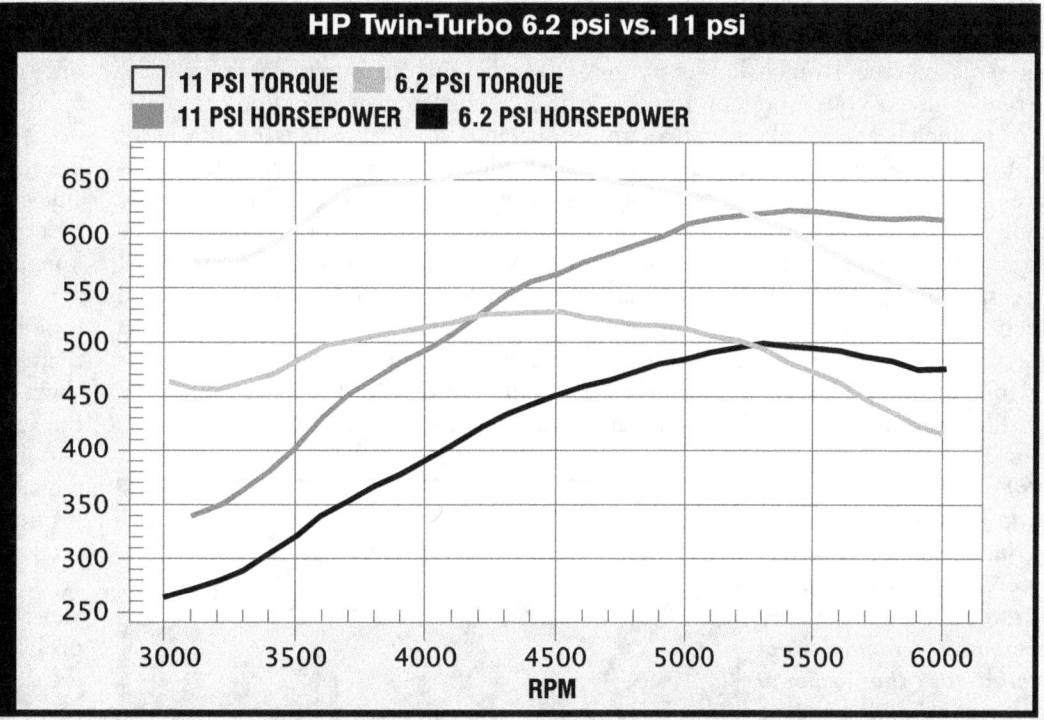

HP Twin-Turbo (6.2 psi):
500 hp @ 5,300 rpm

HP Twin-Turbo (11 psi):
624 hp @ 5,400 rpm

Largest Gain:
131 hp @ 5,800 rpm

HP Twin-Turbo 3-Valve '05 GT: 6.2 psi vs. 11 psi

The great thing about turbo (or blower) motors is the ease at which additional power comes. Increasing the power output was as simple as increasing the boost pressure from the pair of 57-mm turbos. Having already produced 990 hp with these turbos on the 4.6L 4-valve Cobra motor, we knew there was plenty of flow left for this stock 3-valve combination. Upping the boost pressure to 9 psi resulted in a jump to 578 hp, while a step up to 11 psi allowed us to top the 600-hp mark, with a peak power reading of 624 hp. The peak torque was devilishly impressive at 666 ft-lbs.

CHAPTER 9

EXHAUST SYSTEMS

Like the intake manifold, the exhaust manifolds (or tubular headers) are designed to not only allow, but also actually aid, the exhaust flow out of the combustion chamber. The most common misconception about exhaust systems is that bigger is somehow better (a common theme for everything from throttle bodies to cylinder heads). Using this logic, we see that a set of 1¾-inch (primary tube diameter) headers will outflow a set of 1⅝-inch headers. Though this is certainly the case, does this mean that replacing the 1⅝-inch headers you currently run on your mod motor with a set of 1¾-inch headers will result in a gain in power? The answer to this question (like most of the dynamic equations involved with an internal combustion engine) is: it depends. You see the power potential of a given set of headers has much more to do with their overall design (primary length, tubing diameter, and merge points) than the sheer size. Just like an intake manifold, the runner (port) length plays a much more important role than the absolute airflow.

Exhaust manifolds (or headers) are not actually designed to maximize flow. If that were the case, you'd simply build short, large-diameter pipes that offer the least amount of flow resistance. The zoomies used on Top Fuel motors are a good example of maximizing flow without concern for the effect of scavenging. Proper header design will actually evacuate the residual exhaust and even help draw in the fresh induction charge, in effect helping to supercharge cylinder filling. This improved cylinder evacuation (and filling) happens by means of both kinetic energy and reflected pressure wave scavenging. Kinetic energy scavenging occurs by means of the release of pressure from the cylinder just as the exhaust valve opens. The elevated cylinder pressure (from the expansion created by the power stroke) finds the opening created by the recently opened exhaust valve (as the piston approaches BDC). The compression wave created by this flow of the spent gases rapidly displaces the existing column of gas occupying the port. This compression wave increases pressure on the front (leading) side and reduces pressure on the back (trailing) side. Since the compression wave travels through the port (primary tubing in a header) faster than the gas discharge speed (out of the cylinder from the upward moving piston), the low pressure on the trailing side of the compression wave actually helps draw out the remaining spent gases from the cylinder (in essence helping the piston do its job). In addition to improved exhaust evacuation, the low-pressure side of the compression wave also aids in intake flow since the intake valve has opened before the piston reached TDC.

You may be wondering why long-tube headers are so much more effective than the traditional cast-iron (or even short tubular) exhaust manifolds. While the actual flow rates may be comparable between the two types of exhaust systems, long-tube headers improve power production in the same way long runner intakes improve the volumetric efficiency on the intake side. Reflected pressure wave scavenging occurs when the compression wave (that occurred when the exhaust valve opened to release the elevated cylinder pressure) arrives at the end of the primary tube (usually in the collector). Due to the increase in tubing diameter, the compression wave is allowed to expand and spread in all directions. The depression created by

Oddly enough, headers made less of a difference on the higher-horsepower supercharged motors than on the naturally aspirated versions. The tuning effect offered by the exhaust pulse scavenging was less pronounced on the blower motor.

Exhaust Systems

this expansion causes air to rush in from the surrounding area, forcing the negative pressure wave back down the pipe to the awaiting exhaust port. This negative pressure wave helps further scavenge exhaust flow and aid induction flow into the cylinder during overlap. Naturally, the length of the primary pipe has an effect on when (in RPM) this scavenging becomes most effective, as the event should be timed so that the primary reflected wave will arrive at the exhaust port when the piston has just past TDC. Since the reflected pressure waves travel at the speed of sound, the length of the primary pipes determine when the low-pressure wave will coincide with the proper piston position, thus headers are tuned for particular engine speeds.

One of the common misconceptions about headers is that high-horsepower blower motors will require large-diameter headers. If 1⅝-inch headers (of a given primary length) work well on your naturally aspirated 4.6L 2-valve or 4-valve, then shouldn't your supercharged motor work best with larger (free-flowing) headers? The logic seems right, but the reality is actually otherwise, as testing has shown that even on 600+ hp supercharged 4.6L 4-valve Cobra motors, the smaller 1⅝-inch primary headers produced a better overall power curve than the larger 1¾-inch versions. The smaller headers produced slightly better peak numbers, but picked up significant power in the midrange compared to the larger 1¾-inch headers. This header test was run on a '03 Cobra motor equipped with a Kenne Bell blower upgrade. If any combination would respond to the larger headers, you would think that a 600+ hp blown Cobra would, but testing revealed otherwise. Check out Test 6 in this chapter for a rundown on the test results of the 1⅝-inch versus the 1¾-inch headers on this blown Cobra motor.

While I have harped on the fact that exhaust flow takes a backseat to scavenging, in some cases flow is important. If space (or cost) prohibits you from running a tuned header length, you can install a set of "shorty" headers in place of the factory exhaust manifolds. These shorty-style headers offer little or no actual tuning (scavenging effect), but they will improve the flow rate over the factory manifolds. The Ford Racing shorty headers we tested for this chapter showed impressive power gains over the factory manifolds. That they are much easier to install than the traditional long-tube headers can mean a lot to a do-it-yourselfer. The other area where flow is important is in the exhaust system after the headers. Obviously restrictions imposed by the catalytic converter and/or cat-back exhaust system will have a negative effect on power. While regulations usually prohibit messing with the catalytic converters, you can replace the cats with an X-pipe for racing. Aftermarket cat-back exhaust systems are definitely beneficial on higher horsepower motors. Our testing on the Bassani cat-back proved just how restrictive the factory cat-back was. While performance is important, many enthusiasts purchase exhaust systems strictly for the improved sound quality. This is where an X-pipe really shines, as nothing sounds better than a supercharged mod motor with an X-pipe exhaust.

The new 4.6L 3-valve will benefit from long-tube headers as well. These JBA headers featured long primary lengths to enhance low-speed and midrange torque production.

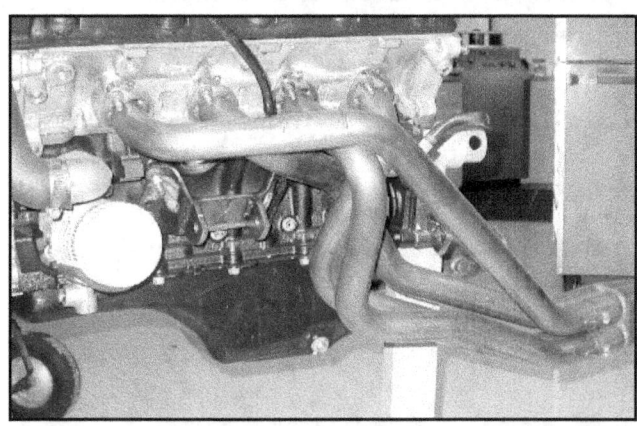

Kooks supplied a number of headers for testing, including these 1-5/8-inch headers for the 4.6L 2-valve motor.

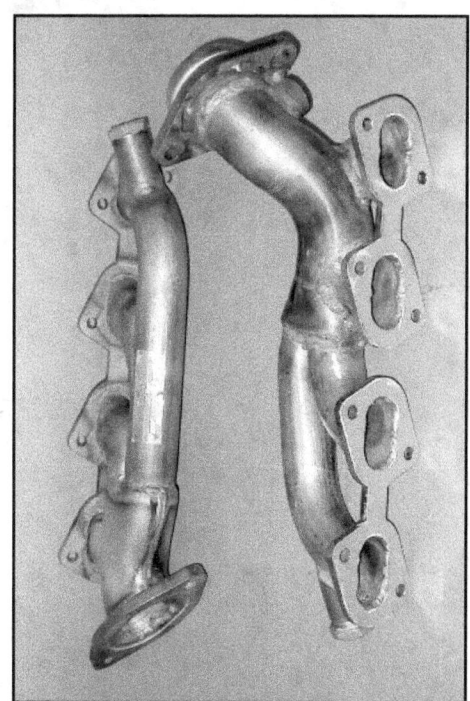

Shorty headers like these stainless steel units from Ford Racing offered as much as 10 hp on a 400-hp naturally aspirated SHM 4.6L 4-valve motor. The Ford Racing short headers are also much easier to install than a typical set of long-tube headers.

Test 1: Early 2-Valve GT: Hooker Long-Tube Headers

This header test was run on the very first modular motor I ever installed on the engine dyno. The '98 4.6L 2-valve GT motor came from Mustang Parts Specialties. Working with the F.A.S.T. fuel injection, Tom Habryzk had the early GT motor up and running in no time. After spending some time tuning the base fuel and timing tables, Tom eventually coaxed peak numbers of 260 hp and 341 ft-lbs of torque. We managed to match the flywheel rating of the new (more powerful) PI GT motors, but before you get all in an uproar about happy dynos and exaggerated power numbers, remember that this reading was taken with long-tube headers, no MAF or air inlet system other than a 3-inch tube and cone filter, and without any of the accessories. The idea was not to exceed the 260 hp offered by the late-model GT motor, but rather to establish a baseline to which we could improve upon. Given the difference between the early and late-model motors, we suspect a later GT motor run in a similar manner would probably be much closer to 300 hp.

Regardless of the actual numbers, we now had an official baseline power reading for the early mod motor. Thanks to the repeatability of the F.A.S.T. management system, back-up runs produced identical power curves. We didn't have to worry about the power changing due to engine coolant or intake air temperature readings, as the changes to fuel and timing based on temperature were effectively zeroed in the programming. This is important as testing on the chassis dyno has shown that power can vary by 10 to 15 hp or more depending on the coolant and/or inlet air temp. To ensure accuracy, we made every effort to run the motor at a constant water, oil, and air temperature. Only then can you ensure accuracy and properly verify the benefits of given performance components. The power output of the '98 4.6L was eventually improved to 307 hp and 345 ft-lbs of torque with a cam swap and Accufab throttle body.

The Hooker Super Comp full-length headers were installed on our engine from the outset, but I was curious to see how much power the headers were worth over the stock 4.6L Mustang exhaust manifolds. To find out, we ran the motor equipped with the Hooker headers and then with the stock manifolds. Equipped with the Hooker headers, the modified 4.6L produced 307 hp at 5,200 rpm and 345 ft-lbs of torque at 4,100 rpm. Like the Hooker headers, the stock manifolds were run with a section of open pipe and no mufflers. The exhaust pipe measured 2.5 inches to match the outlet of the exhaust manifolds. Equipped with the stock manifolds, the power dropped from 307 hp to just 269 hp, a drop of 38 hp. Imagine, adding Hooker headers to your Mustang can be worth as much as 38 hp. Like most flow restrictions (inlet or exhaust), we suspect that the difference in power between the stock exhaust manifolds and the headers would only increase with elevated power levels.

The stock cast-iron exhaust manifolds aren't much to look at. They're designed to last forever and hold in the heat to increase the efficiency of the catalytic converters.

These Hooker Super Comp headers feature more longer primary tubes than the stock exhaust manifolds. A long-tube header like this flows more and offers better scavenging.

Exhaust Systems

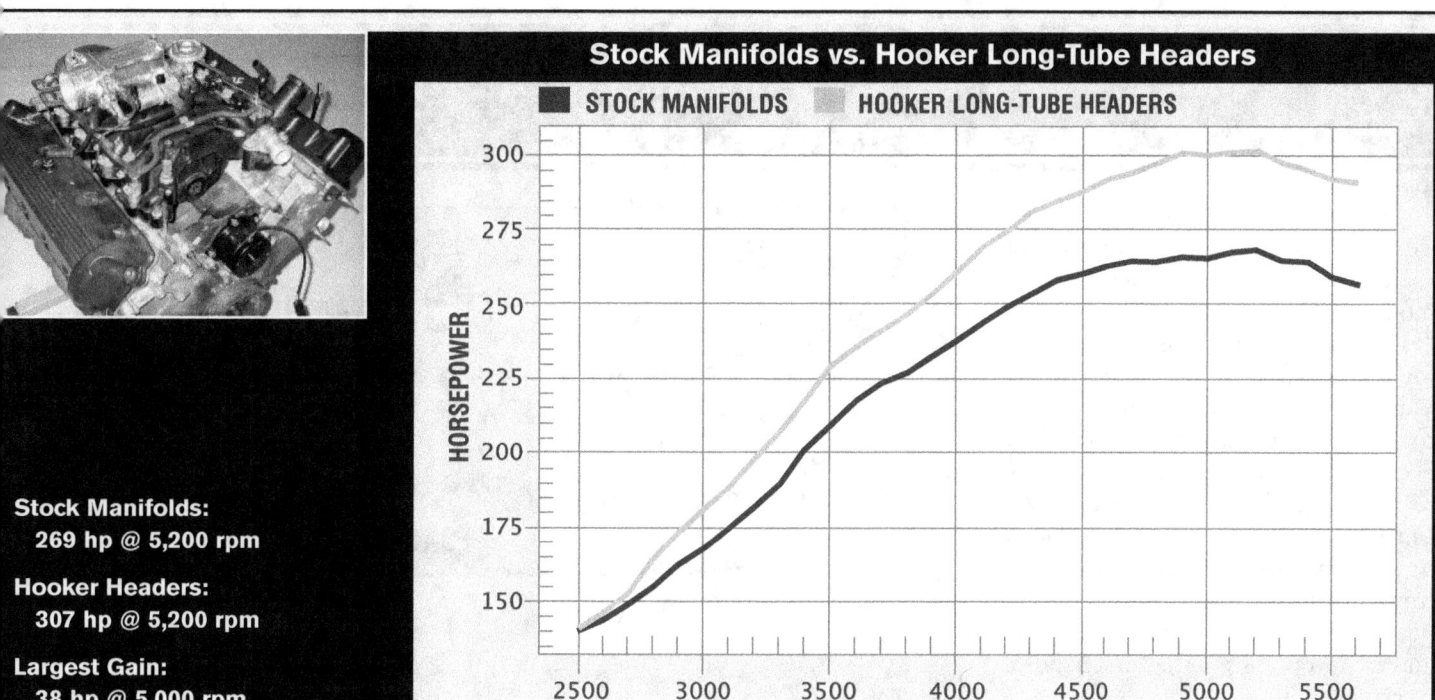

Stock Manifolds:
269 hp @ 5,200 rpm

Hooker Headers:
307 hp @ 5,200 rpm

Largest Gain:
38 hp @ 5,000 rpm

Early 2-Valve GT: Stock Manifolds vs. Hooker Long-Tube Headers (Horsepower)
The Hooker headers were worth some serious ponies on this mildly modified 1998 4.6L. Imagine adding as much as 38 hp to your early GT with just a header swap.

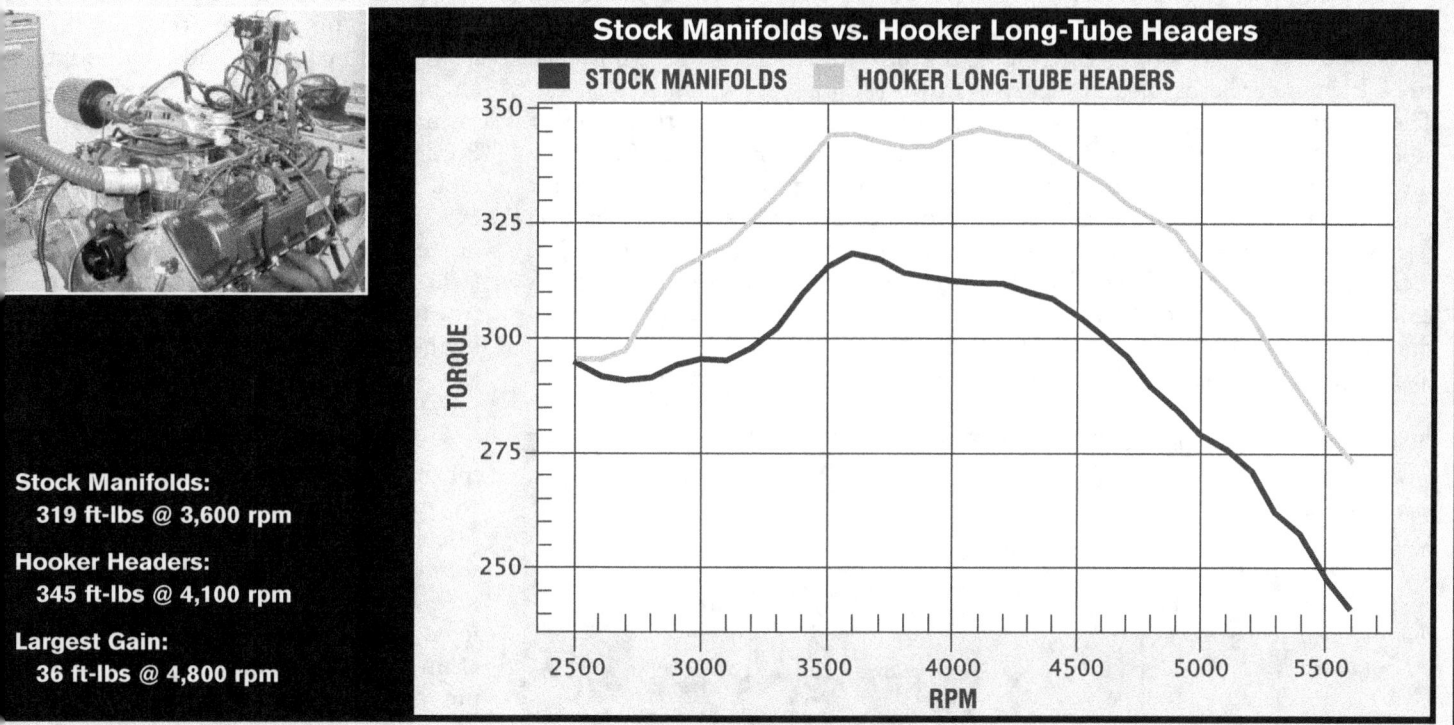

Stock Manifolds:
319 ft-lbs @ 3,600 rpm

Hooker Headers:
345 ft-lbs @ 4,100 rpm

Largest Gain:
36 ft-lbs @ 4,800 rpm

Early 2-Valve GT: Stock Manifolds vs. Hooker Long-Tube Headers (Torque)
The Hooker long-tube headers improved the torque output from 2,500 rpm all the way to 5,500 rpm. The largest gain was an impressive 36 ft-lbs.

Test 2: PI 2-Valve GT: Ford Racing Shorty Headers

Contrary to what you might think, maximum power output is not the desired goal of every performance modification. I realize that the answer, "as much as possible," is standard fare for the question of how much power you are looking for, but the reality is that some of us just want more. Not everyone wants his or her street 'Stang to be able to rip off 10-second ¼-mile times or out-handle a Ferrari. Some of us just want to add a little more performance to what is already a decent performer. If you can have your cake and eat it too, why settle for a handful of crumbs?

For this series of testing, minor modifications were the order of the day. The 2-valve GT mill supplied by Sean Hyland (which we affectionately nicknamed Canadian Bacon) actually featured a forged steel Cobra crank, a set of forged connecting rods, and forged aluminum pistons. The forged pistons produced a stock static compression ratio to go along with the stock PI cylinder heads and camshafts. The remainder of the motor was bone stock as well; from the PI intake and throttle body down to the cast-iron exhaust manifolds. We added an electric water pump, a F.A.S.T. management system, and an MSD coil pack ignition system upgrade. We also took the liberty of installing a set of 36-lb/hr injectors in place of the stock 19-

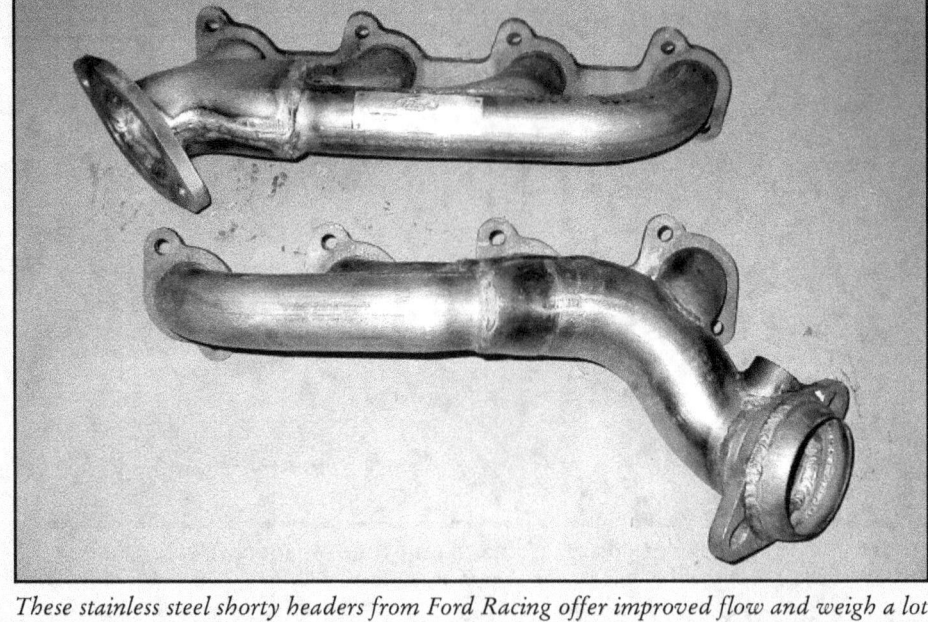

These stainless steel shorty headers from Ford Racing offer improved flow and weigh a lot less than the cast-iron manifolds. They don't add the power of long-tube headers, but they aren't as difficult to install either.

pounders. The injector upgrade was performed in anticipation of the Ford Racing supercharger to be installed down the line (see Chapter 6). Running 26 degrees of total timing and a 13.0:1 air/fuel ratio on 91-octane pump gas, the SHM 4.6L GT motor produced 287 hp at 4,900 rpm and 333 ft-lbs of torque at 4,100 rpm. The torquey GT mill exceeded 325 ft-lbs from 3,500 rpm to 4,500 rpm and produced more than 300 ft-lbs from 2,500 rpm all the way to 5,000 rpm.

With our baseline out of the way, we started on our quest to up the power output of the 4.6L. Our first attempt at adding power came in the form of a set of shorty headers from Ford Racing. Designed as a direct replacement for the factory cast-iron exhaust manifolds, the Ford Racing headers offered improved flow but lacked the primary length offered by true long-tube headers. The Ford Racing headers were constructed of stainless steel to ensure a long life and installed in minutes on the engine dyno (figure considerably more time for installation on the car). As expected, the Ford Racing headers did not offer huge power gains, but were worth 4 to 5 hp and a like amount of torque. The gains were most prevalent from 3,900 rpm to 4,800 rpm and then again past 5,500 rpm. The power output never dropped off compared to the stock exhaust manifolds and the tubular design offered a significant weight savings over the heavy cast-iron pieces.

When you get a close-up look at the stock exhaust manifolds, it's easy to see that there's room for improvement. In this test, we'll see how much of an improvement shorty headers can make.

Exhaust Systems

Stock Manifolds:
287 hp @ 4,900 rpm

Ford Racing Shorty Headers:
287 hp @ 4,900 rpm

Largest Gain:
4 hp @ 4,100 rpm

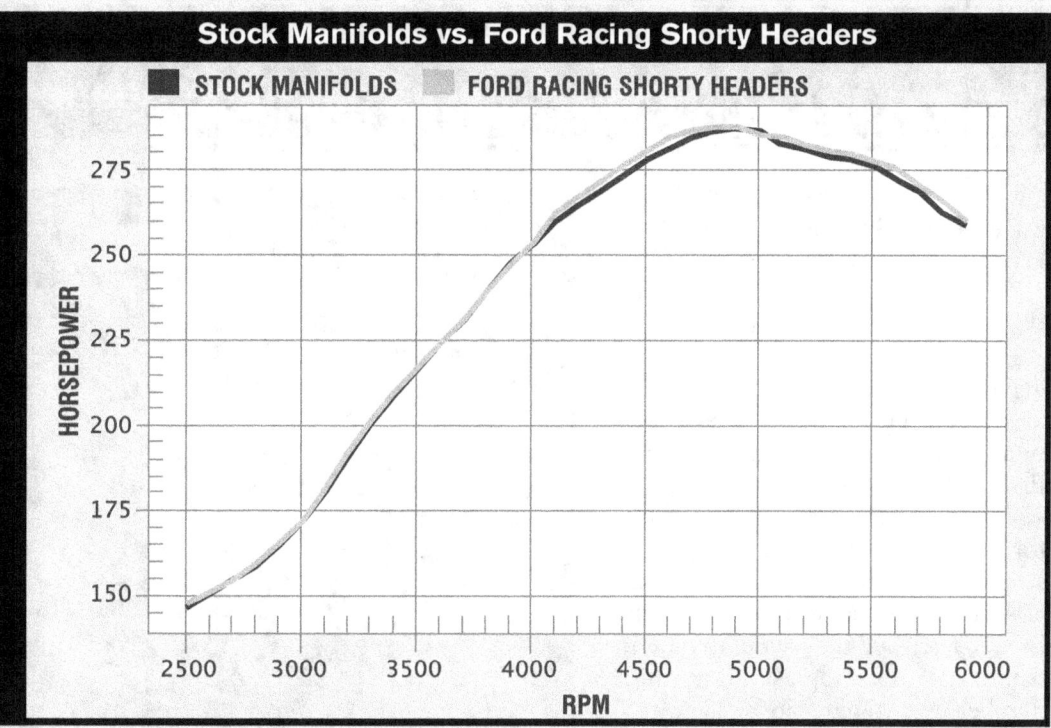

PI 2-Valve GT: Stock Manifolds vs. Ford Racing Shorty Headers (Horsepower)
Given their similarity to the stock cast-iron manifolds, we didn't expect much of a power gain from the Ford Racing shorty headers on this near-stock 4.6L 2-valve combination. The largest gain offered by the Ford Racing shorty headers was 4 to 5 hp between 3,900 rpm and 4,800 rpm.

Stock Manifolds:
332 ft-lbs @ 3,900 rpm

Ford Racing Shorty Headers:
333 ft-lbs @ 4,100 rpm

Largest Gain:
5 ft-lbs @ 4,200 rpm

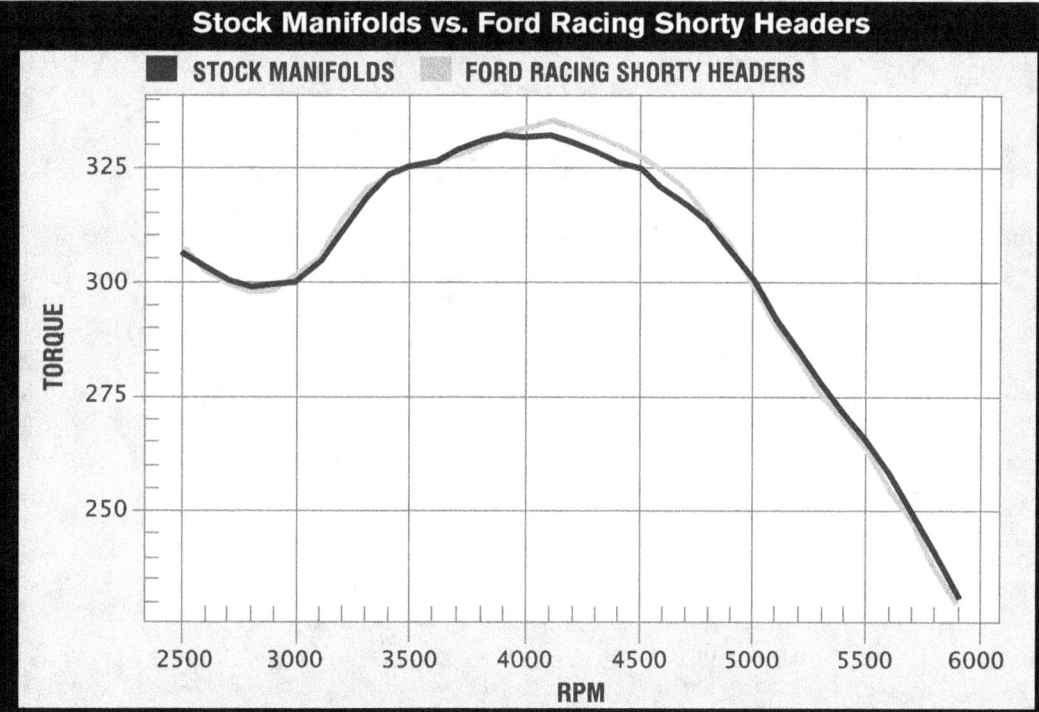

PI 2-Valve GT: Stock Manifolds vs. Ford Racing Shorty Headers (Torque)
The Ford Racing shorty headers offered midrange torque gains and lost no power to the stock cast-iron exhaust manifolds throughout the rest of the rev range.

Test 3: PI 2-Valve GT: Kooks 1⅝-inch Long-Tube Headers

The test motor consisted of a 2-valve 4.6L GT motor from Sean Hyland Motorsports (SHM). The SHM 4.6L was one of the more desirable (1999-up) Power-Improved (PI) engines. It featured a forged reciprocating assembly (but stock compression) topped off with bone-stock PI heads, cams, and composite intake manifold. Essentially, the test mule was a stock 4.6L 2-valve PI mod motor with a forged reciprocating assembly. The strength of the forged internals had no effect on the outcome of this long-tube header test, but they would come in handy later as we applied boost from a number of different blowers and turbos. In addition to the headers, this motor was used to test nitrous, a larger throttle body, and a pair of Comp Xtreme Energy XE262H cams. The results of all those tests can be found in their respective chapters, but know that this SHM 4.6L 2-valve motor was definitely put through its paces.

The SHM 4.6L GT motor was installed on the engine dyno and equipped with 36-pound injectors run by a F.A.S.T. engine management system. The injector size was chosen in anticipation of the eventual Ford Racing supercharger, but worked well on the naturally aspirated motor thanks to the control of the F.A.S.T. system. The SHM 4.6L motor was equipped with the stock exhaust manifolds, an electric water pump, and an MSD coil pack. We tuned it with 28 degrees of total timing and a (WOT) air/fuel ratio of 13.0:1. Equipped with a 2.5-inch open exhaust and the stock 65-mm throttle body, the 4.6L produced 287 hp at 4,900 rpm and 332 ft-lbs of torque at 3,900 rpm. The difference between the 260-hp factory Ford rating and the 287 hp achieved on the dyno can be attributed to the difference in test methods. The 260-hp rating by Ford was achieved with full accessories, full exhaust, and a complete inlet system. Our test motor featured no accessories, an open exhaust, and a free-flowing inlet system. As expected of the stock motor, the power fell off rapidly after 5,000 rpm. The 4.6L did manage to exceed 300 ft-lbs of torque from 2,500 rpm to 5,000 rpm, but dropped off to just 234 ft-lbs at 5,900 rpm.

After running the stock exhaust manifolds, we decided to test a set of long-tube headers. Kooks Custom Headers provided a set of 1⅝-inch long-tube headers designed to fit the late-model GTs. The 4-into-1 Kooks headers featured stainless steel construction and 2.5-inch collectors. Though long-tube header installation would be somewhat more difficult than the Ford Racing shorty headers, according to our testing, your efforts would be well rewarded. Adding the Kooks 1⅝-inch 2-valve GT headers not only improved the peak power output but also upped the power output of the modular motor from 2,500 rpm to 6,000 rpm. Credit the tuning effect of the long-tube headers for the significant power gains, upping the peak power output from 287 hp to 298 hp. The torque peak was up as well, from 332 ft-lbs to 345 ft-lbs, but even more important was the fact that the tuning offered by the Kooks headers enhanced the entire torque curve – always a welcome change.

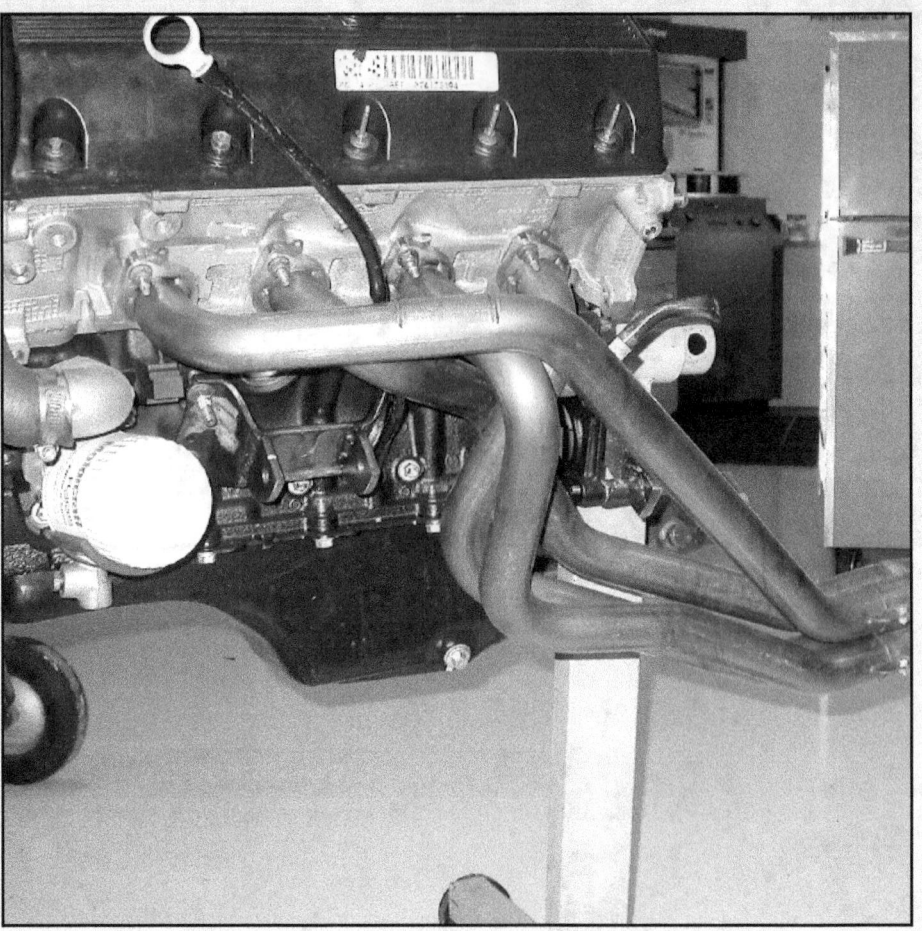

The build quality on these stainless-steel Kooks headers is quite nice. These 4.6L GT headers feature 1⅝-inch primaries and 2½-inch collectors.

Exhaust Systems

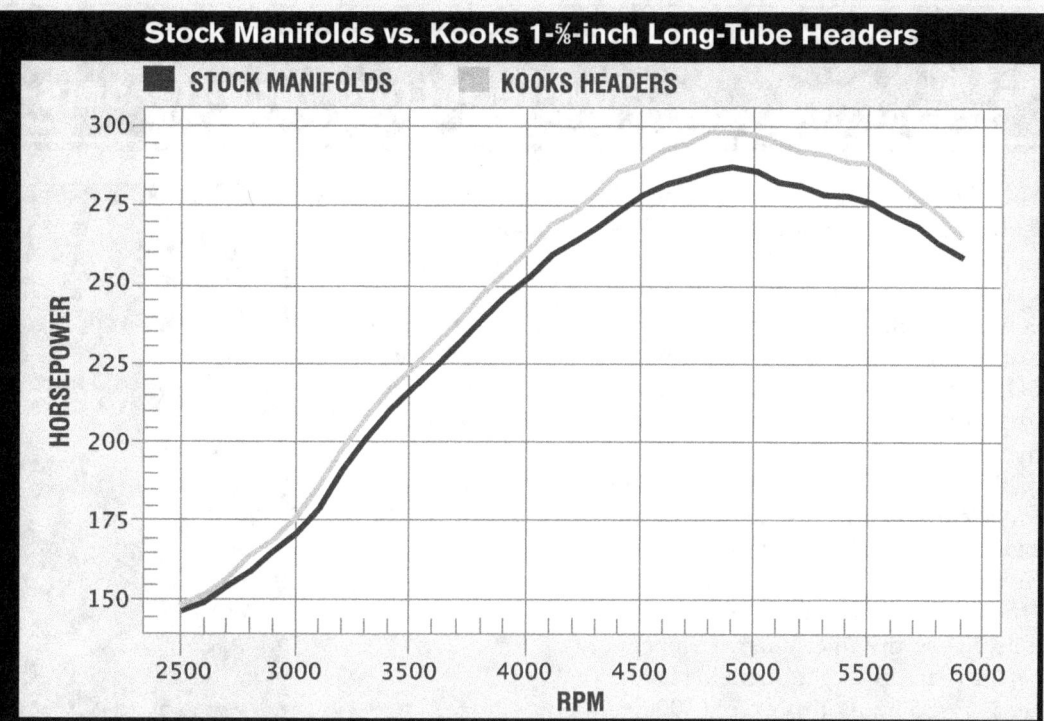

Stock Manifolds:
287 hp @ 4,900 rpm

Kooks 1⅝-inch Headers:
298 hp @ 4,900 rpm

Largest Gain:
12 hp @ 5,300 rpm

2-Valve GT: Stock Manifolds vs. Kooks 1⅝-inch Long-Tube Headers (Horsepower)
When you add a set of headers and are rewarded with an extra 10 or 12 hp, things are looking good. When you add a set of headers that look as good as these Kooks stainless long-tubes, and they add power throughout the rev range, you've really made a wise performance choice.

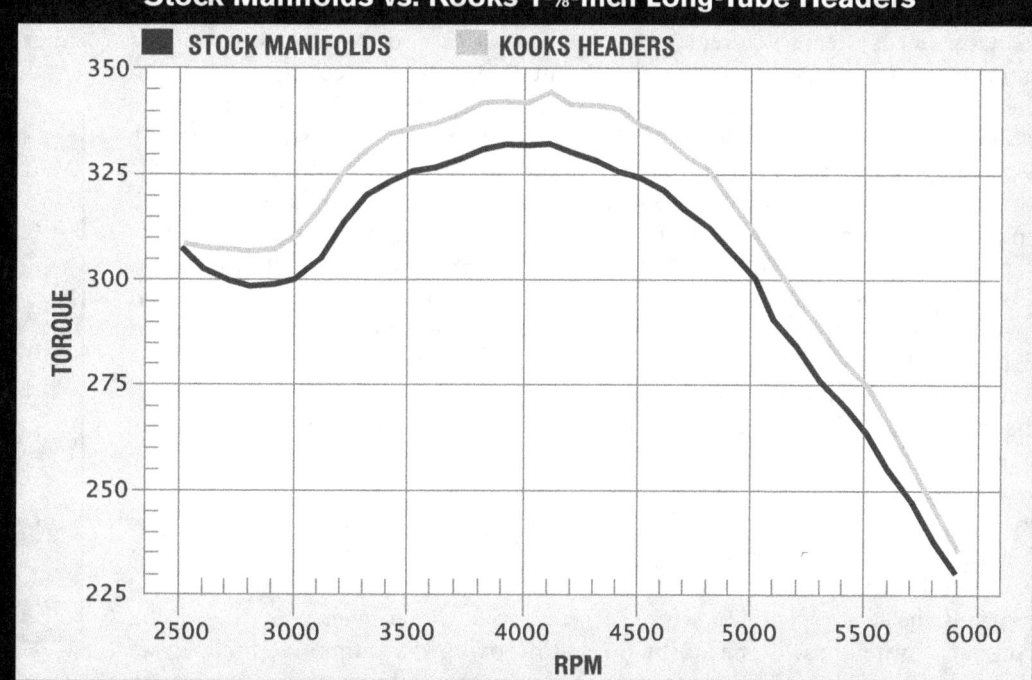

Stock Manifolds:
332 ft-lbs @ 3,900 rpm

Kooks 1⅝-inch Headers:
345 ft-lbs @ 4,000 rpm

Largest Gain:
16 ft-lbs @ 4,400 rpm

2-Valve GT: Stock Manifolds vs. Kooks 1⅝-inch Long-Tube Headers (Torque)
Note that the tuning effect of the long-tube headers offered additional torque right from 2,500 rpm. That means that not only will the Kooks headers improve acceleration, but also throttle response and likely fuel economy as well.

Building 4.6/5.4L Ford Horsepower on the Dyno

Chapter 9

Test 4: Eaton Supercharged 4-Valve '03 Cobra: Flow-Tech Long-Tube Headers

The beauty of the Ford Racing '03 Cobra crate motor was that in addition to every nut and bolt being brand-spanking new, the motor was factory equipped with a number of desirable features, not the least of which was a hefty chunk of forced induction in the form of an Eaton positive-displacement supercharger. While the presence of the supercharger was cause enough for celebration, the real key to the success was the low compression, free-flowing 4-valve heads, and the efficient air-to-water intercooler to help lower the inlet charge temperature to suppress detonation. Having seen '03 Cobra motors exceed 700 flywheel hp, naturally I was anxious to get started.

As expected of Ford Racing, the '03 Cobra motor assembly was shipped complete, including the serpentine drive assemblies (both blower and accessory). Since we planned on running the F.A.S.T. stand-alone engine management system, we removed a number of factory components that were unnecessary. We removed the clutch and pressure plate to facilitate mounting the motor, plumbed water to and from the air-to-water intercooler, and capped the necessary coolant and vacuum lines. Just as with the 2-valve 4.6L GT motors, the F.A.S.T. engine management system allowed us to delete the factory mass-air meter and attending inlet tubing. All that was necessary was the stock throttle body and inlet into the blower, something we would be upgrading later during testing (see Chapter 1). Though the '03 Cobra motor was originally equipped with a coil-on-plug ignition system, we replaced the factory ignition with the coil-pack system used previously on the 4.6L GT motors. This in no way changed the power potential of the motor; it simply allowed us to use an existing management system on the 4-valve motor.

It almost seems like a crime to run stock cast-iron manifolds on an engine like the supercharged '03 Cobra motor. It already features 4-valve heads and a forged bottom end – it's just begging for more power.

One of the very first tests run on the new Cobra crate motor was a set of 1⅝-inch (primary tube diameter) Flow Tech (Hooker) headers. Replacing the stock exhaust manifolds on a 4-valve Cobra motor is no picnic with the motor in the car. On an engine dyno, access to the mounting bolts is much improved. Keeping the ignition timing at a steady 23 degrees and the air/fuel ratio at a constant 11.8:1, we ran the '03 Cobra motor first with the stock exhaust manifolds. So equipped, the supercharged 4-valve motor produced 488 hp and 456 ft-lbs of torque. Installing the long-tube headers and 18-inch collector extensions allowed the supercharged test mule to exceed 500 hp for the first time. The headers upped the peak power to 501 hp, while the torque peak was up slightly to 461 ft-lbs. Interestingly enough, the boost pressure actually dropped with the headers. The reason for this is that the exhaust scavenging helped improve the efficiency of the motor. Improving the pumping efficiency of the motor will result in a decrease in boost (or back) pressure. Installing (the right) cams, ported cylinder heads, or increasing the displacement of the motor will usually result in an increase in power combined with a drop in boost pressure. Please don't be mislead into thinking that I should have increased the boost pressure to compensate for the drop in boost. The real test of the effectiveness of the headers was to install them with no other change.

It will be interesting to see how the supercharged 4-valve '03 Cobra motor responded to the Flow Tech long-tube headers. These headers featured 1⅝-inch headers and 2½-inch collectors.

Exhaust Systems

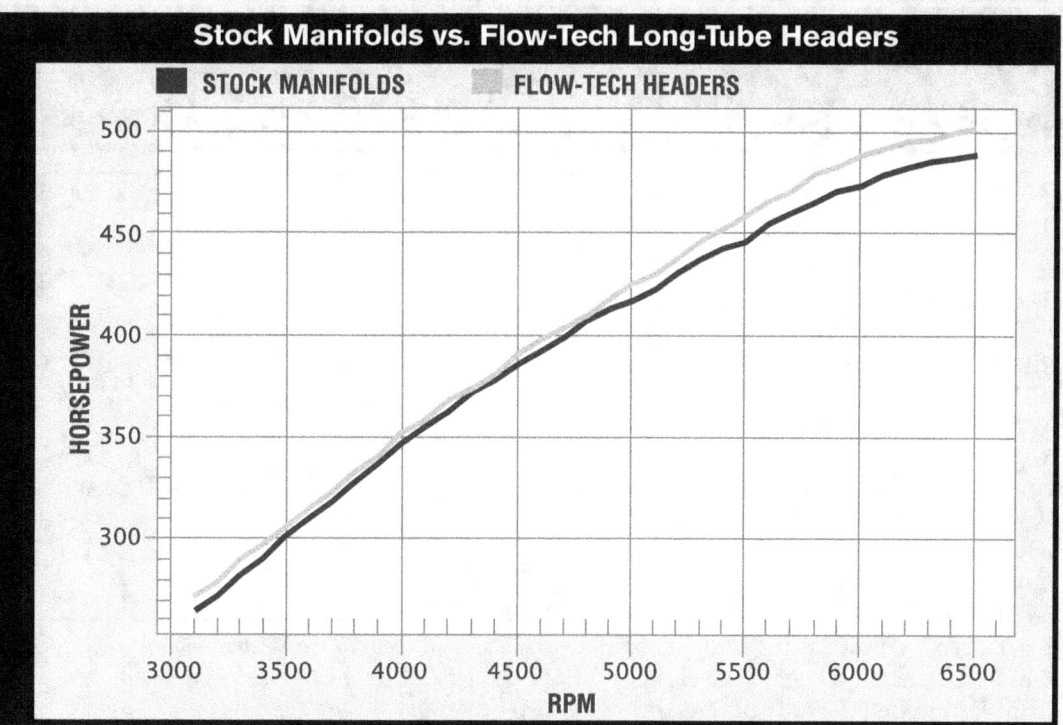

Stock Manifolds:
488 hp @ 6,500 rpm

Flow-Tech Headers:
501 hp @ 6,500 rpm

Largest Gain:
14 hp @ 6,000 rpm

Eaton Supercharged 4-Valve '03 Cobra: Stock Manifolds vs. Flow-Tech Long-Tube Headers (Horsepower)
The Hooker headers showed their worth by increasing the power output of the supercharged 4-valve Cobra by 13 hp, from 488 to 501 hp.

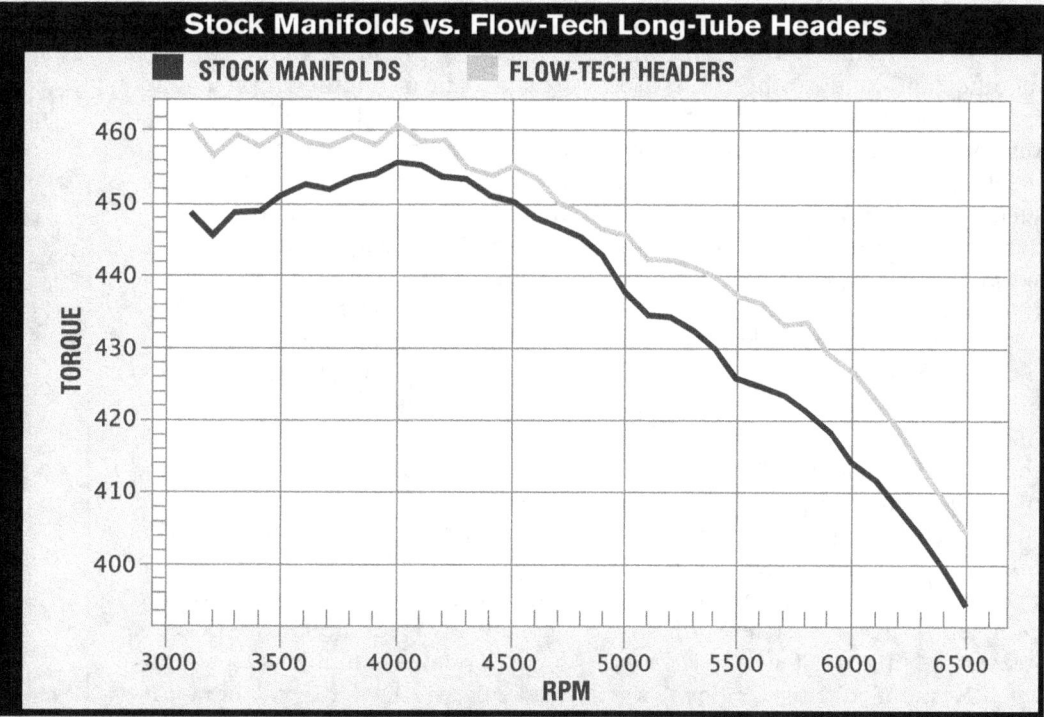

Stock Manifolds:
456 ft-lbs @ 4,000 rpm

Flow-Tech Headers:
461 ft-lbs @ 4,000 rpm

Largest Gain:
13 ft-lbs @ 5,800 rpm

Eaton Supercharged 4-Valve '03 Cobra: Stock Manifolds vs. Flow-Tech Long-Tube Headers (Torque)
Though the majority of the power gains occurred past 5,000 rpm, the headers offered additional torque gains as low as 3,000 rpm.

Building 4.6/5.4L Ford Horsepower on the Dyno

Test 5: Kenne Bell Supercharged 4-Valve '03 Cobra: Bassani Cat-Back Exhaust

This exhaust comparison was designed to test the effectiveness of a Bassani stainless-steel cat-back exhaust system on an '03 4-valve Cobra motor. Unlike some tests run on cat-back systems, this test was performed on the engine dyno rather than the more common chassis dyno. The Westech dyno facility was large enough to allow complete exhaust systems to be installed behind the tried and true '03 4-valve Cobra motor. While factory equipped with an Eaton M112 supercharger, the Eaton was removed in favor of a more-efficient twin-screw design from Kenne Bell. Results of the twin-screw upgrade can be seen in Chapter 7, but it was the more powerful Kenne Bell blower that allowed this '03 Cobra motor to finally exceed 600 hp. In fact, the motor easily exceeded 700 hp with the Kenne Bell, a number only dreamed of with the Eaton roots blower. The Kenne Bell was the only modification to the otherwise stock crate motor. As always, the motor was run with a F.A.S.T. engine management system to control timing and fuel. The timing and fuel control was becoming more and more critical as we increased the power output of this test mule.

To this point, most of the testing performed on our '03 Cobra crate motor involved induction improvements. This is not surprising given that it's supercharged. While more air in is important, more air out is equally important. Originally, we wanted to install a complete factory Cobra exhaust system to compare against a complete Bassani system (including headers). Unfortunately, the factory cat pipe supplied to us (on loan) was clogged. We discovered this only after hooking up the entire exhaust and attempting to run the motor. With the boost gauge showing in excess of 25 psi and the dyno indicating an output

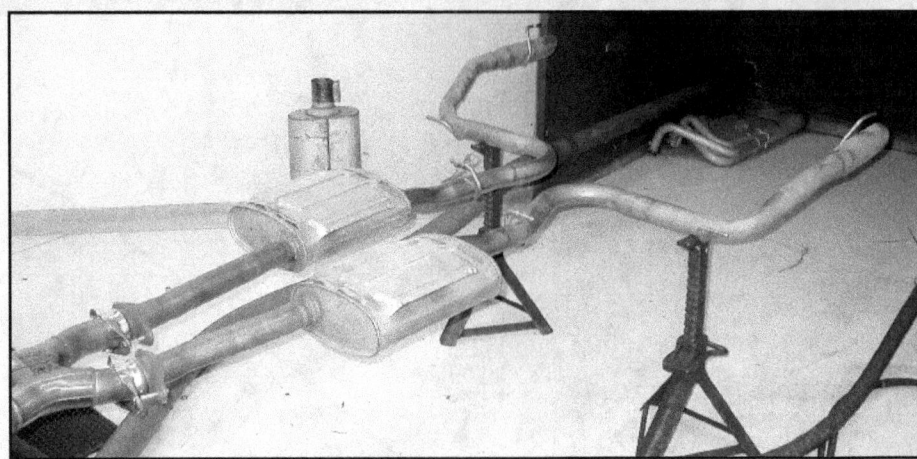

We had enough room in the Westech engine dyno room to test the stock cat-back against a Bassani cat-back. Both cat-backs were tested with a Bassani off-road X-pipe and stock exhaust manifolds.

of less than 200 hp, we knew there was a problem. In the end, we replaced the clogged cat pipe with the supplied X-pipe (no cats) from Bassani, giving us a system that included the stock exhaust manifolds feeding the Bassani X-pipe and the stock Cobra cat-back exhaust. The ordeal took several hours to straighten out, but we finally had a complete system ready to run. Credit the excellent Westech dyno facility for the ability to test complete exhaust systems on the engine dyno.

The Bassani cat-back exhaust test was run with the Kenne Bell supercharger equipped with the 3.25-inch blower pulley and the smaller 7.75-inch crank pulley. Equipped with the stock exhaust manifolds, Bassani X-pipe, and factory cat-back exhaust, the supercharged Cobra motor produced 666 hp and 587 ft-lbs of torque at 17.9 psi. The boost reading is important as improvements to the exhaust system actually lowered the boost pressure. With our baseline numbers repeatable, we replaced the factory Cobra cat-back exhaust with the Bassani 2.5-inch stainless-steel cat-back system. I would be remiss if I failed to point out the fact that the Bassani X-pipe sounded great. I've always liked the effect X-pipes have on the exhaust note and the Bassani system was no exception. Installing the Bassani cat-back upped the peak numbers to 677 hp and 587 ft-lbs, while lowering the peak boost pressure to 17.2 psi. The Bassani cat-back exhaust improved the power output by as much as 12 to 13 hp elsewhere in the rev range.

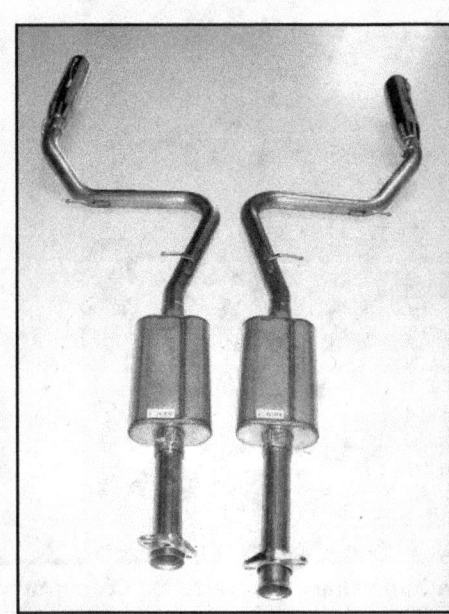

The 2½-inch Bassani cat-back is made of stainless steel and is a direct bolt-on replacement for the stock exhaust.

Exhaust Systems

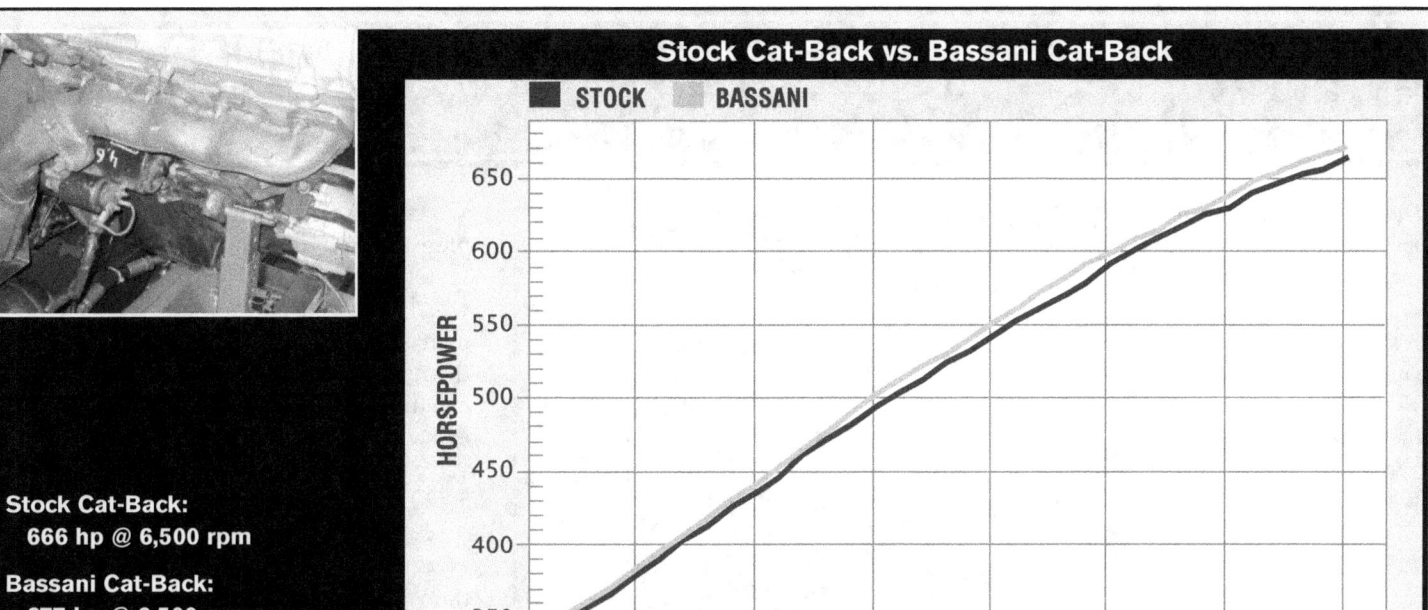

Stock Cat-Back:
666 hp @ 6,500 rpm

Bassani Cat-Back:
677 hp @ 6,500 rpm

Largest Gain:
12 hp @ 5,400 rpm

Kenne Bell Supercharged 4-Valve '03 Cobra: Bassani Cat-Back Exhaust (Horsepower)
Due to the scale, the gain of 10 to 12 hp looks small, but that's because the '03 4-valve motor was producing over 650 hp. Dropping the factory cat-back exhaust netted a sizable gain from 4,000 to 6,500 rpm.

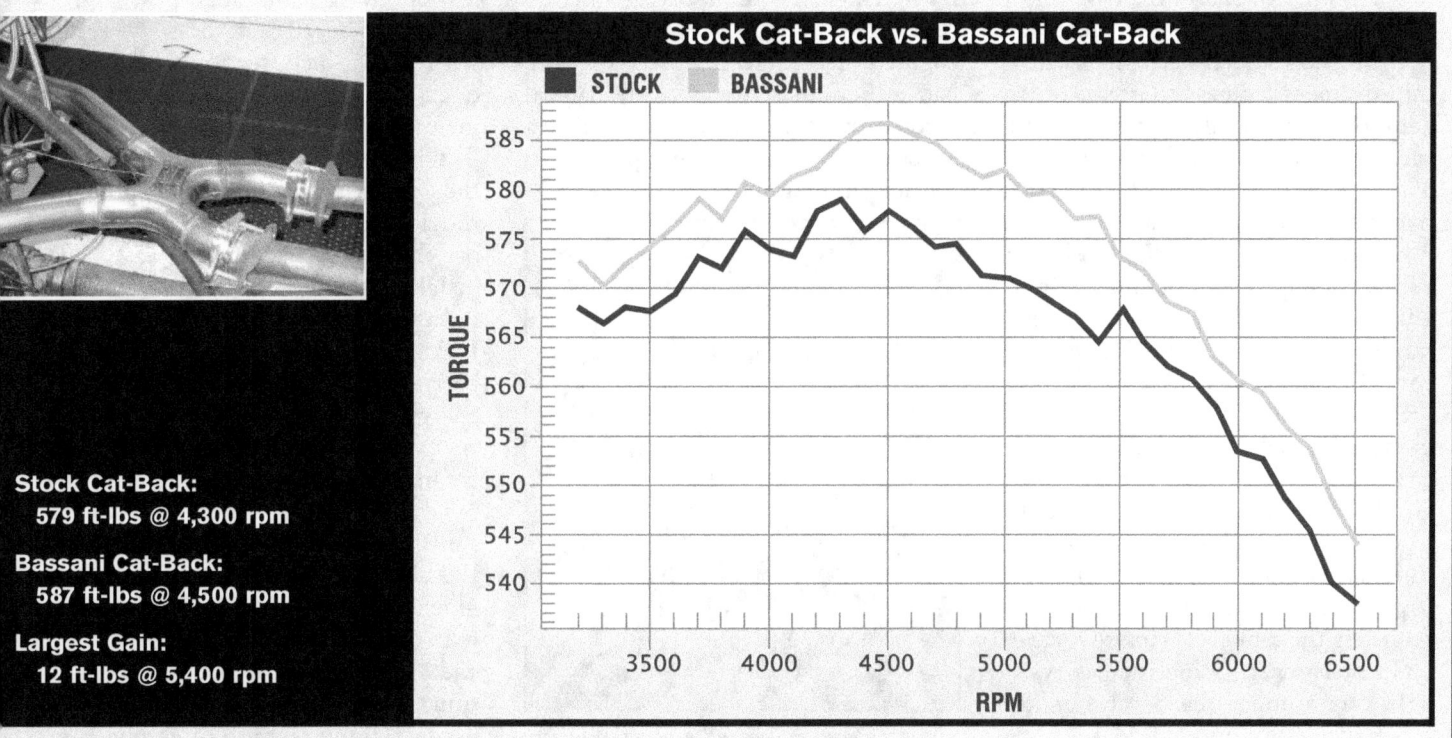

Stock Cat-Back:
579 ft-lbs @ 4,300 rpm

Bassani Cat-Back:
587 ft-lbs @ 4,500 rpm

Largest Gain:
12 ft-lbs @ 5,400 rpm

Kenne Bell Supercharged 4-Valve '03 Cobra: Bassani Cat-Back Exhaust (Torque)
The torque curves show that the factory cat-back exhaust represented a restriction even down below 3,500 rpm.

Test 6: 3-Valve '05 GT: JBA Long-Tube Headers

Though installing any headers on an engine dyno is easy, adding headers to an '05 GT is much easier than it is on '96-'04 GTs. These JBA headers featured 1⅝-inch primaries and 2½-inch collectors.

It can be argued that the new 4.6L 3-valve GT motor is not so much a revolutionary change as an evolutionary one. From the perspective of a Mustang GT, the additional power over the previous 2-valve 4.6L represents huge steps in the right direction. Though the new mod motor shares the basic short block architecture, the top end is all new. The much-needed airflow improvement comes courtesy of an additional intake valve combined with redesigned intake and exhaust ports. The airflow improvements are carried over into the new composite intake manifold, which offers slightly shorter runners, improved (radiused) port entries, and a repositioned (center mounted) throttle body. The new throttle body also featured electronic drive-by-wire actuation. Additional electronic trickery includes variable cam timing; where the cams were advanced and retarded to optimize the power curve at high and low RPM. Traditionally, advancing the cam improves low-speed torque production while retarding the cam events improves top-end horsepower. Using the new variable cam timing, the 3-valve motor offers the best of both worlds.

As good as the new 3-valve motor is in stock trim, I wanted to improve it by installing a set of JBA long-tube headers. The first step was to run the motor in stock trim, or at least in near stock trim, on the engine dyno. The '05 GT motor was supplied by my friends at Vortech Engineering, without whose help, testing on this 3-valve motor would never have happened. A few changes were necessary before running the new 4.6L motor on the engine dyno. First, the drive-by-wire had to be replaced with a mechanical throttle system. Next, we installed a Meziere electric water pump to replace running all of the accessories.

The stock cast-iron manifolds are a slightly better design than previous factory exhaust manifolds, but they still aren't long-tube headers.

We then replaced the factory coil-on-plug ignition system with a coil-pack system from a '98 2-valve GT motor, which allowed us to use the F.A.S.T. management system. Breathing through the stock throttle body and exhaling through the stock cast-iron exhaust manifolds, the '05 4.6L 3-valve GT motor pumped out 356 hp at 5,800 rpm and 384 ft-lbs of torque at 4,200 rpm. The torquey mod motor exceeded 350 ft-lbs from 3,400 rpm all the way to 5,300 rpm.

Next up was a set of new JBA long-tube headers designed specifically for the 3-valve Mustang GT. The JBA headers feature 1⅝-inch primary tubes feeding 2½-inch collectors. The collectors featured JBA's patented Firecone anti-reversion technology to further improve power. The headers featured lengthy primaries, something I expected would greatly enhance low-speed and midrange power production. The JBA headers were run with an 18-inch section of 2.5-inch open pipe (just like the stock exhaust manifolds) and no mufflers. Running in this configuration would eliminate the exhaust system as a possible restriction. Installing the JBA headers on the dyno was pretty easy, and installing them in the new 3-valve GT is easier than the previous GTs. The JBA headers were also supplied with a barrier coating to keep all that heat energy in the tubing where it belongs. As expected, the JBA long-tube headers improved the power output of the 3-valve 4.6L, with the majority of the gains coming below 5,100 rpm. The JBA headers were responsible for as much as 12 hp and 18 ft-lbs of torque, with consistent gains of 12 to 15 ft-lbs and 8 to 10 hp from 3,000 rpm to 5,100 rpm. Oddly enough, the long-tube headers didn't seem to offer any gains above 5,100 rpm, though our inability to alter the variable cam timing may have played a part in that scenario.

Exhaust Systems

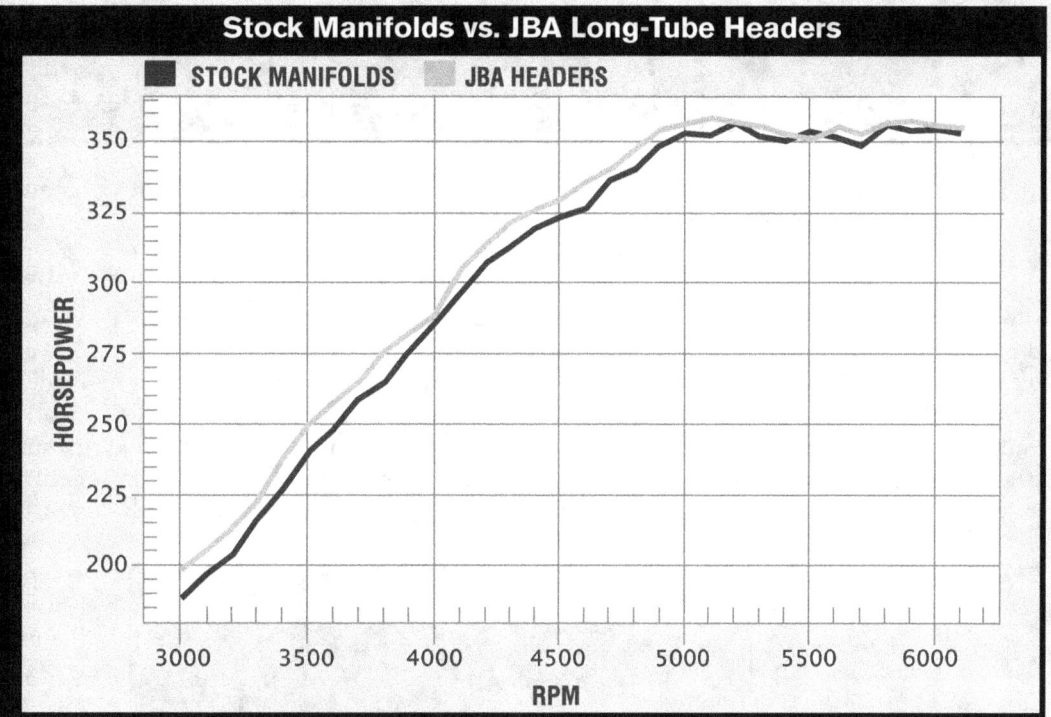

Stock Manifolds:
356 hp @ 5,900 rpm

JBA Long-Tube Headers:
357 hp @ 5,800 rpm

Largest Gain:
9 hp @ 3,600 rpm

3-Valve '05 GT: Stock Manifolds vs. JBA Long-Tube Headers (Horsepower)
The long primary tubes and small collectors combined to enhance power production below 5,000 rpm. The JBA headers were worth as much as 9 hp and showed consistent gains from 3,000 rpm (and lower) to 5,100 rpm.

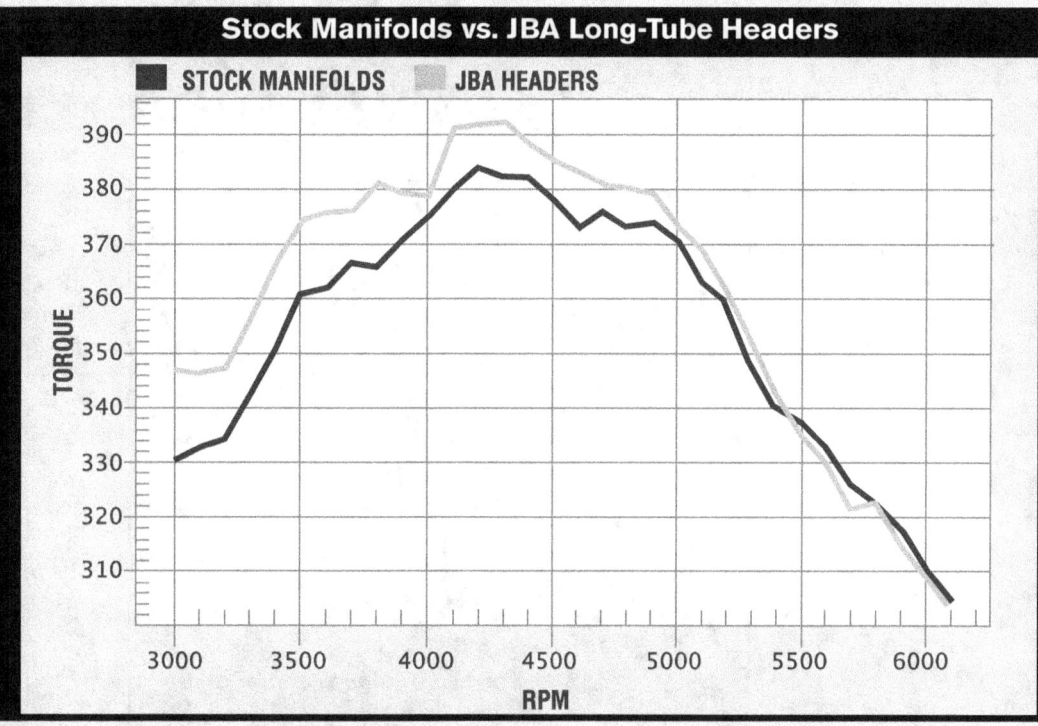

Stock Manifolds:
384 ft-lbs @ 4,200 rpm

JBA Long-Tube Headers:
392 ft-lbs @ 4,300 rpm

Largest Gain:
21 ft-lbs @ 3,100 rpm

3-Valve '05 GT: Stock Manifolds vs. JBA Long-Tube Headers (Torque)
The torque gains offered by the JBA long-tube headers were impressive. I wish I had elected to run the test motor below 3,000 rpm to better illustrate the gains offered by the long primary tubes. A gain of 21 ft-lbs is impressive from a set of headers on an otherwise stock motor.

Building 4.6/5.4L Ford Horsepower on the Dyno

Test 7: Kenne Bell Supercharged 4-Valve '03 Cobra: Kooks 1⅝- vs. 1¾-inch Headers

If you check out the Web sites and postings on the Internet, you'll come across a wide variety of opinions on the subject of exhaust systems for the supercharged Cobra motors. Given the impressive power production offered by the supercharged 4-valve motors, it's understandable that many enthusiasts would opt for the largest header configuration available, in this case a 1¾-inch primary. The bigger is better theme is only exaggerated on modified engines, as all that boosted airflow has to find a way out, right? Unfortunately, there's much more to the exhaust game than sizing. To illustrate this, we performed a back-to-back test on our modified Cobra motor. Equipped with a Kenne Bell supercharger pumping out 10 psi, the modified '03 motor easily exceeded 600 hp. Keeping the timing and air/fuel ratio (as well as air, water, and oil temperatures) the same, we ran a pair of 1⅝-inch and 1¾-inch stainless-steel headers from Kook's Custom Headers (thanks George). This was one of those tests where I could have made a ton of money by betting on the smaller headers. Imagine, picking the 1⅝-inch headers over the 1¾-inch headers on a supercharged motor pumping out over 600 hp.

Both sets of headers featured exceptional build quality and stainless-steel construction, but differed in the primary tubing diameter (1⅝ inch vs. 1¾ inch) and collector size (2½ inch vs. 3 inch). Given the prodigious power potential of the supercharged 4.6L motors, you might immediately assume that the Cobra motor would respond best to the larger headers, but testing actually showed otherwise. Even run at a power level exceeding 600 hp (equipped with the Kenne Bell supercharger pumping 10 psi), the supercharged '03 Cobra produced the best overall power curve with the 1⅝-inch Kooks headers. It should be noted that though the 1⅝-inch headers were equipped with 2½-inch collectors, they were run into the same 3-inch collector extension used on the 1¾-inch/3-inch collector headers. Thus the power differences can be attributed solely to the headers. Check out the supplied power graphs for complete details, but know that the peak power numbers were almost dead even. The major difference between the two header sizes came in the midrange, where the 1⅝-inch headers out-powered the larger 1¾-inch versions to the tune of 8 to 10 ft-lbs from 3,300 rpm to 5,400 rpm. This type of power difference is exactly why I went to great lengths to include complete graphs, not just peak power numbers. Sometimes the power gains or losses were not at the peak, but rather somewhere in the middle.

These 1¾-inch Kooks headers might make you the talk of the Internet, but this test shows how they fair against the Kooks 1⅝-inch headers.

The Kooks 1⅝-inch headers featured 2½-inch collectors and made more torque through the midrange than the 1¾-inch headers.

Exhaust Systems

Kooks 1⅝-inch Headers:
620 hp @ 6,600 rpm

Kooks 1¾-inch Headers:
618 hp @ 6,600 rpm

Largest Gain:
12 hp @ 4,100 rpm

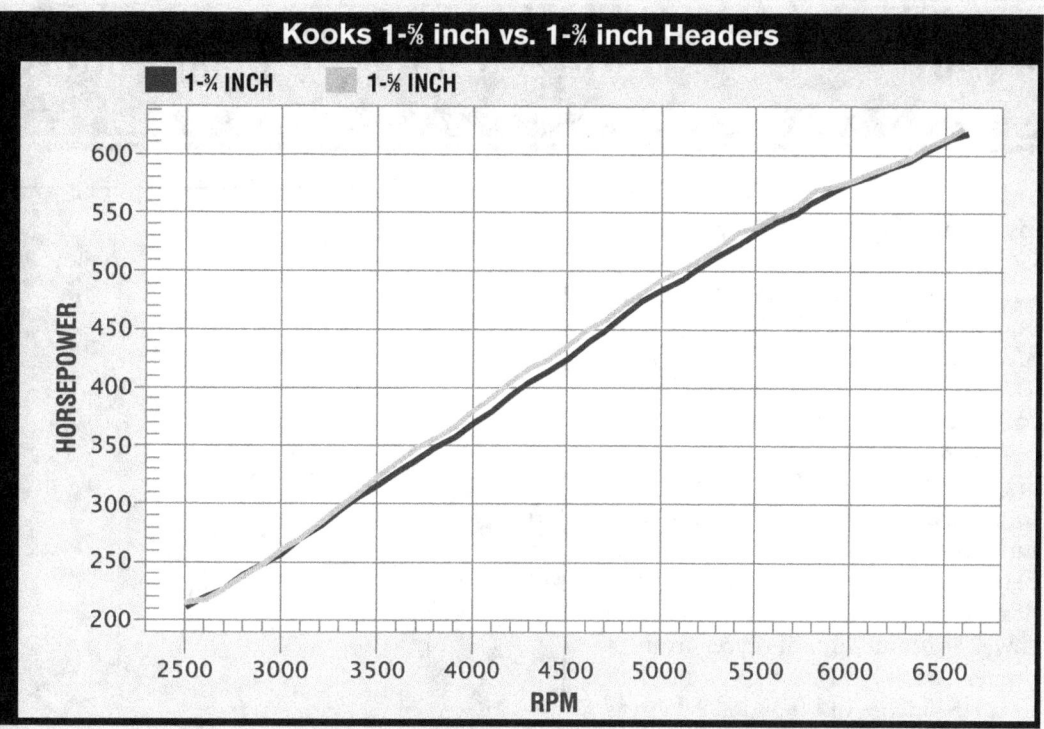

Kenne Bell Supercharged 4-Valve '03 Cobra: Kooks 1⅝- vs. 1¾-inch Headers (Horsepower)
Once again, the scale of the power curve made the power differences seem less dramatic, but the 1 5/8-inch headers handily outperformed the larger 1¾-inch headers from 3,400 rpm to 5,900 rpm, yet lost no power anywhere else.

Kooks 1⅝-inch Headers:
517 ft-lbs @ 5,400 rpm

Kooks 1¾-inch Headers:
510 ft-lbs @ 5,500 rpm

Largest Gain:
13 hp @ 3,900 rpm

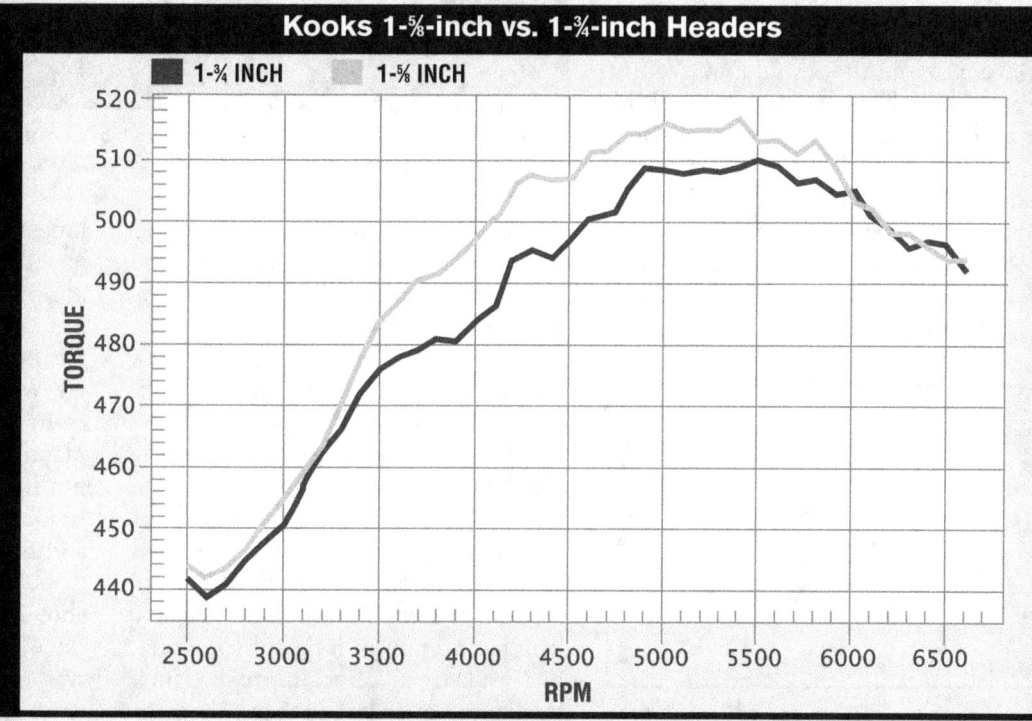

Kenne Bell Supercharged 4-Valve '03 Cobra: Kooks 1⅝- vs. 1¾-inch Headers (Torque)
The Kooks 1⅝-inch headers produced more torque than the larger 1¾-inch headers, while managing to match the peak horsepower numbers. Note the torque gains (as much as 13 ft-lbs) that occurred from 3,400 rpm to 5,900 rpm.

Building 4.6/5.4L Ford Horsepower on the Dyno

Chapter 9

Test 8: 4-Valve Cobra: Ford Racing Shorty Headers

For this test, I relied once again on my Sean Hyland 400-hp 4-valve Cobra motor. The SHM 4-valve Cobra motor was a duplicate of the one used in his book, *How to Build Max-Performance 4.6L Ford Engines*. The 4.6L featured a forged steel crank, rods, and flat-top pistons, mildly ported heads and intake, and a set of Stage 1 SHM cams. The flat-top pistons pushed the static compression ratio to near 10.5:1, which is just about perfect for street use. The flat-top design also provided optimum flame travel without interference from a dome. The Stage 1 cam specs checked in at .452 inches of lift and 209 degrees of duration at .050. The mild cams were designed to offer good midrange power and allow the mod motor to exceed 400 hp on the engine dyno. The 2001 Cobra intake manifold was treated to internal porting. The lower portion of the intake was cut off to provide access to the internal passages. Once ported, the aluminum section was welded back in place. The SHM motor was set up with a stock 4-valve Cobra throttle body and cast-iron exhaust manifolds, and a 2½-inch open-pipe exhaust system. No accessories were used (we ran an electric water pump) and the air/fuel and timing curves were dialed in using a F.A.S.T. management system. After playing with various timing curves, we were finally rewarded with peak numbers of 400 hp and 373 ft-lbs of torque. I guess when Sean says he's sending you a 400 hp motor, he really knows what he's talking about.

The very first test run on the SHM 4-valve motor was to compare the stock exhaust manifolds to a set of Ford Racing shorty headers. Designed as a simple bolt on, the Ford Racing shorty headers lacked the primary length common in long-tube headers, but looked to offer improved flow thanks to better bends than the factory cast-iron manifolds. Installation was a breeze, as access to all of the mounting bolts was readily available (something not the case with many long-tube headers). As I understand it, installing headers with the 4-valve motor in the car is no picnic. It's times like this that I was glad to be working on the engine dyno. The shorty headers were run with the same 2½-inch open exhaust employed on the factory manifolds. As expected, the gains were not huge, but the Ford Racing shorty headers were definitely worth some additional power. From 5,000 rpm to 6,500 rpm, the Ford Racing headers showed consistent gains of 5 to 7 hp. At 6,100 rpm, the power difference was as much as 10 hp, and at 6,500 rpm, the difference was an impressive 15 hp. For the Cobra owner looking to perform the header install at home, the Ford Racing shorty headers might be just the ticket.

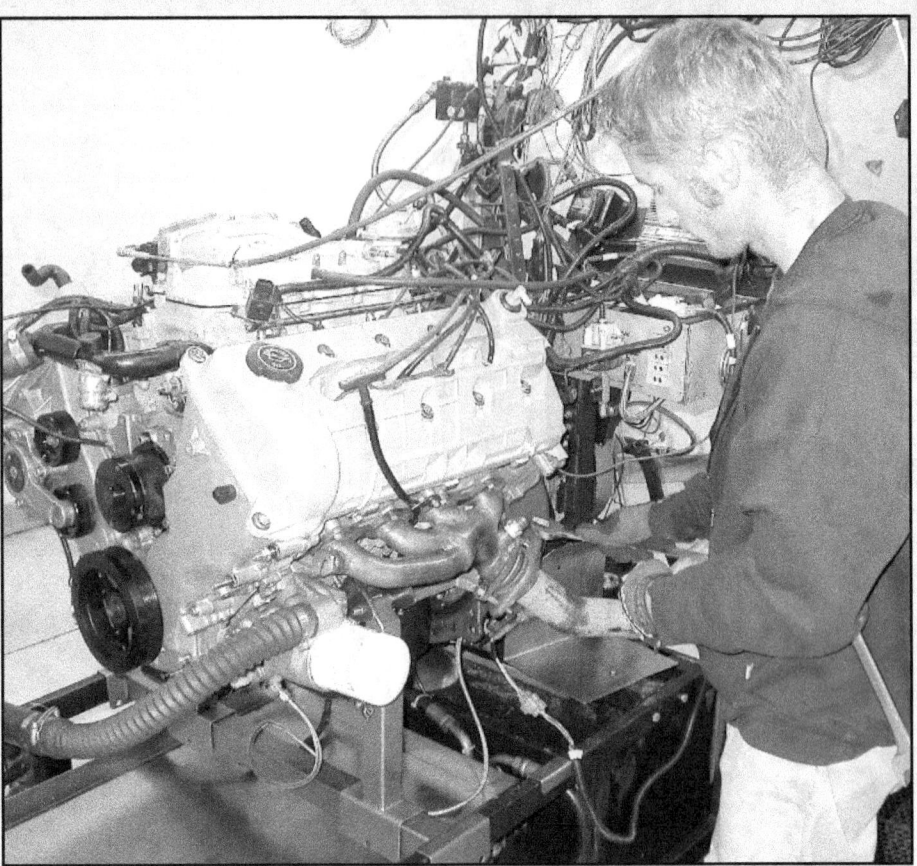

With the stock manifolds or the shorty headers, we ran a 2½-inch open exhaust on the dyno. This ensured that the headers would be responsible for any gains.

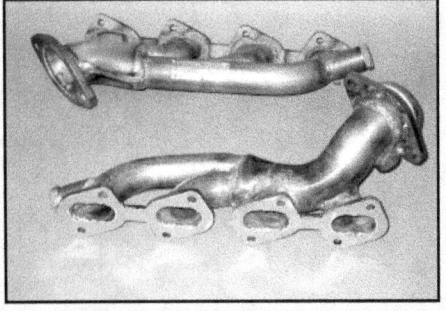

These shorty headers from Ford Racing looked to offer improved flow of the stock manifolds. Though we're testing on an engine dyno, these shorties are easier to install in the car than a set of long tubes.

Exhaust Systems

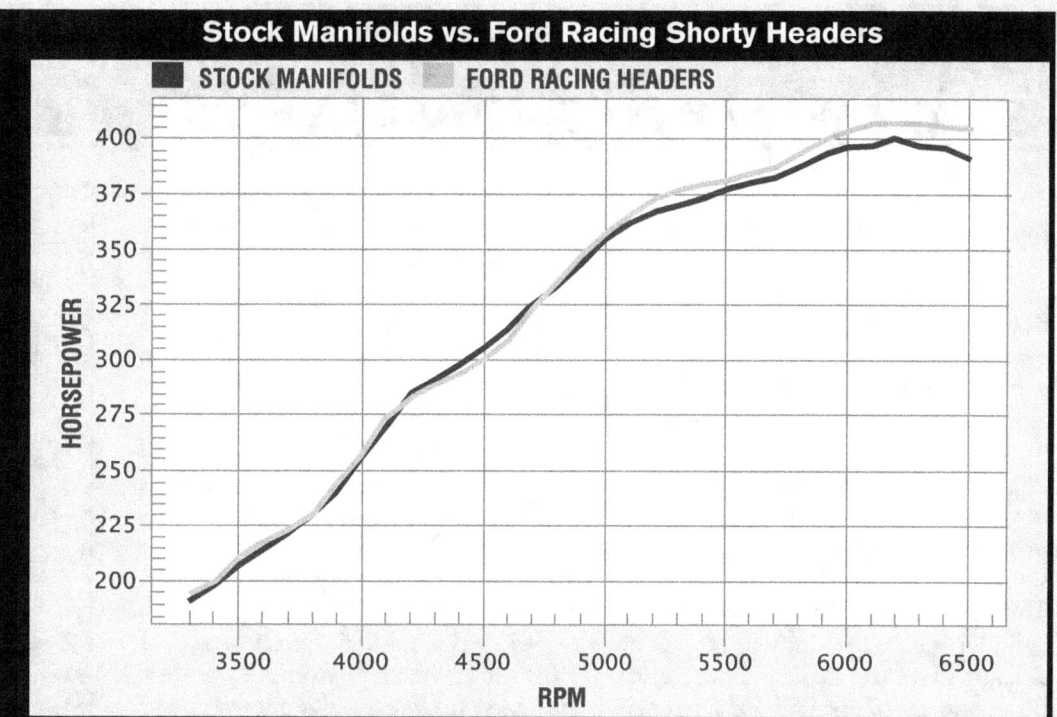

Stock Manifolds:
400 hp @ 6,200 rpm

Ford Racing Shorty Headers:
408 hp @ 6,200 rpm

Largest Gain:
16 hp @ 6,500 rpm

4-Valve Cobra: Stock Manifolds vs. Ford Racing Shorty Headers (Horsepower)
As expected of a simple exhaust flow increase (shorty headers lack the tuning offered by additional primary length), the horsepower gains offered by the Ford Racing shorty headers increased with engine speed. At 6,500 rpm, the Ford Racing shorty headers offered as much as 16 hp.

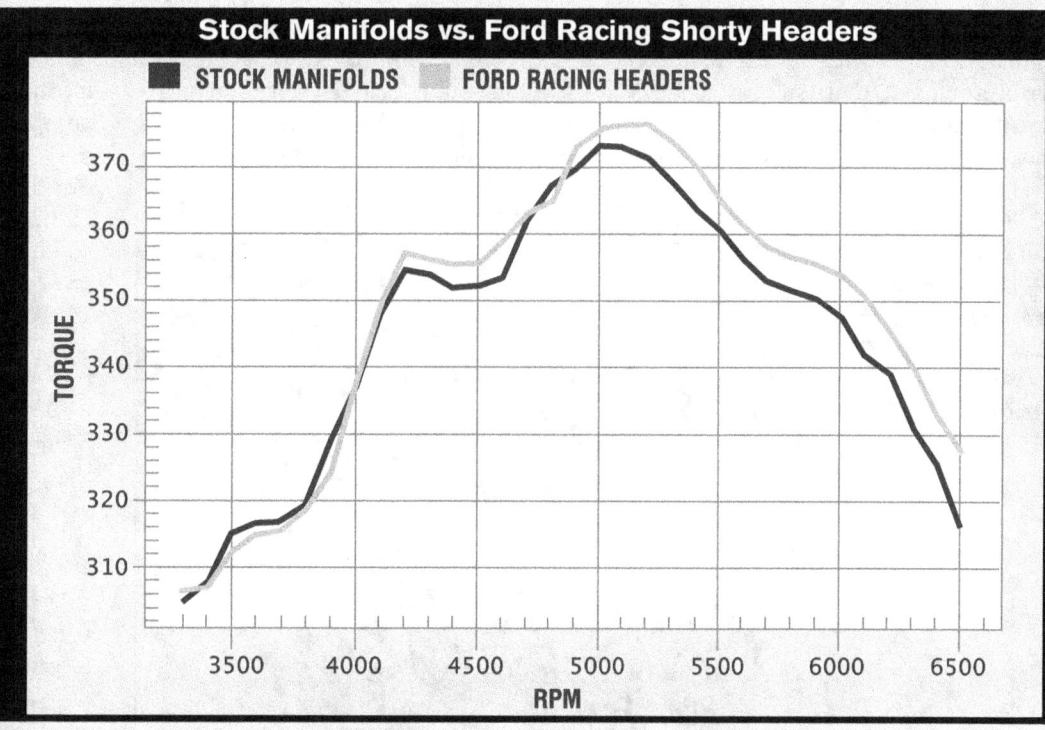

Stock Manifolds:
373 ft-lbs @ 5,000 rpm

Ford Racing Shorty Headers:
376 ft-lbs @ 5,200 rpm

Largest Gain:
11 ft-lbs @ 6,500 rpm

4-Valve Cobra: Stock Manifolds vs. Ford Racing Shorty Headers (Torque)
Most of the torque gains offered by the Ford Racing shorty headers occurred past 5,000 rpm. The shorty header design lacked the long primary length necessary to produce proper scavenging, but the added flow did improve the power output of this modified 4.6L 4-valve motor.

Building 4.6/5.4L Ford Horsepower on the Dyno

Test 9: 4-Valve Cobra: Hooker Long-Tube Headers

Right after running the test on the Ford Racing shorty headers on the SHM 4.6L 4-valve motor, I installed a set of Hooker Super Comp long-tube headers. The long-tube design offers something no factory cast-iron exhaust manifold or even shorty header can. The additional power supplied by long-tube headers is not from improved flow so much as the pulse tuning provided by the length of the primary tubes. Exhaust flow isn't constant; it actually comes out in pulses. Though it happens quite rapidly, each cylinder must fire individually. The exhaust gases from one cylinder must flow out the dedicated exhaust primary pipe before joining the rest of the cylinders (from one bank in the case of a V-8 mod motor) in the collector. Improving the exhaust flow isn't simply a matter of increasing the primary size. If more flow was all that mattered then we would all have shorty headers with 3-inch (diameter) collectors, but that isn't what works best, at least not on a typical performance street motor. The pulses provided by one cylinder actually create a vacuum in an adjoining cylinder. It is this vacuum that helps suck (or scavenge) the exhaust flow from the adjoining cylinder. Scavenging greatly improves exhaust flow from the combustion chamber (not just through the tube). When (over which RPM range) this occurs depends on the length and diameter of the primary pipes, as well as the collector size and shape. This is why it is critical to tune the header to the desired operating range of the motor.

For this test, I chose a set of Hooker Super Comp headers designed for the 4-valve motor. I was actually curious about this test as the long-tube headers showed only minimal gains on the supercharged 4.6L (actually less than on the naturally aspirated 2-valve). While you would think the higher-horsepower supercharged 4-valve motor would benefit greatly from improved exhaust flow, the long-tube headers were not terribly effective. Would the additional compression and the fact that this motor was naturally aspirated change anything? The answer is a resounding yes! Adding the Hooker headers upped the power output by as much as 25 hp, raising our peak number from 407 hp (with stock exhaust manifolds) to 426 hp. The peak torque jumped by 16 ft-lbs from 376 ft-lbs to 392 ft-lbs. The Hooker headers offered consistent power gains from 3,000 rpm to 6,500 rpm, positively indicating the header design does a great deal more than just improve the exhaust flow. The scavenging effect plays a major role in determining the power curve. If you look at the gains, you'll notice that the power curve was simply elevated but not changed. The peak power numbers occurred at the same rpm (+/- 100 rpm), it's just that they were considerably higher with the long-tube headers. Had we elected to run this motor below 3,400 rpm, the power gains would have continued down to 2,500 rpm (or below).

Now that we've tested some long-tube headers on a supercharged 4-valve motor, let's see how they do on a naturally aspirated engine. These Hooker Super Comps feature 1⅝-inch primaries and 2½-inch collectors.

Long-tube headers are a bit of a chore to install on a 4-valve engine in the car, but that's what the engine dyno is for. These Hookers picked up as much as 18 hp and 19 ft-lbs of torque.

Exhaust Systems

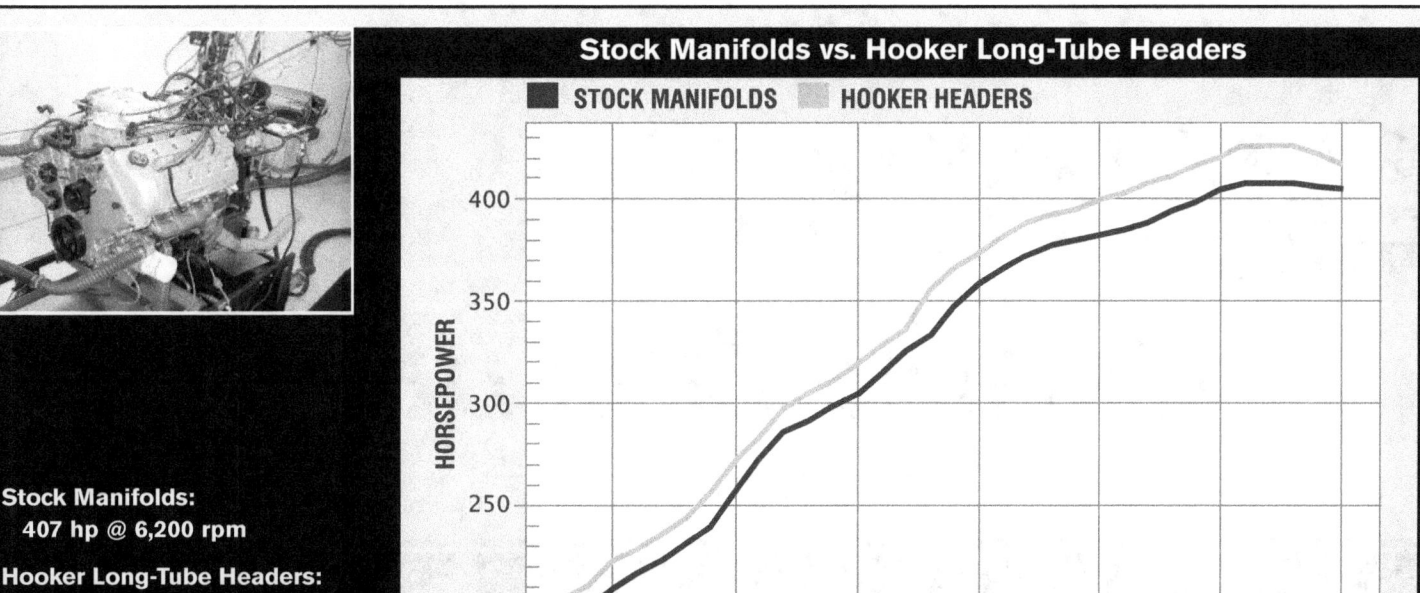

Stock Manifolds:
407 hp @ 6,200 rpm

Hooker Long-Tube Headers:
426 hp @ 6,200 rpm

Largest Gain:
18 hp @ 6,100 rpm

4-Valve Cobra: Stock Manifolds vs. Hooker Long-Tube Headers (Horsepower)
This is the kind of power gains you like to see. While a gain of 18 hp is always welcomed, a consistent gain throughout the rev range will really make a difference in acceleration.

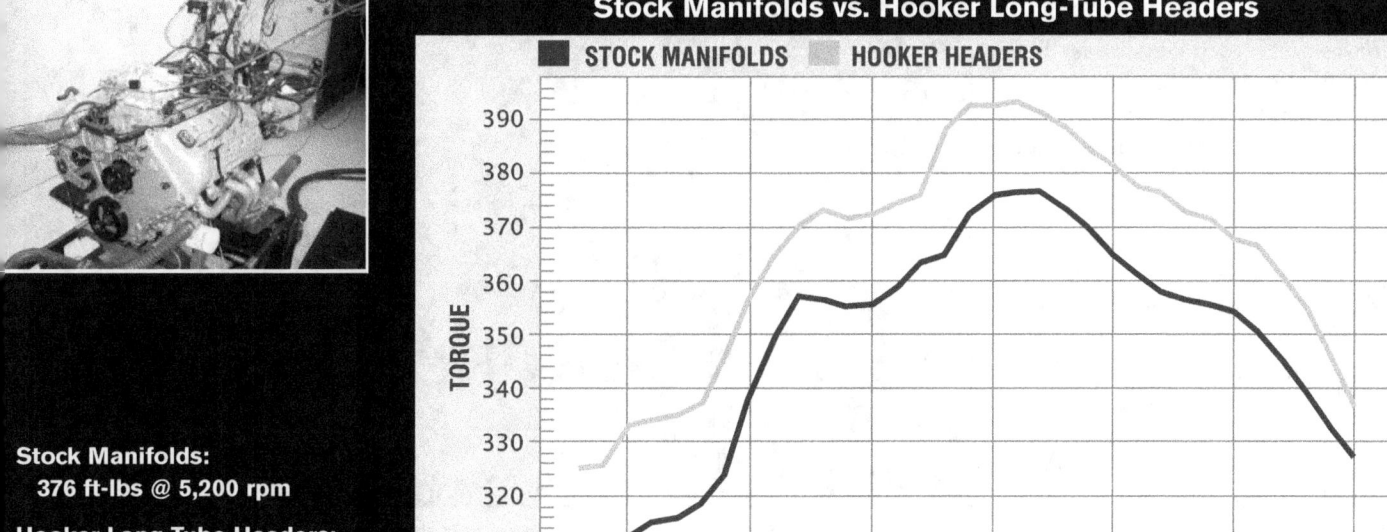

Stock Manifolds:
376 ft-lbs @ 5,200 rpm

Hooker Long-Tube Headers:
392 ft-lbs @ 5,100 rpm

Largest Gain:
19 ft-lbs @ 3,600 rpm

4-Valve Cobra: Stock Manifolds vs. Hooker Long-Tube Headers (Torque)
With an additional 12 to 15 ft-lbs of torque available throughout the rev range, you'll definitely be able to feel the additional power supplied by the Hooker headers. Note that the shape of the torque curve remained consistent and that the headers allowed the 4-valve motor to nearly reach 400 ft-lbs of torque.

CHAPTER 10

ENGINE BUILDUPS

Test 1: 407-hp PI 2-Valve GT

This first buildup was actually an extension of the very first modular motor I ran on the engine dyno. The basis for this 407-hp mod motor started out as a high-mileage '98 2-valve 4.6L. While the early (1996-'98) GT motors don't rank high on the desirability scale, it was perfect for our needs. The early non-PI motors were rated at 215 to 225 hp depending on the year, but it was the short block that makes these early motors so desirable, especially when upgrading to late-model PI cylinder heads. The combination of the early non-PI short block and late-model PI heads has a positive effect on the static compression, upping it by over a full point, from 9.2 to 10.6:1. The late-model PI heads offer improved airflow over the early heads, but the increased compression ratio from the head change can be worth an extra 6 to 8 percent in power. That equates to 18 to 20 hp depending on the original power rating. Bolting on the PI components offers not only improved head flow and compression, but also improved intake flow, as well as a change in effective operating range, thanks to the mandatory use of the PI intake. Now toss in a set of CNC-ported heads and wilder cams and you have the makings of a serious power upgrade.

The 1998 short block was a high-mileage unit, but performed perfectly. When performing the head swap, I upgraded the head gaskets to Fel-Pros and added a set of ARP head studs.

While our non-PI short block offered the promise of additional compression, we wanted to maximize the airflow as well. Ultimately, power is based on airflow, so anything we can do to improve the airflow through the motor will usually result in more power. To cure the airflow bottleneck in the factory non-PI heads, we contacted the airflow experts at Total Engine Airflow (TEA). Known in racing circles for their impressive CNC porting programs, we decided to try a set of their CNC-ported PI heads on our early

Engine Buildups

4.6L. The early and late-model 4.6L heads differ primarily in the size of their combustion chamber. The early heads featured a much larger chamber that was designed to work with a near-flat-top piston. The later PI heads featured much smaller combustion chambers (roughly 7 to 8 cc) to work with a dished piston, thus installing the PI heads on a non-PI short block will result in a significant increase in compression ratio.

While the gain in compression was certainly welcomed, the real power came from the precision CNC porting performed by Total Engine Airflow. The computer-controlled porting upped the flow figures by as much as 50 cfm on the intake side. The TEA-ported heads flowed nearly 230 cfm on the intake and over 200 cfm on the exhaust. Improving the airflow on a factory cylinder head at .500 or .600 inches of lift is easy, but combining those high-lift gains with low- and mid-lift improvements is the sign of a well-designed CNC program. The TEA-ported PI heads showed airflow improvements across the lift range, from .050 through .550 lift (the maximum the valves will see with the available cams).

The motor was further upgraded with a set of Comp XE274H Xtreme Energy cams and PI intake manifold. Though these cams were originally designed for a non-PI motor, they worked well on this PI-headed combination. The XE274H cams offered 236 degrees of intake duration and 240 degrees of exhaust duration. The dual-pattern (more intake duration than exhaust) helped offset a poor intake-to-exhaust flow relationship in the cylinder heads. Unfortunately, this flow imbalance was a negative attribute shared by both of the mod motors and previous 5.0L heads. The XE274H cams offered .500 inches of lift (intake and exhaust) on an idle-friendly 114-degree lobe separation angle. Knowing we planned on revving the motor past 6,000 rpm, we elected to install the Comp Cams valvespring upgrade. The right springs

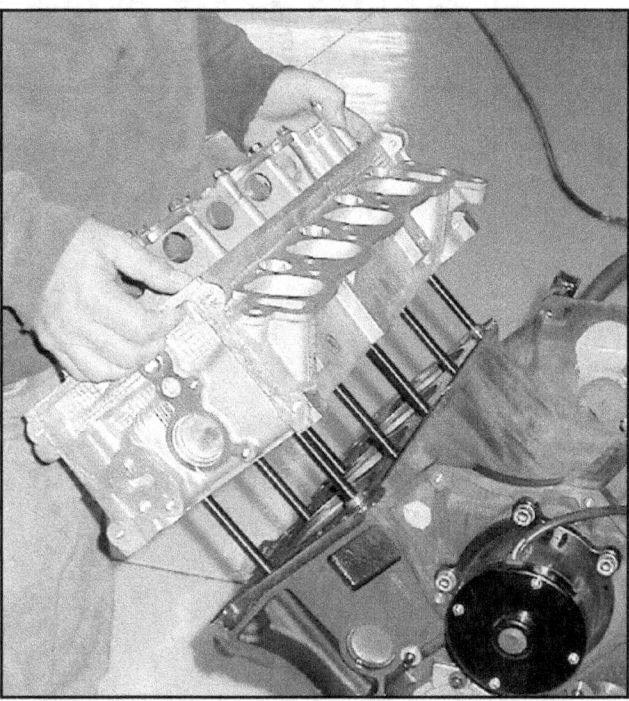

The Stage 2 CNC-ported PI heads from Total Engine Airflow were installed on the awaiting 1998 short block.

Run on the engine dyno, the modified 1998 4.6L 2-valve motor pumped out 407 hp and 394 ft-lbs of torque.

Chapter 10

Part of the buildup included a set of Comp XE274H cams.

are critical for proper valve control and to eliminate coil bind. The spring upgrade ensured that our mod motor could rev safely to take full advantage of the extra power offered by the more aggressive Xtreme Energy profiles.

The PI intake was topped off with an Accufab 75-mm throttle body and matching plenum, while the exhaust chores were handled by a set of Hooker Super Comp headers feeding 3-inch collector extensions. The motor was equipped with an electric water pump and run with a F.A.S.T. management system set to 26 degrees of total timing and 13.0:1 air/fuel ratio. So equipped, the 4.6L 2-valve motor produced peak power readings of 407 hp and 394 ft-lbs of torque. The additional compression ratio provided an exceptional torque curve, allowing the 4.6L to exceed 375 ft-lbs from 4,100 rpm to 5,500 rpm and 350 ft-lbs of torque from 3,350 rpm to 6,100 rpm. In fact, the 4.6L never produced less than 320 ft-lbs of torque from 3,000 to 6,200 rpm. Testing has shown that the factory PI intake was holding the motor back from reaching as much as 450 hp. We tried a Reichard Racing intake on this combination, but it was worth only 10 extra horsepower, and it sacrificed power to the PI manifold all the way up to 6,000 rpm. This test motor needed a custom intake designed to optimize power up to 6,200 rpm, similar to the one used in the next test on the stroker motor.

Test 1: 407-hp PI 2-Valve GT

Block:	Stock 1998 4.6L 2V Iron
Crank:	Stock 1998 4.6L 2V
Rods:	Stock 1998 4.6L 2V
Pistons:	Stock 1998 4.6L 2V
Compression:	10.48:1
Cylinder Heads:	TEA Stage 2 CNC-Ported PI
Cams:	Comp XE274H (non-PI)
Intake Manifold:	Stock PI
Throttle Body:	Accufab 75 mm
Inlet Elbow:	Accufab 75 mm
Injectors:	Stock 1998 19 lbs.
Management System:	F.A.S.T.
Headers:	Hooker Super Comp 1⅝ inch
Exhaust:	3 x 18-inch Collector Extension (No Mufflers)
Fuel:	91-Octane Pump Gas

Dyno Results

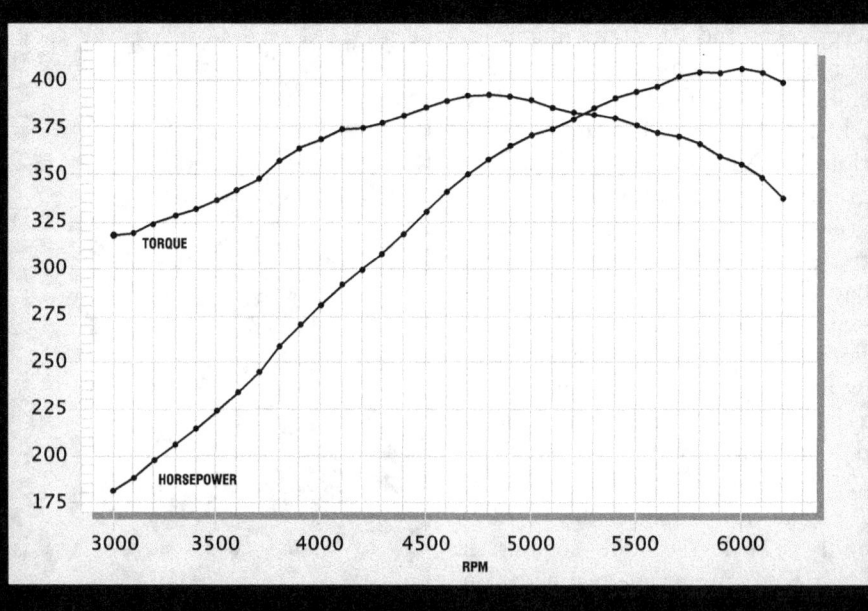

Peak Power: 407 hp @ 6,000 rpm   **Peak Torque: 394 ft-lbs @ 4,800 rpm**

Engine Buildups

Test 2: 490-hp 5.0L Stroker PI 2-Valve GT

The idea behind the buildup was to see how far I could take a 4.6L 2-valve motor without resorting to nitrous or forced induction. Having already topped the 400-hp mark with the previous effort, I wanted to see how far we could push a sensible all-motor buildup. One of the concerns I had while building this particular combination was the induction system. With no aftermarket heads available, I was forced to go the CNC-porting route again. Given my limited success with the available intake manifolds, I decided that this buildup deserved a suitable intake manifold as well. As it turned out, the combination of properly ported heads and a custom intake allowed this 2-valve motor to produce 4-valve power numbers. Sure, there is always more power to be had from even wilder cam timing, higher compression, and race-only components like dry-sump oiling, but I was interested in testing a combination that consisted primarily of off-the-shelf components. The one exception was obviously the intake manifold, but that may be a shelf item by the time this book goes to print.

Given the success I had with the previous set, I was more than happy to give the guys at Total Engine Airflow a shot at this buildup. Unlike the set of PI heads used on the previous 4.6L buildup, these PI heads were given the Stage 3 treatment, including full CNC porting, larger stainless-steel Manley valves, and even combustion chamber polishing. According to TEA, the modifications to the Stage 3 heads upped the flow rate to an impressive 242 cfm on the intake and 204 cfm on the exhaust. Though not quite on par with the 300-cfm number bounced around for hot 5.0L heads (or 4.6L 4-valve heads for that matter), the TEA heads represented the very best I could hope for from a production 2-valve PI casting. It is too bad that a major manufacturer has yet to step up to the complicated machining that is involved with producing an aftermarket 2-valve head. The first one to the market with a set of reasonably priced 2-valve heads that flow 250 to 260 cfm will likely

The 5.0L stroker short block supplied by Coast High Performance featured flat-top pistons with valve reliefs to allow for the aggressive Comp cams.

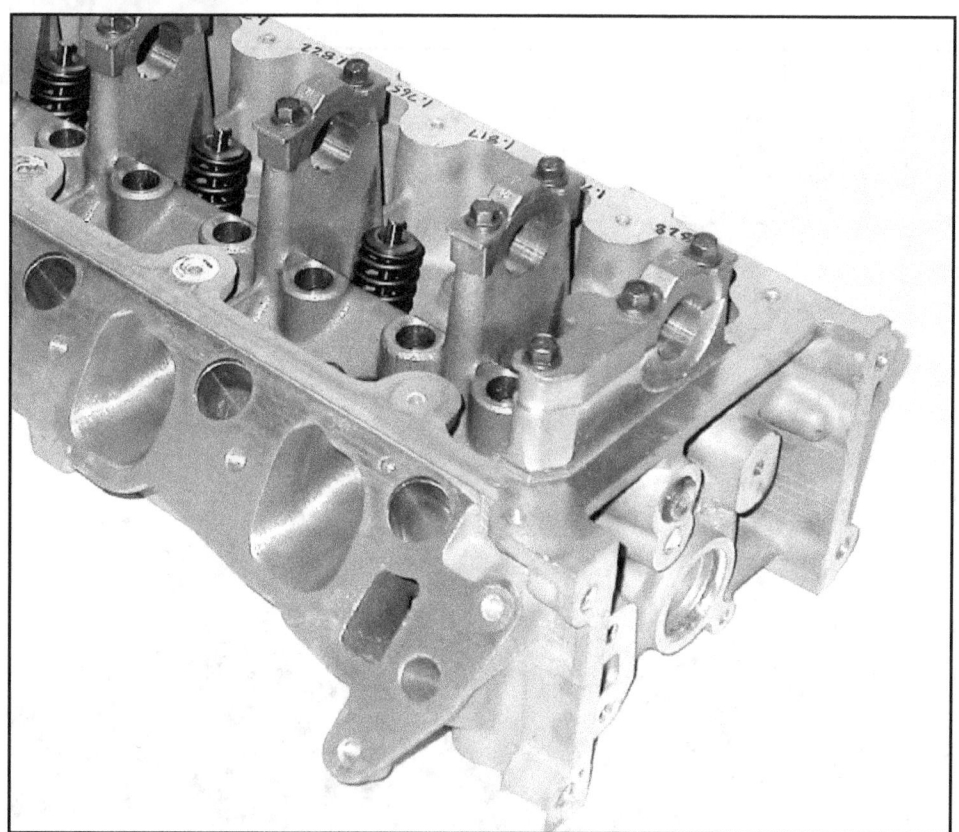

Once again I relied on Total Engine Airflow for a set of PI cylinder heads. These Stage 3 heads offered impressive flow, thanks to the CNC porting and oversized Manley valves.

Building 4.6/5.4L Ford Horsepower on the Dyno

Chapter 10

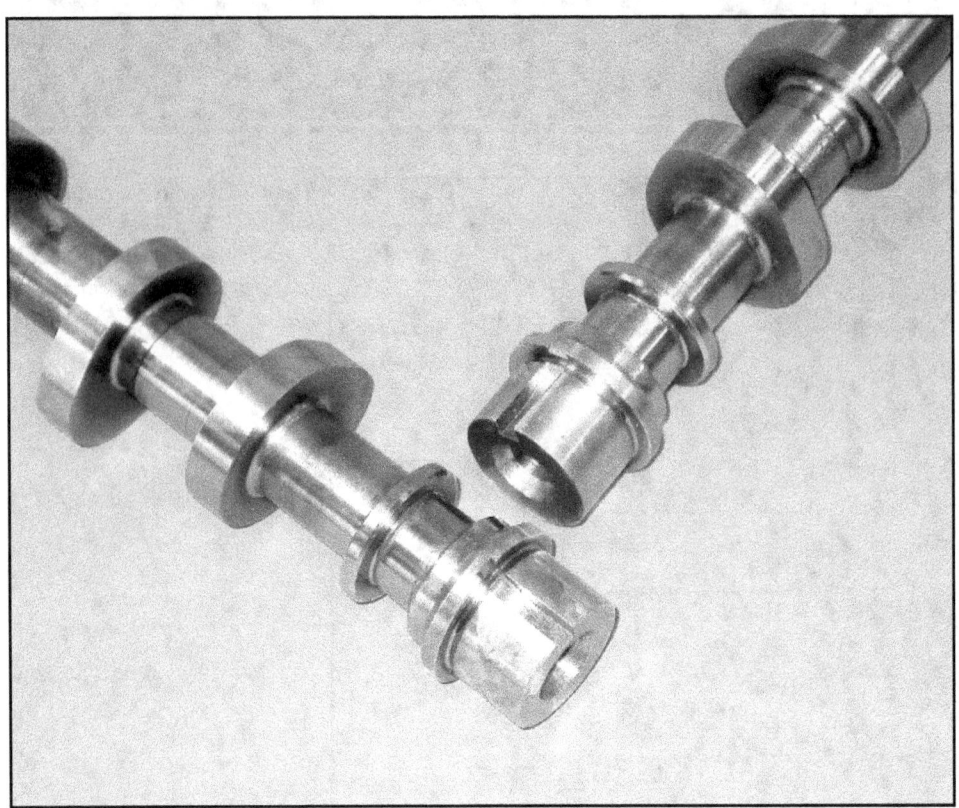
The XE278AH cams were the most aggressive off-the-shelf cams available from Comp Cams.

The custom intake designed by the author had a dramatic effect on power, upping the power output from 426 hp to 490 hp with no other changes.

sell heads by the thousands. Imagine the kind of revenue that might generate.

With the cylinder heads taken care of, I turned my attention to displacement, static compression, and cam timing. It stands to reason that if a 4.6L motor will produce 400 hp, then a 5.0L combination should have no trouble exceeding that number by a sizable margin. With extra displacement (and power) in mind, I turned to Coast High Performance (CHP) for a 5.0L stroker kit. The highlight of the CHP stroker kit was the 3.75-inch stroker crank (up from 3.543 inches). When combined with the .020-over forged pistons supplied in the kit, the result was a jump in displacement from 4.6 to a full 5.0 liters. Though my initial request was a simple stroker kit, CHP supplied a complete (and freshly machined) short block. The CHP short block featured the 3.75-inch stroker crank, a set of forged connecting rods, and a set of forged aluminum pistons. While the stroker kits generally come with dished pistons designed to provide a streetable (or boost friendly) static compression ratio, I opted for a set of flat-top pistons with valve reliefs to provide room for our wild cams. The flat-top pistons elevated the compression ratio of the 5.0L stroker to a lofty 11.55:1, thanks to the 42-cc chamber PI heads.

Next I reached for the largest cam profiles I could find. Down at the bottom of the page in the Comp Cams catalog was a set of XE278AH cams designed for the 4.6L 2-valve PI motor. Like all of the profiles for the PI motors, the XE278AH cams offered .550 inches of lift on both the intake and exhaust. The dual-pattern duration was skewed in favor of the exhaust, with the intake checking in at 242 degrees of duration (at .050) and the exhaust at 246. The lobe separation angle was fixed at 113 degrees. According to the Comp Cams literature, the cams were designed to run effectively to 6,200 rpm (and beyond, I hoped). In addition to the cams, Comp also supplied the necessary valvespring upgrade. Proper valve control is critical for maximum high-RPM performance. The last thing I wanted was to ruin a set of Manley valves with valve float caused by insufficient valvespring pressure.

Engine Buildups

The crowning glory of the 5.0L stroker was the custom intake manifold designed by the author. While conducting research for this very book, I tested every intake manifold available for the 4.6L 2-valve motors. Each available intake had strengths and weaknesses, but in the end, I decided that the maximum-effort stroker deserved a maximum-effort intake manifold. To that end, I fabricated this custom tubular monstrosity that not only provided that Buck Rogers Jet Pack look, but also (hopefully) impressive performance. A great deal of testing went into the design, including extensive calculations regarding the optimum engine speed for effective induction inertial ram charging, induction wave ram charging, and even Helmholtz resonance charging. The three distinct forms of improving the cylinder filling must be calculated and the intake designed accordingly. This is no easy task as the three forms often overlap and care must be taken to eliminate the cross cancellation of effective charge filling.

Finishing touches included a set of Kooks 1⅝-inch stainless steel headers, 36-pound injectors, and a Meziere electric water pump. Wanting to know how the custom intake stacked up against the factory PI setup, I ran the stroker motor with the stock intake before installing the custom job. After sufficient break-in, the 5.0L stroker was tuned using the F.A.S.T. management system and run in anger. Equipped with the factory intake, the stroker produced 426 hp at 5,800 rpm and 427 ft-lbs of torque at 4,700 rpm. Putting my money where my mouth was, I installed the custom intake and the peak power soared to 490 hp at 6,300 rpm, while the peak torque was up to 441 ft-lbs at 5,400 rpm. Equipped with an optimized intake manifold, the stroker exceeded 400 ft-lbs of torque from 3,900 to 6,400 rpm and over 400 hp from 5,100 to 7,000 rpm. The idea behind this stroker buildup was to show it is possible to build a serious 2-valve motor (490 hp qualifies as serious). For those interested in more info on the new intake, check with the guys at HP Performance (505-623-2555), as they expressed interest in marketing the manifold after a slight revision that will allow it to fit under the hood and be run with a single throttle body (it looks even better now as a cross ram).

Test 2: 490-hp 5.0L Stroker PI 2-Valve GT

Block:	Stock 1999 4.6L 2V Iron
Crank:	Coast High Performance 3.75-inch Stroker
Rods:	Coast High Performance Forged
Pistons:	Probe Racing Flat-Top Forged Aluminum
Compression:	11.78:1
Cylinder Heads:	TEA Stage 3 CNC-Ported PI
Cams:	Comp XE278AH (PI)
Intake Manifold:	Custom X Stream
Throttle Body:	Dual Accufab 75 mm
Inlet Elbow:	NA
Injectors:	36 lbs/hr
Management System:	F.A.S.T.
Headers:	Kooks Stainless 1⅝ inch
Exhaust:	2.5-inch Collector Extension (No Mufflers)
Fuel:	100-Octane Rocket Brand Race Gas

Dyno Results

Peak Power: 490 hp @ 6,300 rpm   **Peak Torque: 441 ft-lbs @ 5,400 rpm**

Building 4.6/5.4L Ford Horsepower on the Dyno

Chapter 10

Test 3: 800-hp Vortech Supercharged PI 2-Valve GT

When you go looking for maximum supercharged power, you better make sure the reciprocating assembly is up to snuff. Knowing the stock internals wouldn't cut it, I placed a call to DSS Competition Products, who supplied one of their 4.6L Super Mod short blocks. The DSS Super Mod short block featured a forged steel Cobra crank, a set of forged 4340 connecting rods, and ultra-high-strength forged pistons. To further improve the strength of the bottom end, DSS added a billet main support. The beefy ¾-inch thick main support included ARP fasteners. With the billet main support and a complete DSS forged reciprocating assembly, the iron 4.6L block was about as stout as possible. This same short block can be built using an aluminum 4-valve Cobra or 2-valve Explorer block, but I opted for the added strength of the heavier iron block. After all, it was going to take some hefty boost to reach the 800-hp mark with a 2-valve motor. Two final strength issues were addressed, namely replacing the factory head gaskets with high-performance Fel-Pro versions and the weak stock head bolts with ARP head studs.

With a beefy bottom end, I once again contacted Total Engine Airflow for my 2-valve cylinder head needs. TEA supplied another set of Stage 2 heads that featured full CNC porting to increase the intake airflow from 185 cfm to 235 cfm. The exhaust flow exceeded 200 cfm, giving the heads an intake-to-exhaust flow relationship of nearly 89 percent. Knowing we were going to be installing wilder cam timing, the valvesprings were suitably upgraded. The Stage 2 treatment included CNC porting the combustion chamber, thereby increasing the chamber volume from 42 to 45 cc. Combining the 45-cc combustion chambers with the Fel-Pro gasket and 18-cc dished pistons produced a static compression ratio of just over 9.0:1. While that may seem a tad high for a max-effort forced-induction motor, I planned to employ race

DSS supplied the short block for this 800-hp 2-valve buildup. The DSS combination included a steel Cobra crank, forged rods, and pistons to allow us to really put some boost to it.

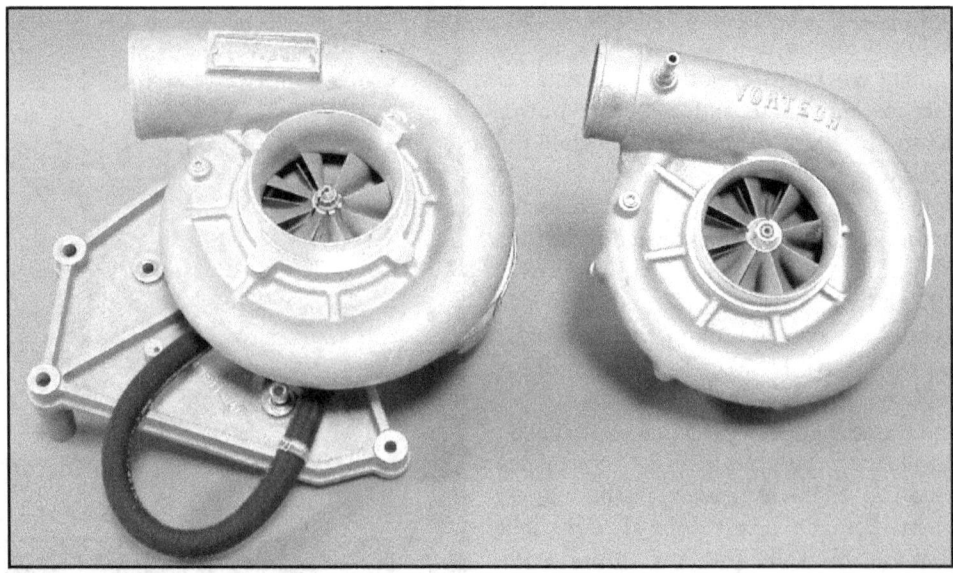

Vortech supplied a T-Trim blower for this buildup but we eventually settled on the larger JT-Trim to reach the 800-hp mark.

200 Building 4.6/5.4L Ford Horsepower on the Dyno

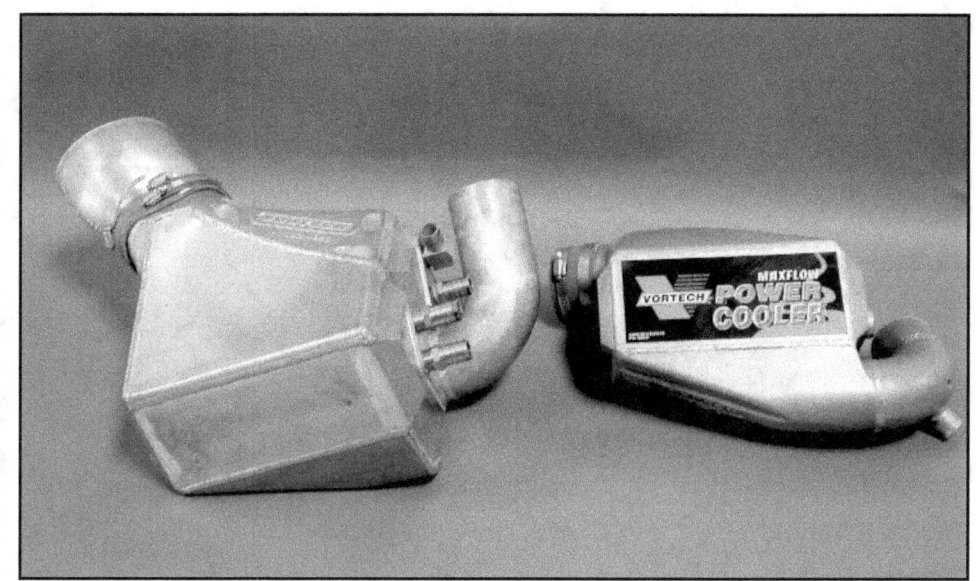

Vortech also fabricated this custom aftercooler that featured a pair of their standard cores. Two cores were used to maximize the cooling effect while minimizing the pressure drop.

fuel, intercooling, and absolute control over the timing and fuel curves to minimize any chance of detonation. The TEA-ported heads were topped off with a Ford Racing Bullitt intake. Before assembly, the Bullitt was treated to Extrude Hone porting to maximize (and balance) the flow rate of each port.

With heads and intake taken care of, I addressed the cam situation. Having had such success with the XE278AH cams on the naturally aspirated stroker, I decide to use them on this supercharged combination as well. Unlike their turbocharged counterparts, supercharged motors (especially centrifugal superchargers) run best with more aggressive cam timing. Remember, a good supercharged combination starts out as a healthy normally aspirated motor. The XE278AH cams offered a 242/248-duration split at .050 and .550 inches of lift (both intake and exhaust). The cams were ground with a 113-degree lobe separation angle. While I expected to trade some low-speed power with the big cams, the duration numbers at .050 ensured plenty of midrange and high-RPM power, while the lift allowed the motor to take full advantage of the flow offered by the CNC-ported heads. Remember, it's important to match the cam lift to the head flow, as it does little good to run a .700-lift cam with a set of heads that sign off at .500 inches of lift. The Xtreme Energy cam profiles offered aggressive ramp rates to maximize lift and power production under the curve.

To ensure adequate fuel delivery to our thirsty supercharged motor, we replaced the stock 19-pound injectors with a set of 65 pounders from F.A.S.T. The injectors were fed by an Aeromotive A1000 fuel pump augmented by a Kenne Bell Boost-A-Pump to increase the supply voltage (and fuel flow rate) if necessary. Finishing up the fuel system was a set of billet fuel rails from Keith Wilson and an adjustable fuel pressure regulator from Barry Grant. If you plan on trying to make 800 hp, your fuel system better

Equipped with TEA heads, Comp XE278AH cams, and an Extrude Hone ported Bullitt intake, the Vortech supercharged 4.6L pumped out 796 hp and 684 ft-lbs of torque.

be up to the task or you can start looking for someone to rebuild the motor. The F.A.S.T. management system was once again employed to tune the supercharged combination. Additional components employed on the motor included Denso Iridium spark plugs, a complete MSD ignition, and Hooker 1⅝-inch Super Comp headers. Though obviously not optimized for normally aspirated power, the 4.6L nonetheless pumped out some impressive numbers. Prepped for boost but minus the Vortech supercharger, the normally aspirated 4.6L produced 397 hp and 382 ft-lbs of torque. Though somewhat aggressive in terms of cam timing, the Xtreme Energy XE278AH cam combined with the long runners in the ported Bullitt intake and efficient CNC-ported PI heads to produce an exceptionally broad torque curve. The torque production of the 4.6L exceeded 350 ft-lbs from 4,300 rpm to 5,700 rpm.

The supercharger came next. Though Vortech offers a number of different superchargers (the standard 4.6L 2-valve kit relies on a V-2 SQ S-Trim), I selected a JT-Trim. According to Vortech literature, the JT-Trim was capable of supporting 1,000 hp, so I knew it was more than enough to feed this 2-valve combination. It was necessary to fabricate a dedicated 8-rib drive system (including crank and blower pulleys) along with a revised dual-core air-to-water aftercooler to take full advantage of the flow potential of the impressive JT-Trim blower. The trick air-to-water charge cooler featured a pair of the standard Vortech cores to ensure plenty of flow and cooling. After equipping the motor with a 7.5-inch crank pulley and 2.95-inch blower pulley, the Vortech supercharger pumped out a peak boost reading of 18.7 psi, where the 4.6L motor produce 798 hp at 6,300 rpm and 684 ft-lbs at 6,000 rpm. Though dyno time was limited while testing this combination (it took a while to get everything sorted), I feel confident that there was more power left in it. Ice water in the charge cooler would surely have increased the power output, as would a cog drive system to eliminate belt slippage. Regardless, nearly 800 hp is pretty impressive from a supercharged 2-valve 4.6L.

Test 3: 800-hp Vortech Supercharged PI 2-Valve GT

Block:	DSS Stock 2001 4.6L 2V (with main girdle) Iron
Crank:	4.6L 4V Cobra Steel (Stock Stroke)
Rods:	DSS 4340 Forged
Pistons:	DSS Forged Aluminum
Compression:	9.0:1
Cylinder Heads:	TEA Stage 2 (CNC) Ported PI
Cams:	Comp XE278AH (PI)
Intake Manifold:	Extrude Hone Ported Bullitt
Throttle Body:	Accufab Oval
Inlet Elbow:	NA
Injectors:	65 lbs/hr
Management System:	F.A.S.T.
Headers:	Hooker Super Comp 1⅝ inch
Exhaust:	3 x 18-inch Collector Extension (No Mufflers)
Fuel:	114-Octane Rocket Brand Race Gas
Blower:	Vortech JT-Trim
Intercooler:	Custom Dual-Core Vortech Aftercooler
Boost:	18.7 psi

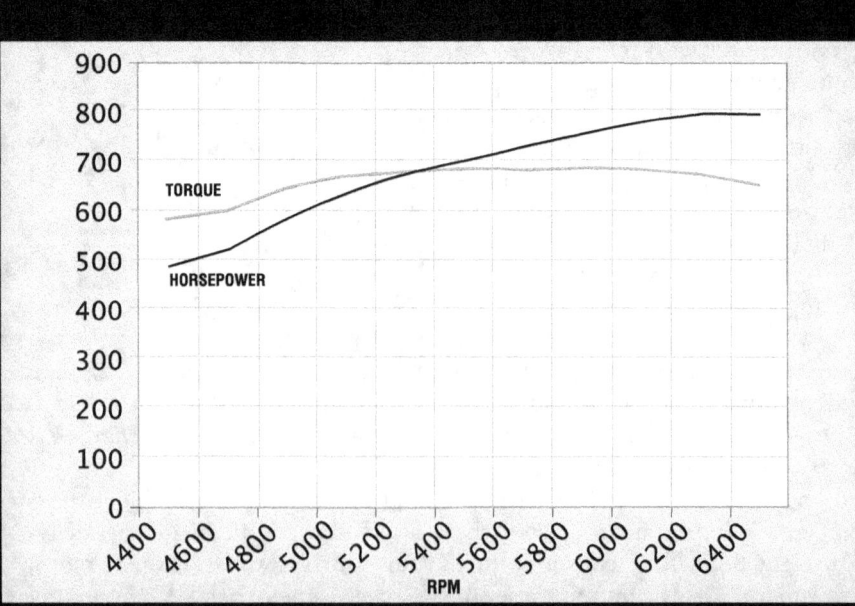

Dyno Results

Peak Power: 798 hp @ 6,300 rpm   Peak Torque: 684 ft-lbs @ 6,000 rpm

Engine Buildups

Test 4: 990-hp Twin-Turbo 4-Valve '03 Cobra

This modular buildup was actually one of the easiest, as it didn't so much involve building a combination; rather, I modified an existing one. The engine started out life as a supercharged 2003 Mustang Cobra engine assembly available through the Ford Racing catalog. Installed as original equipment in the 2003-'04 Mustang Cobras, the supercharged 4-valve motor sported a number of impressive features. In fact, a case can be made that the blower motor might well be the most powerful combination ever offered in a Mustang (so far), eclipsing the real-world power output of even the big-block motors of yesteryear. While most of the attention is focused on the Eaton M112 roots supercharger, the reality is that the Cobra motor is much more than a 4-valve 4.6L with a blower stuffed on top. The '03 and '04 Cobra motors were fortified by the factory for blower usage, meaning they featured a number of components not found in lesser normally aspirated mod motors. The list of blower-specific equipment includes a forged steel crank, a set of Manley forged rods connecting, and low-compression pistons. According to my sources, the cam timing was somewhat milder than the NA motors, something I have come to expect with blower use (at least from the factory). The forged steel crank, rods, and pistons made for a near-bulletproof reciprocating assembly. Toss in the free-flowing 4-valve heads and a trick intake manifold with an air-to-water intercooler and you have the makings of some serious performance potential.

A few years back, the SVT gang went through a bit of a fiasco with power ratings on the 4-valve Cobra motors. Apparently the motors were not producing the promised power levels and steps were taken to appease the Cobra owners with the overrated motors. Apparently Ford and SVT took this episode to heart and came out swinging with the '03 Cobra. Not only did the

Though impressive in stock form, Ford Racing '03-'04 Cobra crate motors offer even more power when you replace the factory Eaton M112 roots supercharger.

supercharged Cobra motor produce the rated power output, but also it seems that the motor was (if anything) purposely underrated. Every one I've tested exceeded the rated output by a significant margin. Rated by the factory at 390 hp and a like amount of torque, I have seen stock Cobras pump out 360 to 370 hp at the wheels on a chassis dyno. That certainly translates to a bit more than the advertised 390 flywheel rating. Need more proof? I ran one '03 4-valve crate motor on the engine dyno to the tune of 485 hp. The motor was bone stock from the throttle body to the cast-iron exhaust manifolds. Of course, the 390-hp rating comes with full accessories, a complete inlet system, and running the factory fuel and timing curves, but know that not only was the supercharged Cobra motor underrated, but the power potential of this combination is staggering, as this test is about to illustrate.

While the factory Eaton M112 blower produced enough flow to push the crate motor near the 600-hp mark, ultimately, the blower itself was the limiting factor. So, off it came to be replaced by a pair of hybrid turbos from HP Performance. Before pressurizing the powerplant, I decided another upgrade was in order. Knowing that the power output of the turbo motor is a function of the power output of the normally aspirated motor, I decided to take steps to improve the normally aspirated power output before applying boost. This is especially true of turbocharged motors, as they tend to add a larger percentage of power than most forms of supercharging. To enhance the power output of the now normally aspirated '03 Cobra

Chapter 10

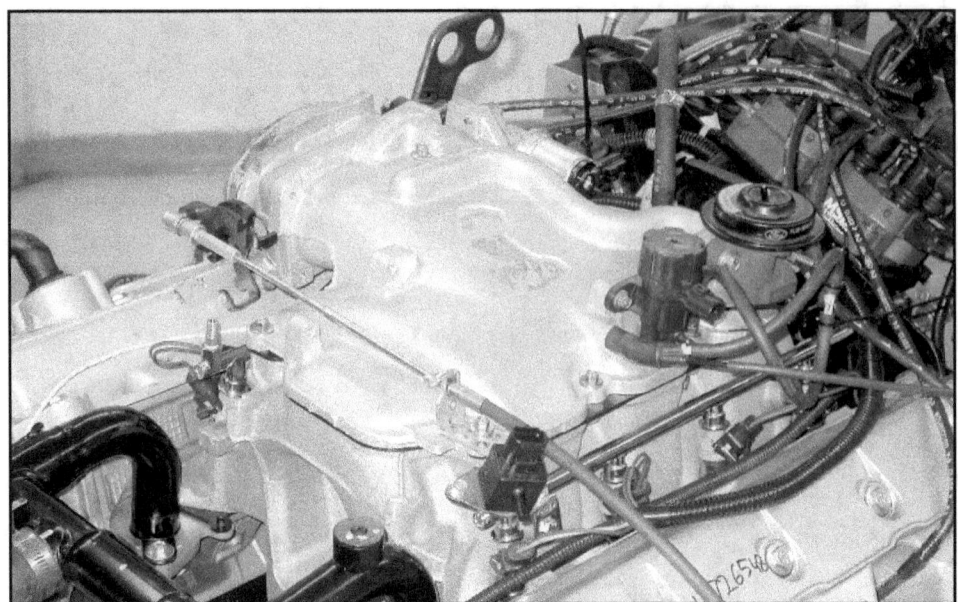

For this test, the blower and lower intake with air-to-water intercooler were removed and replaced with a factory intake from a normally aspirated 2001 Cobra.

Equipped with the twin-turbo system from HP Performance, the '03 Cobra crate motor produced an amazing 990 hp and 911 ft-lbs of torque at just over 20 psi. For those keeping track, that's almost 400 hp more than the factory supercharger.

motor came equipped with not only the Eaton supercharger but also a two-piece intake manifold that incorporated an air-to-water intercooler. The effective intercooler reduced the inlet charge temperature to minimize detonation and allow greater power production. Given the hood constraints, combining the Eaton supercharger with an air-to-water intercooler necessitated very short intake runners. Unfortunately, short intake runners greatly reduce power production in the usable part of the rev range (in this case up to 6,500 rpm). Naturally, when I removed the Eaton supercharger, off came the remainder of the intake and the attending short runners. In the end, I replaced the intercooled Cobra intake with a stock intake from a 2001 normally aspirated Cobra. The NA Cobra intake featured (desirable) long runners that helped promote torque production and allowed the motor to produce an impressive power curve from 3,000 rpm all the way to 6,500 rpm. Since the twin-turbo system included a front-mounted air-to-air intercooler, I wouldn't miss the air-to-water unit under the factory manifold.

Before adding the turbo kit from HP Performance, I ran the normally aspirated '03 Cobra motor with the 2001 intake and Comp cams. The combination produced an impressive 426 hp and 390 ft-lbs of torque. These were pretty impressive numbers considering the low compression and a 281-ci displacement. Now it was time for some boost. Designed also to fit the normally aspirated Cobras, the HP Performance kit includes everything needed to up the boost to 20 psi or more. The kit includes a pair of 57-mm turbos, an ultra-efficient air-to-air intercooler, and all the exhaust and inlet tubing required to run boost from the turbos to the throttle body. The custom header, like the rest of the exhaust and intake tubing, featured Jet Hot coating to keep the heat energy in the tubing where it did the most. The HP kit usually includes injectors and a reprogrammed ECU, but I was running the '03 motor using a F.A.S.T. stand-alone management system and a set of 65-lb/hr injectors. The combination of the 65-pound injectors, Aeromotive

motor, I replaced the stock cams with a set of Xtreme XE262AH cams from Comp Cams. The mild dual-pattern XE262AH cams offered 226 degrees of intake duration, 222 degrees of exhaust duration, and a 114-degree lobe separation angle to go along with the .425-inch lift (both intake and exhaust). The low lift allowed the motor to retain the stock valvesprings, though Comp does offer a valvespring upgrade for the larger (higher-lift) cams. Dyno testing showed these cams to be worth over 50 hp on the normally aspirated, low-compression combination.

Before getting to the turbos, I need to take a look at the intake manifold situation. From the factory, the '03 Cobra

Engine Buildups

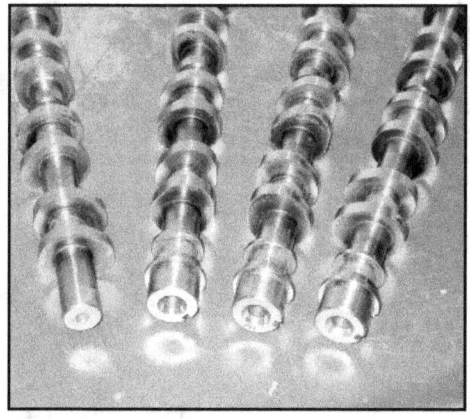

The '03 Cobra motor was also upgraded with a set of XE262AH cams from Comp Cams.

A1000 fuel pump, and Kenne Bell Boost-A-Pump meant we were safe to over 1,000 hp – which turned out to be a good thing.

After installing the kit on the 4.6L motor, I dialed in the boost pressure using a Turbo XS manual wastegate controller. Raising the boost pressure was a simple matter of twisting the small Allen screw in the Turbo XS unit. Run at the minimum wastegate setting of 5 psi, the '03 Cobra motor produced 530 hp and 493 ft-lbs of torque. Stepping things up to a peak of 7.8 psi, the boosted Cobra motor made 670 hp and 576 ft-lbs of torque. The next step was 11 psi, where the twin-turbo 4.6L produced 750 hp and 679 ft-lbs of torque. While we were impressed with the power output at 11 psi, we continued on by upping the boost pressure to 13.6 psi where the twin-turbo motor thumped out 830 hp and 756 ft-lbs of torque. This thing just seemed to be getting happier and happier with each turn of the screw. With the air/fuel and timing still well in the safe zone (combined with the safety of 114-octane fuel), I pushed on to 16.2 psi. Now things were getting serious, as the 4.6L produced 891 hp and 815 ft-lbs of torque. With fingers crossed, I took the boost up in 1-psi increments until finally getting to a peak of 20.8 psi. Running a peak of 20.8 psi (down to 20.4 psi at the power peak), the 4.6L Cobra motor produced an amazing 990 hp and 911 ft-lbs of torque. We suspect the 57-mm turbos were about done at this point, but imagine what an '03 Cobra might feel like with 990 hp!

Test 4: 990-hp Twin-Turbo 4-Valve '03 Cobra

Block:	Stock 2003 4.6L 4V Iron
Crank:	Stock 2003 4.6L 4V Cobra Steel (Stock Stroke)
Rods:	Stock 2003 4.6L 4V Cobra
Pistons:	Stock 2003 4.6L 4V Cobra
Compression:	8.5:1
Cylinder Heads:	Stock 2003 4.6L 4V Cobra
Cams:	Comp Cams XE262AH
Intake Manifold:	2001 4.6L 4V Cobra
Throttle Body:	Accufab Oval
Inlet Elbow:	NA
Injectors:	65 ft-lbs
Management System:	F.A.S.T.
Headers:	HP Performance Turbo Manifold
Exhaust:	Dual 2.5-inch From Turbos (No Mufflers)
Fuel:	114-Octane Rocket Brand Race Gas
Turbos:	HP Performance Twin-Turbo Kit With Dual 57-mm Turbos
Intercooler:	HP Performance Air-to-Air
Boost:	20.8 psi

Dyno Results

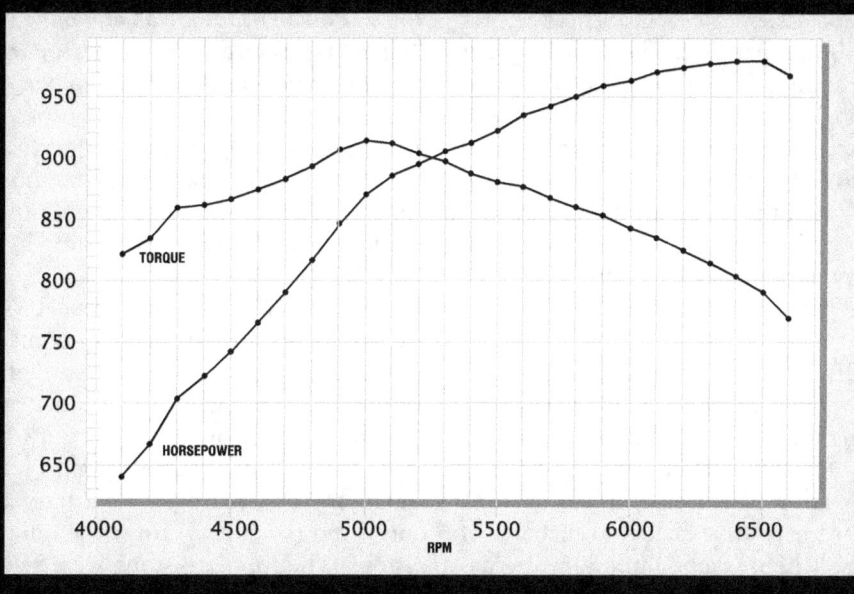

Peak Power: 990 hp @ 6,500 **Peak Torque: 911 ft-lbs @ 5,000 rpm**

Chapter 10

Test 5: 1,350-hp ATI F2M Supercharged 5.4L 4-Valve

It's true that boost pressure is a big equalizer, but making huge power requires more than just a truckload of boost from a big blower. Attempting the excessive boost route on a stock or even mildly modified motor is a surefire recipe for disaster. Exceeding 1,000 hp requires looking beyond boost – in short, you'll need to maximize displacement, engine speed, and boost pressure. This three-tiered approach leaves no stone unturned in the quest for performance. Ford modular motors are available in two different displacements (not counting strokers or big bores). The smaller 4.6L has proven itself powerful, but when it comes to maximum-effort performance, it's always easier to make big power from a big motor. Technically speaking, the larger the motor, the lower the specific output required to reach a given power level. The specific output of any motor is in direct proportion to difficulty and expense. If you're looking to produce 460 hp from a 4.6L, it would require a specific output of 100-hp per liter. Achieving the same output using a larger 5.4L motor requires a specific output of only 85-hp per liter. Believe me, it's a lot easier to reach 85-hp per liter than 100-hp per liter. The added benefit of the additional displacement is low and midrange torque production, as a hike in displacement improves power not just at the power (or torque) peak, but also throughout the rev range. Since races are won not by peak power numbers, but with average power production over the usable range, extra power is always welcomed.

Given the additional power available with the increased displacement, starting this buildup with the larger 5.4L mod motor was a natural choice. The iron block was chosen both for strength and for the relative lack of availability of a suitable lightweight aluminum alternative. The 5.4L block differs from the smaller 4.6L by way of a taller deck height (think 302W vs. 351W). Both

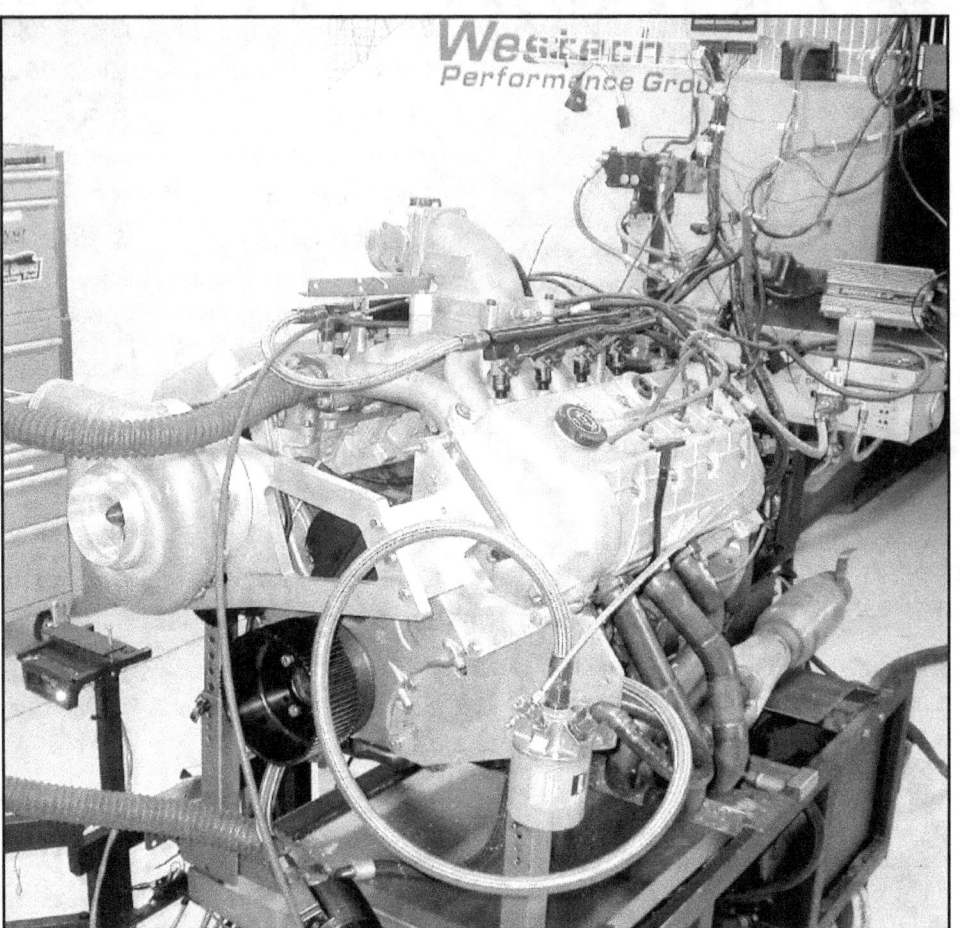
The 5.4L 4-valve motor was equipped with ported 4-valve heads, SHM cams, and a Sullivan intake before being subjected to the rigors of boost. Even in naturally aspirated trim, the motor produced 543 hp and 439 ft-lbs of torque.

mod motors accept the same heads and cams, but intake manifolds are unique due to the width between the opposing cylinder heads. The new 5.4L used in the Ford GT (GT40) super car features aluminum construction, but these blocks are understandably difficult to come by and expensive if you're lucky enough to locate one. The iron 5.4L block was treated to precision machine work and stuffed with a forged steel crank, a set of aluminum connecting rods (drag race only), and (of course) forged aluminum pistons. The forged pistons were selected to achieve a low static compression ratio of almost 12.0:1. While this may seem extremely high for a supercharged combination, the motor runs a steady diet of C16 race fuel, incorporates a serious air-to-water intercooler (with ice water), and was tuned to perfection using the F.A.S.T. management system. When you go racing, why give away the power associated with low compression?

With displacement taken care of, Accufab's John Mihovitz turned his attention to the rpm (and breathing) capability of the mod motor. John knew that producing a solid supercharged motor meant starting with a stout normally aspirated version. To maximize breathing, the forged 5.4L short block was topped off with a set of 5.4L 4-valve

Navigator heads. In stock form, the 4-valve heads out-flowed even professionally ported 2-valve heads, but naturally the 4-valve Navigator heads were not left stock on this buildup. The 4-valve heads were treated to extensive porting (both intake and exhaust) that unleashed another 50 cfm per runner. In addition to the porting, the heads received some proprietary mods to the valve seats, installed heights, and valve job that were the result of extensive testing performed on John's own 6-second mod motor racecar. According to Mihovitz, the 4-valve heads respond to a few tricks that helped unlock not only extra power but also longevity and repeatability (both critical elements in drag racing). The heads were secured using ARP heads, studs, and multi-layer-steel head gaskets.

The other area where Mihovitz's racing experience came into play was with cam selection. John chose a quartet of cams from Sean Hyland Motorsports, including a pair of Stage 2 intake cams and Stage 3 exhaust cams. The thinking behind the larger exhaust cams was that the blower was there to help intake flow while the added exhaust duration helped ensure all of the exhaust found its way out. The Stage 2 intake cams featured .452 inches of lift and 225 degrees of duration at .050, while the larger Stage 3 exhaust cams offered .474 inches of lift and 235 degrees of duration at .050. According to John Mihovitz, the real key to getting the cams to work is to take the time to degree them properly. Given there are four cams, degreeing is a time-consuming process but is a critical element when searching for big power. Both the intake and exhaust cams were installed at 107 degrees. The preload on the new hydraulic lifters was set by adjusting the installed height of the valve and the cam gears were secured using ARP (high-strength) cam retaining bolts. The last thing you want to happen is to have the cam gears come loose at 8,000 rpm!

Given that the motor was intended to run high RPM, the intake manifold was chosen accordingly. The stock long-runner Navigator intake was deemed inadequate for the RPM and power level and was replaced with a new short-

Running 25 psi of boost from any blower will produce excessive heat, so an air-to-water intercooler was employed to drop the inlet temperature. Ice water was used to maximize the cooling effect.

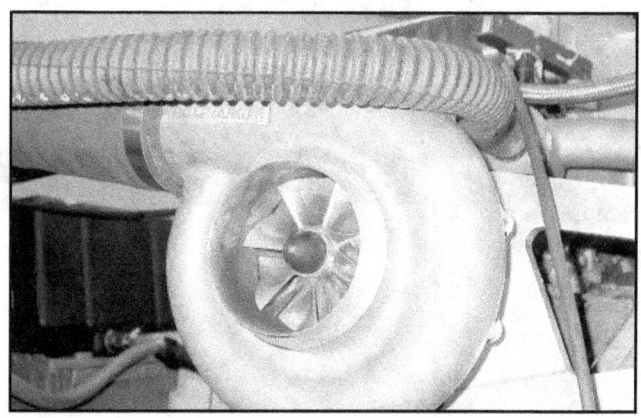

The real power player was the ATI F2M supercharger. Driven using an Accufab cog-drive system, the big blower pumped as much as 25 psi of boost to the 5.4L.

What happens when you push 25 psi through an already impressive 5.4L 4-valve motor? How does 1,350 hp and 1,028 ft-lbs of torque sound?

runner casting from Sullivan. The Sullivan intake was actually designed with a carburetor pad to accept a conventional 4-barrel carb, but the design also included injector bosses to accept an EFI system. The intake was topped with a 90-degree cast-aluminum elbow designed to adapt the carb flange to a 5.0L Ford EFI throttle body. Naturally, John utilized a billet throttle body from Accufab, in this case a huge 90-mm version to maximize airflow to the 5.4L. The 90-mm throttle body ensured plenty of airflow to feed the 5.4L race motor while the short-runner Sullivan intake was designed to shift the torque curve higher in the rev range. A higher torque curve results in more peak horsepower. If all went according to plan, the combination of ported Navigator heads, SHM cams, and Sullivan intake should allow the motor to produce peak power somewhere to the far side of 7,000 rpm. The forged reciprocating assembly would have no trouble running 7,000+ rpm and the ATI blower just makes more boost with engine speed.

Before installing the ATI F2M supercharger, the motor was run in normally aspirated trim to establish a baseline. The 5.4L was equipped with a set of 1⅞-inch to 2.0-inch stepped headers and 3.5-inch collector extensions. The F.A.S.T. management system was employed to control the MSD coil packs and 150-lb/hr injectors. The high static compression allowed the normally aspirated 5.4L to produce 543 hp and 439 ft-lbs of torque. The power curve was just where John wanted it, giving him high hopes for the supercharged power output. The ATI F2M supercharger was installed with a custom cog drive system designed by Accufab to eliminate belt slippage. The cog system featured a 73-tooth crank pulley and 46-tooth blower pulley. Given the expected high boost level (north of 20 psi), an intercooler was employed to reduce the all-important intake charge temperature. Ice water was used to maximize heat rejection through the Spearco air-to-water intercooler. Run with 19 degrees of total timing, an air/fuel ratio of 11.2:1, C16 fuel, and 25 psi, the 5.4L delivered 1,350 hp at 7,200 rpm and 1,028 ft-lbs of torque at 6,500 rpm.

Test 5: 1,350-hp ATI F2M Supercharged 5.4L 4-Valve

Block:	Stock 5.4L 4V Iron
Crank:	Steel 5.4L
Rods:	Forged Aluminum
Pistons:	JE Forged Aluminum Flat Top
Compression:	11.75:1
Cylinder Heads:	Hand Ported 4V Navigator
Cams:	SHM Stage 3 4V
Intake Manifold:	Sullivan
Throttle Body:	Accufab 90 mm
Inlet Elbow:	90 Degree
Injectors:	150 lbs/hr
Management System:	F.A.S.T.
Headers:	Accufab 1⅞ to 2.0-inch Stepped
Exhaust:	4-inch (No Mufflers)
Fuel:	C16 Race Gas
Blower:	ATI F2M
Intercooler:	Spearco Air-to-Water
Boost:	25 psi

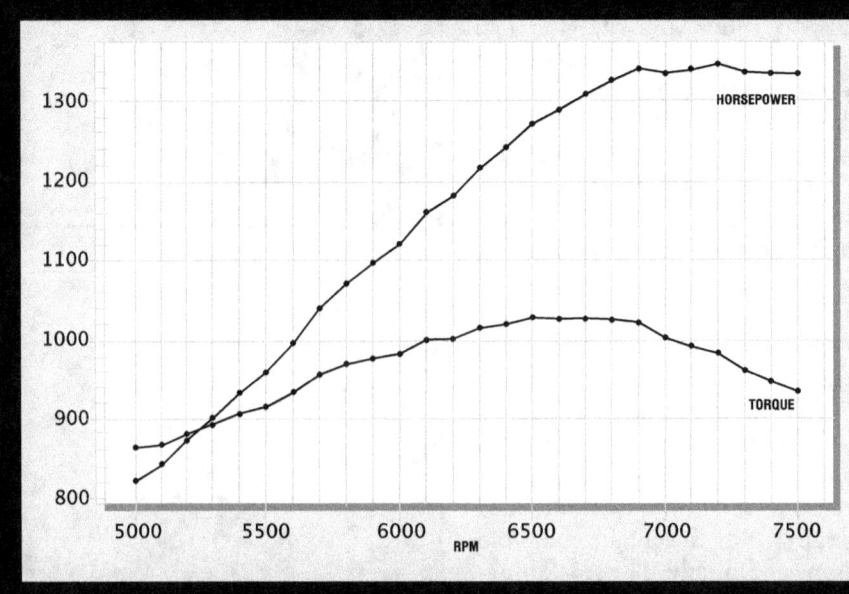

Peak Power: 1,350 hp @ 7,200 rpm **Peak Torque: 1,028 ft-lbs @ 6,500 rpm**

www.ingramcontent.com/pod-product-compliance
Lightning Source LLC
Chambersburg PA
CBHW051404070526
44584CB00023B/3292